SAM HOUSTON

American Giant

SAM HOUSTON

American Giant

By M. K. WISEHART

Robert B. Luce, Inc.

Washington

SAM HOUSTON: American Giant

Library of Congress Catalog Card Number: 62-20000

MANUFACTURED IN THE UNITED STATES OF AMERICA

VAN REES PRESS • NEW YORK

To ROSA, my wife

Preface

IN 1943 when the University of Texas published the last
of eight volumes of a monumental work, *The Writings
of Sam Houston*, a new vista opened to students and a step was taken
toward closing a gap in American history. In an important way this
collection of Houstoniana bears upon a period that has been highly
controversial but never thoroughly understood—those years when
sectionalism was developing and the nation was being drawn into
civil strife.

Writings is Houston's own testament. By virtue of its contemporary origin, authenticity, and scope it takes precedence over much
that has been written and said about him. In many respects he appears in it as a strikingly different man from the one created by
previous assumptions. In the light of this work, the would-be biographer of Sam Houston soon discovers that there are major aspects
of the man's life that call for new understanding, interpretation, and
judgment. Therefore, I have concentrated on revaluating the outstanding traits of character that made him the man he was and the
following major phases of his career: (1) his decision to go to Texas;
(2) his relations as Commander in Chief with the General Council,
the legislative body of the first provisional government; (3) his
plans for defending Texas without sacrificing the Alamo garrison;
(4) his strategy during the forty-day campaign which culminated in
victory at San Jacinto; (5) his anti-war policy as President of the
Texas Republic; (6) his annexation policy; (7) his thirteen years of
service in the United States Senate and his attempts to check the
drift toward war and to heal the breach between North and South;
and (8) his anti-secession policy as Governor of Texas.

Houston had an extraordinary facility for self-expression. He
could talk extemporaneously for two or three hours and hold his
audience in thrall. After sleeping all night on the cold, damp ground,
he could sit on a log and write powerful appeals to stimulate patriotic ardor or eloquent petitions in his own defense. His gift for

expressing himself deserves emphasis. For that reason, it has seemed desirable to give him the floor and let him speak in his own words more often than is usual in a book of this character.

I am grateful to many for assistance along the way, particularly to two notable Texans, Dr. J. Frank Dobie and Dr. Walter Prescott Webb for critical comments on a lengthy prospectus of intentions. Temple Houston Morrow, one of two surviving grandsons of Sam Houston, at great inconvenience to himself, gave me the benefit of numerous letters and conversations which resulted in answers to many of my queries about his illustrious ancestor and about the Houston family. To various advanced students of Texas history who have ransacked the papers of colorful personalities of the period, I am grateful for some quotations which heighten pertinent points in my book and serve as a kind of antiphonal commentary on Houston's strengths and weaknesses.

Dr. Byron Fairchild, Historian, Department of Defense, and Lieutenant Colonel Kenneth E. Kay, U.S.A.F. Staff College, made helpful suggestions on the presentation of the San Jacinto campaign after thoroughly reviewing that portion of the manuscript. To Dr. Charles C. Tansill, long-time professor of American diplomatic history at Georgetown University, and the late Dr. Louis M. Sears, biographer of George Washington and professor emeritus of history at Purdue University, I am grateful for discussions of the "new" Houston which went on for a period of years at the Cosmos Club in Washington, D. C. The unshakeable conviction of Dr. Tansill, a Texas patriot and unreconstructed Confederate, that Sam Houston should have supported the Texas secession movement and followed his state into the camp of Jefferson Davis, inspired a more penetrating inquiry into what Houston actually did.

As the manuscript developed, persistent and helpfully probing queries about it came from the Reverend Herbert J. Clancy, S. J., political historian and associate professor of the history department of Fordham University. Similarly stimulating service was performed by Dr. Robert B. Eckles, associate professor in the history department of Purdue University.

The research and reference staffs of many libraries, particularly the Library of Congress, the New York Public Library, the University of Texas Library, and the Tennessee State Library, were unfailingly courteous and helpful in response to insatiable demands on their time and facilities. Dr. Frank H. Wardlaw of the University of

Texas Press gave encouragement and permission to use various materials. Among others who helped in a variety of ways were Dr. Llerena Friend and Chester V. Kielman, both of the University of Texas Library staff; V. E. Baugh of the research staff of the National Archives in Washington, D. C.; and Robert T. Quarles of Nashville, Tenn., who served for many years as the secretary of the Tennessee Historical Society.

I appreciate my publisher's generous spirit of cooperation and Miss Tadd Fisher's sympathetic criticism and able editing. Of the one to whom this work is dedicated it is not too much to say that without her ability as a researcher and her durability as an inspiring critic this biography could not have been completed.

M. K. W.

Alexandria, Virginia

Contents

BOOK IV

A RULER OF VIKINGS

BOOK V

MAKING CHARACTER

List of Illustrations

(between pages 464 and 465)

BOOK I

TO THE PROMISED LAND

1. *The Truant*

Early springtime found its way through the shadows of the Great Smoky Mountains and into East Tennessee. The natural world budded and bloomed. The air was sweet, and the season characteristically inspired conflicting emotions—nostalgia, joy, hope, despair, restlessness, and lassitude—in all whom it touched. It did not spare sixteen-year-old Sam Houston, heightening the turbulence that was already seething within him.

Sam and the young nation in which he lived had much in common. In 1809, the United States was Sam's senior but it, too, was adolescent, uncertain, brooding, and eagerly pressing on toward still another frontier. The post-Revolution drift to the west had already begun. Ships-on-wheels, laden with families and household goods were threading through the green passes of the Alleghenies.

There were rumors of a possible war with Spain, and James Madison, the fourth President, was striving to avoid war with England. In a log house in Nashville, Andrew Jackson—planter, lawyer, and border captain—was moodily pondering international affairs. During the American Revolution he had been clipped on the head by a British sword for his defiance in refusing to clean an officer's boots. Now he was chafing at his country's tardiness in meeting the challenge of a nation he hated and was praying fervently that the war would begin soon.

But at Baker's Creek, Sam Houston was concerned with immediate problems. It had been two years since his widowed mother, Elizabeth, and her nine children had settled on this well-watered tract of 419 acres. Sam had done his share during those first exciting days when they had squared logs, built a house, and painfully wrested an existence from the stubborn soil. He had willingly swung an ax, dug roots, spaded, hoed, seeded, cultivated, and milked. Now his restive spirit balked at this way of life. He thought he knew what he should and must do, but to whom could he reveal his dreams? Who could give him advice?

Surely he could not turn to his older brothers, James and John. They were disposed to preach and scold, and he scornfully called them the "holy apostles." Ma was the one who understood him. There were times when he thought that he could safely confide in her, but he always decided against it. He wasn't quite sure what he wanted to do yet, although he relished the idea of leaving Baker's Creek, crossing the Tennessee River, and having a look at what was going on in the friendly Cherokee country.

Sam did not mind the backache that accompanied his toil on the farm. What he objected to was that this occupation afforded opportunity for "very little fancy." [1] His aversion to farming and to the dry atmosphere of the local Maryville Academy was earning him the reputation of a scapegrace. He was weary of his older brothers' pointed remarks and of lectures on truancy delivered by well-meaning Dr. Isaac Anderson, the new head teacher of the academy. Provoked by the willful son of an estimable mother, Dr. Anderson said, "I often determined to lick him, but he would come up with such a pretty dish of excuses that I could not do it." [2] Perhaps another factor influenced him; Sam had grown to six feet with the rapidity of green corn on a hot summer night.

The incorrigible truant had also dodged school back in Virginia, before the family had moved to Tennessee, but he had been content to lie on the floor by the fireplace reading books from his father's library. He had become familiar with Brown's *Gazeteer*, Rollins' *Ancient History*, and the big two-volume set of Morse's *Geography*. (The *Geography* was listed as an asset in his father's will.) He found these books much more intriguing than the dull literary fare offered in the academy.

At last, Sam's mother and older brothers agreed with him that his farm duties should be nominal. He could put in regular attendance at the academy and also clerk in the Maryville store, which the

4

Houstons partly owned. From Sam's point of view, the trouble with this arrangement was that clerking offered no more chance for "fancy" than grubbing roots and hoeing potatoes. But he was willing to give it a try.

This was the state of affairs when Sam discovered a book that was different from any he had ever known—Alexander Pope's translation of *The Iliad*. Suddenly, this memorable spring, he was formidably drunk with the excitement, conflicts, and legends of Homer's pagan world. He memorized 500 lines, and then 1,000. In time, he said, he was able to recite almost the entire 500 pages; this was a substantial feat, but Sam's memory was prodigious. Eventually, *The Iliad* shaped and colored his oratorical and literary style and inspired him to give a heroic cast to his activities. Pope's translation has little charm for the modern ear, but it startled young Sam into an awareness of a totally different world.

Sam's minimum contribution of labor was the price for his continued presence at the family board. One day, his brothers discovered him lying on the ground at the edge of a cornfield, enthralled by the tales of Ilium. The team of horses that should have been cultivating the fields was nibbling grass nearby. James and John assailed their brother with raillery and reproofs. He got up from the ground, briefly explained his state of mind, turned his back on his tormenters, and quit the scene. Then he went to Maryville and asked the academy principal to teach him Latin and Greek so that he could read the classics in the original. The principal refused on the ground that Sam had not gone far enough in other studies to justify it.

The next day, without confiding in his mother, Sam did not show up for work in the country store. For several weeks no one knew where he was.

When Sam's mother discovered that he had crossed the Tennessee River and was living with the Cherokees, she sent James and John to deliver her appeal for him to come home. The two boys paddled to Hiwassie Island and found Sam under a tree with his Homer. He recorded later that he received them courteously, standing as straight as an Indian with his back against a tree. He told them that he "preferred measuring deer tracks in the forest to tape and calico in a country store." "The wild liberty of the Red men" appealed to him more than the "tyranny of his brothers." Politely, he asked them to excuse him because he was preoccupied with a translation from the Greek and desired to be left alone to "read in peace." His brothers retreated to carry this news to their mother.[3]

Sam's withdrawal from an environment hostile to his needs of the moment was in the Houston family tradition. It had become more or less standard procedure for the Houstons to break away from unproductive situations and try anew in more promising surroundings.

Sam's great-grandfather, John Houston, Gentleman, traced his line back through the minor nobility of Scotland to Scottish archers who led the way for Jeanne d'Arc from Orléans to Reims. This well-to-do, stocky, rugged man from the highlands was an adherent of John Knox and his fight for "God and Liberty." In protest against the religious and political persecution of the times, John, like thousands of his countrymen, sought refuge in Northern Ireland. His roots were deep in his homeland, but in his mid-forties, he abandoned hope of returning to Scotland and turned toward a new frontier where there was a prospect of freedom. In 1730, he landed in the New World with his wife and six children, his mother-in-law, and a keg of gold sovereigns.

John Houston did fairly well in Pennsylvania, but not well enough. He drifted southward to a sunny valley in the Blue Ridge Mountains of Virginia. Seven miles from Lexington, he acquired land, built a modest homestead, added to his acres from time to time, constructed good roads, and built a stone church in which the valley people worshiped long after he was gone. He left his Timber Ridge plantation to his son, Robert, who was Sam's grandfather. Robert built a fine house with a two-story gallery and square white columns. (There had been a fire during John's time, and it is possible that the first homestead was destroyed, although this is not known.) Robert in turn bequeathed Timber Ridge to Samuel, Sam's father. By then the plantation was prosperous and productive, equipped with farm tools and worked by slaves.

Sam's mother had been Elizabeth Paxton, the beautiful, willowy daughter of John Paxton, the richest man in Rockbridge County. She was eighteen when she married Samuel Houston and went to live with him at Timber Ridge. She, too, was Scottish, and her family's wanderings had also brought them from the highlands to Virginia by way of Ireland.

Elizabeth, who was in her late forties when she was living at Baker's Creek, could readily recall the circumstances that had made the traditional Houston desire for change erupt in her husband. Possessing a powerful physique and outstanding courage, Samuel had served as captain and paymaster of a famous command, Morgan's Rifle Brigade. He liked military life to a notable degree; in fact, Sam Jr.'s most specific memory about his father was his passion for the army.

Samuel, as a postwar inspector of militia, was frequently absent from home. He was promoted to brigade inspector, and then to major. These elevations in rank increased both his satisfaction in his military career and his propensity to conduct his plantation as he thought a gentleman should. His nonchalant disregard of economic facts resulted in the plantation's loss of productivity. Slaves and parcels of land were sold off to make ends meet. For a time, Elizabeth's dowry and her substantial inheritance filled the breach.

While Elizabeth was discovering that her handsome husband was an improvident visionary, her family had been increasing steadily. By February, 1793, when she had been married ten years, she had had four sons and was expecting a fifth child, hoping that the absent inspector would be home in time for the event. As it happened, Major Houston came galloping over the Lexington plank road and arrived at his front door with a few days to spare. The new arrival was the fifth son, Sam, born March 2, 1793. Peggy, the nurse, took charge of him; the major departed for another inspection; and Elizabeth returned to her duties as plantation manager. There were to be another son and three more daughters.

More slaves and land were sold. Major Houston, past fifty, conscience-stricken, and in declining health, faced his day of reckoning. He had to find the best possible way to retrieve the family fortunes. His solution to the problem was the same that had brought his grandfather to the New World—he would move. What lay west of the Alleghenies fascinated those who had not done well enough on the eastern slope to satisfy themselves. Samuel planned to sell Timber Ridge and to take his family to East Tennessee where some of his relatives had prospered. He started negotiations for the sale of what remained of the plantation and for the purchase of a 419-acre tract on Baker's Creek. He bought a new wagon with gear for a five-horse team and made a will providing for the partition of the Tennessee land. Then, while absent from home on an inspection trip in 1807, he died.

Elizabeth disposed of non-transportable household goods and completed the sale of Timber Ridge for £1,000. In addition, she had about $3,600, nearly half in notes and bonds. Debt payments consumed a considerable share of her capital, but she considered herself solvent enough for an adventure that was being undertaken by many persons who were even less well off.

2. A Taste of Paradise

ELIZABETH HOUSTON climbed to the seat of the new wagon on a spring morning in 1807 and picked up the reins of her five-horse team. Fourteen-year-old Sam was on the seat beside her. An older wagon drawn by a four-horse team followed close behind them bearing the rest of the children and more household goods in the care of Sam's older brothers.

Three weeks later Elizabeth's little cavalcade entered Knoxville, the log-house capital of Tennessee—but the logs were squared, a sign of prosperity and progress. Fifteen miles beyond, after fording a river and following a rougher trail, the wagon mistress brought her train into Maryville, the seat of Blount County, where houses were built of unsquared logs and had massive shutters to stop arrows and musket balls.

Then the family began the wildest part of their migration. Along an old Indian trace, hazardous with rocks and bogs, streams to ford, and high brush-grown banks, the Houstons found their way to Baker's Creek Valley. They turned from the main stream to follow a branch, reaching their destination at last. Within sight of the Great Smokies lay the land that the late major had selected.

The journey over the mountains and the early days on Baker's Creek must have been in Sam's mind years later when he wrote of his mother, "a heroine . . . gifted with intellectual and moral qualities

8

which elevated her ... [she] shone with purity and benevolence ... yet ... was nerved with a stern fortitude, which never gave way in the midst of the wild scenes that chequered the history of the frontier settler."[1]

While their new house was being built, the migrants from Virginia accepted the hospitality of Elizabeth's in-laws.

The need for peace and quiet to study his Homer seems to have been Sam's main motive for joining the Cherokees, but there were, of course, other motives. He liked new scenery, places, people. The adventurous migration from Virginia encouraged restlessness. A zest for movement and action had been born in him, as well as a vein of moodiness and introspection that made him long for and sometimes seek intervals of solitude in the forest.

Clerking in the family store had not satisfied his yearning for an occupation with "fancy" in it, but worse was in prospect. His father's will recommended that, at the proper age, his boys learn a trade. Sam found this outlook discouraging. There seems to have been some talk of his going to work in a gristmill and learning the miller's trade.

But in other ways Sam differed from most frontier people: he liked the Indians. He had seen plenty of them. In his *Memoir* he recalls that at this time he was curious about differences between red men and whites, about how they lived among themselves at home, about their inner natures and their beliefs in the Great Spirit. One might think that he was minded to make a kind of anthropologist's survey to find out for himself what he had heard much about, what went on with the band of 300 Cherokees who lived on Hiwassie Island under the easygoing rule of a friendly chief, John Jolly. Perhaps all this was afterthought to explain an event that he himself had not too well understood.

There may have been other factors, but they can all be summed up as curiosity and wanderlust, together with some dissatisfaction with the regime of his older brothers. Whatever his reasons, Houston always believed that fate guided him to cross the river and live with the redskins in preparation for his strange destiny.

Chief Jolly's island was fifty miles from Baker's Creek where the turbulent yellow waters of the Hiwassie River merged with the Big

9

Tennessee. The island, which was mostly level, was a couple of miles wide and a mile long; it was a sylvan paradise laced with deer trails, abounding in game, birds, flowers, wild grapes, honey, and nuts. With the *Iliad* in his knapsack, Sam pulled up stakes and threw in his lot with the red men. He would be connected with them in one way or another all the rest of his life.

Jolly's Indian name Oolooteka (He-Puts-the-Drum-Away) correctly reflected his unwarlike disposition. Like the tall white boy, whose quitting his own people to join the red men amused him, Jolly once had been a wanderer. He had made long trips over the mountains from Georgia to see the sights, observing how other people lived—seeking a better location for himself and his followers. In his mid-forties now, six feet tall and handsome, he saw many of his own aspects mirrored in this fine physical specimen of a white boy, and he liked him. In a matter of days they were close friends.

Probably as a whim after learning that Sam's father was dead, Jolly proposed to adopt him as his son. He was pleased when the white boy welcomed the idea. The deed was done, and the youth was accepted by Jolly's followers. Sam was given the tribal name "Colonneh," the Raven, a sacred symbol of good fortune in Cherokee mythology.

A couple of half-white brothers, the Rogers boys, also took a fancy to Sam and he to them. They taught him things he did not know about trapping. He joined in their water sports and in their ball and pole games, which were similar to lacrosse.

Customs on Hiwassie were not strictly according to the tribal regulations observed by the main branches of the Cherokees. Jolly was rather a law unto himself because he had broken with the main tribe in Georgia and was on friendly but not close terms with the branch that his brother Tallontuske had led to new hunting grounds beyond the Mississippi. Having put the drum away, Oolooteka was weary of the contentious leaders of the tribe who clamored for resistance to the white encroachment on their ancestral lands. He resented the decline of his people, but he saw the alternatives they faced: they could resist and die with pain and grief, or accept and live with reasonable comfort on lands that remained. The Five Nations' talk of union and all-out resistance appeared to him as a fanatical kind of patriotism with race suicide as its fruit.

He invited Sam to sit around the council fire with him and the oldsters with whom he talked over the small problems of his Hi-wassie province. A widow with a charming name, Sun-Shines-on-the-Dewdrop, had lost a cow. A search had to be made because Sun-Shines-on-the-Dewdrop and her three children needed milk; there was a possibility the animal had been stolen and secreted and some-body might have to be called to account.

One Indian's rifle had disappeared. The tribe's collective finger pointed to Bobcat, a recent arrival from the Blind Savannah clan; but the real culprit might be none other than Sharp Knife, whose ways with other people's property did not command great respect in any case. Red Fox was assigned as a kind of detective to unravel this mystery.

After the Green Corn Dance in July the women pounded corn into meal in stumps hollowed out by fire. The meal was made into cakes that were cooked in hot ashes. Some corn, stored in homemade reed baskets which every household kept for the purpose, was saved out for parching in the ear.[2]

Almost a year elapsed before Sam returned home. His mother and sisters, distressed by his wild appearance, wove him a new suit of clothes. His brothers slyly remarked that the family was to be con-gratulated on having a black sheep who might someday be a great Indian chief or governor of the state if he didn't die in a madhouse, which was much more likely. Sam must have ignored these jibes. He had acquired some of the poise and aloofness of his foster father.

During Sam's visit home the Maryville militia, under Captain John B. Cusick, held a muster. It was a lively affair, as musters always were, with whiskey on tap and all kinds of antics. After the festivities Sam and Captain Cusick teamed up for a good time. Nobody seemed to mind until they beat the militia drum under the open windows of the courthouse while court was in session and roughed up the sheriff when he undertook to stop them.

Sam and his playmate discovered that even the frontier had stand-ards of behavior which were enforced. A judicial process was issued by the Blount County court charging Sam Houston and Johnnie Cusick with "disorderly, riotously, wantonly . . . annoying the court with the noise of a drum" and "preventing the sheriff . . .

in discharge of his duty ... against the peace and dignity of the State." A stiff fine was imposed, but it was remitted the next year because Sam was back among the Cherokees and there was no one except his highly respected widowed mother to pay it; on her, it would have fallen as a hardship.[3]

No doubt Elizabeth found an opportunity during Sam's brief visit home to raise some pertinent questions: What was he going to do with himself? Where was this living on Hiwassie going to lead? Would he be satisfied to spend the rest of his life among Indians and be a chief like Jolly?

During his second year on Hiwassie, Sam pondered such questions. He visited his mother's home several times during the twelve months to borrow money for the purchase of blankets, provisions, and trinkets for his Indian friends.

The sap was rising in the stalwart youth. In his *Memoir* he tells that he had favorites among the Hiwassie girls. They must have been astonished when, according to him, he enlivened their walks through the forest with recitations from the *Iliad*. When the *Iliad* didn't suffice, they used sign language and a few words to convey meanings that needed no words at all. Later, and wistfully, Houston described this "wandering along the banks of streams by the side of some Indian maiden, sheltered by the deep woods, and conversing in that universal language which finds its sure way to the heart." [4] But how much love was actually involved is another matter. The Cherokees had a high regard for the chastity of their young virgins and Sam could quickly have worn out his welcome, which he never did.

Houston wrote in his *Memoir* (p. 259), that his youth "was wild and impetuous, but it was spotted by no crime, it was not even soiled by indulgence. His early manhood was filled with earnestness and daring, but it was deformed by no act which lost him the confidence of the virtuous and the doating [sic] love of his mother ..."

He became familiar with the sign language that was universal among the tribes. This knowledge was to prove of real value later, when he rode out alone, covering great distances in a country overrun with savages. He acquired the knack of pithy Indian picture-speech. He would use it later, too, for a great deal of writing that differed from his usual style—sometimes for the pleasure he found in the play of his poetic imagination, but more often to influence his red brothers to sign beneficial trade and peace agreements. He described his Hiwassie sojourn in these words:

> It was the moulding period of life, when the heart, just charmed into the fevered hopes and dreams of youth, looks wistfully around on all things for light and beauty—"when every idea of gratification fires the blood and flashes on the fancy—when the heart is vacant to every fresh form of delight, and has no rival engagements to withdraw it from the importunities of a new desire...." [5]

Charles Edwards Lester, who took down Houston's talks on which the *Memoir* is based, remarked, "Houston has seen nearly all in life there is to live for and yet he has been heard to say that when he looks back over the waste ... there's nothing half so sweet to remember as this sojourn he made among the untutored children of the forest." [6]

Elizabeth's talks with her wandering son on his visits home were eventually rewarded. Sam became aware that he wanted to be somebody and to amount to something. The conviction took hold of him, he wrote later, that satisfaction in life depended upon winning "distinction" among one's fellows. The first step was to restore his standing in the Baker's Creek community by paying his debts. The manner he chose for doing so was characteristic of his frequently displayed ability to meet difficult situations with novel solutions.

He would become an educator, he would open an academy. This idea from a youth whose formal schooling encompassed about six months in Virginia and not more than that in Maryville was sufficiently startling. But he had certain assets to offer, among them his taste for good literature and his knowledge of tracking and fishing acquired on Hiwassie.

He had a printer in Knoxville set up a broadside in impressive black type. S. Houston would open an academy in the log house on John McCullough's farm five miles east of Maryville near the oak that sheltered a fine spring of drinking water. He promised the usual attention to the three R's and deportment and implied his ability to impart special skills. Because of the high quality of the instruction it would be necessary to charge slightly more than prevailing rates.

His charge would be eight dollars for the term, one-third in cash, one-third in corn at 33⅓ cents a bushel and one-third in calico in varied colors—colors suitable, no doubt, for the pedagogue's shirts and for presents to his Hiwassie friends.[7]

Pupils came, slowly at first, then more than he could manage. Besides discipline in the essential R's, he specialized in extracurricular recitations from Homer and Cherokee myths, such as the one about the Great Buzzard that went out after the Flood to seek land and swept so low that its huge wings scooped out the beautiful hills and valleys of the ancestral Cherokee lands.

Sam's academy had long shutters that dropped down inside to admit light. They also served as desks. When cold weather made it impracticable to put them to both uses, the academy was obliged to shut down.

The school was a serious enterprise and indicates one direction in which the twig might have been bent. When he was a United States senator from Texas and had received many other honors, Sam confided in his friend, David Burke:

> When a young man in Tennessee, I kept a country school, being then . . . a tall, strapping fellow. At noon after the luncheon, which I and my pupils ate together out of our baskets, I would go out into the woods and cut me a "sourwood" stick, trim it carefully in circular spirals, and thrust one-half of it in the fire, which would turn it blue, leaving the other half white. With this emblem of ornament and authority in my hand, dressed in a hunting shirt of flowered calico, a long queue down my back, I experienced a higher feeling of dignity and self-satisfaction than from any office or honor which I have since held.[8]

For a while Sam thought that teaching might be his forte and went back to the Maryville Academy to prepare himself, but its masters gave him more Euclid than he could stomach. Mathematics in the abstract was not meant for his type of mind.

President Madison's call to the West to take up arms against the British finally filtered through to Baker's Creek. The war that Jefferson had hoped to avoid and that Jackson had prayed for promised to become reality. In March, 1813, Sam Houston, age twenty, took a walk in Maryville with Willoughby Williams, a friend who was his junior by five years. They watched as a U.S. Army recruiting party with music, a banner, and some well-dressed sergeants wearing white belts crossed over their chests, set up their flag at the four corners.

Fifes tootled and drums rolled. Sam stepped forward and picked up a silver dollar—the token of his enlistment—from a drumhead. As far as he was concerned, he was in the army, but he took home a paper for his mother to sign, because he had not yet reached his majority. His brothers lashed out at him for disgracing the family; they insisted that their father's record in the Revolution entitled Sam to a commission. His calm indifference, broadly hinting at lofty superiority to base calculations, infuriated them. Friends cut his acquaintance, said he was ruined by joining the army as a common soldier. To friends and brothers he made the same answer, his first recorded speech:

And what have your craven souls to say about *the ranks?* I would much sooner honor the ranks than disgrace an appointment. You don't know me now, but you shall hear of me.[9]

3. *Reveille—and After*

WHEN Sam enlisted in the United States Army he was saying goodbye to the irresponsibilities and fancies of Hiwassie as well as any hope of a scholastic career. He accomplished the transition from his fantasy world to the stern activities of army life not only without a jolt but with pride and satisfaction. He was assigned for training to the Seventh U.S. Infantry, and in a matter of weeks was promoted to sergeant. When the Seventh Infantry was consolidated into the U.S. Thirty-ninth Infantry soon afterwards, he was offered an appointment as ensign in the new regiment. Accepting, he was commissioned on July 29, 1813, only four months after enlistment. Five months later he was raised to third lieutenant.[1] The reasons for his rapid advancement are clear from the report made by a qualified observer some twenty-odd years later, when the whole world sud-

15

denly became interested in Sam Houston's military character. Said Thomas Hart Benton from the floor of the U.S. Senate:

> I was the Lieutenant Colonel of the regiment to which he belonged, and the first field officer to whom he reported. I then marked in him soldierly and gentlemanly qualities . . . frank, generous, brave; ready to do, or to suffer, whatever the obligation of civil or military duty imposed; and always prompt to answer the call of honor, patriotism and friendship.[2]

Houston's rather remarkable adjustment was one of the ways in which the Homer-Pope narrative of the tremendous clash of arms on Scamander plain shaped his life, leading him to think that he must cast his life in heroic mold. This influence had already affected the way he wrote and spoke; it would become more pronounced as he realized the usefulness of a definite style in living as well as in speaking and writing.

Courage on a Homeric scale characterized Houston throughout his life. His gallant conduct in his first campaign became a legend and inspired a lifelong friendship between him and Andrew Jackson. In his youth, Jackson had met challenging circumstances with the same high-spirited response. Like Chief Jolly, Jackson could see something of himself in the Houston boy.

Creek braves led by the half-breed, Bill Weatherford, had killed about four hundred men, women, and children with savage brutality at Fort Mims on the Alabama River, August 30, 1813. When news of the atrocity reached Nashville in the early autumn, Andrew Jackson was in bed, weak from loss of blood from wounds inflicted by two enemies in a recent street battle. The Fort Mims horror, inspired, he was sure, by his traditional British enemy, accomplished the equivalent of a resurrection. Haggard, his arm in a sling, he scrambled into the saddle and took the field on October 7.

With a force of callow militiamen and volunteers, Jackson built Fort Strother on the Coosa River in Alabama, from which he sallied forth to win two notable skirmishes. Twice, while based at Fort Strother, he saw his unruly troops in pell-mell retreat before Weatherford's warriors. Jackson asked for a stiffening group of regulars, and the Thirty-ninth Infantry reached Fort Strother on February 13, 1814, with Third Lieutenant Houston at the head of a platoon.

This was Houston's initial contact with the border chieftain. A strapping fellow, he lacked eighteen days of being twenty-one; Jackson was forty-six, tall and bony, with a bristle of yellowish hair. Under Jackson, Houston got his first experience in war.

Jackson was supposed to be a rough backwoods soldier who knew little or nothing of tactics and strategy. But his library contained dog-eared English books on military strategy and translations of French works on the subject; he had explored these same matters with friends who had learned about them in the Revolution under Washington, Greene, and Morgan.

Under Jackson, in this pursuit of Weatherford, Houston learned much about handling men in the field. He saw officers and soldiers put under arrest for drunkenness, the strict attention to the condition of arms, and the control of untrained troops by the example of disciplined regulars.

Weatherford retreated southeast to the Tallapoosa River near its junction with the Coosa. A deep bend in the Tallapoosa known as the Horseshoe inclosed 100 acres covered with small timber and brush. Across the narrow neck of the bend, the Creeks had built log breastworks. On the afternoon of March 26, 1814, Jackson's force of about 3,000 men was in the vicinity of this impromptu fort. Jackson surrounded it and gave the Creeks time to get their women and children off the battlefield. At 12:30 the next afternoon, drummers beat the long roll. The Thirty-ninth Infantry advanced and was first to reach the ramparts. Almost immediately Major Lemuel P. Montgomery fell dead. Houston, just behind him, stepped forward, waved his sword, and called to his platoon to follow.

Arrows, spears, and musket balls were flying thickly. Swords and tomahawks flashed and the yells of savages mingled with the groans of the wounded. Three thousand Indian warriors had been inspired by their prophets to believe that victory would come easily and that their enemies would be swept away. The signal of final victory would come with a cloud from heaven. The cloud did come and it brought rain—but not victory.

Houston vaulted the barricade. His platoon dropped down beside him where, bloodied, he was fighting off a ring of Indians with his sword. An arrow buried itself deep in his thigh. It might have felled a smaller man, but he kept on his feet and led his men on until the enemy abandoned the barricade. Then, failing to remove the barbed arrow himself, he called for aid from a lieutenant who was fighting nearby. The lieutenant, fearful of making the wound worse, did not pull hard enough to draw the arrow out. He told Houston he should find a surgeon.

"Try again," Houston ordered, furious with pain, "and this time, Lieutenant, out with it or by God I'll knock you flat."

The arrow came out, and, with blood gushing down his leg, Houston climbed back over the breastwork and located a surgeon who bound up the thigh and stopped the flow. General Jackson, passing by, recognized the stalwart ensign and told him to stay out of the fight for the rest of the day. Houston had reason to believe that he had acquitted himself reasonably well in the Homeric tradition, but still he was not satisfied.

Creek resistance ended toward night except for sporadic firing from a redoubt, with breastworks and a log roof, in a remote ravine. Gunfire blazed and arrows whistled from the loopholes. Jackson called for volunteers to put this fortification out of action.

No captain reached for this chance for glory, but Houston, still lying on the ground, heard the call. He said later that except for his boast to his brothers about being heard from before he got back, he would not have disobeyed Jackson's order.

Clambering to his feet, he snatched a musket from a man of his own platoon and called all who dared to follow him. A few soldiers trailed behind, down the precipitous side of the ravine. Five yards from a loophole, he felt the shock of two rifle balls in the right arm and shoulder. His arm fell to his side.

Disabled, he called to his men to charge, but they did not respond. Houston remained there, bleeding profusely, on the chance that his presence would inspire the others. When he found himself alone, he painfully worked his way up the rocky slope of the ravine and near the top, out of range, he sank to the ground, unconscious.

The log strongpoint was finally set on fire, and the Indians were forced to abandon it. By the light of a brush fire, a surgeon removed one musket ball from Houston's arm near the shoulder. A second surgeon said it was useless to torture him by trying to remove the other bullet because, after losing so much blood, he could not live until morning. Houston, passing in and out of semi-consciousness, must have heard.

In his account of the battle,[3] he says that he lay there on the wet

18

ground all night, uncovered, alone, without attendance, because he was regarded as one already dead. Through the hours of that ghastly night, racked with pain, he thought of himself as one deserted in his dying hour. But in the morning a spark of life still remained. He was transported sixty miles by litter to Fort Williams and, when the army moved on, he was left behind as a hopeless case. Volunteer Tennessee troops, who had been released to go home, looked after him in their little field hospital. When they were ready to leave, they placed Houston in a crude litter between two horses, and in this fashion—with an agonizing crunch in his shoulder and tortured by the fever of blood poisoning—he was carried through the forest of northern Alabama and halfway across Tennessee.

He cursed his rescuers when the continuous jolting and the pain of his wounds became intolerable and he pleaded to be put down to die where he was. They subdued his howling pain with doses of whiskey. Part of the time, he was mercifully unconscious, but the Tennessee boys did not abandon him. The spark of life continued to flicker.

Two months after the battle, weak and gaunt, assisted by two companions, he walked up the path to his mother's door. His appearance shocked her. She was speechless, not believing at first that the man before her could be her son. Then, she recognized him "by his eyes."

"Don't you know me Ma?" he asked, barely able to speak the words.

Houston ends his own story of Horseshoe Bend with the observation that his conduct that day won him the lasting regard of General Jackson, "who thirty years after ... [with undimmed cheerfulness] sent for General Houston to hurry to his bedside to see him die."

His action at Horseshoe Bend led to Houston's promotion to second lieutenant, May 20, 1814. A convalescent on leave, he went to Washington, D.C., for recuperation and medical care. He reached there in time to observe with solemn reflection the scarcely cooled ashes of the capital, burned in August by the British. His journey in the saddle set him back, and the medical treatment he received did not help. He rode to the home of relatives in the Virginia valley beyond the Blue Ridge and stayed there, gaining strength for his return to Tennessee. One of the old family friends he visited near

Lexington was Captain Alexander Campbell, whose home was near the old Timber Ridge plantation.

In March 1815, back in Tennessee, a couple of months after Jackson's victory at New Orleans, Houston foresaw that the war's end was likely to bring about a cut in armed forces. He applied for a commission as first lieutenant on the ground of meritorious service, but was not hopeful about getting it. On April 25 he wrote to his Virginia friend, Captain Campbell, that he intended to live in Knoxville and look for some "course of livelihood which will not be laborious as my wounds are not near well." He was concerned lest his semi-invalid condition prevent him from someday taking a wife.

> I suppose it will be impracticable for a disbanded officer to marry, for [he] will be regarded as cloathes out of fashion... but I will not despond before I am disappointed, and I suppose that will be some time hence for I will not court any of the Dear Girles before I make a fortune....[4]

A Knoxville army doctor, in charge of the patient, believed that Houston stood a good chance of losing the use of his arm and shoulder unless the second musket ball could be located. In May Houston was transferred to the U.S. First Infantry garrisoned at New Orleans, probably to afford him an opportunity for special medical care. There, an army surgeon located the unretrieved bullet. The young lieutenant drank a swig of whiskey and braced himself with the back of a chair while the surgeon probed and dug. The musket ball was removed, but the ordeal and the attendant copious bleeding sapped what little strength Houston had regained. He spent most of the winter recuperating in a French-built barracks by the river, reading the books that he had brought with him: the Bible his mother had given him, Shakespeare, Akenside's *Poems, Robinson Crusoe, Pilgrim's Progress,* and *The Vicar of Wakefield.* When not confined to the barracks, he took in the colorful life of the city.

But Houston's health still did not command a satisfactory army rating and, in the spring, he was ordered to sail to New York for more treatment. After some weeks he was given a furlough to go home on a visit to his family.

On January 1, 1817, he received orders to report for duty at Nashville under the adjutant general of the Southern Division. Three months later his promotion to first lieutenant came through.

He was required to perform only such light clerical tasks as filling out certificates for the receipt of military supplies. With Andrew Jackson, who was commander of the Southern Division, he had opportunities for reminiscences of Horseshoe Bend, and he learned Jackson's view of what had happened at New Orleans. A more urgent matter they discussed was the prospect of trouble with the Cherokees.

Soon Houston was asked to take on a more important service. In 1816, certain minor Cherokee chieftains had betrayed their tribe by indorsing a treaty; without authority they had signed away thousands of acres of choice lands bordering East Tennessee. When the United States started to take over these lands and, under the unauthorized treaty, to remove the Cherokees to Arkansas Territory, the Indians charged fraud and threatened armed resistance.

General Jackson had other business on hand. He was expecting to be occupied with the Spaniards in Florida and with pacifying the Seminoles in that region. At a time when pacification of the Cherokees might have been a costly diversion, Jackson heard from the trustworthy Indian agent, Return J. Meigs, that Lieutenant Houston was the only man who could prevent a Cherokee outbreak. At Jackson's request, through Tennessee Governor Joseph McMinn, the Washington authorities appointed Houston subagent to the Cherokees on October 28, 1817.

Houston, who believed the Indians had been defrauded, was averse to this new assignment, but soon learned that the government intended to enforce the treaty. After a struggle with his conscience, he decided that the worse of two evils would befall the Cherokees if they resisted instead of accepting the removal peaceably. He put on Indian clothes and joined Jolly's people. He talked earnestly to the young Cherokee braves, trying to convince them that going to Arkansas Territory was the lesser of the evils that confronted them. Chief Jolly invited him to sit with the tribal councilors around their fire.

One of Chief Jolly's objections to leading his followers west of the Mississippi was based on tradition and mythology prevailing among the Cherokees. To his tribe, the West was the abode of Black Evil, death, and misery; the East was the Sun Land, the true home of their gods.

Lieutenant Houston did not conceal his sadness over the business that brought him, but it could not be denied that the tribe's representatives had agreed to the treacherous treaty. He assured his foster father that the whites would treat it as a solemn pledge. He employed the same reasoning that had persuaded him to accept the mission; in substance: If the Five Nations were united and the Cherokees had allies they could put up strong resistance. But there was no chance of this. Without allies they were weak. They had to decide whether to abide by the treaty as if it were sacred; or whether to defy it, remain where they were, and face unceasing war. Under these circumstances how many of his people did Jolly think would survive?

Chief Jolly, quick to grasp the point, addressed his adopted son affectionately. As Jolly put it, Houston had always walked straight with the Cherokees. He was a white man who had learned to think red. Red men had tried, but could never learn to think white.

The Cherokees decided it was wise to accept the new lands of doubtful value in Arkansas Territory and to go without resistance. Chief Jolly's band was the first to prepare for departure. It included 109 braves armed with good new rifles furnished by the government. Well-provisioned flatboats added to the display. But other bands hesitated, and Jolly changed his mind and did not leave immediately.

4. A New Profession

CHIEF Jolly and his people still lingered near the Tennessee River in December, 1817, when Jolly's aged brother, Tallontuske, a virtual king among his people, passed through Knoxville with a delegation of his followers. Tallontuske had long ago broken away from the central Cherokee government and had set up his own branch of the tribe west of the Mississippi. Now he was going to Washington to ask the United States government to recognize his independence.

Governor McMinn, fearing that Tallontuske's dissatisfactions might lead to an outbreak, gave the old fellow kindly assurances, notified Washington of what was coming, and asked Lieutenant

Houston to put on his Indian habit and accompany the delegates. McMinn wrote Secretary of War Calhoun that Tallontuske's band would be accompanied by "Lieutenant Houston by whose vigilance and address they will be most profited." [1]

Secretary Calhoun received the delegation on February 5, 1818, welcoming them with his flawless South Carolina courtesy. Little thinking that this man someday would be his stout antagonist, with the life of the federal union at stake, Lieutenant Houston observed him closely: tall, slender, emaciated, with his grayish thick hair combed straight back from his low, steep forehead. In a dry, metallic voice, Calhoun assured Tallontuske that his people would receive every fair consideration from the Great White Father, President Monroe.

They were filing out when Calhoun detained Houston and demanded to know why the lieutenant had appeared before him in outlandish Indian costume. Houston, who thought he merited praise, was taken aback and explained that it was a matter of tact to maintain prestige with the delegation. True, he was a United States Army lieutenant, but he was also a United States Indian subagent, wearing the costume best suited to his duties.

Calhoun followed up his galling reprimand by demanding an explanation of charges against the lieutenant of complicity with slave smugglers. In retaliation for moves Houston had made against slave-running while he was among the Cherokees, the promoters of the traffic, through congressmen, had accused Houston of being a smuggler himself, guilty of dishonesty and various abuses of power. Houston's straightforward story impressed Calhoun and, at Houston's request, he ordered an investigation. Houston obtained permission from President Monroe to submit his case in person to the executive. He was exonerated.

Nonetheless, he received no apology, no thanks, no regrets, no sympathy, and no appreciation from anybody. This set the young lieutenant thinking. Was he wasting time trying to get ahead in the army? He was not the first nor was he to be the last man to ask this question of himself.

Houston now reviewed a few of the incidents that had discouraged him. Payment of $170.09, due him for expenses as subagent, had been delayed; his account-rendered was being questioned. He needed the money, for he had spent all his resources during the past two or three years trying to regain his health. The claim was not settled until five years after he left the army, at which time it was paid in full.

Houston's lack of progress made him dissatisfied, and he was unhappy over this latest episode. Straws in the wind suggested that a change of vocation was desirable for an ambitious man determined to get somewhere.

It was a solemn business, this necessity of giving up a career in which he had invested health, blood, patience, and five years of effort. But from where he sat, it seemed inevitable. In his Washington lodgings, a few days after his exoneration on charges of slave-running, he wrote a letter to the War Office, March 1, 1818: "You will please accept this as my resignation to take effect from this date," and signed it "Sam Houston 1st Lieut. 1st Infy." [2]

He added a pathetic postscript: "I will thank you to give me my commission, which I am entitled to by my last promotion." The promotion had been granted in May, 1817, ten months before, but he had never received the commission. Months after his resignation, the document arrived, and he preserved it as a souvenir.

Before Sam left Washington he bought a hat and a few other articles of civilian clothing. Then he mounted his horse and rode with Tallontuske and the rest of the Cherokee delegation to Hiwassie in Tennessee. The last of his friends on the island were getting ready to leave for Arkansas Territory. Probably he was too late to say farewell to his foster father or he would have mentioned it in his *Memoir*.

He stopped at Maryville to see his mother, then rode on. The farther he rode the more thoughtful he became. When he reached Nashville he still was thinking about this new problem: What vocation might furnish a sufficient livelihood for him to marry, and a fair chance to win some kind of distinction?

Three months past his twenty-fifth birthday, former Lieutenant Houston stood on the steps of Nashville's new brick courthouse in the hot June sunshine. Directly opposite, there was another recently completed brick building. Log houses were coming down. Already there were a market, three taverns, a post office, and a hardware store. The sidewalks were graveled and curbed with brick.

It was different here ... no New Orleans river smell, no mud, rot, and sweat; no stout-backed Negresses devoting themselves to hairdressing; no silken-clad fancy ladies with complicated coiffures and enticingly displayed bosoms; no threadbare, wistful-eyed French generals lingering over coffee in cafes as they dreamed of Napoleon's plight on the island of St. Helena three years after Waterloo.

In Nashville, a clear air blew down from the mountains. It made Houston's broadcloth tolerable and it appealed to his fastidiousness. He held his new beaver hat in his hand. Yes, this raw, crude frontier outpost with its wharves and warehouses and new steamboat landing had bustle, hustle, and drive. No doubt about its vitality; someday it would be the thriving Philadelphia of the South. If he settled in Nashville, the lively spirit of progress would surely carry an ambitious young man along with it.

Displeased with his futile army experience and not yet happy about his recently acquired civilian status, the ex-lieutenant sauntered across the square and turned into Borough Street. After walking a dozen blocks, he called on Judge James Trimble, a distant kinsman, whose office was in his home. Judge Trimble had a moist, rheumy eye and inflamed patch of broken veins on his right cheek.

Houston came directly to the point. He had determined to practice law and he needed a sponsor and mentor who was, in those days, almost the only key to the bar. In no time, he had pleaded his first case and won it.

Trimble put him through the classics of that day, *Blackstone's Commentaries* and *Coke on Littleton*, and impressed upon him the importance of that great document which laid down the guidelines for the future, the United States Constitution. The law, as practiced on the frontier, was not then a highly technical profession. Even Patrick Henry, one of the greatest of pleaders, knew only his *Coke* when he started.

Trimble was astonished at his pupil's progress. The same power of memory that had made committing most of the *Iliad* a delight came to Sam's aid now. It was easy for him to remember the details of cases, but his intellectual grasp and quick comprehension of basic principles was even more important. The principles once grasped became tools never lost, always stored in that vigorous memory ready for use. In six months instead of the usual eighteen, Trimble concluded that his pupil was ready. He recommended that Sam take

25

the bar examination and was pleased when the fledgling lawyer passed easily, earning the compliments of his examiners.

Houston accomplished his transition from the army to law as smoothly as he had made his earlier change from Hiwassie to the army. His forebodings about the switch in his professional activities faded, but he did not know where he would find the money to keep going until fees came in.

5. *Congressman from Tennessee*

Houston's personal magnetism had attracted persons as widely dissimilar as Chief Jolly and Andrew Jackson. Isaac Golladay, the Lebanon, Tennessee, postmaster, also responded to it. His acquaintance with Houston had hardly begun when he gave proof of his confidence in the young lawyer who had newly come to town. He rented him an office for a dollar a month and lent him the money to pay for it, to buy clothes, to meet the expense of setting up to practice law. Then Golladay went his security with the local tavern keeper for bed and board until fees came in.

Golladay did all this even though he had not so much as a letter of introduction to vouch for Houston's integrity. Whatever Golladay's motives may have been his generosity turned out to be bread upon the waters. Years later in a small town in Texas, Houston, then a United States senator, learned that a stranger who lay in a hotel room critically ill with fever, unbefriended and unattended, was the only son of his "good and true friend," the one-time postmaster of Lebanon. For a time he regularly visited the hotel room to nurse the sick man, feed him, supply the medicines ordered by the doctor, and —over the patient's protest—give the prescribed hot footbaths. Then he took his old friend's son into his home and cared for him until he was well.

Within two years after his start in Lebanon, Houston was elected prosecuting attorney of Davidson County (Nashville) district. The whole town gathered to see him off when he left for Nashville, demonstrating the spontaneity with which people became attached

26

to him. The farewell speeches were flowery and so was Houston's response: "I was naked and ye clothed me, I was hungry and ye fed me; I was athirst, and ye gave me drink...." [1]

With his return to Nashville, Houston was definitely on his way as a rising young lawyer. He performed creditably as prosecutor. Governor Joseph McMinn appointed him colonel and adjutant general of militia, providing him with the prestige of a title. Field officers of the Southern Division bettered this by electing him major general in 1821.

Houston frequently turned in at The Hermitage driveway nine miles east of Nashville, where his old commander's plantation reflected increasing prosperity. The driveway circled an expanse of lawn shaded by large trees, and there were flower beds. The brick and frame house was fronted by a wide two-story piazza supported by small round columns; inside there was a wide central hall with a fine chandelier and a graceful stairway. The place hummed with activity, the goings and comings of relatives and innumerable guests.

Whenever Houston found that the general was unavailable, he enjoyed a homey chat with the general's wife. Soon he called her "Aunt Rachel" and to her he was one of her "boys." Jackson and Aunt Rachel were fond of young people. They were educating a dozen nieces and nephews and others not related, among them the Indian, Lincoyer, a member of a race that the general hated almost as much as he did the British.

Houston's warm, resonant voice and the cadence of his oratory swayed audiences and moved juries. He could talk for hours without notes on any subject about which he was informed. Colorful, impromptu allusions, quotations, and anecdotes swept his hearers with gales of laughter, sometimes intermingled with tears. He had a comic bent and a gift for mimicry. He was active in amateur theatricals and masquerade balls.

Socially disposed, he met often with convivial friends in a corner of the Nashville tavern, and there was no doubt that he drank too much. This activity began to consume entirely too much of his time. Perhaps his growing reputation as a drinker prompted him to reassure potential clients by inserting, in an advertisement for his new law office, the claim that he would be "found there at all times when he should be."

27

Friends once made stayed with him. Indians, wherever they saw him, dropped what they were doing and rushed to embrace him. The half-white Rogers brothers, friends from Hiwassie days and now in Arkansas Territory, traveled hundreds of miles to visit him. His army friends sought him out. He freely reciprocated these friendships. To Governor McMinn, on March 30, 1823, he wrote:

> I never quit a friend until I see a disinclination on his part to be friendly with me. I dearly love my friends because they have been everything to me. I part with them as a Miser does his treasure with anguish and regret.[2]

In 1823, when Houston was thirty, the Ninth Tennessee District elected him to Congress without opposition. Several candidates considered entering the field against him, but withdrew not only because of his popularity but because of his father-son relationship with two politically powerful men which made him invincible. His strongest relationship of this kind was with Jackson, but Governor McMinn had also "adopted" him. Together with Chief Jolly, Houston now had a trinity of spiritual fathers. In a letter to McMinn he referred to himself as one of the governor's two political sons. The other was Daniel Graham, one of those who dropped out of the race for Congress.

Houston could look with satisfaction, almost with awe, at his progress in the five years since he had stood hesitantly on the steps of the Nashville courthouse appraising his future in a new and untried profession.

> I am satisfied there must be a conducting Providence! ... when I advert to my past life and behold the change which has taken place with myself. Five years since I came to this place, without education more than ordinary—without friends—without cash—and almost without acquaintances—consequently without credit. And here among talents and distinction I have made my stand! or the people have made it for me.[3]

Early in 1818 Old Hickory had swept into Florida, then Spanish territory, severely punishing Seminole marauders, hanging two British subjects and seizing Spanish towns. Cabinet and Congress knew nothing of the implicit Presidential instructions under which he acted; they assailed him and threatened him with court-martial,

28

but his forthright action brought roars of approval from the people.
The year before Houston's election to Congress, the Tennessee
Senate had proposed Jackson for the Presidency. Houston eagerly
supported him, writing from Murfreesboro, August 3, 1822:

> You are now before the eyes of the nation. You have noth-
> ing to fear, but everything to expect. The hopes of men in
> Washington will be *frost biten* by the bare mention of your
> name! ... They will strike like the wounded viper.... rather
> than see Integrity ... triumph ... you have been your coun-
> try's Centinel ... when her watchman had been caught slum-
> bering on post ... her Capital reduced to ashes ... you have
> been her faithful guardian ... will not the nation look to you
> again? [4]

This kind of devotion was fully reciprocated. When Houston
went to Washington in 1823 he carried in his saddlebag a prized
letter from the Old Chief to Thomas Jefferson:

> This will be handed to you by General Sam Houston, a
> representative to Congress from this State, and a particular
> friend of mine, to whom I beg leave to introduce you. I have
> known General Houston many years, and, entertaining for him
> the highest feelings of regard and confidence, recommend him
> to you with great safety. He has attained his present standing
> without the intrinsic advantages of fortune or education, and
> has sustained, in his various promotions from the common
> soldier to the Major-General, the character of a high-minded
> and honorable man. As such I present him to you, and shall
> regard the civilities which you may render him as a great
> favor.... [5]

Three giants—Henry Clay, Daniel Webster, and the romantic
John Randolph—dominated the House of Representatives. Houston
modified some of his own histrionic notions as he observed these
more experienced performers. Eager to learn, he absorbed the debates in the House as though they had been assignments from his pre-
ceptor in law, Judge Trimble. A natural and forceful orator with
self-discipline and inspiration, he made some notable speeches but
held in reserve the power that would spotlight him.
For the time being he was content to be the eager student of repre-

sentative government and its principles and procedures, subordinating his own driving ambition to the interests of his constituents and to the support of Jackson. But his part in the work of the House disclosed a remarkable aptitude for industry. He marshaled facts on many complicated subjects. He worked tirelessly on speeches ranging in length from twenty minutes to several hours to make certain they clearly expressed his stand on a wide variety of issues. He displayed the power to draw convincing conclusions from his evidence, although his presentations were often less than concise.

In the Presidential campaign of 1824, Jackson won 99 electoral votes; John Quincy Adams, 84; William H. Crawford, 41; and Henry Clay, 37. Although Jackson received a plurality of votes, he lacked a majority, and the task of choosing a President went to the House of Representatives.

Houston undertook a delicate mission for his friend. In a talk with Congressman Sloane of Ohio, an intimate of Clay, he put forward the proposition: "What a splendid administration it would make with Old Hickory as President and Mr. Clay as Secretary of State." [6]

It appears that the supporters of John Quincy Adams had not overlooked the same possibility. Adams was elected and Clay became his Secretary of State. The Jackson forces emitted the conventional cries of "Foul!" and "Corruption!" and turned their minds to the election of 1828.

Houston was not so busy that he lacked time for a few flirtations and at least one reasonably serious courtship. He was definitely thinking of marriage, despite his earlier promise that he would not marry until he had made his fortune. On January 22, 1825, when he was thirty-two, he wrote a letter of condolence to his friend, A. M. Hughes, who had been "unsuccessful in love affairs." For a quick and beneficial recovery he recommended "taking a new chase!" For himself he said:

> ... I do not know yet the sweets of matrimony, but in March or April, next I will; unless something should take place not to be expected or wished for! To have been married on my way here would not have answered a good purpose. My errand here is to attend to the business of my constituents, and not to attend "honey moons." *Everything in due season!* [7]

Something unexpected must have turned up. Houston did not know the sweets of matrimony by spring. There is one report that his prospective bride turned out to be too fat.

The wind shifted. A year later Houston wrote to a Quaker friend, Major William J. Worth, "I am making myself less frequent in the Lady World than I have been. I must keep my Dignity, or rather I must attend more to politics and less to love." [8]

That was all there was to love-making for the time being. The Old Chief, back in Nashville after retiring as junior senator from Tennessee, showed a disposition to keep his disciple busy. He liked to have Houston do his errands because he got prompt results. One of his requests was that Houston return to Nashville by way of John Randolph's place in Virginia and bring him a filly. He was also to find a free Negro for good wages to look after the stud colts that the general had turned over to the care of a nephew. Houston gladly accepted all these requests as signs of fatherly affection.

Sometimes the assignments were more exacting. In 1826 Jackson heard that John P. Erwin, editor of the Nashville *Banner and Whig,* was to be appointed postmaster at Nashville as the candidate of Mr. Clay of Kentucky. Jackson had his own candidate and Erwin must be stopped. He wrote Houston, with martial brevity, "Attend to this business."

In a letter to President Adams and on the floor of the House, Houston declared that Erwin did not have the moral character necessary for the job. Invited to retract, he declined. A friend of Erwin, General William White, interfered in the quarrel with some remarks about Jackson that Houston thought called for stern measures. He sent a friend to wait on White, a challenge that White later conceded was forced by himself.

Keenly anxious about the pending duel, Jackson was helpful with suggestions while Houston engaged in pistol practice in a meadow at The Hermitage. His final instruction to Houston was to keep a bullet between his teeth to bite on at the moment of firing. He would find that the bite steadied his aim, the Old Chief assured him.

Sobered, anticipating his own death, Houston prepared a letter to be published in case he was killed. "My firm and undeviating attachment to Genl Jackson," he wrote, "has caused me all the enemies I have, and I glory in the firmness of my attachment. . . . I will die

31

proud in the assurance that I deserve, and possess his perfect confidence." [9]

The duelers met at sunrise in a pasture on the Kentucky side of
the state line. White missed his target. Houston bit on the bullet,
shot straight, and hit White in the groin. Kneeling beside the
wounded man, Houston expressed his sorrow about the injury he
had inflicted. The duel, he reminded White, had been forced on him.
White acknowledged this and, believing that he was dying, forgave
Houston.

Houston was opposed to dueling and believed the whole business
of the code was absurd. He was greatly relieved when White recovered. At a political rally, when references to the duel were applauded, he rose and objected. He could not permit himself to be
honored as a duelist. This, he went on, was an unnatural method of
settling a quarrel, and "I thank God my opponent was injured no
worse." [10]

One misconception about Houston has been that in his convictions
and principles he was only a shadow of his Chief. Houston loved and
venerated Jackson as he did no other man, but in some basic principles they stood at opposite poles. Jackson, for example, was against
expansion of the national territory, favoring concentration; Houston became the exponent of an entirely different point of view. He
frequently stood with Jackson when he thought Jackson was right,
but he never hesitated to oppose him when he thought the Chief
was wrong.

During Houston's second term in Congress, the Old Chief, in a
violent mood, went to the brink of another duel, although he still
carried a bullet in his body from an earlier one. The idea that Jackson, again before the country as a Presidential candidate, should resort to the field of honor to settle a quarrel which could easily be
avoided gave Houston some monstrously uncomfortable hours.

Jackson had heard of some unpleasant strictures passed on his
conduct of the Battle of New Orleans by Secretary of the Navy
William Southard. Airing his views in a private circle, Southard
didn't know what dangerous ground he was treading. Jackson addressed a furious letter to the Navy Secretary, and sent it to Houston with peremptory instructions for immediate delivery. Houston

perceived that the letter's tone would surely provoke a challenge¹ unless Southard took the unlikely course of repudiating himself.

The shot that Houston had landed in White's groin was all the experience he wanted with the code. He could not tolerate the prospect of a Presidential candidate risking his life in such a meeting at such a time, and of the public criticism that was sure to follow, whatever the result. Bringing the general to his senses was a task for which he felt qualified, if anybody was. He conferred with other friends and supporters of the general, putting off his reply to Jackson until the Old Chief had time to cool his temper. Then he reported to Nashville that all the general's friends in Washington were in agreement on the issue.

"It is now a desirable matter with all your friends," he wrote to Jackson, "to keep you out of collision . . . I wou'd not suffer your character, as a man, and Patriot to rest under imputations of dishonor!" He would, of course, carry out whatever instructions the general saw fit to give. But the general's authorization for Houston, as his friend, to discuss the matter temperately with Mr. Southard would be better than a letter. In any event, he urged, there should be no thundering ultimatum. "If you shou'd write directly thro me to Mr. Southard, I pray you, to let it be in the mildest, calmest tone of expression—[Southard's] conduct and statement, will most effectually damn him." ¹¹

Houston's calculated delay worked as he had hoped it would. The general's resentment toward Southard alternately subsided and boiled. But in one of his bland moods he wrote an open letter so mild that he was ashamed of it afterward. Houston delivered the letter to Southard, who goggled at it, asked what in the world it was all about, and said the equivalent of Gosh no, he'd never meant to say anything that would reflect on General Jackson's military conduct, of course not.

The affair blew over for the time being and word went around that Houston could handle the old boy. It might have been foreseen that a junior who could calm Jackson when his military conduct was under question would easily distinguish himself where tactful diplomacy was needed. The day would come when he would again achieve some of his finest results in this field and, in a national crisis, would need to use his ability to handle the peppery old gentleman of Nashville.

6. *"I Pray God Grant You a Happy Marriage"*

JACKSON's candidacy for the Presidency made it desirable for him to have a friend at the helm in Tennessee. Governor Billy Carroll, who had been Jackson's second in command at New Orleans, was just completing three successive terms, the limit permitted by the state constitution. Carroll, a wealthy steamboat magnate and cotton shipper, had one great political passion: the governorship of Tennesseee. Publicly he had stated that he would rather be governor of Tennessee than President of the United States.

Near the close of Houston's second term in Congress, he received guarded hints that he should run for governor with Carroll's support but pledge himself to retire after one term, thus making the office again available for Carroll. As his part of the bargain, Carroll would then support Houston for the United States Senate. Houston, as always, subjected this political proposition to cool analysis. He decided that he did not like having his future wrapped up in a neat bundle and handed to him by Governor Carroll. He might want a second term for himself. Brushing aside the suggestion, he ran for governor as a Jackson democrat without a commitment to Carroll.

It was a tough campaign. A revolt against some of Jackson's high-handed methods encouraged the Whigs to put up an opposition candidate, Newton Cannon. In East Tennessee Jackson had lost popularity because he had supported the removal of the state capitol from Knoxville to Nashville. Authorities are divided on whether or not Houston had Carroll's wholehearted support. Most think Houston was backed by Carroll, who was still nourishing hope that Houston would withdraw after one term to run for the Senate, leaving the way open for Carroll to resume the governorship.

Throwing himself into the canvass without depending upon the support of friends to put him over, Houston campaigned energetically in the fashion dictated by Tennessee politics. As a first step he discarded the discreet dress and reserved conduct he had affected in Washington where he had modeled himself after dignified Henry Clay and elegantly pompous Daniel Webster. Now he deliberately dressed himself to enhance the excitement and drama of his appearance at political meetings, barbecues, and barn raisings. He wore a tall, bell-crowned, medium-brimmed black beaver hat, topping a costume described by one observer as including:

> ... shining black patent leather military stock or cravat, incased by a standing collar, ruffled shirt, black satin vest, shining black silk pants gathered to the waistband with the legs full, same size from seat to ankle, and a gorgeous, red-ground, many-colored Indian hunting-shirt, fastened at the waist by a huge red ... sash covered with fancy beadwork, with an immense silver buckle, embroidered silk stockings, and pumps with large silver buckles. ...[1]

On election day, mounted on a superb dapple-gray horse, he made a whirlwind finish covering Nashville polling places. In the final count he did not win by a smashing victory but by a margin that was considered fair to good: 12,000 votes over Cannon. Only a few scattered votes went to a third candidate, Willie Blount.

In his inaugural address Houston emphasized the importance of sustaining the United States Constitution and of opposing the invasion of state authority by the federal government. His first annual message to the legislature recommended public improvements as a proper sphere for state enterprise, and he called for what amounted to an engineering commission to undertake statewide planning. He advocated a canal to by-pass Muscle Shoals in the Tennessee River, providing a southern outlet for Tennessee products.

Throughout his administration his aims were equally sensible and practical. His popularity steadily increased. He definitely broke with the Carroll wing, but he completed many of the projects Carroll had initiated, including periodic examinations of the state banks by auditors and requiring the banks to resume specie payments. The powerful and aspiring ex-governor who was watching all this had plenty of reason to fear that the popular young new governor would not be satisfied with a single term.

Again Houston was thinking of marriage. He wrote to a favorite cousin, "Jack" Houston, "I am not married, but it may be the case

35

in a few weeks and should it—*you* shall *hear* of it, before the newspapers can reach you." [2] He was often seen on his mare coursing to Gallatin to visit the lively plantation home of Colonel John Allen, who was always a cordial host. Colonel Allen had two daughters. Which of them was the object of the Governor's admiration was not at once apparent.

The people seemed to approve when Houston, in the summer and fall of 1828, took an energetic part in the campaign to make Jackson President. He operated what he called a "literary bureau" in support of the Old Chief. His speeches and compositions were effective, and he had to deal carefully with scandalous attacks on Jackson and his wife. The country rocked with campaign violence, perhaps the bitterest it has ever known: Jackson and Calhoun against Adams and Rusk. Old Hickory was lampooned as an illiterate, libidinous wastrel, a lewd and lascivious drunkard, an avaricious gambler and liar, a cold-blooded murderer for his execution of mutineers during the Creek campaign, a homicidal maniac, a bribe-taker, a shyster, a swindler, an atheist, and a slave trader.

These charges were incidental to the scandalous issue that was pressed home with fury: the general's marriage to Rachel Robards some forty years before when, contrary to Jackson's understanding, she had not yet been freed by divorce from her first husband. In this connection Jackson was accused of adultery, cuckoldry, and bigamy.

> *Oh Andy*
> *Old Andy*
> *How many men have you hung in your life?*
> *How many weddings make a wife?* [3]

As one of Aunt Rachel's boys, Houston loved and esteemed her, knowing the whole story. Jackson had aged picturesquely under the stress of financial anxieties, many campaigns, and ceaseless personal conflicts. But Aunt Rachel's radiant beauty had deteriorated, and some saw her as only a dumpy little sixty-one-year-old woman who suffered ill health and bore the marks of sorrow on her face. Her face had browned in the sun and her hands had roughened and calloused from her toil in the cotton and corn fields when she tried to keep the plantation prosperous while the general was absent on his campaigns. However, most people, including Houston, admired her for her good works and for never speaking a word that was intended to hurt, although she herself was repeatedly the object of calumny.

Houston knew that Rachel, should her husband be elected, did not intend to accompany him to Washington. Her health was not good and she feared that she would cut a poor figure in a capital where "society" was becoming constantly more important. But the successful outcome of the campaign and Jackson's persuasion changed all that. Aunt Rachel began making hurried preparations to go. In the flurry and excitement she caught a cold that developed into pleurisy. After an illness of three days she died. The Old Chief always believed that the scandalous campaign killed her.

On a dark and drizzly day Governor Houston led the pallbearers along the garden path to the gash in the earth that had been prepared for her near the house. He saw tears coursing down the face of the Old Chief as they stood beside the grave and he heard Jackson's bitter words, "In the presence of this dear saint I can and do forgive all my enemies. But those vile wretches who have slandered her must look to God for mercy." [4]

The Governor was on hand at the wharf on January 18, 1829, when Jackson boarded the steam packet that would take him on the first leg of the long journey to Washington. The President-elect was near the breaking point that day. The day before he had written to John Coffee, "My heart is nearly broke. I try to summon up my usual fortitude but in vain." [5]

There were political matters that had to be discussed before Jackson left Tennessee. Probably he realized that his hold on the state showed signs of slipping just as he was taking over the national leadership. Carroll's support was weakening because he knew Houston was Jackson's favorite. So Houston was the man to hold Tennessee in line for the administration. In a talk aboard the packet Jackson must have asked Houston when he proposed to announce for re-election. Houston no doubt told him exactly what he had in mind. He expected to be married on January 22, 1829, four days later, and would announce his political intentions soon afterward.

The general knew the Allens, the bride's family, well. "My blessings on you and your bride, Governor," the general said. "I pray God grant you a happy marriage and a long, prosperous life." [6]

7. *Domestic Disaster*

For five years Houston had been a frequent and always welcome guest in the home of John Allen of Gallatin. Thirty miles from Nashville by the turnpike, Gallatin was in Sumner County. Tennessee in those days was said to be like Gaul, divided into three parts: East and Middle Tennessee and Sumner County. The county, to be sure, was in Middle Tennessee, but admittedly it stood apart, distinguished by the wealth and influence of citizens proud of their aristocratic traditions which were consciously modeled on the more mature culture of Virginia's Tidewater communities.

John Allen, a highly respected leader of this select county society, and his invalid wife had been host to Andrew Jackson and Rachel when they were in town for the races. His home, in a bend of the Cumberland River, was surrounded by a lawn of bluegrass; thoroughbreds were in his stables. He served wines and delicacies from New Orleans at his table. Stability was the keynote of John Allen's existence. A proud man, honor was his motto.

Young Congressman Houston was introduced to the Allen household in 1824 by a fellow congressman, Robert Allen, John's younger brother. At that time Eliza Allen, the second daughter, was a fifteen-year-old schoolgirl with blue-gray eyes described as "violet" and braided blonde hair that hung down her back. She was studying literature, languages, and deportment at the Gallatin Academy. Already a fine horsewoman, she skillfully managed her black and white pony that stood twelve and one-half hands high.

In August, 1828, during the Presidential campaign, Houston recognized the growing power of his sentiments for the maturing Eliza. By now she was wearing her hair smoothed down over her ears and fastened in a knot at the back of her neck. She would be twenty in December. As he had done often before, Houston rode to Gallatin for a cozy visit with John Allen, but this time he told Eliza's father of his love for the girl, and John Allen encouraged him.

Though Houston did not know it, family pressure was brought to bear upon Eliza. The Allens stressed her opportunity for a match with

38

a man who had an assured future. Houston already was governor and certain to be re-elected; he was Andrew Jackson's friend and favorite political lieutenant. If Jackson became President, might not Houston be expected to follow in his footsteps? After all, this forecast was being made by many political observers.

Eliza hesitated. She was in love with another man, and the family knew it. Today it cannot be said positively who this favored suitor was. Probably it was the young, impecunious lawyer of good family, Will Tyree, with whom Eliza had danced at Tyree Springs. But in October, on a ride along the Cumberland, Eliza yielded to the Governor's passionate avowals. Shortly thereafter the engagement was announced and the date of the wedding fixed.

At candlelight, on January 22, 1829, four days after his wharfside farewell to Jackson, Houston received his young bride from the hand of her father in the elegant drawing room of the Allen home. The Reverend Mr. Hume, pastor of Nashville's aristocratic Presbyterian church, officiated, and the ceremony was witnessed by an imposing company, consisting mainly of the elite of Sumner County.

These class-conscious guests could hardly have avoided reflecting upon the brilliant prospects for such a union: the bridegroom whose future was widely recognized as promising, and the slender, pretty Allen girl, who must have seemed like the ideal wife for a rising politician. Any onlooker who felt disposed to speculate on the odd chance that this marriage might prove to be a mismatch had only one likely ground, the difference in the ages of the principals. Eliza had passed her twentieth birthday on December 2; the governor would be thirty-six in March.

The morning after the wedding, bridegroom and bride mounted horses and rode toward Nashville in a light snowstorm. The fall increased, and after journeying some miles, they stopped to spend the night at the home of Mrs. Robert Martin, a friend of the Allens. Heavy snow fell during the night, but in the morning they continued on their way.

They paused next at the home of Robert McEwen, one of Houston's two favorite cousins. McEwen's home was only a short distance from the Nashville limits. Here they were entertained for two days; then they proceeded to Nashville and took up residence in a suite on the second floor of the inn overlooking the square.

Nashville society graciously took the newlyweds to its heart. The

Polk (Houston had served in Congress with James K. Polk, later President), Grundy and Peyton families, as well as the rest of the city's select society, gave dinners and receptions in their honor. Comments on their appearance were unanimous: a strikingly handsome pair and one of the happiest ever known. As far as Nashville knew, there were no clouds on the young couple's horizon.

On January 18, 1829, four days before the Houston-Allen nuptials, ex-Governor William Carroll had announced in the Nashville *Banner and Whig* that he would run as a candidate for governor in the coming August election. This did not surprise Houston; he knew the passionate intensity of Carroll's desire to regain the office, but it did not alter his own intentions.

Six days after the wedding, on January 28, the *Banner and Whig* carried Houston's response to the Carroll challenge: "We are requested to announce the present Governor of Tennessee, Honorable Samuel Houston, is a candidate for re-election."

Here was occasion for joy for all who loved hot political combat: two of Jackson's favorite lieutenants in a battle that could conceivably lead to the political death of one. For Carroll and his followers, though they were bitter about it, Houston's announcement was not surprising. While they had hoped that he would choose to run for the Senate, leaving the way clear for Carroll's election without opposition, all signs had indicated that Houston would seek another term. Houston, of course, had nothing to fear. He knew he was doing what the Old Chief wanted and, if necessary, he had every reason to expect aid from that quarter. Jackson, in fact, did offer Carroll a South American ambassadorship to get him out of the competition. Houston, a popular hero, was confident that he could win without any special assistance from the Old Chief.

On April 11, 1829, the rival candidates met in joint debate at Cantrell's Spring, some ten miles from Nashville. A huge crowd gathered from three counties to enjoy the spectacular meeting between the steamboat magnate who had been governor three times and the younger man who was just completing his first successful term.

As Governor, Houston was able to set up a special attraction to draw a crowd—a muster and drill by the militia. At his request, Sheriff Willoughby Williams, his boyhood friend and always loyal follower, passed through the crowd during and after the debate.

Williams reported that all comments overheard strongly favored the Governor, who already seemed to have the Carrollites on the run.

What happened on the night of April 11, after Houston's return from Cantrell's Spring, has always been a subject of speculation. In *Tennessee, the Volunteer State*, John Trotwood Moore suggests that Houston returned home unexpectedly and found his wife burning some old love letters. Apparently she had been weeping over them. Other sources, later discredited, claimed that he had discovered her in another man's arms. It is definitely known that Houston discussed with his wife the cause of their unhappiness. Eliza admitted that she had been cold to him from the first, as he well knew; and she indicated her belief that this state of affairs could not be expected to change. Houston is reported to have told Eliza that she should not stay and be his slave; she should return to her family. If he actually said this, he would have plenty of time and cause to regret his words.

On previous occasions Eliza had suffered from her husband's extreme jealousy. What circumstances this jealousy was based on—apart from Eliza's admission that she was still in love with an earlier suitor—is not known. But it is certain that in the course of this frank discussion Houston made known to Eliza his belief that she had been unfaithful. She denied the terrible indictment and it takes little imagination to conceive the scene dissolving in tears.

Then Eliza made a strange request. She asked her husband to discuss their situation with Dr. John Shelby, a close friend of both the Governor and the Allen family, who had attended Eliza since infancy. But why consult Shelby? Though he had known her since babyhood, he could have known nothing more about her character and background than her husband did. Was there some condition that had come about, say, as a result of a fall from a horse, or from a medical examination, that excited Houston's suspicion as to Eliza's chastity before marriage—a condition that Dr. Shelby could explain?

If Houston's suspicion of Eliza's infidelity originated in something of this kind, he may have been the jealous victim of a strongly held and rather generally accepted view in those days, that a sexual relationship before marriage compromised a girl to an extent that made her an unsuitable wife. At all events, some factor, never to be disclosed, nurtured suspicion and distrust and inflamed Houston with the jealousies and anxieties of a frustrated husband.

It may well be, however, that his suspicions and resentment were totally unjustified. Although well schooled in the social graces, Eliza was doubtless unprepared for the realities of marriage. Perhaps it was too much to expect her to adjust to the unfamiliar surroundings in which she found herself, and to a vigorous, dynamic husband nearly twice her age. Houston, on his part, though deeply in love, could not be expected to appreciate the delicate sensibilities of a young girl going through a difficult transition.

After his talk with Dr. Shelby, the details of which are unknown, he had time to reflect. Whether he was motivated by Shelby's reassurances or by his realization of dangers inherent in domestic discord in the midst of a political campaign, Houston assured Eliza that he was "satisfied." She stood "acquitted by him," and he prayed God he would ever regard her as a virtuous wife. Strange language, to be sure, but there is incontrovertible evidence that these were his thoughts at the time. It amounted to a kind of reservation—innocent because not proved guilty.[1]

During the twelve weeks that had passed since the wedding, Nashville people had been completely unaware of anything unusual in the Governor's domestic situation. Now the storm broke. On April 16, Thursday, Sheriff Willoughby Williams rode into town after five days' absence and went to the Nashville Inn. Dan Carter, the clerk, asked, "Have you heard the news?"

"What news?"

"General Houston and his wife have separated and she has gone home to her father." [2]

Nashville somehow learned of Eliza's abrupt departure before her husband did. She must have gone home by stage during his absence from the inn on executive or political business. By the time he discovered her absence, Nashville was already in an uproar, and all kinds of speculations were in circulation. When presently it became known that the Governor had hastily mounted his favorite dapple-gray mare and followed his wife to Gallatin, the excitement and speculations rose to a feverish pitch.

The Governor arrived at the Allen home with his mare in a great sweat after a frantic ride. He was told that his father-in-law was not at home. Then he asked to see his wife, and permission was granted on condition that the interview take place in the presence of his wife's aunt. Before this unsympathetic witness, Houston begged his wife to forgive his suspicions and jealousy and implored her to return with him to Nashville. During the interview Houston learned, possibly from the aunt, that Eliza had confided to her parents everything that had happened, including her husband's charge of infidelity.

Shocked by his wife's disclosure of what should have been kept a sacred domestic secret and alarmed by the effect that a separation might have on his campaign, Houston lost all composure. According to a member of the family, he knelt and again tearfully implored Eliza to return to Nashville with him. Sustained more than she probably realized by her aunt's presence, Eliza refused to leave the sanctuary of her father's home.

Outsiders did not learn what took place on this occasion until years later, when one of Eliza's nieces revealed the substance in a letter to the Louisville *Courier Journal*.[3] This niece admitted that members of the family had long regretted Eliza's decision. If she had returned to Nashville, as her husband wanted her to, the family believed that they and Eliza would have been spared many years of unhappiness.

On returning to Nashville, Houston wrote his wife's father a letter, an outpouring of a man shaken to a degree that upset his coherence:

> Mr. Allen. The most unpleasant & unhappy circumstance has just taken place in the family, & one that was entirely unnecessary at this time. Whatever had been my feelings or opinion in relation to Eliza at one time, I have been satisfied & it is now unfit that anything should be a[d]verted to. Eliza will do me the justice to say that she believes I was really unhappy. That I was *satisfied & believed her virtuous*, I had assured her on last night & this morning. This should have prevented the facts ever coming to your knowledge, & that of Mrs. Allen. I would not for millions it had ever been known to you. But one human being knew anything of it from me [Dr. Shelby], & that was by Eliza's consent and wish. I would have perished first, & if mortal man had dared to charge my wife or say ought against

43

her virtue I would have slain him. That I have & do love Eliza none can doubt,—that she is the only object dear to me God will witness.

The only way this matter can now be overcome will be for us all to meet as tho it had never occurred, & this will keep the world, as it should ever be, ignorant that such thoughts ever were. Eliza stands acquitted by me. I have received her as a virtuous wife, & as such I pray God I may ever regard her, & trust I ever shall.

She was cold to me, & I thought did not love me. She owns that such was one cause of my unhappiness. You can judge how unhappy I was to think I was united to a woman that did not love me. This time is now past, & my future happiness can only exist in the assurance that Eliza & myself can be happy & that Mrs. Allen & you can forget the past,—forgive all & find your lost peace & you may rest assured that nothing on my part shall be wanting to restore it. Let me know what is to be done[.] [4]

After this attempt to placate his father-in-law the Governor remained in his inn quarters. Friends came to see him, but he did not go out. They reported that street-corner gossips were manufacturing accusations about a grave wrong that the Governor had done his bride and about a terrible accusation that he had brought against her; about his brutal treatment of her, his loose living among Indians, a broken engagement somewhere in his past, and sundry gallantries said to have been commonplace in his colorful experience. Augmenting the crowds that gathered in the square were some of Carroll's deckhands and stevedores.

How could street-corner rioters have got hold of the central fact in the Houstons' domestic situation—that the trouble involved the question of a woman's honor? Had they hit upon a good campaign issue by accident or had John Allen indiscreetly made the disclosure to some of his Sumner County cronies, among whom were a number of Carroll supporters? However it happened, it added impact and despair to the shock from which Houston suffered while he waited for his father-in-law's answer to the query: What is to be done now?

Impelled by the street demonstrations against the Governor, many friends came to assure him of their loyalty and confidence in him. Among them was Chief Justice John H. Overton of the Tennessee Supreme Court, a universally respected man. The judge asked no

44

questions, displayed no curiosity. He said he came solely for such purposes as "philosophy and friendship" could serve in an hour of trial.[5]

Sheriff Billy Williams reported that his office was filled with excited, hysterical people clamoring to know what was back of it all. "What can I say to them, Governor?" he asked.

"There's nothing to say, Billy."

"But you've got to say something, Governor. You owe it to yourself and your friends."

"This is a painful but a private matter, Billy. I do not recognize the right of the public to interfere. I shall treat the public as though it had never happened."

"Oh my God, no!" Billy pleaded. "You can't do that. You'll sacrifice your friends and yourself."

The Governor laid a hand on his friend's shoulder. "Remember, Billy, whatever may be said by the lady or her friends, it is no part of the conduct of a gallant and generous man to take up arms against a woman. If my character cannot stand the shock, let me lose it." [6]

Encouraged by the Governor's refusal to offer an explanation, the Carrollites fanned the fires of scandal into a conflagration. The Governor's least faults were magnified into crimes until presently the growling in the square took a new turn. The frenzied mob yelled that the Governor didn't dare show himself in the street. Even this did not move him. But when the culminating insult came, he responded to the challenge. By the custom of that day he was "posted." Placards proclaimed that Governor Sam Houston—the fearless lieutenant of Horseshoe Bend, the man who had risked his life in a duel for a friend—was a coward. With a few friends Houston walked through the square, glaring at the mobsters. They shrank back. No one approached to back up the posted charge. The Governor turned and walked back to the inn. Had he been attacked that day, he said later, "the streets of Nashville would have flowed with blood." [7]

Soon friend Billy was back again with more shocking news. In John Allen's own bailiwick, the Gallatin courthouse square, a howling mob had burned the Governor in effigy. At this moment, from a window in his living room, the Governor could see a banner carried by the trampling, yelling crowd:

PURITY—IN DEFENSE OF WOMAN'S HONOR—PURITY.

45

The next day the mob in the square became so threatening that the adjutant general, without consulting the Governor, sent militia to disperse it.[8]

While the wild talk and furious accusations continued, a charming lady whose curiosity about the affair was as strong as everybody else's wrote a letter, unknown to Houston, that reflected the public state of mind and her own discreet reservations as well as her inability to spell. Emily Drennen's letter, with its nice feeling for a man overwhelmed by adversity, was addressed to the beloved sister of Stephen F. Austin, Emily Perry, then living in Potosi, Missouri Territory:

> There is a dreadfull stir in the country and town about our Governor . . . a thouseand diferent tails afloat . . . I never can believe he has acted ungentlemanly untill I see him and know the trouth from himself for he was a man so popular I know it must be something dreadfull. . . . He is very sick. . . . And what is more astonishing none of [his wife's] connection has been near. If he was in fault I should think some of them would resent it . . . none of his friends blame him so when you hear repoarts about him you may know they are not so. He has a good menny enemies and a great menny friends. He says time will show who is to blame. The reason he does not tell. . . .

Emily ended her kindly letter on a note that tacitly admitted the failings of all humanity for gossip about the affairs of their neighbors, "I expect you are tyered of this, but I feel so interested." [9]

Believing that his situation was hopeless without complete support of the Allen family, Houston waited anxiously for several days, hoping to hear from his father-in-law. But there was not a word, and not a member of the family came near. Houston's scorn of the jeering mobsters must have mitigated his despair, at least to some extent.

On April 16, 1829, he went to his stand-up writing desk and wrote a letter to General William Hall, Speaker of the Tennessee Senate.

> It has become my duty to resign the office of Chief magistrate of the state. . . .
> That veneration for public opinion by which I have measured every act of my official life, has taught me to hold no delegated power which would not daily be renewed by my constituents,

... And although shielded by a perfect consciousness of un-diminished claim to the confidence & support of my fellow cit-izens, yet delicately circumstanced as I am, & by my own misfortunes, more than by the fault or contrivance of anyone, overwhelmed by sudden calamities, it is certainly due to myself & more respectful to the world, that I should retire from a posi-tion which, in the public judgment, I might seem to occupy by questionable authority.— [10]

The Governor asked Billy to take his resignation to the clerk of the Senate to have it copied. Billy was to bring it back for Houston's signature and then deliver it to the Speaker of the Senate. It was a heavy burden, but Billy carried out the mission.

Houston later described the hours of meditation that preceded his decision to resign. He called them the "darkest" of his life—"the direst hours of human misery." [11] While he was considering what he would do after quitting office, his thoughts turned to his "roving in youth among the Cherokees"; to Chief Jolly who "adopted him as his son, and gave him a corner of his wigwam[.]" Jolly was now "king of the Cherokees" who had moved from the Hiwassie country to Arkansas. Houston and his foster father had not seen each other for eleven years but "they had never ceased to interchange tokens ..." The Governor resolved to turn his face toward his adopted father's home, knowing he "would be greeted there with the old Chief's blessing." [12]

But something deeper than this prompted Houston to go into what he came to speak of as his "self-exile." There was a great unsatisfied yearning in him for solitude in nature that had been latent ever since his taste of paradise on Hiwassie. He still craved what he called "a life of communion with the Great Spirit, and his beautiful creations." This yearning, uppermost at the moment and influential in determin-ing his course, never completely left him. It always returned after intervals, especially in time of trouble; and after the trouble passed he plunged into constructive activities.

On April 23, 1829, a week after his resignation, Houston boarded the steam packet *Red Rover* on which he had booked passage under an assumed name. Dr. Shelby, who had remained loyal after hearing the whole story from Houston's own lips, and Billy Williams accompanied him to the wharf where Houston only a few months before had received Jackson's blessing on his marriage. Passing through the streets he wore an Indian blanket over old clothes. This has usually been considered a disguise. More likely it was a token of his preference for "barbarians" and of his contempt for the "civilization" he was leaving behind.

That same day, after the departure of *Red Rover*, the Reverend Mr. Hume reflected upon the painful transitoriness of all life. "Oh, what a fall," he lamented, "for a Major General, a member of Congress and a Governor of so respectable a State as Tennessee." [13]

With time additional pieces in the Houston-Allen puzzle fell into place. A revealing "inside" story in the form of a letter to a newspaper came from Houston's Washington, D.C., pastor, Dr. George W. Samson, a half-century after the event. According to Samson, his distinguished parishioner told him that during the wedding ceremony he became aware of his bride's hand trembling as it rested on his arm. Soon afterward, distressed for some reason unknown to him, she withdrew from the company and retired to the bridal chamber where her husband joined her. He spoke of her nervousness and told her that he was convinced "some secret had not been revealed."

Samson reported that Houston's sympathy and gentleness together with his assurance that he "would work her no injury," prompted Eliza to confess that "her affections had been pledged to another . . . and that filial duty had prompted her acceptance of his [marriage] offer." Dr. Samson let it be understood that bride and bridegroom "rested" apart that night, Houston on a couch. In the morning the newly married pair agreed to act before the world as if theirs were a normal situation. [14]

In their *History of Tennessee and Tennesseeans*, Hale and Merritt pick up the thread the next day. They say that in the morning before departure from the home of Mrs. Robert Martin at Locust Grove where the Houstons spent the night, Mrs. Martin was watching from a window as the young Martin daughters ganged up on Houston and playfully pelted him with newly fallen snow. Mrs. Martin was observing the good nature with which the Governor let the children get the best of him, when Eliza came downstairs and joined her. In unpublished memoirs, Mrs. Martin narrated what followed.

48

"I said to her, 'It seems as if General Houston is getting the worst of the snow-balling; you had better go out and help him.' Looking at me seriously, Mrs. Houston said, 'I wish they would kill him.' I looked astonished to hear such a remark from a bride of not yet forty-eight hours, when she repeated in the same voice, 'Yes, I wish from the bottom of my heart that they would kill him.' " [15]

Mrs. Martin's explosive secret was kept for many years, until 1913, when Hale and Merritt published their history. The disclosure appears to come from a reliable source. The Martins were substantial people. Quoted portions of her memoirs about life in a Louisiana parish, of family contacts with Lafitte, the Marquis de Lafayette, and several Presidents are discreet and convincing. It is ironical that the only words which can be attributed with any degree of confidence to Eliza Allen about her marriage to Houston are those quoted by Mrs. Martin—"I wish they would kill him."

Assuming they were correctly quoted one inference is obvious— Eliza's resentment of the pressure brought to bear by her parents to forego a genuine attachment and undertake a marriage of prestige was now manifesting itself in feelings akin to hatred of her husband. But allowances must be made for her youth and inexperience and her inability to control her emotions. As she matured, her character developed more admirable aspects and she deplored her earlier behavior.[16]

After the Governor departed from Nashville, speculations were intense for a time, then gradually abated—only to resume later. These ranged all the way from charges that Houston was a lady's man to "brute" and "rake." But one judgment must stand. At the time of the catastrophe Houston was passionately in love with the girl he married. Frenzied by her aloofness, he suffered from jealousy that fostered suspicion regardless of whether it was justified. The desperation that prompted him to seek asylum in the Arkansas forest was that of a man completely crushed by the loss of his bride, the destruction of his domestic life, and the price he had to pay for acting in accord with the dictates of honor.

At Clarksville on the Cumberland two members of the Allen family, believed to be Eliza's uncle, Robert, Houston's one-time fellow congressman, and possibly another uncle, Campbell Allen, boarded the *Red Rover*. Armed and excited, they sought out Houston and declared that his unexplained departure had given rise to a rumor. He was supposed to have said that he had been "goaded to madness and exile" by detecting his wife "in crime." They wanted him to return "and prove it" or to sign a written denial. Houston refused to do either, but, calling upon the captain of the *Red Rover* to witness his statement, he authorized his in-laws to "publish in the Nashville papers that if any wretch ever dares to utter a word against the purity of Mrs. Houston I will come back and write the libel in his heart's blood." [17]

Over the years Houston never permitted an unkind reference to Eliza to be made in his presence without a stern rebuke. If he had been more concerned about his career than about Eliza's reputation Houston could have defended himself against scandal-mongers and political assassins, and he would have had the support of many powerful friends. But this would have meant impeaching his wife by disclosing the nature of the suspicion that had precipitated disaster, which was unthinkable.

On the way down the Cumberland he reproached himself bitterly for his jealous conduct. Years later he told a friend, another pastor, Dr. Rufus C. Burleson, that despondency brought him to the verge of suicide. Reflecting "on the bitter disappointment" he had caused Jackson and all his other friends, he said, "I was in an agony of despair and strongly tempted to leap overboard and end my worthless life." [18]

While the victim was undergoing his agony, the beneficiary and perhaps the chief promoter of the scandal, ex-Governor Billy Carroll, was pressing his gubernatorial campaign with a vigor that assured victory. In a gloating letter he wrote Jackson:

> That fate of Houston must have surprised you ... his conduct ... was very strange and charity requires us to place it to the account of insanity. I have always looked upon him as a man of weak and unsettled mind ... incapable of manfully meeting a reverse of fortune.[19]

This must have deepened Jackson's perplexity into profound grief. It was not his first knowledge of the affair. In April he had written Congressman John J. McLemore, "I have this moment heard a rumor of poor Houston's disgrace. My God, is the man mad?" [20]

8. Forest Exile

Wᴴᴇɴ he left the *Red Rover* at Cairo, Illinois, Houston was accompanied by H. Haraalson, a light-hearted Irishman and a frontier drifter without visible means of support. Haraalson had established his reputation for amusing loquacity and anecdotes with the Nashville Inn's whiskey-drinking coterie, sometimes known as the Monongahela Club, because of a favored whiskey. He satisfied Houston's need of the moment for companionship that could relieve his despair.

They bought a flat-bottom boat for eighteen dollars, loaded it with provisions, took aboard a handy man, a Negro boy, and a dog, and set themselves adrift on the Father of Waters. They soon thought it desirable to replenish their supply of potables and stopped at Memphis, a little village on the east shore, where there were some thirty or more ramshackle cabins, a general store, and three grog shops.

They landed next on the Arkansas shore at Helena, a base for smuggling liquor into Indian territory. The town consisted of twenty cabins and six grog shops. At Helena, Houston evidently encountered James Bowie, although the details of the meeting are unknown. It is reasonable to suppose that Houston was in the leading grog emporium when the massive figure of the redheaded giant darkened the doorway. Probably Bowie ordered the two bristly-haired bear dogs and a huge Negro with whom he customarily traveled to remain outside.

With his brother, Bowie owned a cotton plantation and sawmill in Louisiana. On the side, they had done a little slave-running for the pirate Jean Lafitte. Jim may have been scouting for new land that would make cotton growing easier and more profitable. He already had been to Texas several times. The ex-Governor had little information but some lively ideas about Texas. This fortuitous meeting seems to have stimulated his interest.

At the mouth of the Arkansas river, with Haraalson still in attendance, Houston sold his flatboat and boarded a steamboat that

51

proceeded up the river to Little Rock. This phase of the journey was marked with more attempts to escape reality. Houston indulged "fancy" to the point of irresponsible loquacity. He ranted about future glories he proposed to achieve by establishing—with the aid of Indian allies—"a Rocky Mountain Empire" in the far west beyond the national limits. Or, with the Indians' help, he would conquer Texas and perhaps within a couple of years make himself "Emperor" of that domain. It was loose talk. He had no plans. He was groping toward some future employment.

His presence in Little Rock drew the attention of a young man, Charles Noland, who immediately sat down and wrote to his father to relieve his feelings about a man of Houston's quality going into exile.

> Governor Houston arrived here three days since on his way to join the Indians—Merciful God! is it possible that society can be deprived of one of its greatest ornaments, and the United States of one of her most valiant sons, through the dishonor and baseness of a woman? He converses cheerfully, made a great many inquiries after you. He will stay this winter with the Cherokees and probably will visit the warm spring . . . this summer. He wishes to go to the Rocky Mountains, to visit that tract of country between the mouth of the Oregon and California Bay. He came with a rifle on his shoulder. General Jackson will certainly persuade him to come back from the woods.[1]

From Little Rock, after purchasing horses, Houston and Haraalson rode thirty miles up the Arkansas River valley trail. There they overtook the small steamboat, *Facility*. Houston made arrangements with the captain for passage to Webbers Falls in the Cherokee country. Haraalson rode overland with the luggage, heading for the same destination. Snags and shoals damaged the *Facility*'s paddle wheels; repairs and the necessity to tie up to the bank at night delayed the boat's progress. It never covered more than twenty miles a day.

News that his foster son was coming reached Chief Jolly at his lodge near the mouth of the Illinois River in Cherokee Nation West, some two hundred miles from Little Rock. Apparently one of his tribesmen had heard it at a wood yard where steamboats stopped for fuel.

Hurrying to Webbers Falls, Jolly greeted the ex-Governor when the *Facility* tied up. His moving welcome was recorded by Houston in his *Memoir* (p. 51):

I have heard that a dark cloud had fallen on the white path you were walking, and when it fell in your way you turned your thoughts to my wigwam. I am glad of it—it was done by the Great Spirit.... We are in trouble, and the Great Spirit has sent you to give us council, and take trouble away from us ... you will tell our sorrows to the great father, General Jackson. My wigwam is yours—my home is yours—my people are yours—rest with us.

Pine knots burning in split sticks lighted the guest's way over three miles of woodland trail to Jolly's spacious lodge. Jolly entertained liberally, as became a monarch, slaughtering at least a beef a week the year round for his many white and red guests. When Houston lay down to sleep that night "after the gloom and sorrows of the past few weeks," he felt, he said, "like a weary wanderer returned at last to his father's house." [2]

While the Cherokees had just complaints about the poor hunting grounds that had been forced upon them in exchange for their land in Tennessee, Jolly at least had prospered. His lodge, surrounded by a well-tended plantation, was in a grove of sycamores and cottonwoods on a knoll that separated the Arkansas River from a small stream known as the Illinois. He had three wives, 500 head of cattle and ten servants, including several black slaves. Among his followers he was known as "beloved father."

"Beloved father" had learned some of the white man's tricks. When he signed dishonest papers that profited him without sacrificing the interest of his own people too much, he used his white name. When the integrity of the deal was not in question he signed his Indian name.

Houston was sharing in the council meeting and merrymaking of the Seven Clans when an Osage scout with a crest of bristling hair rode in on a horse which he guided with a one-rein rawhide bridle. The scout brought Auguste Pierre Chouteau's complaints to Chief Jolly and an urgent request for Houston to come at once to his home in the Six Bull River Valleys. For thirty years trader Chouteau had prospered because of his generous treatment of the Osages, and they had repaid him with loyalty such as no other trader commanded.

Houston promptly responded to Chouteau's invitation. Accompanied by Haraalson, who had arrived with horses and luggage, and guided by the Osage scout, he covered 100 miles in two and a half days.

Emerging from the woods and coming to a well-worn trail in the open, he beheld Chouteau's imposing establishment; imposing, that is, for the frontier: a whitewashed, two-story double log house with a large piazza across the front. Excited Negro girls ran to announce the guests to their master. The new arrivals were being surrounded by Negroes, half-breeds, and squaws clamoring welcome and offering services when the dignified, white-thatched Chouteau appeared on the piazza and clapped his hands for quiet.

Houston, Haraalson, and their host had supper in a large open hallway which ran through the center of the house. Masina, the half-breed sister of Chouteau's Osage wife, Rosalie, served the three men. The usual fare was fricasseed wild turkey, roast beef, venison, bread, cake, wild honey, and coffee. After supper the dogs, cats, and chickens slept peacefully at the far end of the veranda while Chouteau told the ex-Governor how the Indians, for whom he had a special regard, were being shamefully robbed by government agents. He urged Houston to report this to his friend President Jackson. And why shouldn't he become an Indian agent himself, Chouteau wanted to know. He could use his influence with Washington to help get rid of corruption.

From Chouteau's, Houston went on a trip of exploration among the Osages, Creeks, Pawnees, and Choctaws to hear their complaints against the Indian agents. If he had any serious intention of setting up a Rocky Mountain Empire this was a good opportunity to investigate the chance of picking up the necessary allies.

A victim of malaria, he returned to Fort Gibson after traveling some six hundred miles through the Arkansas and Oklahoma wilderness in the summer heat. He was alone; what became of Haraalson after he had been at Chouteau's has never been made clear. He had disappeared without trace and Houston did not mention him in the *Memoir*.

Houston opened his campaign in behalf of the Indians with a letter to Jackson's Secretary of War, John Eaton. He recommended the appointment of Chouteau to negotiate a permanent peace between the Pawnees and Osages. He favored Chouteau for this because the trader had the best practical knowledge of Indians of any man he had ever known. He sought no official connection with the proposed peace mission, but volunteered to accompany Chouteau and co-operate without compensation because "this duty would re-create my mind." Though Houston had worked with Eaton as a member of the Nashville Junto for the election of Jackson, Eaton ignored him.[3]

When Houston left Fort Gibson to return to Jolly's lodge about thirty miles distant, he was in the grip of chills and fever. Dismounting at the lodge, he collapsed, fell to the ground, and had to be carried indoors where he rested on a pallet of corn shucks. For more than a month he suffered a near fatal illness. During the crisis someone gave him tea made from the bark of a Peruvian tree. It was quinine. The whites had brought it into the wilderness; from them the Indians had learned of its curative properties.

Rumors of Houston's babblings on his way up the Arkansas River had reached Jackson. They may have been reported by Haraalson to Secretary of War Eaton with whom Haraalson had a slight acquaintance. Haraalson is said to have been prompted by an Irishman's natural urge to tell somebody something; but there is also the possibility that he was a kind of secret agent for the War Department. A gossipy congressman, John Marable, also had heard of Houston's loose talk, and in a letter to Duff Green, who turned it over to Jackson, had attributed fantastic schemes to the ex-Governor.

Some time in August, 1829, Houston received by way of Fort Gibson a letter from Jackson dated June 21. The President, still heartsick for his friend, referred to their farewell at the wharfside.

When I parted with you on the 18th January last . . . I then viewed you as on the brink of happiness and rejoiced. About to be united in marriage to a beautiful young lady, of accomplished manners, and respectful connections, & of your own selection—you the Governor of the State and holding the affections of the people—these were your prospects when I shook you by the hand and bade you farewell. You may well judge my astonishment and grief in receiving a letter from you dated

Little Rock, A. T. conveying the sad intelligence that you were then ... an exile from, your country.

Jackson's soul was in this letter. In it he relieved his anguished feelings in behalf of his friend with exclamations: "What reverse of fortune! How unstable are all human affairs." Jackson ridiculed any notion Houston might have had of using the Cherokees as an instrument of conquest:

> It has been communicated to me [he continued] that you had the illegal enterprise in view of conquering Texas; that you had declared that you would, in less than two years, be emperor of that country by conquest. I must really have thought you deranged to have believed you had so wild a scheme in contemplation, and particularly when it was communicated that the physical force to be employed was the Cherokee Indians. Indeed, my dear Sir, I cannot believe you have any such chimerical visionary scheme in view. Your pledge of honor to the contrary is a sufficient guarantee that you will never engage in any enterprise injurious to your country that would tarnish your fame.[4]

Jackson wanted peace, and Houston, in his letter from Little Rock, had already given him the assurance he desired. But Jackson was taking no chances. What he had heard from gossipers about Houston's loose talk convinced him suddenly his friend was having a dreadful reaction to domestic shock and political disaster. He considered it necessary to protect his administration and the country by putting Houston under military surveillance and having his mail intercepted and read. On May 21, 1829, he entered in his note book:

> As a precautionary measure I directed the Secretary of War to write and enclose Mr. Pope, Govr. of Arkansas, the extract [of Congressman Marable's gossipy report about Houston to Duff Green] and instruct him if such illegal project should be discovered to exist to adopt prompt measures to put it down and give the Government the earliest intelligence of such illegal enterprise with the names of all concerned.[5]

After taking these precautions Jackson made some suggestions about Houston's future employment that were the equivalent of offering a rattle to a troublesome baby. No doubt he desired to be helpful, but it is clear that at this time he was wary of putting their friendship on the old basis. In Washington he was handing out jobs with liberality, but he did not offer Houston so much as a postmastership. Perhaps he was waiting to see what shape Houston's tangled affairs would take. His idea was that in the meantime his unemployed friend might become a missionary to the Indians or build up his influence as a Jackson political lieutenant in Arkansas Territory.

As soon as he was well enough, Houston replied that he lacked the necessary "Evangelical change of heart" for missionary work. As for politics in Arkansas Territory: ". . . there is no field for distinction—it is fraught with *factions;* and if my object were to obtain wealth, it must be done by fraud, and peculation upon the Government, and many perjuries would be necessary to its effectuation!" [6]

Some weeks later, in August, 1829, a heartening letter came to Houston from the man who had been his first regimental commander, Senator Thomas Hart Benton:

> I write to you for the purpose of renewing old friendship, and to request you to call upon me freely if I can be of service to you.
>
> I do not know what your plans may be, but am certain that you have too much energy to be idle, and shall expect to see you in active life before long. [7]

It was the kind of letter to revive an exile's drooping spirits.

On his visit to the tribes before his illness, Houston had learned how they were being defrauded of their annuities by corrupt government agents. He began efforts to induce the government to substitute honest men. In a few cases, he eventually succeeded, but, more or less, it was a losing battle.

There is no doubt that Houston seriously undertook to orient himself to the Indian way of life. During the first summer of exile, he applied for admission to the Cherokee tribe. In October he received his certificate signed by three chiefs, including Jolly. It was granted in recognition of his "past services to the nation" and on account of their "confidence in his integrity and talents." The certificate specified that he was "irrecoverably granted all rights, immunities and liberties" of a Cherokee citizen. In return, he obliged himself to give "obedience to all laws and regulations of the Cherokee nation." [8]

Considering himself an expatriate now, Houston "on occasion of state arrayed himself with the best." He plaited his hair in a long queue and dressed himself according to the customs of the tribe. His garb included a white doeskin shirt worked with beads, ornamented yellow leather leggings, a headdress of eagle or turkey feathers or sometimes a turban of figured silk; in cool weather he wore a bright blanket over this outfit. "He wore his beard upon his chin in a 'goatee,' shaving the rest of his face." [9]

The following spring, 1830, he made a trip to Washington as a member of a Cherokee delegation to complain against the corrupt Indian agents, some of whom eventually were removed. In his bright blanket and buckskin pants, he became a familiar figure on Pennsylvania Avenue, and in these clothes he was received at the President's house. He also sought a contract as provisioner for Indians to be moved farther west, but this fell through and with it his visions of making a large sum of money.

Crossing Tennessee on his way home, Houston was greeted both by small crowds who wanted to show their confidence in him and by renewed attacks from his political enemies. Emissaries of the Allen family proposed a reconciliation, which he rejected but reported in a letter to his friend Major William B. Lewis, with whom he had worked for Jackson's election. "Great efforts, and strong hopes of fame [presumably by political support] were held out to me but, all of no use. Tho' the world can never know my situation and may condemn me, God will justify me!" He also stated that Eliza's family had "sent Mrs. H. to Carthage lest she should come to Nashville, in spite of them, and I would not receive her. If she had come this would have been the case, so I said to my friends from the time I arrived there [in Nashville]." [10]

His refusal of the offered reconciliation brought painful reprisal. Houston had no intention of seeking a divorce at this time, but Eliza's father apparently feared that he might. Colonel Allen formed a Committee of Twelve, all prominent Sumner County men, to investigate and report publicly on the cause of the marital break. William Hall, ex-Speaker of the Tennessee Senate, acted as chairman and Judge Jo Guild was a member. The committee did not talk with Houston because he was in Arkansas, but they interviewed Eliza. Her father furnished them with Houston's letter appealing for a united family stand—the letter that Allen had never answered. This was the only definite evidence that the world would ever have that Houston had brought an accusation of infidelity against his wife, and it was made public by her father.

Meeting in the Gallatin Courthouse to give their status a flavor of authority, the committee formulated its report and included Houston's letter. By implication they charged the ex-Governor with concocting the letter and inventing the infidelity accusation *after* the separation with the object of mitigating charges that he was an "infatuated husband" guilty of extreme jealousy. [11]

Houston's letter, of course, had been an effort to prevent the separation. He pointed this out to the committee in a reply to their report, enumerating their errors and false charges and taking them to task for not concentrating on vindicating Eliza instead of attempting to blacken his reputation. Nothing that befell him during his forest exile cut deeper than the accusation that his conduct was dishonorable. He believed his actions deserved respect and asked the committee to give the same circulation to his letter that they had given to the charges. His request was ignored.

But there was one man to whom Houston could freely pour out his heart and he turned to him in this dark hour. Deeply miserable over the charge that he had trumped up the terrible accusation against his wife, he wrote to Jackson:

> I never sought to injure her with anyone. To you, even *you*, Sir, in whose estimation I have been proud to stand most honorable and fair, I appeal to know of your heart, if I cast the slightest reflection upon her, or her immediate family. I have drank the cup and the dregs only remain for me to consume. I feel well satisfied, nor will I ever permit myself to abandon the ground which I have assumed . . . I have sacrified everything that was Glorious to my peculiar necessities [the need to shield Eliza] . . . & conscious honor, and rectitude only remain as my companions. They are old friends and will not desert me in time to come.[12]

His letter was a pitifully exact statement of his position before the world. Little or nothing remained of his former glories except his own awareness of his honor and rectitude.

Later, on two separate occasions and through two separate channels, other intermediaries tried in Eliza's behalf to bring about a reconciliation. Houston's matured conviction was that the Allens had treated him shabbily and that Eliza had been disloyal. In his judgment, even her youth did not excuse this. He wanted nothing to do with any member of the family. His response was the same as before—he would not receive her, though he always listened courteously and with a non-committal show of interest when friends or busybodies reported her activities and her interest in his welfare and the honors that he had won.

Houston probably realized by now that his attempt to lose himself in tribal existence was doomed to failure, but he made another supreme effort. As a citizen of the Cherokee Nation, he was not subject to the marriage laws of the United States. Among the Cherokees, when a brave and his squaw decided to separate they "divided the blanket," and that was it. Houston took the view that the blanket briefly shared by him and Eliza had been divided and their union severed. By Cherokee custom he married Tiana Rogers Gentry; within the tribe it was a real marriage, not a casual liaison. To Houston and to other whites his wife was known as Diana.

There is nothing to indicate that Diana had come to Houston's notice during his youthful adventure on Hiwassie, but they were bound by mutual recollections of those somewhat idyllic surroundings. She was the widow of a white blacksmith, David Gentry, respected among the Cherokees for his craftsmanship. Her tribal connections were excellent. She was related to most of the important Cherokee families in Arkansas Territory including Chief Jolly's. Her half-brother, John Rogers, was Chief Jolly's logical successor. Her mother was Jennie Due, a descendant of a British Revolutionary officer. Described in her girlhood as tall, willowy, and handsome, Diana, now in her middle thirties, was more than ordinarily attractive.

Houston established himself and his wife in a log house in an apple orchard near the Neosho River, between the Grand River and the Verdigris, thirty-odd miles from Jolly's lodge but near Fort Gibson, where he would have American officers for companions. He called his place "Wigwam Neosho," but it was a house, not a structure of skins and poles. Some little time after setting up this household, he opened a trader's store with goods ordered from Nashville and announced his intention to provide "at honest prices" the things the Indians needed, such as kettles, blankets, bridles, flour, soap, and rope.

Bringing in these supplies involved Houston in a friendly controversy with Colonel Matthew Arbuckle, commander at Fort Gibson. The ex-Governor contended that as a Cherokee citizen he was entitled to carry on trade with his own people without a license from the United States government, just as he was free to marry in the tribe without a white man's divorce. This question, referred to Washington, was decided against him and he was required, just as any other white man, to give bond and obtain from the Indian agent a trader's license.

After they attended a council at Jolly's or came from more remote places, the Indians flocked to share the hospitality of Houston's "pavilion." It was a rickety structure roofed over for weather protection. When his friendly customers settled down for a night's rest in the pavilion, there arose an immense chatter that gave Houston and his bride an experience comparable to living next door to a woodland night club. The good-natured visitors gossiped, chattered, sang, and banged until sleep overcame them; and, if somebody thought of a new joke in the night, then the laughter and chatter started all over again.

When Houston imported nine barrels of liquor, listed in a letter to Colonel Arbuckle as including "five of whisky (four of Monongahela and one of corn), a barrel of cognac brandy, one of gin, one of rum and one of wine," he was again involved in a friendly disagreement with the commandant. Houston wanted to take all of the liquor into his wigwam, where it would be convenient for his personal use. Arbuckle would not permit this arrangement, and, as a concession, Houston proposed to have one barrel of whisky transported to his wigwam and to store the others, subject to his call when wanted, with the sutler at the fort.

He voluntarily pledged himself not to sell or give a drop of whiskey to a soldier or to an Indian. But Arbuckle held that this matter also must be referred to Washington. This time there was discrimination in Houston's favor. He received an order from the Acting Secretary of War on September 30, 1830, which stated that "Genl. Houston may be permitted to take [the nine barrels of liquor] to his own residence" for his personal use.[13]

For some time Houston had been slowly skidding downgrade;

despite his marriage, his generous reception by the Cherokee Nation, and his business, the man who craved distinction could not find peace. The trend became obvious in the late autumn after official permission to store the liquor on his own premises. His sole ambition seemed to be, alone and unaided, to see the bottoms of those barrels.

Houston was popular with the officers at Fort Gibson and often visited them, but this camaraderie aroused painful nostalgia which he expressed in one of his early letters to President Jackson:

> When I left the world, I had persuaded myself that I would lose all care, about the passing political events of the world, as well as those of my own country, but it is not so, for as often as I visit Cant. Gibson, where I can obtain News Papers, I find that my interest is rather increased than diminished. It is hard for an old Trooper, to forget the *note* of the *Bugle!* [14]

The ease with which Houston could tap his huge liquor reserve contributed to his steady downward drift. The Creeks, as they had always done, still called him Big-Holy-Person, but the Osages were now calling him Big Drunk and some whites at the Fort picked it up. Cherokees have denied that his own tribe ever called him that because they loved and respected him when sober, although they deplored his weakness and the many signs of his deterioration. But Big Drunk he was, and at this period, he later confessed, he deserved the name. He put it truthfully and colorfully, though with restraint, writing of himself in the third person: "When this dark cloud fell over the path of Houston, he buried his sorrows in the flowing bowl. His indulgences began with the wreck of his hopes, and . . . he gave himself up to the fatal enchantress. . . ." [15]

At the spring election, 1831, Houston offered himself as a candidate for a seat in the Cherokee Council and to his astonishment was defeated. In his first angry resentment he declared his intention to quit the Cherokees and join the Choctaws. Later he discussed his rejection with his foster father. Evidently, when this talk took place he was in no condition to bear up under the truth. Jolly probably rebuked him for setting a bad example for the tribe. It may have been on this occasion that Jolly said, "A man who is drunk is only half a man." An altercation followed during which Houston, angry and inflamed with alcohol, struck his foster father. The braves who

62

witnessed it seized him, and they were not gentle. He struck back. They knocked him down, and when he still resisted they beat him unconscious. The bruised and dirty white man, pinned to the ground by his red brothers, would have seemed a poor risk ever to pick himself up and become a man again, let alone a great man. But the man in the dirt was Sam Houston.

Before his years of self-exile he had already displayed many of the characteristics needed for leadership in a young and growing nation. He had courage, resolution, tactful diplomacy, the mental powers to grapple with and understand national principles and problems, the personality to attract devoted followers, and a toughly realistic sense of opportunity.

In August, 1831, he went to Fort Gibson only to receive another blow; a letter from Baker's Creek told him that his mother was dangerously ill and not expected to live. He rushed home in time to talk with her and to receive her blessing before she died. In his *Memoir* he recalled weeping at her bedside. Nowhere does he mention the change in himself that seems to have been associated with her death, but a change began when he returned to Arkansas Territory.

He would soon be thirty-nine years old. A man who has reached a dead end at mid-life may feel that hope is empty and aspiration is pointless, but one of Houston's outstanding traits was the buoyancy with which he renewed his struggle against adversity. In the late autumn he told Diana that he was going east on business and might be gone for some time. He had a plan, vague to be sure, but a plan just the same.

Not long after his arrival in Arkansas, he had received two appeals from John Wharton in Nashville. John was the younger brother of William H. Wharton, who, years earlier, had gone to Texas and married the daughter of Jared Ellison Groce, a wealthy leading Anglo-American colonist. "I have heard you intended an expedition against Texas," the younger Wharton wrote. "I suppose, if it is true, you will let your Nashville friends know of it." [17]

Adhering to his promise to Jackson—no illegal filibuster from U.S. territory—Houston had not given the spirited younger Wharton the desired response. Subsequently John had set up his law practice in New Orleans. From there he had visited Texas, and now back in Louisiana, he was preparing to move to Texas permanently. He sent a second appeal to Houston: "I . . . request you once more to visit

Texas," Wharton wrote. "It is a fine field for enterprise. You can get a grant of land, be surrounded by your friends, and what may not the coming of time bring about?"

Houston needed money to test the notion that a man at a dead end with half his life behind him could redeem himself in a new environment. His friends in New Orleans could help with advice on that, so he set out for New York by way of the Gulf port.

9. *The Flogging*

At the mouth of the Arkansas River two days after Christmas, 1831, Houston boarded a steamboat for New Orleans, where he hoped to see his two friends, John Wharton and William Christy. He was glad that, traveling by way of the Gulf, he could avoid Tennessee. Writing in the third person (*Memoir*, p. 62), he said that "sight of the spot where he had seen the bright hopes that had greeted his early manhood, crushed in a single hour, only awakened associations that he wished to forget."

His companions, a party of Indians in bright-colored blankets and feathered headdresses, were on their way to ask the government once more for protection from dishonest Indian agents. Houston was not a member of the delegation, but an unofficial adviser and friend. Two European tourists on board noted the former Governor's run-down appearance.[1] He wore a rumpled buckskin coat, shrunken from wetting, with a frayed beaver collar given him by an Indian. His plight was worse than the strangers realized. He did not even have funds for his board bill in New York should he be detained for any length of time.

In March Houston had long talks with James Prentiss, a financier prominent in the affairs of the Galveston Bay and Texas Land Company. This company already had vast holdings in Texas and was selling land and scrip to venturesome investors. Houston discussed his plan to locate large acreages in Texas that might be acquired in bulk and sold off in parcels with good profits.

Houston, knowing little about the situation in Texas, was not certain that he would undertake the hazardous journey. Prentiss did not know whether he could persuade friends to join him in backing the venture, or whether he would do so himself. But when Houston left New York for Washington, negotiations were definitely under way for some kind of a survey trip to Texas, and it was understood that discussions would be continued by letter.

Three days after his arrival in Washington, Houston picked up a copy of the *National Intelligencer*, April 3, 1832, and read the report of a speech made by Congressman William Stanberry of Ohio in the House of Representatives. Stanberry asked this question, "Was the late Secretary of War [John Eaton] removed in consequence of his attempt fraudulently to give to Governor Houston the contract for Indian rations?" The imputation of the question and of Stanberry's general remarks was clear: Houston and Eaton were accused of fraud and the honor of the Jackson administration was challenged.

Houston knew and Stanberry could easily have found out that Eaton had resigned voluntarily in a situation growing out of a Jackson-Calhoun quarrel. Eaton had become involved in it by suppressing a pamphlet that was intended to put the quarrel at rest. A contributing factor in his resignation was the scandal concerning his wife Peggy O'Neill, a tavernkeeper's daughter with a questionable past who had been socially ostracized by Vice-President Calhoun's wife. Squabbles over Peggy, and Jackson's firm support of Eaton, had weakened the prestige of the administration in some quarters.

The ration matter referred to by Stanberry concerned events in the spring of 1830 when Houston was in Washington as a member of a Cherokee delegation. At that time the government had under consideration the so-called Indian Removal Act. If, as anticipated, the Indian tribes were moved farther west, large quantities of provisions would be required for their journey.

Houston had sought a contract as provisioner without bidding. Bids were customary in some cases but were not required by law. Anti-Jacksonites got wind of the fact that Jackson and Eaton seemed disposed to favor Houston, and started an uproar, whereupon Eaton put the contracts up for bidding. Houston and a partner, John Van Fossen, entered a bid of thirteen cents per ration. The lowest bid was eight cents, but Eaton refused to let the contract on the ground that expected bids from Ohio had not arrived in time to be considered. The anti-Jacksonites charged that the real reason was the administration's desire to favor Houston. While the question was being knocked about, the Indian Removal bill failed to pass, the need for rations ceased, and the whole matter was dropped. With the collapse of the Removal Act, Houston lost what he regarded as a chance to pick up a fortune.

From Houston's viewpoint, Stanberry's attack was crucial on two other counts. He later charged in his *Memoir* (pp. 55-56), that Stanberry was a brazen scoundrel, one of a large clique in the House inspired by a conspiracy of Arkansas Territory swindlers to "ruin Jackson as a public man by calumny" and to "cover Houston with infamy." Their motive, he explained, was to prevent Jackson and Houston from interfering with fraudulent practices involving Indian annuities and other matters.

There was an equally important fact that Houston did not confide in his *Memoir*. It could be especially damaging, at this critical moment when the exile in his shabby buckskin coat enjoyed the prospect of mending his fortunes and regaining respectability with the aid of New York financiers. If it went unchallenged, it would wreck his promising connections and place a further stain on his name.

In his room at the Indian Queen Hotel, Houston wrote a note to the Honorable William Stanberry. After referring to what he had read in the *National Intelligencer* he said: "The object of this note is to ascertain whether my name was used by you in debate, and, if so, whether your remarks have been correctly quoted . . . I hope you will find it convenient to reply without delay." [2]

As Houston's "friend," Cave Johnson delivered the note to Stanberry, who responded promptly with a note addressed to Johnson: "The object of the note [delivered by Johnson] is to ascertain whether Mr. Houston's name was used by me in debate, and whether my remarks were correctly quoted. I cannot recognize the right of Mr. Houston to make this request." [3]

Infuriated by this haughty rebuff, Houston let it be known that he proposed to chastise the congressman at the first opportunity. From this time, whenever he went on the street, Houston carried a heavy hickory walking stick, cut from a tree at The Hermitage.

Learning of this, Stanberry's friends urged the congressman to go armed.

On the evening of April 13 Houston paid a social call on Senator Felix Grundy of Tennessee in company with Congressman John Blair of the same state and Senator Alexander Buckner of Missouri. The three visitors left Grundy's together. At about eight o'clock, on Pennsylvania Avenue, as they were passing opposite Stanberry's boardinghouse, Blair saw the congressman crossing to their side of the moonlit street. Anticipating trouble, Blair turned abruptly and disappeared in the shadows. Houston and Senator Buckner waited until Stanberry came up.

"Are you Mr. Stanberry?" the ex-Governor asked politely.

A man of large impressive physique, Stanberry answered that he was. Instantly excited, Houston exclaimed, "Then you are the damned rascal!" and he struck Stanberry over the shoulder with the hickory cane.

With the cry, "Oh don't!" Stanberry started to run. On account of his Horseshoe Bend wound, Houston was weak in the shoulder. He could not hold the congressman and flog him at the same time. He leaped on Stanberry from behind, attempting to use his weight to pull his victim down. Stanberry staggered but carried Houston's 180 pounds a considerable distance.

In his testimony later, Senator Buckner was unable to say whether Stanberry managed to free himself or Houston "thrust Stanberry from him." At any rate, when Stanberry's hat fell to the ground, he stooped to pick it up, tripped, and fell. Rolling over on his back, he lifted both feet while loudly emitting sounds that Buckner described as "hallooing." Houston continued the as-yet-unfinished business of belaboring Stanberry's exposed posterior. Buckner was about to intercede—so he testified—when he saw Stanberry, on his back, "put out both hands." Buckner said that he did not see what was in Stanberry's hand, but "I heard a sound like the snapping of a gunlock, and I saw particles of fire." If there was a weapon it did not discharge. Buckner said he thought he saw Houston seize the weapon and then continue to whack Stanberry with his stick. Still on his back, Stanberry put up both feet again, and Houston battered that part of his anatomy later described by Buckner as "elsewhere." [4]

Then, satisfied that justice had been done, Houston stopped. Stanberry, after lying still for a moment, apparently expecting more of the same, scrambled to his feet and fled across the street to his quarters.

Afterwards, when asked how he felt while punishing Stanberry, Houston said, "Meaner than ever I felt in my life; I thought I had gotten hold of a great dog, but found a contemptible whining puppy." [5]

Confined to his bed, Stanberry wrote to Speaker Andrew Stevenson the next day, charging that he had been "assaulted and knocked down" by a "bludgeon and severely bruised and wounded by Samuel Houston. I request that you lay it before the House." [6]

A resolution calling for Houston's arrest and punishment was promptly introduced. Congressman James K. Polk, the future President, argued correctly that the House did not have the power of arrest in such matters, but the resolution passed with a shout of enthusiasm, 145 to 25.

Arrested and brought before the bar of the House of Representatives, Houston walked down the aisle in the custody of the sergeant-at-arms, wearing his rumpled coat with the worn beaver collar and carrying his hickory cane. Speaker Stevenson read the arraignment, charging that Houston had "waylaid" Stanberry.

The accused denied that he had assaulted Stanberry in the manner charged, but admitted great indignation because of what he had read in the *Intelligencer*, "imputing to the accused by name a gross offense." The dissemination throughout the country of such falsehoods, affecting "his honor and character," had prompted inquiry, he said. Stanberry had refused to answer, aggravating the initial offense. At the moment of encountering Stanberry, Houston said, he was not seeking or expecting to see him, but "thus excited ... on accidentally meeting Stanberry ... himself unarmed with nothing but a walking stick while he believed that Stanberry carried pistols ... he did assault and beat him." [7] But he denied that he intended to commit contempt of the House or that he had breached any of its privileges.

When informed that his version of the encounter was regarded as equivalent to a plea of "not guilty," Houston protested that the matter was not within the jurisdiction of the House but he would defend himself. He asked for twenty-four hours to prepare his defense. He was granted forty-eight hours.

All other news ceased to be of national interest. Anti-Jacksonites seized the opening to attack the President. The *United States Telegraph*, owned by General Duff Green, formerly a friend but now a political enemy of Jackson, charged on April 21, 1832: "We have long seen, that tactics of the Nashville school were to be transferred to Washington and that the voice of truth was to be silenced by the dread of the assassin...."

Niles' Register, specializing in such news of Congress as it considered fit to print, omitted columns to make space for the spectacular case. Fantastic reports circulated. One said that President Jackson had expressed the wish that there might be "a dozen Houstons to beat and cudgel members of Congress." Though Jackson had had his troubles with that body, what he actually said was, "After a few more examples of the same kind, members of Congress will learn to keep civil tongues in their heads." [8]

On the second day after arraignment, in his shabby coat, Houston presented himself at the bar of the House, this time accompanied by the illustrious counsel, Francis Scott Key. The galleries and aisles were crowded. Congressman Phillip Doddridge, an intimate of Stanberry, led off by objecting to the prisoner being in the "mere personal custody of the Marshal... eating and drinking the public wine." [9] Since the prisoner must be fed at public expense, Doddridge argued, he should be kept in jail. Not enough members concurred in this proposal, so Houston continued free in the custody of the marshal.

The prosecution offered Stanberry as the first witness. He displayed an assortment of lumps, bumps, welts, and bruises, excepting only those on the "elsewhere" portion of his anatomy. All this effectively proved what the defense already admitted—that Houston had done a thorough job.

On cross-examination Stanberry was asked what, if any, evidence he had to support his charge of fraud. Objections that this was an attempt to put the plaintiff on trial instead of the defendant were overruled by a vote of the House, 101 to 82.

Stanberry then testified, "It was no part of my intention to impute fraud to General Houston." Later, though, he did attempt to prove that Houston had been guilty of fraud.[10]

The prosecution closed its case after a week and Key opened for the defense. Key had drunk too much and was not in good form. His argument was feeble and his presentation wandered and sagged. Houston was not happy about the gentlemanly quality of Key's speech but, unlike his peppery friend in the President's house, he was not disposed to make an issue of it.

The President sent for Houston, who was exhilarated to behold Jackson in a worse rage than he had ever seen before. With blistering invective, Jackson lashed out at his enemies in Congress. "It's not you they wish to injure, Sam," he said. "They wish to injure your old commander." He said that Houston must prepare his defense and must dress like a gentleman when he presented it. From a drawer he withdrew a long silk purse containing gold pieces and offered it to Houston.[11]

Houston's pride rebelled, and he declined, saying that he had no means of repaying the money. Jackson insisted.

Most of the money in the purse, but not quite all, went for clothes of the kind that Jackson would have approved. Houston had a tailor measure him for a knee-length coat of a fine material and trousers cut in the latest style; he also supplied himself with a white satin waistcoat and other appropriate items for a gentleman's wardrobe.

After Key's fiasco, Houston more or less managed his own defense. With perfect courtesy he cross-examined Stanberry and questioned some of his own witnesses. One of these was Senator Buckner, who supported Houston's claim that the meeting with Stanberry was accidental and by no means an ambush. He told of seeing the sparks that he supposed came from Stanberry's pistol. The defense did not produce the weapon nor ask to have it produced. In behalf of Defendant Houston, Counselor Houston proceeded with extreme leisureliness. On May 6 he was notified that he must close his case the next day.

On the evening of the sixth Houston gave a party and opened a jug. Apparently the affair was financed by a small surplus remaining from Jackson's gold pieces. The friends who gathered were all from Tennessee except House Speaker Stevenson. Years later, Houston described the evening to a group of friends in Texas, including Judge

Alexander W. Terrell, later ambassador to Turkey in the Grant administration.

At midnight Speaker Stevenson was snoring on the sofa. Senator Grundy had ceased to be interested—or interesting. Congressman Baillie Peyton suffered from a low level of visibility. Congressman James Polk left early. It may have been on this occasion that Houston good-naturedly described his friend Polk as "a victim of drinking water as a beverage."

Though he drank deeply that night, Houston told Terrell "he could not feel intoxicated." Nevertheless, he doubted that he would be sufficiently well ordered in the morning to present a summing-up that would favorably impress his hearers and the sanctified old gentleman in the President's house. For ascertaining his potential capacity for the day's performance after a night's carouse, he had an established procedure which involved morning coffee. He called a bellboy and ordered him to wake up a barber and bring him. When the barber arrived, Houston instructed him to return at sunrise with his "shaving traps" and a cup of coffee. Then he opened a drawer and showed the barber a pistol and a purse. "If the coffee does not stick when I drink it," Houston said, "take this pistol and shoot me, and the gold is yours."

In explanation of this procedure, Houston dwelt at length in his account to Terrell—who became a chronicler of Houston memorabilia—on the hopelessness of his position before the world. He was on the bottom rung of the ladder, he said, and he would rather die than make a failure of his summing-up speech. He was sure he would fail if the coffee sickened him.

Terrell's recollection of Houston's narrative concludes with this: "The next morning the coffee agreed with him, and being dressed for the occasion he appeared at the bar of the House in custody of the sergeant-at-arms at the appointed time." [12]

10. *Applause for the Accused*

AT NOON on May 7, 1832, Speaker of the House Andrew Stevenson, who had been a guest of the defendant the previous evening, went to his dais. At his back was a figure of Liberty above a marble eagle with wings spread in flight, and on either side of the eagle were flag-draped panels with likenesses of Washington and Lafayette. The House chamber, under its sixty-foot high glass dome, was jammed with an expectant audience; in addition to members, there were government officers, army and navy personnel, diplomats, socialites, and the press.

Every seat on the floor was occupied, and chairs in the aisles accommodated part of the overflow; other spectators pressed together between the columns along the walls. In the front row sat Counselor Key and near him Junius Brutus Booth, one of the best known actors of the day, who was in attendance to give his moral support to an old friend, the accused.

Houston faced the assemblage after a respectful bow to the speaker. His poise, dignity, and elegant attire contradicted the current tales of debauchery and degradation. Few had any idea of the phenomenon they were witnessing: the defendant's extraordinary ability to stage a suave performance after the conviviality of the night before. In a resonant voice carrying to every part of the chamber, Houston confessed embarrassment at being arraigned for the only time in his life on a charge of violating the laws of his country. He asked that the actions for which he stood accused be "pursued to the motives" that inspired them. If, himself deeply wronged, he had trespassed upon the prerogatives of the House or his country's laws he was prepared to accept responsibility. Even though the House was exceeding its authority under the Constitution, he would abide by any judgment and penalty that this body chose to inflict.

He assured the House that he did not underestimate the charge against him.

[It] is one of no ordinary character [he said]. If I shall be convicted of having acted from the motive alleged by my accuser [waylaying, with intent to kill] lasting infamy must be the necessary consequence. The darkest dungeons of this Government, with all the pains and penalties of treason, [are trifling] compared with that load of infamy which must attach itself forever to my name.

He immediately attacked the legality of the proceedings:

I admit that the members of this House have privileges ... [but] it is idle to say that ... it goes with a member and remains with him while outraging the rights of citizens....

If such a discretion [as this trial] is in your hand, the power of punishment must extend to life itself ... over a man who had not, in any way, interrupted your deliberations. If you can arrest him, you may not only fine him, and imprison him, but you may inflict upon him torture and death. When a member of this House, entrenched in his privilege, brands a private citizen in the face of the whole nation, as a fraudulent villain he ... renders himself answerable to the party aggrieved....

Gentlemen have admitted that the power they claimed is not found in the Constitution. Then where is it? [1]

All members of the House who had any sense of responsibility for their official conduct must have felt uneasy as Houston made it clear to the assemblage and thus to the nation that the House, without a vestige of authority, was exercising the powers of grand jury, prosecutor, jury, and judge. Throughout his summation he relentlessly emphasized the extraordinary character of the proceedings.

Houston reminded his hearers that Stanberry under cross-examination had declared it had not been his "object to impute fraud" to the defendant, but later had changed his position arguing to the contrary. The "unfounded surmises and flimsy affidavits submitted in support of this contention were dismissed by Houston with a fillip of ridicule as unworthy of serious discussion. This cleared the way for his emphasis on what he desired to have accepted as the main issues: the illegality of the proceedings and its destructive effect upon his reputation and character. At moments, he wandered from these issues but always returned to them. For more than an hour his eloquence enchanted his friends and disgusted his opponents, and he had another hour to go.

A member had alluded "to the Constituent and National Assembly

73

of France" as a precedent for the action of the House. Houston seized upon this to emphasize the manner in which the House had breached its constitutional powers. Referring to the National Assembly, he said:

> What legislative bodies could have been more corrupt than they? ... they themselves had usurped the power they exercised—and terror struck the hearts of men who had no home, no country: for where there is no security to the citizen there is neither home nor country.... Bonaparte was used to say that it was not he who seized the thrones of Europe, but it was the people of Europe who had thrown themselves under his feet. ... Let the House do its duty within the Constitution, and they will find, throughout every portion of this people, a spirit of the deepest reverence to sustain their rights.

He turned his attention to fears expressed by some members that they would become the victims of "immolation" similar to that suffered by the Hon. Mr. Stanberry unless Houston was severely dealt with.

> Some of the gentlemen have thrown out the idea that... some rude, ferocious bully might assault them for the remarks they had offered on the floor. If these remarks ... refer to me I ... can assure them that I have not merited such a reproach. ... I have never thirsted for the blood of my fellowman.... I never have been engaged in riots, or guilty of bullying any man ... nor have I ever assailed anyone unless when deeply wronged. ... I made no resistance to [my illegal apprehension] ... yet it has been deemed not sufficient to rely on the constitution ... personal feelings of members have been appealed to ... to induce the House to act under the influence of partiality and to sacrifice its duty, the law, and the Constitution to merely personal consideration.... It is not my rights alone, but the rights of millions that are involved here....

From mild persuasion he turned to indignation:

> But while standing at this bar, have I not been branded with the epithet of assassin? ... Will the annals of judicial proceeding exhibit another instance where such language has been permitted to be applied to an individual in custody? Yet ... in the eyes

of this whole nation I have been traduced by the epithet assassin. ... I bore no dagger when I met my accuser! ... I could not but think of the ... rebuke administered to the high priest of the Jews by the Apostle Paul, when he stood in bonds before him; and the high priest ordered him to be smote upon the mouth. 'God shall smite thee, thou whited wall, for sittest thou to judge me according to the law, and commandest me to be smitten contrary to the law?'

The prosecution had dropped big names such as the Earl of Shaftesbury and Sir Alexander Murray in connection with cases involving legislative immunity and more or less irrelevant statutes under Anne, George II, and George III had been cited. With his wide reading in history and law, Houston could deal with this kind of competition. He ornamented his discourse with similar allusions marshaling an impressive list of tyrants: Draco, Caligula, Caesar, and Cromwell among others. The illegalities of which they had been guilty had brought serious consequences. In the same way, he said, the tyranny and illegality of which the House was guilty in this case would reflect upon it.

In the midst of his discourse Houston paused, and there was a touch of the ominous about it. It was no mere oratorical effect. He wanted strict attention and he was rewarded with hushed silence. He reminded the House of his voluntary pledge to abide by its judgment and penalty in spite of its illegal procedure. But he wanted members to know that there were limits beyond which he would not permit any man to violate his rights no matter what the cost.

Here he was referring to something that the House itself had regarded as improper and had stricken from the record. Members had referred to his marital troubles in a manner which Houston denounced as "wanton." The exact terms of these attacks are not available because they were eliminated. What is known about the incident comes from Congressman Baillie Peyton who related the circumstances to Alexander Terrell.[2]

Peyton said that Houston took up this matter in the House with "might and majesty." Brushing aside tact and mild persuasiveness, the accused informed the House that he had an announcement to make. He stood at his full height, straight as an Indian, with no suggestion of humility or compromise in his bearing. He cautioned every member who might be tempted to indulge in unwise comment to bear in mind that the defendant was not on trial for his marital difficulties and tragic sufferings. The proceedings related to a single substantive offense, and gentlemen should restrict their comments to the issue.

"That man Stanberry," he thundered, "has slandered me through the columns of a newspaper, and refused even to answer a polite note, and I chastised him as I would a dog, and I will visit the same punishment on the shoulders of anyone who insults me, even though it be one of you who now sit in judgment on my conduct."

Stirrings of sympathy rippled through the galleries, followed by a thunder of applause. Speaker Stevenson pounded the gavel in vain. When the assemblage finally became silent, a Washington belle in the gallery rose, tossed a bouquet at the defendant's feet, and in a startlingly flute-like soprano voice called out, "I had rather be Sam Houston in a dungeon than Stanberry on a throne." Terrell reports:

He [Houston] told us that when he stooped down to take the flowers and looking up bowed his thanks to the fair lady he felt a thrill of joy like that he experienced in the flush of victory at San Jacinto.

Houston went on:

Though the ploughshare of ruin has been driven over me and laid waste my brightest hopes...I have only to say to those who rebuke me...when they see adversity pressing upon me...

I seek no sympathies, nor need;
The thorns which I have reaped are of the tree
I planted; they have torn me, and I bleed.[3]

Houston had reached that moment when an orator realizes that his audience is in his hand; the skill of his performance fascinated even hostile members of the assembly. He discarded argument and switched to emotional effects: "Though it may have been alledged that I am a man of broken fortune and blasted reputation, I never can forget that reputation, however limited, is the high boon of heaven. Perhaps the circumstances of adversity, by which I have been crushed, have made me cling to the little remains of it which I still possess, and to cherish them with the greater fondness."

Two years and six months before, on Christmas Eve, 1829, the accused, in Indian dress, accompanied by a delegation of his red brothers, went up the Mississippi on his way to Washington. He was stirred by the sight of the shore of Tennessee, to which he referred as his "homeland." Stricken by memories of the disaster that had led to his exile and contemplating his ruined fortunes and his various failures since he had retired to the forest, he had been inspired to a poetic thought. The thought gave birth to a long poem of five stanzas on a theme that dominated his whole life: no matter how far down in the scale of human values adversity plunged a man, that man could look upward with hope and trust that someday his aspiration would come true.

Without naming the source of the lines, Counselor Houston in behalf of Defendant Houston quoted Poet Houston for the benefit of his profoundly attentive audience:

> There is a bright undying thought in man,
> That bids his soul still upward look
> To Fame's proud cliff;
> And, longing, look
> In hope to give his name
> For after ages to admire
> And wonder how he reached
> The dizzy, dangerous height,
> Or where he stood, or how.

He pointed to the American flag over the portrait of Lafayette. "So long as that flag shall bear aloft its glittering stars . . . shall the rights of American citizens be preserved safe . . . till discord shall wreck the spheres—and the grand march of time shall cease—and not one fragment of all creation be left to chafe on the bosom of eternity's waves."

With a gesture and a bow of courtesy to the speaker, Houston indicated that he had finished. The gallery applauded, then gave him a standing ovation. Again Speaker Stevenson gaveled for order in vain. The accused took his seat near Counselor Francis Scott Key. Actor Junius Brutus Booth, an authority on great performances, leaned over and said with feeling, "Houston, take my laurels!" [4]

11. *Bread upon the Waters*

AFTER four days of debate, with Houston present in the custody of the marshal, the House voted against discharging him without penalty. Then, by a vote of 106 to 89, he was deemed "guilty as charged," and was sentenced to be reprimanded by the speaker.

May 14 was set for carrying out the sentence, and on that date the chamber was crowded again. The speaker asked the defendant to stand before him. Houston took his place with a respectful bow. At some length, with deliberate emphasis, the speaker complimented the guilty man upon his character and intelligence. Briefly he added, "I forebear to say more than to pronounce the judgment of the House which is that you... be reprimanded at this bar by the Speaker... and... I do reprimand you accordingly."

The reprimand, which included commendation of the accused, was applauded. True to his promise and with another bow to the speaker, Houston accepted the judgment of the House. But he asked and was granted leave to file a protest in the House *Journal* that the sentence as well as the proceedings were "unwarranted by the Constitution." [1]

The event launched him on a period of triumphant rehabilitation. After his long series of mishaps and defeats, Houston enjoyed the sensation of victory. He shed his buckskin coat; with it went the remnants of Big Drunk. Houston's conduct was circumspect in every way. Anti-Jacksonites assailed him, but their tone was milder. Editorial comment throughout the nation expressed approval and joy when he embraced anew the country that he had quit with bitterness.

Houston went to live in the President's house. Jackson offered him any one of a number of appointments. But Houston declined office on the ground that he might still be a handicap to the Old Chief, and also because, since his talks with Prentiss in New York, he entertained new and attractive ideas about Texas.

Congressman Stanberry liked the outcome of Houston's trial in the House as little as he did the flogging. But now he put up more of a fight. He persuaded the House to appoint a committee to investigate the ration matter. This inquiry took several weeks; Houston was in attendance most of the time. Witnesses came from far away, one being Auguste Chouteau from Arkansas Territory. The majority report stated, "John H. Eaton and Samuel Houston do stand entirely acquitted from all imputation of fraud."[2]

Stanberry next attempted to have Houston denied the privilege of the House floor to which he was entitled as a former member. Congressman Polk went into action in Houston's behalf and the resolution failed by 101 to 90. Then Stanberry took his case to the Federal Court of the District of Columbia where it should have gone in the first place. Houston was indicted on a charge of criminal assault. This development attracted little attention; but Houston, eager to set out for Texas, was frustrated by delays and postponement of the trial date and proceedings.

All that spring and summer, while his two trials were in progress, Houston exchanged communications with Prentiss about the Texas project.[3] Back in April, three days after he read Stanberry's first fraud imputation in the *National Intelligencer*, Houston received his first letter from the financier. Prentiss said that hourly he expected a packet to arrive "with important intelligence that [may] require your sudden departure on the business of which we lately conversed. . . . are [you] still inclined to embrace the object?"

Houston answered promptly on April 8:

It will be convenient for me [after my trial] to repair to New York at any time and with very little delay . . . repair to TEXAS, and assume any duties in relation to the Agency, which may be assigned to me. . . .

Since I saw you I have concluded to visit TEXAS at all events this Spring or Summer, but will go by way of Nashville [unless the company requires otherwise].

Six days before his memorable summation in the House, Houston again assured Prentiss that as soon as the case was disposed of "and matters could be arranged . . . I will set out for the *land of promise.*" He underscored it. The land of *promise!* Expectations were mounting, a driving force urged him to be off for the sunlit land, and he was full of optimism.

Throughout the correspondence there are shadows and forecasts of changes that might be expected in Texas. On a note for $1,594.20 Houston bought from Prentiss certificates representing one-half interest in the Dominquez grant. Soon afterward, he wrote Prentiss, "The land which I bought, to be candid with you has claimed not much solicitude of me. I looked to other matters."

Other matters? Something of more importance than a mere acquisition of 25,000 acres? It was frankly admitted between the correspondents that the value of the acres purchased depended upon whether Texas continued under the sovereignty of Mexico or came under that of the United States. Such matters were always referred to as a "change" that might be expected in Texas. Financiers, speculators, adventurers, and ambitious men did not use such blunt terms as "insurrection," "revolution," or "filibuster." The language employed was more in keeping with a cautious weather report: *a "change" in prospect, possibly stormy. Change . . . a key word.*

While his second trial was in progress, Houston received a long letter, dated June 2, 1832, from John A. Wharton in New Orleans. Wharton was jubilant about the outcome of the House trial.

> . . . from all that I have read and heard you certainly have lost nothing [by your affair with Stanberry], but on the other hand your conduct has been approved by a large majority throughout the Union; so far as I am concerned (and I profess to feel most deeply in your welfare) I do most sincerely and heartily rejoice at your whipping the puppy and I read with pleasure and pride the account of your bearing throughout: this is the case with all of your friends here. . . .

Wharton stated in this same letter that a Virginian, Dr. Branch T. Archer, who had been in Texas for twelve months, had just returned and was "of opinion that there will be some fighting there next fall, and that a fine country will be gained without much bloodshed, he is very desirous that you should go there, and believes that you can be of more service than any other man." Wharton expected to go to Texas in August to visit his brother William. He urged Houston to come too. "Texas does undoubtedly present a fine field for fame, enterprise, and usefulness, and whenever they are ready for action I will be with them." [4]

Houston's impatience to get started was further excited by this letter. But he still was detained by court delays. On June 16, his affairs still dragging, he wrote to Prentiss: "I am in haste to be off. I am very poor, and I will only expend money here. Indeed, I must and will be off soon—if I have to walk to some large water course, and make a raft to float upon!" The possibility of his resorting to a raft for transportation arose from his extreme lack of money. Prentiss had promised him an advance which he had not received.

On June 28, 1832, Houston was convicted of criminal assault and fined $500 and costs by District of Columbia Court Judge William Cranch. Houston called the verdict "tough." But the Court gave him a year to pay and never tried to enforce it. Finally on July 3, 1834, some two years after imposition of the fine, it was remitted by President Jackson on the ground that it was excessive.

His case disposed of, Houston put off for Nashville where President Jackson had gone immediately after the adjournment of Congress. From there, on August 18, he wrote to Prentiss about recent disturbances in Texas, of which he had heard rumors. He regretted not having been there, presumably because he would have liked to participate. Also he reported the latest news from friends recently returned from Texas about the glories of that place.

I have seen several friends here lately from Texas, and all represent it in the most prosperous state, and say it is a lovely region! Thousands would flock there from this country, if the Government were settled, but will not venture without it!

My opinion is that it would be of vast importance to have persons there who could look at matters, with a view, to [make] changes, which are necessary, and must [take] place, before long in that country, and without which it can never be, what it ought to be, for the benefit of those interested.

He added other news that gave him pleasure:

Several persons have said to me that I was looked for, and earnestly wished for by the Citizens of Texas. . . . The people look to the Indians on Arkansas as auxiliaries, in the event of a change—So I will pass that way and see my *old friends*. I will ride to the Hermitage this evening, and see the Old Chief. . . .

The expense money from Prentiss, which he had expected in Washington, failed to overtake him in Nashville. To make the exploratory land survey which he and Prentiss had agreed upon, he had to have money from somewhere because his cash resources were extremely limited. He was beginning to suspect the New Yorker of leading him on without seriousness of purpose. He wrote a letter of rather sharp criticism, betraying the fact that he felt he had been hoodwinked. "My hopes were ardent in the prosperity of that country, but they are less so at this time. You know that hope deferred maketh the heart sick! ... I have no doubt but what you will act in good faith. ..."

A hard blow came with Prentiss' letter in mid-August. A new obstacle had arisen to interfere with his Texas plans. Cholera, the plague that medical science could not stop, had come down the Champlain Canal from Montreal. Victims, weakened from vomiting, in a single day, succumbed to the agonizing pains of bursting stomachs, turned blue, and were taken away in hearses. The plague moved down the Hudson on passenger boats and freighters. In New York the afflicted died by the dozens each day. Doctors knew nothing to do. Newspapers recommended, in addition to prayer, staying away from crowded places.

In a letter, also written on August 18, Prentiss reported from the stricken city:

> The cholera is yet dreadful & more so than appears from our daily reports—burials are double the number of reported deaths by cholera. ...
> This awful calamity has prevented any movement in our Texas affairs since I last wrote. ... I talked with our mutual friend ... & urged him to make the needful advance ... to which he replied he was not able at this most distressing moment to do more than for himself. ...

Disappointed in his hope for financial backing from New York, Houston went to The Hermitage. Jackson may have lent him money, as much as $500, to help him on his way.[5] In any case, Houston received a passport that had been issued at Jackson's request by Acting Secretary of War John Robb, under date of August 6, 1832. It described "General Sam Houston. ... a citizen of the United States. Thirty-eight years of age, Six feet two inches in stature, brown hair and light complexion. ..." The passport requested "all the tribes of Indians, whether in amity with the United States, or as yet not allied to them by Treaties, to permit [him] safely and freely to pass through their respective, territories. . . . and in case of need to give him all lawful aid and protection." [6]

The passport was the result of conversations between Houston and Jackson in Washington about Houston's proposed visit to Texas. It has been the basis of mistaken assumptions that Houston went to Texas either as Jackson's personal agent or as a government agent with an understanding, direct or implied, that he was to promote revolution. For over a century historians have made exhaustive efforts to unearth evidence of such an arrangement, but have produced nothing to justify this conclusion. Jackson believed that the Choctaws, Chickasaws, and Creeks could promote their westward migration by signing a treaty of peace with the Texas Comanches whose power the other western tribes feared; as far as he was concerned, Houston's mission in Texas was to see that this was accomplished. "A confidential mission" with "little known of its history," Houston described it in after years.[7]

Another subject must have figured prominently at The Hermitage meeting. Houston's spirited behavior in the Stanbery trial had revived his popularity in Tennessee. His friends had rallied. A movement was on foot to make him governor again. Houston had no thought of abandoning his exploratory trip to Texas, even though his political prospects had improved and Prentiss had disappointed his financial expectations. But on September 15 he wrote a final letter to Prentiss, saying, "The matter of Texas, has to my mortification, not turned out, as I had hoped and believed, but I shall 'cast my bread upon the waters, and look for its return after many days.' Tomorrow morning I am to set out for there!"

When he set out "for there" he went roundabout by way of Wigwam Neosho. Anticipating a long absence either on account of his Texas business or of political activity in Tennessee, he settled up his Cherokee domestic affairs with finality. Diana may have understood from the first that the tribal ceremony was intended to raise the status of their relationship above the level of a mere liaison, but she must have realized that if he ever resumed public life in the States she could not go with him.

Their relations appear to have been resolved in accord with the tribal rule that when a white man separated from his Cherokee wife she should be "compensated for her pain and anguish." He gave her the Neosho property with its fields and two slaves. He stripped himself of his last good horse and kept only "Jack," a bob-tailed mustang. From Diana he received a power of attorney which identified her not as his wife but as the "widow of David Gentry." The use for which this power was intended is not clear, but it may be surmised that it was in lieu of a divorce. The designation of Diana as Gentry's "widow" was something tangible to indicate that the married relationship had terminated.

When he left the Cherokee country, Houston was accompanied on the first stage of his journey by a friendly, celebrated character, United States Marshal Elias Rector, formerly a peddler, later known as the Arkansas Traveler. They shared spiritual exaltations and liquid refreshments. Rector seems to have felt obligated to this distinguished man who furnished such rare companionship and high-grade entertainment.

Houston was acutely aware of his loss of dignity by riding a wretched tailless mustang that let his feet almost touch the ground. A legend put words into his mouth that are almost as good as anything Houston could have devised. To his companion, who was riding a fine big horse, he is reported to have said:

> This damned bob-tailed pony is a disgrace. He is continually fighting flies, and has no means of protecting himself, and his kicks and contortions render his rider ridiculous. I shall be the laughter of all Mexico. I require a steed with his natural weapon, a flowing tail, that he may defend himself against his enemies as his master has done. . . . you *must* trade.[8]

Whether or not these were Houston's actual words, Rector was persuaded and generously agreed to the proposed exchange. When they parted, Houston rode off on a horse that was up to his standard.

Legend also has it that, not satisfied with this generosity, Rector threw in a razor, and Houston is supposed to have said to him, "I accept your gift and mark my words if I have good luck, this razor will sometime shave the chin of the President of a republic." [9] Too pat for credence, this observation does not coalesce with good evidence as to what was actually in Houston's mind at the moment. On December 2, 1832, at Fort Towson, near the Red River, just before

84

he crossed over this "muddy Rubicon" he wrote to "Dear Jack."
Jack was his favorite cousin, John H. Houston of Washington.

> I have been for weeks past in the Indian Country, and, of
> course, no writing, but now, as I am about to enter Texas, I will
> just give you a touch. My health and spirits are both good, my
> habits sober, and my heart straight.
> ... friends have announced my name as a candidate for next
> Governor of Tennessee. Shou'd I live, I must be back by the
> first of April, or last of March and see how the land lies for
> such business. My friends are sanguine of my success. I do not
> doubt it, if I should run! as I think I shall.
> My business in Texas is of some importance to my pecuniary
> interest, and as such, I must attend to it! [10]

Thus, when according to unfounded legend, Houston is supposed
to have been thinking about himself as the president of an as yet un-
born republic, he was actually looking over his shoulder with a sharp
eye on his chances of being re-elected governor of Tennessee. On
the practical side his view of his future was that of a land speculator
much in need of financial rehabilitation; and he was still the same
idealistic opportunist eager to distinguish himself by some kind of
service.

In his *Memoir* he recorded that "one look" at Texas and the situation of the people was enough to convince him that this was the
place for him. But that one look consisted of a ride of twelve hundred miles or more, talks with many people, a meeting with Stephen
Austin, and a variety of other activities. He soon gave up completely
any idea of resuming politics in Tennessee. In time, Houston discovered that Texas needed him as much as he needed Texas.

BOOK II

THE FIVE-POINTED STAR

1. North and South of the Rio Grande

TWELVE years before Sam Houston crossed the Red River into Texas, Moses Austin, a Connecticut Yankee, traveled a thousand miles through wild and dangerous country to San Antonio de Béxar, capital of the Spanish province of Texas. As a maker of lead products in Virginia and a miner of lead in Missouri, he had been dogged by a bad fate. But his faith in the frontier remained and he dreamed of establishing a colony.

Governor Antonio de Martinez, influenced by Austin's friend, Baron de Bastrop, a German officer in the service of Spain, supported Austin's petition. From the authorities of the Eastern Interior Provinces of New Spain, Austin received permission to bring in three hundred families.

On his midwinter homeward journey, Austin rafted rivers and was unable to prevent dampness from reaching his gunpowder supply. Unable to shoot game, he lived on roots and acorns. Exposure brought on pneumonia, but he managed to reach the home of his daughter in Missouri before collapsing. He died June 10, 1821, at fifty-six.

His deathbed plea, addressed to his wife, Maria Brown Austin, was that their son Stephen Fuller Austin, a university-trained lawyer, continue what his father had begun. In his dying hour he prayed that God would help Stephen go on with the colonization in the same way he would have done.

Stephen, born in Virginia on November 3, 1793, was then twenty-seven years old. Physically frail but a spiritual giant, he had gone forehandedly to New Orleans to arrange for colonists and supplies so that he could share in the undertaking if his father succeeded in getting the grant. On learning of his father's dying request, he hesitated only momentarily because of the immensity of the task; then decided to carry out his father's wishes.

In San Antonio, Governor Martinez received him cordially and gave him permission to bring in 800 families. He also authorized Austin to govern his colony as he thought best. The beautiful region that Austin was to settle lay between the San Jacinto and Guadalupe rivers, extending eighty miles inland from near the coast and including the lower parts of the Brazos, the San Bernard, the Colorado, and LaVaca rivers.

In newspapers of the Mississippi Valley, the *empresario* published announcements of the terms he would allow settlers: 640 acres for each male colonist over twenty-one; 320 acres for a wife; 160 acres for each child; and 80 acres for each slave. Mechanics and men of capital would be allowed additional land and privileges in proportion to their capacity to produce. In return they must take an oath of allegiance to the Mexican government, pay Austin 12½ cents an acre to cover his expenses, and settle and cultivate a part of their grants by January, 1823. All settlers must give proof of moral, sober, and industrious character.

Austin's first settlers were a few families from Nacogdoches. After he advertised in the States, the movement was brisk—at first. Then Austin was obliged to spend a year in Mexico City to persuade the government to confirm the grant he had already received and to pass a colonization law. In the States the movement was held back by reports of disaster to Austin's early settlers, suspense about land titles, accounts of Indian attacks, severe droughts, and the necessity to depend on lean deer and mustangs for a steady diet.

Even so, 150 families reached Texas while Austin was absent in Mexico making final arrangements. After that, the growth of Austin's colony was still more rapid; an official census in the fall of 1825 showed 1,800 persons, 443 of whom were slaves. The colonists were mainly land-hunting Americans dissatisfied with the land policy of their own country. Early arrivals suffered from continual depredations—murder, robbery, horse-stealing, cattle-killing, destruction of hogs and crops. Austin's difficulties as administrator were innumerable. He had much to learn about dealing with colonists, but he learned rapidly. He discovered that the people who had joined his venture were by and large a rough lot. Considering the temper and disposition of some of them, he felt that he "had fared well," for "among ignorant . . . Americans," he said, "independence means resistance and obstinacy, right or wrong. This is particularly true with frontiersmen." [1]

By 1825, interest in Austin's project was widespread in the United States, particularly in Tennessee and Kentucky. A tabulation of 800 applicants from the United States between July, 1825, to July, 1831, showed 200 from Louisiana; 111 from Alabama; 300 from Arkansas, Missouri, and Mississippi; and others from New York, Kentucky, Ohio, Georgia, Pennsylvania, and Virginia. Only 20 were from New England. Growth encouraged Austin to seek and colonize other grants. Census figures showed 2,021 in 1828; 4,248 in June, 1830; 5,665 by 1831.

Inspired by Austin's example and attracted by Mexico's favorable colonization laws, other land-hungry Americans obtained grants. Among them were men whose names would have a special place in Texas history—Robert Leftwich, Haden Edwards, Green Dewitt, Benjamin R. Milam, and David G. Burnet.

The original grant to Moses Austin was a reversal of the Spanish policy of excluding foreigners. Moses Austin received special consideration because his passport showed that he had once been a Spanish subject. Then too the recent revolution in Spain resulted in a somewhat more liberal government.

Why Mexico for a time after winning independence from Spain continued the policy of encouraging American colonists is clearer than why Spain did so in the first place. The Spanish viceroys had failed to protect Mexican settlements in Texas as well as in some of their territory south of the Rio Grande. Mexican authorities welcomed the possibility that this wild, disordered region, which was constantly being raided by Indians, particularly the Comanches, and by desperadoes, might be tamed by American frontiersmen.

Before Sam Houston set foot on Texas soil, all that region north of the Rio Grande twice was declared to be an independent republic. Texas territory reaching to the Rio Grande was included in the Louisiana Purchase, made by Thomas Jefferson in 1803. This claim was maintained until 1819. That year Spain's need for money prompted her to consent to the sale of Florida. President Monroe, somewhat absent-minded about the complications he was creating, forfeited the American claim to Texas as part of the price for Florida. The Monroe treaty made the Sabine River the boundary between Texas and the United States. Many Americans resented the surrender of Texas in this debonair fashion, among them Henry Clay and Dr. James Long. Clay worked off his resentment with an eloquent filibuster opposing the treaty. Long carried his resentment to the court of last resort—war, albeit, a private war.

A volatile son of tempestuous Tennessee, Long had fought under Jackson at New Orleans. He collected seventy-five bold, irresponsible followers and marched from Natchez, Mississippi, to Nacogdoches. After capturing the town with little or no resistance, he announced the existence of a free and independent Texas. He moved on to Galveston and from there was planning to proceed to take San Antonio when the news came early in 1821 that Mexico had won independence from Spain. Long's invasion collapsed.

The second effort to establish an "independent Texas Republic" was known as the Fredonia Rebellion. It had more serious consequences than Long's attempt, leaving in its wake suspicion and hate that powerfully affected Mexico-Texas relations later.

After it became known in the United States and Mexico that Austin's extensive land grant was but a small part of Texas' fertile soil, Americans and Mexicans hurried to Mexico City seeking similar concessions. One of them was Haden Edwards. He spent an expensive and vexatious year in the Mexican capital. After a hard tussle, on April 18, 1825, he finally succeeded in wangling a grant of 100 square miles of the finest fertile lands in East Texas. On its west boundary, along the Navasota and San Jacinto rivers, it bordered Austin's colony. It included the area around Nacogdoches and was populated by a few settlers, most of them Mexicans.

The old-time squatters whose claims bordered Edwards' or were included within his boundaries, numbered in all about sixteen hundred. They had set up their own system of local government, and few had any technical claim to the lands they occupied. They were a colorful band of settlers—Spanish and French Creoles, the usual collection of rough American frontiersmen and adventurers, Indians of various tribes, and a few substantial planters. Long before the

Edwardses came, land claims had been in conflict. Now squatters and title holders alike, fearing displacement, banded together in a kind of conspiracy to protect what they regarded as impairment of their rights by the new *empresario*.

Edwards' contract required him to protect the rights of all who claimed to be original owners of land within the bounds of his grant. It also authorized him to organize and command militia to control the situation. In the hands of an indiscreet man such powers could lead to trouble, and they did.

Haden's brother, Major Benjamin W. Edwards, was associated with him in carrying out his contract. Having invested considerable sums, they were eager to get their money back, and they wanted it fast. Within a month after his arrival in Nacogdoches in the late spring of 1825, Haden Edwards posted notices at street corners announcing himself military commander. All who claimed land within his territory were required to present themselves and show titles or documents. Those who had valid titles would have "to bear the cost of proving them." The lands of those who did not conform to these requirements would be "sold to the first person that occupies them." [2]

The squatters whose just claims Edwards was supposed to protect fought back. Many had what they believed to be good claims, though they lacked the documents to prove their claims. Some were Mexican citizens who feared being dispossessed by this arrogant, rawboned, hustling administrator who lacked the tact, gentleness, and devotion that had contributed to Stephen Austin's success.

Edwards sold an American some land held by a Mexican who could not produce a title. The storm broke; the claimant petitioned the legislature. Mexicans sided with their countrymen, and some Americans sided with Edwards. In a letter to Austin, Edwards boasted that in response to this opposition: "...I came out in a Herricane (sic).... Sounded the trump all around bidding defiance to all their threats and bidding them to leave the lands or...make arrangements to pay for them." [3]

Austin advised in response that Edwards was behaving imprudently and was on the road to disaster. "You do not understand the nature of the authority with which you are vested...." Austin wrote. "Continuance of [your] imprudent course...will totally ruin you, and materially injure all the new settlements." [4]

Forty squatters rode into town, seized Edwards, took him into court and invited complainants to testify against him. No one dared respond, fearing reprisals by the forceful Edwards clan. So some of the Edwardses' associates were tried, convicted, and declared deserving of death, but sentence was commuted to eternal disbarment from office. All this was unofficial terrorism, a kind of lynch law that stopped short of hanging.

On the advice of Austin, Major Edwards sent a report to the political chief of the Department of Texas at San Antonio, Don José Antonio Saucedo, outlining the controversy between the Mexican who had been displaced from his claim and the American who had bought it. Edwards was astonished and angry when the matter was decided in favor of the Mexican.

Major Edwards then appealed to Don Victor Blanco, the governor of the dual state Coahuila-Texas at Monclava. He was amazed and angered by the governor's reply of October 2, 1825:

> In view of such proceedings, by which the conduct of Haden Edwards is well attested, I have declared the annullment of his contract, and his expulsion from the territory of the [Mexican] republic.... He has lost the confidence of the Government, which is suspicious of his fidelity; besides, it is not prudent to admit those who begin by dictating laws as sovereigns. If to you or your constituents these measures are unwelcome and prejudicial, you can apply to the Supreme Government; but you will first evacuate the country, both yourself and Haden Edwards....[5]

Evacuation, to be followed later by an application for redress, did not appeal to the Edwardses as a likely road to justice. Backed by some of their American followers, they prepared for war. They called themselves "Fredonians," appealed to colonists in other localities to join their cause, and informed the Mexican government that they would not "concede one inch, short of [the government's] acknowledgement of their entire, free and unmolested independence from the Sabine to the Rio Grande." [6] Then, on December 16, 1826, the Edwardses declared the Texas portion of the dual state Coahuila-Texas independent, and named it the Republic of Fredonia.

Local anti-Fredonians attacked the Edwards stronghold and succeeded in gaining possession of Nacogdoches on January 4, 1827.

With a few losses, the Fredonians succeeded in driving the squatters out and regained possession of the town. They appealed to Austin to aid their rebellion. Loyal to his oath to Mexico, he refused. Early in January, with 300 men, Colonel Mateo Ahumado, on his way to put down the Edwardses, marched through San Felipe. With several hundred armed colonists and two four-pounder cannons, Austin joined him. Ahumado's force, thus supported, approached on January 27, and discouraged the Fredonians, who slipped out of town. Retreating toward the United States, they crossed the Sabine on January 31, 1827.

The curtain fell on what had the appearance of mere *opéra bouffe*, but the episode had serious consequences over the long term. Austin's part in furnishing the two four-pounders and leading a group of organized colonists against the Fredonians increased his standing with the Mexican government, though it was resented by some colonists. The affair frightened Mexican officials and caused a strong garrison to be set up at Nacogdoches and a general tightening of frontier controls. Its worst effect was the suspicion it left in the minds of all Mexican officials. On the other hand, many Texans believed that the Mexican government had dealt unfairly with the Edwards brothers and were persuaded that Mexican officials should not be relied upon for a just administration of the law.

Events that took place in Mexico were even more exciting and had a powerful impact on Texas history. Spain intended her colonial policy to be enlightened, but power was corruptly used for profit and exploitation. The government was the only source of initiative in the colony, yet the people received no training in governing themselves. A wide gulf developed between the privilged well-to-do and the impoverished. The decade beginning about 1810, before independence from Spain was achieved, was one of rebellion repressed by terror. The hard fighting in behalf of the people was led by patriotic Catholic priests. Father Miguel Hidalgo y Costilla, known as Mexico's George Washington, was a "kindly, public-spirited, mockingly irreligious and frankly immoral priest." [7]

Betrayed by his followers, Hidalgo and his lieutenants were captured and hanged. The leadership of the insurgent forces was taken over by Father José María Morelos and then by Father Mariano

Matamoros, both of whom met the same fate as Hidalgo. The fighting was fiendish on both sides. It set precedents of conspiracy, treachery, torture, hate, wholesale destruction, and murder which were bound to affect the course of events during the early years of the country's self-rule.

The resistance of the royalist forces to the liberation movement brought into prominence one of the most brilliant and precocious characters in Mexican history. Born at Jalapa on February 21, 1795(?), Antonio López de Santa Anna was a youth of extraordinary capacities. At fifteen, he enlisted in the royalist army. On August 18, 1813, he served as a cadet under General Joaquin de Arredondo who triumphed over the revolutionary general, José Alvarez Toledo, on the Medina River in Texas. Seven hundred and fifty Anglo-Americans who aided the revolutionists were slaughtered there in an ambuscade.

Back in Mexico, operating on the coast near Veracruz, in a clean-up after the Hidalgo rebellion, the young Santa Anna showed such persistence and courage in digging out and finishing off insurgents that he was promoted to captain. This youth, who began his career by exterminating aspirants to liberty, would grow up to call himself "protector of the people" and "the Napoleon of the West." He had what Sam Houston recognized as elements of genius and greatness, but his performance as soldier and statesman was erratic. At all events, he had the ability to become master of Mexico, not once but nine times.

Next to Santa Anna, the most important character brought to light by the early disturbances was a "handsome, dashing man with brown hair and reddish sidewhiskers... Augustín de Iturbide." He had offered to lead Hidalgo's revolutionary army, but Hidalgo distrusted him. So Iturbide, with greed and bloodthirstiness, fought on the royalist side and helped put down Hidalgo's rebellion. A "genial, good-natured, witty and greedy wastrel," Iturbide wrote the Spanish viceroy on Good Friday, 1814: "In honor of the day, I have just ordered three hundred excommunicated wretches shot." [8] In that massacre women were treated the same as men. Iturbide lived to become president of Mexico and received the homage of the people. Turmoil, treachery, and bloodshed continued for the balance of the decade.

Having wasted his wealth in self-indulgent living, Iturbide was desperate. He presented himself as the would-be champion of the royalist government against liberalism, and described himself as without ambition or self-interest. By this deception he obtained a government command, then persuaded the revolutionist, Vincente Guerrero, to join him.

The young Santa Anna, recently made a lieutenant colonel of the royalist forces by the viceroy, also joined Iturbide. All of his troops came with him. With these supporters Iturbide was strong enough on February 24, 1821, to declare Mexico independent of Spain by an edict known as the "Plan of Iguala." This plan proposed to make independent Mexico a limited monarchy under a Bourbon king. It set up Roman Catholicism as the sole religion and gave all office-holders rights to their existing posts. Spaniards, Mexicans, Creoles, and Indians were all declared united in a fraternal union. A committee (junta or regency) was set up to govern the country provisionally.

Officials, troops, prelates, and the people swallowed Iturbide's bait. He rode his black charger into Mexico City and received the golden keys. He was cheered by the people as "the Father of Independence." Iturbide, as the victorious general, chose the regents who were to govern; in turn they elected him to the executive power. He opened the government purse to claimants of all kinds; and on July 21, 1822, he proclaimed himself "Emperor of Independent Mexico."

Santa Anna, now twenty-four years old, hailed Iturbide's elevation with joy, but his joy soon waned, and he turned against the emperor charging that Iturbide represented "imperialist reaction." With his genius for attracting followers, Santa Anna then precipitated a revolution to establish a republic. Iturbide's generals deserted him, and, with the army, supported Santa Anna. The slender forces that remained loyal to the emperor were conquered. The people, who had formerly admired the red-whiskered "liberator," had come to detest his claims to imperial majesty. They, too, went with Santa Anna. Iturbide's abdication and banishment followed.

The talented Santa Anna did not consider it opportune, as yet, to take center stage; he was too young, and the chances were too many that he would be disposed of by the same kind of turnabout by which he disposed of others. On March 31, 1823, he cooperated in setting up a regency of three men—Pedro Celestino Negrete, Guadalupe Victoria, and Nicholás Bravo.

Since there was no monarch, some kind of governmental system had to be devised. Under the regime, sentiment for what was called "republicanism" gained ground, but neither Santa Anna nor his followers understood that this form of government derived authority from the people and operated on a representative basis. A congress to create a republic and provide a constitution met on November 7, 1823. Men whose experience was mainly with intrigue, tyranny, and treachery were now called upon to decide the weightiest problems of statesmanship.

In the congress that enacted this so-called liberal constitution on January 31, 1824, Texas was represented by a delegate whose name would appear later in the annals of Texas, Erasmo Seguin. Members of the assembly were men who had also framed a constitution as part of Iturbide's plan for independence. The congress now declared Iturbide's election as emperor illegal, and it went even further, undertaking a feat of omnipotence by announcing that Iturbide's empire never had existed.

Dreading further tyranny, the members conceived of liberty in high-flown transcendental terms that echoed slogans of the French Revolution. They were also beguiled by the prospects of offices for all. Nothing was more remote from their experience than the system of government they were undertaking to form. A single individual was appointed by the Congress to draft the constitution, using that of the United States as a prime example. Other models were consulted—the Spanish constitution of 1812 and that of the French Republic. It took him three days to produce the required document.

The new constitution mixed privilege, intolerance, and reaction with democracy, liberty, and progress. A basic difference between the Mexican and the United States constitutions was that the American one was adopted by the people, then by the states, and could be amended only by a convention of the people or by the states. Mexico's constitution was a mere statutory enactment and could be amended or repealed by Congress at will. It neither provided for a supreme court, nor recognized the rights of trial by jury, habeas corpus, petition for redress of grievances, or peaceable assembly.

Moreover, it recognized the fact of perpetual revolution by providing the president with loosely stated extraordinary powers which seemed to authorize him to rule as dictator whenever he considered that a crisis required it.

The regency that Santa Anna had helped set up continued to rule for some fourteen months after the constitution was enacted. On May 7, 1824, by a statute which actually amended the new constitution, Texas was made a partner in a dual-state arrangement with Coahuila: the new state to be known as Coahuila-Texas. Most Mexicans in Texas, including the colonists, objected to this combine, fearing that the new state government would be controlled to their disadvantage by the more powerful and popular Coahuila.

There were two reasons for the new arrangement. The population of Texas was at that time considered too thin for the state to stand by itself. However, Mexican authorities were beginning to fear the consequences of rapid immigration. To brake any opposition, the statute declared the arrangement temporary and promised that the merger would be dissolved when "Texas possessed the necessary elements to prove [the ability to carry on as] a separate state of herself." [9] This meant, of course, that Texas could expect some day to become a separate state within the Mexican federation.

On April 1, 1825, Guadalupe Victoria, a member of the three-man regency set up with the support of the young Colonel Santa Anna, was inaugurated president after an election. His four-year term was a bright period for the Mexican people, who were relieved of violence. Colonists in Texas had few troubles during his regime except with Indians and the Fredonia Rebellion. Monclava became the capital of the dual state and its constitution was enacted on March 21, 1827. Provisions satisfactory to the colonists were incorporated in the constitution, such as a limited bill of rights and other provisions for public education. Citizens could vote for municipal officers and for electors for higher officers. The only trouble was that these provisions were never put into effect. Soon the colonists complained that the dual-state setup was being used to frustrate equitable judicial procedures and to prevent economic progress in the Texas portion of the compound state.

Manuel Gomez Pedraza was elected president in 1828 to succeed Victoria. The brilliant Santa Anna, now thirty years old, perceived that if Pedraza lasted out his full term he would be difficult to unseat. In consequence, Santa Anna made a great to-do about popular rights, attacked President Pedraza for being reactionary, and denounced the election as illegal.

Another competent revolutionary operator, Vicente Guerrero, joined Santa Anna. Displaying audacity and quickness of movement in the campaign to overthrow Pedraza, Santa Anna held his troops together by permitting brigandage and distribution of spoils. The insurgents triumphed, and the "vile Pedraza," as he was now called, fled to the United States on April 1, 1829. The Mexican Congress, which had declared Pedraza elected, voted the office vacant and made Santa Anna's fellow conspirator, Guerrero, president on the grounds that his revolt had succeeded.

Santa Anna had become a popular hero at the age of thirty-one. For the time being this was better than being president and having his career nipped too soon.

Guerrero's vice-president was General Anastasio Bustamante, a "heavy, dull, rather kindly and fairly honest aristocrat, though nominally a moderate Federalist." Guerrero made the tactical error of putting Bustamante in command of the army at Jalapa. Taking farewell of his president, Bustamante exclaimed, "Never will I unsheathe my sword against General Guerrero." [10]

Santa Anna had demanded that Guerrero make him minister of war. Knowing the treacherous propensities of his former commander-in-arms, Guerrero had refused. Santa Anna then offered his services to the vice-president, but Bustamante, also fearing the consequences of the proposed association rejected it. Instead, regardless of his pledge never to take up arms against Guerrero, Bustamante launched a revolution against his former chief. Then Santa Anna decided that the best he could do would be to support Guerrero. In the field, Bustamante's forces won against the combined fighting power of Guerrero and Santa Anna. Santa Anna retired to his home, from which he ventured to make appearances for occasional popular ovations, and held himself ready for the next chance.

Bustamante took office on January 1, 1830, two months after Sam Houston, in Arkansas, was formally admitted to citizenship in the Cherokee nation and three days after he wrote his friend John H. Overton a letter of gratitude for sustaining him in his "darkest, direst hour" before his departure from Tennessee after his domestic tragedy. Houston knew little or nothing about these explosive events south of the Rio Grande, but they would have a good deal to do with his future.

Bustamante's foreign secretary, Lucas Alamán, a Mexican patriot who deserved the title of statesman as much as any man in the country, had studied politics in Europe, and had excellent powers of analysis and reasoning. Alamán studied a report from another patriot, General Manuel Mier y Teran, on what Mexico must do to save her Texas territory. Teran was one of a group of five or six distinguished Mexicans most bitterly antagonistic to the colonists. His report recommended the establishment of numerous military posts in Texas. He proposed to relocate large numbers of Mexicans there and encourage convicts to take up residence in Texas after their release from Mexican jails. The report contained this passage:

"... these measures involve the safety of the nation and the integrity of our territory ... [we have] no choice of measures in this matter. Either the Government occupies Texas now, or it is lost forever, for there can be no possibility of reconquest when our base of operations would be three hundred leagues distant while our enemies would be carrying on the struggle close to their base. . . .[11]

Impressed, Secretary Alamán supported General Teran's recommendations with a memorandum describing in detail what he conceived to be the deliberate methods used by the United States for encroachment:

They commence ... in the territory they covet upon pretense of commercial negotiations, or of the establishment of colonies, with or without the assent of [their] Government. These colonies grow, multiply, become predominant ... they begin to set up rights ... founded upon historical facts which are admitted by nobody ... then follow discontents and dissatisfaction calculated to fatigue the patience of the legitimate owner ... when things have come to this pass, precisely the present state of things in Texas, the diplomatic management commences.[12]

Alamán's arraignment of the United States was not without some justification. It was based in part on three attempts by the United

States to buy Mexico on March 26, 1825, on March 15, 1827, and again on August 25, 1829, only a few months before Bustamante became president. This last offer was for $5,000,000.

What the Mexicans did not understand was that early efforts to buy Texas were largely prompted not by territorial ambition but by the desire to impose peace on a neighboring region that was overrun with uncontrolled Indians and desperadoes. Efforts to purchase Texas were made without consulting the colonists or considering their wishes. Though the United States did not intentionally prejudice relations between the colonists and Mexico, this was the result, and it brought on harsher measures of oppression by the Mexican government with sharper resistance by the Texans.

Alamán failed to realize that the colonists were not responsible for these activities and that large numbers of them seriously desired to keep their oaths of loyalty to Mexico and to continue under her sovereignty. But this desire to continue with Mexico was contingent upon Texas' being allowed to sever relations from Coahuila and, as a separate state, to set up decent judicial and education systems and enjoy profitable commercial relations and other advantages. Prompted by his study of General Teran's report, Alamán formulated and promoted a new colonial policy that was bound to make trouble. It was the basis of what became known as Bustamante's Law of April 6, 1830, and it burst upon Texas with hurricane force. This mandate provided for stern military occupation, settlements peopled by Europeans and Mexican convicts; new customs duties, closer trade ties with the rest of Mexico, and reduced trade with other nations.

As a climax, it prohibited immigration and suspended all land grants unless 100 colonists had already settled in the areas allotted. Only Austin's first grant and the Green Dewitt colony just west of it had qualified under the new edict.

Though Stephen Austin considered the law cruel and unjust, he tried to quiet the fears of his settlers by assuring them that the law would aid Texas trade and industry. He argued hopefully that the heavy Mexican troop movements, then beginning, were for frontier protection only and not directed against the colonies. But hotheaded settlers raised loud outcries for the immediate seizure of Texas. Anti-Mexican propaganda broke out in the American press. Pressure by Washington representatives in Mexico to buy Texas increased.

Mexicans saw the North as a giant stealthily expanding at their expense.

In support of Bustamante's law of 1830, Mexico spent half a million dollars building military posts and garrisoning them with 1,300 troops, most of them convicts, and then proceeded with the plan of customs collections. The Mexican government apparently had no suspicion that these measures made a powder keg of Texas. Stephen Austin wrote the Mexicans a warning which, if heeded, might have saved Texas for Mexico:

> I have informed you many times, and I inform you again, that it is impossible to rule Texas by a military system. . . . From the year 1821 I have maintained order and enforced the law in my colony simply by means of *civicos* [civil decrees], without a dollar of expense to the nation [Mexico]. . . . Upon this subject of military despotism I have never hesitated to express my opinion, for I consider it the source of all revolutions and of the slavery and ruin of free peoples.[13]

General Teran, originator of the repressive program, was now military commander of the Eastern Provinces, including Texas. His headquarters were at Matamoros. In 1831 he stationed Colonel John D. Bradburn in the brick fort at Anáhuac at the mouth of the Trinity River. Bradburn, a Kentucky adventurer who had fought for Mexico against Spain, was both military commander and customs collector. Being rash-tempered, he promptly put Anáhuac and Liberty, thirty miles up the river, under martial law. He roused further resentment in Texas by imprisoning two Mexican officials whom he charged with assisting American colonists to enter the territory illegally.

Next, a group of colonists who complained to Bradburn about the misbehavior and depredations of Mexican convict soldiers were rebuffed. Finally, in May, 1832, William Barret Travis, an aggressive young lawyer from Georgia who would earn fame at the Alamo, and several companions took matters into their own hands and punished a couple of Mexican soldiers for bad behavior. Bradburn ordered the Texans arrested and they were confined in the fort.

Alarm spread. Colonists gathered from a hundred miles or more, with Frank W. Johnson their elected leader. From the Brazos River district 100 men came to his support. On their march to Anáhuac they captured a detachment of Mexican dragoons. Johnson and his followers surrounded Bradburn's fort and demanded the release of Travis and his companions. In turn, Bradburn offered to exchange them for the prisoners Johnson had taken. After the exchange the Johnsonites withdrew to Turtle Bayou, five miles from Anáhuac on the Liberty road, and held a meeting.

On June 13, 1832, the Texans at Turtle Bayou adopted the Turtle Bay Resolutions, as they were called. In them, President Bustamante was condemned for violating the constitution of 1824, and the colonists declared their intention to support the man who had promised to defend it: General Antonio López de Santa Anna, the agile-minded "people's protector." The Turtle Bay Resolutions were the colonists' first formal declaration of opinion on political affairs of the Mexican government.

Just before the Turtle Bay Resolutions, Santa Anna had called upon the people of Mexico to take arms against the tyrannies of his former associate Bustamante. As he had betrayed Iturbide, Guerrero, and others, he now turned on his old friend. The colonists were overjoyed by the good news that Santa Anna's revolution against Bustamante was progressing. In their enthusiasm for him they went to war against Bustamante's forces in Texas.

At Velasco, John Austin, a captain in the coast trade, asked the Mexican commander, Colonel Domingo Ugartechea, to permit his schooner, with cannon aboard, to pass the fort without interference. He was en route to support a new attack by the colonists at Anáhuac. Ugartecha refused. The fort was surrounded on the night of June 26 and taken in a battle that lasted all the following day.

On June 29, Ugartechea signed a capitulation, received the honors of war, and marched out at the head of his force. He was allowed to lead his men home to Matamoros. This was victory number one in outright civil war in support of colonists' rights and of the revolutionary general, Santa Anna. The losses: seven Texans killed, 17 wounded; Mexicans, 35 killed, 15 wounded.

Then Colonel José de las Piedras, commander of the Mexican garrison at Nacogdoches and a known adherent of Bustamante, made himself obnoxious by stimulating trouble between whites and Indians. Seven hundred colonists collected and organized under John W. Bullock as colonel. Bullock presented Colonel Piedras with a demand that he renounce Bustamante and pledge his loyalty to Santa Anna. Parlaying for time, Piedras retired his force from the Old Stone Fort to the church. On August 2, 1832, Bullock's force occupied the town, defeated a Mexican sortie, and kept up an intermittent fire on the fort all night. In the morning the Mexicans withdrew toward San Antonio, and were attacked twenty miles to the west on the Angelina River.

In a truce talk, Colonel Piedras refused to declare himself loyal to Santa Anna, and transferred his command to Major Francisco Medina, who made the required profession of faith. Piedras was sent first to Velasco and from there was allowed to go to Tampico. The remaining officers and soldiers were taken by James Bowie to San Antonio. Losses in the engagement on the Angelina: Texans, three killed, five wounded; Mexicans, 47 killed and about the same number wounded. The action finally cleared the colonies of all Bustamante's soldiers except those at San Antonio and Goliad. A considerable number of colonists questioned the wisdom of these successful affronts to the Mexican military authorities. After the capture of the garrisons at Anáhuac, Velasco, and Nacogdoches, they separated into what was known as Austin's "peace party" and Wharton's "war party."

Many Texans hoped the revolt would bring stability. They expected that, with Santa Anna's support, the bonds between Texans and Coahuila would be severed and the law of 1830 abolished. But instead, from this point on, the war snowballed from combat to combat and convention to convention.

And all this time Sam Houston was still in the United States, hearing rumors of a disturbance but never really knowing what lay behind it. Though he did not cross the Red River until months after the colonies had been cleared of Bustamante's soldiers, he has often been held responsible for "plotting," "provoking," or "improvising" the Texas Revolution.

On August 22, 1832, while Sam Houston was in Nashville arranging his affairs to finance his speculator's trip to the Promised Land, the officials of San Felipe township issued a call for a convention to meet on October 1. Seventeen townships responded with fifty delegates. The members of this convention elected Stephen F. Austin by a two-to-one vote over William H. Wharton, to preside. It was the first political meeting held by delegates from all Texas colonies. They were brave men. The conviction was growing (and without help from Sam Houston, who was not even in the country) that the intermittent civil war between Mexico and Texas had left wounds too deep ever to heal.

Of the many committee reports adopted by this convention, two were most important. One was an argument for repeal of Article Eleven of the Law of April 6, 1830, which prohibited immigration from the United States and suspended practically all colonizing contracts. The other report was reviewed by a special subcommitte of three members including William H. Wharton and Stephen F. Austin. They approved a petition to Mexican authorities for a Texas state government separate from Coahuila.

No delegate opposed the content of the petition, but members did question its advisability on the ground that, instead of boldly seeking the well-known object, the expedient thing was to ask permission of the Mexican government to submit the petition. This would have been correct procedure under Mexican law and precedent. But this precaution was not adopted. When the petition was forwarded, the Mexican authorities interpreted it as another revolutionary act.

Four weeks later, on November 8, 1832, Austin was warned by the political chief of San Antonio that holding a public meeting without permission was illegal under existing laws. This epitomized one of the basic differences between two opposing systems that had developed north and south of the river. Austin underscored the deepening rift by referring to the Anglo-American concept of the inherent right of peaceable assembly to seek redress of grievances.

The ferment continued. Soon disappointment and bitterness were expressed because the convention of October 1 had failed to defy the mother country by drawing up a constitution for a separate state, electing officers, and submitting a *fait accompli* to the Mexican government. So, in January, 1833, a citizens' committee, again ignoring the Mexican contention that such activities were revolutionary, issued a call for the election of delegates to still another convention to meet April 1. The members of this committee knew that Santa Anna, whom they still regarded as their patron saint, was a candidate for the presidency in Mexico. Confident of his election, they were firm in their conviction that he would befriend them.

When Sam Houston crossed the Red River in December, 1832, it was just three months before the next convention was to meet. For an adventure-minded speculator and opportunist, primarily concerned with advancing his financial interests but at the same time eager for a call to some inspiring kind of service, this timing was a favorable coincidence. Houston would have an opportunity, however brief, to familiarize himself with the current situation before he was called upon to participate as a delegate in the upcoming convention.

2. *Lone Rider*

Houston spent his first night in Texas in a settler's cabin on the road that stretched from the Red River to Nacogdoches. In Texas, horsemen usually traveled together for protection, but Houston, accustomed to covering long distances alone in the States, did not hesitate to go his way in solitude. Safe at Nacogdoches after a ride of 180 miles, he paused briefly for rest, reported to the authorities, and looked up two friends, Henry Raguet and Adolphus Sterne.

From there Houston turned westward following the *Camino Real*, the ancient Royal Highway. La Salle had informed his sovereign a century and a half before that this road from San Antonio de Béxar to the Sabine River was as good as the one from Paris to Orléans. But Houston now rode along a weed-grown track with bogs and sinkholes, no longer a splendid highway.

After crossing several smaller streams he came to the Trinity River, where he probably crossed at Robins Ferry. Turning southwestward from the San Antonio road, he followed Middle Road to Austin's colony. This took him through the bottomlands of the Brazos River, a meandering stream to which the Spanish had given the name *Rio del Brazos de Díos*, River of the Arms of God. Houston estimated that this region was capable of supporting 10,000,000 persons. The brilliant sunshine, the bracing air, the clear waters, and the well-stocked larders of the settlers radiated promise.

Houston reached San Felipe on the west bank of the Brazos early in the afternoon of a crisp December day when the sun was shining over the raw, crude buildings. This community of thirty families had been planned by Stephen Austin as a Spanish-American town, but it had developed without a plaza; its houses, stores, and a town hall were straggled along a single street. The main thoroughfare, worn by cartwheels and hoofs, had pawing holes in front of the hitch rails. The houses and the town hall were unpainted and weathered, attractive and quaint; but Stephen Austin's dream of a beautiful city had not been realized.

A sign, rattling in the breeze under the gallery of the Virginia House, promised that guests would not be bothered by rats or fleas. On the other side of the street a long, bare pine building, the New England Retreat, advertised baked beans, doughnuts, codfish—and Mexican lotteries.

Houston discovered that Austin was absent somewhere within his vast domain. On the veranda of the Austin home, he encountered another disappointed visitor and shook his hand. The visitor was James Bowie, the reddish-haired giant with whom Houston had downed several mugs of whiskey nearly four years before at Helena, Arkansas, when he was on his way to the Cherokees. Bowie had joined the Catholic Church and had married Ursula Veramendi, the beautiful daughter of the vice-governor of the state of Coahuila-Texas. He had two children, nearly three-quarters of a million acres of land acquired by the politically unpopular hundred-league grants, and a fine home near Saltillo in the Coahuila section.

Houston and Bowie rode together to San Antonio. In the Comanche country beyond that city Houston met with the tribe's chiefs. He obtained their promise to go to the United States in about three months to visit the Indian commissioner at Fort Gibson for a peace conference with other tribes and whites in accordance with the mission he had undertaken for President Jackson. He gave the chiefs messages from the Great White Father and presented them with a medal bearing Jackson's likeness. He was entertained in the home of Bowie's father-in-law and, while there, explored the charming stone and adobe town of San Antonio, that, in its second century, dozed in limpid sunlight. He enjoyed its aura of poetry and indolence: the glimpses of colorful patios; the cadences of the guitars; the flashing garments of *señoritas;* the picturesque garb of the *señores.* Then, traversing the same route by which he had come, he returned to San Felipe to see Stephen Austin. It would be his first meeting with this extraordinary man.

Houston and Austin had in common certain qualities of mind and temper, but basically they were from different molds. Both had been born in Virginia and in the same year. Austin, seven months Houston's junior, was lightly built and of medium height; Houston was six-feet-two, with a powerful frame and muscular physique, capable of enormous endurance. Austin's tastes and temperament did not fit him for frontier life. Gentle by nature, he loved order, poetry, music, and all the other advantages of a cultured society; he perferred to dress well, to dine with cultivated men and women, and to dance afterward. But devotion to his colonizing ideal led him to give up these things, along with his desire for a wife and family. In a retrospective mood, Austin wrote a friend that from the day of his arrival in Mexico "I bid an everlasting farewell to my native country, and adopted this [country] and in so doing I determined to fulfill rigidly all the duties and obligations of a Mexican citizen." Then, looking ahead, he had taken as his motto, "The redemption of Texas from the wilderness, fidelity and gratitude to my adopted country, inflexibly true to the interest and just rights of my settlers." [1]

Austin, understandably suspicious of newcomers, may have rated Houston as a militant adventurer. No doubt he feared that so restless a character would incline toward the Wharton war party. He could not then have known that caution, as well as fire and devotion, was a basic ingredient of Houston's character.

Houston made known his desire to purchase a league of land in one of Austin's grants. For approximately 4,428 acres on Karankawa Bay, the price agreed upon was $375, with an exchange of horses a part of the transaction. Thus Houston achieved one of his aims in coming to Texas. By Austin's grant of a headright in his colony on December 24, 1832, Houston became a landowner.

His destination after leaving Austin was beyond the Sabine, but on this ride he again paused at Nacogdoches. Before he left, his friends asked him to let them put him up for election as a delegate to the April 1 convention at San Felipe, and he consented.

At Natchitoches, Louisiana, he wrote Andrew Jackson a letter that could not be trusted to Mexican mails. But before writing it, he wrote Henry L. Ellsworth, United States Indian Commissioner at

Fort Gibson, reporting that the Comanche chiefs had agreed to be there for a peace conference in about three months. Then he told Jackson about the great distances that he had traveled in Texas, and reported his opinion that "nineteen-twentieths" of the people of Texas favored its acquisition by the United States, but he gave no authority for his information. No doubt he had encountered numerous Texas patriots. He may have talked with one of the Whartons, or with William Wharton's father-in-law, Jared Groce, or with Henry Smith of Brazoria. He also reported to Jackson that Texans were determined to have a separate state government and, unless order was restored, would break away from Mexico. He then pictured a possibility that he knew was well calculated to make Old Hickory's hair stand on end: If Texans could not borrow money in the United States to aid their movement "away from Mexico," they might appeal to England.[2]

Returning to Texas by the Sabine River ferry, Houston traveled westward for a few miles and paused at the ancient village of San Augustine, where Philip Sublett had developed a plantation and a comfortable home. Sublett had been with Houston at Horseshoe Bend and had admired his gallantry there. After a short visit with this man, who would remain one of his devoted friends through life, Houston rode some thirty miles westward to Nacogdoches.

Only forty-seven miles from the Sabine, with its stone mission rising on a knoll between two streams, Nacogdoches had been for two decades a center for adventurers who slipped across the Louisiana border into the Redlands. Floaters had stayed behind after various raids and after the Fredonia Rebellion led by Haden Edwards. Some had become gamblers and land grabbers while others had become substantial citizens.

When he arrived in town, Houston learned that his candidacy as delegate, announced by his friends, had been well received, and his election was certain. With a glow of friendliness, he reciprocated this cordial proof that he was a welcome citizen. He had a number of other reasons for fancying Nacogdoches as a place to make his home. Its population was large enough to support a law practice, and it was a good base for the kind of land speculations that he had discussed with Prentiss. Besides, there were two good friends living here.

Henry Raguet, a Pennsylvanian born in Bucks County, of Swiss-French descent, had been with Houston in New Orleans more than a year before. While others at that time were urging Houston to make Texas his home, Houston had made the same recommendation to Raguet. After prospecting the Texas situation on horseback, Raguet had moved his wife and six children to Nacogdoches and had opened a store to deal in clothing and other merchandise. Already he was a respected commercial figure; the first man to sell cloth by the 36-inch yard instead of the 33-inch Mexican yard.

Adolphus Sterne, a little rosy-cheeked Jew, was a friend of even longer standing from Nashville days. Born in Cologne, Germany, Sterne had emigrated to New Orleans at sixteen. He had now been established in Texas for eight or nine years. He had assisted the Fredonians in their futile rebellion by smuggling in munitions secreted in bales of dry goods. Tried by a military court and sentenced to death, he had been saved by the influence of the Masonic order of which he was a member. On parole and pledged not to participate in any rebellion against Mexico, he was the *alcalde internio*—something like a justice of the peace pro tem, and holder of the municipal funds.

As a peddler and storekeeper prospecting for a better location, he had visited Nashville and there, a member of the tavern's afternoon whiskey-drinking coterie, he had made the acquaintance of attorney Houston when Houston's star was rising. Sterne's wife, Eva Catherine Rosine, had come to America from Germany with her parents when she was six years old. Both parents had died of yellow fever while going up the Mississippi and Eva had been adopted by Placide Bossier and his wife, wealthy French Catholics of Natchitoches, Louisiana. She had been raised a Catholic. Twenty-three years old, she was devoted to her religion. Adolphus had adopted it and sometimes attended Mass.

A few weeks after becoming a resident of Nacogdoches, Houston was elected a delegate to the April 1 convention. Again he mounted and rode westward to San Felipe. Delegate Houston knew that his constituents were dissatisfied with the inconclusive results of the preceding October convention and desired their representatives to take a firmer stand. He supported the election of William H. Wharton against Stephen Austin for presiding officer. This time the war party was in the ascendant, and Wharton won. Houston served as chairman of a committee that framed a constitution for the separate state of Texas which the party advocated. David G. Burnet, served as chairman of a committee to prepare a plea to the Mexican authorities for approval of the document that Houston's committee was writing. The convention decided that three men should be sent to Mexico City to present the petition and the proposed constitution.

Houston discovered that Austin's enemies intended to exclude him from this mission. Strongly in favor of a separate state government for Texas because of what he had learned about the bad effects of the Coahuila-Texas combination, he foresaw that without Colonel Austin, there was no hope of success. He supported Austin as one of the emissaries, and Austin was elected along with James B. Miller and Erasmo Seguin. The three chosen men considered that they had been elected to the dismal privilege of sticking their heads into the lion's mouth. Austin vigorously disapproved the convention's procedure, believing that the colonists should have asked the Mexican regime for permission to submit a petition and proposal. Nonetheless, with his usual sense of duty, he alone accepted the risk and ten days later set out for Mexico City.

Before Austin left San Felipe, Houston had a friendly confidential interview with him. He wrote of it later:

> ... I assured him if he succeeded in obtaining a State Government, that I would never oppose him, for any Civil office in the state, but render him my cordial support thereafter. This I was induced to do because he was aware that I had not supported him for the Presidency of the Convention and while he was absent he might suppose that I would countenance intrigue against him, which I resolved not to do, but to support and to sustain him in his absence.[3]

Immediately after the convention adjourned, Houston, still alone, continued westward on the mission for which President Jackson had provided his passport. In the Comanche country beyond San Antonio he met once more with the chiefs and again reminded them of their pledge to attend a conference at Fort Gibson. A month later he himself was back at the fort in Arkansas, only to be disappointed that neither the Indians nor Indian Commissioner Ellsworth put in an appearance.

These arduous journeys across Texas and through the Oklahoma and Arkansas wilderness aggravated his old Horseshoe Bend wound. He went to Hot Springs to rest and recuperate, and on July 31, 1833, he was able to write his cousin Jack (John Houston) that the inflammation had subsided and bone fragments had "escaped." "Texas," he rhapsodized, "is the finest portion of the globe that has ever blessed my vision," adding that he intended to settle in Texas, where extraordinary prospects had come to him both as a lawyer and a landowner.[4]

Back in Nacogdoches in the autumn, he moved from Brown's Tavern into Adolphus and Eva Sterne's home. Sterne once noted in his journal that so much was left over from every meal that he and his wife had decided they might as well take a paying guest. Houston no doubt was glad to leave the flea-ridden tavern and its bad food. Gentle Adolphus' home was one of happiness and devotion. Situated on the edge of town not ten minutes from the plaza, it was approached by a walk up a little hill to a gate that opened onto a kind of patio with paths of sand and gravel and beds of rich soil lined with red tile. In one of these the attractive *Señora* Sterne had her jumping-bean shrub; in another was her "patli" bed of medicinal herbs. The main flat stone path meandered from the gate to a roofless stone veranda at the door.

Houston was now actually practicing but without having become a citizen as the law required. No one complained. It was obvious that for court work he had to know some Spanish. He began to pick up odds and ends of the idiom from Adolphus and Eva, but a pleasant opportunity for learning more of the language presented itself. The third child and eldest daughter of Henry and Ann Raguet was seventeen-year-old Anna who, from her twelfth year, had attended the best schools in Philadelphia. A talented linguist, she spoke and wrote Spanish, French, and German. Under the young girl's instruction Houston made some further progress in colloquial Spanish and began dropping an occasional Spanish phrase in his letters. However, he apparently did not concentrate with the effort necessary for a man of forty to become proficient in a new language; or possibly he was distracted from this pursuit by the charms and attractiveness of his teacher.

By the time she was eighteen, Anna was the belle of the old mission town. One of her suitors was a handsome man of twenty-seven, Dr. Robert Anderson Irion, born in Paris, Tennessee. Until the previous year he had practiced medicine in Vicksburg, Mississippi. His profession made him a welcome addition to the Nacogdoches community. With his cultured manner and warm personality, he was a welcome visitor at the Raguet home and an acceptable suitor for Anna's hand. Later Houston and Irion, in a kind of Miles Standish and John Alden relationship, became keen but always friendly competitors for Anna's preference.

Perhaps Houston's association with the young and charming Anna reminded him of Eliza Allen and suggested that he might do well to erase the last traces of that affair. On November 30, 1833, he engaged Jonas Harrison, a local attorney, to file his petition for divorce. The plea was based on his four-year separation from Eliza and the impossibility of a reconciliation.

A few weeks after filing his divorce petition, Houston took a new name, Samuel Pablo, and was baptized at the local Catholic mission. Adolphus Sterne stood as his godfather and Eva as his godmother. The Mexican law that only Catholics could be landowners and serve as lawyers may have had something to do with his "conversion."

By the spring of 1834 Houston believed that war between Texas and Mexico was a definite probability, and he was certain that in the coming struggle Texans must look after their own interests without help from outsiders. In April he returned to Washington, D.C., and took lodgings in Brown's Indian Queen Hotel. While there he resumed negotiations with the New York financier, James Prentiss, to whom, on April 24, he wrote a prophetic letter:

> I have written to you just my *opinions* on the course which things must, and will take in Texas. She cannot, and will not remain as she now is. Keep my predictions, and see how far they are *verified!* ...
>
> You need not hope for acquisition (if ever) by this Government of Texas during the Administration of Genl. Jackson— If it were acquired by a Treaty, that Treaty, would not be ratified, by the present Senate—!!!
>
> Texas, will be bound to look to herself. ... This present year, must produce events, important to her future destiny. *I think*, greatly beneficial to her prosperity. I depricate the necessity,— and however favorable the result, may be for her—Still if Mex-

ico had done right, we cou'd have travelled on smoothly enough.[5]

If Mexico had done right! At the moment, Mexico had fanned the smoldering rebellion. After nine months in Mexico presenting the proposed Texas constitution and the petition for its enactment, Stephen Austin had been arrested by General Santa Anna's agents at Saltillo, January 13, 1834. The petition had been rejected and he was on his way home.

Austin had told Acting President Farias, a bitter enemy of the colonists, that his people would not submit to further delay with regard to separation from Coahuila. Farias had taken this as a threat. Austin, disappointed by the failure of his mission, had written the *Ayuntamiento* (municipal government) of San Antonio on October 2, 1833, urging all municipal governments in Texas to get in touch with each other and organize "a local government for Texas as a state of the Mexican Federation according to the law of May 7, 1824 so as to effect the organization in union and harmony as soon as the [Mexican] Congress has refused its approval." [6]

Mexican government agents had intercepted this letter and Austin's arrest for treason followed. He was taken back to Mexico City and lodged in a dark dungeon of the Inquisition, 13 x 16 feet without windows, and kept solitary and incommunicado. Father Muldoon, a friend and confessor of Santa Anna, together with William S. Parrott, an American merchant, tried in vain to arrange for his stay under bond at the *Casa Mexicana*, a boardinghouse. Acting President Farias issued orders that he was to be prevented from talking or writing. Food was furnished through a slot in the door, and on bright days a ceiling skylight admitted enough light for reading. Father Muldoon sent him food, but for a month Austin had no books. Austin wrote in his diary that he preferred "bread and water with books to the best eating without them." [7]

He was kept in solitary confinement from February 13 to May 1, 1834, when he was transferred to another prison and held until Christmas, 1834. Then he was released on $300,000 bond put up by a Mexican, Pascual Villar, but his movements were restricted to the federal district. The conditions of his life were greatly improved, and he was relatively happy but much concerned about events in Texas.

This harsh treatment of Austin was one of the events Houston had in mind when he wrote James Prentiss that things would have gone smoothly "if Mexico had done right." On learning of Austin's arrest and the circumstances of his incarceration, all Texas flamed with anger and then judiciously quieted down. During 1834 there were no conventions, and rebellious acts were frowned on out of fear that consequences would be visited upon Austin. Mexican officials took a more conciliatory attitude during this period.

It has been traditional to say that Houston was at this time fomenting or improvising revolution, but actually he easily accommodated himself to the mood of the country and enjoyed his law practice, his land acquisitions, and an interval of quiet and a pleasant social life with his friends the Raguets and their winsome daughter Anna.

3. *"Down with the Usurper!"*

THE BREAK in Houston's political career, his frustration following his self-exile, and many other disappointments had taught him patience. He had come to believe that events developed with a kind of inevitable ripening. Discreet opportunist, he could wait.

He perceived that courage and boldness, common enough in Texas, were spawning unprofitable and dangerous recklessness. Texas had a desperate shortage of men with experience in government or military matters. He had both. When, "with the coming of time," as John Wharton had expressed it, the need arose for men of his kidney, he would be ready.[1] Part of his readiness was his sound perspective on what lay ahead for the Promised Land. For the moment, his role was that of an intensely interested spectator aware of but not part of the latent revolutionary forces beneath the surface.

Old-time colonists resented attempts to stampede them into precipitous action. They became indignant when newcomers, uninvited, attempted to take over the leadership. Fully aware of this, Houston conducted himself accordingly.

As he showed in his summing up in the Stanberry case, Houston was familiar with Roman history. His much-thumbed copy of Caesar's *Commentaries*, supposed to have been carried in his saddle-bags, has survived to become a museum item. His favorite Roman character was Caius Marius (c. 155 B.C.-86 B.C.), a general, who had also been in exile. Among his other virtues as general and states-man, Marius displayed patience and the ability to recover after set-backs. Following his exile, he organized a well-disciplined army out of unpromising material and a demoralized soldiery and inflicted two decisive defeats on invaders. Houston especially admired Mar-ius' ability to make a comeback. In 1831 on a brief excursion from Arkansas to Tennessee during his own forest exile, Houston had his portrait painted as Marius. The picture showed him standing in bare feet among the simulated ruins of Carthage, dressed in a toga-like garment that exposed one shoulder.[2]

In time of excitement, when an impetuous man such as Mosely Baker came to Houston demanding action, Houston told him to quiet down. Houston realized that all newcomers, among whom he included himself, would do well to keep their mouths shut because a large proportion of East Texas was definitely opposed to warlike doings. The Nacogdoches civil government had recently refused to send delegates to a convention.

He busied himself with normal private pursuits, keeping an eye out for the best lands that could be bought at the cheapest price. He did well at it and also at his law practice; his coming to the Promised Land had already proved more than satisfactory. In his letter of July 31, 1833, he had reported enthusiastically to cousin Jack that he had received a retainer of $750 in one case and a retaining fee of $2,000 a year in another. With two men who put up the capital he had "pur-chased about 140,000 acres of choice land in which I am equally interested—beside this I own and have paid for 10,000 [acres] which is, I think, the most valuable land in Texas"—all this in less than a year.[3] On May 5, 1835, he received title to a headright, another league of land (4,480 acres) in the David G. Burnet Colony.

Besides busying himself as a speculator, he was defending criminals on assignment from the authorities and serving clients in litigation over defaulted payments. He was enjoying the hospitality of the Raguet home and trying to make a favorable impression on Anna. He had made a friend of that fine young man Dr. Robert Irion, who would be close and of great service to him in the troubled years ahead; and he began what proved to be a lifelong friendship with a twenty-nine-year-old Georgian, Thomas J. Rusk.

Rusk, who would some day serve Texas as secretary of war, had just arrived in Nacogdoches. He had carelessly invested in a Georgia gold mine and the manager of the mine had decamped to Texas with Rusk's money. He pursued the embezzler, only to discover that the stolen funds had been lost in a card game. Rusk liked the country and decided to settle.

Don Samuel Pablo Houston, now his formal name as a practicing attorney, appeared in Rusk's behalf before Alcalde Berry, successor to Alcalde Adolphus Sterne. He supported a petition for citizenship for "the foreigner Rusk" who "desires to dwell under the wise and just government which offers the protection of its beneficent laws to honest and industrious men." [4]

In Mexico, General Antonio López de Santa Anna was crowding his fate. His philosophy, or his lack of one, did not permit him to wait. Still only thirty-six, he thought he had passed the season when he could afford caution and delay. There were times when, in the words of an able historian, he assumed a kind of "beneficial divinity." "Tall, thin, apparently feeble but capable of great exertion on occasion, with a head that bulged at the top, a swarthy complexion, brilliant and restless eyes," he had "a clear-cut voice and a voluble tongue." The American consul in Mexico reported to Washington concerning him, ". . . Can read somewhat." But Santa Anna was not concerned with lessons from literature or history. "Were I made God," he is said to have declared, "I should wish to be something more." [5] Whether or not he said it, and he probably did, he was hustling along the road to "something more."

With the army at his back he had had himself elected president on April 1, 1833, the same day that Houston met with the other delegates to the second convention at San Felipe. Thus Santa Anna had been president nine months when Stephen Austin was arrested at Saltillo and confined in solitude in Mexico City. For most of this time the new president had left civil affairs in the hands of Vice-President Valentin Gomez Farias, who served as acting president while Santa Anna busied himself at the head of the army putting down disorders and consolidating his power in anticipation of the next step toward "something more."

118

His tactics were similar to those of Iturbide whom he had run out of the country: frequent liberal proclamations preliminary to *de facto* dictatorship.

On April 12, 1834, he resumed the civil duties of the presidency. Nine months later, on January 1, 1835, he dispersed the Congress and convened a new one whose members were selected from his loyal following. This Congress by statutes that nullified provisions of the so-called liberal constitution of 1824 gave him all the powers he asked. He was now dictator, absolute monarch, in all but name. For protesting against this betrayal of the constitution, Vice-President Farias was denounced as a traitor and banished. In his place Santa Anna set up Miguel Barragan.

Driving hastily for supreme power in every last corner of his realm, the dictator had Barragan issue a decree abolishing all state legislatures throughout the Mexican federation, including that of Coahuila-Texas, and provided for the appointment of governors by the supreme government. This government was Santa Anna himself.

Most states south of the Rio Grande submitted without objection, but a few protested. Zacatecas organized for resistance. After the citizens of this liberal state refused to surrender their weapons, several prominent officers loyal to Santa Anna pretended to desert him and joined the insurgents. The Zacatecans received them with open arms. Betrayed, they surrendered on May 11, 1835.

Santa Anna ordered rigorous punishment for the rebels. His soldiers burned and destroyed, pillaged and robbed. Many men, women, and children were slain or tortured in one of the bloodiest massacres that had yet taken place in the Western Hemisphere. Estimates of the number slaughtered run as high as 2,500.

Even in Mexico, Mexicans ventured to denounce the self-styled "people's protector" as the "worthy son of the father of lies," as an "unrivaled chameleon," and as "a shameless hypocrite, atheist and blasphemer." A Mexican periodical, *El Crepúsculo*, on May 16, 1835, wrote ... "with the tranquillity of a tiger, which, sated with the flesh of its prey, reposes on what it does not wish to devour, Santa Anna reports his victory [in Zacatecas]." [6]

As his answer, Santa Anna announced to the nation that his life was entirely devoted to the freedom and happiness of the people and to preservation of the federal system. But Mexican pamphleteers painted the picture in different colors. "The vile and traitorous

Santa Anna wishes to be Emperor," one declared. Another pamphleteer echoed, "Depravity and ambition make up the character of that miserable Proteus." [7]

As for Texas, Santa Anna believed with General Teran and the patriot Alamán that if the colonists were allowed to stay longer they could never be dislodged. They should be forced back to the United States or exterminated. This called for haste. His intention was not announced publicly, but it soon became apparent.

As a first step toward "something more" in Texas, Santa Anna assigned his brother-in-law, a charming, cultivated young man, General Martin Perfecto de Cos, to command Mexico's northern and eastern provinces including Coahuila-Texas. Soon, at Monclava, the capital of the dual state, Cos disbanded the legislature and arrested the governor. Texans at this remote capital, fearing capture and punishment, fled for their lives.

The colonists had no loyalty to the corrupt dual state government and cared nothing at all what happened to it. But its repression by Cos disclosed that Santa Anna, who previously had inspired their trust as the "people's protector," was but another aggressive dictator, determined to impose new wrongs rather than right old ones.

At Anáhuac, in January, 1835, Andrew Briscoe, a respected merchant, resenting enforcement of the new tariff because he was informed it was not enforced elsewhere, expressed his feelings freely, and even played practical jokes on the guards at the customs house. With a friend, he was tossed into jail on the order of Captain Antonio Tenorio, one of Cos's commanders who was also the Anáhuac customs collector.

A small unofficial group of twenty-five disturbed citizens (Sam Houston not among them) gathered at Stephen Austin's capital, San Felipe, on June 21, 1835, to discuss what should be done about Tenorio. While assistance to Briscoe was being considered, a courier with dispatches from Cos to Tenorio was captured and relieved of his mailbags.

One of Cos's letters disclosed Santa Anna's ripening strategy. Cos acknowledged Tenorio's complaints against the colonists and indicated that presently Tenorio's request for more troops would be satisfied. Another letter announced that the behavior of the rebellious colonists would soon be corrected. With consternation the twenty-five men pondered these words:

> In a very short time the affairs of Texas will be definitely settled, for which purpose the Government has ordered to take up the line of march a strong division composed of the troops which were in Zacatecas.... These [Texas] revolutionists will be ground down,...[8]

Troops from Zacatecas! Revolutionists to be put down! Only two months before, terror-stricken fugitives had come across the border with the tales of blood-drenched vengeance exacted upon the people of Zacatecas for refusal to surrender their weapons. Now, from Cos's dispatches, the Texans knew that Santa Anna planned for them the same bitter fate that he had dealt out in Zacatecas. Spontaneously 200 angry men gathered at San Felipe on June 22 to consider this threat. In the heat of their anger they organized a force of twenty-five young daredevils who declared themselves ready to proceed to Anáhuac and settle with Captain Tenorio forthwith. No action they might take would dispose of the threat by Santa Anna, but it would be some satisfaction to punish the captain. The twenty-five chose as their leader an impetuous twenty-six-year-old lawyer from Georgia who was always more eager to fight than to conduct law cases—William Barret Travis.

At Harrisburg, a small settlement at the head of navigation on Buffalo Bayou, Travis seized the sloop *Ohio* and put a small cannon aboard with some powder and the one available cannon ball. On June 29, 1835, off Anáhuac, he fired the shot. It hit the fort, raised a cloud of dust, but caused no damage.

On the strength of this single shot, Travis boldly demanded immediate surrender. Captain Tenorio asked for one day to consider; Travis haughtily gave him one hour. Knowing from experience that a large force of angry colonists would soon gather, Tenorio surrendered his 50 men to Travis' 250. With no facilities for safeguarding or feeding his captives, Travis accepted their pledge never again to fight against Texas, and paroled them. They were ordered to march to San Antonio and were furnished with arms to protect themselves against Indians.

Possibly Travis' private little one-shot campaign should be regarded as the second stroke of the Texas Revolution following the earlier conflicts of Anáhuac and Velasco. Santa Anna proceeded on the assumption that war had begun. But the colonists generally regarded it as unfortunate, premature, and dangerous. All the Texas municipalities promptly passed disapproving resolutions. They declared their loyalty to Mexico and condemned the Georgia lawyer for rashness. They were not ready and were still uncertain about the best course to take. The disappointed newcomer Travis indignantly rejected the censure of his fellow citizens:

> Being highly excited by the circumstances ... I volunteered in that expedition, with no other motives than that of patriotism & a wish to aid my suffering countrymen in the embarrassing strait to which they were likely to be reduced by military tyranny. I was casually elected the commander of the expedition without soliciting the appointment. I discharged what I conceived to be my duty to my country to the best of my ability. Time alone will show whether that step was correct or not. And time will show that when this country is in danger that I will show myself as patriotic & ready to serve her as those who to save themselves have disavowed the act & denounced me to the usurping military.[9]

Santa Anna's officials pretended to believe that the colonists were sincerely penitent over Travis' unauthorized behavior. In that case, they said, the colonists should be glad to surrender Travis himself and four other troublemakers: Lorenzo de Zavala, a Mexican fugitive from Santa Anna's wrath; and three Texans, Francis W. Johnson, James B. Miller, and Robert M. Williamson. The colonists, after deliberation, answered that unfortunately the named gentlemen had left and their whereabouts were unknown.

The demand for the arrest of Travis and others set the war party in motion. The party grew in strength, but a minority held control over all meetings, insisting that aggressive acts be held in restraint until Stephen Austin's release.

Repercussions from William Travis' one-shot victory had not died away when Austin, after a year and seven months of imprisonment and detention, was released by the Mexican government. He had been put on trial for treason, charged with the design to separate Texas from Mexico. On May 3, 1835, the Mexican Congress passed an amnesty law, apparently to relieve some of the pressure of dissatisfaction building up against the dictator. Austin's counsel managed to have the amnesty law interpreted to cover his case. He was released and on July 11, 1835, received his passport. He left the following week for New Orleans. On September 1, he arrived at Velasco, where a committee from Brazoria invited him to a public dinner "to express their approval of his public services and their respect for his virtues." [10]

Simultaneous with Austin's landing at Velasco, news reached the colony that Santa Anna was outfitting ships to bring supplies to Texas and already had collected 3,000 men south of the Rio Grande in preparation for an invasion. In his speech at the Brazoria dinner on September 8, Austin expressed regret at finding Texas in commotion. But now, though he had long been an advocate of peace, he recognized that this turmoil was the "fault" of a "revolution" provoked by "imprudent measures of the [Mexican] federal and state governments." During his imprisonment his views had changed: he believed that the time for action had come. The people should decide whether they were willing to submit to tyranny and give up their rights under the long-disregarded 1824 constitution. He called for a general consultation "of the best, calmest, and most intelligent men. . . . Let this consultation decide what to say to the central government," he urged; and he asked all municipalities to send five delegates. In each delegation there should be at least one man who could remain after the consultation to form a new state government. [11] To Mexicans the word "convention" meant a plan for military insurrection. For the usual term, Austin had substituted "consultation."

In defiance of Mexican law the citizens of Nacogdoches promptly called a mass meeting, elected Sam Houston chairman, and supported Austin's proposal. The meeting then elected Houston a member of the Committee of Vigilance and Safety. This committee in turn appointed him Commander in Chief of the department's military forces and authorized him to raise and organize troops, issue proclamations, and sustain the principles of the constitution of 1824.

The hour had struck. Patient waiting for what the "coming of time" might bring was now rewarded. On October 5, 1835, Houston wrote a letter to Issac Parker, an American from Illinois, and a red-hot Texas patriot. It was virtually a message for the American people. Flaunting it, Parker dashed across the Sabine into Louisiana, broadcasting Houston's inspired war cries:

> ... *War in defence of our rights* ... *is inevitable, in Texas!*
> If *volunteers* from the United States will join their brethren in this section, they will receive liberal bounties of land. ...
> Let each man come with a good rifle and one hundred rounds of ammunition, and to come soon.
> Our war cry is: "Liberty or Death."
> Our principles are to support the constitution, and *down with the Usurper!!!* [12]

The same spirit flashed in his General Orders to Nacogdoches troops and prospective volunteers on October 8:

> The time has arrived when the revolutions in the interior of Mexico have resulted in the creation of a dictator, and Texas is compelled to assume an attitude defensive of her rights, and the property of her citizens.
> Volunteers are invited to our standard. Liberal bounties of land will be given to all who will join our ranks with a good rifle and one hundred rounds of ammunition.
> The morning of glory is dawning upon us. The work of liberty has begun. Our actions are to become a part of the history of mankind ... millions will sympathize in our struggle, while nations will admire our achievement. ... Let your valour proclaim to the world that liberty is your birthright. We cannot be conquered by all the arts of anarchy and despotism combined. In heaven and in valorous hearts, we repose our confidence.[13]

These orders, signed by Houston, were carried by Adolphus Sterne to New Orleans to expedite delivery to William Christy. Five days after receiving it, Christy presided as chairman of a committee which raised funds for two companies of infantry, one under the command of Captain Robert C. Morris. Both companies soon would be on their way to Texas in gray uniforms that gave them the name "the New Orleans Grays."

Tennessee, Kentucky, Georgia, Alabama, and Mississippi responded to the same call with men and money. Who could doubt that the friend of Andrew Jackson, the boyish hero of Horseshoe

Bend, an ex-governor and general of Tennessee, and the man who had flogged Stanberry and, in the House of Representatives, had valiantly defended his reputation, would make a good leader?

On September 22 General Cos landed 400 men at Copano on the coast. He marched them to the north and west and by October 4 was approaching San Antonio. He sent General Domingo de Ugartechea with a force of dragoons to demand that the citizens of Gonzales surrender an old cannon that had been given to the town four years before for defense against Indians.

The demand was absurd, but it was part of the Mexican dictator's plan for exerting authority and tightening control. Gonzales citizens, believing that it was a pretext to cover a sudden attack, refused to give up the artillery piece. Ugartechea asked for reinforcements and Cos sent more troops under Lieutenant Francisco Castañeda. But the people of Gonzales did not scare easily. A regiment quickly formed under Colonel John H. Moore, Lieutenant Colonel Edward Burleson, and Major Alexander Somervell.

Moore and his staff decided to attack before Castañeda could be reinforced. They cut up a liberal supply of iron horseshoes for ammunition, then loaded the cannon aboard the ferry, crossed the river, and marched on Castañeda's camp. Their attack, however, was delayed by a dense fog.

Castañeda sent a captured Texas horseman to inform the enemy that he had no orders to fight. The Texans sent back a message that if Castañeda didn't want to fight he could surrender. Castañeda formed his men. Whether this was for defense or attack, the Texans did not know, but they were taking no chances. Colonel Moore ordered the cannon into action.

This worthy piece had once been spiked, and then the spike had been driven out. With a touch hole as big as a thumb, it couldn't throw a cannon ball twenty yards. Plugged with powder and loaded with cut-up horseshoes, it went off with a terrifying bellow as the Texans charged, some with pikes made by attaching sharpened files to poles. The Mexicans ran. The colonists' cavalry numbered only a third that of the retreating enemy, and they did not pursue.

It was discovered that some of the prisoners the Texans captured were ex-convicts who had been promised three dollars for the expedition. Half-starved wretches, they had had little to eat except corn for days past. But the courage of the hastily gathered Gonzales regiment was incontestable, for they could not have known of the hopeless lack of morale in the Mexican command.

If the hostilities at Anáhuac and Velasco were the actual beginning and William Travis' one-shot campaign was the continuation of the Texas Revolution, this affair was the first round of a war now recognized as "inevitable" by both sides.

Stephen Austin as current chairman of the Texas Central Committee of Safety sent out the following communique from San Felipe on October 3:

> For the information of everyone.... the people of Texas are informed that their fellow citizens at Gonzales *have been attacked—the war has commenced!* They will also perceive that General Cos has arrived with a reinforcement of troops, and is preparing for a campaign of extermination against the people of Texas....[14]

Before the end of the month the republican government of Mexico had been abolished and President Santa Anna was in command as absolute dictator. Texas volunteers, gathering in the vicinity of Gonzales and not quite realizing the scope of the effort Santa Anna was launching against them, made a daring decision. They concluded that their best move, now that they were in open revolt, would be to capture the Mexican force commanded by the dictator's brother-in-law at San Antonio.

Houston, still in Nacogdoches, did not agree with this decision when he heard of it. He was convinced that San Antonio could not be taken without heavy artillery and better-trained troops than were available. It was the conservative opinion of a cautious one-time regular army man. But with his responsibility limited to the forces at Nacogdoches, he could make no move to prevent the undertaking.

4. *Preparations for Freedom*

ELECTED delegate to the Consultation of November 1, Houston placed subordinates in command of the Nacogdoches troops and went to San Felipe. He reached there on a golden afternoon in late October.

Austin had made preparations for receiving guests. On returning to San Felipe in September after long imprisonment in Mexico, he had found his belongings scattered, his house stripped and unfit for occupancy. In a letter to his brother-in-law, James F. Perry, he spoke of his need for supplies because he must "receive visitors" and he "must be a little decent" for them. He went on:

> I want a barrel of salt beef, one of salt pork—some flour—some boxes of wine ... two beds and bedding—a barrel of good whiskey—some spoons—some rice—some beans ... if Mrs. Williams can spare the oxen and wagon I wish to keep it until I can buy one—and some cows for milk, for I have nothing. I want a bricklayer to build the kitchen chimney, which has fallen down in the great rain ... one set of bed curtains ... I have no blankets or bedding at all. ...[1]

As for the cost, it would have to come from where the money for his trip to Mexico had come—from where much more would have to come as he proposed to continue to serve his country—his own pocket.

Houston rode into Austin's corral and turned his mare over to the Negro, Job, with instructions to cool her out and let her stand in a lean-to protected from the wind before she was fed; then he followed the weedy path to the front of Austin's house. On the dirt-floor veranda he found a dozen men in checked calico or brown duck shirts sitting in cowhide-bottom chairs or talking quietly in two's and three's. He saluted them. They responded cordially with a certain deference, calling him "Governor" or "General."

One of them was the Alabamian Richard R. Royal, an early settler in Matagorda and a power in his community. He had been made chairman of the temporary Central Committee that Austin left in charge of civil affairs when he went to the front.

After the battle over the old cannon and Austin's message to the people that war had begun, eager volunteers had flocked to Gonzales. Calling themselves the Volunteer Army of Texas, they had sent word to San Felipe that, ready to march on San Antonio, they wanted a general to command them. Austin told the delegates who were beginning to arrive that he himself would go to the front to take command, and he asked for volunteers. Every delegate on hand declared himself eager to go. But Austin insisted that at least twenty had to stay behind, so they drew lots. The unlucky ones were to remain with Dick Royal to carry on until the full membership of the Consultation assembled.

Another delegate in the group was Henry Smith, a man of slight physique, a Brazoria neighbor and strong supporter of William Wharton and the war party. Smith was known for his vivid opinions and shrewd judgments, his peppery temper and lack of tact. The colonists were accustomed to seeing him in the same attire summer or winter: a black suit with close-fitting coat, tightly buttoned from the neck down; a high collar, and a black stock.

James Robinson, an Ohio-born lawyer and a fellow delegate of Houston's from Nacogdoches, was also on hand. When Robinson happened to be holding a twig or whip he had the unpleasant habit of slapping his boot with it as if he were an overseer.

The most outstanding member of the group had suffered more at the hands of Santa Anna than any other man present. This was Lorenzo de Zavala, a Mexican, one of five delegates from the town of Harrisburg. He had supported General Santa Anna's campaign to overthrow his predecessor, the tyrant Bustamante. Later Zavala had been disillusioned. His heart had ached for his fellow countrymen and he had held himself in part responsible for their anguish when Santa Anna tortured and butchered the people of Zacatecas after their unsuccessful attempt to preserve their state government.

Zavala had ventured to sign a protest against Santa Anna's conduct and an appeal to Mexicans to oppose him as they had earlier despots. In reprisal, Santa Anna had confiscated Zavala's substantial Yucatán estates. With his wife and son he had escaped to Texas, settling north of Buffalo Bayou near Harrisburg. With Santa Anna now demanding that the colonists surrender him, Zavala had unreservedly thrown in his lot with Texas, supporting the colonists' demands for schools, a judicial system, and constitutional procedures.

Zavala was the only man in Texas with more experience than Houston in legislation and administration. While Houston had been studying and practicing law, Zavala had studied medicine in the best schools of the United States and Europe. He had practiced in Mérida, the Mexican town where he was born. When elected to the *Cortes* of Spain, he had crossed the ocean to serve. During his 1820-1822 term in this embryonic parliament, with its powers limited by monarchic whims, he had learned during the rebellion under Ferdinand VII how cruel revolutions can be. Later, he had served in the Mexican Congress as Yucatán's representative and had twice been governor of the state of Mexico. While governor, he had served his country as national finance minister and had spent two years as Mexican minister to France.

Short, chubby, swarthy, with softly glowing eyes, Zavala had extremely small hands; his boots were the tiniest that General Houston had ever seen on a man. His movements were birdlike, his hands expressive with restrained gestures. He spoke excellent English with a trace of accent. He had been at Gonzales when the skirmish over the old cannon had taken place, and he filled Houston in on the details of that curious episode.

Shortly after his arrival in San Felipe, the delegates left behind by Austin complained to Houston that their number was insufficient for a quorum and hence they could carry on no business. Houston replied that he would go immediately to the front to bring back enough delegates for the Consultation to get on with its work. From Austin's larder he filled his saddlebag with food, went to the lean-to where his horse was cooling out, saddled and bridled her, and within an hour or two was on his way west again.

Late in the afternoon of the following day, in rolling country near Cibolo, some twenty-five miles east of San Antonio, Houston caught up with the Volunteer Army of Texas. After assembling at Gonzales following the cannon fight, they had loosely organized in groups according to the sections from which they came. Under Austin's command their number swelled during the march to between 500 and 600. Being volunteers, not a regular military body, they were not required to take oath, and felt free to withdraw at will. Sometimes they left in squads and, after attending to their home affairs, drifted back to the army in two's and three's. At the moment they numbered about 400.

After saluting Austin, Houston rode to the front of the straggling line and wheeled his mount to the side of the road, where he could inspect them as they passed. They carried buffalo robes, store blankets, checkered counterpanes, and bed quilts. Few had boots or shoes. Many wore moccasins and sombreros or coonskin caps with long tails. Some had stiff nankeen breeches; others wore new yellow buckskin breeches and coats. Most of the buckskin he saw was hard, stiff, old, and greasy—a sure sign of hard living in the saddle and around campfires. They carried double gourd canteens, Indian-style, and had frying pans slung from their packs.

About half were mounted, riding Spanish and Indian ponies which were shaggy and caked with dust and mud. Some rode drooping, lanky brown and gray mules saddled with scraps of ragged leather. Occasionally a half-broken mustang dashed wildly for freedom. Riders sometimes dismounted to give foot soldiers a lift. Their weapons ranged from muskets, shotguns, squirrel guns, Kentucky long rifles, and horse pistols to broadswords, butcher knives, bowie knives, and tomahawks.

Austin had been compelled many times to issue orders to stop promiscuous shooting from the ranks to save ammunition. But even as Houston watched, a flock of blackbirds flew overheard and several guns blazed jubilantly from the ranks. He was reminded of Jackson's stern discipline to establish "subordination" at the beginning of a campaign. Inevitably the barefoot troops suggested the bloody footprints at Valley Forge. Badly as they needed discipline and training, Houston was sure that better-spirited men never were seen in ranks. The equipment, not the quality, of the troops disturbed him.

That night, beside Austin's campfire, Houston heard what had happened since Austin had taken command. He had awarded a number of commissions; he could remember only six, though he was not certain of the ranks assigned. The six Austin remembered were Erastus ("Deaf") Smith, James W. Fannin, William Wharton, William B. Travis, Dr. James Grant, and Edward I. Burleson. Burleson, hardly able to write his name, was an experienced Indian fighter with a home on the Colorado River. The others were also qualified in one way or another. Austin believed that any one of them knew as much about leading troops as he did. To their credit, they had all clamored to take commands into action.

Austin also told Houston that James Bowie had joined him. Bowie had come galloping into camp on a small gray mare with six volunteers from Louisiana, his knife in his sash and a rifle slung from his saddle. He, too, wanted a commission and Austin had given him one; but Austin could not be sure whether he had made Bowie a colonel or a major. Bowie had lost his wife and children in a recent yellow-fever epidemic and he was drinking heavily. His former despair had seemingly been replaced by a constant state of excitement.

Bowie had quickly made friends with Fannin, a Georgian who had spent two years at West Point in the class of 1823 alias James F. Walker and had resigned because of illness in his family. In joint command they had left camp with ninety men of the Harrisburg Volunteers and Brazos Guards to scout the roads around San Antonio. A report had reached Austin that the two men had quarreled and separated after dividing their troops. Where they were now he did not know.

It was with the mixed feelings of an old soldier that Houston listened to this strange report from the commanding general. Austin, always willing to do his best for the colony, made no pretense of being fitted for command. Moreover, he did not seem well; he was racked by a cough that had not left him since that long solitary confinement in his damp cell in Mexico. He felt the cold and drew his coat closely around him, though the evening was mild.

When Houston raised the question of sending delegates back to carry out the urgent business of forming a government, Austin readily agreed that this was desirable; but, he contested, the troops must be given the reason for the departure, lest they think themselves deserted by frightened and fleeing delegates. Next morning Austin called the troops together and made a speech, announcing that it was as desirable and necessary to form a government as it was to fight. Houston, William Wharton, and Branch T. Archer made similar pleas.

The troops then voted on whether the delegates should return or stay with the army; all except a dozen favored the delegates' going back to set up a government. Two days later Houston reached San

Felipe at the head of enough delegates, together with those already on hand, to make a quorum.

In the town hall, a small, one-story frame building with neither ceiling nor plaster, fifty-one delegates from thirteen counties met on November 3 and elected Wharton's man, Archer, to preside. He took his place at the head of a long rough board table. Outside, the weather was chilly; inside, warmed by human bodies, the room was at first comfortable and then hot. The delegates loosened their shirts at the neck. The room smelled strongly of horses and human sweat.

Taking the floor, Wharton moved that Texas declare herself an independent country. Zavala, the Mexican idealist, opposed Wharton with quiet dignity. Such action, he pointed out, would offend all liberal Mexicans, adding that it would prevent sympathetic Mexican states from coming to the aid of Texas in putting down the despot. He believed that if the delegates were satisfied to set up a separate state government within the Mexican federation, liberal Mexicans would be attracted to the cause.

A group of delegates led by the exceptionally able Don Carlos Barrett, a lawyer and politician, opposed even considering the idea of separating from Mexico. Houston, on this occasion, must have been impressed by the man's way of presenting his convictions. He later rated Barrett as one of the most competent men in Texas, but also one of the worst because he "was so capable and all his capability was turned to harm." [2]

Supporting Zavala, but with some qualifications, Houston argued for support of the Mexican constitution of 1824 and introduced a resolution to this effect. He proposed that a complete record of the colonists' grievances against the Mexican government be prepared with care and presented for the consideration of the civilized world. A pioneer, to be sure, but also rather well traveled in the States, he was conscious of the world that lay beyond the frontiers of Texas.

Every Texan was familiar with the offenses that Houston enumerated: sudden arrests, shootings of colonists, denial of the right to assemble, interference with commerce, and arbitrary acts of all kinds by civil and military authorities in the Redlands, San Antonio, Saltillo, and Mexico City. There was no adequate school system or judicial system; intolerable delays vitiated all legal proceedings.

Tyrannical acts by hostile and corrupt officials were common. Houston emphasized that for diplomatic reasons it might be unwise to declare independence at this time. Such a step, he said, would be an invitation to instant annihilation, the equivalent of adding ten thousand men to Santa Anna's forces. He feared that such action taken now would jeopardize future success. His resolution on the subject was opposed by Wharton, and he withdrew it.

The vote on November 6 to establish a provisional government was decisive, but opposed by a surprisingly large minority, 33-14. The next day's declaration of purpose was equivocal. To avoid alerting Mexico, it was slanted as much toward continuing the connection with that country as it was toward independence. With this objective it was agreed that the provisional government would be established upon the principles of the constitution of 1824.

The delegates spent about a week drawing up their plan for a provisional government, which they called the organic law. It provided civil and military laws and for a governor, a lieutenant governor, a general council, and a major general who would be commander in chief of all forces during war. The council was given legislative powers.[3]

While it was vaguely assumed that the new state might exist within the Mexican confederation, it was also understood that setting it up might lead to war, or even that the war had already begun. And finally it was recognized that the hastily drawn plan was defective. Later it was stipulated that another convention to perfect it should meet in about three months at Washington-on-the-Brazos, farther from the frontier and the impending Mexican invasion. Thus the matter of independence was shelved until the next meeting.

In the election for governor, Houston supported Stephen Austin, but Henry Smith, the Wharton man in the tight-buttoned black coat who had shown sympathy with Houston's more conservative approach, was chosen. Houston's fellow townsman, James Robinson, was elected lieutenant governor. Houston was elected major general. Article II of the plan specified that the major general was to be "Commander in Chief of all the forces called into public service during the war"—a clear assumption that war would follow separation from Coahuila.

A courier arrived from General Austin with news and a message for the delegates. A Mexican force of 300 cavalrymen, 100 infantry, and two artillery pieces had pushed down the river bottom to Concepcion in an early dawn fog and attacked Bowie's advance patrol. Bowie's men had seized a Mexican brass six-pounder and driven the Mexicans back with their own canister. When Austin's force arrived on the double from Espada Mission, the Mexicans broke and fled, but Colonel Bowie did not pursue. Austin had reproved him for not following the Mexicans to the walls of San Antonio. Bowie, insubordinate if not insulting, had blamed Austin for not arriving sooner.

Austin announced to the Consultation that he wished to be relieved of command and suggested that his successor should be "A man of robust health ... more competent ... my worn out constitution is not adapted to a military command, neither have I ever pretended to be a military man.... it is an office ... I never sought and tried to avoid." [4]

The convention accepted Austin's resignation and appointed him, William Wharton, and Archer commissioners to go to the United States to sell a bond issue of a million dollars and to raise volunteers and supplies for the Texas army.

Before adjournment on November 14, 1835, Houston addressed the members, expressing his pride and satisfaction in the trust shown by his election as Commander in Chief. He was stirred, and when he was stirred he was eloquent. His speech made a strong impression, but no stronger than the one he had made on November 4 in support of his committee's declaration of causes why Texas must be prepared to take up arms. Gail Borden, Jr., a revolutionary newspaper editor of Galveston (who would some day be distinguished for his revolutionary process for condensing milk), had heard Houston's speech on the fourth and the next day wrote Stephen Austin: "Had a conversation with Genl. Houston today. I believe he has the interest of our country at heart. He made the best speech yesterday I ever heard; the whole tenour of it went to harmonizing the feelings of the people and to produce unanimity of sentiment." [5]

A majority of the members of the Consultation were "old settlers." Houston, having been in the country a little less than three years, was still regarded as a newcomer and had not passed all the tests. His military capacity was still an unknown quantity. But some, like

Borden, were learning to respect his sincerity. Houston's eloquent speech in accepting the command showed there was no doubt in his mind that he was both ready and adequate for the task ahead.

5. The Intrigue

THE first government paper signed by the fiery-tempered little man in the tight-buttoned coat was a commission designating Sam Houston Major General and Commander in Chief. Next, Governor Smith addressed a strong message to the General Council which was received on November 15, 1835:

> ...no common duties devolve upon you. You have to call system from chaos; to start the wheels of government, clogged and impeded as they are by conflicting interests....Without funds, without the munitions of war; with an army in the field contending against a powerful foe. These are the auspices under which we are forced to make a beginning....[1]

General Houston set up his headquarters in the front room of the Virginia House, preferring to take a chance on its rats and fleas rather than risk the codfish menu of the New England Retreat. His landlady, a fat, motherly soul, waddled in and out of his headquarters. Always a believer in symbols of authority to command proper respect for the officers of a properly organized regular army, Houston undertook to locate some gold braid. Probably his landlady improvised it from doilies or portieres; something that at least looked like braid was sewn to the shoulders of his velveteen jacket.

Houston immediately concentrated on the defense of Texas against impending invasion from the south. He ignored the activities of the volunteer army at San Antonio because they were irrelevant to this immediate objective. He soon discovered that, though he had been appointed Commander in Chief, he had no real authority because the Council had refused to cooperate in organizing the regular army.

But before the basic disagreement arose between him and the

Council, he undertook to move available men into positions where they could be most useful. One of these was Captain James W. Fannin of the Volunteer Army, which was encamped just outside San Antonio. His two years' training at West Point promised to make him valuable in the recruiting and training department. Houston knew that the Georgian was ambitious, quarrelsome, and of a somewhat dubious background. At thirty-one, after a varied career as a smuggler and slave-runner, he had come blazing into Texas with funds for speculation. Desiring to put all of Fannin's talents to use, Houston sent a courier to San Antonio with a letter, offering him an appointment as inspector-general of the army with rank of colonel and asking him to come to San Felipe as soon as he could.

The same courier brought back Fannin's answer asking Houston to have the Council appoint him brigadier general, next in rank to the Commander in Chief. "I am well satisfied," Fannin wrote, "that I can fill either of the posts *better than any officer*, who has yet been in command." He emphasized his self-confidence by underscoring.[2]

Soon afterward Fannin put in his appearance at San Felipe. A tall, dark, loose-jointed, overbearing man with a nervous manner and shifting eyes, he presented himself at headquarters protesting that the appointment offered him did not measure up to his experience and ability, and he demanded that Houston ask the General Council to commission him brigadier general. But Houston asked the Council to make Fannin a colonel, not a brigadier general. Behind the Commander's back, Fannin immediately began the manipulations and intrigue within the Council that ultimately led to disaster for himself and Texas.

By November 21, when Houston had been Commander in Chief one week, the New Orleans Grays, the volunteer force financed by William Christy and his New Orleans friends, reported for duty to Stephen Austin's command at San Antonio. They brought two cannon that Austin had been waiting for.

That same day Austin proposed to his officers that his planned assault on the Mexican-held town take place the following morning. Colonel Ed Burleson and Lieutenant Colonel Philip Sublett reported in writing that officers and men were opposed to the assault and unwilling to attempt it.

Austin accepted this blunt response as the proper finale for his attempt at military leadership. Three days later he paraded the troops and announced the news that had just reached him from San Felipe: With Wharton and Branch he had been appointed to serve as a member of a commission to the United States to raise loans and other support. He called for an election, and the men voted for Colonel Burleson to take over the command. Austin quit the front on his way first to San Felipe and then to New Orleans.

The troops that Burleson took over occupied positions where Austin had placed them in readiness for assault on the town. Some held an offensive position near the powder house, 1,000 yards east of the Alamo, an old chapel-fort; the rest were camped near the old mill in a bend of the San Antonio River about 800 yards north of the Alamo. Trenches built on the San Antonio River bank were manned with infantry. A battery placement had been erected at night. The Mexicans under the young General Cos held two positions, one in the town and another in the Alamo itself.

Winter nipped at the troops now under command of the wily old Indian fighter, General Ed Burleson. They did not even have tents and could not be expected to camp in the open. On December 3, 1835, Burleson called a council of war which decided to retire the army to winter quarters at Goliad or Gonzales. Then a Mexican lieutenant deserted to the Texans and reported that the defenses of San Antonio were weak. Burleson's adjutant general, Colonel Francis W. Johnson, a loud-spoken man of thirty-six but a shrinking violet when it came to this kind of fighting, turned to Colonel Benjamin R. Milam and said that the time had come to call for volunteers. When Johnson side-stepped the opportunity to call for volunteers himself, most of the army was gathered around the headquarters of General Burleson.

"Who will go with Old Ben Milam into San Antonio?" Milam called out.[3]

Milam was only forty-four, but "Old" was a common title of distinction with a connotation of merited esteem, resolution, and mature judgment. He had recently escaped from prison in Monterrey while the army was still commanded by Austin. He had arrived in camp half starved, haggard from imprisonment, and dressed in clothes much too small, with sleeves six inches above his wrists and ragged trousers far above his ankles. Now, having found more suitable clothing and having fed on corn and good tough beef and some of the liberal supplies of liquor furnished the army by Dick Royal, he was himself again.

No great rush followed Milam's call, but a respectable number of men did step forward and Milam ordered them to assemble at the old mill at dark to organize. Two columns, one commanded by Milam and the other by the canny Frank Johnson, were formed. On December 5, Colonel James C. Neill was ordered to place a battery north of the Alamo Mission and to open fire at 5:00 A.M. to divert attention while the columns advanced on the town. The advance made some progress, capturing a few houses on the outskirts. At 9:00 A.M. Neill withdrew to his camp at the old mill, where the enemy attacked him without success.

On December 6 the Texans discovered cloth in one of the captured houses and made sandbags to protect their artillery while firing on the town. The next day they found that the Mexicans had thrown up a redoubt outside the Alamo. The Texans forced the Mexicans to abandon this position, but during the night the enemy strengthened their force in a building between the town and the Alamo. Early in the morning the Texans forced Mexican withdrawal by concentrated artillery and rifle fire.

On December 8 all positions occupied by the Texans were bombarded by the enemy. Ben Milam and a small storming party had gained entrance into a house. Fearlessly he came out to observe the enemy and was shot through the head. Johnson took over command of the storming parties. Under cover of darkness that night, the enemy was reinforced by troops under the command of Ugartechea.

On the morning of December 9, which was cold and wet, the enemy's fire slacked off. All that day and during the early part of the following night the Texans were busy driving holes with crowbars through the mud, stone, and adobe walls of houses nearest the enemy. They had begun this work several days before. Now they crawled through these holes and from advanced positions made rushes under cover of darkness, but they were checked by heavy fire. With the light of morning, a white flag had replaced the Mexican flag flying above the town. Firing ceased and Johnson sent for Burleson. General Cos and the Texans appointed commissioners to draw up articles of capitulation which were signed December 10, 1835.

A few hundred Texans with hunting knives and rifles, together with a detachment of New Orleans Grays with two small cannon, five hundred men in all, had defeated more than a thousand well equipped Mexican soldiers in a well fortified position. Casualties: 12 Texans killed, 18 wounded; 150 Mexicans killed, wounded unreported.

Austin's intention to take San Antonio by direct assault after a siege of two weeks had been courageous but probably would not have had this favorable outcome. After his departure the siege had lasted two weeks more and the city was finally taken by a slow five-day advance, part of it through house walls.

Now the Texans were confronted with the unforeseen problem of feeding and guarding Mexican prisoners. General Cos and all his men gave their solemn paroles never to fight against Texas again. Then Cos was permitted to return across the Rio Grande, his troops taking their muskets and one cannon with ten rounds of ammunition for protection against Indians. All other public property was left behind.

With the Mexicans marching toward the Rio Grande, most of the Texas volunteers went home. Colonel J. C. Neill was placed in command of the Alamo with a garrison of about one hundred Texans and several hundred volunteers from the States, who were now pouring in.

In parts of the colony thoughtless persons believed the war was over. Sensible men saw otherwise. The Commander in Chief sent congratulations from San Felipe to the front but he distrusted the course of events. Early reprisals could be looked for to offset the victory at San Antonio. This was a time, he urged in letters to Governor Smith, while actually directing his remarks to the Council, when Texas should be vigorously preparing her regular army for defense against the oncoming invasion—a time for recruiting, drilling, learning tactics, and acquiring discipline.

While the fighting was going on at San Antonio, Houston had completed his plan of defense against impending invasion from below the Rio Grande. He knew that President-General Santa Anna was collecting large forces at Saltillo and Monclava. It was possible that he had already moved some of them to the Rio Grande. To meet the invasion Houston proposed to have his defense line based, on the north, at Gonzales, east of the Guadalupe River. On the south it was to be based at Victoria, some sixty miles from Gonzales and on the east bank of the same river. From Victoria he planned to send scouting parties and armed detachments southeast as far as LaVaca Bay. The scouts would report on the movements of the Mexican column which he expected to advance from Matamoros to penetrate and devastate the Texas coastal area. The detachments would be assigned to harry the invader in this area.

His plan called for importing supplies and volunteers in unarmed vessels to Copano and Dimitt's Landing. He also laid out a plan for the recruitment and organization of a regular army. Troops, scattered under various small commands, were to be concentrated to begin training. Too little time had elapsed for scouts to bring back reliable information on the president-general's movements, but Houston anticipated that Santa Anna's invasion would come with "the rise of grass." The surrender of Cos and the capture of San Antonio convinced Houston that he could not go wrong in assuming that General Santa Anna as his first objective would undertake the recapture of that city to restore Mexican prestige.

Houston had no intention of defending San Antonio. He thought that Santa Anna must be met in the field and defeated in one battle; otherwise Texas would risk being overwhelmed by numbers. Defense-in-place—a fight by men shut up in a fort—was no part of Houston's scheme. His often-stated belief was that Texas could not afford to undertake such an enterprise against an enemy who could bring up unlimited reinforcements for siege and assault. She must depend upon quick flexible movements. Instead of defending San Antonio, he hoped to prevent Santa Anna from reaching it. To accomplish this objective, he proposed to take the field himself and lead the attack on Santa Anna's advancing column when it came.

With considerable precision, he planned his operation against the Mexican general. He would take command of more than a thousand volunteers who, coming from Texas and the States, would collect at Copano on Copano Bay, then being used as a port of entry for Refugio and San Patricio. He would employ the volunteers to destroy, capture, or rout the Mexican column that was expected to advance northward along the coast from Matamoros. This self-imposed assignment should not be too difficult because he foresaw that the Mexicans would be harried on the way by scouts and other mounted groups. He calculated that his rear echelon would be safe when the enemy's coastal invasion force had been taken care of. Then he expected to turn and, with some addition to his numbers, intercept Santa Anna before he reached San Antonio. Houston anticipated that Santa Anna's force would also be demoralized by its long march, short provisions, and winter weather, thus increasing the odds in favor of the Commander's success.

But he had a supplementary plan in case his calculation for a fairly easy victory went awry. He would concentrate his main force of several thousand volunteers and regulars, equipped with all kinds of available arms, at Gonzales on the east bank of the Guadalupe. If he did not prevail over Santa Anna, he would retreat to Gonzales, with the Mexicans presumably following him; there he would fight the one big battle that he hoped would topple the Napoleon-of-the-West, establish the success of Texas arms, and liberate the country. It was neat, practical, and it made sense. The Commander in Chief was quietly confident that his plan for a regular army supplemented by volunteer commands to carry out this strategy deserved the support of the provisional government. He soon discovered that this was exactly what he lacked.[4]

The Consultation had directed the Council to give immediate attention to setting up the regular army. But by Article VIII of the plan of government, it had made the mistake of putting the appointive power for regular army officers in the hands of the Council. Governor Smith was charged only with commissioning them. This was the reverse of the American system by which officers would have been appointed by the governor and confirmed or rejected by the General Council.

While Houston was concentrating on preparations to meet the spring invasion, he was hampered by the Council's deliberate preoccupation with irrelevant matters. Though the members behaved as if oblivious of the emergency, he did not at first suspect treachery. There was imperative need of haste, but the Council spent its time in futile debate over new names for old municipalities and in laying out the boundaries of new municipalities. Prompted by Houston, the governor warned the Council that they were not performing the main duties laid upon them by the Consultation, and still, with less than three months before invasion was expected, the Council showed itself indifferent to the crisis.

By letter to Governor Smith on December 6, Houston again appealed to the Council for prompt establishment of the regular army. He pointed out that the Council was responsible for naming the officers of companies, regiments, brigades, and corps and added:

> ...It is required of me to raise the Regular Army without delay. I feel the responsibility of my Situation at a time when every effort should be exerted and means used for the accomplishment of an object so necessary to the defence & happiness and I apprehend, the Salvation of Texas. I must remain under the conviction, however, that all essential power is withheld from me to meet the requisitions of the Organic Law.
>
> It is true the company of officers of the Infantry Regiment have been appointed by the Hon. General Council, but the field officers proper to command ... the several recruiting Rendezvous have not been appointed....
>
> ...Unless the officers are appointed at an Early day it will be impossible to have an army at the opening of the Campaign which can not, in my opinion, be delayed with Safety to the country longer than the 20th of February or the first day of March, at farthest.... We must have an army or abandon all hope of defending the Country!
>
> ...an army of the enemy amounting to 10,000 men, with suitable munitions of war, must be met and vanquished or Texas will be overwhelmed for years to come. Union and confidence among ourselves, and a generous support of the Army, will achieve everything that is desirable to Freemen! ...
>
> Permit me to implore you most earnestly to give your attention to the Subjects herein very respectfully Submitted.[5]

Distraught by delay and frustration, he apparently did not realize that assurances of vigorous use of the regular army under a willing Commander in Chief was exactly the way to inspire opposition and delay.

But finally, on December 7, the Council yielded to part of Houston's demands, and field officers were elected: J. W. Fannin, colonel; J. C. Neill, lieutenant colonel; William Oldham, major. Officers for the artillery were D. B. Macomb, lieutenant colonel; W. B. Travis, first major; and T. F. L. Barrett, second major. These officers were immediately assigned to various duties by Houston.

After Fannin was sworn in and given his commission, Houston

ordered him to open a recruiting station at Matagorda and to acknowledge receipt of this order in writing. Fannin did neither; he
vanished from San Felipe. The next the Commander in Chief heard
about him he was in Velasco on the coast. Houston sent orders for
Fannin to report to headquarters, but he did not return.

The Consultation had had members of unusual ability, but the
Council members were inferior and inclined to be casual about attending meetings. Most of the competent members had been obliged
to go home to look after their families. After John A. Wharton and
Almanzon Huston resigned to serve as staff officers on assignment to
New Orleans to raise funds and ship supplies, the Council did not
have one man left who was both able and loyal to the plan of
government set up by the Consultation, although all members took
oath to support it. Without authority for doing so, the Council
passed an ordinance enlarging its membership from 13 to 24. Its
loyalty was not to Texas but to an inner clique of intriguers within
the Council. Frequently the Council acted without a quorum.

After electing the field officers in response to Houston's repeated
demands, the Council busied itself with various futile activities. The
most urgent matter that Houston submitted—an estimate of expenses
for recruiting—was not acted on. Houston was without funds. Meanwhile, the Council was appropriating money for strange causes. On
December 3, it appropriated $500 for Colonel José Maria Gonzales,
a Mexican revolutionist, who offered his services as a spy. He took
the money, disappeared, and was never heard from again.

On December 9, over Governor Smith's veto, the Council accepted the services of General José Antonio Mexia. He was authorized to draw upon the government for all necessary funds and to
proceed to San Antonio to further the revolution. Earlier in the
year, Mexia, a shady character, had left the United States with
twenty-two young Americans, who had been recruited in New
Orleans as emigrants to Texas. Though they were supposed to land
at Velasco or some other Texas port, Mexia took them to Tampico.
He had some plan in mind that was never disclosed. A detachment
of Santa Anna's troops from the Tampico garrison seized the Americans. Mexia managed to escape and fled. The Americans were
charged with invading Mexico, condemned without trial, and shot.
On the edge of the grave, eighteen of them signed a denial, declaring

with their dying words that "No intention to invade Mexico had existed in our minds." [6] To this man who had recently returned from Tampico, the Council voted liberal funds, but denied the Commander in Chief an appropriation for recruiting. Mexia collected the funds and disappeared from Texas, vanishing in the night without reporting at San Antonio.

This was not the last of the Council's peculiar conduct. Mexia's courier, Captain Julian Miracle, was granted an appropriation to serve as a spy. He collected the money and hastily followed Mexia's footsteps, never to be heard from again. The motives behind the Council's strange conduct were mixed, but mixed motives did not prevent the intriguers from agreeing on their objectives.

Don Carlos Barrett, a lawyer and politician, defended by his partisans as a patriot, but described by Houston as the "worst man that ever was in Texas," had exceptional ability.[7] He was a member of practically all committees set up by the Council, including the all powerful military committee. In the Consultation, Barrett had led an assertive minority which vigorously opposed separation from Mexico. Nothing had happened to change his conviction. When certain members of the Council proposed to set up an unprecedented office to be known as military agent, he fell in with it. These military agents were to serve as commanders in the field and be responsible solely to the Council and not to the Commander in Chief. This, of course, was illegal and unauthorized by the organic law from which the Council received its authority.

Richard Royal of Matagorda, a warm friend of the ambitious and egotistical Fannin, was another vigorous supporter of the military agent principle. He was eager for Fannin to have unrestricted authority to lead an attack on Matamoros with the object of taking spoils that would defray expenses of war. This put Royal on the side of the intriguers against the governor and the Commander in Chief, both of whom stood for strictly legal procedure and for a vigorous policy of preparedness to resist invasion.

Wyatt Hanks aspired to the job of army sutler which Houston said would mean $10,000 a year to him. To get it, Hanks pleaded by letter for Houston's support while conniving to get similar support from members of the Council. This threw him into the intriguers' camp. As chairman of the military committee he conspired against the authority of the Commander in Chief and secretly wrote letters to officers at San Antonio urging them to undertake a campaign against Matamoros.[8]

Intriguers in the Council also had the support of Lieutenant Governor James W. Robinson, who presided over all Council sessions. In the end he was one of the most active in the insurrectionary movement which overthrew the provisional government.

These four men—Barrett, Royal, Hanks, and Robinson—were the core of the intrigue. Other members of the Council were merely rubber stamps. Propositions favored by the intriguers were passed when only a handful of members, no quorum, was present. Finally, to further their objective and to end Houston's stubborn demand for action in support of the regular army, the Council's inner clique decided that the Commander in Chief had to be removed from the scene.

On December 16, a Council order directed Governor Smith to instruct General Houston to move his headquarters to Washington-on-the-Brazos, a small town, raw and new, hardly worthy of a name, fifty miles by a difficult road from the San Felipe capital. Houston later commented in his *Memoir* (p. 80): "It was evident they believed the success of their intrigues depended upon getting the Commander in Chief as far off as possible."

On December 17, Houston wrote a letter to Governor Smith stating his intention to comply with the Council's order. He charged that Chairman Hanks of the military committee "interposed every possible obstacle to the organization of the army." Hanks, he pointed out, had been so incensed with the Commander in Chief for demanding speedy organization of the army that in a report to the Council he had "used remarks of a personal character toward myself . . . deemed so indecorous [by the Council] that they were stricken out of the report." In this same letter he spelled out the Council's responsibility for preventing organization of the regular army:

> In the meantime, I do most earnestly solicit the attention of your excellency to the subject of an appropriation to cover the recruiting contingencies of the army. . . .
> More than a month has now elapsed since the adjournment of the consultation, and the army is not yet organized; and, though I have ordered some officers on the recruiting service, it has been on my own responsibility.

He had reason to suspect looseness in the Council's handling of the liberal contributions that were flowing in from the States: "I would beg leave to suggest ... establishing a system of accountability in all [the Council's] disbursing departments; requiring ample security of all officers ... entrusted with funds, agreeably to the system established in the United States, if provisions of the organic law are not sufficient." [9]

Though he fully understood why the Council had moved his headquarters to the backwoods, and foresaw the evil consequences, he stated his intention to be guided by the will of the civil authorities. Privately Governor Smith seems to have suggested to Houston that if the Commander would collect the necessary troops he would be given orders to disperse the Council and put an end to its subversive activities. But Houston's attitude was that his oath permitted him to resign if dissatisfied, but not to rebel against the civil government. Probably he foresaw that if he engaged in a wrangle or physical struggle with civil authorities his later usefulness would be impaired. He might well be charged with a desire to become a dictator. This would have affected his standing in the convention that was to meet on March 1. Obedience to civil authority was the keynote of his policy.

The intrigue of the inner circle to render the provisional government ineffective and to get all military and financial power into their own hands was now well under way. They had not yet accomplished their major aims, but soon would—with clever traps laid for the downfall of the hot-tempered governor and the obedient Commander in Chief.

6. The Council Fires a General

WASHINGTON was some forty miles north and a little to the west of San Felipe and, like it, was situated on the bank of the Brazos River. It had a few settlers' cabins along a single street that was cut through the woods; the tree stumps were still standing. In addition, there were some shanties and an unfinished barracks-like building that had been hastily thrown up the preceding fall when it was supposed that the Consultation would meet there.

A few days before Christmas, Houston, leading a pack mule, rode into his new backwoods headquarters. He was a general-in-exile, shunted from the center of power by the General Council. But in Washington he found Captain Peyton S. Wyatt, a native of Huntsville, Alabama, and fifty-six volunteer Alabamians. They had brought with them fifty first-rate United States muskets. Captain Amon B. King was there, too, with eighteen men from Paducah, Kentucky. They had come in response to Houston's first eloquent appeal from Nacogdoches for volunteers to share "the morning of glory." Because the Council had openly discussed its intention to deprive him of authority over volunteers, he felt embarrassed about accepting the services of the newcomers; but he decided to do so "for the good of the country." [1]

Wyatt's and King's men were greatly discontented, and disappointed by their reception, the lack of arrangements for them, and reports they had heard of squabbling in high places. Houston explained matters as best he could and persuaded them not to abandon the cause. He ordered them to proceed to Refugio for a rendezvous with other volunteers who were expected to land at Copano and Matagorda.

The Commander in Chief set up a rough board table at one end of the unfinished barracks, drew up a bench, spread out his scanty office supplies and went to work. He wrote to Governor Smith about Wyatt and King. On the day after Christmas, he reported to the governor that a courier had arrived with a report from San Antonio, "All quiet but no discipline." [2] Then, as he could not serve by organizing the army, he turned to correspondence to help the cause.

He wrote President Jackson that Texans would show themselves worthy of every trust. He sent similar reassurances to William Christy in New Orleans, John Overton in Nashville, and many others. Over his signature as Commander in Chief, he asked them to give every assistance that seemed appropriate to those Texas commissioners who were already in the States. No hint of the unsatisfactory state of affairs within the government appeared in his voluminous and eloquent correspondence.

He wrote a number of letters to Don Carlos Barrett, a member of the Council. In one on January 2, he said:

> I am ... pressed with business; and thank God my Christmas times are over, and I am most miserably cool & sober—so you can [say] to all my friends. Instead of Egg-nog; I eat roasted Eggs in my office. There was no *fuss here* on yesterday [*i.e.*, no drunkenness to celebrate the New Year], and I trust you had none in San Felipe, for if so our country, will be ruined—the world is now looking on us, and by our fruits, we shall be judged. Union & harmony will make up everything that we could wish to be. Dissension will destroy Texas. . . .[3]

Then, throughout the settlements, he appealed to outstanding men who were likely to be delegates to the March convention. He urged them to come promptly and to be prepared for decisive action. The Commander in Chief needed instructions from new civilian authorities. Presently he was cheered when Stephen Austin sent a letter from the United States reporting his belief that a declaration of independence by the March convention would lead to an influx of volunteers with supplies and money.

Before the Council had ordered Houston to his backwoods headquarters, they had directed him to make a treaty of neutrality and peace with the Cherokee Indians in northeast Texas. Now he wrote Barrett that as soon as he returned from this duty he would "proceed to the *frontier;* and organize the army for a prompt movement in the Spring." [4] Whether the Council would permit him to do this was another question.

He was ready to leave for the treaty-making on January 6 when a courier rode into camp with a letter from Colonel James Neill, commander of the garrison at San Antonio. Inspired by Francis W. Johnson and Dr. James Grant, the volunteers had organized a regiment to march on Matamoros, an important city on the lower Rio Grande. They had elected Johnson, colonel; Dr. Grant, lieutenant colonel; and Robert C. Morris of the New Orleans Grays, major.

Johnson and Grant, quitting the fortress with their followers, had stripped the garrison of all horses, blankets, provisions, and medicines, leaving behind eighty sick and wounded in distress. They set out for Goliad and Refugio on the route to Matamoros, taking with them the crack New Orleans Grays and fifty rifles donated by

Adolphus Sterne. Neill reported that the weakened garrison was in a pitiable plight and begged for instructions and help.

Houston knew that Johnson, the burly Indian fighter, had been intriguing in the Council for an illegal appointment to independent command outside the jurisdiction of the Commander in Chief. Dr. Grant, a shrewd and unscrupulous Scot, who had been dispossessed of his rich mines and land holdings in Mexico, stood to recover some of his lost wealth by a successful raid on a prosperous Mexican city. Major Morris, commander of the Grays, was doubtless an innocent dupe of Johnson and Grant. And somewhere in this scheme, Houston was convinced that the hand of another insubordinate plotter, James W. Fannin, would appear. Under terrific stress, he wrote to Governor Smith on January 6, 1836:

> I have the honor to enclose to your excellency the report of Lieutenant-Colonel J. C. Neill.... I may be permitted to hope, you will attend in person, that ... the government may deliberate, and adopt some course that will redeem our country from a state of deplorable anarchy. Manly and bold decision alone can save us from ruin. I only require orders and they shall be obeyed. If the government now yields to the unholy dictation of speculators and marauders upon human rights, it were better that we had yielded to the despotism of a single man [Santa Anna]....
>
> Within thirty hours I shall set out for the army, and repair there with all possible despatch....
>
> No language can express my anguish of soul ... send supplies to the wounded, the sick, the naked, and the hungry, for God's sake....[5]

Now he believed that it was a mistake for the October convention not to have proclaimed the independence of Texas. No other cause could unite, harmonize, and banish selfishness and lift the acts of men above the shameful levels of intrigue, ambition, and insurrection. He concluded his letter to Governor Smith with the question: "What would the world think of the authorities of Texas? Prompt, decided, and honest independence, is all that can save them, and redeem our country...."

It was a frank confession of error by a man who had opposed "independence now" and had argued successfully for a state government as a diplomatic blind to cover preparations for defense and independence later. His policy of postponing independence to avoid reprisals had collapsed. Now he was for independence at the earliest possible moment as a stimulus to harmony and united effort. Governor Smith immediately responded with an order instructing Houston to proceed to the frontier and to do everything in his power to stop the Matamoros expedition.

George Hockley joined Houston at Washington-on-the-Brazos during the last week in December. On January 2, 1836, he carried a letter from Houston to Don Carlos Barrett, now the most influential member of the Council. In the letter, Houston requested that Hockley be commissioned as a major in the regular army. Barrett ignored the request, and Hockley returned to Houston's headquarters empty-handed.

This was an important reunion. Hockley was a friend of long standing; he would be at Houston's side constantly during the exciting events of the next few months and the years to come. They had met in Washington, D.C., when Houston was a young congressman and Hockley was a War Office clerk. In 1828 Hockley had moved to Tennessee when Houston's star was rising and he was Governor. Houston had assisted Hockley in getting established commercially. The younger man (he was now thirty-three and Houston was forty-two) had joined his friend in Nacogdoches in response to Houston's stirring cry that the morning of glory was at hand and the battle would be for liberty or death. In the provincial Nacogdoches force, Hockley had served as a major under Houston's command.

Lacking official standing of any kind, Hockley went along as friend and confidant when Houston left for Goliad on a cold and windy day, January 8, 1836. On the way they met Captain Phillip Dimitt, who told a distressing story. Johnson's and Grant's disorderly followers had forced twenty of Dimitt's men to dismount and had seized their horses, each the property of its dispossessed rider. General Houston said that if he had his way the owners would be compensated.

They reached the Goliad mission on the night of January 14. An appeal signed by Colonel James W. Fannin had been posted where the troops could see it. Fannin called for volunteers to join an expedition to "reduce Matamoros." Over his signature as "Military Agent" of the General Council, he promised: "the troops *should be paid out of the first spoils taken from the enemy.*" Houston knew that Fannin, trained at West Point, could not be ignorant of the implication of such a statement, and he underscored it in his report.[6]

From Major Morris of the New Orleans Grays, who had been left in command at Goliad, he learned that Dr. Grant had departed for Refugio with some of the two hundred men from the Alamo, leaving Morris to bring the remaining troops after twenty-four hours. Johnson had disappeared, no doubt to go to San Felipe to get authority from the General Council for the Matamoros project. The next morning, standing on the gray stone wall of the Goliad presidio east of the mission, General Houston appealed to the troops to refrain from participation in Johnson's and Grant's lawless enterprise.

His impassioned appeal, addressed them as honorable and intelligent men and implored them to understand the nature of the proposed attack on Matamoros. Their would-be leaders promised that they would be paid out of the first spoils taken from the enemy. What effect would a declaration of this kind have on the civilized world? On the enemy? On the citizens of Matamoros? It most certainly would convince them that their city, if taken, would be given up to pillage, and it most certainly would cause them to resist desperately. The people of Matamoros were not aware of the high-minded and honorable men who filled the ranks of the Texas army. The appeal by promoters of the Matamoros expedition to the soldiers of Texas to accept payment out of the first spoils taken from the enemy divested the campaign of any character save that of a piratical, predatory war.

Johnson and Grant had persuaded the troops to believe that the Matamoros expedition was authorized by the provisional government and would have the cooperation of liberals in northern Mexico. Houston told the troops that the expedition was not authorized. He also informed them that all appeals to other states of the Mexican confederation to join Texas in resistance to Santa Anna had been unsuccessful. Even the inhabitants of Zacatecas, the most liberal of all the Mexican states and the one that suffered most under Santa Anna's tyranny, had made no movement to support Texas.

Houston was convinced that, after the disloyal behavior of the Council, a campaign for all-out independence was the one course that could unite and save Texas. He advanced this conviction publicly for the first time in his address to the men:

> Since it is impossibe to call forth any sympathy from our fellow Mexican citizens ... and as they let us, the smallest of all the provinces, struggle without any aid, let us then, comrades, sever that link that binds us to that rusty chain of the Mexican Confederation; let us break off the live slab from the dying cactus that it may not dry up with the remainder; let us plant it anew that it may spring luxuriantly out of the fruitful savannah. Nor will the vigor of the descendents of the sturdy north ever mix with the phelgm of the indolent Mexicans.... Two different tribes on the same hunting ground will never get along together. The tomahawk will ever fly and the scalping knife will never rest until the last of either one tribe or the other is either destroyed or is a slave.[7]

On journeys through the province, he told the soldiers, he had learned "the wishes of our countrymen... 'Texas must be a free and independent state' is the general word." Then he implored them to disarm the illegal enterprise and support the cause of independence.

> A general convention of the representatives of the People will be held at Washington on the first of March of this year. It is the duty of the army to send several representatives; and I hope that my comrades will elect only men who will vote for our independence, will fearlessly proclaim our separation from Mexico, and what they decide upon, comrades, we will defend with our arms....[8]

As the result of this talk, a large number of men refused to take part in the Matamoros expedition, and the project was ruined for the time being.

At Goliad, Houston's speech to the men was interrupted by the arrival of a courier from Colonel Neill, commander of the Alamo. Neill's message disclosed that one of his scouts, sent out before Johnson and Grant had stripped the garrison of its horses, had returned from the border, reporting that two of Santa Anna's generals had led separate columns across the Rio Grande. Colonel Neill appealed for help to defend the Alamo and asked for a furlough so that he could go to the aid of his sick family.

Houston had hardly finished reading this dispatch when Colonel James Bowie rode up. Although Bowie had left six hours behind the other courier, he had all but overtaken him. His purpose was to lead back to the Alamo all the men who were willing to help defend it against the invader. Far from keen about any strategy involving a defense of forts, Houston explained the situation to the troops and called for volunteers. Perhaps he was not as eloquent as he would have been in behalf of a project in which he believed. Only thirty men responded; a few others indicated they would think it over.

To Bowie, a man whose courage and judgment he respected, Houston disclosed his reluctance to immobilize an army in a fortification threatened by greatly superior forces. Bowie believed that one hundred men could defend the Alamo against any number the Mexicans could bring.

Houston wrote out an order and asked Bowie to take it to Colonel Neill. The first part of the order was imperative; it granted Neill's furlough and instructed him before he left to remove all cannon from the Alamo and abandon the place after demolishing the fortifications. Houston emphasized, "We must annihilate the invader in the field." But he added a discretionary statement: Since Colonel Neill was at the Alamo and knew the situation better than anyone, he should use his own judgment.

Then Houston wrote a hasty letter to Governor Smith outlining his own projected movements:

> In an hour I will take up the line of march for Refugio Mission with about 209 efficient men, where I will await orders from your Excellency....
> I would myself have marched to Bexar but the Matamoras rage is so high that I must see Colonel Ward's men. You have no idea of the difficulties I have encountered. Patton has told you of the *men* that make the trouble. Better materials never were in ranks....[9]

Captain William H. Patton, who had joined the army recently, was not yet familiar with the quality of the men in the ranks. Later, as aide-de-camp to Houston, he would become better acquainted with their merits. Not the *men* but the commanders who usurped authority and seduced the men were the culprits.

When Major Morris, feeling himself obligated to the insurrectionary leadership of Johnson and Grant, started his troops for Refugio on January 15, General Houston and his aide accompanied him. It is likely that the General talked to the troops on the way, in language soldiers could understand, about the absurdity of a few hundred poorly equipped men undertaking an unauthorized expedition against an important and well-defended town of a nation easily capable of putting twenty thousand troops in the field. Perhaps he told them that six to ten thousand Mexicans already had gathered near the border and that at least two columns had crossed the river. But his main purpose in going to Refugio was to contact commanders of the volunteers who had been instructed to rendezvous there, particularly Colonel William Ward, commander of a Georgia battalion that had landed at Copano some two weeks before.

At Refugio, Houston was shocked to learn that Fannin had seized command of Ward's battalion, thus preventing Ward from carrying out orders that Houston had given him. Houston hardly had time to digest this when Francis W. Johnson, the bustling bluff settler, six years Houston's junior, presented him with an order relieving Houston from command of the volunteers.

The Matamoros project focused the insurrectionary, counter-revolutionary activities of the Council. Grant had fathered the idea to feather his own nest. Fannin and Johnson, ambitious for independent commands, had promoted the enterprise with the Council. The military committee had recommended Johnson to command all the troops he could raise for the expedition. This recommendation, passed by the Council, subverted the authority of the Commander in Chief. The committee had argued that its plan to take Matamoros would "carry the war into the enemy's country; and with the vessels that will be floating in the service of Texas in one month, will give us the entire command of the Gulf from Matamoros to New Orleans over our enemies." [10]

While Johnson, at San Antonio, had been preparing to take command of the venture, the Council had appointed Fannin as joint commander. Fannin had been at Velasco organizing the volunteers arriving from the United States. His powers also were in total conflict with the authority of the Commander in Chief. He had been made an agent for the provisional government of Texas, and had been granted the right to make loans and to impress property. Johnson at first refused but later agreed to share the command with Fannin.

Fannin had prepared an appeal to appear in the *Telegraph and Texas Register* on January 9, 1836, "ATTENTION, VOLUNTEERS! An expedition has been ordered by the General Council . . . Volunteers from Béjar (San Antonio), Goliad, Velasco and elsewhere are ordered to rendezvous at San Patricio. . . ."

Johnson had also issued a lengthy proclamation, "Our first attack will be on the enemy at Matamoros. . . ."

On January 7, the day before Houston left Washington-on-the-Brazos for Goliad, the violent feud between Governor Smith and the Council had terminated in events of a revolutionary nature. The Council had refused to submit their measures concerning Matamoros, the military agents, and other matters for the governor's approval or veto, as required by the plan of government. Governor Smith, without the least hesitation, had informed the Council that he regarded them "as debased human villains," and had ordered them to adjourn until March 1. He had had no more authority for this order than the Council had for many of its illegal acts, but his provocation had been great, and he was in a fight. He had closed his angry indictment of the Council with the inflammatory statement that, "A convention has been called which will afford a sovereign remedy to the vile machinations of a caucussing, intriguing and corrupt council." [11]

The Council had promptly retaliated with its final all-out revolutionary act. It ordered the governor to "cease the functions of his office," and appointed Lieutenant Governor James Robinson to succeed him. Then, usurping complete military authority, the Council had ordered a change in the command: "General Houston is relieved of command of all volunteer forces." Colonel J. W. Fannin and Major F. W. Johnson had been named as the Council's military agents, subject only to the orders of the Council itself. They were given joint command of all volunteers and instructed to proceed with the expedition to Matamoros.[12]

Governor Smith's only sin had been bitter and angry words; the Council's had been treacherous and evil deeds. First by intrigue and then by insurrection the Council had accomplished all their main objectives. They had removed the Commander in Chief, taken over the exclusive direction of military affairs, and wrecked the provisional government. For the moment, the Council was supreme; they had accomplished their ends by lawlessness in violation of their oaths.[13]

In San Antonio on January 26, a group of soldiers and citizens met to adopt resolutions condemning the Council. They charged the Council with misappropriating "money lent Texas to pay the San Antonio garrison" and praised the governor for "firmness in the execution of his trust." [14]

The Council's unfaithful acts were to result in many appalling consequences.

After Houston read the Council's orders dismissing him and elevating Johnson and Fannin to supreme command except over the regular army (which did not exist), Johnson wanted to know if Houston proposed to interfere with his authority. Houston assured him that he had no such intention. Later Houston explained the promptness with which he accepted the changed situation. Had he remained with the forces illegally commanded by Johnson and Fannin, he would have risked being held responsible for the disasters that he believed were bound to follow.

Houston paraded the troops and addressed them briefly and cautiously, taking care to avoid saying anything that could be interpreted as seditious. He read them the commission he always carried with him in which the governor had assigned to Houston's command all troops—volunteers, regulars, and militia. "But now," he explained, "orders have been issued by the Council that conflict with the governor's. The Council, in my opinion, does not have the authority to issue such orders. I intend to recognize the authority of Governor Smith. Your new leaders—military agents—on the other hand recognize the authority of the Council. You must decide for yourselves which you accept."

Confused by changes in command, by glowing forecasts of spoils to be taken and shared, and by all kinds of rumors about the brawling government and the oncoming columns of Santa Anna, the troops sent an informal committee to ask the General what he thought they should do. He would not place himself in the position of inciting insurrection or disobedience in any force sponsored by civilian authority, even an "illegal" authority such as the Council. But he thought that the soldiers were entitled to more specific guidance than he had yet given them.

"If you believe," he told them, "that the Council has deposed the governor and withdrawn command of the volunteers from the Commander in Chief illegally then you are justified in concluding that your new commanders have no authority over you. As volunteers you might consider yourselves privileged to go home. If you do, I suggest that you keep your rifles in good shape and practice marksmanship if you can spare the ammunition. Equip yourselves with good boots that will stand hard wear, and enjoy a comfortable furlough. Soon after the March 1 convention I promise you plenty of fighting. Our cause will be just and a noble one and well understood by all. Till March, then, I bid you farewell, and God bless you." [15]

The volunteers talked this over. Two hundred announced that they would not go to Matamoros, and left for home. The other 200, by following the military agents, sealed their own fate.

The General, with Hockley and two other loyal officers, left for San Felipe in the evening after his talk with the troops. On that ride he learned of Governor Smith's removal by the insurrectionary Council. Through the night and most of the next day, he despaired of the Texas cause. More than two months had passed since the Consultation had set up a provisional government, and not one effective step for defense had been permitted by the Council. By bloodless insurrection the provisional government had been destroyed, and the government that survived had no legal foundation whatever.

Dejected, he was assailed by doubts and uncertainties. Years later, speaking of himself in the third person to his collaborator on his *Memoir* (p. 85), he described the terrible darkness of this hour, his agonizing reappraisal of his personal situation:

All the way to San Felipe, he was troubled by the most painful suspense—whether to withdraw once more from the treacheries and persecutions of the world, and bury himself deep in the solitude of nature, and pass a life of communion with the

Great Spirit, and his beautiful creations—or whether he should boldly mark out a track for himself, and in leading a new people to Independence, trample down all opposition. During most of the [following] day he rode along in silence, and none of his companions disturbed his reveries. Towards evening he addressed them ... and dwelt with enthusiasm upon the future prospects of Texas....

His purpose was fixed. He would not resist the Council with violence, but he would stay with the cause. He would boldly mark out a new track.

7. A Cry from the Alamo

At Washington the long barracks-like log and board house with mud and stone chimney had been completed, and a dozen new shanties had been thrown up. A few stumps had been removed from the main street.

Colonel William Fairfax Gray of New Orleans was there on a special mission. He had been in the Louisiana city when Stephen Austin and his fellow commissioners had raised a $200,000 loan with the help of an enthusiastic committee promoted by William Christy. Gray's mission was to report back to New Orleans whether the ability and spirit displayed by the delegates to the March convention justified another loan of equal amount.

At San Felipe, Colonel Gray had witnessed brawls between the General Council and the fearless, determined Governor Smith, and now he was not favorably impressed by proceedings in Washington. He advised his New Orleans sponsors that their first loan to Texas, from a sound financial viewpoint, had been ill-advised and that a second would be folly. But Colonel Gray did not leave the scene after dispatching this opinion to New Orleans.[1]

Vital questions agitated the delegates during the days late in February before the convention assembled. What should be done about members of the perfidious Council who represented themselves as official delegates? A number of the troublemakers had put in an appearance, among them Richard R. Royal of Matagorda, one of the most active plotters, and an obscure member, John McMullen. If these and other insurrectionary councilmen hoped to spread the poison of sedition in this gathering, they must be stopped. Later, the convention brusquely denied seats to Royal and McMullen.

Governor Smith and Lieutenant Governor Robinson were also on hand. Smith was eager for a hearing, wanted to explain the revolutionary behavior of the "wicked" Council and justify his violent attacks on their "villainous" aims. There was some sympathy for Smith among the delegates, but little else. They were too busy at this time to bother about the battle that had waged between the governor and the Council. So, along with Royal and McMullen, Smith was brushed aside.

James Robinson, acting as if he thought he were still governor, was there, too. The delegates were prepared to deal with him in good time. Presently they would send a committee to Smith and Robinson to inform them that their duties as provisional officers had ceased. When asked to surrender all papers connected with the late provisional government, Robinson refused, and disappeared from the convention.

Don Carlos Barrett, most influential of all the late conspirators, was conspicuously absent. He vanished when it looked as if the fighting might begin, and would not be heard from for many years— not until Sam Houston would take care of him.

The delegates fully expected that Texas would declare her independence. But who would be president of the new nation? William Wharton was the logical man, but he was absent in the United States and, besides, he did not want the post. It was well known that Wharton had written Governor Smith, "In the new organization I will have nothing to do with the executive post. I prefer the post I am now in to any other if they (the delegates) choose to keep me in it." [2]

Houston seemed to be the best man available for the post of Commander in Chief under the new government. The delegates respected him because he had shown respect for the civil authorities—even for the authority of the General Council which had insulted and abused him and appeared to have betrayed the best interests of the country.

But where was General Houston? The voters of his home town—Nacogdoches—had rejected him as a delegate. Why the voters had turned down Houston was not definitely known, but there were many possible reasons. Houston had not been in Nacogdoches to explain his position. He might have been defeated by the activity of land grabbers who resented the resolution he introduced and supported annulling the tricky land grants made by the legislature of Coahuila-Texas. Naturally the land grabbers who held these grants were incensed.[3]

Houston's friends in Refugio, hearing of his defeat, had promptly elected him from their district. So he was expected as a delegate to represent them. But where was he?

Colonel Gray observed that a non-delegate, a well-set-up man with a spade beard, was buttonholing elected members of the convention. The man was assuring members that others might be reluctant to serve as president, but that he could be counted on to fill the vacancy even if it meant that Santa Anna would put a price on his head. This man was David G. Burnet, a former New York bank clerk. Noah Smithwick, a gunsmith at San Felipe, had known Burnet a long time. He had noted in his diary that there was nothing noticeable about Burnet's appearance except that he had a "twist in his face." [4]

In a spirit of adventure, Burnet had taken part in an expedition to free Venezuela. He had traveled alone among the Indians of the North American west. For a decade he had had a big land concession in the Texas redlands, and now he was a land lawyer and a two-weapon man; carried a pistol in one hip pocket and a Bible in the other. He did not drink or swear, but nobody called him timid. He had served in the April, 1833, convention at San Felipe along with Houston. The delegates seemed satisfied that if the presidency was to go by default, Burnet might as well have the post as anyone. Burnet's pre-convention electioneering was to pay off. Among the officers of the new nation presently to be elected, he would be the only one who had not been a member of the convention.

Another question that agitated the delegates: Where was the

invader? Had he got beyond the Rio Grande? Or would he postpone his advance until the "rise of grass." In the south, near the Rio Grande, the grass must be rising now.

Santa Anna, in fact, had encountered and, by persistence, was overcoming his worst troubles. Well past the Rio Grande, he was progressing with his luxurious marquee, his fine camp equipment, and his chest of gold, to carry out his angry determination to exterminate the upstarts who sought to break off a huge part of his imperial realm. He drove his troops relentlessly, marching them with reduced rations during the harshest weather. Somehow he inspired them with loyalty and zeal, though he scoffed at the sufferings of the sick who filled his wagons. Retreating settlers burned the grass, and stock died from disease and from eating burned vegetation.

But Santa Anna, General Cos (his brother-in-law), and General Joaquin Ramírez y Sesma (his second-in-command), were moving ever nearer to San Antonio when a bone-chilling norther struck their troops. Santa Anna suffered as his troops did; but he pressed on. Cos, by returning to Texas to fight, was breaking his parole.

The freezing wind of this same wet norther, rising to a gale, struck the delegates at Washington. In twenty minutes the temperature sank fifteen degrees, continuing to fall slowly for several hours. The delegates gathered around camp fires or sought shelter in the shanties. The second day it was worse. Two days later, in the tradition of the norther, the storm ceased and permitted mild weather to return.

And still, Colonel Gray noted, the convention did not get down to business. Provisions were running short; they were down to bread and pickled pork. Gray thought the prospect of starvation would spur the delegates to get on with their business, but they continued to mark time. Apparently they were waiting for the delegate from Refugio. Many seemed to think that the action to be taken depended more upon him than upon any other man.

Late on the twenty-sixth or the morning of the twenty-seventh, a messenger dashed in. He brought a letter, dated February 24, 1836, from Colonel William B. Travis, commanding at the Alamo. Governor Smith had transferred Travis from recruiting duties to command the Alamo while Colonel Neill was on furlough. Travis was well remembered for his one-shot victory at Anáhuac. His message was a cry for help:

> To the People of Texas & All Americans in the world—
> Fellow citizens—& compatriots—I am beseiged, by a thousand or more of the Mexicans under Santa Anna—I have sustained a continual Bombardment & cannonade for 24 hours & have not lost a man—The enemy has demanded a surrender at discretion, otherwise, the garrison are to be put to the sword, if the fort is taken—I have answered the demand with a cannon shot, & our flag still waves proudly from the walls—I shall never surrender or retreat Then, . . . come to our aid, with all despatch.
> . . . If this call is neglected, I am determined to sustain myself as long as possible & die like a soldier. . . .

VICTORY OR DEATH.

> P.S. The Lord is on our side—When the enemy appeared in sight we had not three bushels of corn—We have since found in deserted houses 80 or 90 bushels & got into the walls 20 or 30 head of Beeves—[5]

A collection was taken up for the courier, and he sped on his way to tell colonists to the east of the Alamo's need. Some of the delegates wanted to go to the aid of Travis, but there was nobody to organize them. Again they anxiously inquired for the delegate from Refugio. Probably they learned from Governor Smith that General Houston had gone to a treaty-making in the redlands. Surely, they were encouraged to hope, Houston could be expected any day now.

Back in November 1835, the San Felipe Consultation had received reports of a threatened outbreak by the Cherokees in northeast Texas. The tribe had become resentful because land grabbers had trespassed on some of their best-watered hunting grounds and threatened to take possession. It was also believed that Mexican agents were seeking to enlist them as armed allies against the colonists. If the Cherokees joined the enemy, Texas would face a desperate situation—war in the northeast as well as in the south and west.

Houston was made chairman of a committee to report on how

this situation should be handled. His committee recommended that a treaty be drawn to confirm the Cherokees' claim to the choice lands granted them by the Mexican government in 1819, before grants to white settlers had become common. This recommendation had been favorably acted upon. The public faith of Texas was pledged to support the Cherokee claim.

On December 28, 1835, Governor Smith had appointed Houston and two others to serve as commissioners to negotiate a treaty of peace and neutrality with the Cherokees and the numerous minor tribes associated with them. On returning to San Felipe from Refugio after the Council had illegally stripped him of command authority, Houston had conferred with Governor Smith. Smith, also stripped of his authority, had stated that he would continue to consider himself the only legal governor of Texas. Again, he was ready to disperse the Council if Houston would provide the necessary troops.

But Houston was firm in the stand he had previously taken; he wanted no part in any military action against civil authorities, but assured Smith that he would support him as the one rightful and legitimate governor. To make the best use of Houston's services pending the Washington convention, Governor Smith directed him to proceed with the other commissioners who had been appointed to negotiate a Cherokee treaty.

On his way to the treaty-making, Houston enjoyed a brief respite from winter travel in the home of his friends Henry and Ann Raguet. For a time he was again in the company of the girl who had once undertaken to teach him Spanish, the lovely Anna Raguet, now in her twentieth year. Before he left for the village of his old friend Chief Bowl, head of the Texas branch of the Cherokees, General Houston told Miss Anna that he regarded war with Mexico as a certainty. What would she give him as a token of her esteem and her wishes for his success in any duty that the Washington convention might see fit to assign him? She promised to knit him a silken sash, the kind that officers wore under their sword belts. He thanked her and told her he would stop for it on his way back to the convention.

In mid-February he arrived at Chief Bowl's village with Commissioner John Forbes; Hockley, now a colonel; and several young couriers. The third commissioner, John Cameron, did not attend. Houston and his fellow commissioners found the Indians in such a state of excitement that negotiations could not begin at once. He settled down in a house in Bowl's village and spent his time calming his red brothers. The Indians had been so aggravated by the whites that it took all of Houston's arts of friendship and brotherhood to placate them. He talked to them in the sign language and Cherokee tongue he had learned on Hiwassie Island and in Arkansas. He used the vivid picture-speech to persuade them that their best chance of happiness would come from following the path of peace with the colonists.

Gradually the excitement quieted down and things began to come his way. A day was set for negotiating the treaty, but on that day the excitement again was too intense to make progress possible. Houston began again. The dissidents finally yielded to persuasion, influenced by his past connection with the tribe and his adoption by Chief Jolly. Chief Bowl, their revered leader, assured them that this red brother was a white man whose word could be depended upon. Houston pledged his sacred honor and all his authority as Commander in Chief to support the treaty which would bring peace to the tribe forever if the Cherokees would sign.

The next day, February 23, 1835, the treaty, which would have many important consequences, was completed with Fox Fields, a half Indian, acting as interpreter. It declared "a firm and lasting peace forever" between Texas, the Cherokees, and twelve other tribes. It confirmed that, substantially, the Indians were to have the lands they had received by grant from Mexico. In exchange for land they relinquished, other land was granted to them.

Houston and Forbes, as commissioners for Texas, signed the treaty. Then Bowl and seven other chiefs, among them Big Mush, Corn Tossle, and The Egg, signed for the Indians. Fields and Hockley, with five other whites, signed as witnesses. The whites got the guarantee of peace and neutrality they needed, and Houston saw to it that the terms were fair to the Indians. Undoubtedly he told the chiefs that the treaty would not go into effect until ratified, and he certainly believed that it would be ratified. To the chiefs, on the other hand, signing the treaty was the final act that made it good.[6]

Houston returned to Nacogdoches and the Raguets. While Anna's family looked on, she tied around his waist the silken sash that she had knitted.

After leaving Nacogdoches, freezing weather and high water compelled Houston and his companions to lay over for the better part of a day in a settler's cabin. He reached Washington late on February 27, hours after the courier had delivered Travis' appeal for aid. The delegates swarmed around him, and somebody handed him the message from Travis. He read it and passed it to Hockley. Some of the delegates asked him to lead them to San Antonio. Others wanted his opinion on what should be done. He advised them to organize the convention and get on with the business of setting up a government.

This was the first news that Houston had of Santa Anna's presence at San Antonio. From Governor Smith, he knew that Travis had succeeded Neill at the Alamo. Travis' plight confirmed his belief that defending the Alamo was futile. What had forts to do with defending the vast area of Texas against a foe that had the troops necessary to besiege and starve out a dozen forts? He wondered if his discretionary orders to Colonel Neill to abandon the place had been passed on to Travis.

Houston's directives to demolish the fortification in Béxar and to carry the cannon to Gonzales were qualified in a way that left execution to Neill's judgment. Letters in the Texas State Library from Neill, Bowie, and Travis show that they all believed that the Alamo must be defended because the abandonment of San Antonio would leave a wide open road for the Mexicans into the interior of the colonies. Travis, who arrived at the Alamo on February 3, 1836, agreed with this decision made earlier by Neill and Bowie. Houston never criticized the defense of the Alamo in the light of the circumstances. But as long as he lived, he felt keenly and with bitterness that the acts of the faithless Council had deprived Texas of a properly organized army for defense. Such an army, he believed and repeatedly asserted, would have made the defense of the Alamo unnecessary.

On February 29, Colonel Gray recorded in his diary (p. 121): "Gen'l Houston's arrival has created more sensation than that of any other man. He is evidently the people's man and seems to take pains to ingratiate himself with everybody. He is much broken in appearance, but has still a fine person and courtly manner."

Houston had been through more than six weeks of almost incessant travel and had met one crisis after another. He had had an attack of malaria. He had been assailed continuously by keen anxiety for the future of his adopted country. He had traveled more than six hundred miles in winter on the swing around the circle from San Felipe to Washington; to Goliad, Refugio, and back to Washington; then on to Nacogdoches and Bowl's camp; and finally back to Nacogdoches and Washington, with sundry side trips. He had spent long hours writing urgent letters, reports, and a treaty.

In their half-finished convention hall the delegates elected Richard Ellis president and H. S. Kimble secretary. A committee was instructed to draw up a declaration of independence, an anonymous version of which had already been circulated. The points made in the declaration's indictment of Mexico were similiar to those Houston had made in his address to the San Felipe Consultation. The declaration was passed unanimously on March 2, 1836; by coincidence, on Houston's forty-third birthday. That same day he issued a communique as Commander in Chief under his old commission.

> Let the citizens of the east march to the combat. The enemy must be driven from our soil, or desolution will accompany their march upon us. *Independence is declared....* Immediate action united with valour, can alone achieve the great work. The services of all are forthwith required in the field.
> P.S. It is rumored that the enemy ... have entered the colonies. The fate of Bexar is unknown.... The patriots of Texas are *appealed to in behalf of their bleeding country.*[7]

He was tired. It was the prose of a weary man, without the directness and fire that Houston had formerly displayed when he was stirred.

The next day, March 3, 1836, delegate S. H. Everitt moved that the convention proceed to elect a commander in chief and instruct him to take the field. Though Everitt did not mention Houston's name, the resolution seemed to point to him. Houston arose and said that if he was to be considered for the post, the delegates should know on what terms he would accept it. Therefore, Everitt himself

166

moved to table the resolution. After the session Houston talked with a number of the most influential delegates and reminded them that the General Council had frustrated his attempt to organize an army and prepare for the country's defense. If he assumed the same responsibility again, it must be with the definite understanding that the new government would sustain him as long as he showed himself worthy of confidence.

On March 4 James Collinsworth, chairman of the military committee, introduced a resolution as specific as Houston could have wished. It appointed him "Commander-in-chief of all the land forces of the Texian army, both regulars, volunteers and militia ... and endowed [him] with all the rights, privileges and powers due to a Commander-in-chief in the United States of America." It authorized him forthwith "to proceed to take command, establish headquarters and organize the army accordingly." [8] He was to continue in office until suspended by the government. Several delegates spoke in favor of the resolution, and it was adopted on March 5, 1836. The only dissenting vote was cast by Robert Potter of the landowner's clique in Nacogdoches.

Houston rose to explain briefly his former course as Commander in Chief and the delicate position the decrees of the Council had placed him in. He expressed confidence that he would have the full support of the new government, and accepted his appointment with feelings of "solemn obligation."

It was Saturday and the session adjourned until Monday so that the important committees could prepare their reports. But early on Sunday, March 6, an alarm sounded and President Ellis called the delegates into special session. He told them he had "a communication of the most important character ever received by any assembly of men." He read another appeal from Colonel Travis, who wrote:

> I look to the *Colonies alone* for aid: unless it arrives soon, I shall have to fight the enemy on his own terms.... A blood-red banner waves from the Church of Bejar, and in the camp above us, in token that the war is one of vengeance against rebels; they have declared us as such, and demanded that we should surrender at discretion, or that this garrison should be put to the sword. Their threats have had no influence on me, or my men... *God and Texas—Victory or Death!!* [9]

To rouse Texans to the need for action a thousand copies were ordered printed for distribution in handbill form. Then delegate Robert Potter proposed an adjournment so that all delegates could hasten to the relief of the Alamo. Without formality, Houston quickly took the floor. Every eye turned on him. The delegates waited expectantly. His voice vibrated. "This proposal is mad. We have declared ourselves independent but we have no organization. There must be a government. It must have organic form. Without it we would be nothing but outlaws, and can hope neither for sympathy nor the respect of mankind. The country is in peril. I advise you to sit calmly and firmly and cooly pursue your deliberation. Be wise. Be patriotic. Feel no alarm. I pledge myself to proceed at once to Gonzales where we hear that a small corps of militia have rallied. I will interpose them between this convention and the enemy. While you choose to sit in convention I promise you the Mexicans will never approach unless they march over my dead body. If mortal power can avail I will relieve the brave men in the Alamo." [10]

This was Houston, stirred.

Without waiting for the delegates to vote on his recommendation the General hurried from the hall to prepare for his early departure. He was delayed more than an hour waiting for his commission, for which Chairman Collinsworth's resolution, indorsed by President Ellis, had to serve. Then, on that memorable Sunday, March 6, 1836, when the state of affairs at the Alamo was as yet unknown, he set out on the 115-mile ride west to Gonzales. With him were George Hockley, already appointed inspector-general of the army; aides-de-camp Richardson Scurry, Captain Albert C. Horton, an Alabama youth, and Verne Cameron, a spirited lad of eighteen, who was taken along as a courier.

They rode hard that day, stopping late at night only to rest their horses. They had reached open prairie. At dawn, Houston walked alone to some distance from his companions and listened. Travis had said in one of his letters that as long as the Alamo could hold out signal guns would be fired at sunrise. For some days past the signal had been heard for a distance of 100 miles. The day before, Houston had been told that "a dull rumbling murmur had boomed over the prairie like distant thunder."

In his *Memoir* (p. 91), he wrote that he "listened with an acuteness of sense which no man can understand whose hearing had not been sharpened by the teachings of the dwellers of the forest."

But he heard "not the faintest murmur floating on the calm morning air." He knelt, his ear to the ground. Then he returned to his companions and told them that he could detect no sound of cannon. He expressed no fears, but let them draw their own conclusions. They mounted. For some time Houston rode on in gloomy silence.

In the aura of excitement created by the latest alarm from the Alamo and the Commander in Chief's burning appeal before his hasty departure, the convention members discussed the projected constitution.

On March 12, a resolution by George W. Childress was passed. It provided "that a single star of five points, either of gold or silver be adopted as the peculiar emblem of this republic: & that every officer & soldier of the army and members of this convention, and all friends of Texas be requested to wear it on their hats and bosoms." [11]

That same day a resolution by J. W. Taylor was also adopted. It made the five-pointed star a part of the Texas flag with one letter of "Texas" in each of the five points. It was the launching of the Lone Star, the inspiring symbol which, as an emblem of the Republic, had not yet appeared in any sky.

BOOK III

FORTY DAYS AND NIGHTS
THAT CHANGED THE WORLD

1. *The Fall of the Citadel*

COLD, rain, muddy roads, washouts, and swollen streams delayed the progress of Houston's small cavalcade on its journey to Gonzales. The troops passed many fugitives who had abandoned their homes and were fleeing eastward, panicked by Santa Anna's advance from the south. None could tell the Commander in Chief what had happened at the Alamo; and Houston wrote later, "None turned about, joined our party and faced the hazards of the westward journey." He feared the Alamo had fallen. But Houston did not accept his inability to hear cannonading as final proof of the citadel's fate.

After crossing the raging Colorado River on Wednesday, March 9, 1836, Houston sent young Verne Cameron with a dispatch to Colonel James W. Fannin. With the New Orleans Grays and other volunteers, Fannin had taken refuge in the fort at Goliad. Houston hoped that the disloyal colonel would now recognize his authority; he informed Fannin that he had received a new commission as Commander in Chief from the Washington Convention and instructed him to abandon the Goliad fort immediately. He was to march all troops to the Gonzales crossing at Cibolo Creek twenty-five miles east of San Antonio. If he followed these instructions, Fannin would be able to help Houston and the Gonzales volunteers relieve the Alamo garrison.

At 4 P.M. on Friday, March 11, 1836, Houston rode into the

volunteers' camp on the Guadalupe near Gonzales, 76 miles from San Antonio. He found 374 men, 50 of whom were mounted. They had gathered in four groups in response to Travis' appeals. The groups were led by Ed Burleson, who had conducted many daring forays against Indians on the Colorado; Alexander Somervell, a modest and reliable man; James C. Neill, who had been prevented by the presence of Santa Anna's troops from rejoining the Alamo garrison after the expiration of his furlough; and fiery Captain Sidney Sherman. Sherman had just marched his company of Kentucky and Ohio volunteers more than four hundred miles from Natchitoches Landing on the Red River in Louisiana.

Though reluctant to yield command of his group to Houston, Burleson promptly recognized the Convention's authority. Houston ordered him to parade the troops. The condition of the troops was deplorable—not much better than that of the "Volunteer Army of Texas" when Houston had seen it advancing on San Antonio under Austin the previous autumn. Some of the men had no weapons; others had weapons but no ammunition. Houston was told that there were provisions for only two days. He read them the declaration of independence; his commission; and his instructions, signed by Richard Ellis, president of the Convention, and by Chairman Collinsworth of the military affairs committee. The troops cheered, but without any special enthusiasm. Burleson was the better known and more popular man.

Houston's instructions gave him sweeping authority. But in all Texas this was the single organized force under his control; and these men and boys had gathered for relief of the Alamo. They had not committed themselves for any other service. If the men could be induced to stay, they must be organized; once organized, they must be trained. Even so, they would not constitute an army equal to the country's needs. The hour was long past for beginning such an undertaking. The vicious intrigue within the General Council to prevent formation of a regular army had seen to that.

Houston directed Burleson to organize the men into a regiment of battalions and companies the next day, Saturday, at 11 A.M. He set Sunday as the day for electing officers, but quickly learned that he was moving too slowly. Just after dark on the day of his arrival, two Mexicans reached Gonzales with news that the Alamo had been captured and the garrison massacred. They said Santa Anna had ordered his attack on the citadel at 3 A.M. the previous Sunday and that by 8 A.M. the fight was over. The bodies of the defenders, on Santa Anna's orders, were being burned in the public square.

Within a matter of minutes after the two Mexicans told their story, thirty women of Gonzales, whose husbands had gone to the Alamo on March 1 in response to Travis' appeals, learned that they were widows. Their outcries and those of other civilians were heard in the nearby camp. General Houston had the Mexicans brought to him. On the way, they retold their story, creating tremendous excitement among the troops.

Houston tried to restore order by instructing Hockley and other officers to circulate among the men to tell them that the Mexicans were spies, that their stories were false and intended only to frighten. Half believing his own propaganda and hoping it was true, he put the two Mexicans under arrest. While he was privately questioning them, twenty men quit camp. They told Burleson they were going home to look after their families. Houston, then and ever afterward, called them deserters, even though they had not taken a service oath.

Houston decided that the substance of the Mexicans' story must be true, but remained skeptical of some details. Before he finished questioning the Mexicans he asked Burleson to send out a small company of scouts to get as near San Antonio as possible and to report the situation there. Then he sent new orders to Colonel Fannin at Goliad, with a letter:

> Anselmo Borgara states . . . that the Alamo was attacked on Sunday morning at the dawn of day, by about two thousand three hundred men, and carried a short time before sunrise, with a loss of five hundred and twenty-one Mexicans killed, and as many wounded. Colonel Travis had only one hundred and fifty effective men out of his entire force of one hundred and eighty-seven. After the fort was carried, *seven men* surrendered, and called for Santa Anna and quarter. They were *murdered* by his order. Colonel Bowie was sick in bed, and also murdered. . . . The bodies of the Americans were burnt after the massacre. . . . Lieutenant Dickinson,[1] who had a wife and child in the fort, after having fought with desperate courage,

175

tied his child to his back and leaped from the top of a two-story building. Both were killed by the fall.

I have little doubt but that the Alamo has fallen—whether above particulars are all true may be questionable. . . .

In a postscript he added:

In corroboration of the truth of the fall of the Alamo, I have ascertained that Colonel Travis intended firing signal guns at three different times of each day until succor should arrive. No signal guns have been heard since Sunday. . . .[2]

Houston's previous order, if obeyed, would have put Fannin within twenty-five miles of the Alamo, at the mercy of the victorious Mexicans. His new order instructed Fannin to turn away from the crossing on the Cibolo and fall back immediately to Victoria, taking a position east of the Guadalupe River where he could support the commanding general and be supported by him. Fannin also was to blow up the fortress at Goliad and to complete its destruction before he left the vicinity. Finally he wrote: "The immediate advance of the enemy may be confidently expected as well as a rise of water. Prompt movements are highly important."

On Saturday morning, Houston hurriedly completed the regimental organization. The men elected Ed Burleson, colonel; Sid Sherman, lieutenant colonel; Alexander Somervell, major. The Commander in Chief spent the remainder of Saturday instructing officers and companies in drill and tactics. His anxiety for news from Burleson's scouts increased hourly. On Sunday morning he learned that two extraordinary men, Erastus ("Deaf") Smith and Captain Henry Karnes, were in camp and he had them brought to headquarters.

Karnes, from Tennessee, was twenty-four. As a boy in Arkansas he had been trained in hunting and trapping by his father. An attachment had developed between Karnes and Deaf Smith, who was forty-nine. They had gone together into San Antonio with Ben Milam the preceding December when General Cos had surrendered. Karnes had seen Smith on the roof of the Veramendi house, the home of James Bowie's father-in-law, when Ben Milam was killed. At about that same time, Smith had been wounded. Until then

Smith's loyalty to the Texas cause had been under question because of his family affiliations. For fourteen years he had lived in San Antonio after marrying a young Mexican widow, *Señora* Guadalupe Ruiz Duran; they had three daughters.

It was clear to Houston that, in a prolonged game of hide-and-seek with an enemy capable of assembling well-organized and greatly superior forces, he must rely upon men as skilled as these to serve as his eyes and ears. When he talked with them about the experience that fitted them for scout duty, Karnes seemed to defer in everything to his squat, stocky, older comrade. Smith's knowledge of Mexican customs, language, and manners made him invaluable. Houston was struck by the fact that Smith's loss of hearing, caused by disease in infancy, had apparently sharpened his other senses; it was said that he could detect the presence of people or animals before others could see or hear them. His eyesight was especially keen. Deaf Smith's modesty, as well as his confidence, appealed to Houston. Obviously his deafness had made him sensitive; he was reticent and answered all questions laconically in a high squeaky voice.

Houston explained that it was vital to learn within the shortest possible time what had happened at the Alamo and about Santa Anna's intentions and movements. He asked whether Smith and Karnes wanted other men to go with them and how long they would be gone. With a gesture, Karnes indicated that Smith would answer for the team.

Smith said that he and Captain Karnes could move faster and do better if they went alone. Then, after a moment's thought, he said that they should get within sight of San Antonio and back within three days. The General wished them good luck, again stressed the importance of their mission, and told them to pick the best horses in camp and hurry.

After Smith and Karnes left, Houston made the minutes count. He prepared his first report to Chairman Collinsworth of the Convention's military committee, enclosing a copy of his order to Colonel Fannin and the letter that accompanied it about the probable fate of the Alamo.

The enclosed statement [about the fall of the Alamo], which came here a few moments after my arrival, has induced me to adopt a course very different from that which I intended before the information was received. The enclosed order to Colonel Fannin will indicate my convictions, that, with our small unorganized force, we cannot maintain sieges in fortresses, in the country of the enemy. Troops pent up in forts are rendered useless; nor is it possible that we can ever maintain our cause by such policy. The want of supplies and men, will insure the success of our enemies. . . .

On seeing the various communications of Colonel Fannin at this point, I could not rely on any co-operation from him. . . . I am using all my endeavors to get a company to send in view of the Alamo; and if possible, arrive at the *certainty* of what all believe—its fall.[3]

In this report he expressed doubt that such a company could be formed because of the scarcity of horses. Moreover, a group of men who had got within eighteen miles of the Alamo (before Houston arrived at Gonzales) had been repulsed by Mexican cavalry. Then he added: "This moment Deaf Smith and Henry Karnes have assured me, that they will proceed in sight of Bexar (San Antonio); and return within three days." In closing he expressed his fear that Goliad was in siege.

On their first assignment as Houston scouts, Smith and Karnes succeeded beyond expectations. They were both back later that same Sunday. Less than twenty miles out, they had met Lieutenant Almeron Dickerson's widow, Susannah, who had been with her husband in the Alamo when he had been killed. Mounted and carrying her fifteen-month-old child, Angelina, she was being escorted by a Negro guide.

After the firing in the Alamo died away, Mexicans had found Mrs. Dickerson in the chapel. The only Texan or "Anglo-American" woman among the defenders, she had been put with two Mexican women in a small room to the right of the main entrance. A Mexican officer had come calling for her by name, telling her to speak up if she wanted to save her life. On her way to Santa Anna's quarters, she believed she saw the mutilated body of David Crockett between the church and the long barracks.

Santa Anna was kind to her and took Angelina in his lap. He tried to persuade Mrs. Dickerson to let him send her to Mexico

City where Angelina could be brought up properly. When she protested, he appointed an American Negro, Ben, the orderly of Santa Anna's aide, Colonel Juan Nepomuceno Almonte, to accompany her to Gonzales. The President-General told Mrs. Dickerson that he had just returned from an inspection and had seen the bodies of three perfidious men, Travis, Bowie, and Crockett.[4]

Ben was a clumsy Negro who had served as a ship's steward and was the butt of sharp complaints when he served Santa Anna and Almonte. When he and Mrs. Dickerson left San Antonio mounted on horses furnished by the Mexican general, Ben carried Santa Anna's proclamation offering pardon to all insurgent Texans who would lay down their arms. Those who did not were warned that they would meet the same fate as the Alamo defenders.

Ben and Mrs. Dickerson set out on March 11, making slow time because of the baby in her arms. They had left San Antonio some miles behind when they were joined by Travis' robust, twenty-three-year-old Negro boy, Joe. He also had been in the Alamo, and had been routed out from his hiding place by Mexican soldiers and taken to Santa Anna. His Excellency told him that he was not waging war on Negroes and that he would be freed if he would point out the bodies of Bowie and Travis. Joe had done so.

Joe was allowed to attend a review of troops and he got the exaggerated notion that there were more than 8,000 of them. Distrustful of Mexican promises concerning his welfare and having been tapped by a Mexican soldier's bayonet, Joe had slipped out of San Antonio on foot before Mrs. Dickerson and Ben departed. He surprised them east of the Salado River when he suddenly appeared from the roadside brush where he had hidden from possible pursuers, and joined their little cavalcade.

As the party continued toward Gonzales on March 11 and 12, Joe shuffled alongside Mrs. Dickerson's horse. On Sunday, March 13, two horsemen approached, and Joe again darted into the tall grass, seeking concealment in fear of Indians. But the horsemen turned out to be Deaf Smith and Karnes.[5]

After a brief recital by Mrs. Dickerson, Smith directed Karnes to gallop on ahead while he followed at the fastest pace possible for Mrs. Dickerson. Sometime in the early evening, Karnes reported to Houston, confirming the fall of the Alamo on the basis of Mrs. Dickerson's eyewitness story, and reporting that Santa Anna was preparing to move on Gonzales with a strong force.

Houston had been in camp just about fifty-two hours. Things were moving fast. One of Burleson's scouts came in, and Houston received another report that Santa Anna's army was moving toward Gonzales. The scout said that on Friday night—the same day that Houston reached Gonzales—an army, supposed to be commanded by Santa Anna, had camped on the Cibolo after a forced march of twenty-four hours. The scout said the enemy had planned to camp Saturday at Sandy. From there he would head directly for Gonzales and should reach there late Sunday night or early Monday morning.

Even on the strength of this, Houston did not act precipitately. He had matters of tactics and strategy to decide. His troops had increased in number in the past two days to about four hundred men. Did that justify making a stand? If a stand was not made here, what plan should be adopted? At about eight o'clock in the evening, Smith arrived with Mrs. Dickerson, Angelina, Joe, and Ben. The Commander in Chief's *Memoir* tells the story:

> Houston was walking alone, a few hundred yards from the camp, at the moment this stricken and bereaved messenger arrived. He returned soon after, and found that her fearful narrative of the butchering and burning, with some of the most stirring details of that dark tragedy, had already struck the soldiers with a chill of horror; and when she told them that 5,000 men were advancing by forced marches, and their artillery would soon be heard at Gonzales, the wildest consternation spread through the camp. Their alarm soon reached a pitch of desperation. Some were stunned with silence—others were wild with lamentations. . . .
>
> He then addressed the soldiery in the most fervid manner, and they all gathered around him, except a few who had at the first impulse fled for their horses. He detached a guard instantly to intercept fugitives, and more than twenty were brought back to the camp. But a few good runners made their escape to the settlements, and carried panic in every direction.[6]

From Ben, Houston received Santa Anna's paper warning settlers of their fate if they did not lay down their arms. He spoke of it contemptuously and put it where he could lay hands on it to send to the military committee. Smith and Karnes's timely encounter with the little cavalcade from the Alamo encouraged him to believe that his scouts were lucky as well as competent. From this time on, out of respect for the older man, he called Smith either by his last name or referred to him as "the wonderful Mr. E." "E" was for Erastus.

In a matter of minutes after hearing Mrs. Dickerson's brief story, he ordered Colonel Burleson to break camp in haste. At 8:30 he decided that his men should be ready to march at 11:30.

So Houston's gloomiest forebodings proved correct. Defense of the Alamo had cost Texas some irreplaceable men, and Santa Anna was still at large with a force many times more powerful than Texas could get into the field on short notice.

For a century and a quarter, it has been emphasized that the slaughter at the Alamo yielded some real benefits, and no one paid higher tribute to the courage of the defenders than Houston. After the frustration of Houston's attempt to recruit and train a regular army, the defense of the Alamo had delayed Santa Anna's advance for two weeks during which the Convention completed and signed the declaration of independence and reappointed Houston Commander in Chief. The volunteers who had gathered at Gonzales to go to the aid of the Alamo—which fell before Houston reached Gonzales—became the nucleus of his army.

These were undeniable benefits. But they were coincidental, and Houston regarded the Alamo as the tragic and unnecessary consequence of the Council's treacherous destruction of the first provisional government. When that government had charged him with recruiting and training a regular army, he had planned to meet Santa Anna with adequate force and defeat him in the field before he reached San Antonio. There never had been any doubt in Houston's mind that he could have accomplished this object. For him, the Alamo would always be the battle that should never have been fought; he remained unchanged in his belief that static defense of isolated strong points was not the way to liberate Texas.

Confirmation of the Alamo's fall and the mistaken report that Santa Anna himself was in command at the Cibolo changed Houston's plans for advancing toward San Antonio. He decided to fall back and camp on the Colorado near Burnham's Ferry.

If circumstances were favorable he planned to fight somewhere along the Colorado River. But this was his short-term plan. His long-term plan took shape while Burleson was getting the army ready to fall back. Houston believed that at all cost he must keep this little force intact—as a nucleus about which Texas could rally. He would avoid conflict with any superior force unless circumstances gave him compensating advantages. He would be ready to take on any reasonably comparable enemy force that parted from its main body. If such opportunities failed to arise, he would continue to retreat right up to the Louisiana frontier, getting "as near to Andrew Jackson and the Old Flag" as he possibly could, with the expectation that there he could reorganize with Texas and American volunteers surging to his standard.[7]

The Commander kept this long-range strategy to himself. He especially did not want anyone to know that he was prepared to retreat to the border to save his force if that became necessary. There were jealous and willful officers in his command; these daring spirits were imbued with the same desperate courage that had inspired the men in the Alamo. He soon became convinced that some of his officers were so eager to fight that they would go into combat regardless of the odds for or against victory.

But the report by Burleson's scouts, which had induced Houston to fall back, was only partially correct. A large force of Mexicans, reported to include about 2,000 infantrymen (but actually including only about 600) and 150 cavalrymen with light artillery under the command of General Joaquin Ramírez y Sesma, had reached the Cibolo. The well-equipped force, exceeding Houston's in number, was reported to be driving for Gonzales. The scouts misinformed Houston about an important particular: Santa Anna was not in command of this advancing force. He had ordered General Sesma to march through San Felipe and Harrisburg on his way to conquer and devastate the colonies of East Texas. The route would take Sesma across the Guadalupe River to Gonzales where he was to wipe out the nest of vipers that had collected under some unidentified commander—Houston, of course.

Intoxicated with his success at the Alamo and the several successes of one of his commanders, General José Urrea, in the coastal area, Santa Anna "supposed that the enemy would not dare to show his face again and thought that the war was over." [8] He promptly furnished his subordinates with a complete strategic plan for the subjugation of Texas; he himself expected to return to Mexico City. Early in March, after crossing the Rio Grande on his advance to San Antonio, Santa Anna had learned that rebellion had broken out in Mexico. He had ordered a naval vessel to pick him up at Matagorda and take him to Veracruz about April 1, so that he could put down the rebellion.

Although Santa Anna believed that actual resistance had ended in Texas, he planned to devastate the colonies by execution, burning, and plunder; he would wreak the same vengeance on Texas that had scourged the Zacatecans. All rebels found with weapons in their hands were to be executed unless they surrendered. If they surrendered they were to be executed anyhow. Civilians were to be stripped of their possessions and treated in a way that would make them seize any chance to put themselves beyond the Sabine. This carefully planned strategy was to be executed by three divisions operating in three separate zones.

To insure the accomplishment of the plan during his absence, Santa Anna had transferred his command to General Vicente Filisola. Filisola was a competent officer experienced in putting down rebellion. The assignment that Filisola was to carry out required General Sesma, after disposing of the Gonzales rebels, to proceed through San Felipe and Harrisburg to Lynch's Ferry at the junction of the San Jacinto River and Buffalo Bayou. This ferry was a gateway to an important section of eastern Texas. Sesma's final mission was to take station at Anáhuac to support General Urrea after Urrea had advanced through the coastal country from Matamoros.

Sesma commanded the division in the central zone; Urrea commanded the right zone. In the left zone, General Antonio Gaona, with 700 troops equipped with all available arms, was to march by a more northerly route through Bastrop and Washington-on-the-Brazos to take station at Nacogdoches. Thus, Santa Anna's orders comprised a capable—even brilliant—plan for the total subjugation, extermination, or expulsion of the Anglo-American colonists. For this three-zone campaign covering all colonies in Texas, Filisola would have a total of about 6,000 men.

Houston's retreat placed him in the central zone where General

Sesma was operating. This was a fortuitous circumstance which Santa Anna had not counted on. When Santa Anna devised the plan he did not know that Houston would command the force gathered at Gonzales; and when Houston began his retreat, he did not have the slightest inkling of the president-general's three-zone campaign or of his intention to return to Mexico.[9]

2. The Long Retreat

THERE was much confusion in camp after Houston ordered Burleson to prepare the army to move out within three hours. The townspeople, too, were instructed to get ready; they were to be taken along so that they could be protected from the invader's vengeance.

For transport, the army had only one wagon drawn by four oxen. Other wagons and horses, mules, and oxen were collected from the town. The Commander in Chief reserved the army's wagon for baggage and munitions. All the others were detailed for the use of women, children, and old people. Infantrymen were instructed to carry all possible supplies. Two brass cannon were sunk in the river. The townspeople, struck with grief and terror, were slow in selecting the small treasures they wanted to save and in taking their places in the wagons. Some of the townspeople were unaccounted for, and Burleson estimated that about twenty volunteers had recently quit camp to take care of their families. But at the specified hour, he reported that the army was ready.

Fearing that the disorganized camp might be struck by a fast-moving detachment of the enemy's main force, Houston told Burleson he would not delay the movement beyond midnight for the sake of civilians. He ordered a mounted rear guard of Texans, and friendly Mexicans commanded by Juan Seguin, to bring the rest of the panicky civilians as soon as they could be organized. So the army, ahead of the ox-drawn ammunition wagon, pulled out under cover of an overcast sky a few minutes before midnight. It was

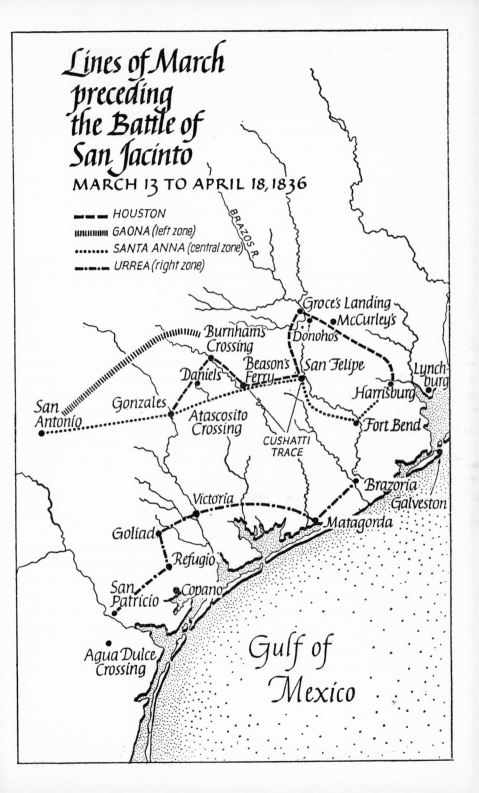

Lines of March preceding the Battle of San Jacinto

MARCH 13 TO APRIL 18, 1836

- – – – HOUSTON
- ▥▥▥ GAONA (left zone)
- ········ SANTA ANNA (central zone)
- –·–·– URREA (right zone)

BRAZOS R.

Groce's Landing
McCurley's
Donoho's
Burnhams Crossing
Beason's Ferry
San Felipe
Lynchburg
Daniels
Harrisburg
San Antonio
Gonzales
Atascosito Crossing
CUSHATTI TRACE
Fort Bend
Victoria
Brazoria
Galveston
Goliad
Matagorda
Refugio
San Patricio
Copano
Agua Dulce Crossing

Gulf of Mexico

Sunday, March 13, 1836, the first day of the long retreat. Houston had ordered the army to follow the trail east to the crossing at Peach Creek.

Shouts of protest and ridicule came from the ranks because some of the soldiers resented Houston's order for the army to depart, leaving the civilians to follow later. Houston, who had provided protection for the civilians, ignored the complaints. He urged the men to move on, step lively! This army was not an army; it was an untrained and unruly mass of boys under twenty, farmers, herdsmen, settlers, and volunteers from the States, but it was the only army that gave hope of saving Texas. Houston would not risk a delay of even fifteen minutes. He told officers to let the men know that the rear guard would look after laggard civilians.

An oak forest several miles east of town engulfed the army ankle deep in sandy soil. Some cursed the luck that had taken their horses from them for civilian use. Houston went to the rear to lend a hand in getting the ammunition wagon out of a sandtrap. By daylight the army had gone ten miles and then paused to refresh in a wood at Peach Creek. The men slept.

They were awakened by loud explosions. Some said it was Santa Anna's artillery firing on the rear guard. Others, who claimed to be able to distinguish sounds, said that barrels of whiskey in the burning stores of the town were exploding. Houston accepted this theory; informed that citizens had put poison in the whiskey, he had ordered it destroyed. The liquor had indeed exploded—in two conflagrations; the rear guard, without orders, had set fire to the whole town.[1]

The civilian caravan caught up with the army at Peach Creek and the women helped the men cook breakfast. They made thin, brittle pancakes of flour and water without shortening, but to the hungry men, the cakes tasted good. Before the army left Peach Creek, Houston organized commissary procurement under command of Juan Seguin. The main mission of Seguin's squad was to gather beeves for slaughter along the line of march.

After breakfast the mixed caravan moved on. As Houston rode along the column, a young officer saluted in a fuzzily uncertain fashion. Houston suspected that not all the liquor at Gonzales had been blown up, and waited at the side of the trail until the sutler's wagon came along. He ordered the sutler to produce all the liquor he had; several jugs were broken on the rim of one of the wheels. The delicious fumes that arose did not weaken Houston's resolution to abstain from drinking until the campaign was over. He had provided his own private method of control over his yearning for alcohol by holding a small vial of salts and hartshorn (then used as a source of ammonia) to his nostrils. Perhaps he recalled the severity with which Jackson had dealt with drunkenness on the march from Fort Strother to Horseshoe Bend.

Late in the afternoon of Monday, March 14, the weary army made camp at Daniel on the east bank of the LaVaca River. Houston sent one of his aides, Major William Austin, from here the next day, to appeal to the citizens at Columbus to send munitions and supplies at once—and men and artillery if they could. These were to be sent in turn to Burnham's Ferry on the Colorado River.

A courier from Goliad delivered a dispatch from Colonel Fannin. Fannin reported that he had held a council of war since receiving Houston's orders and had determined, contrary to instructions, to defend Goliad. He had changed the name of the place to "Fort Defiance" and was prepared to accept responsibility for his disobedience.

General Houston answered immediately with peremptory orders for Fannin to obey instructions and retire to Victoria. He confirmed that the Alamo had fallen, pointed out that his own departure from Gonzales left Goliad dangerously exposed, and warned Fannin that disaster was certain unless he moved promptly.

On Tuesday, March 15, the army camped on the Navidad River. Houston wrote to Chairman Collinsworth informing him of Mrs. Dickerson's arrival and her confirmation of the fall of the Alamo. By now Houston had had time to talk with Mrs. Dickerson at great length. Besides giving him her eyewitness account of the slaughter, she corrected the story Borgara had told about her husband's suicide. Lieutenant Dickerson could not have leaped to his death with their daughter on his back; Angelina was their only child and she was there in camp to prove Borgara's tale was false.

The facts that Mrs. Dickerson gave her grandchildren, refuting the off-repeated tale, are that her husband, ranking officer of the artillery, came to her that fatal Sunday morning in the room they had occupied, and told her the end was near because the Mexicans were within the walls. He kissed her, told her to do everything she could to save the life of Angelina, and then returned to his guns. This was the last time she saw him.[2]

After his talk with Mrs. Dickerson, Houston ordered a cradle made of a box lined with grass and cloth so that Mrs. Dickerson would not have to hold Angelina in her arms.

His letter of March 15 to the military committee was prompted by his concern that the civilians at Washington, busy with the formation of a government and inexperienced in war, might assume that his withdrawal was prompted by lack of resolution instead of by sound military considerations. He clarified his policy for Collinsworth and the committee, informing them of the swift march of Santa Anna's army toward Gonzales on the eleventh with an infantry force reported to number at least 2,000 men. He reported:

Upon this statement of facts, I deemed it proper to fall back and take post on the Colorado, near Burnham's, which is fifteen miles distant from this point. My morning report, on my arrival in camp, showed three hundred and seventy-four effective men, without two days' provisions, many without arms, and others without any ammunition. We could have met the enemy [at Gonzales] and avenged some of our wrongs; but, detached as we were, without supplies for the men in camp, of either provisions, ammunition, or artillery, and remote from succor, it would have been madness to hazard a contest. . . . If starved out, and the camp once broken up, there was no hope for the future. By falling back, Texas can rally, and defeat any force that can come against her. . . .

I am fearful Goliad is besieged by the enemy. My order to Colonel Fannin, directing the place to be blown up, the cannon to be sunk in the river, and to fall back on Victoria, would reach him before the enemy could advance. That they have advanced upon the place in strong force, I have no doubt; and when I heard of the fall of the Alamo, and the number of enemy, I knew it must be the case.

Our forces must not be shut up in forts, where they can neither be supplied with men nor provisions. Long aware of this fact, I directed, on the 16th of January last, that the artillery should be removed, and the Alamo blown up; but it was prevented by the expedition upon Matamoros, the author of all our misfortunes....

Had it not been for the council, we would have had no reverses.[3]

This communication was from a General with a point of view and a definite plan. He wanted his men to fight not only with valor, as men had fought at the Alamo, but under conditions that would give them a chance of surviving to enjoy the fruits of victory. If necessary, for lack of an opening for such a battle he would retreat to the Louisiana border and reorganize there. But he was still keeping this possibility strictly to himself.

3. *Open-Air Headquarters*

ON the fourth day out from Gonzales, Houston's caravan—foot soldiers, mounted men, plodding oxen, and wagon loads of women, children, and old people—sloshed through mud and chilling rain. They made the last fifteen miles to Burnham's Ferry in twelve hours, a normal day's march for unencumbered infantry. Houston praised the troops for their dogged perseverence and their phenomenal accomplishment in convoying civilians over all but impassable roads. But on the bank of the swollen Colorado, he encountered more than a thousand civilians, frightened by the wild tales about the Gonzales deserters and frantic to cross the river. Husbands, wives, and children who had been separated were wildly searching for one another.

Houston rode into this bedlam with calm demeanor and soothing words. He reduced the disorder to manageable proportions by promising that the soldiers would man the ferry and put all civilians safely across before a single armed man stayed on the east bank. That night he reported to Collinsworth that, during the four-day march, 200 men, willing to fight but ill-equipped, had joined his force which now numbered about 600. He added:

It pains my heart that such consternation should have been spread by the deserters from camp...if only three hundred men remain on this side of the Brazos, I will die with them or conquer our enemies. . . .

Let the men from east of the Trinity River rush to us! let all the disposable force of Texas fly to arms! . . .

. . . not a man in the Alamo but what, in his death, honored the proud name of an American. Let the men of Texas avenge their deaths! Rouse the Redlanders to battle! Ratify the Indian treaty; and let the Camanches be approached. . . .

I know that the government will do all in its power for the army.[1]

The several hundred American volunteers under Fannin were Houston's constant anxiety. If Fannin had persisted in his stubborn determination to defend Fort Defiance, his force was still in the heart of enemy-occupied country. Houston could only hope that Fannin had obeyed repeated orders to retreat to Victoria. Assuming that Fannin had obeyed, he directed the colonel to fall back on the main army if he found his position at Victoria untenable.

All of the civilians were ferried over the Colorado. Then the army crossed, and Houston held his troops for two days on the east bank as a shield for the civilians who were making their way to San Felipe. Apart from convoying civilians, he had accomplished his military purpose by putting the Colorado River between him and the enemy. This provided his small force with a better means of defense against an enemy of superior force. It also gave his army a chance to rest.

He moved the army from Burnham's Ferry on the morning of March 19, 1836, making a sharp right-angle turn southward along the east bank of the river toward Beason's Ferry—a destination twenty-five miles downriver at the present site of Columbus. He reached it late the next day, knowing that, with Mosley's Crossing above and Atascosito below, Beason's Ferry gave him command of three crossings on the Colorado.

His purpose was twofold. He was eager to engage the enemy wherever he could find it in force approximately equal to his own. However, if he was greatly outnumbered and had to retreat from Beason's Ferry, he could make his next move toward San Felipe over the Cushatti Trace. The trace was on higher ground and furnished better conditions for marching; the army could avoid the flooded, difficult terrain that Houston had passed over on his way from the Convention to Gonzales.

There was no sign of the enemy at Beason's Ferry, but Houston believed some of its forces were nearby. He issued a communique which was intended to stiffen morale, declaring that victory was inevitable if unity of action and discipline were preserved. The enemy's numbers were small as yet; unless reinforcements arrived soon the defeat of the Mexicans was certain. In a skirmish, Texas spies had already checked one of the enemy's reconnoitering parties.

The skirmish had occurred twenty miles away at Rocky Ford on March 20 when Captain Karnes and a detachment of five men had met an enemy reconnoitering force of greater strength. When the Mexicans fled, the Texans pursued them, killed one, took one prisoner, and captured three horses and a pair of saddlebags. One saddlebag contained an article of clothing belonging to an Alamo defender.

This skirmish, followed by others in which Deaf Smith and his scouts participated, impressed the Mexican command with the stubborn fearlessness of the Texans on the Colorado. The encounters were factors in a change of plan made by the Mexican high command which eventually altered the character of the whole campaign to the advantage of Texas.

Two days later Karnes and Smith reported that General Sesma was on the opposite bank three miles above Houston's camp near Mosley's Crossing. Sesma had 600 infantry, 150 cavalry, and two pieces of artillery. His troops, badly clad and suffering from cold, were building boats to cross the stream. Everything indicated that Houston would have what he was looking for—a chance to do battle on the Colorado.

Having left the Convention on March 6, Houston did not know that a new provisional government had been elected until he received a dispatch on March 23. David Burnet was President; Lorenzo de Zavala, Vice-President; Thomas J. Rusk, Secretary of War; and Robert Potter, Secretary of the Navy. Houston wrote a cordial letter of congratulation to Rusk, his young Irish friend and client of Nacogdoches, assuring him that he would find the Commander in Chief "a worthy subaltern." [2] He appreciated receiving good news for a change and thought that the new government held a promise of stability, but the first letter from Rusk tempered his optimism.

False reports that Santa Anna's cavalry had crossed the Colorado had demoralized the government officials. The Cabinet had voted to transfer the capital to Harrisburg as a place of greater safety. In disorder and excitement, the solons had pushed down the Brazos to Groce's Landing and then on to a temporary capital at Harrisburg on Buffalo Bayou. Houston did not know that the government's flight placed it directly in line of Sesma's advance.

Suddenly, Houston knew that his hopeful assumption that Fannin had promptly obeyed orders to demolish and abandon the Goliad fort had been vain. On March 23 he received an express from Victoria stating that Fannin had abandoned the Goliad fort on March 19. A few miles from the town, Fannin had been attacked and surrounded by a Mexican army an hour and a half before sundown. The outcome of the battle was unknown. Houston, fearing the worst, wrote Secretary of War Rusk on March 23 a long letter with a variety of anxious observations:

> You know I am not easily depressed but, before my God, since we parted, [at the Washington Convention] I have found the darkest hours of my past life! My excitement has been so great, that, for forty-eight hours, I have not eaten an ounce, nor have I slept. I was in constant apprehension of a rout; a constant panic existed in the lines: ... All would have been well, and all at peace on this side of the Colorado, if I could only have had a moment to start an express in advance of the deserters [from Gonzales]; but they went first, and, being panic struck, it was contagious, and all who saw them breathed the poison and fled. It was a poor compliment to me to suppose that I would not advise the Convention of any necessity which might arise for their removal. I sent word and advices, the first moment of leisure to the Convention; and all was calm in my communications to Mr. Collingsworth....
>
> The retreat of the government will have a bad effect on the troops, and I am half-provoked at it myself.... If what I have heard [of] Fannin be true, I deplore it, and can only attribute the ill luck to his attempting to retreat in daylight in face of a superior force. He is an ill-fated man....[3]

Peter Kerr, a Mexican, came into camp on March 25, 1836, with more disturbing news. Fannin had finally retired from Goliad without destroying the fort as he had been ordered to do. He had led the garrison—less than 300 men—out in a heavy fog. Six miles from Goliad Mission he had encountered 1,000 Mexicans commanded by General Urrea. Kerr was suspected of being a spy, but after the Commander in Chief examined the matter fully, he was obliged to conclude that Fannin had been overwhelmed. The number of survivors and the fate of the prisoners were unknown.

The "flight of the wise men," as Houston ironically called the government's dash to Harrisburg; the report of Fannin's capture; and new reports about the heavy Mexican build-up on the west bank had a bad effect on morale. Some men quit camp. Houston countered by informing the troops that any man who left without permission would be treated as a deserter. He advised the government that he had taken this action with regret; but if the cause of Texas was to be defended it was necessary that every man who joined up should realize that he was in for the duration of the war. The men grumbled, but for the time being did not desert.

Houston again felt obliged to bolster low morale by subterfuge. He recalled a courier who was leaving with dispatches for the Secretary of War, and with the stub of a pencil wrote a hasty postscript on the outside wrapper: "With reenforcements soon to arrive the force in camp will be more than fifteen hundred men." This postscript, as anticipated, became known to the men before the courier left camp and had the desired effect.[4]

Houston had relaxed camp and marching discipline while the troops had been convoying civilians. Now he warned his men that he would not tolerate insubordination. Since the river's flood tides temporarily protected him from attack, he began training the army. He ordered drills and ceremonies and encouraged the officers to meet for military discussions. During one of these meetings, the officers asked the Commander in Chief to set up a council of war. He answered that, for the present, strategy was his business, and theirs was to build an army that could stand steady in emergencies. He formally complimented the men on their parade formation, for mounting guard promptly, and for marching without confusion. Then he informed the military committee that the discipline prevailing in his camp was excellent and did credit to the officers and men. His statement may have been a trifle exaggerated, but he desired to encourage government confidence in the army.

Houston took the camp's single drum into his own custody to prevent the possibility of its use in a moment of panic to beat an alarm. He himself beat the morning and evening tattoo: only three light taps that could not be heard by the enemy or lurking spies. He informed Rusk about his personal situation on March 24:

> I am writing in the open air. I have no tent, and am not looking for out for the luxuries of life. I am only looking out to be useful to my country and the cause of liberty. Do devise some plan to send back the rascals who have gone from the army and service of the country with guns. Oh, why did the cabinet leave Washington? [5]

"The wonderful Mr. E." and Karnes came to Houston's open-air headquarters under a tree, bringing with them a couple of prisoners and a captured communication from General Sesma addressed to Santa Anna at San Antonio. The prisoners' information was neither clear nor convincing. One thing they said was that Sesma's force had been increased by reinforcements to 1,500 men. Houston did not believe this and said so in a letter to the Secretary of War.

But the prisoners had come closer to the truth than Houston thought. Sesma's latest reinforcements consisted of several hundred infantrymen dispatched from San Antonio on March 16 by order of General Santa Anna. They were commanded by General Eugenio Tolsa, who also had a generous complement of dragoons.

From Sesma's dispatch, Houston learned that Santa Anna's main divisions were operating in concert and that Sesma was in communication with Generals Urrea and Gaona. The dispatch did not disclose the movements of the other two generals, but Houston had reports on them from scouts.

Urrea with 1,500 men was in position to cross the Colorado at Wharton, 40 miles below Houston. Gaona with 700 men was preparing to cross the Colorado at Bastrop, 60 miles above Beason's Ferry. Houston realized that Gaona could move to attack him on one side, while Urrea attacked the other, and Sesma advanced toward the Texans across the Colorado. Houston's knowledge of this situation was sufficient to prompt new considerations. Vaguely, the Commander in Chief was beginning to see that behind the operations of Santa Anna's divisions there was a master plan which could overwhelm Texas. It made him all the more determined to keep his own small command safe.

Houston was in doubt as to Santa Anna's whereabouts, even though Sesma's dispatch had been addressed to San Antonio. Where was Santa Anna? That question was uppermost in Houston's mind. In one letter to the War Department he expressed the belief that Santa Anna had returned to Mexico; in another, he surmised that the Mexican general was still in San Antonio. Only time could solve that riddle.

Houston's position was safe for the moment, but he knew that it could become precarious. His plan to preserve the army and save Texas was intact and workable: to fight, if he could get into a favorable situation, against an enemy force not unreasonably superior. Otherwise, he would fall back to the border, if necessary, to reorganize, get reinforcements, and then make a new advance. He believed that his troops were capable of defeating the enemy against odds of three-to-one. But a victory of this kind could hardly be repeated against columns that could reinforce each other indefinitely. Common sense and his passionate desire to save his little force dictated continued retreat.

In various letters to Rusk and the government he explained his reasoning. He had been prevented from fighting on the Colorado by high water, the low morale of his men following the flight of the government, the capture of Fannin, and the arrival of strong enemy reinforcements. Instead of receiving the reinforcements and artillery he had expected, he had been obliged to reduce his numbers by granting furloughs to men who had to take care of their families. It was perfectly clear to Houston that, if he stayed on the Colorado, he would risk his army and the outcome for Texas. He was reluctant to announce another withdrawal, but what else could a responsible and cautious commander do?

4. "I Will Do the Best I Can"

HAVING decided to withdraw from the Colorado over the Cushatti Trace to San Felipe, Houston proceeded with extreme caution. To prevent Sesma from seizing a chance to attack, he reinforced his outposts and sent scouting parties along the river to attract the enemy's attention and give the impression that an attack was imminent. While this diversion was going on, the troops loaded the wagons, making ready to break camp when darkness fell.

With satisfaction, Houston learned from Smith and Karnes that Sesma, alarmed by these movements up and down the river, had drawn his lines farther back into the timber. At dark, he ordered his men to light bright camp fires. When the rest of the troops slipped quietly away, eastward, toward San Felipe only infantry outposts were left behind. This movement from Beason's Ferry took place on March 26, 1836. Houston had had less than six full days in camp to carry out his ambitious plans for training the army, but the sacrifice of training was part of the price for another retreat.

Five miles east of the Colorado, he ordered a bivouac without fires and sent mounted men to recall the covering outposts. As soon as they were in, the march was resumed. Scouts brought word that Sesma's pursuit was under way, but their information was incorrect. Sesma did not venture across the Colorado until the fourth day after the Texan army departed from Beason's Ferry; he had been intimidated by Houston's pretense of an impending attack. But Houston assumed that the scouts' report was accurate and rode along the column, as he had when leaving Gonzales, urging the men to step lively.

The eastward march was through sparse country and, except for beeves, supplies were short. Sometimes there was nothing but beef for the commissary crew to bring in. Spring rains continued around the clock, and the nights were cold. There were no tents for either the Commander in Chief or his troops; they could find shelter only in dry spots under the trees.

But they were able to make excellent time over the high ground of the trace. It was fifty miles to San Felipe; the army covered half this distance in one day, reaching the Brazos woodland on March 27. The next day—their sixteenth on the march from Gonzales—the Texans arrived in San Felipe.

At San Felipe, Captain Mosely Baker, an impetuous company commander, was found to be spreading a report that if General Houston ordered another retreat his successor would take over the next day. Certainly such mutinous talk would justify a court-martial, but this was hardly practicable under the circumstances. Houston passed the word to the troops that they would soon have all the fighting they wanted. He had also discovered that the Texas steamboat *Yellow Stone* had passed up the Brazos for a load of cotton at Groce's Landing. This presented a possible solution for his main quandary: how to cross the flooded river if crossing seemed best before engaging the enemy.

A number of officers ventured advice when it appeared that Houston intended to continue the withdrawal northward along the west bank of the Brazos. Some wanted to make a stand at San Felipe, others wanted to cross over to the east bank, and still others urged withdrawal south along the west bank to Fort Bend some forty miles below. Houston listened courteously, said he would think it over, and would give the orders in the morning. He asked them to be ready.

In the morning, Houston ordered the column to proceed north along the west bank of the Brazos. Baker's company and one commanded by his confederate, Captain Wyly Martin, refused to march. Houston adopted diversionary tactics to avoid a head-on collision. He ordered Baker to cross over to the east bank, intrench, and remain behind with his men to delay the enemy's advance. Houston sent Wyly Martin and his company to Fort Bend for similar duty. He told both men to destroy the ferryboats if there was any prospect that the enemy would get hold of them. These were hazardous fighting assignments, and the vigorous advocates of "Let's fight now!" could not refuse.

On the march northward along the west bank of the Brazos, Houston's wagons stalled and the troops floundered in driving rain.

197

During the crossing of Mill Creek, which emptied into the Brazos, a soldier died of fatigue and exposure; his was the only death so far from this cause. After passing Mill Creek, Houston was obliged to rest his troops, and he took the opportunity to write to Secretary Rusk:

> On my arrival on the Brazos, had I consulted the wishes of all, I should have been like the ass between two stacks of hay. Many wished me to go below, others above. I consulted none—I held no councils of war. If I err, the blame is mine. . . .
>
> There was on yesterday, as I understood, much discontent in the lines, because I would not fall down the river. If it should be wise for me to do to, I can cross over at any time [at Groce's Landing], and fall down to greater advantage and safety. . . .
>
> For Heaven's sake, do not drop back again with the seat of government! Your removal to Harrisburg has done more to increase the panic in the country than anything else that has occurred in Texas, except the fall of the Alamo.[1]

After two more days of slogging through mud and rain, Houston made his camp opposite Groce's Landing on March 31. He immediately took possession of the *Yellow Stone* in the name of the Texas government and found Captain Ross completely cooperative. Houston reported to the War Department that he would wait at this camp for promised reinforcements and supplies. He wanted flour, sugar, coffee; and he wanted them sent by pack horses, not wagons. "My horses and baggage-wagons in camp give me all the care I have, except my general solicitude." [2]

He wrote Rusk that conflicting reports from scouts left him uncertain about movements of the enemy, but "Mr. E. [Deaf] Smith is out, and, if living, I will hear the truth and important news." He added:

> The reinforcements promised to our army never arriving, has kept us in a mood not so enviable as could be wished for. Send daily expresses . . . I must let the camp know something, and I want everything promised to be realized by them. I hope I can keep them together; I have, thus far, succeeded beyond my hopes. I will do the best I can; but, be assured, the fame of Jackson could never compensate me for my anxiety and mental pain.[3]

198

In the intensity of his loyalty to his adopted country and his anxiety for her, the last drop of adventurer-speculator blood had been squeezed from Houston's veins. A Texas patriot had emerged from the ordeal. He now thought, wrote, and spoke of his adopted country as if he had never known any other.

5. *The Goliad Massacre*

HOUSTON's camp on the west side of the Brazos gave him a sense of security. It was virtually a moated castle, well up on a rise above the flooded river and creeks. If the enemy tried to approach the camp from behind or on either flank, they would have to struggle through rain-soaked bottom land, heavy forest, and swollen streams, swamps, and lakes. In some places, they would have to wade through water that would reach to their waists or even to their necks.

The dry ground at the top of the rise was suitable for drill, so Houston resumed the training that he had begun at Beason's Ferry. Once more he set up instruction schools for officers and encouraged discussions of military subjects. When the tedious drill made the troops pray for a fight, the Commander in Chief patiently explained that standing and drilling shoulder-to-shoulder and sharing communal subordination under a drill master helped to make a man a soldier.

Reports of disasters had been coming in piecemeal to the Council's military agents ever since Houston had left the Convention. He had hoped they were exaggerated, but confirmation had always been worse than the original reports.

Johnson and Grant's campaign against Matamoros had collapsed. They had recklessly entered and pillaged territory occupied by Mexican troops. One of General Urrea's detachments, operating along the coast, had ambushed Grant who, with most of his men, had been shot in a skirmish at Agua Dulce Creek. All prisoners had been executed.

Johnson's force had been surprised in a predawn attack at San Patricio because he had failed to put out sentinels. He explained later that the men were poorly clad and he did not want to expose them to the cold. Johnson had escaped with only twenty of his men. Then, before Houston's army had left Beason's Ferry, Johnson had abandoned his few remaining followers and had gone to his home beyond the Trinity River. Of the Council's six independent commanders, only Johnson deserted his men to seek safety.

After a fight at Refugio, another detachment of Urrea's coastal command had captured and executed that honorable but unfortunate man, Captain Amon King, and his company of volunteers from Kentucky. At Refugio, Urrea had also captured Captain William Ward and the survivors of his Georgia battalion. Houston did not know what had finally happened to them, but Santa Anna's no-quarter policy was a source of sore anxiety to him.

Fannin and his several hundred followers were still unaccounted for. From Peter Kerr's incomplete report, Houston knew only that Fannin had belatedly abandoned Fort Defiance and, with about three hundred volunteers who were very much needed by the main army, had set out for Victoria. He knew that Fannin had encountered a superior force commanded by General Urrea. Though Kerr had been unable to tell him the outcome of this engagement, Houston had assumed the worst because he considered Fannin "an ill-fated man." He feared that Fannin and his men were prisoners of the enemy. This turned out to be the case, and, on Sunday, April 3, Houston received an express from Victoria which, as usual, disclosed that the situation was worse than he had imagined.[1]

In the fog, six miles from Goliad, Fannin had met Urrea's greatly superior force on the open prairie, and his men had fought bravely for two days inside a square protected by wagons and baggage. In this battle, March 19 and 20, 1836, known as "Fannin's Fight," seven Texans were killed and 60 wounded. Urrea had 1,000 men the first day and received 400 reinforcements on the second day. His report exaggerated Fannin's losses and minimized his own, but his losses are conservatively estimated to have been 200 killed and wounded.

On March 19, Fannin had been wounded in the thigh. The next day, after consulting his officers, he had decided that he could save his wounded only if he surrendered. He sent out a white flag, and the enemy responded with another. Fannin and Urrea signed a formal surrender agreement, stipulating that all Texans who capitulated would be treated as prisoners of war and, within eight days, would be returned to the United States by way of New Orleans. Urrea sent Fannin and the other surviving Texans, including the wounded, back to Goliad for confinement in the same presidio where General Houston had stood on the wall to plead with the troops to recognize Governor Smith's authority rather than that of the Council and its military agents, Fannin and Johnson.

A few days after Houston had received the express about Fannin's defeat, several men who knew what had happened at Goliad arrived in camp and reported a horrible sequel. The presidio guards had robbed the prisoners of their blankets, forcing the captured men to lie uncovered on the damp, windswept ground. The men suffered from lack of water and had only a trifling amount of beef to eat raw or to cook over small twig fires. Almost all of them were young men from the United States, in their early twenties. They had been away from home for six months. Several had flutes and when they played "Home, Sweet Home" many of the others wept openly. Soon they were crowded by the arrival of Major William P. Miller, commander of 80 Tennessee volunteers, all of whom had been captured while landing at Copano; and Captain William Ward with 85 men who had been taken at Victoria. Altogether in the presidio, there were 430 prisoners, including more than 70 wounded.

Under guard, Fannin and Adjutant Joseph M. Chadwick were taken from Goliad to Copano to arrange for passage to New Orleans. A few days later Fannin returned to Goliad and, in all sincerity, told the men that arrangements for their return home had been completed.

At dawn, on Palm Sunday, March 27, 1836, the prisoners were awakened. Mexican officers formed all but the wounded for marching, and told the prisoners they were to be freed on parole. A vessel would take them to New Orleans. Then some 350 unsuspecting men were divided into three divisions and marched out under guard. They included prisoners who had been taken without arms in their hands and who had not been in battle. They passed some Mexican women, collected near the entrance, and heard them say, "*Pobrecitos! Pobrecitos!* ("Poor fellows!")

One division was herded down the road leading to the lower ford of the river, another along the road toward San Patricio, and a third along the road toward San Antonio. Guards marched in double files on both sides of the three columns. Half a mile from town the guards halted the squads and filed around to face them from one side. Somebody from the prisoners' ranks shouted, "Boys, they're going to shoot us. Run for it!" Musket locks clicked along the Mexican line; the volley sounded immediately afterward.[2]

Those who were not hit made a run for it and many were shot as they ran. A few escaped into the woods. On the ground, the wounded were bayoneted or killed by the lances of the dragoons. The bodies lay in heaps. The number of those killed appears to have been well in excess of 330. A Mexican report, following the usual practice of misrepresenting Texas losses, reported 445 dead. A Mexican officer, who commanded one of the firing squads, wrote in his diary:

> This day, Palm Sunday, March 27th, has been to me a day of most heartfelt sorrow. At six in the morning, the execution of ... American prisoners was commenced, and continued till eight, when the last of the number was shot ... what an awful scene did the field present, when the prisoners were executed, and fell in heaps! And what spectator could view it without horror! They were all young, the oldest not more than thirty, and of fine florid complexions. When the unfortunate youths were brought to the place of death, their lamentations and appeals which they uttered to Heaven, in their own language, with extended arms, kneeling or prostrate on the earth, were such as might have caused the very stones to have cried out in compassion.

The official report of Colonel Nicholas de la Portilla, who carried out the execution order was cool and formal. But in his letter to his immediate superior, General Urrea, who later claimed that he had protested against the order to General Santa Anna, wrote, "... a scene enacted in cold blood ... has filled me with horror. All I can say is, that my duty as a soldier, and what I owe my country, must be my guaranty." Portilla was less restrained in his *Diario*. He told of "a great struggle of feeling among the officers and soldiers ... at having been concerned in so painful an affair." On March 26, 1836, he noted: "At seven o'clock in the evening arrived a courier extraordinary from Béxar, from his Excellency Gen. Santa Anna, notifying me that the whole of the prisoners who had surrendered by force of arms, were immediately to be shot, with regulations as to the manner in which the order was to be executed." Portilla's report, letter, and *Diario*, removed any doubt about official responsibility for the mass murders.[3]

From the woods, the escaped survivors heard the sound of heavy firing in the presidio. They knew that Fannin and the other wounded men were being gunned and bayoneted to death. At least one of the few survivors was concealed and sheltered for a few days by a friendly Mexican family before he started for Gonzales.

To prevent panic at Gonzales, Houston had tried to conceal the worst about the Alamo. Now, believing that the army was growing up, he encouraged his men to talk about the Goliad massacre. It was a story to make men out of boys, and only six men quit camp because of it. This encouraged Houston's belief that a splendid transformation had come over the army in a few short weeks.

When General Houston walked through camp, he permitted the soldiers, after saluting, to approach and address him informally. They wondered why nearly 400 unwounded men had not overpowered the presidio guards and attempted to escape? The only possible answer was that for more than six months those men had been in a land that was not their own. They had come to help because of liberty. They had been told that they would soon be liberated from the presidio and they had reason to fear that infractions of discipline would delay their release. On Palm Sunday morning, starved, chilled, and ragged, they had relied on the promises of officers who spoke a language they did not understand and they never suspected imminent mass murder. Furthermore, they had not had the main army's advantage of training and discipline. Houston pressed home his great object lesson, discipline, and used his favorite word, "subordination." Confidence in one another makes an army, he said.

The men talked of nothing but Goliad—and vengeance. They were bitterly angry; mad through and through and burning for a fight. Houston hoped they would stay that way. He concluded his report to Secretary of War Rusk about the Goliad tragedy with these words:

> Will not our friends rush to the conflict, and at once avenge the wrongs which have been inflicted on our dauntless com-

rades! The day of just retribution ought not to be deferred. Send expresses to the coast and to the United States.[4]

Soldiers returned from furloughs, and new recruits joined up, including 80 men from East Texas. Other men, who had left without permission to relieve distress at home, came back. Houston welcomed them, although he sternly warned that if they left again without leave, he would treat them as deserters. There were now nearly 1,000 men on the rolls—more than at any time since the retreat from Gonzales—but Houston reported to the War Department his estimate that at least 4,000 men had fled beyond the Sabine into Louisiana. However, on April 13, 1836, after sending 150 men to support Wyly Martin at Fort Bend and another small force to aid Captain Baker at San Felipe, he reported to the department that he had only 523 effectives.

Houston's authority was virtually absolute. The rank and file believed in him and resented criticism of "Old Sam," as some called him. He had become their protector and friend and was preparing them so that they would not share the fate of the men at Goliad. At least, under his command, they would die with weapons in their hands.

From President Burnet at Harrisburg, General Houston received an undated dispatch, probably written on April 2, 1836:

The enemy are laughing you to scorn. You must fight them. You must retreat no farther. The country expects you to fight. The salvation of the country depends on you doing so.[5]

Burnet was a civilian official who had not been anywhere near the front; he knew nothing about the high water and poor conditions for marching, and apparently was unable to weigh the military considerations that guided the Commander in Chief. If Houston had discarded his own policy and immediately carried out the order, his troops would have had to wade toward the enemy through flood waters up to their necks. Burnet's jeering tone had been inspired by Houston's sharp criticism of the government's disorderly flight from Washington. On April 6, Houston answered the provisional president's letter with dignity and restraint:

To D. G. Burnet Esq., President of the Republic of Texas:
    Sir: I have kept the army together under most discouraging

circumstances, and I hope a just and wise God, in whom I have always believed, will yet save Texas, and that confusion and dismay may yet seize upon her enemies, and chastise them for their cruelties and oppression. I am sorry that I am so wicked, for "the prayers of the righteous shall prevail." That you are so, I have no doubt, and hope that Heaven, as such, will help and prosper you, and crown your efforts with success in behalf of Texas and humanity.

I am very truly your friend—Sam Houston.[6]

Houston continued to drill and discipline his soldiers. Two men were court-martialed; one for desertion, the other for mutiny. At Houston's suggestion, a surgeon recommended mercy for one man, and the court-martial recommended mercy for the other. He welcomed the opportunity to grant the pardons, but warned that thereafter he meant to carry out death sentences imposed for desertion or mutiny.

One day, as he looked over the mail that was about to leave camp, he discovered a letter addressed to Secretary of the Navy Robert Potter, who was a close friend of President Burnet's. It had not been submitted to him in accordance with his rule that letters must never leave the camp unless he had examined them. Opening it, he found a dozen pages written by Lieutenant James Hazard Perry, one of his aides. Perry, a New Yorker, had joined Houston's camp at Beason's Ferry after presenting a letter of strong indorsement from Potter. At the Washington Convention, Potter had cast the only vote against Houston for Commander in Chief.

Perry described Houston's camp as filthy from neglect; he said that the men were undisciplined, and that no effort was being made to train them. Houston, astonished, read on:

Agreeably to your request I embrace the earliest opportunity of giving you the information you desire with respect to the army....

...the greater part of the officers...betray a most culpable disregard of their duties to their country....Many of the men of whom I speak are high in office and have the management of the affairs of the army....

We are now within striking distance of the enemy, and there are no signs of moving; our men are loitering about without knowing more of military tactics at evening than they did in the morning, while the General, either for want of his customary excitement (for he has entirely discontinued the use of ardent spirits) or, as some say, from the use of opium, is in a condition between sleeping & waking which amounts nearly to a constant state of inanimity ... men are leaving us every day, by tens and twenties, dissatisfied with the unhealthy situation of the Camp & disgusted with the inactivity & want of energy in the General. ... [P. S.] I should not be surprised if we are not ordered to retreat still further.[7]

This was one of several intimations Houston had that a coalition was forming against him, perhaps in retaliation for his strictures on the government's flight. He summoned Perry to headquarters—a pile of saddles under an oak tree—and read portions of the letter to him. He told Perry that his falsehoods were calculated to injure the service. Perry had not only betrayed his commander's confidence, he had ministered to the malignity of the commander's enemies without serving any useful purpose. The indignant general spoke with self-control and elaborate firmness, saying that Perry's behavior warranted turning him over to the troops and letting them run him out of camp. But no, he went on, he would do nothing of the sort. He was so little disturbed by the spying and machinations of his enemies that he would keep Perry right there in camp where he could keep an eye on him.

6. *"On Whom the Burden Must Rest"*

THE Goliad horror was still fresh in Houston's mind when he was heartened by the arrival of a new recruit, Lorenzo de Zavala, Vice-President of the Republic. Zavala, whose son had joined Houston's camp on the Colorado, was disgusted with Robert Potter's spying and the government's intrigue against the Commander in Chief.

On the evening of the day following Zavala's appearance, Houston was informed that another man was signaling his desire to cross over from Groce's Landing on the east bank of the Brazos. Houston sent a Negro to ferry the man across the river in a rowboat. The Negro returned with Secretary of War Thomas Rusk. Like Zavala, Rusk wanted nothing to do with the cabal against the Commander in Chief and had come to see for himself what kind of conditions prevailed at the front. Houston's cordiality and his assurance that Rusk's presence was an inspiration to the troops made the secretary decide to remain with Houston for the balance of the crisis.

Scouts brought news that the Mexicans had reached San Felipe. Captain Mosely Baker had retired his force to the east bank of the Brazos opposite San Felipe and had intrenched, following orders. He was prepared to resist if the Mexicans attempted to cross.

In brief special orders, Houston informed the army on April 7, 1836:

> The advance of the enemy is at San Felipe. The moment for which we have waited with anxiety and interest is fast approaching. The victims of the Alamo, and the names of those who were murdered at Goliad call for <u>cool</u>, <u>deliberate</u> vengeance. Strict discipline, order, and subordination will insure us the victory.
>
> The army will be in readiness for action at a moment's warning. . . .[1]

In effect, he was telling the army for the first time, that there would be no more retreats. But the Commander in Chief was not yet ready to move—not until he knew more about what was going on at San Felipe and Fort Bend.

A couple of days later Houston received a dispatch from Captain Baker, who informed him that the enemy was busily collecting materials for boats. One of Baker's men, John Bricker, had been killed by a cannon shot, and Baker requested immediate reinforcements for his 95 men. Houston sent him 45. Four days later, on April 11, a scout reported that the Mexicans seemed to have given up the idea of crossing at San Felipe; they were going downriver with the possible intention of crossing at Fort Bend. If this report was true, Houston's west-of-the-Brazos camp was no longer secure. A hostile force might appear in front of him on the east bank, and, if high water subsided, another Mexican force might approach him from the rear. The time had come when he might have his first opportunity to engage an enemy force of numbers approximately equal to his own.

On April 11, Houston ordered all officers commanding outposts on the river to put their forces east of the Brazos and to report at Donoho's where two roads intersected, one being the main highway from Groce's Landing to Harrisburg. The next day he issued final orders to all of his camp commanders to prepare to cross as soon as possible. Colonel Burleson's command, a horse guard, was to look after the rear until further notice. These orders brought an end to his much-prized opportunities for training his men. Altogether, he had had only eighteen days to prepare the troops for combat; the rest of what they needed to know would have to be acquired on the march.

When Houston set up his west-of-the-Brazos camp, he had arranged to use the *Yellow Stone* whenever he decided it was advisable to cross the river. His agreement with Captain Ross stipulated that the Texans would pay the owners for damages and for detention and use of their property. For services in ferrying troops, each of the crew would "be entitled to one-third league of land" (nearly 1,500 acres), and officers "to a proportionately larger quantity." The crew would not be required to bear arms.[2]

The army started to move across the swollen river on April 12 with about 100 sick men, 200 horses, and 10 ox-drawn wagons containing ammunition and baggage. Houston crossed with the first contingent and asked Rusk to remain behind to supervise and then to follow with the last load.

When the Commander in Chief stepped ashore, he saw an inspiring sight: two fine cast-iron, six-pounder cannon in perfect condition. They were a gift from citizens of Cincinnati, and had been forwarded to Houston by the Texas government. Nine men were needed for each gun crew and forty responded to Houston's call for volunteers. He made Colonel Neill, who had preceded Travis as commander of the Alamo and had been with the army since Gonzales, commander of artillery. The gun crew were organized and immediately began training. Curious soldiers surrounded the two cannon, gazed admiringly upon them, and promptly christened them "The Twin Sisters."

On April 13, while supervising the unloading and making his dispositions on the east bank, the Commander in Chief received another taunting letter from President Burnet. It was dated April 12 and stated that there was nothing to stop the march of the enemy to Harrisburg or Galveston. The country expected something from its Commander in Chief; the government looked to him for action. The time had arrived to determine whether the country should be given up—abandoned—or whether the enemy should be met and at least one struggle made for the sake of boasted independence. These harsh words came from a panicky president, but they cut.

By the light of his evening fire, Houston dictated to Colonel Hockley his reply, which he addressed to Acting Secretary of War David Thomas. He patiently reviewed the military reasons for the long retreat, described the difficulties of the crossing, and then expressed his reactions to personal ridicule:

> Sir ... I have the honor to remark, that taunts and suggestions have been gratuitously tendered to me; and I have submitted to them without any disposition to retort either unkindness or imputation. ...
>
> I do hope that my last envelope to his excellency the president, will show you on *whom* to rely, and on *whom*, for a while, the burden must rest. ...
>
> I beg leave to assure you that I will omit no opportunity to serve the country ... for the love of it, without ambition, or ulterior views into which selfishness can enter. I have, under the most disadvantageous circumstances, kept an army together ... but I cannot perform impossibilities. These remarks are not in anger ... but arise out of the pressure of difficulties which you cannot appreciate, because they are unexplained to you. ... I write in much haste, pressed by business, and engaged in the contemplation of matters, I hope, not distant.[3]

On April 13, he also received news of a threatened outbreak among the Cherokees in northeastern Texas. In the midst of all his other business and the confusion of debarkation, he sat down to write to Chief Bowl and remind him of his treaty obligations:

> My friend Col. Bowl. I am busy and will only say, how da do. To you! You will get your land as it was promised in our Treaty, and you, and all my Red brothers, may rest satisfied

that I will always hold you by the hand, and look at you as Brothers and treat you as such!

You must give my best compliments to my sister, and tell her that I have not wore out the Mockasins which she made me; and I hope to see her and you and all my relations, before they are wore out. Our army are all well, and in good spirits. In a little fight the other day several of the Mexicans were killed, and none of our men hurt. There are not many of the enemy now in the country. . . .

Sam Houston   Colonneh [4]

This letter was the hasty product of a weary, distracted man and lacked the colorful phrases Houston ordinarily addressed to his red brothers. But he hoped it would make Bowl and the other chiefs honor their treaty of neutrality and stand firm against Mexican enticements. He knew that a report of even a small military success would bolster the Indians' morale and believed that his fraternal assurances would help, too.

Then he composed a sharp rebuke to the "citizens of Texas." He called it an "appeal" and sent copies for distribution to the settlements.

You have suffered panic to seize you. . . . You will now be told that the enemy have crossed the Brasos, and that Texas is conquered. Reflect, reason with yourselves, and you can not believe a part of it. The enemy have crossed the Brasos, but they are treading the soil on which they are to be conquered. . . . Then march forward; and with the confidence of men determined to conquer, join the troops now in the fields, and your enemy is certainly in your power.[5]

The appeal brought a number of badly needed volunteers into Houston's new camp.

For three days the *Yellow Stone*, fueled with green wood cut by the troops, belched heavy black smoke as it puffed from shore to shore. On the night of April 15, the army camped at Donoho's farm three miles from Groce's Landing and waited for the outposts to draw in from their stations.

Donoho, whose sympathies were with Mexico, protested against the army camping on his land and cutting his timber for firewood. The General's patience was wearing thin. Detachments were marched and halted beside a long rail fence. Houston gave no orders, but the army took the hint that cutting down Mr. Donoho's trees was useless labor and they promptly used Mr. Donoho's rails for firewood.

Wearing a torn leather jacket, General Houston was supervising the blacksmith who was cutting up horseshoes and old iron for the Twin Sisters. A new recruit brought in a rifle that had a broken lock and asked Houston to repair it. The General told him to leave his weapon and call back in about an hour. When the recruit came back he was brimming with apologies; a comrade had told him the Commander was a blacksmith. Houston laughed, and said the recruit had been correctly informed. He was, indeed, a very good blacksmith and there was the rifle with its lock in good order to prove it.

Word passed along that General Houston, who was hell for discipline and tough marches, was also an excellent blacksmith and could take a joke. The skills Houston had acquired on Hiwassie Island and in the Arkansas forest were paying dividends now. The army was behind him.

During breakfast on the morning of April 16, Houston received reports that the enemy had crossed the Brazos at Fort Bend and was marching toward the improvised seat of government at Harrisburg. In his scathing letter, Burnet at least had not exaggerated the government's danger. Houston immediately ordered marching formation, which caused a commotion because some of Wyly Martin's undisciplined troops from the Fort Bend outpost had come into camp on empty stomachs. They wanted their breakfast and were not about to move until they were ready.

Houston was in no mood to humor mutineers. He ordered them to fill their bellies and get out of camp as fast as they could. He gave them a choice: they could either go to East Texas beyond the Trinity River and revive the courage of fugitives from West Texas who had gathered there, or they could go plumb to hell. The troublemakers chose East Texas, and both Houston and the troops were glad to see the last of them. Even though some of his officers still criticized him, his action cemented the growing confidence and mutual reliance existing between himself and his troops.

7. A Cautious Commander

WHILE Houston was still on the west bank of the Brazos, reports made by his scouts and outpost commanders helped him to deduce Santa Anna's three-zone strategy. At that time, as he wrote later, he knew the "strength, position and designs" of each division in each of the three zones. "The plan of campaign," he said, "gave evidence of the superior ability of Santa Anna and showed the man [I] had to deal with." He believed that if the three-zone project could not be broken up "Texas would be swept by three rolling streams of fire." [1]

But Houston did not know Santa Anna's present position or the part he was playing in executing the three-zone conception. He knew that the Mexicans' central-zone army had been in command of Sesma on the Colorado, but he assumed that Santa Anna was now in active command. This temporarily mistaken assumption led to no error on Houston's part; it merely increased his caution. When he was east of the Brazos, his assumption became reality, although he had no positive proof either from prisoners or captured dispatches. After a delay of several weeks, Santa Anna had caught up; he was not actually directing operations in the central zone but was leading a force in advance of the central zone's main army.

A curious sequence of events, unknown to Houston, had made Santa Anna reverse his decision to return to Mexico City to put down rebellion there.

For almost three weeks after Houston's midnight departure from Gonzales, Santa Anna had continued to make his headquarters in San Antonio. Sesma, in a dispatch sent to Santa Anna from the Colorado opposite Beason's Ferry, had related that his troops had been halted at the river by a large and intrenched force of revolutionaries on the east bank—Houston's force. The dispatch had been written after Sesma's scouts had suffered considerable losses in a sharp encounter with thirty Texans under Deaf Smith and Captain Karnes.

Preparing to depart for Mexico by April 1, Santa Anna had relinquished supreme command to General Vicente Filisola, a competent and experienced soldier. An Italian by birth with a long record of service in the Mexican army, and loyal to Santa Anna, Filisola had disagreed completely with his chief's strategic conceptions. Filisola realized that under Santa Anna's supposedly brilliant three-zone strategy no two of the columns would be within supporting distance of each other. He did not regard operations in three widely separated zones without contact between divisions as a stroke of genius. He also objected to Santa Anna's returning to Mexico. With all his deficiencies, Santa Anna was beloved—an inspiration to his troops.

Filisola had discovered that advice irritated his chief, who refused to listen to anything not in accord with his own ideas. Considering this attitude dangerous in the extreme, Filisola persuaded Colonel Juan Almonte, Santa Anna's most trusted aide, to assist him. They bolstered their criticism of the three-zone plan by referring to the rebels' stubborn stand on the Colorado. They stressed that Urrea's easy victories over Johnson, Grant, and Fannin would not be repeated; they had been won against volunteers from the United States. Now Mexicans would have to deal with a tougher breed—Texans who would be defending their homes—and the fighting would be desperate. Filisola proposed that small garrisons be left at Bexar, Goliad, and Copano to protect the army's rear while all other forces should march as a consolidated body until the main force of the enemy was defeated.

Santa Anna was not convinced. His victory at the Alamo and Urrea's easy triumphs over badly led Texans had left him in a state of exultation and he was contemptuous of Texan valor. However, he did defer to Filisola and Almonte in one respect. He decided that his southern empire would have to wait. He resumed full authority and once again made Filisola his second in command to carry out the strategy that his aides had condemned.

Santa Anna left San Antonio on March 31, 1836. On April 2 he was at Gonzales, accompanied by Filisola, Colonel Almonte, other staff officers, and an escort of dragoons. There he discovered that high water had prevented Colonel Augustin Amat from crossing the Guadalupe with 500 infantrymen sent from San Antonio to support Sesma on the Colorado. Leaving Generals Filisola and Cos at Gonzales to assist Amat's column in crossing the river, Santa Anna and his dragoons rafted the stream and hurried on to the Colorado by approximately the same route that Sesma had taken. Filisola and Cos were to follow him later.

On April 5, Santa Anna crossed the Colorado a few miles below Houston's abandoned camp site at Beason's Ferry. The next day he overtook Sesma who, intimidated by the stand Houston had made on the Colorado, was proceeding cautiously toward San Felipe. The more impetuous Santa Anna detached about 700 infantrymen, 70 dragoons, and a 12-pounder cannon from Sesma's force. By forced march he reached San Felipe on April 7. After attempting to dislodge Mosely Baker's force on the opposite bank, he decided it would be unwise to cross the river at that point.

He left orders for Filisola to have General Cos and 500 infantry reinforcements join the commander at Fort Bend and bring 50 boxes of musket cartridges with them. Then he marched 30 miles downriver, reaching Fort Bend on April 11. Mexican sympathizers informed Santa Anna that Houston was commanding the rebels who were hiding about 30 miles above San Felipe on the west bank of the Brazos, and that the rebels had transferred their capital to Harrisburg. Without waiting for Cos, but leaving orders for him to follow with the reinforcements, Santa Anna crossed at Thompson's Ferry. Using a repaired ferryboat, the Mexican force completed their move on April 14, one day before Houston's army was safely across the river at Groce's Landing. Thus, by April 15, both forces were east of the Brazos.

This circumstance changed the whole character of the campaign. In his *Memoir* (p. 107), Houston noted that if the ferryboat used by the Mexicans had been destroyed with the "vigilance enjoined" on Wyly Martin by the Commander in Chief, Santa Anna would have been detained on the west bank for weeks in order to build a replacement.

Santa Anna had made only superficial inquiries about Houston's capabilities as a commander, and what little he knew did not impress him. He took it for granted that Houston was just one more of those incompetent rebel leaders who could be destroyed at his convenience as easily as Urrea had disposed of the defunct Council's "independent" commanders. So the information received from Mexican sympathizers about Houston's position did not make it worthwhile to seek an encounter. In fact, Santa Anna did not know yet that Houston had crossed the Brazos; Houston might still be in hiding west of the river.

Santa Anna contented himself with sending Houston a message by a Negro who had helped in repairing the ferryboat. He instructed the Negro to go to Houston's camp and tell him that General Santa Anna would return and smoke him out as soon as he had administered satisfactory punishment to the rebel government at Harrisburg. Having satisfied his vanity and expressed his contempt for the enemy in this boastful message, Santa Anna began a forced march for Harrisburg with the intention of capturing the rebel government and executing its officials if they were armed.

Then an episode occurred which, if Houston could have witnessed it, would have revealed fatal weaknesses in his antagonist's character—erraticism and instability. Just as Santa Anna was emerging from the Brazos' timbered bottom land into the open prairie, he came to a small creek over which a large fallen tree formed a bridge. The infantry crossed it nicely. Ammunition was passed over by hand. In a tremendous hurry to catch up with the rebel government, Santa Anna directed that the baggage and commissary mules plunge in fully loaded. The stream rose above their pack saddles. Several mules, after getting a foothold on the opposite bank, slid back down into the water, producing a jam of officers and dragoons, pack mules, and horses. Several officers and dragoons fell into the water; stores were damaged, and two mules drowned.

During this episode His Excellency, still in an exalted state, stood on the bank laughing heartily, infinitely amused. One of his officers, Colonel Pedro Delgado, later wrote an account of the affair and noted that the incident struck him as an ominous commentary on Santa Anna's ability to command.[2]

While Houston was disposing of the "little mutiny" at Donoho's on the morning of April 16, scouts brought into camp the Negro who carried Santa Anna's message. The Negro said he had been captured by the Mexicans and released to act as a courier. Houston was skeptical about the sender's identity. Was it reasonable to suppose that, as the Negro reported, the Mexican president-general would separate himself from his main army and proceed in advance of it with a force of 700 or 800 infantrymen, one cannon, and a small force of dragoons? The message called for study. What was back of it? If Santa Anna had actually sent it, thus fearlessly disclosing his intentions, it indicated something more than mere confidence —overconfidence, perhaps, as well as contempt for his antagonist. This suggested that Santa Anna's force might be larger than the Negro estimated; or perhaps Santa Anna expected to be in touch with reinforcements.

The communication also betrayed discrepancies in the information supplied by Santa Anna's scouts. He appeared to believe that Houston's army was still west of the Brazos. Always doubtful of news that affected carefully laid plans, Houston weighed the possibility that the message was a ruse.

With a Mexican force driving for Harrisburg under an unknown commander, conceivably Santa Anna, Houston had reason to ponder upon the readiness of his troops and the amount of sickness in his camp. Like every general, he would have liked a little more time to whip his men into shape and he would have liked more of them. But he had done the best he could with drill, parade, discipline, rebukes, and emphasis on subordination. There was no time to set up another training school. Whatever the army was to be when it met the enemy, it was today.

Before the march got under way from Donoho's, Houston had one more duty to perform. A devastating outbreak of measles had hit the army, and he had provided a guard of sixty men for a hospital camp directed by Dr. William Smith. While the march was forming, Houston rode to the sick camp to see that everything was as satisfactory as possible.

Periodically, it had rained heavily for weeks. Now, when the army was starting off in hot pursuit of the enemy, it rained, the troops said, as it had never rained since Noah. The sky darkened to sooty black, and a twilight gloom settled over the prairie; a whisper of wind, rising to an ominous roar, rushed ahead of a dense gray curtain of water, and suddenly the deluge was upon them. It came cascading down in solid diagonal sheets, drenching the men in a second. This was merely a prelude. With growing fury the storm pelted, whooped, thrashed, and roared at the plodding column.

In his report to the government, the Commander in Chief called the prairies "a quagmire." The troops slogged on, slipping, sliding, and falling to their knees. The cavalry dismounted to save their horses, and wagon wheels sank into the mud above their hubs. The loads had to be manhandled across treacherous bogs while other troops lifted the empty wagons so that the oxen could drag them out. Houston, dismounted, took off his coat, and lent his weight and the strength of his one good shoulder to the task. He did this eight times in the course of a few hours.

During the long, violent storm, as he forged through the mud and bogs, Houston was preoccupied with a profound question. Where was the Mexican advance, and was Santa Anna with it?

8. *Birth of a Battle Cry*

IN spite of the storm, the army succeeded in slogging through to McCurley's, near the present site of the town of Hockley, on the night of April 16, 1836. The next day they came to Cypress Creek, and on April 18—thirty-seven days since Gonzales and the third day of their pursuit of the enemy—they reached Buffalo Bayou opposite Harrisburg. They had covered fifty-two miles in two and a half days under conditions about as bad as could be imagined, averaging nearly six miles a day more than was normal for infantry under fair conditions.

Houston was expecting to cross the Bayou to go to the defense of the government when scouts brought word that the provisional government, warned of the enemy's approach, had slipped out of Harrisburg barely in time, and the enemy had burned the town. This news still did not solve Houston's major quandary. Was Santa Anna actually in command of the enemy's advance?

Santa Anna had reached Harrisburg on April 15. There he had learned that the rebel government, warned in time, had fled by boat toward Galveston. Without much deliberation, he had ordered Colonel Pedro Delgado and a small force to burn the town and then to follow him in quest of the fleeing government.

When he left the Brazos, Santa Anna had expected to dispose of Burnet and his cabinet by a quick sally and to be back at Fort Bend within three days to rejoin Sesma. But the narrow margin by which the Texas government had escaped beguiled him into an unpremeditated change of plan. From Harrisburg he set out in pursuit of the government toward Morgan's Point (New Washington) on April 17 at 3 P.M., frustrated by the same storm that was impeding Houston's army.

Soon after he left Harrisburg, his twelve-pounder and its team of draft mules began bogging down in holes said to be as deep as ravines. Finally it was stalled at a narrow bridge that could not support cannon and mules and had to be diverted around the head of a small bayou by a detached company commanded by General Manuel F. Castrillon, who had directed some of the important action at the Alamo.

Colonel Delgado caught up with his chief at 10 P.M. that same day after putting the torch to Harrisburg. He stated in his account later that the marching column was delayed by a violent storm and wandered from its course. "So," wrote Delgado, "His Excellency ordered a halt requiring every man to stand in the ranks without shelter from the rain." [1] These harsh tactics were invoked to keep the soldiers from getting lost or deserting.

Thus on April 18, while Houston was cautiously calculating how much he dared risk on the chance that Santa Anna was actually with the Mexican advance and could be overtaken and defeated, Santa Anna had reached Morgan's Point, which was eighteen miles from Harrisburg.

Deaf Smith and other scouts brought information to Houston about the movements of the Burnet government. Warned of the Mexican general's approach, members of the government had escaped on horses and mules to a steamboat landing on Buffalo Bayou where they had boarded the small steamboat *Flash*.[2] They had traveled down the narrow, choked channel, apparently heading for Galveston. From Galveston where would they flee? Houston did not dwell on this; the movements of what he called the "self-preserving government" were unpredictable.

While Houston was still in doubt about the identity of the commander of the Mexican advance, the incredible Mr. E. crossed Buffalo Bayou with three men on a raft and was again at the right place at the right instant. He captured three Mexicans, Captain Miguel Bachiller and two privates, who had been entrusted to carry a buck-

218

skin bag filled with letters addressed to General Santa Anna. Smith brought them to Houston at once.

One of the dispatches was from General Cos. It assured Santa Anna that, pursuant to instructions, Cos was coming on with all possible speed to support His Excellency's advance and was following him toward Galveston. Now Houston knew as much about Santa Anna's intentions as His Excellency did—and he knew more about Santa Anna's promising prospects for reinforcements. This was knowledge he could use and he was ready to put it to work.[3]

As usual, though, Houston did not know Santa Anna's present whereabouts. Not having definite information, he assumed that the Mexican might have been delayed by the storm and might be somewhere near, perhaps within a few miles.

Before Houston made his final decision on the basis of General Cos's letter, he reviewed what he knew about the situation so that he could determine the risk involved in pursuing Santa Anna. He knew that the main Mexican army in the central zone was being strengthened at Fort Bend and estimated that it included about 1,000 men. Actually 4,000 infantrymen and dragoons were collecting there under Filisola's command. Sesma was with Filisola. Houston also knew that Gaona, commanding the left (northern) zone was west of the Brazos. (Actually, Santa Anna had ordered Gaona to depart from previous instructions and swing southeast to San Felipe.) But Houston concluded correctly that Gaona was not in a position to give him trouble.

As to that veteran commander and executioner, General Urrea, Houston had no reason to believe that he was operating anywhere except along the coast in the area where he had achieved many successes. Actually, Santa Anna had ordered Urrea to abandon his station at Victoria and proceed to occupy Matagorda and Brazoria. By April 13, Urrea had occupied Matagorda and taken possession of valuable supplies intended for the Texans; on April 15, while Houston was at Donoho's, he had marched to Brazoria. High water would keep him from ever getting beyond the Brazos.

The Commander in Chief had no worries about Santa Anna's ability to overtake the agile Texas government. He was confident that if the Mexican general pursued the refugees into the Galveston marshes he would find himself extremely vexed. The government had displayed marvelous dexterity in getting into dangerous spots and out again. Houston could make his decision without concern on that score.

His analysis occupied only a few minutes after he had studied the dispatches. Then he confided his decision to Rusk who had also read the dispatches and knew what was at stake. Rusk listened gravely and nodded in agreement when Houston said, "We need not talk. You think we ought to fight, and I think so too." [4]

Houston and Secretary Rusk believed the encounter might be close, a matter of hours, not days. They agreed upon a communique to alert all Texas that Armageddon was at hand. It was dated April 19, 1836, from Harrisburg, although the Texans were then on the opposite side of the bayou. The first part of the two-part communique was signed by Rusk:

> *Fellow Citizens:* Let me make one more appeal to you ... to rally to the standard of your country. The army reached here yesterday late in the day.... From the prisoners we learn that ... Santa Anna himself is just below us, and within sound of the drum.... We are ... marching upon him. He has a reinforcement of about one thousand men upon the Brazos, about forty miles from here. A few more hours will decide the fate of our army: and what an astonishing fact it is, that, at the very moment when the fate of your wives, your children, your homes, your country, and all that is dear to a free man are suspended upon the issue of one battle, not one-fourth of the people [men] of Texas are in the army! ... are you freemen? If you are, prove your blood and birth by rallying at once to your country's standard! Your general is at the head of a brave and chivalrous band, and throws himself, sword in hand, into the breach, to save his country....
>
> Rise up at once, concentrate, and march to the field! ... A different course disgraces and ruins you; and what is life worth with the loss of liberty? May I never survive it!

The second part was signed by Houston:

> We view ourselves on the eve of battle. We are nerved for the contest, and must conquer or perish. It is vain to look for present aid: none is at hand. We must now act or abandon all

hope! Rally to the standard, and be no longer the scoff of mercenary tongues! Be men, be freemen, that your children may bless their fathers' names!

Colonel Rusk is with me, and I am rejoiced at it. The country will be the gainer, and myself the beneficiary. Liberty and our country! [5]

While copies of the communique were being prepared for the Redlands courier, Houston, sitting on a log before his campfire, penciled a letter to Secretary of War Rusk:

> This morning we are in preparation to meet Santa Anna. It is the only chance of saving Texas. From time to time I have looked for reinforcements in vain. The Convention's adjourning to Harrisburg struck panic throughout the country. Texas could have started at least four thousand men. We will only be about seven hundred to march, besides the camp guard. *But we go to conquest.* It is wisdom growing out of necessity to meet and fight the enemy *now*. Every consideration enforces it. The troops are in fine spirits, and now is the time for action. We will use our best efforts to fight the enemy to such advantage as will insure victory, though the odds are greatly against us. I leave the result in the hands of an all-wise God, and I rely confidently upon His providence. My country will do justice to those who serve her. The right for which we fight will be secured, and Texas shall be free.[6]

This letter was Houston's defense against possible charges of rashness in risking his country's fate on the outcome of a single battle. In case he lost, he wanted it understood that his attack against a superior foe was not prompted by the same impetuosity and recklessness that had brought destruction to the forces of Grant, Johnson, and Fannin. If he was killed, he wanted the circumstances to be on the record. For this reason, he had two copies of the letter made. The original went to Rusk. He gave a copy to Hockley and asked him to preserve it, and dispatched the other copy to Henry Raguet at Nacogdoches.

Near his bivouac on the bayou, General Houston had set up a camp for 150 men who, like those left behind at Donoho's, were suddenly stricken with measles, causing a serious depletion of his force. When he asked for volunteers to remain with the sick, not a

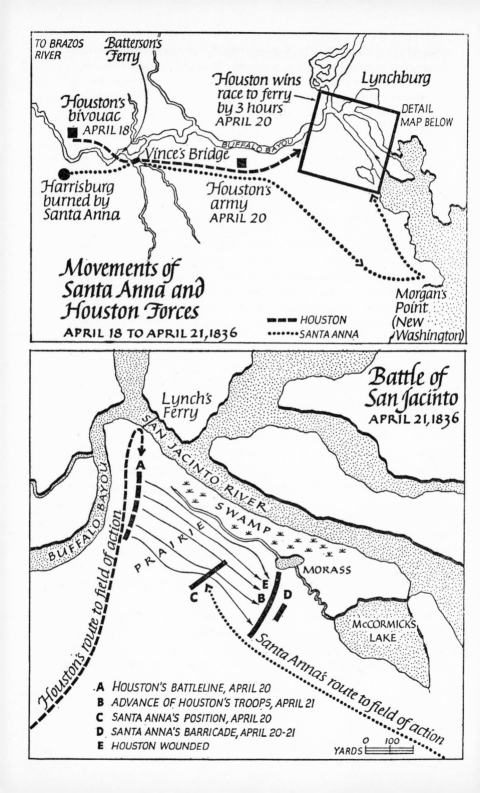

TO BRAZOS
RIVER

Batterson's
Ferry

Houston's
bivouac
APRIL 18

Houston wins
race to ferry
by 3 hours
APRIL 20

Lynchburg

DETAIL
MAP BELOW

BUFFALO BAYOU

Vince's Bridge

Harrisburg
burned by
Santa Anna

Houston's
army
APRIL 20

Movements of
Santa Anna and
Houston Forces
APRIL 18 TO APRIL 21, 1836

Morgan's
Point
(New
Washington)

- - - HOUSTON
·········· SANTA ANNA

Battle of
San Jacinto
APRIL 21, 1836

Lynch's
Ferry

SAN JACINTO RIVER

SWAMP

BUFFALO BAYOU

Houston's route to field of action

PRAIRIE

MORASS

McCORMICKS
LAKE

Santa Anna's route to field of action

A HOUSTON'S BATTLELINE, APRIL 20
B ADVANCE OF HOUSTON'S TROOPS, APRIL 21
C SANTA ANNA'S POSITION, APRIL 20
D SANTA ANNA'S BARRICADE, APRIL 20-21
E HOUSTON WOUNDED

YARDS 0   100

man stepped forward. The General gladly accepted this as an indication of fighting spirit and assigned the guard himself.

He ordered the men to travel light, and all the army's train, except one ammunition vehicle, to be left behind before the new advance began. Houston had to get his army across Buffalo Bayou to be on the side where the Mexicans were, but, at his camp site, the stream was wide and there were no ferries. Therefore, he marched his troops to Batterson's Ferry, two miles east of Harrisburg. This embarkation point offered few advantages over the former one, and conditions there made the crossing a critical task. The bayou was 350 feet wide and 15 feet deep; the ferryboat, half filled with water, was sinking.

Houston dismounted, called for an ax, and went to work hewing wooden planks with which to make repairs. While the repairs were in progress he fashioned oars out of rails. After the first small company went aboard, an accident dislodged the new planks and the boat threatened to sink. Houston leaped aboard to mend the damage. Then he crossed with the first contingent, leaving Rusk behind as in the Brazos crossing, to come with the last group.

A cavalryman called from shore to Houston, "We can't get your horse down the bank."

The bank was high and steep. All the cavalrymen were having trouble goading their mounts into the stream. Houston stepped to the stern of the boat, clapped his hands, and called his horse by name. She plunged into the stream and followed her master to the other shore. In his *Memoir*, Houston remembered the well-disciplined, loyal behavior of the faithful horse he had left on the bank at Batterson's. She had carried him during the past hard winter and so far this spring.[7]

Then the crossing was delayed because the boat drifted downstream with the current. The General directed the men to make a cable of *cabriestas* (horsehair rope) and other materials. He helped to construct it and had it fastened on opposite sides of the stream. The boat, attached to the cable by a pulley arrangement, was prevented from drifting.

After that, the passage back and forth went rapidly, but the ferry was small, and Houston shared some anxious hours with Rusk as the two men superintended the operation from opposite banks. They feared that the enemy's column might appear at any moment while the Texans were divided by a deep stream and some of the cavalry horses were still swimming in it.

By sundown, without loss, all infantrymen in light marching order, a squadron of cavalry, and the Twin Sisters were on the same side of the bayou with the enemy. The repaired boat was giving way, and four men were bailing constantly when Rusk went over with the last trip, his feet ankle deep in water. Apprehensive of surprise and glad to be reunited on the same side of the stream, the two leaders clasped hands and exclaimed fervently, "Thank God—we are at last safely over!" [8]

Houston called the men together in formation just before dark on April 19, 1836. Up to this point, he had made no speeches to the army, but now he told them that a collision with the enemy could not be delayed for long. This one man, Santa Anna, Houston told them, was responsible for their troubles and sacrifices. With officers and men who slaughtered Travis and his men, Santa Anna, cut off from support, was not at the mercy of the army of Texas. A decisive battle was at hand; some would be killed. Any man who was afraid should fall out.

Again he was using subterfuge for the sake of morale. He told the army Santa Anna was cut off from support, although he knew that Cos, with reinforcements, was already on the way. He waited. Not a man moved. A little over a month before, some of the men had deserted when Santa Anna's approach was rumored.

"This is our battle cry," Houston said. "Remember the Alamo! Remember the Alamo!"

The men picked it up and shouted back in chorus, "Remember the Alamo! Remember the Alamo!"

Again the General gave the cry, and they repeated it. In his *Memoir* he noted, "This watchword . . . was caught up by every man in the army, and one simultaneous shout broke up into the sky . . . and the green islands of trees in the prairie sent back the echo." [9]

9. Suddenly the Twin Sisters Barked

HOUSTON resumed his march, anticipating contact with the enemy at any moment. A mile from Batterson's Ferry the army crossed Vince's Bridge over Vince's Bayou, a stream flowing into Buffalo Bayou from the south. On the low side, east of the bridge, the land was flooded, and the troops waded through water to better footing on the prairie. Beyond the flooded area were the remains of camp fires which, according to Mr. E., signified that Santa Anna's troops had passed that way not long before, but rain had made it impossible to tell how old the coals were. Nevertheless, the dead fires were evidence of Santa Anna's nearness and inspirited the troops who were achingly weary from the day's exertions.

As Santa Anna slept under a marquee on a rise overlooking San Jacinto Bay, Houston rode along his column on the night of April 19, goading his tired marchers with words of encouragement. He urged them on until they began stumbling and falling in the ranks; then he turned them from the trail into the shelter of thick timber and let them rest for two hours. He took no rest himself but remained on the alert against the ever-present possibility of surprise.

While the army slept Houston cogitated. The scouts that he had sent toward Morgan's Point had not returned, so he had nothing definite to guide him. But he was still confident that Santa Anna would not succeed in overtaking the exceedingly mobile Burnet government. Deprived of his quarry, frustrated again, what would Santa Anna do? His Excellency might decide to pursue the government farther, or he might turn to rejoin his army at Fort Bend. Houston concluded that a third course was more likely; in all probability the Lynchburg ferry would be the Mexican's objective. This seemed a reasonable deduction because if Santa Anna was unopposed at that point, the ferry there would open the way for him to proceed into the Redlands to spread his "stream of fire" as he had done at the Alamo, at Goliad, and in his own state, Zacatecas.

From Morgan's Point, Santa Anna was somewhat nearer the ferry than Houston was; there was no telling when he might start for it. He might be moving in that direction at this very moment. Houston decided that he must press the Texans on, regardless of their discomfort. Having previously switched from retreat to pursuit, he now conceived himself to be in a race for the ferry.

On the camp drum, which was always in his custody, Houston sounded his usual three beats for assembly. The sleepy men staggered to their feet and resumed the march in the dimness of predawn on April 20. Mercifully, the rain held off as they pushed forward.

Santa Anna's actual thoughts during these hours were not recorded, but they can be reconstructed from knowledge of his situation, his actions, and his character. Surely, the last thought in his mind was that he was involved in a race for the ferry. The night of April 19 could not have been an altogether restful one for him. Before turning in he had sent out a trusted scout, Captain Marcos Barragan, with a few companions to reconnoiter. He would decide his next move when Barragan reported back in the morning, although he had pretty well made up his mind that he would turn toward the Lynchburg ferry. Still, he was not absolutely certain; there were other possibilities even though he had sent orders for Cos to join him at the ferry. He had not yet sent orders for Filisola to come with all of his men and arms, but that too was a possibility. He might hear from Cos, which also would influence his decision.

On April 18, when Santa Anna had approached Morgan's Point at noon, he had discovered that Burnet, who had been there before him, had escaped again. Alerted by a Negro, who was herding horses, President Burnet and his suite had fled by boat to Galveston Island.

Santa Anna was aware of the ticklish problems involved in pursuing the rebel government into the Galveston marshes, where there would be no boat handy for him. Should he proceed to cross the ferry and settle accounts with the rebels in East Texas or turn and seek out the swamp rat on the Brazos, or wherever he happened to be? The more or less undecided president-general slept, a little uneasily to be sure, but he slept. In moments of tension such as this one he was accustomed to chew a small piece of opium. This aided him in getting to sleep.

A little after sunrise on April 20, Houston's army passed over a knoll and beheld the outlines of Lynchburg a mile and a half away.

They kept on. Standing knee deep in lush green grass on a crest, the General saw a flatboat tied up at a point of land that jutted into the San Jacinto River. As he stood there, scouts reported that the enemy was not in the immediate vicinity and had not crossed the river. But the Mexican sympathizers at Lynchburg had loaded a boat with supplies for Santa Anna's use. Obviously the president-general was expected.

A small force of Texans went out to capture the boat. Supplies, mostly flour, were brought into camp. When Juan Seguin and his commissary rustlers drove some of settler Vince's beeves into camp and slaughtered them, breakfast got under way. Soldiers used the flour to slap together some dough for cakes. Everything indicated that the army had time to enjoy a leisurely breakfast; the scouts who had been assigned to get close to Morgan's Point had not returned.

Santa Anna had awakened from his uneasy sleep to face the day of his decision. He ordered his men to burn the fine warehouse at Morgan's Point and all of the houses in the town. He personally supervised the destruction of Colonel James Morgan's choice orange grove.

At about eight o'clock, Santa Anna sent scouts on ahead to look over the road to the ferry; everything appeared to be ready for the army to march. Then, as Santa Anna, General Castrillon, Colonel Delgado, and other members of the staff were taking a last look at the smoldering ruins of the settlement, Captain Barragan dashed in at full speed. Barragan's horse was lathered with sweat, and the Captain was wildly excited. Colonel Delgado later gave an eyewitness account.[1] Barragan shouted that Houston was close behind Santa Anna and that the Texans had captured, disarmed, and executed some Mexican stragglers.

Much to his regret, Houston had not overtaken any Mexican stragglers that night. His course east and north to the ferry had veered away from the one Santa Anna had taken east and south to Morgan's Point. Barragan and his companions had had an encounter with Houston's scouts and managed to escape on their fleet horses before ascertaining that they had not met Houston's main army.

Near the site of the burned settlement there was a dense wood with a narrow lane running through it for about half a mile. The lane was just wide enough to permit passage of a single file of loaded pack mules or of a double file of mounted men. According to Delgado's account:

> Upon hearing Barragan's report [His Excellency] leaped on his horse and galloped off full speed for the lane, which, being crowded with men and mules [already started for Lynch's Ferry] did not afford him as prompt an exit as he wished. However, knocking down one, and riding over another, he overcame the obstacles, shouting at the top of his voice, "The enemy are coming! the enemy are coming."

Santa Anna's excitement terrified the troops. "Every man thought of flight," Delgado wrote, "or of finding a hiding place, and gave up all idea of fighting."

Having progressed frantically through the lane, His Excellency came out into open prairie. Here, says Delgado, "His Excellency did me the honor to place me in command of the artillery and ordnance. ... [Our] officers having dismounted and taken their stations in front of their commands, we moved in search of the enemy, with flankers on both sides to explore the woods."

The Mexicans did not find the enemy. It was decided finally that Houston's army was nowhere near and that Captain Barragan had been guilty of a false alarm. The march continued at snail's pace. Santa Anna, eight miles from the ferry, was hampered by his large brass field piece and moved at less than a mile an hour across the rutted, boggy prairie.

Houston's men were still smacking their lips over beef and dough cakes when his scouts reported that they had had a light skirmish with Mexican scouts, exchanging shots a short distance from Morgan's Point. Houston realized that what he had been hoping for was coming true; Santa Anna was approaching the ferry over the road from Morgan's Point.

About three-quarters of a mile back on the line of march Houston had noticed a long skirt of heavy timber along the east side of Buffalo Bayou and had marked it as a good battle position. He ordered march formation, and the troops snatched up meat from the breakfast kettles as they ran to fall in. When they reached the new camp site, Houston put guards around it. Since concealment was not his purpose, fires were lighted and the men resumed their cooking. More dough, made from the captured flour, was rolled on sticks and baked into cakes. But the artillerymen's breakfast was interrupted again when Houston directed Colonel Neill to move the Twin Sisters out into the prairie far enough to be seen by an approaching force.

At 2 P.M. on April 20, 1836, Santa Anna's advance scouts discovered pickets in the edge of a wood. They were Houston's, of course, but His Excellency was not certain about this. In a state of considerable tension, he found things confusing. It was difficult to believe that the Texas swamp rat who had been hiding in the Brazos bottom lands could have marched his army through mud and rain such as his own troops had contended with. Perhaps the pickets were from a large force from East Texas that had collected west of the ferry without being detected by the Mexican scouts.

Those two guns posted out there in plain sight with no evidence of support—where did they come from and what did they mean? An invitation to attack by a powerful force lurking in ambush? His Excellency doubted that Houston had managed to bring two six-pounders over the same terrain that had made such difficult going for his own twelve-pounder.

Hastily, without being very discriminating about his position, Santa Anna formed his infantry and cavalry from column into line, intending to feel out the enemy with cannon before attack. Through his large marine spyglass, he saw that his twelve-pounder was cutting limbs from the trees that sheltered the opposing force.

Suddenly the Twin Sisters barked and spewed canister, grape, and cut-up horseshoes. It was the first time that the gifts from the Cincinnati citizens had been fired; they had not been put to the test even during practice. The men had been curious about what kind of bang the cannons would reward them with for all their work and trouble dragging the six-pounders through mud and rain. This explosion was entirely satisfactory, particularly in its effect upon the enemy.[2]

A captain reported to Santa Anna that Captain Urrizia was badly wounded. His horse had been killed. The enemy's cannon had shattered the ammunition chest on the limber. Another hit killed two mules.

Disturbed by the accuracy of the enemy's fire, Santa Anna sent an infantry charge to take the opposing artillery. The Twin Sisters barked again. Some of the attacking Mexicans fell, and the rest retreated. Loud cheers came from the force concealed in the wood behind the guns. During the sharp but brief artillery duel, Houston rode among his men, urging them to cheer as loudly as they could to give the Mexicans the impression that they were opposed by a confident and overwhelming foe. Cannon balls severed the branches above his head. One shot hit the bit of his horse's bridle. The animal bolted but was quickly brought under control. She bled badly and later had to be destroyed.

Colonel Neill was wounded in this same duel with the enemy. Houston put Hockley in charge of artillery to replace Neill, but said that he would miss Hockley's services as an aide.

Late in the afternoon Houston was well satisfied with the business of the day. He wanted the army to eat and to rest in readiness for tomorrow. He believed he could defeat the enemy now, but with the Mexicans on the alert and arrayed for a fight, victory would exact heavy losses. He was thinking hard—how to take the enemy by surprise.

Colonel Sherman of the Second Regiment, who had marched his followers from Natchitoches to join the volunteers at Gonzales, reported to the Commander and asked leave to use his cavalry to capture the Mexican field piece. Houston refused but instructed Sherman to use his cavalry to reconnoiter. Houston gave him "positive orders not to advance beyond the timber, or endanger the safety of his men." [3]

The reconnoitering party had just disappeared from view when Houston heard firing. Defying the Commander's instructions, Sherman had emerged from the woods and charged the Mexican line with the object of capturing the field piece. But Santa Anna's dragoons galloped up, and drove Sherman back in a sharp, brief encounter. Several horses were killed. Cavalryman Olwyn J. Trask was killed and two other cavalrymen, Devereaux J. Woodlief and Walter P. Lane, were wounded. Lane, dismounted, was so badly disabled he could not walk. A Georgia cavalryman, Mirabeau Buonaparte Lamar, who recently had joined Houston at Groce's Landing, saw Lane's plight. Lamar was a poet with longish hair, pleated pants, a keen sense of rhythm, and a thirst for acts of gallantry. He dashed toward Lane, dismounted under fire, lifted the wounded man into his saddle, climbed up behind him, and brought him into camp. The troops cheered the rescue.

Houston rode out and met Sherman coming in. He blazed with indignation, believing that Sherman had deliberately intended to bring on an engagement which the Commander in Chief did not want at that time. He reproved Sherman for violating orders while succeeding in nothing but "sacrificing the life of the brave Trask and disabling the intrepid Woodliff [Woodlief] both of whom were now being borne back." [4] The rebuke was merited, but it made Sherman his enemy for life. For political purposes Sherman later charged that Houston showed cowardice at San Jacinto.

When he returned to camp Houston praised the fearless poet, Lamar. On the spot before the men, he made Lamar a colonel, and gave him command of the cavalry. He hoped that prompt reward for gallantry would offset any damage Sherman's fiasco had done to the army's morale.

10. *Eve of Combat*

ACTIVITIES ceased on both sides. Santa Anna had grave suspicions about the number of men concealed in the timber. If they were Houston's rebels and usurpers who had eluded Sesma at Gonzales, they must have been strengthened by new recruits and probably exceeded his own force of less than eight hundred men.

At first he was inclined to countermarch to General Cos, who already should be on his way to join Santa Anna. On second thought, it seemed likely that if he retreated, the enemy would pursue and attack him. He hurried a dispatch to Filisola urging him to come up with his force at all possible speed. Then His Excellency went to look for a suitable camping ground—and a better battlefield.

The site he chose along the shore of San Jacinto Bay faced the northwest and placed the enemy on his right, at long musket range. On the southeast, the rear of his army would be sheltered by an extensive grove of trees, which was bounded on the south and east by a wide stretch of impenetrable marshland. Between the grove and the marshland was a tiny stream, a rill in which the tide ebbed and flowed, making it, in effect, a miniature bayou. The soggy marsh, with its small bayou covered all the territory between the grove and San Jacinto Bay. It was an unlikely camp site or battle-ground for a force that might find it necessary to retreat. But Santa Anna's choice accomplished his aim; he wanted to make sure that he was well protected from surprise attack on his flank.

The Mexican camp was on slightly rising ground three-quarters of a mile from the enemy's camp. Santa Anna placed his dragoons to protect his left and shielded his right with infantry stationed in timber some four hundred yards from the enemy's force. In the center, he threw up breastworks and built a five-foot parapet of pack saddles and baggage to protect his cannoneers; he also gave them infantry support on each flank.

Colonel Delgado discussed with General Castrillon the camp and battle site chosen by His Excellency. Castrillon was a man of experi-ence; he had been chosen by his chief to rescue the invaluable twelve-pounder cannon from its plight at Sim's Bayou, which flowed into Buffalo Bayou. At the Alamo, early on March 6, his troops had silently moved toward the citadel. He had directed the placing of scaling ladders; some of his men mounted the shoulders of others, and he had encouraged them until they had made a lodgment in the upper part of the Alamo. Now, Delgado pointed out to Castril-lon that, in case of a reverse, His Excellency had left no room for retreat. The camping ground of His Excellency's selection was, in all respects, against military rules: "Any youngster would have done better," Delgado said and reported it later.

"What can I do, my friend?" Castrillon answered. "I know it well, but I cannot help it. You know that nothing avails here against the caprice, arbitrary will, and ignorance of this man."

Delgado and Castrillon gloomily agreed that His Excellency appeared to have put himself in a box and to have slammed the lid down over his head.

That night, after munching a small piece of opium, Santa Anna slept soundly within a short distance of San Jacinto Bay, well pleased with his dispositions and serene in his confidence that Cos would be up in the morning, and that Filisola would follow later.

There were no signal taps for Houston's troops that night. Word passed from headquarters when it was time for camp fires to be out; and the men were ordered to have their arms close at hand for the always anticipated "surprise" attack.

Fatigued to the limit of endurance after thirty-eight days and nights of constant vigilance and exertion without one good long unbroken sleep, the General varied his nocturnal routine. He asked Hockley to take over for him and make sure that the sentinel outposts remained on the alert. He also entrusted the drum—which had never before left his custody—to Hockley, with these instructions: If the Commander did not waken early in the morning, no matter; the men were to be roused for the stand-to with the usual three taps. His resting place was a well-drained spot under a tree. Between him and the ground there was nothing, not even a blanket. The rain had stopped, but a chilling wind blew. Usually he slept with his head on his saddle which he covered with a small blanket. But today he had given his blanket to the men for cannon cartridges—cloth bags containing powder attached to the cannon ball for firing. His head rested on a coil of artillery rope.[1]

Drifting off to sleep Houston pondered the morrow's plans. A lawyer and something of a student of history, who by force of circumstances was adept at making war, Houston had studied his adversary for several years, following Santa Anna's progress and reverses south of the Rio Grande. He was concerned with every shred of evidence that bore on the kind of man who had chosen a battlefield—or at least an encampment—backed and flanked by timber, a swamp, and a river.

It was significant that the man sleeping out there in his elegant marquee had undertaken to establish a dynasty on the throne of Montezuma. His attempt had achieved marked success, but what had he done with it? He had not seized the imperial title as Iturbide had done, but he had made his authority absolute over a rich country and 7,000,000 people. His congress was at his feet; his will made the law. He could have blessed his country with enlightened policies if he had been an enlightened man, but he had subverted all the liberal provisions in the federal constitution of 1824 and enforced his authority with the bayonet.

Zacatecas was the bloody answer to the secret nature of the man who called himself the Napoleon of the West. When Zacatecas

233

refused to bow to his will, he had marked it for vengeance, marched upon it, and reduced it—not by force of arms, but by sending a hired traitor and spy. The spy had been ordered to go with his back lacerated as if driven from his own camp; he had obtained command and drawn the Zacatecans into a trap, leading to the capture of their city. The scenes of cruelty that had followed were beyond description.

Now Texas with some 25,000 souls—whites, Negroes, and peaceful and hostile Indians—had been marked for similar chastisement. Part of it had already been inflicted at the Alamo and Goliad. The disasters and cruelties that Texas suffered caused Houston sharp mental anguish as hard to bear as actual physical pain.

The man out there nicely sheltered from the cold wind of the norther was at best a riddle. It was said that his behavior was flamboyant and his dress extravagant. But others reported that he dressed quietly and was gentlemanly; they said his odd-shaped head and his melancholy black eyes in his sallow face gave him a sad, humble expression. Although he had his human impulses, it was apparent that victory intoxicated Santa Anna to the point of hysteria. His blood-thirstiness suggested instability, lack of confidence. This might make him more vulnerable than his battle position. Perhaps he could be intimidated.[2]

Houston was confident. He knew these youngsters under his command; they had hardened under discipline and prolonged ordeal. Under today's fire, they had behaved well. He rated them veterans now. Their response to the battle cry he had given them after the crossing at Battersons' Ferry showed he had the flint to ignite them with fury. If tomorrow the enemy should outnumber him as much as three-to-one he would not hesitate.

The president-general had been ready to fight today—reason enough for Houston to hold off. But would Santa Anna be ready tomorrow or would he wait for Cos? When would Cos come up? In the dispatch captured by Mr. E. there was no indication of the speed Cos hoped to make. Anyhow, what was true of most Mexicans must be true of Santa Anna. They had to have their siesta. This was the cautious Commander's cue for tomorrow's surprise.

11. *The Battle*

The Commander in Chief's sleep was undisturbed during the night and continued despite the sounds of the camp stirring to life next morning. Hands strange to the drum—Hockley's—sounded the three taps for the predawn reveille, and the sleepy, bone-weary men lurched to their places in the ranks. When Houston finally awoke the sun was shining full in his face. He rose hastily and walked to the edge of camp. A brisk breeze whipped the Mexican encampment flags that stood out in the brilliant sunshine. At last, the rains had ceased.

Ever since Smith captured the buckskin dispatch bag, Houston had known that Cos was on the way. This morning Mr. E. reported that late yesterday he had got near enough to study Cos's camp. He estimated that Cos had a force of about 550 men, which would certainly bring Santa Anna's force to more than 1,300. After another close study of Santa Anna's camp, Houston decided that Cos had not arrived during the night.

Later, at about ten o'clock, with Rusk and his own youngest aide, Lieutenant Alexander Horton, Houston rode out a short distance for another observation. No change was apparent in the enemy's camp; but there, coming over the rise of the prairie, from the direction of Harrisburg, was a marching column.

He regarded the sun as a good omen and, as he wrote later, determined, "Today the battle shall take place." [1] Cos's arrival did not change his decision, but strengthened it. However, the appearance of the Mexican reinforcements produced excitement in the Texan lines. Houston quelled the apprehension by coolly informing the troops that these were the same men they had seen the day before. These Mexicans "had marched round the swell in the prairie and returned in sight of the Texan camp to alarm their foe, with the appearance of an immense reinforcement—for it was very evident Santa Anna did not wish to fight. But it was all a *ruse de guerre* that could be easily seen through—*a mere Mexican trick.*" [2]

Colonel Hockley and Colonel John Wharton reported that the field officers desired a council of war. Houston had sometimes attended the officers' classes to exchange views on military subjects; but he had never discussed his duties as Commander in Chief with subordinates. But his officers were about to command in battle, and he could not ignore their natural anxiety. Moreover, some of them had been exceedingly caustic about his earlier refusal to go out of his way for a fight, and he was interested to know what their views were now.

He held the council of war at noon under the headquarters oak. It consisted of six field officers and Secretary of War Rusk. After some discussion, Houston formulated the proposition the field officers wished to vote on, "Shall we attack the enemy in position, or receive their attack on ours?"

In accord with custom he called first on the two junior officers, Major Lysander Wells and Major Joseph L. Bennett. They voted to attack. The four senior officers (Burleson, Somervell, Millard, and Sherman) had previously discussed the matter with Secretary Rusk and agreed with his opinion. Because Rusk was a sincere and trusted friend, Houston listened to his comments sympathetically and with interest.

Rusk said, "To attack veteran troops with raw militia is a thing unheard of; to charge upon the enemy without bayonets, in an open prairie has never been known; our situation is strong; in it we can whip all Mexico." Thus the council, including Rusk but not Houston, stood five to two in favor of a defensive position. Houston accepted this as the majority opinion and said immediately, "Gentlemen, you are adjourned." He withdrew without informing them that prior to the meeting he had resolved that the Texans would attack that very day. The field officers may have inferred his intention when he instructed them to remain in close contact with their commands.[3]

The situation he had observed the day before at Vince's Bridge had been in his mind continually since his decision to make this a day of battle. The bridge was the most direct means for additional reinforcements to join Santa Anna or for the retreat of a beaten force. Obviously, destruction of the bridge would prevent either army from retreating in that direction and delay further reinforcements to Santa Anna.

The Commander and some of his officers had observed that the lower bank of the bayou near the bridge was flooded. Concerned about a means of retreat in case of disaster, the officers had recommended the construction of a floating bridge at that point. This was the exact opposite of the General's desire. But, wishing to avoid anything in the nature of what he called "army polemics," he kept his intentions to himself.

After the council he sent for commissary-general John Forbes, whom he had come to trust when they were fellow commissioners in making the Cherokee treaty. He directed Forbes to secretly place two sharp axes beside a certain tree which he pointed out on the edge of the nearby timber.

Some time later he sent for Mr. E. and directed him to choose a well-mounted companion for an important mission and to come to the tree where Forbes had concealed the axes. In a few minutes Smith was there with redheaded Private D. W. Reeves, a cavalryman. Houston gave them the axes and told them they were to cut down Vince's Bridge and burn as much of it as they could, making sure that it was damaged beyond possibility of use. Smith's leathery face wrinkled into a grin of delight.

"This looks a good deal like a fight, General," he said in his squeaky falsetto.

"Unless you hasten," Houston answered, "you will find the prairie changed from green to red on your return!" [4]

Smith and his companion slung their axes from their saddles and rapidly rode away.

Then the General sent for a young soldier who could beat martial time on a drum, although he could not roll it. The youth informed him that one of his comrades had a fife, and the General sent the drummer to fetch him. When the fifer came he confessed that he could play only one tune, a popular song of the day: "Will You Come to the Bower That I Have Shaded for You?" The General smiled grimly and said this would do perfectly for what he had in mind. He told the drummer and the fifer to remain together and to keep in touch with headquarters for their instructions. This completed his preliminary preparations. Now his task was to prevent any act, deliberate or otherwise, that would give an alarm before the enemy's siesta hour.

At three o'clock that afternoon Houston ordered assembly and roll call. A good many men reported sore feet from marching without shoes or moccasins. Some were shaking with an ague that may have been malaria; others were pale and sickly. After ordering the sick out of ranks he had 783 "effectives"—260 more than he had when he crossed the Brazos.[5] The additions were men who had come in from outposts and recruits who had responded to the appeals of the Commander in Chief and the Secretary of War. Houston believed that he was going into battle outnumbered two-to-one, reckoning that Santa Anna had upwards of 1,500 men. But in this he was mistaken; Mr. E.'s estimate had come close to official figures. With Cos's reinforcements, Santa Anna's force numbered 1,360.

After the men had taken refreshments, Houston ordered the officers to form the army for an advance. They were to do so in camp to avoid evolutions near the enemy.

The cavalry, sixty-one men under the long-haired Georgia poet, Lamar, was posted about a half mile to the right, up the bayou. A grove would screen them from the left of the Mexican line, but Lamar could see the Commanding General when he waved his hat. The infantry's advance from camp began in columns of two, marching first to the front, then to the left. It, too, was screened from the enemy by a grove; the battle line was formed with the Texas infantry opposed to the enemy's infantry, artillery to artillery, and cavalry to cavalry. Burleson's regiment held the center. Slightly forward and a little to the left were the Twin Sisters under Hockley. Four companies of infantry under Millard would support the artillery on the right. Lamar's cavalry formed the right wing, and Colonel Sid Sherman's Second Regiment the left.

While the troops were getting into battle formation Houston closely watched the Mexican camp. He saw no evidence that the movements of his Texans were observed. A little after 3:30 P.M. the General waved his hat. His cavalry advanced, passing the head of a shallow dry ravine. Infantry and artillery passed through the steepest part of the ravine and up a slope on the far side.

The Mexican pickets discovered the cavalry as it passed the head of the ravine. They could be heard shouting *"Centinela alerta! Centinela alerta!"* (Sentinels, alert!)

Mexican infantry and artillery began firing, but their aim was much too high. The artillery fire crashed into the branches of the timber. The distance was too great for the musket fire which could not be effective at more than 100 yards.

Hockley hustled his guns ahead of the infantry line to within 200 yards of the enemy breastwork and commenced a hot fire with canister, grape, and cut-up horseshoes. His shots scattered the enemy's loosely stacked barricade and opened a breach. Bursts of orange-colored fire came from behind the Mexican breastworks.

Captain Bob Calder had never imagined anything like this could happen—the Texas line silently advancing under fire without returning it. He thought this must be more terrifying to the Mexicans than if the Texans had advanced with shouts and yells. He looked to his right and there was the General, tall and upright on his horse, fully exposed to enemy fire, the zest of battle on his face.

The Commander in Chief had given strict orders to keep silent until after the first volley; and this volley was not to be fired until ordered. Because it took at least a minute to reload after firing, the General could count upon but one volley from the infantry and, to be deadly, it must be at close range.

Smith galloped onto the field and told the Commander that he had accomplished his mission. Houston dashed in front of Burleson's regiment and announced that Vince's Bridge—the Mexicans' best means of escape—was down. Later, gunner Ben McCulloch reported that he had to refrain from firing one of the Twin Sisters because the Commander in Chief was directly in the line of fire. Smith rode back and forth across the field behind the advancing line waving his ax and echoing the General: "Vince's Bridge is down! They can't get away, men! Victory or death!"

A couple of trigger-happy Texans blazed away.

Houston cursed. "By the Mother of God men, hold your fire! God damn it, I say hold your fire! Now hold it! Keep low!"

Crouching low, the Texans went rapidly through the tall grass to Houston's continued chant: "Keep low, men! Hold your fire!"

With the Mexicans fully alert, Houston signaled the drummer and fifer to come in at their loudest and shrillest. In march time the

239

drum thundered and the fife shrilled "Will You Come to the Bower That I Have Shaded for You?"

Twenty paces from the barricade Houston ordered the volley. "Kneel! Shoot low! Fire!"

The volley was low; it killed and disabled many. Then waving his hat so that the flank commanders could see it, Houston ordered the charge. "Forward! Charge! Remember the Alamo! Remember Goliad!"

Infuriated by their own war cry and nerved by the suspense of their silent advance, the center column surged through the breach the Twin Sisters had opened in the barricade. Elsewhere men went over the top, still yelling, "Remember the Alamo! Remember Goliad!" As they shouted, they swung their ten-pound rifles as clubs. Only a few had bayonets.

When the charging infantry masked the Twin Sisters, Hockley's gunners abandoned their guns and joined the charge. Mounted artillery officers led them through the broken line. The enemy's gunners were overwhelmed before they could fire the last round they had rammed into their twelve-pounder.

Colonel Sherman drove the enemy's right toward the center. Lamar's cavalry, advancing on the enemy's left, had encountered the Mexican dragoons leisurely riding their horses bareback to water. In a headlong charge, the Texans drove the dragoons toward the center. This doubled and trebled the confusion there. The Mexican center was a seething mass of demoniacal men and neighing horses; heads were bashed with rifle butts, bellies ripped with knives.

Houston declared afterward:

> It would be a gross mistake to suppose that the Mexicans played the coward that day—for they were slain by hundreds in the ranks where they stood when the battle began—but the fierce vengeance of the Texans could not be resisted. They fought as none but men can fight, when they are striking for their homes, their families and their dead kindred. The Mexican officers and men stood firm for a time, but the Texans stamped on them as fast as they fell, and trampled the prostrate and the dying down with the dead, and clambering over the groaning, bleeding mass, plunged their knives into the bosoms of those in the rear.[6]

On their knees the Mexicans cried, "*Me no Alamo!*" But all had been at the Alamo and were now paying for the shrill *degüello*, the "no quarter" bugle call which had sounded the fate of that garrison. When they found that "no quarter" ruled here, too, they rose and sought in flight the safety denied them by the rifle butts, knives, and bayonets of the Texans.

When the Texans came within sixty paces, a general flash, orange in hue, issued from the Mexican line, which was drawn up in perfect order. This was the enemy's only concerted volley. At that moment, Houston was at the head of his own center column. The volley was too high to have much effect, but several balls hit the Commander's horse in the breast. At the same time Houston was struck by a copper ball from a Mexican *escopeta*, a kind of musket with a bell-shaped muzzle. It cut through his boot and shattered the front portion of the leg bone an inch above the ankle, severing arteries and veins. He felt the shock, but mildly because of the moment's tremendous excitement. His horse shuddered, lurched, but remained on its feet. Houston spurred the animal and it responded. He surveyed the line from left to right.

In the center, the rout was well under way. Off to the right he saw that 48 Regulars, all there were, part of Colonel Millard's command, were in confusion. He galloped over, and asked Millard the cause of delay. Millard replied that his horse was wounded, and a moment later his mount plunged to the ground.

A column of about 100 enemy infantrymen began to advance in good order toward Millard's force. Houston quickly assumed command of the Regulars and led them to meet the approaching column. About 30 yards from the enemy he ordered the Regulars to halt, kneel, and fire. One volley sent the Mexicans in flight. This ended organized resistance on the field. The rest was pandemonium, hand-to-hand struggle, and headlong flight.

After the Regulars routed the last Mexicans, Houston discovered a detachment of inactive Texas cavalry a little farther to the right. He ordered them to pursue the enemy and prevent them from reorganizing.

Most of the fugitives scattered to the west and south toward Vince's Bridge. The pursuing Texans managed to get west of them. Many of the Mexican dragoons had to flee on foot because they could not mount their frightened horses. The Texans could mount anything that had hooves. They captured the horses and joined their own cavalry in the pursuit. For miles dead bodies were scattered over the prairie and along the road to Vince's Bridge.

Had the Mexican fire been lower, Houston declared afterward, the Texans, advancing in broad daylight, would have been mowed down and the fierce fighting at the center would never have taken place. About eighteen minutes after the fight at the center began, the rout was complete.

This moment had been long in preparation. It was the thirty-ninth day since Gonzales.

Houston's assault at the siesta hour had paid off well. Santa Anna was asleep in his marquee when the attack began. The reinforcements Cos had brought were sleeping off the fatigue of their long march of the day before. When a Mexican bugler on the right signaled the advance of the enemy's opposing wing (Sherman's force), His Excellency and staff were awakened. Colonel Pedro Delgado, in his account, described the situation at this moment. "His Excellency and Staff were asleep; the greater number of the men were also sleeping; of the rest some were scattered in the woods, in search of boughs to prepare shelter. Our cavalry was riding bareback to and from water." Delgado stepped up on some ammunition boxes to observe the enemy's movement. As the Texans silently advanced he became aware of the total confusion in the Mexican camp. "General Castrillon shouted on one side," he wrote. "On another Colonel Almonte was giving orders; some cried out to commence firing; others to lie down to avoid grape-shot. Among the latter was His Excellency."

This was the situation as Delgado saw it from near General Santa Anna's marquee: Everything was in confusion but there was no lack of courage; the Mexican sentinels died trying to rally their men. But soon, Delgado saw Mexican soldiers flying in all directions. He endeavored to collect enough men to put up a fight but the effort was futile. "The evil was beyond remedy," he wrote, "they were a bewildered and panic-stricken herd."

Then Delgado saw the enemy, meeting no resistance, "dash, lightning-like, upon our deserted camp." A moment later:

242

...I saw His Excellency running about in the utmost excitement, wringing his hands and unable to give an order. General Castrillon was stretched on the ground wounded in the leg. Colonel Trevino was killed, and Colonel Marcial Aguirre was severely injured. I saw, also, the enemy reaching the ordnance train, and killing a corporal and two gunners. . . .

At this moment of extreme disorder, wearing red worsted slippers and a blue linen dressing gown over a white shirt, His Excellency (as he said in his own report) mounted a speedy horse and dashed off in the direction of Vince's Bridge. Delgado decided that he should follow the example of His Excellency, since everything apparently was lost. He later justified his flight by stating that a further attempt to rally the troops would have been in vain. "It is a known fact," he wrote, "that Mexican soldiers, if once demoralized, cannot be controlled unless they are thoroughly inured to war." This trait, he might have added, was by no means limited to Mexicans.

Delgado tried to mount his own horse, but the firing made the animal frightened and fractious. Giving up, Delgado led the excited animal from the field. His objective was the grove between the battlefield and the marsh, on the bay shore only a musket shot from camp. Many, from what Delgado called "our disbanded herd," had already rushed for cover there. The "herd," he noted bitterly, "rushed for the grove to obtain shelter from the horrid slaughter carried on all over the prairie by the bloodthirsty usurpers."

These fugitives had first sought to escape southwestward from the battlefield over the prairie, no doubt with Vince's Bridge in mind. Cut off in that direction by Texans who were busily avenging the Alamo, and not having heard the word that all who surrendered were to be spared, they had turned back to seek shelter in this grove that Delgado was now headed for. To get to it, Delgado and many of the fugitives had to cross the narrow bayou, swollen by the tide and the recent rains. Near shore the water was shallow; at the center its ten-foot depth was masked by muddy water. In desperation many fugitives had plunged in and, mired, had been shot from the bank. Delgado was not wrong when he stated that here "the greatest carnage took place." The Texans on shore were so close that they could hardly miss; more than one hundred died on this spot.

When Delgado reached the narrow bayou, he saw Colonel Juan Almonte, Santa Anna's aide and interpreter, swimming across with his left hand holding up his sword in his right. At this critical moment, Delgado suddenly leaped into the saddle, taking his horse by surprise. With two bounds, the horse carried him near the opposite bank before he bogged down. Delgado slid off and sank in mire up to his waist. Pulling himself up by the grass, he struggled toward shore, abandoning his horse and leaving his shoes behind in the mud. "I made an effort to recover them," he wrote, "but I soon came to the conclusion that, did I tarry there, a rifle shot would certainly make an outlet for my soul." He reached shore and, barefoot, made for the grove. There he joined a number of other officers with whom he "wandered at random, buried in gloomy thoughts upon our tragic disaster."

Slightly unsteady from loss of blood, Houston rode out on the battlefield after his little foray at the head of the Regulars. He spoke to both officers and men, again ordering them to stop the killing, and placed Colonel William Allen in command of a fifteen-man squad to catch up with the pursuit and inforce the order against wanton killing. He told Allen that the Alamo had been avenged and all who surrendered should be brought into camp. Several times he stated that this order must be observed.

After dispatching Allen's squad, Houston followed for some six hundred yards the route that many fugitives had taken. Then, turning back, he came to the spot where Almonte and Delgado had succeeded in crossing the narrow bayou and where many of their comrades had been slain. Houston called the small bayou "a deep morass," and later described the sight he beheld there.

... multitudes, in their desperation, had rushed to this spot as a forlorn hope. They had plunged into the mire and water with horses and mules, and, attempting to pass, had been completely submerged; every one who seemed likely to escape soon received a ball from the murderous aim of a practiced rifleman, and the morass was literally bridged over with carcasses of dead mules, horses, and men.[7]

As the General rode up, a number of Texas infantrymen were standing there considering what to do next because their ammunition was exhausted. Thinking the General intended to plunge into the morass, they called out to him. They were equally concerned that he should not get mixed up with the corpses under water.

The General, in fact, was somewhat dazed from fatigue and loss of blood. The shouting caused him to rein his horse sharply, and the animal fell dead. It was found later to have been "pierced" with five bullets but none in a spot that was immediately fatal. Presumably it had bled to death. Houston believed one bullet went through a kidney. As the horse fell, he narrowly saved himself from being pinned under. Several soldiers rushed to his aid. Seeing that he needed support, they "sustained him on one leg." This was the first that anyone except the General knew that he was wounded. Adjutant Lynch, nearby, dismounted, put his stout roan at the General's disposal, and with assistance from the men lifted him into the saddle.

Just then, across the bayou, Houston and his companions saw a considerable force of Mexicans marching in reasonably good order —240 men who had collected under the command of Colonel Almonte. Evidently the Mexicans intended to attack.

The Texans made a rush to pass around the bayou to get at the marching force. The General ordered them to halt and form, not to advance upon the enemy in disorder. They obeyed. Then he directed Deaf Smith to make contact with the enemy and inform them that if they surrendered they would be treated as prisoners of war. He asked Secretary Rusk to follow Smith and receive the surrender.

The band of Mexicans had already surrendered. Colonel Delgado, beneficiary of the General's stop-the-killing order, was a member of this same party. They had all been wandering aimlessly in the grove when they were overtaken by Colonel Allen's little squad and saved from execution at the hands of zealous troops.

Before he left the scene, General Houston ordered Captain Amasa Turner of Company B to march a group to the battlefield to prevent pillage. Then, mounted on Lynch's roan and accompanied by Rusk, he started for the Texas camp. Returning over the battlefield, he was surrounded by a swarm of soldiers who trudged along at his side. They had a new reverence and affection for him. All his detractors, the jealous aspirants who had wanted to replace him in command

and had preached discontent and rebellion, had been answered today. The men stroked the General's borrowed mount and affectionately patted their Commander's boots.

One Texan asked if Houston liked the work his men had done that day. He answered that they had covered themselves with glory and would receive the spoils as a reward for their valor. He would not take any of the spoils himself, he said, but would share the honors of the triumph with them.

A soldier's hand bumped against the General's wounded leg, forcing an exclamation from Houston and making him lurch in his saddle. The soldier looked at his wet hand, told the General that he had been hit and that his boot was leaking blood. The word spread that the General was wounded.

At his oak tree headquarters, Houston, still mounted, was issuing some necessary orders when General Rusk presented a prisoner, Colonel Juan Nepomuceno Almonte, Santa Anna's aide. It was the first time the General and Almonte had met. The General later recorded, "This seemed to give a finishing stroke to the victory." [8]

Completely exhausted from fatigue and loss of blood, Houston fell from his horse. Colonel Hockley caught him in his arms and laid him at the foot of the oak tree.

12. *The Splendor and Miseries of Victory*

THE morning after the battle dawned clear and warm. Soggy prairie and swollen streams were the residue of the norther's chilling blasts and torrential downpours that had vexed both armies.

Under his headquarters oak, General Houston lay on a cot taken from the enemy's stores. The arms victory was complete, but he knew that the campaign would not end until Santa Anna was captured or his fate was definitely known. After a wakeful night caused by the pain of his wound, Houston's one great concern was that Santa Anna, if captured, be brought into camp alive and unhurt. He had not received any report from the parties that had been searching for Santa Anna all night, and he decided to send out others even though he did not want to weaken the guard around the 500 prisoners in the camp. The new detail of searchers was allowed to choose the best from 200 captured Mexican horses. They were instructed to treat Santa Anna courteously if they found him and to bring him immediately to the Commander.

Early that afternoon Sergeant James A. Sylvester and four other men were on the bank of Buffalo Bayou near where Vince's Bridge had been destroyed. On the west side of a small branch they saw five deer. Sylvester rode toward them, aimed at the buck, and was about to fire when the herd took fright and dashed off. Looking about to discover what had alarmed them, Sylvester saw a man moving toward the destroyed bridge. The Mexican dropped into the tall grass. Ordered to get up, he hesitated before rising and extending his hand to Sergeant Sylvester, who took it. The Mexican pressed Sylvester's hand warmly and kissed it, and asked where General Houston was.

The prisoner wore what Sylvester called "common clothes" and declared himself to be a private soldier. Incredulous, Sylvester pointed to the prisoner's soiled but elegant shirt. Sylvester, in reporting the incident, said the Mexican burst into tears and replied that he was an aide to General Santa Anna.

In a mild tone Sylvester said, "Don't grieve. You won't be hurt."

On the way to camp the little party passed a large group of Mexican prisoners sitting under guard on the ground. They suddenly scrambled to their feet and saluted.

"*El Presidente!*" they murmured, "*El Presidente!*" [1]

The news rippled through the Mexican camp: the president-general was a prisoner like the rest of them. Sylvester and his men found it hard to believe that this tearful, complaining little fellow was actually the dreaded Alamo butcher. Colonels Hockley and Forbes took charge of the prisoner and conducted him to headquarters.

Houston was dozing fitfully, probably under the influence of an opiate that Surgeon General Alexander Ewing had given him. The pain of his wound was severe. Looking up, Houston beheld the oddly dressed captive, who announced in Spanish: "I am General Antonio López de Santa Anna, President of the Republic of Mexico, and a prisoner at your disposition." [2]

Instantly wide awake, Houston sat up. He waved Santa Anna to a box that stood nearby, and Santa Anna sat down. After some time, with apparent emotion but with great composure compared to what Houston expected under the circumstances, Santa Anna proposed a negotiation for his liberation.

Houston was elated, thrilled, tingling with excitement; thoroughly delighted that he had Santa Anna alive and unharmed. He had reason to believe that he could end the war here and now, with Texas independence guaranteed.

There was still another reason for his elation, as he pointed out. Had he not destroyed Vince's Bridge, Santa Anna, on a fast horse, might easily have been marching back at this very moment with his reserve force to redeem his disaster and release the prisoners.

Houston observed Santa Anna's keen eye occasionally glancing around the camp. With a timid expression the prisoner pressed the sides of his breasts with both hands and gave two or three half-suppressed groans, like a man who was suffering deep pain. At this moment, General Rusk came up accompanied by Lorenzo de Zavala, Jr., son of the vice-president of Texas. Santa Anna recognized young Zavala at once and advanced to meet him with great cordiality, exclaiming, "Oh! My *friend*, my *friend*, the son of my *early* friend," as he embraced young Zavala, dropping a tear, as Rusk reported.

Young Zavala returned the greeting with the deference that would have been due to Santa Anna's "former rank and power," but, says Rusk, his "look seemed to wither Santa Anna." Staring him full in the face, Zavala said with restraint, "It *has* been so, Sir." Santa Anna was unable to conceal his mortification.[3]

Colonel Almonte, who had been sent for to act as interpreter approached the captive general with a show of respect and grief. During the conversation that followed, Houston lay on the ground, resting on his elbow. Almonte acted as translator. The talk appears in the *Memoir* with the assurance that great pains were taken to get as nearly as possible the exact words of the speakers.

Santa Anna (after embracing Almonte, and recovering perfectly from his embarrassment, rose, and advancing with the air of one born to command, said to General Houston— "That man may consider himself born to no common destiny, who has conquered the Napoleon of the West; and it now remains for him to be generous to the vanquished."

Houston.—"You should have remembered that at the Alamo."

S. A.—"You must be aware that I was justified in my course by usages of war. I had summoned a surrender, and they had refused. The place was then taken by storm, and the usages of war justified the slaughter of the vanquished."

H.—"That *was* the case once, but it is now obsolete. Such usages among civilized nations have yielded to the influences of humanity."

S. A.—"However this may be, I was acting under orders of my Government."

H.—"Why, YOU *are the Government* of Mexico."

S. A.—"I have orders in my possession commanding me so to act."

H.—"A Dictator, sir, has no superior."

S. A.—"I have orders, General Houston, from my Government, commanding me to exterminate every man found in arms in the province of Texas, and treat all such as pirates; for they have no Government, and are fighting under no recognized flag. This will account for the positive orders of my Government."

H.—"So far as the first point is concerned, the Texans flatter themselves they have a Government already, and they will probably be able to make a flag. But if you feel excused for your conduct at San Antonio, you have not the same excuse for the massacre of Colonel Fannin's command. They had capitulated on terms proffered by your General. And yet, after the capitulation, they were all perfidiously massacred, without the privilege of even dying with arms in their hands."

Those who were present say that when Houston came to speak of the Goliad tragedy, it seemed impossible for him to restrain his indignation. His eye flashed like a wild beast's, and in his gigantic effort to curb in his wrath, cold sweat ran off from his brow in streams. [Interpolation probably by Charles Edwards Lester.]

S. A.—"I declare to you, General (laying his hand on his heart), that I was not apprised of the fact that they had capitulated. General Urrea informed me that he had conquered them in a battle, and under this impression I ordered their execution."

H.—"I *know*, General, that the men had capitulated."

S. A.—"Then I was ignorant of it. And after your asseveration I should not have a shadow of doubt, if it were not that *General Urrea had no authority whatever to receive their capitula-*

tion. And if the day ever comes that I can get Urrea into my hands, I will execute him for his duplicity in not giving me information of the facts." [4]

Angry soldiers passed the headquarters sentinels and gathered close around their General and his prisoner. Scowling and fingering the knives and pistols in their belts, they were walking armories equipped with Mexican weapons.

Santa Anna lost his composure and raised a nervous hand to his face. He said he was suffering from a slight indisposition and asked for a small piece of opium which was furnished by Dr. Ewing. Houston ordered the soldiers to withdraw and their prompt obedience gratified him as much as it did Santa Anna.

Santa Anna's guilt merited death, but was it wise to exact this penalty? Houston could think of several reasons to favor a different course. The western settlements were broken up and the fugitive settlers were camping out—a burden on East Texas. Texas could have raised 4,000 men but only 1,000 had responded. The hysterical government was dashing about unwilling to consult the Commander in Chief on the best location for its safety. The number of prisoners taken was almost equal to the only existing organized army. They had to be guarded in the open and they had to be fed. On Texas soil, there were four Mexican forces under four experienced generals —Filisola, Urrea, Sesma, and Gaona. With reasonably good leadership they could concentrate to avenge Santa Anna's defeat before Texas could assemble and train an adequate force. The past forty days and nights had clearly demonstrated that Texas could win in the end, but at what cost?

Suspension of hostilities with peace and independence guaranteed by a dictator held as hostage seemed the wisest course.

Santa Anna proposed a treaty of peace to be signed by General Houston and himself. Houston refused on the ground that this was not his responsibility but that of the civilian government. Santa Anna protested that he did not like dealing with civilians and would prefer to make a treaty with the Commander. Again Houston refused and peremptorily, without promise or condition, demanded that Santa Anna sign an armistice—hostilities to cease, all Mexican forces to withdraw from Texas, a permanent treaty of peace to be drawn later between Santa Anna and the Texas government.

Almonte, at his general's direction, wrote out the necessary order to Filisola and through him to the other Mexican generals:

The small divisions under my immediate command having had yesterday evening an unfortunate encounter, it has resulted in my being a prisoner of war in the enemy's hands, but all possible considerations have been shown to me, therefore I command you to cause General Gaona to countermarch to Béjar to wait there for orders. Your Excellency will also return to the same place with troops under your command, ordering at the same time General Urrea to retreat with his division to Guadalupe Victoria, because an armistice has been agreed upon with General Houston, until some negotiations are arranged, by which the war is to cease forever.[5]

General Houston sent Smith with a small party to deliver the order to Filisola. Colonel Burleson was instructed to follow with 250 men to observe how Filisola acted and to protect Smith if necessary.

Houston states that Colonel Almonte showed a disposition to continue the conversation with him and asked the victorious General why he had not attacked the Mexicans the first day the armies met. Said Almonte:

"You had reason to suppose we should be reinforced. And yet if you had risked a battle that day you would have had another story to tell, perhaps, for our men were *then* ready to fight, and so anxious for the battle to come on, that we could hardly keep them in their ranks. Why did you wait till the next morning, General?"

"Well," replied Houston, "I see I was right. I *knew* you expected I should bring on the battle that day, and were consequently prepared for it. Now if I *must* be questioned by an inferior officer in the presence of his General, I will say *that was just the reason why I did not fight;* and besides, I thought there was no use in having two bites at one cherry." [6]

Santa Anna had become interested in the conversation, and Almonte related to him what had been said. The Mexican general, transported with rage, cursed Almonte for losing the battle.

Houston ordered Santa Anna's marquee set up near headquarters, and restored his personal baggage to him. He thus protected Santa

Anna from threats or demonstrations and encouraged good behavior on the part of the prisoners.

That same afternoon he sent a hurried dispatch to the fugitive government leaders whose whereabouts he did not definitely know. Assuming that they might be at Galveston, he addressed his dispatch to them there. It was not a mere report of the battle but an announcement of victory with a suggestion that the government join him at his headquarters near the San Jacinto River.

During the night three of Deaf Smith's men returned with General Cos, several other officers and Santa Anna's secretary. In the morning Santa Anna asked for another conference, and Houston granted it. The Mexican general appeared in elegant dress, referred to Houston as his "host," and inquired politely about his wound and general health. Houston received his dapper prisoner in an old black coat, snuff-colored pantaloons, a black velvet vest, a fur cap, and a worn-out boot on his left leg. His right leg was bandaged with rags.

Santa Anna expressed a desire to negotiate for his liberty, and Houston sent for Secretary of War Rusk. In Rusk's presence, Houston explained that he could take no action on the Mexican general's proposal because Texas was ruled by a constitutional government.

Santa Anna wanted to know where the government was. Houston evaded, indicating there was some uncertainty about this. In his *Memoir*, he remarked that the government had "fled from the scene of danger, and scattered to the four winds of heaven." [7]

From his cot, Houston directed the distribution of spoils. He had Santa Anna's treasure chest brought to headquarters and looked on as a guard stood over it and counted about $12,000 in specie, mostly Mexican silver. All the money went to the soldiers; none to Houston or to officers. There were less than $20 for each man—not enough to cover the government's promises to its soldiers.

It took four days to bring in the captured stores and distribute them to the soldiers. Colonel Delgado watched the proceedings with anguish, and later wrote in his "Account":

> It was hard to see them breaking our trunks open and everyone of them loaded with our shirts, trousers, coats, etc., whilst we remained with what we had on our bodies.

I saw my boots going, while my blistered feet were wrapped up in pieces of rawhide.

To make up for our cloaks, overcoats and blankets...they favored us with the great-coats of our own soldiers, which were so lousy that we had the greatest trouble to rid ourselves of the vermin....

The saddle and pack-mules belonging to our division were also distributed among the conquering officers and soldiers.

They [the soldiers] would adorn them [the mules] with the green and red cords which our Voltigeurs and Grenadiers wore on their caps, placing them on their ears, necks, or backs.

Delgado was deeply pained when the young Texans, adorning their mules with trappings, mixed their colors—white, yellow, and crimson—without the least regard for harmony. But he was delighted when saddles were placed on long-eared mounts which "knew nothing beyond the pack" and the "poor Yankees," taken by surprise, were tossed sky high.

Delgado suffered a gnawing fear that he and his comrades were to be executed in retaliation for the Alamo. With a large number of other prisoners he was marched into the woods where a huge fire was burning. Bitterly, he reflected that he would consider it an act of mercy to be shot first before he was tossed into the flames. He recorded his surprise when a little later, he was prodded with the butt of a rifle and told to get closer to the fire where he could warm himself and dry out his clothes. Delgado seems to have wondered if, like green wood, he was to be seasoned before he was cast into the flames.

No doubt things were going on in camp that the Commanding General did not know about. In his report, Delgado related how three of Houston's soldiers, speaking broken Spanish, told the prisoners about a meeting of Texas soldiers to decide whether the captives should be executed immediately or when the Commanding General got around to ordering it. Delgado went cold as ice a little later when, at a short distance from camp, more than a hundred Texans formed in line and carefully and deliberately loaded their guns. To him it was perfectly obvious that those soldiers who favored immediate execution had won the argument. "I crossed myself and committed my soul to God," he wrote. But again he was dumfounded when the men who had so ostentatiously loaded their guns went off to relieve the guard. He never did appreciate this grisly joke.

On the third day after the battle General Houston completed his report to the government, regretting the delay due to his "situation." He did not mention his wound but described the action and praised his staff and certain officers including Deaf Smith, Karnes, and Lamar ("whose gallant and daring conduct on the previous day had attracted the admiration of his comrades"). He praised Rusk for being on the field and "continuing his activity . . . until resistance ceased." He reported Texas losses as two killed and 23 wounded, six of whom died. The enemy's losses he reported as 630 killed, including one general, four colonels, two lieutenant colonels, five captains, and 12 lieutenants. He listed 730 prisoners. The stores and arms taken were vast in quantity, including 600 muskets and several hundred horses and mules.[8] He gave written instructions to the courier who carried his dispatch to the government, supposed to be at Galveston: "Tell our friends all the news and that we have beaten the enemy . . . tell them to come on and let the people plant corn." Already the Commander was looking ahead to the purpose for which he had fought his epic battle—the building of a self-reliant nation.[9]

Deaf Smith overtook Filisola on April 28, on the West Bernard River, 30 miles west of the Brazos and 70 miles from San Antonio. He brought Filisola's reply back to General Houston; it was addressed to Santa Anna. After reading it, Houston handed it to the Mexican general:

As soon as I was informed by some dispersed officers and soldiers of the unfortunate encounter which your Excellency communicates to me . . . I made the movements proper for concentrating the army . . . but in attention to the said communication of your Excellency, I am going to repass the Colorado, and will cease hostilities, should the enemy not give occasion to continue them. . . .[10]

The dictator's eyes filled with tears. Houston consoled him with the suggestion that if Filisola had not had the wisdom to obey his superior's orders he would have been cut to pieces by Smith and

Burleson, for Filisola was badly mired, whipped, and beaten by Generals Mud and Rain.

The General ordered out burial squads who found that deterioration of the corpses had been rapid because the weather had turned so warm. They sent a delegation to the General to tell him they would prefer another battle to carrying out this assignment. Headquarters was so near the battlefield that the General had no difficulty in appreciating the weight of this protest. After their long ordeal of forty days and nights, he did not have the heart to impose this further burden on them.

A Mrs. McCormick, who owned the farm on which the battle was fought, called at the headquarters of the Commander in Chief and asked him to get the stinking Mexicans off her land.

The General tried to mollify her. "Madam, your land will be famed in history as the classic spot upon which the glorious victory of San Jacinto was gained! Here that latest scourge of mankind, the self-styled 'Napoleon of the West' met his fate!"

"To the *devil* with your glorious history," madam replied. "Take off your stinking Mexicans." [11]

A strange sight was witnessed on the battlefield at dusk; a figure moved from corpse to corpse, although the dead soldiers' clothing had already been searched for loot. The phenomenon was explained when it was discovered that a Yankee dentist was collecting teeth from the corpses, not for the gold, because Mexican troops did not have that kind of dental work, but for use in artificial dentures.

Proximity to the battlefield became intolerable. The General ordered his headquarters and both camps, Texan and Mexican, moved to a distance of a mile and a half. The removal was just being completed when members of the government arrived from Galveston aboard the *Yellow Stone*, under command of that same Captain Ross who had so handily assisted the army to cross the Brazos.

Houston relinquished custody of Santa Anna to the government along with copies of the Mexican general's orders to Filisola. He explained that these orders had been issued after an agreement for a temporary armistice pending a treaty of peace to be negotiated between the dictator and the Texas government.

For the government to retrace its steps after panic flight was embarrassing enough. But now to face the fact that the General they had taunted and jeered had achieved a phenomenal victory and already had negotiated the retirement of all Mexican troops was downright painful. Conceivably, with his devoted army at his back, this unpredictable man might make himself dictator and send the government flying again. As soon as they found that Houston was not disposed to do anything of the sort they treated him with less consideration than before.

The motive behind their hostility was obvious. Unless Houston's character was blackened and his courage and achievements depreciated, his fame as a hero would become established and the government leaders would suffer a loss of reputation for their panic flights and their treatment of him. An attempt to deflate Houston's reputation with the army failed; then the government stooped to personal harassment. Bluntly it demanded delivery of the specie found in Santa Anna's treasure chest. Houston answered that the money had been distributed to the men in lieu of payments and unfulfilled promises.

Mr. Burnet said he needed the money for the government. Houston did not doubt this. Secretary of the Navy Potter declared that he needed it for his department. Houston conceded that this was also true, but he added that the needs of the men were as great as anybody's and they were entitled to much more than they would ever get. No attempt was made to force the troops to surrender their shares.

In battle, Colonel Almonte had ridden a fine black stallion he had received from settler Vince, and Karnes had captured it after the rout. Because of Karnes's admiration for the General, and in recognition of the General's loss of his own horse, Karnes presented the mount to him. Houston declined the gift at first and had the animal paraded for auction; the proceeds were to go to the troops. The men objected. They led the animal back to headquarters and insisted that the General keep it.

Although informed about how the stallion had come into the General's possession, the government demanded its surrender. Houston complied without a murmur. The government returned it to the original owner, settler Vince, who was mildly in sympathy with the Mexicans and, as Houston wrote later, "a man who had never done anything for the country." [12]

At a Cabinet meeting Secretary of the Navy Potter proposed Houston's dismissal from the service; Houston's distribution of the captured Mexican specie to the troops was Potter's principal item of alleged misconduct. Secretary of War Rusk opposed this, indignantly warning that it would be futile for the government to try to alienate the sympathy of the troops from the Commander in Chief.

Volunteers were now rushing to the battlefield from all quarters. Some were fugitives who had fled in panic; others came in response to appeals from Houston and Rusk on the eve of battle, but they arrived too late. An active, vigorous, and firm Commander was needed, but Houston was helpless because of his wound. He was unable to stand even with the aid of crutches of stout saplings that had been made for him. Foreseeing that he would be unfit for service for a considerable time he recommended to the government that Secretary of War Rusk take over as acting Commander in Chief. Rusk was the one man who would have been acceptable to the troops. The government appointed him Brigadier General and gave him the temporary post. The poet and cavalry captain, Lamar, was appointed to fill Rusk's place in the Cabinet.

General Houston was not invited to a Cabinet meeting called to discuss the fate of Santa Anna. Rusk explained Houston's view that Santa Anna was worth more to Texas alive than dead. Rusk, asked to obtain Houston's opinions on the terms of a possible treaty in case Santa Anna's life was spared, made his inquiry by letter. Houston promptly answered:

> I have not the pleasure to know on what basis the Executive Government contemplate the arrangements with Gen. Santa Anna, but I would respectfully suggest.... The recognition of the Independence of Texas should be a sine qua non. The limits of Texas should extend to the Rio Grande, from the mouth, pursuing the stream to its most north western source, and from thence north east to the line of the United States. Indemnity for all losses sustained by Texas during the war. Commissioners to be appointed for ascertaining the fact. One Mexican, one Texian, and one American. The guarantee to be obtained from the United States, for the fulfillment to the stipulation on the part of the contending parties. Gen. Santa Anna to be retained as a hostage, until they [the terms] are recognized or ratified by the Mexican government. Immediate restoration of Texian or

Mexican citizens, or those friendly to the cause of Texas, who may have been retained with their property. Instantanious withdrawal of all the Mexican troops from the limits of Texas. All property in Texas to be restored, and not molested by the troops or marauders in falling back. Cessation of all hostilities by sea and land. A guarantee for the safety and restoration of Mexican prisoners, so soon as the conditions shall be complied with. Agents to be sent to the United States to obtain the mediation of that government, in the affairs of Mexico and Texas.[13]

Numerous other provisions were suggested for repatriation of citizens, restoration of seized property, and mediation by the United States in disputes between Texas and Mexico. Houston was as thorough in suggesting terms for a peace treaty as he had been in his military preparations.

On May 5, 1836, the *Yellow Stone* was being readied to take the government leaders, and Santa Anna and his suite to Galveston. The army under Rusk was preparing to march to the west where the settlements had been broken up by the Mexican invasion and there was some fear of renewed hostilities.

Surgeon Ewing was worried about the General's wounds; inflammation was excessive, discoloration was spreading rapidly, the pain was intense and Ewing had no medicines or materials for dressings. Advised that it was imperative to get to New Orleans as soon as possible for treatment and possibly for an operation to remove fragments of bone, Houston, too weak to stand, wrote his farewell to the troops and had it read as an army order.

COMRADES: Circumstances connected with the battle of the 21st render our separation, for the present, unavoidable. I need not express to you the many painful sensations which that necessity inflicts upon me. . . .

The enemy, though retreating, are still within the limits of Texas; . . . Discipline and subordination will render you invincible. Your valor and heroism have proved you unrivalled. Let not contempt for the enemy throw you off your guard. . . .

At parting my heart embraces you with gratitude and affection.

SAM HOUSTON, Commander-in-Chief.[14]

The next day Houston learned that the government had refused permission for him to sail on the *Yellow Stone*. Ewing believed that if the General was not permitted to sail, he would die within sight of the San Jacinto battlefield. The surgeon general made formal application to the government for Houston's passage. The application was refused. The General was advised that his place was with the army, though the army was on the eve of marching west and the General was unable to stand without assistance. Dr. Ewing reported the government's attitude to Captain Ross. Ross retorted in salty language that the *Yellow Stone* would not sail until General Houston was aboard.

Late in the afternoon of May 7, President Burnet, Vice-President Zavala, War Secretary Lamar, Navy Secretary Potter, and other government dignitaries boarded the *Yellow Stone*. At 5 P.M. Santa Anna, Cos, Almonte, Delgado, some officers of lower rank, and as many Mexican privates as could be accommodated, went aboard under guard. Shortly afterward, General Houston was carried aboard on his cot by Rusk, now acting Commander in Chief, and Rusk's favorite younger brother, David.

The government made no attempt to prevent the Commander in Chief from boarding; they realized that at a gesture from him the troops were eager to take charge of the situation. However, with the authority of the Cabinet, the new Secretary of War, Lamar (now a close friend and adviser of President Burnet and already a candidate to succeed Houston as Commander in Chief) summoned Surgeon General Ewing and informed him that he was not authorized to leave the army to accompany General Houston. If he did so, he would be discharged from the service.

When Ewing reported this to Houston, the General responded, "I am sorry, my dear fellow, for I have nothing to promise you in the future, and you know I am poor, so you had better not incur the displeasure of the new Secretary of War."

But Ewing said that he would stick with the General. Later, after Ewing's dismissal from the army, Houston praised him as a "magnanimous man . . . [who] would not desert a friend . . . in the hour of need." [15]

On the morning of May 8 the *Yellow Stone* started toward Galveston. Undoubtedly Houston saw, as did many others, an incident that only Delgado reported:

259

As the steamboat passed opposite the battle-field of San Jacinto, the troops on board were formed, facing to the field, and presented arms, the drums beating a march. They remained in that position until they had lost sight of the field. What was their object?

Delgado could not fathom this spontaneous act of the troops. The troops had their General's word for it: they had won their country's independence, their place in history was assured, the ages would remember them. Without realizing that their victory, in terms of immediate decisiveness, would be honored in the annals of human warfare, they respected themselves for their part in a memorable event. This field which had witnessed their valor and in years to come would be the scene of many reunions inspired solemn reverence.

A panel on the memorial shaft at San Jacinto, taller than the Washington Monument because Texans willed it that way, tells the remarkable story with brevity, restraint, and accuracy:

> MEASURED BY ITS RESULTS, SAN JACINTO WAS ONE OF THE DECISIVE BATTLES OF THE WORLD. THE FREEDOM OF TEXAS FROM MEXICO WON HERE LED TO ANNEXATION AND TO THE MEXICAN WAR, RESULTING IN THE ACQUISITION BY THE UNITED STATES OF THE STATES OF TEXAS, NEW MEXICO, ARIZONA, NEVADA, CALIFORNIA, UTAH AND PARTS OF COLORADO, WYOMING, KANSAS AND OKLAHOMA. ALMOST ONE-THIRD OF THE PRESENT AREA OF THE AMERICAN NATION, NEARLY A MILLION SQUARE MILES OF TERRITORY, CHANGED SOVEREIGNTY.

In his *Memoir* (p. 135), Houston's own account of the battle closed with these words:

> On that well-fought field Texan Independence was won. It was not a struggle for the aggrandizement of some military chieftain—nor was it a strife for empire.... They were fighting for all that makes life worth living, or gives value to its possession....
> But the sublimity of the spectacle is lost, unless the eye has scope for a wider field of vision. There *are* events whose consequences can be measured by no estimate into whose calculation *centuries* do not come.

Houston realized early that San Jacinto and the independence of Texas were the prelude to a continental change of vast scope that would affect the world power balance. It was the beginning of the end of Mexican-Spanish dominion north of the Rio Grande.

In Galveston harbor, a government schooner, the *Liberty* (four guns; George Wheelwright, captain) was about to sail to New Orleans for repairs. Dr. Ewing applied to the government for passage for his patient. This request was refused. Granting the General permission to sail on a government vessel would have been the same as giving him permission to leave the country—an informal kind of furlough. The Cabinet preferred the General to appear to be leaving in defiance of the government. Plans had already formed to replace Houston as Commander in Chief with Secretary of War Lamar.

A small dirty American trading schooner, the *Flora*, was also in the harbor, about to sail for New Orleans. At Houston's request, her captain came to call on him aboard the *Yellow Stone*. Houston explained that he wanted passage for himself and his staff but, unfortunately, was unable to advance a dollar in payment because neither officers nor men of the Texas army had been paid during the campaign. Houston had given all the funds he carried to the widowed mothers and children of the Alamo defenders. The *Flora's* captain readily assented to deferred payment.

After the General moved to cramped quarters aboard the *Flora*, Dr. Ewing kept him in touch with developments on land. Soldiers who had fought with Houston, refugees who had gathered from all parts of Texas, and recently arrived volunteers from the States, held a meeting to discuss their future now that the war seemed to be over. Addressing this meeting, President Burnet made some indiscreet remarks that reflected on the character of the Commander in Chief. This was the beginning of a campaign of defamation in which Burnet and his allies participated more or less consistently for two decades with charges of cowardice, Indian orgies, opium eating, immorality, and drunkenness.

Infuriated, the veterans and refugees seemed to feel that a ride on a rail or a ducking in Galveston Bay would be appropriate for some members of the government. Houston took notice of these threats and disorders in an appeal which he addressed as special orders to the army and had posted in a prominent place in town:

The Commander-in-Chief, having in consequence of his wound retired from active duty for the present, earnestly requests that the troops now on Galveston Island, and those which may hereafter arrive, will cherish towards each other mutual confidence and respect, that they will render obedience to the commands of their officers, and that the strictest order and subordination may be be maintained. He has heard with regret that some dissatisfaction has existed in the army. If it is connected with him, or his circumstances, he asks as a special favor, that it may no longer exist.... Obedience to the constituted authorities and laws of the country is the first duty of a soldier. It will adorn his virtues and qualify him for the highest rights of citizenship.

The General in taking leave of his companions in arms, assures them of his affectionate gratitude, and enjoys an assured confidence that they will not neglect the advice of a fellow soldier, who will be proud to reunite with them, at the first moment when his situation will permit.[16]

The pledge of reunion filled the troops with elation. Burnet's government dropped the idea, for the time being, of ousting the General and making Lamar commander in chief.

When the *Liberty's* captain learned of the government's refusal to grant Houston passage on his ship, he invited the General to sail with him secretly. Houston felt obliged to refuse this offer because acceptance would be inconsistent with his own appeals for subordination and obedience to the civilian government. But the *Liberty's* captain seems to have had doubts about the seaworthiness of Captain Appleman's *Flora*. Even a government that refused its wounded General passage when in need of medical aid could hardly complain if the *Liberty*, in case of accident to the *Flora*, extended assistance.

When the leaky *Flora* put off on May 13, did the schooner *Liberty*—also leaky but in better condition than the *Flora*—serve as a convoy? The record does not show it and the government certainly did not authorize it; but it appears that both vessels left the harbor at about the same time and the *Liberty* may have been hovering in the distance with promise of rescue and survival for the feverish semi-delirious man of many pilgrimages who was now returning to his native land, a miserable and humiliated hero of world renown.

BOOK IV

A RULER OF VIKINGS

1. *Frustrating the Swashbucklers*

A FTER a stormy nine-day passage, the *Flora* docked at
New Orleans on Sunday, May 22, 1836. An expec-
tant crowd waited on the levee, alerted by a messenger from the
pilot house in the lower harbor. In New Orleans, as elsewhere, early
reports of the victory at San Jacinto were discredited. Then came
Houston's battle report and Santa Anna's statement that he was a
prisoner of war. Overnight Houston's military fame matched Jackson's.

For a month Houston had been "without medicines or poultices."
He was weak and gaunt from lack of food and, during the last days
of the voyage, he had fainted whenever he was moved. When the
Flora docked, Houston was lying on the open deck. Although he
was disturbed by semi-delirious fantasies, he was able to recognize
the voice of William Christy who had brought Doctors Kerr and
Cenas. The wounded General knew that he was among friends;
indeed so many people impetuously jumped aboard the little boat
that she listed. Captain Appleman begged them to leave before his
craft foundered.

An unsuccessful attempt was made to lift Houston to the dock;
the torture was unbearable for him. Then with a tremendous effort
of will he seized his crude crutches and got over the gunwale without assistance, standing up in view of the wildly cheering crowd. His
hair was matted, a tangle of beard framed his bloodshot eyes, his
leather jacket was in tatters, and part of a blood-stained shirt was

wound loosely around his ankle. As he lay down on the litter that Christy had brought, he lost consciousness.

Day after day anxious citizens gathered in front of Christy's home in Girod Street, eager for news of the General's condition. Houston's recovery was doubtful until Dr. Kerr removed numerous splinters of bone and drained the wound. Then the threat of gangrene abated and improvement was rapid. Twenty-one years before, this same surgeon, then in the U.S. Army, had removed the bullet that had prevented young Lieutenant Houston's Horseshoe Bend wound from healing.

As soon as reports of Houston's recovery circulated, citizens, who had already passed resolutions in his honor, offered a testimonial dinner. The General answered:

> My health at present would compel me to decline the generous offer of a public dinner. . . . I would consider that I should be wanting in proper respect for my adopted country, and the cause in which my fellow citizens are engaged, if I were to unite in any festive entertainments whilst Texas contains one individual hostile to her liberty; . . .[1]

Letters of congratulation poured in. One from United States Congressman Ben Currey, an intimate of President Jackson's White House circle:

> You are by Genl Jackson, Mr. Van Buren, Maj Lewis, Colo Earle etc ranked among the great men of the earth. . . . Hays is abusing you for not putting Santa Anna to death. . . . Genl Jackson says he is rejoiced at your prudence. . . .[2]

A letter from Jackson's own hand added a leaf to Houston's laurels. Houston had won a victory greater than the one at New Orleans; he had attacked but Jackson had stood on the defensive. Jackson said that he personally had contributed as much as he could spare to a fund being raised for Texas.

Vague reports of misbehavior in the army reached Houston. He feared that the fruits of a victory won by caution might be lost by rashness, but his anxiety to return to Texas was firmly curbed by Dr. Kerr. Then a rumor came that the provisional government was again planning to remove him from command. He contented himself with a letter to acting Secretary of War Lamar: "My wound has improved. Some twenty or more pieces of bone have been taken out of it. My general health seems to improve slowly. It is only within the last four or five days that I have been able to sit up any portion of the day." [3]

More bad news from Texas. Burnet's provisional government lacked firmness. There was wild talk, and some preparations were being made to invade Mexico. Matamoros again was the objective. Houston was convinced that his immediate return was imperative and set out for Texas despite the protests of Christy and the doctors.

On the journey up the Red River to Natchitoches, Louisiana, he suffered a setback; his wound began draining and his leg swelled. He sent word of his condition to his Nacogdoches friend, the youthful Dr. Irion, who arrived on June 26, cleaned and dressed the wound, and accompanied the General on horseback to San Augustine. There, as a guest of his old friend, Philip Sublett, Houston was obliged to undergo another period of convalescence.

On crutches, the General attended a Fourth of July barbecue and appealed for steadiness rather than haphazard adventures. Afterward he wrote friends that he was eager to get back to the army but could not do so without jeopardizing his life. He cautioned them not to let this become known; it would be better for discipline if the dissatisfied army continued to expect him in the near future.

Sources close to the provisional government charged that the General was skulking, that his wound was trifling, and that he was magnifying the extent of his injury for political purposes. The provisional government was on the move from day to day and little could be learned of its whereabouts or activities. The army, under temporary command of Thomas Rusk, was off somewhere near San Antonio.

At Velasco on May 14, Burnet's government had signed not one but two peace treaties with Santa Anna. One, at Santa Anna's insistence, was to be kept secret. It stipulated that the dictator, in behalf of Mexico, acknowledged the complete independence of Texas; the Rio Grande, from its mouth to its source, would be the boundary between the two countries. In turn, the provisional government pledged Santa Anna's immediate safe return to his own country so that he could try to persuade the Mexican Cabinet to ratify this secret treaty as well as another that was to be made public.

Under the terms of the public treaty, Santa Anna agreed not to take up arms against the Republic of Texas "during the present war for independence." All Mexican troops would be evacuated from Texas territory to the southern side of the Rio Grande. Thus, by implication the public treaty recognized the Rio Grande as the boundary and that the war between Texas and Mexico was over.

In making two treaties and insisting that one remain secret, Santa Anna was playing political poker. He knew that his commitment to recognize Texas independence would anger the Mexican people—hence the secrecy. On the other hand, he wanted to appease the Texans sufficiently to win his freedom and return to Mexico as soon as possible. Houston, at San Jacinto, had suggested the important terms in the treaties, including the boundary, in the memorandum he prepared for the government at Rusk's request. But returning Santa Anna to Mexico as soon as the treaties were signed was exactly the opposite of what he had recommended. He had stressed the importance of retaining Santa Anna and other officers as hostages until the treaty was recognized or ratified by the Mexican government.

On June 1, Santa Anna, Colonel Almonte, and several other Mexican officers were escorted aboard the Texas naval vessel, *Invincible*, for passage to Veracruz. Adverse winds detained the *Invincible* at anchor off Velasco for three days. On the third day the steamboat, *Ocean*, donated to Texas by the citizens of Mobile, arrived at Velasco with several hundred volunteers under the command of a North Carolinian, Thomas Jefferson Green. Another North Carolinian, Memucan Hunt, shared the command with Green.

Green claimed the rank of brigadier general for services in the Texas Revolution. According to the later testimony of General Houston, Green had never got near enough to the action actually to see an enemy. Anyhow, Green's behavior on this and later occasions gave him a bad name in Texas; he became known as "Dog" Green. As for Hunt, he was totally unfamiliar with conditions in the republic and probably had never before set foot on Texas soil.

On the day Green and Hunt landed, they and their disorderly followers joined a crowd in front of the house occupied by President Burnet to protest Santa Anna's return. Green and Hunt made inflammatory speeches and the crowd became a mob, shouting demands that Santa Anna be turned over to them. Burnet appeared and insisted that Santa Anna be returned to Mexico in conformity with the terms of a properly executed treaty. William Wharton and Attorney General Peter Grayson, one of the signers of the treaty, also defended the agreement and demanded that the faith of the nation be preserved. Wharton was especially bitter in denouncing interference with the government by members of the army and by strangers who had just come to Texas.

Undeterred, Green and his associates boarded the *Invincible* and demanded that Captain Jeremiah Brown turn Santa Anna over to them, but the captain refused to release him without a requisition from the government. Brown did agree that he would not sail on orders from the government but only on those from Green. Then, under pressure of the mob, Burnet signed a requisition authorizing a small armed force to bring Santa Anna ashore. According to evidence that Houston gathered later (and reported to the U. S. Senate), Green, with what he called his "brigade," boarded the *Invincible*, seized Santa Anna, showed him handcuffs, and made him shout, "Hurrah for Texas." [4]

Captain William H. Patton, a Tennesseean who had served with the rank of major as Houston's aide-de-camp at San Jacinto, commanded the force that was responsible for bringing Santa Anna ashore and protecting him from the mob. Patton landed the dictator at nearby Quintana and marched him and his aides through a menacing crowd to Velasco. A few days later, under orders from the provisional government, Patton took Santa Anna and his aides to Columbia, twenty miles up the Brazos. When a plot to poison Santa Anna was discovered, the dictator was moved twelve miles from Columbia and kept under protective custody.

Then, for reasons known only to themselves, members of the provisional government followed Santa Anna to Columbia. There, amid inadequate surroundings, they set up a capital.

Houston learned of these events while he was recuperating in San Augustine. He perceived that the independence and future peace of Texas had been jeopardized by the government's failure to retain Santa Anna and his entourage as hostages until the treaty pledges had been fulfilled. But, since the treaty had been formally executed, he publicly stated that its terms should be observed. He sharply criticized the behavior of the swashbucklers who had tried to kidnap Santa Anna and childishly demanded that he cry, "Hurrah

The Republic
of Texas
1836-1846

for Texas." Later, Houston censured the government for its lack of courage and resolution to control the mob.

The coming of Thomas Jefferson Green and his followers was the beginning of a new affliction for Texas. Theodore Roosevelt, in his *Life of Thomas Hart Benton*, maintained that the liberation of Texas was accomplished by men of the lawless, sea-roving Norsemen type—Vikings. But the cautious, meditative Houston was no Viking. The old settlers and their sons and the volunteers who extinguished Santa Anna's "streams of rolling fire" were not Vikings. Those who truly deserved the name were the reckless adventurers, thirsting for excitement and glory and greedy for spoils, who came swarming into Texas after the liberation.

What the country needed most was administrative ability—the firm sway of constitutional law, as Houston put it—and sound judgment in the conduct of its domestic and foreign affairs. The Vikings could not supply these things. They brought rashness, confusion, anarchy, and an infectious spirit of lawlessness. This lawlessness led to seditious activities by leaders of the army, pillaging by army volunteers, raids on peaceful settlers, the theft of government property on a large scale, and the defiance of court procedures.

Houston referred to the adventurers in this way: "All new States are infested, more or less, by a class of noisy, second-rate men, who are always in favor of rash and extreme measures. But Texas was absolutely overrun by such men. There seemed to be few of that class who give character to the institutions of new States, which spring suddenly into power,—men who are brave enough for any trial, wise enough for any emergency, and cool enough for any crisis." [5]

During most of the nine years that Texas existed as an independent constitutional republic, this spirit of insubordination and rashness was his biggest problem.

While in San Augustine, Houston was advised by Rusk that two insurgent army colonels were inciting the troops to demand that Santa Anna be tried and executed. Houston responded with a thundering appeal addressed to Rusk but written for the benefit of the army and the public:

> ... disregard if you will our national character and place what construction you please upon the rules of civilized warfare

we are compelled by every rule of humanity and morality, to abstain from any act of passion or inconsideration that is to be unproductive of positive good, execute Santa Anna and what will be the condition of the Texans, who are held as prisoners by the Mexicans? ... Doubtless torture will be added to the catastrophe ... Texas to be respected must be considered politic and just in her actions. ...

Looking to the future, he added:

The affairs of Texas connected with Genl Santa Anna ... have become matters of consideration to which the attention of the United States has been called ... for Texas, at this moment, to proceed to extreme measures ... would be treating that government with high disrespect and I will respectfully add, in my opinion it would be incurring the most unfortunate responsibility for Texas, I therefore, as commander in chief of the army of the Republic do solemnly protest against the trial sentence or execution of Genl Antonio Lopez de Santa Anna—President of the Republic of Mexico until the relation in which we are to stand to the United States shall be ascertained.[6]

This communication had its effect. The demand for revenge on Santa Anna, stimulated by the example of Thomas Jefferson Green and his followers at Velasco, was postponed. It was Houston's first success in countering disorders promoted by swashbucklers.

Stephen Austin shared Houston's concern for the reputation of Texas; he suggested to Santa Anna that he ask the President of the United States for aid in obtaining his release. The dictator readily complied. In a letter, Santa Anna assured President Jackson that he desired to return to his native land to assure recognition of Texan independence and to facilitate the annexation of Texas to the United States. Jackson disregarded the political questions and stressed the humanitarian aspects in a letter to Houston:

Nothing *now* could tarnish the character of Texas more than such an act [Santa Anna's proposed trial and execution] at this late period. It was good policy as well as humanity that spared him ... his person is still of much consequence to you. ... He is the pride of the Mexican soldiers and the favorite of the Priesthood and whilst he is in your power the priests will not furnish the supplies necessary for another campaign, nor will the regular soldier voluntarily march when their reentering Texas may endanger or cost their favorite Genl. his life, therefore preserve his life and the character you have won.[7]

Rusk reported to Houston that Mexican leaders contemplated a new invasion. Six thousand troops were said to have been collected at Veracruz, 4,000 at Matamoros. The Texas army needed supplies. Confusion prevails in the country, Rusk wrote. When would Houston place himself at the head of the troops? If his coming was long delayed, Rusk feared for the consequences of the grumbling that had laid hold of the soldiers.

With rumors of invasion sweeping the country, hundreds of citizens converged on San Augustine, apparently in the belief that Houston's presence somehow guaranteed their safety. Though Houston had declined a dinner in his honor, he did consent to attend a meeting to discuss the problem of defense, where he urged courage and firmness. During the next two days, inspired by his eloquent plea, 160 men organized as a military force and marched to the front.

Houston worried less about the Mexicans that he did about the noisy extremists from the States. Before his leg infection had healed, he undertook the thirty-mile ride to Nacogdoches, made himself as comfortable as he could in his old quarters, and again shared the bountiful table of his godfather and godmother, Adolphus and Eva Sterne. Now he was nearer to the capital at Columbia and could receive news from there more promptly.

Burnet was proving as weak in the conduct of government as he had been in dealing with the Velasco riots. His one plan for supplying an empty treasury was to sell land scrip in New York. Bids sank to one cent an acre. The plan was canceled, and Burnet had no substitute to offer.

Again the unpaid army became a prey to adventurers. Thomas Jefferson Green swaggered into camp, revived the Matamoros project, and boasted in a letter to Rusk that he intended to march immediately to burn the town, destroy anyone who resisted him, and retreat before the townspeople recovered from their panic.

Rusk's report to Houston on Green's activities seemed to suggest sympathy with the undertaking. Houston responded immediately with a vigorous lesson in the elements of grand strategy: caution

273

when one's position is weak. But weeks later he heard that the army was getting ready to move. This time he appealed directly to the army through the acting commander. He told the soldiers that he could see no reason for the Matamoros undertaking—"this mad, impolitic, and hazardous project"—which would repeat the error that had led to disasters at Goliad and the Alamo.[8]

His straightforward appeal halted the project for the moment. Burnet's authority collapsed; the army scoffed at his appeals for order. The refugees, gathered by thousands in camps on their way back to burned settlements and deserted ranches, derided official proclamations. Stealing and pillaging continued. Burnet charged that General Houston was fomenting this disorder to discredit him.

The measure that Burnet finally conceived for the solution of his problems was to send Secretary of War Lamar to replace Rusk in command of the army. Lamar went to the front and appealed to the men with fervent oratory. He assured them that the voice of man made generals but God alone made heroes. If the army did not desire him as commander, he would enter the ranks and lead the van to victory, guided by the flash of his sword.

Finally, Lamar told the men that he would not be content to take command without a visual demonstration that they desired him to assume the post. All those willing to accept him as commander were to march to the right; all others were to step to the left. Fifteen hundred men briskly stepped off to the left; 170 stepped to the right.

After this overwhelming disapproval, Lamar quit camp, and Houston's friend Rusk remained in command. Houston's letter to the army had achieved its purpose.

2. *From Commander to President*

PRESIDENT BURNETT called a general election under the Texas constitution for September 5, 1836. Stephen Austin promptly announced himself for the presidency, and Henry Smith, the man in the tight-buttoned coat who had served as governor under the Council, followed suit.

Smith was more popular with the army than Austin, who labored under a variety of criticisms—some of them unjustified. The one well-based charge concerned his ineptness as a military commander. But the charge that he had opposed Texas independence and had not done all that he could as a commissioner to win support from the United States, was unjustifiable and unworthy. Members of the army waited to hear from the Commander in Chief before making a decision and were disappointed when Houston did not announce himself.

Houston was in no hurry. He was familiar with the weakness of both candidates. From the sidelines in Nacogdoches he pondered the question: was either candidate capable of dominating the lawless adventurers in Texas and those who were swarming into it from across the Sabine? Could either man win the support of the opposing party in setting up and maintaining a government? He was afraid that the election of Austin or Smith would result in a continuation of the weakness and disorders that existed under the ad interim government.

Friends urged Houston to enter the contest. A petition with 600 names demanded that he serve. A handbill, widely circulated and reprinted in the *Telegraph and Texas Register* of August 3, 1838, asserted that "The people have a right to require the services of General Houston."

But Houston was not ready to declare himself. Instead he wrote Rusk saying that he realized Rusk was popular with the army, had few enemies, and had the ability to be president. After thinking it over for ten days, Rusk answered that he felt flattered Houston should think him worthy of the presidential chair, but his age precluded him from running. At thirty-three he was considerably younger than most of the men then prominent in Texas affairs.

Houston still waited. Undoubtedly he was attracted by the opportunity to lead a new nation through its early struggles, but he believed that his greatest usefulness might be with the army. As the Austin-versus-Smith campaign developed, he saw the matter in a new light. In a shrewdly reluctant letter "To a Gentleman of the Army"—Inspector General George Hockley—he announced his candidacy:

> You will learn that I have yielded to the wishes of my friends in allowing my name to be run for President. The crisis requires

it or I would not have yielded. Duty, I hope, will not always require this sacrifice of my repose and quiet.[1]

Years later Houston explained the reasons that finally prompted him to seek the Presidency:

> After the capture of Genl Santa Anna, I was compelled to go to New Orleans in the Month of May, for Surgical, as well as Medical aid. On my arrival I met a number of Texians there, and they requested me to become a candidate for the Presidency. This, I positively refused to do. From that time up to within fourteen days of the election, I refused to let my name be used. ... but there were two parties in Texas, known as the "Austin" and "Wharton Parties". . . . Govr Smith was the ostensible head of the "Wharton Party." So far as I could judge the parties were pretty equally balanced. In this posture of affairs, I was firmly impressed with the belief, that if either of the Gentlemen should be elected, it would be next to an impossibility to organize and sustain a Government, as whoever he might be, he would be compelled to fill all the offices with his own friends, and those of the opposite feelings, would of course, oppose the administration, which in the then condition of the country could only be sustained by the united efforts of the Community. Not being identified with either of the Parties, I believed, I would be enabled to consolidate the influence of both, by harmonizing them so as to form and sustain an administration, which would triumph over all these difficulties, attendent upon the outset of the Constitutional Government in Texas.[2]

Hockley posted copies of the letter he had received from Houston where the army could read it. The troops rejoiced. Throughout the settlements, Henry Raguet circulated many copies of the *Telegraph* that contained the General's letter. Ad interim President Burnet and Secretary of War Lamar resented the General's intrusion into politics. Henry Smith withdrew from the candidacy and supported Houston; he understood that the crisis required a man of strong personality to rule the Texans—later described by Theodore Roosevelt as a people whose "virtues and faults alike ... were those of a barbaric age."[3]

In the election, the people were to vote for a president, a vice-president, senators, and representatives. In addition, three questions were put to the voters: adoption of the constitution; authority of Congress to amend the constitution; and annexation to the United States.

Houston knew that the constitution was by no means a perfect or even sound document, although it has often been praised as comparable to the Constitution of the United States. Its defects were inevitable in view of the manner in which it was created. Leaders agreed generally that, with Texas threatened simultaneously by internal disorders and by invasion from Mexico, this was not the time to distract the public with a new convention to write a constitution.

The election of September 5, 1836, passed off without major incident except for the painful humiliation of Stephen Austin. Austin, who had remained in the campaign, received only 587 votes; Henry Smith, who had withdrawn, received 743. Houston was overwhelmingly elected President with 5,119 votes. Mirabeau Buonaparte Lamar was elected Vice-President. The constitution was adopted unanimously. Only 223 voters were willing to trust the Congress with the right of amendment, so this proposal failed. More than 6,000 favored annexation, and only 93 opposed it.

President-elect Houston immediately announced his Cabinet, which was chosen, he said, for two purposes: to get men of ability and to harmonize factions. He extended the olive branch to the Austin party by nominating Austin for Secretary of State, and to the Wharton party by calling Henry Smith to serve as Secretary of the Treasury. He made a gesture towards Burnet's following by naming James Collinsworth as Attorney General. He proposed Thomas Rusk for Secretary of War, and S. Rhodes Fisher for Secretary of the Navy.

Collinsworth announced that he would not serve under Houston, so the attorney general's post went to a young, rich, handsome, and able lawyer from North Carolina, James Pinckney Henderson. Houston greatly admired Henderson for his intelligence, ability, and passionate devotion to his adopted country. Austin, astonished and hurt by his small vote, at first declined to serve, protesting ill health. Houston ignored this protest, sent Austin's nomination to the Senate along with the others, and privately brought pressure to bear on Austin to change his mind. If Cabinet appointments, well distributed among the important factions could accomplish it, Texas was assured of a united effort to build a new nation.

The constitution specified that the President was to take office on the second Monday of December. But the "wise men," as Houston called the creators of the Texas constitution, had failed to set a date for convening the First Congress. Then, President Burnet called it for October 3, 1836, at Columbia, the new capital of the Republic. This meant that the constitutionally elected Congress would begin its functions while the ad interim President was still in office, creating policy complications during a time of crisis.

Lorenzo de Zavala, the fine-spirited Provisional Vice-President who was always ready to act for the stability and dignity of his adopted country, set an example by resigning on October 21. President Burnet followed the next day, and at 4 P.M. that same afternoon President-elect Houston was inaugurated.

Part of the ceremony took place at Columbia under a huge live oak—"the inauguration tree"—near two rough unfinished cabins that were to serve as meeting houses for the Senate and House. Rain drove the officials indoors, where the ceremony was completed around a blanket-covered table in an old store house.

Houston laid aside his crutches, but he still limped badly. He wore a new broadcloth suit, a fancy brocaded maroon waistcoat, and the sword that he had carried at San Jacinto. His upper lip, chin and cheeks were shaved clean; there were traces of close-cropped side-burns. His body was thin, his face lined, his bronze hair beginning to show gray; but his voice was mellow and resonant. He pleaded for cooperation and unanimity in the development of the country.

"Futurity," he said, "has locked up the destiny which awaits our people . . .

"A country like ours is environed with difficulties, its administration frought with perplexities.

"I shall confidently anticipate the establishment of Constitutional liberty."

Henry Raguet was in the audience, and William Christy, who had come from New Orleans to attend his friend's induction, was invited to sit with the retiring officers. Houston pointed to Christy, saying, "He was the first in the United States to respond to our cause. His purse was ever open . . . his presence among us . . . will inspire new efforts in behalf of our cause." Then Houston unfastened his sword and laid it on the table. "Should the danger of my country again call for my services I expect to resume it [the sword]."

His opponents long caricatured this gesture as a piece of Houstonian histrionics, but it appropriately contradicted their forecast that Houston, as President, would become a dictator. His gesture dramatized the needs of the country: tranquility and the end of military adventures.

Just before the close of his inaugural address, he referred to the fact that in the recent election the people "with a unanimity unparalleled," had declared their desire to be united with "the great Republican family of the North. The appeal is made by a willing people. Will our friends disregard it? They have already bestowed upon us their warmest sympathies. We are cheered by the hope that they will receive us." [4]

One able young man, Francis Lubbock, whose name was to become well known in Texas had left his bride in New Orleans while he went to attend Houston's inauguration. He was so impressed by the President's personality, manner, and speech that he hustled back to New Orleans and soon returned with his bride. He found Columbia filled with people. Lubbock ate with Fitchett and Gill, tavern keepers, and slept under the inaugural oak, "the lodging place of many." (Presumably his bride also enjoyed sleeping outdoors.) He felt himself part of a promising new world when he rubbed elbows on the street with the President, senators, representatives, military leaders, and many notables, including Stephen F. Austin, the Wharton brothers, Ed Burleson, Thomas Rusk, Albert Sidney Johnston, and Vice-President Lamar. Lubbock left a verbal portrait of the vice-president which enumerated these features: a man of French type; five feet seven inches tall; dark complexion, rather curly long black hair, and gray eyes; peculiar dress—"he wore his clothes very loose, pants very baggy with large pleats, looking odd as he was the only person in Texas who dressed in this style." [5]

Houston did not stand well with Lamar. The poet vice-president, who had been given his start in Texas when Houston promoted him for gallantry at San Jacinto, complained of the President's informal drinking and mingling with the masses.

Houston wrote to a friend that he came into office at a gloomy hour. The army had one day's supply of breadstuffs. The men, unpaid for months, were sullen, resentful, and in a state to follow the lead of agitators. The recent recruits were the most bitter and uncontrollable; they wanted their pay and they wanted Santa Anna to be tried and executed or executed without trial. The treasury was empty and the Republic had no credit. The public debt contracted during the revolution amounted to $1,250,000. Two Texas war vessels, *Invincible* and *Brutus*, were detained in New York because Treasurer Smith was unable to pay their repair bills, and there was not enough petty cash to buy stationery for the President and the Cabinet. Accommodations for members of the government were so lacking that business could not proceed "unless Congress will adjourn to some point, where ... greater conveniences can be speedily obtained." [6]

The Senate and the House each had a rough unfinished shack for their sessions. Local families had promised to lend chairs and tables from their own houses to Congress, but the families were still sitting in the chairs and eating at the tables, so the members fashioned crude substitutes. Twenty-seven rooms in ten houses had been pledged for the use of congressmen and government officers, but these pledges were unredeemed, and since most of the rooms were still occupied, the government leaders slept in blankets on the rough board tables and floors of their meeting rooms. In good weather some preferred to sleep on the ground under the inauguration oak.

A one-room office with a small fireplace in the home of a settler was provided for the President. At Mrs. Sledge's, his meals of milk and bacon were plentiful—at times—although his teeth were strong and he would have enjoyed tough fried beef. For the duties of his office, he lacked the most necessary facilities. He did not have and never would have an authentic copy of the constitution. The government archives consisted of a lot of loose papers which had been tossed into an old trunk. The two vital treaties signed at Velasco were missing until a search turned them up.

The President was obliged to delay signing his first batch of commissions for want of a pen. He used a cuff link for an official seal. The terrible stringency was relieved somewhat when the Congress granted him authority to borrow $50,000 from a patriotic commercial firm, McKinney and Williams, which had already advanced unsecured funds to the provisional government for three times that amount.

3. Unorthodox Diplomacy

HOUSTON clearly saw the appalling situation of a country that existed somewhere in the background of the family of nations. With his customary keen analysis he separated the problem into essentials. At the top of his list he placed recognition by the United States. But he could hardly ask recognition for a country whose boundaries were unknown. One of the first things he did was to prepare a bill declaring the Texas boundary to be that which he had recommended in his battlefield memorandum to Burnet and which had been adopted by the Treaty of Velasco: the Rio Grande from its mouth to its source and thence northeast to the boundary of the United States.[1] Congress ratified the bill and Texas became a nation with definite boundaries—if it could maintain them.

The President's next move was an attempt to honor the Velasco Treaty, even though he disapproved of it, and to return Santa Anna to Mexico. Texas could not afford to deny the terms of the treaty. Houston asked the Senate for approval to release Santa Anna and his aide, Colonel Almonte.

President Houston informed the Senate of his belief that the Texas climate and Santa Anna's present mode of life as a prisoner were so different from those to which he was accustomed that he feared the general might "die within the present season" and if he did, "Would Texas, as a people, escape the imputation of having poisoned him? Or may not some rash person (as has been attempted) take his life by violence?" In that case "Texas would experience the moral effect of such an occurrence." Santa Anna could not properly be held as a hostage for fulfillment of the Velasco Treaty because the treaty provided for his release.[2]

But the Senate was dominated by those who wanted Santa Anna executed, and passed a resolution directing the President not to

281

release the Mexican without the advice and consent of the Senate. In a second message Houston stated his reasons for not being able to concur in the Senate's resolution. He had hoped for the Senate's participation in Santa Anna's release as an "exhibit to the world" that Texas had "a civil and not a military Government." But the Senate's response to his request, he felt, put improper restraint upon his "executive functions." He argued that the sweeping powers given him as Commander in Chief by the Washington Convention authorized him to deal with a prisoner who had been captured in the field. This, he reasoned, gave him exclusive authority over the final disposition of the prisoner.[3]

This message actually explained action that Houston had already taken. He had withheld it long enough to accomplish Santa Anna's release without risking interference from the unruly Vikings.

Houston had written Jackson that he might have doubted the wisdom of releasing Santa Anna except that his Old Chief had urged it. He may have been influenced by his desire to persuade Jackson to recognize Texas. Actually, Houston now believed that, if Santa Anna returned to Mexico, he might keep that unhappy country in commotion for years and impede rather than accelerate an attempt to reconquer Texas. However, he considered the national faith committed beyond question by the Velasco Treaty to the Mexican president's release. Santa Anna might be seized and executed at any minute by a band of roving adventurers; the result would be a lasting stain on Texas. A way must be found to get him out of the country safely.

A discreet exchange of letters between Jackson and Houston produced an unorthodox solution. The President of the United States would assist the President of Texas to rid his country of the President of Mexico. The first step in this plan called for sending Santa Anna to Washington to meet with Jackson at the President's House.[4]

Preparations to get Santa Anna on his way were conducted secretly. Houston presented him with a fine horse for the journey. Then he placed him in the custody of three trusted men: Colonel Hockley, Colonel Barnard Bee, and Major Patton, who twice before had saved the prisoner's life from threatening mobs.

Before the cavalcade quietly departed for Washington, D. C.,

President Houston gave Santa Anna a letter of introduction to Jackson.

> The distinction, and character of Genl Santa Anna will super-
> cede the necessity of my saying anything in his favor ... as his
> reputation is a portion of the history of mankind! As an in-
> dividual, I claim leave to recommend him to your manly, and
> generous regard. ... [5]

To reveal his true intent, Houston gave Hockley two more letters to take to Washington. One, addressed to Jackson, was not to be seen by Santa Anna; the other was to be delivered to the Mexican minister. In the confidential letter to Jackson, Houston said:

> My great desire is that our country Texas shall be annexed to
> the United States. ... It is policy to hold out the idea (and
> few there are who Know to the contrary) that we are very able
> to sustain ourselves against any power who are not impotent,
> yet I am free to say *to you* that we cannot do it. Do not under-
> stand me as yielding to any unfounded apprehensions in behalf
> of Texas—
> Whenever I see that the crisis has arrived I will repair to the
> van of danger and show to the world that I can act and fall
> as a man.
> Your wishes are regarded by every patriot in Texas, and did
> I not believe by liberating Santa Anna I was acting in accord-
> ance with your wishes I might distrust the measure. ...
> To you, Sir, I confide the course and the measures so far as
> may be in your power of making a free and happy people I hope
> with our kindred people of the United States. ... [6]

This was Houston's first appeal since his inaugural address for the annexation of Texas by the United States. With reason, he believed that Santa Anna's release would influence Jackson toward granting recognition, which was the first step toward annexation.

In his letter to the Mexican minister, Houston offered advice about how Santa Anna should conduct himself during negotiations with President Jackson: "In all cases ... let him assume the style of a President, and head of the Mexican Republic." Houston suggested that the dictator, before presenting himself at the White House, write President Jackson "an official letter ... such as Diplomacy requires ... a confidential official letter to General Jackson assuring him that he is willing to countenance or to contribute to the annexation of Texas to the U. States . . . if this is done at the instance of General Santa Anna, General Jackson can be induced to furnish a national vessel of the U. S. for Genl. Santa Anna to sail in [for] the Coast of Vera Cruz. . . ." [7]

A ship to take Santa Anna home in style without having him touch Texas soil again was part of the unorthodox solution.

On the way to Washington, Barnard Bee provided Santa Anna with money to buy suitable clothes. The blood-stained tyrant was beautifully attired when he went to dinner at the President's House. His appearance bore out Houston's description of the fallen dictator —his "fine face—a rather long, but well shaped head—black hair and eyes, and a *perfect form*—he is about five feet and eight or nine inches high—his elocution is rich, and characterized by considerable fire—his eye is quick but firm, and his manners and address are worthy of a prince." [8]

At dinner, Santa Anna made a good impression. He talked fast, saying what he knew would be agreeable to Jackson. He conceded that Mexico could never conquer Texas; if Mexico succeeded in overrunning it she "could not hold it without standing garrisons of twenty thousand soldiers," which his country could not support even if raised. Santa Anna assured Jackson that the invasion of Texas now threatened by Generals Urrea and Bustamante would "end in smoke." If returned to Mexico, Santa Anna would immediately put a stop to the proposed invasion. He would show the world that what he had promised in captivity in Texas he would fulfill in the capital of his nation.

The talks between Jackson and Santa Anna were "secret," but each reported them in detail to William Wharton, one of the Texas agents in Washington. Wharton reported them to the Texas government at Columbia, and observed:

> I thought he [Santa Anna] took a sound view of the matter, at least, it corresponded with my own. How far, he was candid and sincere, you are as well able to judge as myself.

At the conclusion of his report to Wharton, Santa Anna remarked that the United States had "an overflowing treasury, about which, there was much debate and squabbling. . . ." He hoped that Wharton would not raise obstacles to obtaining "a few millions" from the government of the United States for a quit claim to Texas. This would enable him to make a treaty satisfactory to Mexico, "securing at once and forever, the independence of Texas, or her annexation to the United States...." [9]

President Jackson, never deceived by the smoothness of the Alamo-Goliad butcher, cooperated in all except the payment to the Mexican's treasury. He had Santa Anna escorted to Norfolk, Va., and installed in comfortable quarters aboard the *Pioneer*, a United States naval vessel bound for Veracruz. This completed one of the most extraordinary diplomatic actions in history: a defeated dictator was escorted by his conquerors on a long journey to negotiate with the head of a powerful neutral state who, in turn, at the request of the conquerors, sent the ruthless tyrant home with honors.

4. *War between the Brigadiers*

AFTER Santa Anna departed from Texas, Houston turned to countless pressing problems. He obtained authorization from Congress for a $5,000,000 bond issue and sent agents to the United States to place it. With the assistance of Secretary of War Rusk he worked out detailed instructions for militia officers in case Mexico followed up her unceasing threats of renewed hostilities. He dislodged from the payroll so many useless officials inherited from the ad interim government that he aroused the enmity of their friends in Congress. He drove his Cabinet to work day and night to build up their departments.

Some contractors were cheating on supplies to the army. Houston made war on them by issuing a set of forty stringent regulations for department heads, auditors, commanders, and government agents, thus plugging so many loopholes that he let himself in for heavy criticism. The contractors charged that "Old Sam" was aiming at a dictatorship and interpreted the regulations that frustrated profiteering as a sign that his reign had begun.

Disturbing news came from the army on the frontier. President

Houston had relieved General Rusk of his army command so that he could serve as Secretary of War. He had assigned Felix Huston to succeed Rusk temporarily with rank of brigadier general until a permanent appointment could be made. This assignment seemed a "natural." Huston, a Kentucky lawyer in his late thirties, had rushed to Texas in 1835, given considerable service to the cause, and contributed $40,000 to raise and equip a company that fought at San Jacinto, although he had not been there himself. He was a tall, handsome, blond daredevil whose fiery eloquence ignited his followers. A cast in one of his gray-blue eyes gave him a mysterious expression and he had a compelling fascination for the troops.

But Houston learned that his new brigadier general was reviving Dr. Grant's old dream of seizing and pillaging Matamoros. Huston was promising the troops victory and unlimited spoils if they would march with him to the Rio Grande; first they would march to Columbia and sink the "do-nothing Houston government"—the President and the Congress—in the Brazos River. In Huston's insurrectionary activities, President Houston saw a threat that had to be dealt with promptly. He appointed a senior brigadier, Albert Sidney Johnston, and sent him to take over Huston's command. Huston was designated junior brigadier. Johnston, it seemed, was another "natural." Graduated with honors from West Point, he had resigned from the United States Army in deference to the wishes of his young wife; after her death, he had joined the Texas revolutionists to fight as a private.

Johnston presented his orders to the junior brigadier. Huston's pride and honor were wounded. He denounced his newly appointed superior, President Houston, and the Texas Senate with abusive language. He refused to yield the command and challenged Johnston to a duel. Instead of arresting his subordinate, as he should have done, Johnston felt that honor compelled him to fight. In a chivalrously punctilious battle, on February 7, 1837, beside the LaVaca River, the warring brigadiers exchanged five shots before Johnston fell. He was seriously wounded. The repentant Huston rushed to him, expressed regret, acknowledged him as his superior, and promised loyalty. He soon violated his pledge; Huston was a Viking who could tolerate no superior.

Writing to Albert Sidney Johnston, he expressed mortification and regret over the duel, urging Johnston to maintain harmony in camp and by all means to prevent dueling in future. He sent two doctors and medicines for Johnston, but before the senior brigadier was able to resume his duties the President was informed that drunken troops were pilfering and interfering with citizens in San Antonio. Brusquely, Houston ordered that all such infractions of discipline be stopped forthwith and commanded in most positive terms that all ardent spirits in San Antonio should be instantly destroyed and spilled on the ground.

Shortly thereafter, disturbed by reports of inadequate and lackadaisical guards, he informed Johnston that he suffered from intense anxiety and would continue to do so until the country was tranquil. While it appeared that Mexico was not in a condition to make good her current threats to invade and conquer Texas, Houston warned Johnston that he must at all times remain on the alert.

For the moment, Houston's duties at the capital prevented him from visiting the army. He was hastening the organization of mail routes; feed for the post horses was hard to get and he had to arrange for credit by giving his personal guarantee. He was conferring with Attorney General Henderson about setting up a judicial system and choosing a chief justice, judges, and officials for each of twenty-three counties. With Secretary of State Stephen Austin he was working on instructions for the Texas agents in Washington, D. C., regarding tactics to be employed in pressing for recognition—or preferably annexation—by the Jackson administration. As soon as these various matters had developed to the point where they did not demand his hourly attention, he went to the army, making his appearance suddenly and unannounced.

Old-timers from the San Jacinto campaign affectionately crowded around Houston. They took his horse by the bridle and touched the rider as they had done when returning from the victorious battle. The President visited the hospital and reviewed the army, talking to the men like a devoted father. His voice soared out over the ranks as he assured both veterans and recruits that the eyes of the world were upon them. Their nation was taking definite form. He urged them to remain sober and not to let themselves be inspired to an injudicious march for plunder and spoils. They should subordinate themselves to the will of the civil government. In this way they would disprove calumnies that were spreading abroad against

Texas. They had a great responsibility. He wanted their promise—no wild, fantastic schemes, no long marches, no invasion of Mexico until their old commander saw fit to lead them.

They cheered the prospect of Houston taking command. He told them that he accepted their response as a promise. Then, alone with Junior Brigadier Huston, he settled the matter of command. He wanted it understood that the junior brigadier was subordinate to the senior brigadier. Huston shrugged, screwed up his mouth, and looked sidewise out of his eye with the cast. His whole manner deprecated this idea. He said the senior brigadier was not in condition to command. Houston declared that the senior brigadier would not be superseded at this time by the junior brigadier. For the moment, he felt obliged to leave the matter there.

He returned to Columbia, meditating upon the best method of getting rid of the insubordinate junior brigadier without disrupting the army. When he arrived, Houston learned that Secretary of War Rusk was favorably disposed toward Huston's plan for a "campaign of conquest." He made known his displeasure and accepted Rusk's resignation.

As Rusk's successor, he chose William S. Fisher, a Virginian, who had settled in Gonzales before the revolution and had organized a company that had joined General Houston's retreating army on the Colorado River. An adventurer, secretly eager for a filibuster against Mexico, Fisher outwardly subscribed to the administration's cautious military policy of remaining on the defense without rashly provoking Mexico.

Although hostilities between Texas and Mexico were suspended, with the exception of sporadic border raids, peace had not been agreed upon. Mexican leaders continued to threaten an invasion to terminate the short life of the Republic. But President Houston confided to Secretary of War Fisher his belief that action by Mexico was less inimical to the safety of Texas than the disorderly excesses of the country's own unruly elements.

One of these elements was Junior Brigadier Huston, who was still plotting to seize the army and invade northern Mexico. The President, attending to many urgent duties, kept an eye on him, figuring out when and how it would be possible to get rid of him. Huston had acquired such power with the army that his abrupt removal might call for a show of strength. The President wanted to avoid this, so he left matters as they were while he planned his strategy with care.

The close and friendly cooperation of the President and Austin— the man who had been humiliatingly rejected for the top office— excited the admiration of observers. Houston and Secretary of State Austin agreed that recognition by the United States, a first step toward annexation, should be the keystone of Texas foreign policy. With Houston's concurrence, Austin had given William H. Wharton and Memucan Hunt official status as Texas diplomatic agents in Washington, D. C. The President was in constant conference with his Secretary of State and he closely followed reports that came from Wharton and Hunt.

Recognition proved to be a far more ticklish question than Houston had anticipated. Many in the United States assumed that it would be followed inevitably by annexation. Within a week after news of the San Jacinto victory reached Washington, John C. Calhoun had taken the floor in the United States Senate to speak in favor of recognition. It was generally suspected that the South Carolinian's purpose was to encourage the acquisition of new slave-holding territory; at least that was how his remarks were interpreted in the North, particularly in New England. Consequently, great pressure was exerted upon President Jackson to withhold recognition.

Wharton's first report reflected the violent division of opinion in the United States. Before Jackson had shown the slightest inclination to grant recognition, John Quincy Adams, a former President and now a congressman from Massachusetts, denounced him for conspiring to bring it about. Adams went even further, charging Jackson with a "conspiracy" to force the United States into the Texas-Mexican war in the interest of slave holders. Reporting this, Wharton remarked that the North would greet Adams' charge "with a universal shout of applause." Another Wharton dispatch ended on a less discouraging note.

The Northern Abolitionists and fanaticks will of course always oppose annexation.... [but] When the North has ... lost her political ascendency she will not object to indefinite extension of the agricultural interest of the south and West.... .

I believe that this Union will dissolve should the North obstinately oppose the annexation of Texas. . . .[1]

Southerners were as ready as the Northern extremists to stake the fate of the nation on the Texas issue.

Another dispatch from Wharton disclosed to the harassed President on the Brazos that his Old Chief on the Potomac was indeed in hot water over the question of recognition. Already recognition was tied not only to annexation but also to slavery. Wharton reported what Jackson believed must be done to help override the objections of the North before Texans could seriously hope for recognition:

> Genl. Jackson says that Texas must claim the Californias on the Pacific in order to paralyze the opposition of the North and East to Annexation. That the fishing industry of the North and East wish a harbour on the Pacific; that this claim of the Californias will give it to them and will diminish their opposition to annexation. He is . . . anxious on this point . . . and says we must not consent to less. This is in strict confidence.[2]

Like the Texas President, Secretary of State Austin had official quarters in a half-open, two-room clapboard shack which lacked windows and shutters and was heated by a small fireplace. Unwell, he did what he could to keep the affairs of his office in good order. His last important duties were to send instructions to Wharton and to draft a proclamation against the slave trade.

On Christmas Eve, 1836, he worked over his papers, felt chilled, and went out into the raw, bitter night for a brisk walk along the town's muddy street. He saw the candlelit windows of the log cabins and the Christmas greens on the doors and heard sleigh bells and carols. Without wife or family, he may have been consoled by the knowledge that Texas had achieved a kind of independence even if peace was unstable. When he returned to his cabin, his teeth were chattering.

On Christmas Day, Austin's Negro servant called in Dr. Phelps. Delirious and suffering from pneumonia, Austin held out until December 27 when, at forty-three years of age, he died on a pallet on the floor. Up to the day of his death, dispatches from Texas agents in Washington had contained hardly a line of encouragement about the outlook for recognition, but during a moment of consciousness Austin had said, "Texas recognized. Archer told me so. Did you see it in the papers?" [3]

His admirers grieved that he did not live to reap the deserved fruits of a harvest sowed with unremitting selflessness and loyalty. His biographer has proposed that words he wrote a short time before his death should be his epitaph: "The prosperity of Texas has been the object of my labors, the idol of my existence. It has assumed the character of a *religion*, for the guidance of my thoughts and actions for fifteen years." [4]

With heavy heart, President Houston issued General Orders for mourning to the army, the navy, and the people:

> The father of Texas is no more. The first pioneer of the wilderness has departed. General Stephen F. Austin, Secretary of State, expired this day at half past twelve o'clock at Columbia.[5]

He directed commanding officers to fire twenty-three guns, one for each county in the Republic, as soon as they received his order. Then the President and his Cabinet went down the Brazos River aboard the old *Yellow Stone* and crossed to the home of James Perry, the second husband of Austin's beloved sister Emily. They stood beside the rough casket in a little Presbyterian church where Austin, born a Catholic, was buried in a tomb of homemade bricks.

5. *Two Sides of Recognition*

HOUSTON returned to Columbia a lonelier man for the loss of one whose true worth he had come to appreciate. It was the second tragic loss for the Republic within six weeks. The preceding November, Lorenzo de Zavala, who had served as vice-president of the provisional government, had capsized in a rowboat and drowned while crossing the flooded Buffalo Bayou.

Now Houston called back into service the man he had removed from office because of a disagreement about military policy. Thomas Rusk briefly succeeded Austin as secretary of state. He did the paper work; Houston gave the instructions. The President frequently consulted his shrewd Attorney General, J. Pinckney Henderson, on strategy regarding recognition and annexation. The wealthy North Carolinian, who had abandoned a thriving legal practice to throw in his lot with Texas, was deeply devoted to his adopted country. Houston pondered how he could put Henderson's devotion to best use. Anticipating that Henderson would be useful as a representative in Europe, Houston appointed him Acting Secretary of State in December, 1836.

Wharton's latest dispatch showed that he still did not know of Austin's death and that he had felt cut off from communication and proper instructions during the months when Austin's health was failing. In his bitter complaint Wharton uttered a prophecy that already had been fulfilled:

> Not a line from home up to this date. How long must this continue to be the beginning, middle and end of my communications? How long must I be compelled to suffer the great embarrassment which this silence of the grave inflicts upon me![1]

With Rusk and Henderson, Houston picked up the recognition problem where Austin had left it. They reviewed Wharton's discouraging dispatches. Even friends of Texas opposed annexation, Wharton reported, but they did so on entirely different grounds from those that influenced the abolitionists. Some Southerners believed that a "destiny brighter than annexation" awaited Texas, and Wharton said that Southern radicals were not thinking of Texas as an independent country or as a state within the Federal Union but as a member of a Southern slave-holding confederacy to rise on the ruins of a dismembered Union.

This kind of talk was not to President Houston's liking, but it was one of the many inescapable complexities of the recognition-annexation question. He feared that agitation by the advocates of discordant viewpoints would darken the outlook for early action by President Jackson. Another dispatch, heavy with portent, came from Wharton, dated December 11, 1836.

> Already has the war ... violently commenced even on the prospect of annexation. The Southern papers those in favor of the measure are acting most imprudently.... Language such as

the following is uttered by the most respectable journals.... The North must choose between the Union with Texas added— or no Union. Texas will be added, and then forever farewell abolitionism and northern influence. Threats and denunciations like these will goad the North into a determined opposition and if Texas is annexed at all it will not be until after the question has convulsed the nation for several sessions of Congress.[2]

The President and his advisers anxiously awaited every scrap of information from Washington, D. C. Dispatches were delayed or sometimes arrived before ones sent earlier. They came by special courier, but the couriers might take sick or dally on the way.

Angry and bewildered, Wharton commented on a message President Jackson had sent to Congress including the statement: "Recognition [of the independence of the Texas Republic] at this time ... would scarcely be regarded as consistent with the prudent reserve with which we have heretofore held ourselves bound to treat all similar questions."[3]

Wharton, in dealing with President Jackson, was already bearing down heavily on the commercial advantages that the United States would lose by failing to grant recognition. Jackson was also being reminded that, if the United States continued to hold off, Texas must naturally turn to England for friendliness and assistance. Such suggestions were in accord with Houston's desire, and he gave Wharton positive instructions so that the agent could work effectively.

Houston knew that the domestic political situation had a good deal to do with Jackson's apparent reluctance to grant recognition. This knowledge was borne out by another dispatch from Wharton, who reported that Secretary of State John Forsyth had told him that the abolitionists were embarrassing the administration. It would be better, Forsyth said, if a Northern President took responsibility for recognition.[4]

Wharton reminded President Jackson that if he adhered to this policy he would be deprived of the glory of granting recognition and that Van Buren would garner it. Jackson was sick and tired and was not remotely moved by the prospects of losing the glory. He declared that it was a matter for Congress, but Wharton would not be diverted. Congress would not act without a special message, he suggested.

Jackson was averse to sending a special message. Wharton pursued the matter. To his colleagues on the Brazos he reported the ensuing conversation. Houston and Henderson read it together and with immense relish, surprised by Wharton's aggressiveness and daring. He pulled no punches:

> I told him [President Jackson] that his message had done us as much injury as he could possibly do us unless he were to unite his arms with Mexico and invade us. That it struck at the root of our credit. That without recognition we were begging off our public lands with great difficulty at fifty cents per acre, that with it we could dispose of any quantity at one dollar per acre. That we could get what supplies we wanted, build vessels, etc etc, with recognition. That we could immediately negotiate our 5 millions loan etc That he was mistaken in supposing that a delay to recognize would do neither party any harm. Of course it would do Mexico no harm, it would please and animate her. That the Mexicans would have his message printed on Satin and circulated through all the Country ... That nothing but God himself could defeat our ultimate independence, but that his message would make our road to the attainment of it longer and more thorny.

This was hair-raising stuff, even for the sturdy men on the Brazos. Eagerly they read on:

> ... He [Jackson] became as I was convinced dissatisfied with the position in which his message placed both him and Texas. My object was to obtain his assent to a move in Congress by his friends recommending to him the immediate recognition of our independence. In this I have succeeded.... He said ... he doubted the power of the President to recognize of himself he wished the sense of Congress on the subject and would immediately concur if a majority recommended it. This was all I wanted. His friends will move on the subject during the coming week.... [5]

Wharton saw to it that Jackson's friends in Congress moved fast. But their move, though helpful, was not quite in the manner that Jackson had suggested. Congress inserted an item in a general appropriation bill providing a salary for and expenses of an "outfit" for "a diplomatic agent to be sent to Texas when the Executive is satisfied of her independence." This passed the buck back to Jackson.

In Texas, the grass was rising and trees were leafing; warm March days and spring brought hope. Good news came in another dispatch from Washington. On March 3, one day before he ceased to be President, Jackson, already packed to return to Nashville as soon as he had turned over the office to Martin Van Buren, had invited Wharton and Hunt to the White House for a glass of wine. When they arrived, he referred to the congressional authorization to appoint a chargé d'affaires to Texas whenever he was satisfied about Texas' independence. Jackson told Wharton he regarded the authorization as a "virtual decision of the matter," making it his duty to "acquiesce."

"Gentlemen," the President said, rising. "I have the honor to announce that I have sent to the Senate the nomination of Alcee La Branche, of Louisiana to be chargé d'affaires of the Republic of Texas." He proposed a toast to the independence of Texas, and, thrilled, Wharton and Hunt drank to it. At last the Republic had gained recognition.[6]

The bells tolled in Texas, but dolefully. Texas wanted to be let in, and the door was not ajar. Recognition without annexation came as hope deferred—a bitter pill.

President Houston wrote to Henry Raguet without excitement or jubilation that Texas was recognized as a nation. To Dr. Irion he sent a scribbled note that was slightly less restrained:

... You will have learned that we are Independent, and recognized by the U. States ... the last official act of Gen'l Jackson's life. This alone is a cause for joy, but annexation wou'd have rendered me truly happy, and secured all that we contended for. My only wish is to see the country happy—at peace and retire to the Red Lands, get a fair, sweet "wee wifie" as Burns says, and pass the balance of my sinful life in ease and comfort (if I can).

... My health, under your Esculapian auspices, thank God, is restored, and my habits good....[7]

Houston was grateful, but not elated. He had not really anticipated that annexation would accompany recognition, although he had

295

asked and hoped for it. In April, 1834, while on a visit to Washington, D. C., he had written to James Prentiss, "You need not hope for the acquisition by this Government of Texas during the Administration of Genl. Jackson. If it were acquired by a Treaty, that Treaty would not be ratified by the present Senate. Texas will be bound to do for herself...." [8]

Just the same he was saddened. The day came when he wrote that he and Jackson had been lifelong friends but the Old Chief had never been able to do anything for him.

That competent observer, Colonel William Fairfax Gray, who had reported the Washington-on-the-Brazos Convention for New Orleans sponsors, happened to be in Texas when the epochal but disillusioning recognition news arrived. He recorded:

> ... recognition does not give much pleasure to President and Cabinet of Texas. All persons are disappointed. Their hopes have been so highly raised of a speedy annexation ... that they can't at once be reconciled to the new state of things presented by recognition. Texas independent, and compelled to fight her own battles and pay her own debts, will necessarily have to impose heavy burdens [on] her citizens. [9]

Another contemporary Texas observer, John Ford, agreed that failure to win annexation was a painful blow because Texas finances were in bad condition, the treasury was empty, and it would be difficult to keep the army in the field and the little Texas navy afloat.

President Houston's days were fuller and his responsibility more burdensome. If Texas hoped eventually to achieve annexation, her first step must be to meet the requirements of her new independent status. This would tax her self-restraint and require the development of a stable national character. Was she equal to it? Could Houston hold in check the aggressive adventurers who were eager to displace him? He was still pondering strategy to get rid of the junior brigadier.

6. *Boom Town Capital*

In an early message to Congress the new President warned that the complicated business of nation building could not be carried on efficiently under the existing conditions in Columbia. Many members of the government were sick and some had died. Good men were quitting because of their wretched accommodations. Houston asked for immediate action on choosing a permanent site for the capital. He favored Groce's Landing, although he did not mention it in his message and never pressed for it.

The Congress was slow to act on his recommendation, but the slack was taken up by a firm of enterprising real estate promoters and speculators. The energetic Allen brothers, Augustus C. and John K., had recently arrived from the United States and bought some four thousand acres on Buffalo Bayou. It was an eligible location at the head of navigation on the bayou and near the battlefield of San Jacinto. Otherwise, it was a wild and desolate stretch of badly drained prairie and alligator-infested swampland with the usual abundance of mud and mosquitoes. The Allen brothers engaged youthful Gail and Thomas Borden to develop an impressive map showing a city of sixty-two square blocks and a public square set aside for an imposing capitol building.

They proposed to call this community-on-paper Houston City in honor of their renowned President. The promoters agreed to erect the capitol at nominal cost with the understanding that it would revert to them and their heirs if Houston City ever ceased to be the capital. As promoters will, they promised to have the capitol and adequate housing ready at an early date, by May 1, in about five months.

Congress adopted the Allen plan and moved that the next session, following the December adjournment, should meet in the new capital on May 1. It occurred to the President that the Congress was hazardously relying on the promise of real estate promoters, but the Allens were charming fellows, and Houston already had had too many conflicts to oppose Congress unless compelled to do so.

On January 20, 1837, prompted by natural curiosity about the city that would bear his name and by concern over its being ready when promised, he visited the site. The progress that he beheld was stupendously short of what the promoters had promised. He saw three small log cabins, one saloon, and a dozen persons who, like himself, were just looking things over.

He was too busy with government affairs to check on the capital's progress again before he left Columbia for good in mid-April and went to Houston City, stopping first at Harrisburg, which was twelve miles from the new capital by the narrow, winding, log-obstructed bayou, or six miles by muddy roads. Mosely Baker, Francis Lubbock, and their wives were his fellow passengers in the rowboat that took him on to Houston City. Baker was the difficult army captain whose rebellious activities Houston had checkmated on the long retreat. Young Lubbock and his wife by now had settled themselves permanently in this exciting new country.

This time a busy, stirring scene greeted the President in Houston City. There were two stores and six saloons. Streets had been laid out and named; they were wide and handsome, though deep with mud, watered by undrained rivulets, and paved with stumps. Forty cabins lined these thoroughfares. The square walls of a two-story capitol had been erected, but the building still lacked a roof. One story of Ben Fort Smith's City Hotel (planned for two stories) presented a hopeful aspect on Franklin Avenue between Main and Travis Streets. The most amazing thing of all was the increase in population. Attracted by the skillful advertising of the Allen brothers and their glowing promises, nearly five hundred people had come to find permanent homes in this city that had forty cabins. On the outskirts, a tent city had sprung up where veterans had gathered to celebrate San Jacinto Day on April 21, six days distant.

In pantaloons and boots, the President sloshed through the mud of Main Street to the office of the promoters. Major John Kirby Allen, a tall handsome man with a somewhat pompous manner of speech, received him with deference and cordiality, appropriately expressing the hope that this settlement with its great future would honor the name it bore. He conducted the President to the executive mansion, a log cabin with two rooms separated by a "dog trot" —an open hall similar to a modern breezeway. One room was intended for the President's sleeping chamber; Lubbock reported that it had no fireplace but only a small clay furnace over which the President could bend and warm his fingers Indian fashion. The floor was made of earth and puncheons—slabs with the smooth side up and the curved side down. The room contained a cot with a tick filled with Spanish moss. A lean-to at its back was to serve as combination kitchen and living quarters for servants.

The dog trot was designated as the reception room. The second inside room was to be the President's drawing room. It also was equipped with a roughly constructed cot which could be sat upon until chairs were provided. Both rooms had small rough tables.

The President probably slept in the executive mansion that night, and undoubtedly experienced the loneliness he had forecast for himself. Before leaving Columbia he had written to Dr. Irion, "How sad the scenes must be at my Leevees, no Mrs. H—— there, and many who will attend can claim fair dames as theirs!!!" [1]

The very next day he had evidence that the capital city was already blessed with one of the inevitable signs of advancing civilization. A newspaper, the *Texas Telegraph and Register,* was thrust into his hands fresh from the press, the ink not yet dry. Dr. Francis Moore, Jr., and his associate, Jacob W. Cruger, had moved their newspaper from Columbia and had been able to get out an early edition.

Invitations to the San Jacinto Ball on April 21, the anniversary of the battle, were printed on white satin and were sent to all the settlements within one hundred miles. Good accommodations were promised for the ladies. Emissaries were dispatched to bring girls on horseback or in wagons from Oyster Bay, Caney Creek, and Brazos Bottoms.

The President ordered a new black silk velvet suit from New York for this important occasion. Happily, the coat was lined with white satin, conforming to the keynote color and fabric of the celebration. His trousers were trimmed with gold lace, his cravat was tucked inside a crimson waistcoat, and a military plume was in his large hat. The men had agreed to wear white dancing slippers, but the President, because of his still troublesome wound, was obliged to wear boots; they were red-topped and silver-spurred.

He walked to the ballroom with Major Allen and J. T. Crawford,

the British Consul from Veracruz. Crawford was on hand to represent the commercially alert British Empire in acquiring any trade
advantages that might ensue from being on the scene early. Later,
he wrote to the British minister in Mexico City, commenting respectfully on President Houston's appearance and character.

To the strains of "Hail to the Chief," the President led the Grand
March with Mrs. Mosely Baker. He had tactfully chosen the wife
of one of his most ardent antagonists, but told her truthfully that
he had done so because she was the most beautiful woman there.
Mrs. Baker wore a white satin gown with a black lace overdress.
Mrs. Sidney Sherman, wife of the troublesome colonel whom Houston had rebuked for aggressive conduct on the day before the San
Jacinto battle, was charming in a bouffant white velvet. Other ladies
wore soft, white billow-skirted mull gowns with low necklines, their
glamour heightened by touches of rich white satin.

The ball was impaired by only one unpleasant incident. Shrill
cries of excitement and sympathy arose when a mounted messenger
arrived and informed the two Cooper sisters that their brother had
been killed by Indians on the Colorado River.

After the dancing everybody went to the City Hotel and sat
down for a late supper of turkey, venison, coffee, cakes, and wine
in the two finished rooms which were lighted by an improvised
wooden chandelier holding two-score candles. There were many
toasts, much "spreeing."

The opening of Congress was postponed for five days until May
5, 1837, to permit erection of a temporary covering to keep the
sun out of the roofless capitol. President Houston delivered his
greeting to the legislators in person. Of recognition he said, "We
now occupy the proud attitude of a sovereign and independent
Republic; which will impose upon us the obligation of evincing to
the world, that we are worthy to be free." This would be accomplished, he assured them, by wise legislation, maintenance of the
nation's integrity, and the redemption of all pledges. He said that
the position of Texas on annexation had not changed since the
adjournment of the last session, but he hinted that enemies of the
new Republic made the outlook for a happy solution of that question
uncertain. He urged the Congress to legislate not only for emer-

gencies but for a "permanent system" that would anticipate the nation's future growth.

He outlined about twenty of the nation's major requirements, such as revising the existing land act "that is not adapted to our situation"; agreeing upon the limits of the northeastern boundary with the United States; ending the sale by United States agents of arms and ammunition to the Indians; and maintaining discipline in the army, which was now strong enough for the country's needs.

He gave prominence to the immediate financial crisis. The treasury had been unable to meet demands upon it because the agents to whom Congress had issued land scrip were legally beyond the control of the Executive. These agents had refused to recognize drafts properly drawn against them. It was important for the Congress to act at once to correct this; the commission sent to the United States to negotiate a loan of $5,000,000 had failed.

Under Texas law slaves could be brought in only from the United States. With regard to the flourishing illegal slave trade, Houston expressed an attitude that made him many personal enemies:

> ...It cannot be disbelieved that thousands of Africans have lately been imported to the island of Cuba, with a design to transfer a large portion of them into this republic. This unholy and cruel traffic has called down the reprobation of the humane and just of all civilized nations.—But abhorrence to it is clearly expressed in our constitution and laws. Nor has it rested alone upon the declaration of our policy, but has long since been a subject of representation to the government of the United States, our ministers apprising it of every fact which would enable it to devise such means as would prevent either the landing or introduction of Africans into our country.[2]

Among those who listened to this address was Dr. Ashbel Smith, a rather short wiry man of thirty-two, who wore a spade beard after the fashion of former Provisional President Burnet. Smith told J. Pinckney Henderson that Houston's words had impressed him favorably, and Henderson immediately proposed that they call at the President's house.

After the introduction, Henderson filled the President in on Smith's background. Smith had A.B. and A.M. degrees from Yale College and wore a Phi Beta Kappa key. His health had broken while studying law. After a prolonged convalescence in North Carolina, he had gone to Europe to study medicine. When he returned, Henderson had talked with him about going to Texas, but Smith had put off coming and was a recent arrival. Dr. Smith still had not decided to make Texas his home, but he liked what he had seen so far.

The President cordially declared that Dr. Smith was exactly the kind of man that Texas needed to counteract the noisy, troublesome adventurers who predominated in the waves of immigrants from beyond the Sabine. He invited Smith to make use of the spare room and cot on the other side of the dog trot; it was the auspicious beginning of a life-long friendship. Smith's disciplined mind, sharp wit, and sympathetic comprehension of the President's difficulties made him an inspiring companion.

Among the many complicated affairs of state in which Dr. Smith became involved, first as a confidant and later as confidential adviser, was the critical military situation. On the frontier near San Antonio, Texas had an army of 2,250 men, volunteers who had swarmed in from the United States, leavened with a small minority of disciplined San Jacinto veterans. Most of the troops and many of the officers had never known Texas as a cause, but were soldiers of fortune—potential Vikings—eager to find adventure beyond the Rio Grande. General Felix Huston had reneged on his pledge to accept General Johnston as his superior and put his friend, a Colonel Rodgers, an extreme Viking insurgent, in command while he went to the capital to entice the veterans to join him in a filibuster.

The veterans were still collected in the nearby tent city where Huston circulated among them with promises of wealth and glory to be won by a march on Mexico. While he was doing so, President Houston received a report from General Johnston that Colonel Rodgers was stirring up the army with promises that they would soon march on Houston City, "chastise the President" for his failure to provide for the country's defense, and "kick Congress out of doors." [3]

The President knew that this must be an appealing program to the lusty insurgents. He was aware that Huston was also button-holing senators and representatives, assuring them that a march on Matamoros and other Mexican cities would bring glory to Texas. One of Huston's persuasive arguments was how much easier it would be to meet the financial needs of the new nation with spoils from Mexico than by taxes to be paid by Texans. He was making headway with his proposal for a law instructing President Houston to put himself at the head of the army to lead an invasion of Mexico. This proposal was accompanied by a broad suggestion that if the President refused—as was likely—a competent substitute would be available in the person of General Felix Huston himself. The insurgent volunteers' unreliability and the legislators' infatuation with aggression below the Rio Grande threatened the good character and survival of the Republic. The Mexicans, aware of the troublemakers, might decide to wage all-out war while Texas was weak and unready.

The President asked Ashbel Smith to cooperate with him in carrying out his strategy for getting rid of Huston. He invited the general to stay at the executive mansion, vacated his own cot for Huston, and moved in with Smith. In the President's absence, Smith encouraged Huston to talk at length about his ideas on invading Mexico and the quantity of men and equipment that would be needed. General Huston logically concluded that the President was coming to see things his way; he was gratified to believe that the President was apparently considering him to lead the enterprise.

When his guest was sound asleep, the President quietly left the executive mansion and walked a quarter of a mile to the one-room cabin occupied by Acting Secretary of War William S. Fisher. Fisher, his tall figure draped in a long muslin nightshirt, got up and lighted a candle. Houston instructed him to mount his horse by daybreak, get to San Antonio as fast as he could, and exercise all of the judgment and firmness at his command to execute the orders he was to carry. Fisher was to furlough the entire army for thirty days with the exception of 600 men. One group of furloughed men would go to Dimitt's Landing, a second to Velasco, a third to Galveston, and others to various points along 200 miles of coast. To be sure, this might produce an uproar from the army and Colonel Rodgers might try to interfere; but that situation, if it arose, must be overcome with finesse.

Fisher was to inform the troops that, at the end of the thirty days, any man who did not report for duty promptly when summoned would be considered a deserter. He was to say that the President wished them to enjoy their furlough because he would be obliged to assign them to arduous and unaccustomed duties when they returned. Marsh land must be drained and railroads must be built. With so many tasks to be done, the President was unwilling for the army to live in idleness at the expense of the people. In short, Fisher was to do his best to persuade the volunteers that desertion was preferable to the duties that would be assigned upon their return.

General Fisher proved equal to his task; the three furloughed groups of troublesome volunteers from beyond the Sabine marched to the coast. As soon as the President learned that his orders had been executed, he directed General Huston to return to the front to await orders. At the front, Huston found that the entire army, except 600 old reliables under General Johnston, had melted away. Disgusted, General Huston also took off for Galveston. There, he stamped the mud of Texas from his boots before sailing for New Orleans. He considered the President's action a dirty trick.

Ashbel Smith did not think it was a dirty trick. He regarded Houston's solution of the problem as the most marked evidence of statecraft that he had ever observed. Houston assured Smith that he believed tranquility would best advance the cause of Texas. He would use such means as he could devise to impose peace on all who would plague Texas with insurrection and hazardous military ventures.

Impressed by Houston's determination and resourcefulness, Dr. Smith decided to cast his lot with Texas. The next day, the President sent in his nomination of Smith for Surgeon General of the Army.

The army was recruited back to strength without "volunteers" from the United States. Houston's cup was running over with administrative problems when he was informed of another attempt to alienate the army. This time the mischief was being done by a once loyal man who had suddenly developed a Viking streak. Major Thomas G. Western, commanding the cavalry at San Antonio, had picked up the siren song sung by Dr. Grant and General Huston: a raid on Matamoros and other towns of northern Mexico would produce unlimited bonuses and spoils for the conquerors. He began by stimulating the troops to demand military action by the government against Mexico. From this he advanced to a demand that the feeble, one-horse Houston administration be overthrown by the army.

Western's word carried considerable weight because he had proved himself a patriot by excellent service in the Revolution. He had raised a company of forty-eight men for the duration of the war and personally had been a victim of Mexican troops who had burned his home and buildings and his mercantile establishment at Goliad.

Houston had enough evidence to warrant the court-martial of Major Western, but such disciplinary procedure against a "revolutionary patriot" was impractiable. It was necessary to frustrate Western by "statesmanship" without risking insubordination in the ranks. Houston learned that William H. Patton was in the capital, about to leave on private business for San Antonio. Patton had served as an aide-de-camp at San Jacinto and he was one of the three commissioners that Houston had assigned to accompany Santa Anna to Washington. For the mission at hand, the President needed a man who had a strong inclination to gossip. On this score, Houston believed that he could rely on Patton's impulse to disclose anything that had been imparted confidentially.

He called Patton in and told him that he was thinking of sending an envoy to London and Versailles. The man he had in mind was said to have cultivated manners and diplomatic skill equal to those of the American President, Martin Van Buren. Did Patton think that Major Western was qualified for the post? This was all confidential to be sure; not a word to Major Western.

When he was certain that Patton had had time to reach San Antonio, Houston dispatched a courier with urgent orders to Western to report to Houston City. The President cordially received Major Western but dropped no hint of any forthcoming appointment to the Court of St. James's. A week passed. Major Western finally asked Surgeon General Smith, who was known to be close to the President, if he had heard Houston mention anything about his appointment as ambassador. Dr. Smith could not recall having heard it mentioned. In fact, he was quite sure it had not been mentioned because, confidentially, the President was about to announce the appointment of J. Pinckney Henderson to that post. Major Western found this hard to believe, but Henderson's appointment a few days later made it official.

Upon his return to San Antonio, Western found orders removing him to a different post; another officer was in command of the cavalry. He joined General Huston in denouncing the President for a dirty trick. His reprisal was similar to that of other Vikings who knew of Houston's weakness. He charged that never, positively never, was the President known to be sober. Meanwhile, an enormous flow of shrewd, pungent, and powerful state papers continued to emanate from the executive mansion.

7. At Odds with the Colossus

THE President's burdens became almost unbearable. He often worked until after midnight and sometimes until two and three o'clock in the morning. To the girl who had become his confidante, Anna Raguet, he wrote on May 20, 1837, "It is past midnight. The toils of the day have passed by and all the recollections of friendship and affection recur...." [1]

At dawn he washed his face in a bucket of water on a bench behind the executive mansion. Looking into a piece of broken mirror fastened by wood pegs against the wall, he shaved with Elias Rector's gift razor. When he did not arise before the rest of the population, interested spectators who occupied the nearby cabins observed his matutinal ablutions.

Battling the country's money problem was now the President's greatest burden. It involved him in constant difficulties with Congress. In a message on June 6, 1837, he asked Congress to avert a situation that he called truly deplorable. On its own credit the government was unable to obtain supplies necessary for the army:

> ... The executive has been compelled to give his individual obligation for supplies for the army, endorsed by some of the honorable members of your body. This was done at a time when a part of the army was in an actual state of mutiny, from want of every kind of provisions....
>
> Since the commencement of the constitutional government, no public officer has received any salary. Their personal expenses

are great, from the fact of their having to pay an exhorbitant price for board. . . . They have tendered me resignations from time to time, induced by their actual necessities, . . . [to] obtain the means of subsistence. The Executive since he has come into office, has received into the treasury, and disbursed, only five hundred dollars for provisions for the troops. . . . the aid which it is in your power to give, is most sincererly and earnestly invoked.[2]

This was only the beginning of shortages and hardships, of Presidential pleas, and of controversies between the Executive and the lawmakers. The Republic's debt, mainly for war costs, when Houston's administration took over, amounted to $1,250,000. Creditors were restless. With a stubborn world depression taking hold in 1837 and an equally stubborn Congress to manage, it was a trick to get good men to act as department heads.

The country comprised an area of about 238,000,000 acres. After allowing for all grants to individuals by Spain and Mexico (26,280,-000 acres) and for extensive land bounties to volunteers and settlers, there remained a vast acreage of unappropriated public domain. Congress hastily passed a land bill for a general land office. Houston, fearing that the prevailing disorderly conditions would result in preference for false claims, vetoed it on June 8, 1837. Congress authorized him to employ New Orleans agents to sell land scrip in the United States at fifty cents an acre. There were no takers for the 700,000 acres put on the market. Then Congress gave him authority to seek $5,000,000 in foreign loans. This created a huge bubble of glowing expectations followed eventually by disillusionment. Of all the expedients tried, a tariff proved the most reliable and paper money issues the most disastrous.[3]

The executive mansion was crowded with department heads conferring with the Chief, getting instructions, and seeking advice on the framing of bills. In years to come they would write letters and reminiscences about how, stripped of all their clothes except their shirts, they sweated through that hot spring and summer working in the President's cabin.

Unhappy about the lack of progress toward annexation and drawn homeward by the illness of his wife, William Wharton quit as Texas Minister Plenipotentiary in Washington in May, 1837. He sailed for home on the Texas warship, *Independence*, which, after a fight, was captured by two Mexican war vessels. A prisoner of war, Wharton was taken to Mexico City.

Wharton's imprisonment meant trouble for Houston. Many persons demanded aggressive action against Mexico, but the President believed this would be dangerous in view of his country's situation. He sent John A. Wharton with thirty Mexican prisoners to treat for his brother's release. At Matamoros, when John presented himself under a flag of truce with a written proposal for an exchange of prisoners, he was thrown in jail. This further increased the President's embarrassment. The brothers Wharton neatly extricated him from this dilemma by escaping their jailers and returning to Texas.

The episode brought to light the existence of divided councils in the President's Cabinet. It also generated enthusiasm in Congress for a naval war against Mexico, notwithstanding the fact that the Texas navy had only three ships and lacked funds for maintenance. Houston scorned the jingoists who favored offensive war when their own country was weak and divided. He dismissed Secretary of the Navy S. Rhoades Fisher, who, without authorization, had ordered two Texan vessels on a cruise for reprisal against Mexican shipping. This policy of discretion cost Houston the support of some of his following. He was attacked on a number of issues; his failure to accomplish annexation, his land and financial policies, his liberal treatment of Indians, and his purely defensive war policy.

Struggling with his country's financial problems, Houston was giving close attention to the most promising solution: annexation to the United States. On June 26, 1837, through Robert Irion, who had succeeded Henderson as Secretary of State, Houston sent urgent instructions to Plenipotentiary Memucan Hunt, who had succeeded William Wharton. In the existing situation, the unvarnished truth would be of utmost use to Minister Hunt. Houston dictated the portions of the instructions that described the young Republic's distress and need. Irion wrote:

> Another subject and by far the most important of all on which I have been instructed to communicate is that of *Annexation*. You will renew the application ... and urge as speedy action ... as possible.
>
> On the success of this measure our permanent prosperity, and,

perhaps, existence as an organized Government, mainly depends.
... It is useless for us to deceive ourselves on this subject, and it
becomes my duty to inform you that the situation of the country is deplorable. We are without credit abroad and our resources are exhausted at home; and things generally are vering
towards anarchy, violence and insubordination. Annexation is
the remedy, and it is expected that you will exert yourself to
effect it.... Under every aspect of the case it is necessary that
a speedy decision of the U. S's Government on the subject
should be known.

Irion went on to say that conditions in Texas "imperiously demand that we must be intimately associated with some strong power.
..." To this power would be granted "an advantageous treaty" with
"important concessions of privileges...." He added, "Our Agent,
Gen. Henderson has gone to Europe whose instructions will depend
much upon the course adopted by the U. States."
Then Irion resumed in the voice and manner of Houston:

Such candor and my duty ... require me to inform you is our
situation. Visionary schemes of a glorious Republic are less
calculated to advance the true interests of our Country than
the practical common sense proposition to become a part of a
great nation firmly established....[4]

Hunt was also advised to refer for further information to the instructions that the late Secretary of State, Stephen Austin, had issued
on November 18, 1836, to Texas Agent, William H. Wharton. These
detailed instructions, prepared after consultation between Houston
and Austin, became part of the strong policy to be pressed by Hunt
in 1837.
As Texas agent in Washington, Wharton had been instructed to
advise the United States, as Hunt was to do, that the desire for annexation could not be expected to last indefinitely if action was not
taken soon. This continued pressure for immediate action was
prompted by the desperate plight of the new Republic. The country
which Houston, for diplomatic reasons, was trying to persuade the
world to accept as a free, upstanding, prosperous nation with commercial advantages to offer her friends, was on her knees beseeching
succor.
The idea that Texans might change their minds about annexation

if it was not accomplished speedily was simply a tool put in Wharton's hands to hasten the objective. It had proved impotent. Now Hunt would try his luck with it.

On August 11, 1837, Hunt, writing from Washington, informed President Houston of a great misfortune:

> I have ascertained beyond a doubt that Mr. Forsyth, Secretary of State of the United States, is violently opposed to annexation!! I could not avoid proclaiming on hearing of it 'and you too Brutus' knowing it as I did to be 'the unkindest cut of all.' [5]

Secretary Forsyth unequivocally rejected Hunt's formal annexation proposal with an explanation that stirred Hunt's ire. It would not be constitutional, Forsyth said, "to annex a foreign power." In reply, Hunt referred to the acquisition of Louisiana and Florida. Forsyth also expressed the fear that annexation would make the United States a party to the still-smoldering war between Mexico and Texas.

Hunt and Houston were able to infer many things that Forsyth left unsaid. That unpleasant fellow, Congressman John Quincy Adams, was widely advertising his belief that annexation probably meant war between North and South and the breakup of the Union because New England would secede. Obviously President Van Buren did not wish to make himself the target of the bold and relentless abolitionists.

The anti-Texas phase of the American Anti-Slavery Society's campaign had been going on since June of the previous year. One of the members' arguments was that Texas, once admitted, would be split into six or eight states as large as Kentucky. This, they claimed, would enable the South to dominate the nation and take away the rights of petition and free speech which the abolitionists relied upon in their campaign against slavery. Therefore, New England would resist annexation; dissolution of the Union could be one of the consequences. Some foresaw the agricultural South overthrowing the protective tariff, crippling Northern manufacturing, and seriously injuring Northern shipping.

Petitions and resolutions against the annexation of Texas poured into the Foreign Affairs Committee of the American House of Representatives in large quantities. William Lloyd Garrison's *Liberator* reported that memorials of protest with 600,000 signatures were presented at a single session of the United States Congress. Vermont joined Massachusetts in arguing that recognition followed by annexation would give the slave-holding interests such weight that the free section must either dissolve the Union or be "degraded." Northern abolitionists contended that slave owners were capable of any crime. Adams predicted that the annexation of Texas would have the infernal consequence of consecrating the United States to a bloodstained, ruinous career of aggression in behalf of slavery.

President Houston received the story of the opposition in fragments from his Washington agents, newspapers, and returned travelers. Like the members of his Cabinet, he was shocked by the storm that the plea for annexation provoked. The whole nation, said a member of the U. S. Congress, "was in a state of agitation, working like a troubled sea." [6] But, Houston asked, could not those who presumed to speak for the Colossus of the North understand that something beyond their immediate interests was involved—nothing less than the destiny of a continent? Presiding over the most turbulent realm on earth, he deplored the dominance of passion and prejudice in the affairs of men.

During the months that had passed since Houston became President, there had been progress in some directions. But it was qualified by the adverse influences of a deepening world depression and a stubborn Congress that refused to back paper currency issues with the one resource of the nation—public lands. Anarchy prevailed in some sections; ex-soldiers and volunteers from the United States were asserting the power of "impressment" and seizing the goods and property of settlers.

On November 16, 1837, Houston wrote to Henry Raguet:

Today I will commence my annual message which has been deferred, only on account of my health. My situation ever since I came into office has been most disagreeable ... not one comfort ... and subject to every exposure of season and weather—at last a house has been purchased by the Government, and is ordered to be fitted up for future use—so you see I will be in order for a Levee or Soiree. [7]

When his health was poor Houston drank more heavily. Reports about it may have been exaggerated. His friends were embarrassed and his opponents seized the opening to charge that he was unfit for office. Colonel James Morgan, a salty character, who had suffered heavy losses when Santa Anna destroyed Morgan's Point, kept up a running commentary on Texas affairs with Samuel Swartwout, one of Houston's friends in New York City. He reported that President Houston was so unpopular that he would spare Swartwout the details. Morgan disliked Houston at this time, but later he became a convert, believing Houston was the one man who could control the excesses of a turbulent country.

As foreseen, the annexation resolution offered in the United States Senate by Senator W. C. Preston on January 4, 1838, was frustrated in June when it was tabled by a vote of 24-14. Waddy Thompson's counterpart resolution in the House of Representatives was filibustered to death by Congressman John Q. Adams, who gave a three-week talk on it, beginning on June 16, 1838. Unexpectedly, Daniel Webster of abolitionist Massachusetts issued a warning from the floor of the Senate to his anti-Texas colleagues. Denial of annexation, he said, might arouse England's interest in Texas and cause her government to take steps that would be detrimental to American interests.

Houston believed the warning was fully justified and was amazed that it had attracted so little attention. His own opinions had crystallized. Without annexation, developments were bound to occur that would cause the United States great anxiety. Texas had no recourse but to seek the protection of stronger powers. England and France must be courted. Their influence with Mexico must be brought into play. That was not all. In seeking annexation immediately after winning independence, Texans had been moved by fear of invasion and the country's unstable situation. If a treaty could be achieved with Mexico, England, and France, public opinion might change and Texans might prefer permanent independence to annexation. As an American, Houston believed this would be deplorable; as a Texan, he knew that some such change in the status of the new nation was necessary as soon as possible. To effect this change, Texas must cease to be a rejected suppliant in the outer portals. Her appeal for annexation should be withdrawn.

Former Surgeon General Anson Jones of the Texas army, dreaming of the day when he would be president of an independent Republic, was now chairman of the Committee on Foreign Relations of the Texas House of Representatives. In the House, Jones had introduced a resolution that the Texas annexation offer be withdrawn unconditionally. Unfortunately the President in support of this resolution could not reveal the strategy that was taking shape in his mind, and it was voted down.

Asserting his executive authority over Texas foreign policy, Houston sent instructions to Texas Minister Memucan Hunt on May 19, 1838, to withdraw the annexation proposal unconditionally. By the time the instructions reached Washington, Hunt had resigned and was on his way to New Orleans. Houston's instructions, sent to Hunt's temporary successor, Peter W. Grayson, on June 12, restated the previous directive: "Should the present session of the Congress of the U. States adjourn without having acted finally on this subject, you will immediately . . . withdraw the proposition." He also instructed Grayson to inform "our Diplomatic Agent, Gen. J. P. Henderson, near the Governments of Great Britain and France" of this action so that he may be in possession of the fact at the earliest possible moment. "I have informed him that such action will be given." [8]

The purpose of this instruction was to give the Texas government a freer hand in the execution of an alternative plan involving France and England if annexation by the United States was finally refused. This plan was carried a step near consummation on June 25, 1838, when Houston named Anson Jones Minister Plenipotentiary to succeed Hunt.

On reaching the United States capital, Jones found Attaché Fairfax Catlett in a quandary, puzzling over how to "withdraw unconditionally" an annexation proposal that already had been rejected by the United States. To Jones this situation presented no insuperable difficulty. He called on Secretary of State Forsyth and stated emphatically that members of the Texas government had changed their minds, had withdrawn the proposal, and had no intention of renewing it. Forsyth received this intelligence with an affable nod of complete indifference. To Jones, the new situation was altogether satisfactory. In his journal he wrote exultantly, "Annexation is at an end . . . how glorious will Texas be standing alone and relying upon her own strength." [9]

But all Texans did not agree with these sentiments. Houston was brooding deeply over the kind of a foreign policy that might compel the United States to reconsider, or at any rate would give Texas strong allies with commercial relations and military support.

8. *An Eager Reach across the Sea*

IN his namesake capital, Houston observed that Major Allen's workmen had not been imbued with the idea which, as President, he had advocated for the benefit of the entire country: that Texas should lay her foundations deep and strong and build for permanence. Already, in 1838, the executive mansion showed the ravages of wind, heat, rain, and sun. The roofless porch sagged and the front stoop was askew and scarred by a broken board. The leaky roof had been patched. The walls, from which the mud chinking had fallen, had not yet been boarded over to cover the cracks.

Back in June, 1837 the unique condition of the President's house had come to the attention of the celebrated naturalist, John J. Audubon, when he visited the city as a sightseer and was conducted on a tour by the Secretary of the Navy. After his visit, Audubon described the President's bachelor circumstances.

We approached the President's mansion wading in water above our ankles. This abode ... is a small log house, consisting of two rooms and a passage through, after the Southern fashion. ... We found ourselves ushered into ... the ante chamber; the ground-floor, however, was muddy and filthy, a large fire was burning, and a small table covered with paper and writing materials, was in the centre; camp beds, trunks, and different materials were strewed around the room. We were at once presented to several members of the Cabinet, some of whom bore the stamp of intellectual ability....[1]

Since the President was busy, the Navy Secretary took Mr. Audubon for a stroll around the city. They went to the capitol where

314

they found the roof leaking on disgruntled members of Congress. Before he left town, Audubon was introduced to "His Excellency." He reported that the President was not dressed in an Indian blanket, but wore a handsome velvet suit and a cravat somewhat in the style of 1776. Houston talked with his guests briefly in the reception room and then invited them into his crowded private chamber.

He introduced Audubon to his friends and staff, who were sitting on stools and camp beds, and then asked his visitors to drink with him. Audubon, with glass raised, wished success to the Republic; the President with a nod and a gracious word thanked him. Considerately, the naturalist made his visit brief because he saw that the President and his advisers were working under pressure. Afterward he wrote that he never would forget the impression made on him by President Houston, his place of abode, and the men around him.

Audubon had reason to be impressed with the intellectual quality of the men around Houston. On the day of his visit, the President was in conference with Dr. Robert Irion, Ashbel Smith, and J. Pinckney Henderson. Immediately after Audubon left, the President resumed his discussion with these three. He expressed regret over the reluctance of the United States to annex Texas. It was necessary at once to counter this setback by seeking friends abroad; he had decided to send Henderson as Texas agent to the Court of St. James's and to Versailles to seek recognition and obtain commercial treaties. As soon as recognition was granted, Henderson was to become Minister Plenipotentiary.

Steps were taken that day that, in 1838, produced promising results in Europe which somewhat offset the failure to accomplish annexation. The conversation between the four men was reflected in written instructions that Houston later gave to Henderson.[2]

On June 25, 1837, through Secretary of State Irion, Houston instructed Henderson to inform Her Majesty's Government in Britain and His Majesty's Government in France that Texas has "a civil and military government in successful operation," and has "a right to expect to be recognized on the basis of reciprocity, and placed on ... the footing of the most favored nations;—on which conditions you will uniformly insist."

Houston and the members of his government feared Britain and

France might be prejudiced against the Republic because of the constitutional provision permitting slaves to be brought into Texas from the United States. The President's instructions covered this point:

> On the subject of slavery you can speak with candor and truth, admitting that its institution was cruel and impolitic, that under existing circumstances, owing to the peculiar organization of the Government, the nature of the climate, the habits of the people and the locality of the country, it *must* continue as provided by the constitution and laws: at the same time it is a striking fact that the condition of slaves in this Republic is far more tolerable than in the U. States, from whence alone they can be introduced. Why then should their emigration be discouraged?
>
> By emigration their condition is greatly ameliorated without increasing the number of slaves.

Neither Houston nor Henderson was quite satisfied with this attempt to offset probable condemnation of slavery by British statesmen. On a later occasion Houston excused himself from the exercise of further ingenuity on the subject by authorizing Henderson to present any other effective argument that occurred to him in defense of the wretched institution. The President's instructions to Henderson continued:

> In the event of success in obtaining the recognition of independence you will then present your credentials as Minister Plenipotentiary, and ascertain as correctly as possible the nature of treaties into which that Government will be inclined to enter with this. . . .
>
> It is the desire of the President that you will make the necessary inquiries relative to a Loan, and advise this Government whether it can be effected in Europe, and if so, on what terms.
>
> The President directs that you express to that Government very friendly disposition of the citizens of this Republic towards the people of England, and their high regard for the Sovereign who presides over that powerful Kingdom.
>
> Should you deem it advisable to visit France for the purpose of soliciting the recognition of our independence by that Power you will observe the same policy as that indicated in regard to England.

Further emphasis was laid on exploring the possibilities of a loan.

In London, Henderson was promptly received in audience by Her Majesty's Foreign Minister, Viscount Palmerston on October 13, 1837. Later, negotiations were so long delayed that he lost patience. With the impetuosity of youth, he submitted further requests for interviews in terms that virtually demanded action at peril of his leaving England for France. In due course Lord Palmerston responded affably.

Henderson's communications to Lord Palmerston presented a glowing picture of progress in Texas that made excellent reading. They reflected information supplied by Irion who wrote under the influence of President Houston's sunny optimism. Henderson was informed that the threatening attitude of Mexico, which was said to be causing the British Cabinet to withhold recognition, was "but vain boasting on paper." A regular flow of immigration had increased the population to 150,000. Relations with the Indians were pacific. Laws were administered as regularly and as perfectly as in the United States. Public gaming had been prohibited. Financial affairs were in excellent order; the new currency was at par. The increase in Texas commerce was amazing.

Much in this glorious picture, as presented to Her Majesty's Foreign Minister, would have been news to Texans. "Star money" was wavering at 65 cents on the dollar. Some Indians were on the warpath, but that was always the case. The population estimate was inflated ten per cent more than the actual population would be in another decade, but was somewhat justified because immigrants were arriving daily. On occasion, the President himself had relied on prophecy rather than fact when he spoke of Texas. He appreciated an envoy of comparable flexibility and congratulated him on his masterly presentations.

Houston learned that further congratulations were in order. Henderson's resolute prodding of Lord Palmerston and his glowing presentation of the situation in Texas were effective. Palmerston granted him an appointment, and the interview was cordial, lengthy, and promised results.

Houston was delighted to learn of Palmerston's affable admission that the matter of Texas recognition was regarded as important to Her Majesty's Empire. Palmerston inquired about the status of relations between Texas and the United States. Feigning ignorance that the United States had recognized Texas, Palmerston asked many questions about the size of Texas, her seacoast, rivers, and harbors. Suddenly he inquired why Texas had applied for admission to the United States.

Henderson, falling back on the art of diplomatic deception, readily explained that this had been the result of momentary distress and uncertainty when Texas was not in a position to meet the Mexican threat of reconquest. But now, he alleged, all that was past; Texas was fully capable of maintaining herself. Henderson assured the foreign minister that, after recognition, treaties could be arranged that would enable England to remove the products of all other nations, including the United States, from Texas markets.

Impressed, Palmerston observed that he believed Texas had abolished slavery. This was provocative; Palmerston believed nothing of the kind. In accord with instructions, Henderson explained how Texas found herself in her present peculiar situation with regard to slavery. Palmerston remarked that the matter would have to be considered by Her Majesty's Cabinet in deciding on recognition.

On December 21, 1837, seven weeks after Henderson's arrival in London, Palmerston informed him that Britain would not extend recognition because there seemed to be a possibility that Mexico would reconquer Texas. Henderson countered by asking for a promise of recognition if Mexico did not subjugate Texas within a few months. Then Palmerston hedged, warning that if Texas desired consideration from England she must "look well" to her "slavery conditions."

Henderson accepted this rebuff politely. As the next best thing, he wrote a letter, hoping to persuade Palmerston to enter into an informal commercial agreement. Again, the British dragged their feet. Henderson pressed for another interview and, receiving no response, applied again. When this request was ignored he adopted a blunter tone, reminding Palmerston that more than a month had passed since the question of Britain's opening her ports to Texas vessels had been taken under consideration. Palmerston promptly invited Henderson to an interview, during which he agreed that Texas vessels could enter British ports, although this action was not to constitute recognition. Texas vessels would be regarded as Mexican.

"But these ships will have only Texas papers," Henderson responded.

"Her Majesty's Government will overlook that," Palmerston conceded coolly.

Palmerston's concession involved a complicated diplomatic situation. England was anxious for trade with Texas, but Palmerston had reasons to stay on the good side of Mexico—after all, Mexican trade was important, too, and England was Mexico's creditor at the time. It would be unwise to antagonize the Latin nation by formally recognizing Texas.

Henderson had taken an important step forward, and Houston congratulated him again. But was there not danger that Henderson might venture too far too fast? The President, expressing his satisfaction with everything that had happened so far, cautioned Henderson to be extremely careful not to offend Palmerston. Then he quickly qualified this suggestion. Henderson was the man on the spot; and in the end he was the best judge of what should be said and how to say it.

The tangible result of Henderson's six months' work in London was a written agreement with Palmerston covering the entry of each nation's ships into the ports of the other. Final results, not yet accrued, were many, although there was no indication that England would grant a loan to relieve the plight of distressed Texas.

Henderson discounted Palmerston's statement that the British refusal to recognize Texas in 1838 was based on doubt of the new country's ability to maintain independence and resist Mexican attempts to reconquest. He believed that three other reasons were of equal or greater force: uncertain political conditions in England; fear that recognition of Texas would jeopardize British-Mexican trade relations and the payment of debts to British creditors in Mexico; uncertainty as to the course the United States might pursue on annexation, and the possibility that Texas would abandon her independence to achieve it. If annexation took place after England recognized Texas, Palmerston said his country would be the laughing stock of all Europe.

Having accomplished all that was possible for the time being, Houston's diplomatic agent proceeded to France in April 1838.

After spending several months in Paris, Henderson perceived that Count Molé, President of the Council and His Majesty's Minister for Foreign Affairs, required the same kind of approach that had been successful with Lord Palmerston. Daringly but with punctiliously elaborate propriety, he submitted to Molé on September 26, 1838, an accurate account of broken appointments and unanswered communications, and referred to embarrassing and unmerited delays, to tardiness and indifference to the dignity of a country that sought favored-nation treatment. Thus prodded, Count Molé received him. They talked of recognition, commercial treaties, and a loan. Henderson wanted recognition to come first so that he could discuss commercial treaties as the representative of a nation equal with France. Molé firmly rejected this proposal. Talk of a loan was not opportune. References to it were of the vaguest character.

For the time being recognition was postponed.

9. *A Rejected Suitor*

Houston City developed a society as quaint as any that has ever existed on American soil. A wild, picturesque, cosmopolitan boom town, it had a population of some two thousand men and two hundred women of mixed nationalities: American, German, Dutch, French, Irish, English, Portuguese, Italian, Negro, and Indian. A hundred Mexicans, captured at San Jacinto, had chosen to remain in the Republic rather than return to their native land.

On the streets were cotton planters, doctors, merchants, clerks, tailors, boatmen, teamsters, auctioneers, carpenters, scouts, gamblers, veterans, and ex-military men from the United States looking for adventure. A score of lawyers were finding plenty of business in this new city where title disputes were common.

Billiard rooms and horse races attracted patrons. A wealthy planter made a bet with a gambler; they staked their horses, and when the planter lost he argued that such a debt should not be paid. The dispute did nothing to prove whether or not a gambling debt is a moral obligation, but it did prove that the gambler, with fatal effect, was quicker on the draw. When the gambler was brought to trial on a murder charge his friends broke up the proceedings with a raid on the court.

A channel had been cleared in the bayou. Two steamboats that plied between Galveston and Houston City supplied a diversion for eager crowds that gathered to watch immigrants or traders arrive. Accommodations in the city were so scarce that passengers were allowed to remain on board overnight.

The capital lacked wells to supply drinking water. A roadway was scraped out to a sandbar where the drivers of drays and carts could fill their barrels with bayou water which they peddled by the bucket from house to house. Much sickness resulted, and Francis Lubbock proposed that the legislature provide $500 so that he could go to New Orleans and bring back 10,000-gallon cypress cisterns which could be filled with rain water. The Congress agreed, and the new source of drinking water had an excellent effect on the health of the town.

Houston observed the population growth with pleasure. On January 12, 1838, he wrote to Anna Raguet, his "peerless Miss Anna," the "Belle of Nacogdoches":

> ...Now for the place and the people where I am yet fated to pass some eleven months in empty splendor and magnificent misery. No place has ever within my knowledge improved as this has. I presume that not less than one hundred souls arrive by sea each week that passes, and generally of the better sort of folks—bringing wealth, worth and intelligence into the country.[1]

When fall came with its bitter sleety "northers," the citizens had two alternatives for keeping warm. They could go to bed in their clothes under all the blankets they had, or they could join their shivering fellows around huge bonfires in the streets, usually in front of an open saloon.

President Houston was as fond as any private citizen of having his shanks and backside warm. He frequently mingled with the crowds around the bonfires; but on the night of February 1, 1838, he stayed indoors suffering from the cold. In a scrawl that suggests he was chilled to numbness, he wrote to Miss Anna:

> It is late at night, and I am freezing in a miserable open house; four windows in it, and not one pane of glass nor shutter—three

doors, and shutters to but two—no ceiling and the floor loose laid. Is not this a "White House" with a plague to it? The Palace [a new house for the President] is not finished, but it is said to be in progress and will soon be completed.

People are daily arriving by twenties and fifties in this city. . . .[2]

The second year of Houston's Presidency, 1838, was the fifth year of a pleasant, increasingly serious, but far from satisfactory flirtation with Miss Anna. Houston was lonely. In letters to friends he spoke of his desire for home and family. Undoubtedly intentions of serious courtship were in his mind if all went well between him and the flaxen-haired, blue-eyed girl from Nacogdoches who had once woven him a silk sash for his sword.

His garland of laurel leaves with a note awarding her a share of those won on San Jacinto battlefield had brought no encouraging response. In semi-humorous terms he had asked her, while he was recuperating from his wound at Philip Sublett's in San Augustine, to take pity on a wounded veteran and to come to visit him. This request had fallen upon stony ground. His offer to give her the honor of making the first Lone Star flag to fly from the mast of the "capitol" at Columbia had proved futile and, of course, excusable because she was absent from home on a visit to New Orleans.

During most of this year he was too busy with government affairs to journey to East Texas and was obliged to conduct his affair with the charming Anna by letter only. Discreet and reserved, but at the same time pointed and revealing, his letters disclosed admiration and warmth of feeling. The deeper significance of his tone did not escape Miss Anna. She was twenty-two now, clever, well read, a conversationalist in four languages, and mature for her years. With the situation well in hand, she reserved decision. Reports reached her about the President's drinking and of occasional conduct that was not altogether elegant. She had other reasons for reserve. The President was only one in a large field of competitors.

Houston's tone of light banter varied with a kind of irony and self-satire. He would imply a hope of seeing Miss Anna in the capital and then would add: "And as you have such an *aversion* to *Houston*, I cannot hope to meet you there." [3] Sometimes he conveyed his admiration in letters to her father: "I was charmed the other day at receiving by your care, a very interesting letter from Miss Anna. . . . One of the most intelligent, sensible and best written letters that has ever met my eye from the hand of a young lady." [4]

At other times he wrote her hoping perhaps to discover how his suit would prosper if he became serious.

> . . . By the Bye, I am told that it is reported that I am married to Mrs. Long! I never saw her but twice. . . . Besides she has one or two pretty Grand Children, which wou'd argue that she was older than I am!
>
> I will not marry until I can once more go to Nacogdoches and see how my matters are there! . . . [5]

He received no intimation that his "matters" would go favorably if he put in an appearance at Nacogdoches. Realizing that Anna must have heard current reports of his heavy drinking, he touched on the matter lightly, suggesting that he was a reformed character. In a postscript written on the margin of one of his letters he wrote: "——— [name missing] and myself are reformed; neither gets 'tight!' . . . 'I never drinks nothing.' " [6]

He was broadminded about her other suitors, conscious perhaps that the real battle for Miss Anna's hand would be waged by younger men. In almost every letter he referred handsomely to suitors that he knew enjoyed her favor; to Dr. Irion, as "the noble Irion" or "Doct. Irion, the best of men, sends best regards to all." Sometimes he brought to her attention a highly desirable possible suitor: "By the Bye, General Henderson, Secretary of State, is a bachelor, young, noble, and rich—a man of genius. Note this, will you, and look out!"

Many times, unsuccessfully, he solicited an invitation to visit her in her home. He needed no invitation to visit his good friends, the Raguets, but he hoped for one from Anna as evidence of his status with her.

> I shou'd be extremely happy to see you in your fathers house, and spend, as I have so often done, some happy hours, free from the cares of Revolution. If we have peace, and war is ended soon, I will endeavor to be in Nacogdoches, by the last of this month, or some time in April; and spend a few days—if not, it will be impossible for me to be there until the adjournment of Congress.[7]

In answer, he received not an invitation but a letter from Miss Anna about the policies that she thought would be most advantageous for Texas.

An important letter to Houston sent by "private conveyance" from Washington, D. C., was long delayed but finally reached him. It was from United States Congressman John Campbell, an old Nashville friend who had been a fellow supporter of Andrew Jackson and was a distant cousin of Eliza Allen Houston. Just before leaving Tennessee, Campbell had spent two or three weeks at his brother's home in Lebanon. Mrs. Houston also had been in Lebanon visiting friends. Campbell was present at a gathering when Houston's victory over Santa Anna came up for discussion. He reported on Mrs. Houston's behavior:

> ... She showed great pleasure at your success and fairly exulted.... No subject... was so interesting to her as when you were the subject of the conversation; and she shew evident marks of displeasure and mortification if some person was to say anything unfavorable of you.... Some of her friends wanted her to git a divorce; and she positively refused; and said she was not displeased with her present name; therefore she would not change it on this earth; but would take it to the grave with her. —she has conducted herself with great surcumspiction and prudence and with great dignity of character so much that she has gained the universal respect of all that knows her She is certainly a most estimable woman; to have sustained herself as she has under all difficulties she has had to encounter.—I have dwelt on this subject as I believed it to be one that would not try your patience.... [8]

Campbell's letter was plain intimation that the way to reconciliation was open. Soon Houston received a second letter on the same subject, more definitely pointed, from his cousin, Robert McEwen. In the matter of reconciliation, McEwen conceded that Houston had the right to the last word and the door remained open. "Your wife desires such an event," McEwen said, and pointed out that many of Houston's friends felt that it would suitably crown Houston's Texas triumph. Cousin Bob concluded: "You occupy the position of a second Washington," and he was "gratified to learn that you have become a sober man." [9]

Prolonged reflection was not necessary to determine Houston's position on reconciliation. He had no unkind word, then or ever, for any member of the Allen family. But, as on the occasion of their first reconciliation offer, he wanted nothing more to do with any of them, and this included the girl, now a grown woman, who had kept silent when her family had abandoned him to the malice and scandal of political partisanship.

The net result of the letters from Campbell and McEwen was a definite move by Houston to clear up his marital status. His petition for divorce, filed in Nacogdoches before the revolution, had been lost, and the attorney who had filed it was dead. Houston retained a lawyer, W. G. Anderson, to investigate what had happened to it.

Anderson succeeded in locating the papers and discovered that nothing had happened. He pressed the matter in a court action before District Judge Shelby Corzine in San Augustine. The petition was based on the length of separation and the impossibility of reconciliation. Eliza and her family were represented by attorney Townsend at the proceeding before Judge Corzine. Formal papers granting the divorce are not available, but Houston was advised of the successful outcome by his attorney.

He had suffered, but he was able to forget. In years to come when anyone had the temerity to mention his first wife, he listened with obvious interest but made no comment. He never voluntarily opened the door he had closed on the past. For Eliza it was different. Although she married and had children, her first marriage was her tragedy until the day she died, March 3, 1862.

Years later when interested persons sought to find Eliza's grave, all traces of it had vanished. Weathered stones in the Gallatin cemetery marked the graves of her parents, brothers, sisters, and many in-laws, but that of the girl whose broken marriage had made history was unmarked. The same persons learned that two of Eliza's children had died before her.[10] Descendants of the family report that before her death Eliza destroyed every daguerreotype or painting that would have permitted posterity to gaze upon her features.

The peerless Miss Anna heard reports about the divorce and complained to others, among them possibly her father, about the President's "addressing" her when he was not free to marry. Anna's indifference or coldness had prevented Houston's "addresses" from taking a too-serious turn, so she scarcely would have been justified in making a serious protest to the President himself. A flirt, she was indulging her privilege of pique.

The President was embarrassed when he learned about Miss Anna's state of mind. He could handle troublesome dictators, frustrate absurd proposals of Congress, and devise a shrewd policy to embarrass the United States, all with diplomatic finesse and a triumphant degree of aplomb. But in the letter in which he tried to square himself with the belle of Nacogdoches he flopped hopelessly.

"Miss Anna," he wrote on June 4, 1838, "Having learned that by some agency you were induced to believe that I had presumed to address you at a time when I must have been satisfied in my own mind that legal impediments lay in the way of my union with any lady. ..." He stopped right there. It was a beginning that got nowhere. He abandoned the effort, put a period where there might have been a dash, and went on, miserably: "This may have been the fact as to your belief, and yet the result as to my hopes and my attachments [was] not changed so far as your choice was concerned and my wishes or destiny involved."

This may have meant something but exactly what it was is difficult to say. The President must have paused over it. If it meant anything at all it was a veiled admission that he had addressed her significantly "with hopes" of a serious "attachment" before he was divorced.

"But one thing would still remain for me to reflect upon," he continued, still looking for a way out. "You (I assert it with great pleasure) and myself have been friends, and I so highly appreciated your worth as to believe that you would not assume to be the friend of anyone whom you did not believe possessed the most undoubted honor and sense of rectitude."

Here was an interesting contribution to logic. His best evidence that he had not been guilty of an offense against her was the fact that she had esteemed him as a friend. This left him in a bog and the only solution was to lunge manfully for the other shore. He went on: "Then had I addressed you or sought to win your love when I was aware that the same must have taken place at the expense of your happiness and pride and peace and honor in life, I must have acknowledged myself a 'lily liver'd wretch! ! !'"

326

If Miss Anna really cared for him she certainly would protest that he was not "a lily liver'd wretch." She never did.

At this time, he had been divorced for about a year. Anna's complaint related to attentions and addresses that antedated the divorce. Referring to the application for divorce which he had filed in 1833 soon after coming to Texas—a matter which he had never followed up—he declared, apparently unaware that this was the one argument on which he should have taken his stand:

"I believed I was as free from all legal or moral hindrance to any union which might be created as the mountain air which I so much delight to breath. I was *honest*. . . I was *devoted! ! !* Of *this* enough." He added in conclusion: "This much I have felt bound to say to you on the score of old friendship and a desire to evince to you that I have merited the esteem with which you have honored me in by gone days." [11]

Anna was not concerned about the legality of the President's divorce but with "addresses" paid to her before the divorce. Nevertheless, the President was moved to send with his letter of June 4 to her several memoranda from some "gentlemen eminent in the profession of the law" testifying to their belief that he had now been legally divorced. One such letter received by Houston from his attorney, W. G. Anderson, dated April 8, 1837, must have astonished Anna, who could make herself understood in several languages. The letter from Anderson to his client closed with this statement:

> I . . . take great pleasure in saying to you that a [decision] was made and that from hence you are absolved from Marital obligations into which you have heretofore entered, so far as it is in the power of the Court, the powers of which, taken in connection with the Legislative enactments of the Country I conceive to be amply sufficient for & to all intents and purposes, I have done with this.[12]

So Anderson was through and apparently glad of it. Houston and Anna were almost through. Anna's aloofness and pique were reminiscent of his earlier experience with "coldness." He never again wrote her with the same freedom and confidence. His letter certainly made it plain that Anna could take his past "addresses" seriously if she wanted to, and they could have gone on from there. But Anna did not grasp the opening, and Houston was embarrassed by her complaints to others about the impropriety of his courtship when he was not divorced. Their correspondence lapsed while Anna thought it over. Then her letters became more frequent as if, after all, she had not yet quite made up her mind. Sometimes he apologized for not answering her letters for a month or more, and he continued to speak highly of "Doct. Irion." When Irion and Anna became engaged, there was not the slightest break in Houston's friendship with the doctor. It continued after Irion and Anna were married. Eventually, the first-born of the happy pair was one of more than one hundred infants in Texas who were named after Sam Houston.

10. *Periwig and Knee Pants*

ONE way or another things got done. Nation building went on day by day, with energies transferred from annexation to the pursuit of recognition by England and France. In mid-summer of 1838 the President was able to announce that a commercial agreement had been reached between the Republic and Her Majesty's Government, providing for admission of ships of either country into the ports of the other. Henderson had received inquiries from the ministers of Belgium and Holland and from agents of the Hanseatic Cities about prospects for commercial arrangements. The outlook for recognition was hopeful.

President Houston was nearing the end of his term (limited by the constitution to two years for the first president and to three years thereafter). Texas already had the aspect of a nation. A capitol building, with a colonnade of square pillars, was nearing completion. Constitutional procedures were established with John Birdsall of New York presiding over the Supreme Court. Immigration was continuing; the mails were operating.

Taxes had been levied and accepted. A tariff produced the greatest amount of revenue. Tonnage dues, port fees, a direct property tax, poll taxes, business taxes, and land fees were imposed and collected by the government's agents. Agitators had been subdued, at least for the time being. The army supported the President and there was no immediate danger that it would be lured into hazardous enterprises south of the Rio Grande.

Next to minimizing currency fluctuations, one of the President's greatest problems was minimizing his intake of alcohol. This presented baffling difficulties in a country where thirty or forty toasts were common at public dinners. On January 1, 1837, he had made a New Year's resolution. It was formalized as a bet on the seventh with one of the founders of Houston City, Augustus C. Allen, a man of small stature and great energy, who was a friend to Houston and a foe of liquor. Their wager agreement, signed, sealed and witnessed, read:

AGREEMENT.– The conditions are these: A. C. Allen alleges that Sam Houston will not abstain from the use of ardent spirits, wines and cordials; and should said Sam Houston do so, then said Allen is to pay to said Houston, a suit of clothes, which shall cost and be worth $500.oo; said Houston alleges that he is not to use any ardent spirits, wines or cordials, and is only to use malt liquors, and should he violate this agreement, then, he is to pay the said Allen a suit of clothes worth $500.oo. This agreement is to expire on the 31st day of December, 1838. The clothes are to be paid immediately thereafter.[1]

A month after this contract was signed, a Virginian, W. T. Brent, called on the President. They discussed the exaggerated reports of the President's drinking that were being circulated by his enemies. Afterward Brent wrote to a relative in his home state, saying that he had called on the President, found him in good health, and determined not to touch ardent spirits until the first of January next.

Ashbel Smith had gone to Philadelphia to purchase army medical supplies. During a side trip to Virginia, he wrote to President Houston about being entertained by President Van Buren in Washington, D. C. Van Buren believed that annexation was unlikely under present conditions and was convinced that the effects of many falsehoods circulated by the detractors of President Houston would be impermanent.

Inquiries had come to Smith from the New Orleans *True American* as to the truth of the charges circulated about President Houston's conduct, his drinking, his "beastliness," and his general erratic behavior. Smith responded with a tribute to the man he knew well. It was reprinted in the *Texas Telegraph* of February 24, 1838:

> He has been represented as an imbecile in body and intellect:— a moral and physical wreck. Never was calumny more false. His health has certainly been impaired by privations and exposures; but he possesses at this moment more physical force—despite his severe attack of the congestive fever last summer,—than ninety-nine able bodied men out of one hundred; and he is still capable of enduring fatigue, privations, and watching in a most extraordinary degree. As regards his mind, he is still in the pride of his intellect. . . . His bearing is that of the most lofty and princely courtesy; and he is singularly endeared to his personal friends; and despite all that has been said to the contrary, I believe him the most popular man in Texas. The statements of his being a madman and cutting tall antics before high Heaven and man, are utterly and gratuitously false.

There is no evidence that Houston ever bought the $500 suit for A. C. Allen.

After a long absence, Vice-President Lamar returned to Texas and announced himself a candidate to succeed President Houston. David G. Burnet joined forces with him as a candidate for the vice-presidency. With the zest of a crusader and the polished phrases of an experienced troubadour, Lamar based his campaign on the necessity of giving Texas "a new character." He expressed contempt for the administration's effort to bring about annnexation and declared that Texas was able and worthy to stand alone. He poured vitriol on the President's attempt to persuade the Senate to ratify the treaty of peace and neutrality with the Cherokees. He made it clear that, if elected, he would sweep Houston's policies into the dustbin. Money would be made easier, duties abolished, and taxes reduced. By these means he proposed to give the nation its new character. Not a trace would be left of the previous administration that had woefully impaired the nation's exalted prestige.[2] The deaths of two opposing candidates during the campaign left Lamar and Burnet in the field unopposed. They were elected by a substantial vote.

A considerable body of opinion in the United States viewed the

330

Houston policies with the same distaste professed by Lamar. The New Orleans *Picayune* (December 19, 1838) summed it up:

> He [Lamar] appears to be unanimously popular with the people of [Texas], and will, no doubt, prove to be the best chief magistrate that could have been selected. It is certain that he is strenuously opposed to *annexation*. He wishes Texas to stand as she is—a free and independent republic, alone and unconnected with any nation. He will also form an entirely new Cabinet; and it is expected that almost everything will be changed for the better.

"Changed for the better . . ." The phrase galled Houston. He retired from office taking with him some of the ingratitude customarily displayed by republics toward their servants. He was denounced by the politically ambitious and by the various anti-Houston factions for having saved the life of Santa Anna, for his opposition to an invasion of Mexico, for his methods of preventing it, and for favoring annexation as the best solution of the Lone Star's many troubles. But he still believed he commanded the loyalty of the people.

By promising to give Texas "a new character," the President-elect had adroitly reflected upon Houston's character and the character of the Republic under his administration. Houston had kept silent during the campaign of detractions, but after Lamar's election, he had to decide whether he could afford to surrender his office without restating his policies and the reasons behind them. Having decided to present his views to the electorate again, he had to consider how this could best be done.

He discovered that as the outgoing executive, he was scheduled to preside over the sumptuous inauguration ceremony of his successor, but an opportunity had not been provided for him to say even a few words of farewell. He hit upon an ingenious method for rectifying this possibly accidental but probably intentional oversight. From somewhere he obtained a costume of the kind that had been worn in the days of George Washington, knee breeches with silver buckles, pumps with buckles, a silk coat, and a powdered wig. In this regalia, on December 1, 1838, he took the chair of state fully aware of the probable effect of his simulated appearance as the Father of His Country. It excited the enthusiasm of the huge crowd that gathered

331

in front of the capitol. There were cheers for "Old Sam." Many voices demanded a speech—a demand for which he was ready.

He reviewed at length his policies which were under criticism. This took time. But it did not take long to dispose of the troubles he had had with Congress. The Presidency, he said briefly, had been "a pillow of thorns," and he begged the Congress to treat his successor better than it had treated him. He was by turns sharp, good-natured, witty, wise, and savagely satirical. Nobody was bored.

As the President's speech went on into its second hour the crowd stayed with him. No doubt he was aware of the effect that his interminable valedictory was having upon the chronically weak digestive system of President-elect Lamar, who suffered acutely under the strain of three hours of Houstonian oratory. In conclusion, the retiring President expressed his sincere good will for the incoming administration that was to give Texas "a new character." Then with a broadly generous wave of his widespread arms, he beckoned President Lamar to the chair of state.

Lamar took his carefully prepared address from an inside pocket of his coat and rose to speak. But internal dissensions, simultaneous stomach and intestinal spasms, warned that this was not his day. He handed his manuscript to Algernon Thompson, Clerk of the Senate, who read to the exhausted audience in an uninspiring monotone a speech replete with grandly rhythmic passages. The "new character" had come out definitely second best in its first conflict with the old.[3]

The outgoing President concluded his participation in Lamar's inaugural with a levee in the refurbished executive mansion now sometimes called the White House. New curtains and carpets had been provided for this event. The rooms were overflowing with guests. Ashbel Smith was impressed by Houston's distinguished bearing. He wrote to his friend, William Locke, ". . . it was worth while to behold the elegant form and manly proportions of General Houston, to listen to the promptness and variety of his colloquial powers his facility and great tact to appropriate compliments as . . . he received the greetings of beauty and of talent."

Lamar's incoming was celebrated by a ball in the capitol. Here Smith beheld the "elite of the land its beauty and worth . . . a large and overflowing assembly of noble and accomplished dames, of soldiers scholars and chivalrous gentlemen."[4]

Anson Jones commented on the inaugural as a *"grand affair"* and added concerning Lamar's ball... "tis said there was some excess of riot, and some shameful spreeing, towards the breaking of the day." [5]

Dr. Moore's *Texas Telegraph*, substantially a David G. Burnet organ now, had found little to admire in Houston's administration and much to deplore. But "Old Sam's" departure from the scene provoked some second thoughts and a kind of nostalgia bordering on repentance for the abuse to which the retiring President had been subjected.

"The day will come," the *Telegraph* said, "when his name shall appear in the pages of the Texian story, unsullied by a single stain— his faults... forgotten, his vices buried in the tomb...." [6]

Ex-President Houston did not think highly of this premature committal of his vices to the tomb. It was too obviously a way of getting rid of him. Much remained to be done in this country which, in large part, was his creation. Besides, he was intensely curious to observe the efforts of Lamar and of Burnet to give Texas "a new character."

At least the Houston-Henderson operation in Europe was not to be short-circuited by the new administration. The youthful, aggressive Henderson had proved to be as popular in France as he had been in England, and Count Molé asked Lamar to continue Henderson at his post. Lamar did so.

BOOK V

MAKING CHARACTER

1. Margaret

FREE from government responsibilities for the first time since the revolution, General Houston turned to one of the purposes that had brought him to Texas—land speculation. He joined Philip Sublett, George Hockley, and four others as a co-proprietor of a real estate development, Sabine City. At their request he wrote the prospectus, which was printed as an advertisement in the *Texas Telegraph*.

> ... The attention of the adventurous, the enterprising, and the capitalist, is invited to the most elegible point ... easy of access ... possessing a good anchorage ... as rich soil and dense population as any other portion of Texas. All the country east of the Trinity River, must ship their products through the Sabine Pass....
> ... shares can be had by application to the stockholders and lots for buildings and dwellings, from the agent of the city.[1]

His interest in the venture declined almost as fast as the ink dried. He disliked assuring clients that they could get rich overnight by investing in a project that he knew to be risky. He gave less attention to real estate promotion and put another iron in the fire, establishing a law partnership with John Birdsall on January 8, 1839. The terms of the partnership were expressed in exactly thirteen words, "The copartnership is equal, and to continue during the pleasure of the parties." [2]

337

Before coming to Texas, Birdsall had completed a judgeship to which he had been appointed by Governor De Witt Clinton of New York. He had been chief justice of Texas during Houston's presidency, and his mind was more systematically trained in law than Houston's. Houston believed he could benefit from this association; it promised to be both lucrative and enjoyable.

His co-proprietors persuaded him to postpone his practice of law until he had made a trip to the United States to interest capital in Sabine City. This would fit in with a plan he had long been considering—a visit with his Old Chief in Nashville. It would also give him an opportunity to select some blooded stock for a ranch at Grand Cane on the Trinity River where he owned an extensive tract that had cost him 12½ cents an acre.

Preparing for his mission, he dressed to play the role of a conservative promoter. He shaved clean, with the exception of neat sideburns, and put on a new black broadcloth suit, ready-made, from New York. In scrip dollars the suit cost him as much as the one that he had pledged in his wager with Major Allen.

Just before he started for New Orleans, he received a cordial letter from Anna. He answered with reserve, maintaining his usual affability and mentioning a matter that rankled: The new chief of state had promised to give Texas a new character. This hurt Houston because it cast reflections on his administration.

In New Orleans he called on William Christy. No doubt he asked Christy for names of prospective land purchasers, and Christy may have mentioned several in Mississippi and Alabama. Houston's activities in New Orleans and Mississippi came under the observing eye of his one-time minister to the United States, Memucan Hunt. Hunt's rise during Houston's administration had not been as rapid as he thought he deserved; his request to be made secretary of war had been refused. Houston's opinion of Hunt, expressed in one private letter was, "Hunt is a good fellow—all told!" In another he said, "Although General Hunt is naturally a gentleman in feeling he does not know at all times how to conform himself to his destiny." [3]

Hunt was now an anti-Houston man, serving as President Lamar's secretary of the navy. He was visiting friends, not trailing the ex-President. Their paths crossed by accident, and Hunt took pleasure in forwarding gossipy reports about Houston to Lamar. From New Orleans, Hunt wrote that Houston received little or no attention there; a report had circulated that after giving a temperance lecture, Houston had become intoxicated and burned off his coat tail. Hunt claimed that Houston had been seen on the day of his arrival going to his lodgings wrapped up in a large cloak, presumably to conceal the condition of his coat tail.

At Hickman Lewis' farm in Alabama, Houston was pleased by a chestnut filly, Proclamation, priced at $2,000. He bought Proclamation and other fillies, but did not complete the transaction until August when he was on his way back to Texas after visiting Nashville.

In Mobile, he called on William Bledsoe, a tobacco and merchandise broker who received him cordially. Bledsoe expressed interest in the Sabine City project and seems to have suggested that his mother-in-law, Mrs. Nancy Lea, the widow of a Baptist minister and a shrewd business woman herself, might also be interested. He invited the General to visit his home in nearby Spring Hill and offered to assist in arranging for him to address a Mobile audience on annexation and, incidentally, on promising land developments in Texas.

On a May afternoon Bledsoe brought General Houston to his stately home. His eighteen-year-old wife, Emily Antoinette, was entertaining the ladies of the local Baptist church. Mrs. Bledsoe's twenty-year-old sister, Margaret Moffatt Lea, passed strawberries and cream.

Margaret was dressed less strikingly than her dark-eyed sister; she was taller and fairer than Emily and had brown hair and placid violet eyes. She had kept abreast of General Houston's activities since his arrival in New Orleans, hoping, it is said, that she would some day meet him. The time had come; Houson bowed low over her hand and, with more than casual warmth, said he was charmed.

Family legend is the source of details about this encounter. General Houston, having been introduced to Mrs. Bledsoe's numerous guests, became slightly confused as to identities and a little later mistook Margaret for her sister. When Margaret, engaged with her social duties, passed near Houston he said to another guest, "If she were not already married I believe I'd give that charming lady a chance to say 'no.' "

"But that's not Mrs. Bledsoe," was the answer, "that's the older unmarried sister. So you're free to give her that chance, General." [4]

When Margaret finished serving her sister's guests, she accompanied the General on a walk along an azalea path. Emily was amused because she saw little more of them that afternoon.

The General stayed with Bledsoe a week, during which he addressed two enthusiastic Mobile audiences in the interests of annexation and the possibilities of rising land values in Texas. In the parlor of the Bledsoe home, Margaret sang prettily for him, accompanying herself on her guitar. He frequently walked with her in the azalea garden. Ten years had passed since his disastrous marriage to Eliza Allen. Now he was forty-six, and this girl who charmed him as he had never before been charmed was twenty-six years younger than he. Her health, he imagined, was delicate. Could she stand primitive conditions and the demands that would be made upon her as the wife of a lawyer, politician, promoter, and stock raiser?

One evening he pointed to a lone star that was low in the heavens. He referred to it as a star of destiny and asked Margaret to gaze at it after he was gone—to meditate upon its possible significance. She was to remember what he had told her about life in Texas; it was the most beautiful country in the world but not without hardships. Perhaps he was a man who was never to know tranquility because his future was bound up with the future of Texas. Much as he longed for peace, he seemed to be destined for strife. He told her that he would send her tidings from Nashville. They would be important tidings, and he would be anxious to know how they were received.

The Hermitage had a new banjo-shaped driveway different from the approach in 1829, encircling a lawn with trees and flowers. The house was not the same, either. Some five years earlier, in 1834, a spark from the dining room fireplace flue had ignited the roof. Portions of the walls had been saved and used in the reconstruction. The new façade had taller pillars and was more imposing than the old. The interior was somewhat like the original plan, but the old furnishings looked a little seedy.

The most notable change Houston observed was what time had done to the Old Chief. Jackson's brow was more deeply furrowed, and the lines from the base of his nose to the corners of his mouth were more pronounced. His eyesight had dimmed; anything he read, he held close to his right eye. His ample crest of hair had turned almost pure white. His voice, though milder, still had a vibrant ring. He was much leaner and weaker in the flesh, but still strong in spirit.

From the windows of his bedroom at The Hermitage, Houston looked out over Rachel's garden toward her tomb which was a short distance from the house. He recalled the day when, with the other pallbearers, he had walked the cotton-strewn path carrying her casket. An eighth of a mile to the east was Tulip Grove, the home of Jackson's nephew, Andrew Jackson Donelson.

The two old soldiers had much to talk about—Horseshoe Bend, the Battle of New Orleans, and San Jacinto. Jackson was glad to get the truth about the long retreat from Gonzales. He thought Houston was smart to take the enemy by surprise at their siesta, and he was proud of him for choosing the prudent course and not sacrificing Santa Anna.

Houston must have pleased his Old Chief when he said he would always regard his success at San Jacinto as the result of his familiarity with Jackson's tactics in the campaign against the Creeks. He also praised Jackson's handling of the 1833 nullification crisis in South Carolina. He believed that the Old Chief's way of coping with it had strengthened national bonds. The country was indebted to Jackson for that.

Their talk turned to graver and more contemporary matters. Jackson believed annexation would work itself out. The United States couldn't afford to have another "Canady" under British dominion on its southwestern frontier.

In a long letter to Jackson the previous summer, Houston had described the outbreak of a small-scale war in the Nacogdoches area when land grabbers had violated the treaty which Houston had negotiated with the Cherokees two months before San Jacinto to keep them from siding with the enemy against the settlers. The affair was typical of the trouble he was having in combating disorderly, lawless elements. Later letters suggest that, while he was in Nashville, there was a great deal of talk about his difficulties in influencing Texas to be the kind of country he wanted it to be. Jackson shared Houston's respect for legal and constitutional procedures, and Houston credited the Old Chief with inspiring him with these ideals.

For Jackson the years of stress and turbulence were past. When he quit office after his second term he was more popular than when he had entered it—the first President to have that experience. The years of quiet and peace had begun, a period in which he figured as an elder statesman, the Grand Nabob of Nashville. The destiny of Texas was the only disturbing question on the horizon.

Houston had come to The Hermitage with a desire for spiritual refreshment in communion with his Old Chief. He received it in abundance.

Soon after his arrival at The Hermitage, Houston wrote a letter to Margaret Lea. Either this letter has not survived or its publication has not been permitted, but from Margaret's answer we know its character. Houston made it clear that his heart was touched, his soul aflame. At last he had met one who could not be other than his final fate, and he would rejoice to find it so. He reminded her that he had asked her to look at the Lone Star and meditate upon its possible significance for them. The vital question may have been plainly put. At all events it was clear that he wanted her to be his wife and would wait anxiously for her response.

Mails were slow. With mounting anxiety he had to wait several weeks for his answer. Jackson left him much to his own resources as he did all his guests, but they visited frequently. After a lapse of weeks Margaret's letter came. It was dated July 17, the year, 1839, was omitted. The first few words told him he could not have asked for more. She had been disappointed because the letter he had promised to send her from Columbus was never received; she had concluded that the mail miscarried: "... however, I have heard from you and the tidings are truly welcome I assure you. My answer may be taken as strong evidence of that, for it is the first I have addressed to any gentleman."

It was the letter of an innocent, sheltered girl, eager and thrilled to find herself in love for the first time. The glow in her heart prompted her to describe the natural beauty of the green hills, groves and bowers of her home in Marion. Then:

> I am in the midst of my childhood's friends, and greeted on every hand with gentle words and soft endearing epithets and I am happy; Quite happy? Ah no ... there are those absent whose station within my heart remains unfilled.

She was so happy that she suffered from constant dread lest some link in this "grand union of tender associations" be severed. She was sitting in the library, a favorite resort:

Now in the early morning it looks out upon a range of wild hills, still slightly obscured by the mist of the night, and in the evening, the sunset rays will beautifully gild their rich verdure. . . . I am in the midst of a band of heroes, ideal and real, and sages with their wisdom and philosophy are here and orators and poets. . . . And yet though it may seem sacriligious, my heart is not with them today. It is like a caged bird. . . .

Last night I gazed long upon our beauteous emblem the *star of destiny*, and my thoughts took the form of verse, but I will not inscribe them here, for then you might call me a romantic star-struck young lady. . . .

She regretted that it would not be possible to see him at the home of her brother-in-law, but Bledsoe and Antoinette would be there and would be delighted to see him. Bledsoe and her mother were planning to go to Texas in October, but they were unwilling to have her accompany them until General Houston had visited her at home in Marion, and she had felt obliged to agree.

During their walk along the azalea path, Houston evidently had told her that she was his Esperanza—the one hoped for. Now she reminded him of this. If he did not make the journey to Marion on his way home he would not see "his Esperanza *for ages (months I mean)* to come." [5]

Nothing was lacking. The one hoped for acknowledged her identity and welcomed her destiny. This was his answer—she would be his wife. After that, what could have kept him from visiting Marion on his way home?

He returned to Alabama in late August. Margaret received him with radiant happiness; her mother and brother, with the respect and warmth due a distinguished man who was honoring their family by joining it.

Margaret and the General walked along the azalea path that led to the bench where they had observed the evening star. She tucked her hand inside his arm and smiled up at him. The promise implied in her answer to his "tidings" was made definite here. He took her in his arms.

A practical, sensible woman, Nancy Lea had reason to be an uneasy mother. Had her daughter succumbed to a passing infatuation for this world-renowned General? Was her lovely, proud, reserved, poised, home-loving Margart pursuing an indiscretion that she might regret? Why, Margaret scarcely knew Houston unless one took into account what she had read about him in New Orleans papers as a victorious general and president of a new country. And Mrs. Lea had heard certain stories about the General's domestic troubles in Tennessee and about his heavy drinking.

Though troubled, she did not think it wise to interfere—and not for lack of courage either. As the wife of a Baptist preacher who had had to subdue many factional strifes in his congregation, she had been well trained in courage. At the propitious moment, she was ready to talk straight out to the ex-President of Texas. Mrs. Lea made no effort to deal with the delicate question at this time, but evidently considered the engagement as tentative. The next step would be determined when she went to Texas in the spring with her son-in-law to look at lands which she might possibly be interested in buying.

When General Houston left Alabama, he and Margaret considered themselves definitely engaged with nothing tentative about it. Years later, Houston's first biographer, the Reverend William C. Crane, asked Margaret how she had dared to make such an important decision on such brief acquaintance, commit herself to a life in a wild country, and risk unhappiness and misfortune by linking her destiny to a man given to excesses. She answered that it was because the General had "won her heart." [6] She also confessed that she had conceived the idea that she could reform Houston and meant to devote herself to that work. Margaret Moffatt Lea had found a career. While Houston turned his hand to making character for Texas, she would help the General make character for himself.

2. The Gentleman from San Augustine

HOUSTON returned to Texas by the Red River route in September. At Natchitoches, he either bought a horse or picked up one that he had left there with a settler. Then he rode to San Augustine where many surprises and some grief awaited him. His law partner, John Birdsall, had died of yellow fever late in the summer, ending a close association which Houston had looked forward to renewing with happy expectations.

He learned that Houston City would soon cease to be the capital. The new administration was transferring it far out on the western frontier to a place named after Stephen Austin. The legislative act sanctioning the move specifically eliminated Houston City for all time as a site for the permanent capital. The administration wanted to prevent Houston's name from being permanently associated with the nation's capital; it also wanted to placate western settlers who believed they were entitled to the prestige of having the capital in their region and desired it as a step toward their protection against Indian raids.

One of Houston's pleasant surprises was the discovery that, during his absence, his friends in San Augustine had promoted his election to the Texas House of Representatives. Thus he was officially back in politics and fully disposed to accept the opportunity for further service. He still considered Nacogdoches his home but was complimented that San Augustine voters had adopted him.

But his victory was outweighed by the number and variety of unpleasant surprises. The worst was Lamar's failure to recognize the Cherokee treaty which Houston and his fellow commissioners, Hockley and Forbes, had negotiated in February, 1836, just before the Lone Star Republic was born. This treaty guaranteed that the Cherokees could "enjoy forever" all lands "granted them by the Spanish Provinces" in exchange for a pledge of everlasting peace. The treaty terms had been suggested by the General Council and the Cherokees had observed them faithfully. As Houston pointed out, they had refrained from attacking undefended settlements in East Texas at a time when they might easily have tilted the balance against the colonists.

Early in his presidency, Houston had submitted the Cherokee treaty to the Senate and earnestly pleaded for its ratification. A committee appointed to report on it had recommended that the Senate refuse to ratify the treaty, even though Texas already had benefited substantially by its terms. The committee had acknowledged that the treaty complied with directions from the San Felipe Consultation and the Council, but these instructions, it held, had been issued upon wrong premises. Despite numerous appeals from Houston, the Senate had refused to ratify.

Houston believed that no people in the country had a better right to their lands than the Cherokees. Before the whites had come streaming in, the Spanish authorities had invited Chief Bowl and his people to abandon their settlements along the Red River in Arkansas. They had been granted a choice strip of land 130 miles long by 60 miles wide in the Nacogdoches district. This strip, substantially intact, had been guaranteed them by the treaty.

Threats and attacks on the Cherokees had occurred in the summer of 1838 when Houston was in Nacogdoches on vacation visiting the Raguets and other friends. He had received letters of alarm and anguish from Chiefs Bowl and Big Mush, both of whom had signed the treaty after persuasion by him. They were alarmed when white men threatened to kill them and were stricken in their hearts that such threats could be made despite the sacred treaty promises. In one of his letters to Houston, written for him by an Indian agent, Bowl had said, "... my people from the Bigest to the least have a little dread on their minds," he besought Houston to come to see him or, if he could not come, to send reassurance.[1]

Houston had reassured him that same day:

Before the surveyor could get time to run the line [the boundary line as agreed in the Cherokee treaty], the fuss began, but it will not stop on that account.... I wish it well done, that it may stand always....

The words of good men should never be forgotten.... I have given an order that no families or children of Indians shall be disturbed or have troubles, but that they shall be protected and even the Mexican families, and property shall not be troubled! That war may cease everywhere is my wish, ... Tell my Sister, the children, and all my red brothers to sleep in peace....[2]

To quiet the anxiety of Big Mush over white aggressions, he had written at about the same time:

I wish you to stand by the Treaty which I made with you & my Red Brothers. I will never lie to that treaty while I live, and it must stand as long as [a] good man lives and water runs. I will build it up; and all men shall see it.[3]

He had thus given the most positive reassurances that his picture-talk vocabulary was capable of. In addition, he had urged the chiefs

346

to put their trust in General Thomas Rusk, who "will protect you. Look to him as a great friend."

These communications had quieted the Cherokees and the trouble had subsided. All had been calm when Houston left the country to visit Jackson.

President Lamar hated Indians. He may have acquired this antagonism as a participant in harsh actions against the Cherokees in Georgia. Seizing the opportunity of Houston's absence from the country, he made his first move to give Texas a more forceful character than it had enjoyed under his predecessor. Abandoning Houston's policy of peace and trade, he had launched a series of small Indian wars, beginning in the west. In retaliation, the Comanches had joined other tribes in raiding the frontier. Settlers suffered massacres and the destruction of their homes by fire. Undeterred by these minor wars, the administration decided that the Cherokees must leave the country or be exterminated.

Now, with humiliation and sorrow, Houston learned of the fate that had overwhelmed the red men who had kept faith and had acted in accord with his reassurance. It was all the more bitter because it had happened while he was discussing with Jackson the principles and policies that brought honor to a nation. From talks with a number of participants, he familiarized himself with the details of the Cherokee War. John H. Reagan, a native of Tennessee, was probably one of his informants.

At twenty-one Reagan was a deputy surveyor of Texas Republic lands and had witnessed important events in the Cherokee War. Later, he recorded them in his reminiscences.

Lamar had permitted surveyors for speculators to intrude provocatively into Cherokee territory and set up measuring lines and stakes in the gardens and yards of Chief Bowl and his lesser chiefs. The Cherokees had objected vigorously but without violence, compelling Lamar to look elsewhere for a pretext to wage war and expel them. He found it when a few renegade members of Chief Bowl's tribe were captured on the Colorado River. They were returning from Matamoros in company with a Mexican bandit, Manuel Flores. Lamar's followers falsely charged that these men had represented Chief Bowl in recent negotiations with Santa Anna against the peace of Texas.

Lamar sent Martin Lacey, an experienced Indian trader as Indian agent, with a five-man commission to treat with Bowl and his allied chiefs. Among the members of this commission were ex-President Burnet, whose land claims conflicted with those of the Cherokees; Secretary of War Albert Sidney Johnston; and Thomas J. Rusk, whose participation in the outrage scarred his friendship with Houston. While the commissioners were negotiating, troops were readied under General Burleson and Major General Kelsey H. Douglas. They knew that, regardless of the outcome of the negotiations, the Cherokees had to go.

Reagan reported that Chief Bowl courteously invited the president's commissioners to confer beside a spring a few rods from his house. The commissioners charged Bowl's people with murder, theft, and treachery. Bowl denied the charges, but admitted that the Cherokees who had joined the renegades might have been guilty of misdeeds. Probably they were the ones who had been captured with the Mexican bandit. Bowl's people had instructions to show no mercy to these men and to kill them wherever found. Bowl was as anxious to have them brought to justice as the whites were.

This report did not alter Lamar's determination. He ordered a company under Major Benjamin C. Waters to occupy land bordering the Cherokee country. Actually it was land that belonged to the Cherokees under old agreements. Bowl protested and threatened war if the troops built a fort there, as they intended to. Lamar justified his course by claiming that the Cherokee land had become a center for conspirators.

Bowl defended himself and his people in prolonged negotiations until he was weary. Finally, resigned in spirit, he told Lacey that he was eighty-three years old. Whatever came of this could not matter to him personally, but he feared for his three wives and his children. If he fought the whites, they would kill him; if he refused to fight, his own people would kill him. He had led his people a long time and had resolved to stand by them.

General Johnston planned the campaign with the assistance of General Hugh McLeod, Lamar's brother-in-law. McLeod commanded the major regiment. Reagan, who had been present during some of the conferences with Bowl, told in his reminiscences of being impressed by the chief's dignified behavior and frankness.

Reagan regretted it when the order came to attack on July 15, 1839, but he participated in the action.

In the first day's fight, two whites and eighteen Indians were killed. On the second day, the battle lasted two hours. Bowl was conspicuously mounted on a "paint" horse; he wore a black military hat, a silk vest, a sash, and a sword—probably the battered old sword that Houston had given him. Bowl exposed himself recklessly, riding up and down in the rear of his line while telling his warriors that if they would charge, the whites would turn and run.

But the Indians retreated under heavy fire. Bowl was shot in the thigh and his horse was disabled. Bowl dismounted and was limping off the field when he was shot in the back. He walked a short distance and fell, then rose to a sitting position directly in front of John Reagan's company.

Remembering the Bowl's dignity and force in council and his devotion to his tribe in sustaining their decision for war against his own judgment, Reagan endeavored to save him. As Reagan ran toward Bowl Captain Robert Smith approached from another direction with drawn pistol. "Captain, don't shoot him," Reagan pleaded. But Smith fired, and the bullet went through the back of the old man's head, killing him instantly. The troops pursued the other Indians, driving old and young, women and children, sick and wounded to the Arkansas boundary to seek the protection of Chief Jolly.[4]

From San Augustine, Houston rode to Nacogdoches where he was cordially welcomed by Henry Raguet and the Sternes. A meeting of leading citizens was called at the town hall. A large number attended, curious to know what the former President might have to say about Lamar's Cherokee adventure.

After expressing his indignation over the Cherokee outrage, Houston mounted his horse again and started his long journey westward to take his seat in the House of Representatives. His speech had embittered and angered some of his closest friends in Nacogdoches; they resented his charge that the Cherokee War was an act of bad faith. Years passed before they forgave him.

Some two years later, on October 20, 1841, Adolphus Sterne noted in his diary that General Houston had addressed a crowd in the court house. He added: "There exists at present no difference between the people of this County and Gen. H except the Cherokee question among those who differ with the General upon that I am One." [5]

The new capital at Austin was a difficult three to five day journey from the old capital, depending upon weather and conditions of the roads. Its alleged charm and scenic beauty did not alter the fact that it was dangerously exposed to Mexican and Indian raids. Then, too, Houston learned that the decision to relocate the capital had been made under pressure of promoters who believed they could make money selling lots in Austin.

One feature of the new capital testified to the soaring fancies of a lyric poet. President Lamar had provided himself with a splendid although flimsy two-story residence where he entertained lavishly, sending the bills to the Treasury. While most settlers were enduring extreme privations, he had begun equipping the president's house with imported furnishings, decorated dinner services, maple bedsteads, rocking chairs, luxurious carpets, astral lamps, center tables, and sideboards with marble tops at a cost of more than $10,000.

Under fair November skies in 1839, the main street promised a magnificent vista some time in the future when the newly planted trees had grown larger. Meanwhile the mud was as formidable as that in Houston City. Within an hour after rainfall began, the drivers of ox-drawn vehicles were reduced to prying out wheels with the fence rails they always carried for that purpose. The Hall of Congress, on an elevation just off Congress Avenue, was a modest one-story affair. The one-room shack that sheltered Houston had a dirt floor and a small clay fireplace.

The chill of December had come before Houston took the initiative in a campaign of his own to give a new character to the Republic. On the floor of the House, he denounced the removal of the capital to "the most unfortunate site on earth," without a house between it and Santa Fe.[6] The exposed location invited raids by Indians and Mexicans who were inflamed by Lamar's provocative policies and by the hostile acts of irresponsible individuals.

Although it bore his name, he would not defend Houston City as a desirable site; but it had been chosen by the Congress under an agreement with the town proprietors that the capital should remain there for a term of years not yet expired. Did not the government intend to respect promises? It was well understood, he said, that members of the government and Congress were interested in land transactions. Did the government intend to become a speculator in city lots as one might expect a Mexican government to do? He proposed that at the right time the people be given a chance to say where the capital should be located. This proposal enraged the border citizens, and Houston was attacked by their representatives.

Before a crowded House whose members had been forewarned of his intention, Houston introduced a bill providing that all lands recently owned and occupied by the Cherokees should be treated as if owned by the government, sectionalized into 640-acre tracts, and offered at private sale. His argument on the subject really began three weeks before he introduced the bill, in a speech on December 3, 1839, when he described the injustice of the campaign against the Cherokees. He stated that the Cherokees had been defrauded and unjustifiably driven from their lands by the government, which had acted in bad faith.

> ... The blood shed on that occasion will not be unavenged; and the time is not distant when the Indian war cry shall be heard upon our border, and the country will learn the bad effect of making enemies of *tried and faithful friends*.

During the seven years that he had lived on the border the Cherokees "had never stolen a horse *nor drawn one drop of white man's blood*. Letters ... had been written to them, to incense them to join the Mexicans. They never acceded to it. And they were friendly up to the time they were driven from their homes and country. By the treaty they were not bound to fight for us—they were only bound to keep the peace, and they kept it."

The land speculators and their supporters wanted their pre-emption of Cherokee lands legalized. If, as Houston argued, the Cherokees had legal title to their lands, then speculators' claims were null and void. In that case, the land from which the Cherokees had been expelled belonged to the government and could be opened up for private sale. Houston later stated that "less than $3,000,000 it could not bring," and he thought "it would bring nearer eighteen millions than three. Its value could not be computed—there was not an acre that would not redeem ten Texas dollars."

He urged that money received from the sale of the Cherokee land should go to the Treasury to "provide a sinking fund for the redemption of our bonds. . . . The war . . . was produced by the encroachment of the speculators—[their] locations were not made in good faith—and if we now confirm them in their illegal locations, the blood shed in the Cherokee war will rest upon our own shoulders."

Spokesmen for the speculators bitterly opposed the measure on the grounds that the land never had belonged to the Cherokees. Houston referred to various grants, treaties, and agreements to show that the Cherokee title had been complete until they had been illegally expelled. He charged: "There has been a party in the Country who have always endeavored to suppress the light, and throw as much darkness and mystery about it as possible. This party have been engaged in extensive land speculations, and would fain have monopolized all the Cherokee lands, to their own unhallowed purposes."

He had been called the Indian's friend, he went on, and had been accused of greater lenity toward them than he had shown to his own countrymen. These accusations did not intimidate him. He would pursue the course necessary to preserve the country's reputation, safety, and prosperity. He hoped the time had arrived when the question could be decided on its merits; that each member would reach his verdict as members of a jury did, deciding between man and man. It was too late to do the Indians justice, but at least their claim should be acknowledged. His moderation and restraint on a subject so close to his heart impressed some of the representatives.

Then President Lamar's Adjutant General, Hugh McLeod, presented Chief Bowl's large black military hat with a bullet hole in it to Houston. It was to be Houston's share of the Cherokee War plunder. The hat had been supplied by the fiery patriot and vindictive Indian fighter, Ed Burleson. The bitter irony of the presentation maddened the San Augustine representative. He charged that the government was a tool of land speculators, and laid the basis for later attacks on Vice-President Burnet's claim that his title to land in the Cherokee country was better than the earlier grant to the Indians by Mexico. This was the first time Houston had mentioned Burnet as a backstage participant in the Cherokee outrage.

Closing his discussion, he said he doubted that he had convinced the House of the justness and expediency of the measure. But he had expressed the honest convictions of his heart, he assured them, and he believed that the future would credit him for integrity of purpose no matter how Congress decided upon the bill.

When it came to a vote, members of the House dared not reject a measure obviously favoring the whole people against the speculators. In January, 1840, Houston's bill for disposal of the Cherokee lands "passed by almost an unanimous vote." According to Senator Francis Moore's *Telegraph*, February 5, 1840, Houston's remarks in support of the measure had excited not only the reproach of his enemies, but the grief and shame of his friends.

3. *A Trio of Dreamers*

HOUSTON's victory with the Cherokee land bill was possible because President Lamar's political fortune was slowly changing. Lamar was in trouble. While he had been indulging in dreams of ridding Texas of Indians and of expansion and conquest, his administration had been falling to pieces. Only ten of his supporters who had been elected in 1838 were returned in 1839 when San Augustine sent Houston to the House of Representatives.

Nonetheless, he announced his intention to carry on the Mexican war with vigor. He disapproved of Houston's attempts to bring about annexation and declared that Texas, if left to herself, would prosper. In a message to Congress he urged that the issue be allowed to expire. His diplomatic agent to Mexico had been rebuffed. The Congress had promptly appropriated money for a company of Texas Rangers and three companies of militia to protect the frontier against Mexicans and Indians. But results were negative, because there was not enough money to support the troops. Outraged by Lamar's aggressive policies, the Indians continued their murderous raids.

Deterioration had set in on the frontier, particularly in Robertson County. Settlers who had the means of getting away moved out. Some were unable to leave because their horses had been stolen. Without protection by the government, those who remained had to stay in their houses; without protection from Indians, they could not even plant corn.

Like his fellow President, Martin Van Buren, Lamar was unfortunate in the conditions that existed when he took office. The entire world was suffering a prolonged economic downtrend that statesmen could not control. The United States, as a result of President Jackson's mistaken financial policies, was particularly hard hit and unable to grant loans.

So Lamar now faced even more acute financial difficulties than Houston had encountered. But Houston had moved with caution, putting limited amounts of interest-bearing promissory notes into circulation.[1] He was no financial genius, but common sense told him that paper, used as currency, had a better chance of maintaining worth if backed by a tangible asset such as the country's public lands. President Lamar, on the other hand, boldly issued large sums of non-interest-bearing currency known as "red backs." Unsupported by any kind of security, the red backs tumbled to 16¢ on the dollar the first year and 12½¢ the second year. They rose to 35¢ on the strength of a false rumor of a big loan from France. When this rumor exploded, Lamar's financial dream collapsed. His red backs fell again to 12½¢.

Lamar was a tragic figure despite his many engaging qualities. His truly lyrical gifts were displayed in several volumes of verse; he knew the thrill of letting imagination take wing. In beautiful prose, he also sang of education as the guardian genius of democracy. He believed that his administration was the propitious hour for Texas to lay the foundation of a great moral and intellectual edifice which after ages would hail as the chief ornament and blessing of the country. Toward this ideal he asked the Congress to set aside land for the use and support of a school system. But he lacked administrative ability and tact in dealing with men. He lived apart from realities. Already he was dreaming of a great conquest to ameliorate the economic sickness of his country. He expected this vast project, an expedition to Santa Fe, to win prestige for himself, give Texas a new character, and place his name in history. He nourished this dream for months before he gave any intimation of it to the Congress or to his fellow citizens.

Absorbed, he became oblivious to his surroundings and was conspicuous for his absent-mindedness. He passed friends on the street without recognizing them. As he approached the capitol one morning, a group of state employees decided that it would be a good joke to interrupt his reverie. They surrounded and saluted him with a salvo of lusty good mornings. Astonished, he awoke from his dream, removed his hat, made a low bow, and responded, "Good morning, gentlemen, in the name of God, good morning to you all." Immersed in his dream, he passed on, unaware of what had happened.[2]

Houston's dream at this time was of limited scope, severely practical. He looked toward a stable government and a self-contained, contented people; trade with the Indians, peace with Mexico, readiness for defense, increased production from the land, a good mail service, good schools, sound court procedures, an enforceable tax system, and a stable currency. To accomplish Houston's objectives, Texas needed a certain type of man in the executive office. Houston thought he knew an available man of exactly the right type—himself. He dreamed that the day would come when Texas would listen to his warnings of dangers ahead; he hoped that day would come soon. But, having criticized Lamar for his Cherokee War and various other measures, it seemed advisable to adopt a policy of reasonable skepticism, watchful waiting, silent incredulity. His moderation as a critic did not impress Lamar and his supporters, but it chagrined Senator Anson Jones.

Senator Jones was a wily New Englander whose career, like Lamar's, had been marked by strange forces. One way or another, almost every move he had made to advance himself had suffered cruel frustration.

A native of Great Barrington, Massachusetts, born of an exceedingly poor family, Jones had made extreme sacrifices to get a medical license in his own state. To support his early practice, he obtained merchandise on credit and opened a drug store. This enterprise failed because friends to whom he was financially indebted for his education turned against him and seized his stock. He salvaged enough from the wreck to pay for one term of study at Jefferson Medical College in Philadelphia.

In 1832 he opened an office in New Orleans. Doctors were at a premium because of a yellow fever epidemic. His fees soon gave him a taste of economic independence, and the future seemed bright. Then Jones was stricken with the fever. Again his financial resources were wiped out, partly because of the high fees he had to pay for medical care.

From this disaster, he saved enough to pay for steamboat passage to Texas. With fifty dollars' worth of drugs, his sole capital, he landed at Brazoria. One look after he went ashore persuaded him that he had made a mistake and he returned to his ship to negotiate passage back to the States. But Brazoria's leading citizen, William Wharton, heard of the newcomer and his profession. He tried to convince Jones that Brazoria was his opportunity. Jones yielded to the extent of agreeing to stay over until the next steamboat. His prosperity began at once, and Brazoria became his home.

Jones was one of the doctors left by Houston to look after the sick in the measles camp at Harrisburg during the San Jacinto campaign. He was also one of those who had urged Houston to take the offensive before he was ready to do so. Back in October, 1838, when Houston was president, Jones had served as Texas minister to the United States.

Temperamentally, Senator Jones was strange and "twisted." One of his twists was his distrust and hatred of Houston, who had befriended him and given him opportunities. Jones was possessed by a compulsive notion that he could manage the Texas Republic better than either Lamar or Houston, that he deserved to be president, and some day would be. It is possible that he was generally familiar with Lamar's vast project. There is no doubt about his disapproval of Lamar as an administrator.

It was Jones's custom to record thoughts and opinions in diary-like memoranda. Of Lamar he wrote:

> Gen. Lamar may mean well—I am not disposed to impugn his motives—he has fine belles-lettres talent, and is an elegant writer. But his mind is altogether of a dreamy, poetic order, a sort of political Troubadour and Crusader, and wholly unfit by habit or education for the active duties, and the every-day realities of his present station. Texas is too small for a man of such wild, visionary, "vaulting ambition."[3]

The paths of General Houston and Dr. Jones became more and more intertwining. At the moment, with his eye on the presidency, Jones managed politically to keep a foot in both the Lamar and the Houston camp. Privately he disapproved of Houston as much as he did of Lamar. Houston's ability to play a waiting game particularly distressed him. A policy of caution always seemed to work out in

356

Houston's favor; this, together with his outrageous good luck, brought him rewards that Jones thought were undeserved.

In short, Houston was not striking out at the Lamar regime with the bitterness and violence that Jones desired. Jones's secret hope was that "Old Sam" would attack the administration so vindictively that an irreconcilable quarrel would result in a compromise on Dr. Jones to succeed Lamar. Jones jotted diary-like entries and comments on letters, envelopes, and official memoranda. Every night he recorded his own good deeds and the evil doings of others. Some of the latter concerned Houston's shortcomings. For years the doctor secretly impugned the character of the man who perhaps was a little suspicious of Jones but respected him for his ability and supposed him to be a friend. In his diary, Jones explained the basic "viciousness" of Houston's temperate behavior toward the Lamar Administration:

... Gen. Houston, I fear, does not care how completely L---r ruins the country, so that he can hide the errors, the follies and widespread ruin of his own past administration, and have it to say, "I told you so; there is nobody but Old Sam after all."

Then again, one wintry night during the 1839-1840 session, Jones recorded his belief that—

Gen. H. is not so strong in what he does himself, as in what his enemies do: it is not *his* strength, but *their* weakness—not his *wisdom* but *their* folly. Cunning, Indian cunning is the secret of his success. Old Bowles ... learned him all he knows though he has native tact, was an apt scholar, and learned *Indian* well.

Each of this trio of dreamers would leave his mark on the Republic.

4. Resolute Lady

GENERAL Houston learned more about the virtue of patience by waiting for letters from his Esperanza. The post was always delayed, but Margaret's letters were never disappointing when they arrived. They breathed devotion and revealed that Margaret was exactly what she called herself in one of them, a resolute young lady with no weakening in her determination to join the General and to make Texas her home.

Writing to her in the evenings, the General responded with all the fervor of his nature. So that they could be married at the earliest possible date, he pleaded with her to come to Texas in the spring when her mother and William Bledsoe were going to inspect land that he had recommended for purchase. In answer, Margaret named the approximate date on which she expected to arrive in Galveston. Two days before the House adjourned, the representative from San Augustine mounted his horse and rode to the Gulf port.

With the thought presumably, that the arrival of an ex-President's bride deserved some public notice, the General made known to his friends the purpose that brought him. A tremor of excitement ran through the town. A few caustic remarks about the ex-President awaiting the arrival of his bride were dispatched to President Lamar by one of his staunch supporters, James Love, a lawyer from Kentucky.

The boat from New Orleans, bearing passengers from Mobile, came up to the Galveston bar at midnight. Shortly after dawn, she moved into the harbor and anchored. The weather was fair and the scene that greeted the newcomers was favorable. Travelers always spoke of the early morning charm of the harbor—sloops and schooners floating at anchor, sea gulls soaring, curlews singing, and cranes screaming. They were also likely to be impressed by the number of shipwrecks alongshore. A high hurricane tide had inundated part of the island, destroyed a number of frame houses near the wharf, and driven some ships ashore. Some of the wrecked ships, with their masts still standing, were in use as dwelling houses. In a new country everything had to be put to use.

The General went out to the vessel in a dory and found Mrs. Lea and Bledsoe on deck. Just as he was greeting them, a cannon of the shore garrison boomed and startled Mrs. Lea. The General hastened to assure her that it was not a sign of hostility, but a salute. His friends in the garrison were taking this means of announcing their pleasure in the arrival of his bride-to-be. Then he asked if Margaret's absence was the result of indisposition from the voyage.

"General Houston," Mrs. Lea said firmly, "my daughter is in Alabama. She goes forth in the world to marry no man. The one who

358

receives her hand will receive it in my home and not elsewhere." [1]

The gentleman from San Augustine—former President, victor of San Jacinto, confidant of Jackson—promptly bowed his acquiescence, recognizing these as proper terms emanating from a perspicacious mother. In impassioned letters to Margaret and to Robert Irion, Henry Raguet, Ashbel Smith, George Hockley, and others, Houston had confessed his loneliness for the sweets of the fireside. Terms far more exacting than Nancy Lea's would have found him ready. Her terms represented her own capitulation. Mrs. Lea liked the General and had no desire to stop the marriage, but she still was a little skeptical about whether this exciting country was a suitable homeland for Margaret.

As for Margaret, having yielded to her mother's wishes, she had plenty to occupy her at home while Mrs. Lea and Bledsoe were sizing up the country that was to be her home. On April 25, 1840, in a letter to her mother, Margaret wrote that she had been working on her trousseau. She had made herself a white satin dress, a purple silk, and a blue muslin.

General Houston and Margaret Lea were married at the home of her eldest brother, Henry, in Marion, Perry County, Alabama, on May 9, 1840. After the ceremony a group of Margaret's girl friends sang an original ode, to the tune of "*The Old Oaken Bucket.*" It celebrated the bridegroom's fame and in the final stanza made a notable comparison:

> *Our Washington's name has been hallowed in story,*
> *As founder of Freedom's retreat in the West.*
> *Another has risen to share in his glory—*
> *The Texian Patriot—our honored guest!* [2]

From Mobile the Houstons took a boat to New Orleans where they transferred to the *New York* to go to Galveston. There is a family legend that, during the passage, Margaret told the General her views on temperance. Probably she had been reluctant to discuss the subject earlier lest it appear to be an attempt to strike a bargain. Now she told her husband of her fervent hope that he would give up drinking.

Margaret was not satisfied with assurances about past conduct. She was looking toward the future. For a girl of twenty-one who was dealing with a forty-seven-year-old, strong-willed man of established habits, she handled the matter effectively and with delicacy. Without pledging himself to total abstinence, the General agreed that he would never again drink to excess. Margaret's ultimate object was to persuade the General to commit himself to total abstinence and she was prepared to proceed tactfully by degrees.

When reports first circulated that Houston intended to marry, his friends had dismissed them as incredible; then, when the news was confirmed, they were shocked and grieved. George Hockley had written Ashbel Smith that he feared this marriage would be the General's death warrant—i.e., if it ever occurred. He would only believe it when he heard that it had been perfected. Smith, if he had misgivings, confided them to no one. Barnard E. Bee wrote Smith that he had learned "with great pain" of "the marriage of Genl. Houston to Miss Lea! I had hoped it would never be consummated— in all my intercourse with life I have never met with an individual more totally disqualified for domestic happiness. . . ." [3]

Behind his friends' concern was the fear that another marriage would end as the Tennessee affair had done, and plunge Houston into another period of despair and heavy drinking.

Many times Houston's poor health and broken appearance had been attributed to drinking when he was actually convalescing from malaria. But he was a heavy drinker; most men were in those days. The chances were slim that he could change in a community where heavy drinking was a feature of every social occasion. But no one could estimate the power of the tall, poised, serene girl with fine slender figure, lovely eyes, lustrous hair, and a beguiling simplicity and directness. The bold character she had married had his mission, as she knew perfectly well. And she had hers. She accepted hers with unquestioning faith, never doubting that she could save her husband from his weakness.

Ashbel Smith saw a good deal of General Houston and his bride in Houston City. His answer to Barnard Bee's pessimistic prediction gave Bee much to think about. He reported that the Old Chief's health was excellent. Houston was indulging in no conviviality with his friends and was a model of conjugal propriety. Smith had had dreadful misgivings about Houston's marriage, but so far they had not been borne out. Not only Houston's health but all his ways were infinitely mended. Would it last? Smith was hoping for the best.

On the way to San Augustine to mingle with Houston's constituents, the newlyweds stopped at Nacogdoches. The edginess of Houston's old associates over his eulogy of Chief Bowl and his denunciation of some well-known local citizens as unscrupulous speculators was apparent at first, but it was blunted before the couple left. Margaret's charm and compelling beauty, her natural warmth, her pride in the General, and her pleasure at being with him among his old friends were irresistible.

Nacogdoches relented sufficiently to honor the Houstons with a barbecue. The couple encountered a good deal of what passed for humor. A crowd, exhilarated and hilarious, surrounded them when a local wit, Nat D. Walling, asked Mrs. Houston if she had ever been in Shelby County.

Young Mrs. Houston could not assure him that she had, and Walling advised her that she certainly must go there because General Houston had forty children in Shelby County. Margaret dealt with this by tucking her hand inside her husband's arm and looking up at him, smiling and confident, as if to suggest that at this point he had better take over.

Walling explained that he meant the General had forty children in Shelby County named after him. Good-naturedly, the General said that he would be obliged if Walling would connect his sentences more closely.

On this occasion, the General drank only cold water, although liquor was plentiful.

In San Augustine they attended a number of barbecues, dinners, and meetings at which the General spoke. Margaret's charm impressed George Hockley and the General's abstinence dumfounded him. Hockley noted that even when Margaret was not with Houston while he was campaigning for re-election, he did not touch the liquor that flowed in abundance. Then Hockley wrote to Ashbel Smith, qualifying his earlier opinion that marriage would be the General's ruin. All observers, he said, agreed that Houston's estimable wife would accomplish his reformation if it could be accomplished by anyone.

Houston was re-elected on September 7, 1840, to serve in the Fifth Congress. With his bride, he returned to Houston City where they stayed in the Lubbocks' ample two-story house in a healthy spot across the bayou. It was a pleasant interlude. In his memoirs, Lubbock told how he and his wife, who was only a few years older than Margaret, enjoyed the visit of Houston and his beautiful bride.

The General's visit was interrupted by a request from the Galveston Bay and Texas Land Company for him to take charge of some important title suits coming up in the San Augustine court. Margaret had a touch of the fever, and the Lubbocks were happy to have her stay behind with them. Rumors of her husband's conduct—not in accord with his pledge never again to drink to excess—drifted back to her. They originated with Memucan Hunt, now President Lamar's Secretary of the Navy. Houston answered Margaret's anxious letter of inquiry about these reports with affectionate reassurances and a renewal of his pledge.

> My Love. I do sincerely hope that you will hear no more slanders of me. It is the malice of the world to abuse me, and really were it not that they reach my beloved Margaret, I would not care one picayune—but that you should be distressed is inexpressible wretchedness to me!
> My dear! do be satisfied, and now in your feeble health be cheerful for that is all important to you, and my dear, if you hear the truth you never shall hear of my being on a "*spree*."
> . . . My heart embraces you, my dear! Thine Ever Truly Houston.[4]

Then he received word that Margaret's fever had taken a turn for the worse. Agitated, he rode at once to her side, finding her a little better, although the fever still ran high. He felt guilty for having exposed her to the Texas scourge.

Houston believed that wooded land he owned at Cedar Point which jutted into Galveston Bay was healthier than any in the vicinity of Houston City. He had already arranged to build a simple summer cottage, but it would not be ready until spring, and meanwhile furniture must be selected and bought. He had agreed with his wife that it would be best not to build an all-year home until they had adequate funds in hand and knew whether the capital would remain in Austin.

Depressed because she felt herself a hindrance instead of a help, Mrs. Houston suggested that her husband go back to his law cases in San Augustine. When able, she would go home to her mother, recover her health, and come back as soon as possible to join him. They adopted this plan, but instead of returning to San Augustine immediately, Houston waited until Margaret's fever had abated and then took her to Galveston and put her on the boat.

5. *A People if Not a Government*

In San Augustine, Houston completed two court cases, winning both. The land company paid him with a substantial draft on a United States bank. He sent it to Margaret for expenses and for things for the Cedar Point home.

In his *Memoir* (p. 200), he did not describe in detail the conditions that he encountered on the way to Austin for the December session of Congress, but dismissed them with one angry stroke, "[Lamar's] treatment of the Cherokees and other tribes spread scenes of rapine and murder from the Red River to the Rio Grande."

Houston took his seat in the House, pulled out his pocket knife and whittled toys from soft pine—heads of horses, dogs, and Indians, or grimacing medicine men—to give to settlers' children. Whittling was a sign that he was deeply preoccupied with important problems. Conditions had been bad in 1836 when he had taken over the government after Burnet's failure. They were far worse now. What could be done?

Gloom and despair pervaded the western borders. Immigration had slowed down. Settlers feared the frontier was breaking up, and numbers had moved out; four years of poverty and renewed onslaughts by Indians, Mexicans, and white marauders had completed their disillusionment. No one knew when the Mexicans might make a serious effort at reconquest.

Houston frowned over his whittling. President Lamar was holding court, entertaining, and dreaming about his Napoleonic coup. He was too busy to ask Congress to call out the militia and restore order. Anyhow, he had used up in the Cherokee War the entire sum that Congress had appropriated for defense. That outrage, Houston thought scornfully, must be rated as the administration's biggest achievement to date, although Lamar had announced many other projects: one day a great national bank, the next a great national road, and then a system of education described in glowing prose. Each prospect was lost to sight as soon as the next began to bloom. Meanwhile, such everyday needs as mail routes, schools for settlers' children, and courts were neglected. With many new incumbents on the pay roll, expenses were mounting.

Congressmen from all parts of the country reported that trade was at a standstill except in such necessities as bootleg gin, rum, and whiskey which brought in no revenue. Within six months a congressman's salary in red backs would not be worth crossing Congress Avenue to pick up.

After failing to win Mexican acknowledgment of Texas independence by diplomatic means, President Lamar asked Congress for a declaration of war against Mexico. When a joint committee of the House and Senate reported favorably on a war measure, Houston laid aside his whittling and fought the resolution on the floor. Above everything, he declared, Texas needed peace and time to gain prosperity and consolidate. Some of Houston's usual supporters deserted him, but the vote sustained his position and the resolution was beaten.

Houston returned to his whittling and waited for the next move. It came with a speed that was appropriate to its grandeur. President Lamar brought his grand project out into the open; he asked an appropriation for an expedition to Santa Fe to establish the claim of Texas to 2,000 square miles of territory in New Mexico ceded by the treaty of Velasco but not actually occupied by Texas settlers.

In his November, 1839 message, he had proposed undertaking trade relations with that region as a solution of the Republic's financial ills, but Congress had blocked it. Lamar believed that the project would prosper because there was revolutionary heat in New Mexico. Congress did not share this view. To the Fifth Congress of 1840 and the country at large, Lamar proposed a more detailed and ambitious plan. He announced the project as a peace mission, although troops were to accompany its members. A territorial government would be set up with a governor, customs officers, and military commandant. To Houston, "peace mission" seemed a disingenuous description of a venture that was intended to subjugate territory still occupied by

Mexico, although claimed under the law that established the Rio Grande as the national boundary.

In the southwest, Mexican citizens of El Paso del Norte were busily cultivating the grapes of a choice Asiatic variety that had been introduced by the Franciscans along with raisins and other fruits for drying. Paso wine and brandy went out by way of Chihuahua up through "new" Mexico (a large part of it claimed by Texas but occupied by Mexico) and east over the Santa Fe Trail. Duties and charges on the trail were a lucrative source of revenue for Mexico. Under the Lamar plan, customs paid to that country would be seized, and Texas would be saved from insolvency.

This argument brought Houston to his feet again, with the shavings of his whittling clinging to his breeches. Gentlemen would be out of their minds, he declared, to take this proposal seriously. An unsupported expedition, 1,000 miles through wilderness, prairie, and mountains, could endanger the future of Texas. The Republic had not proved its ability to maintain peace within the territory that it already occupied. Convinced against their will, the congressmen refused to approve the measure. President Lamar's project had met its first setback, but his determination to carry it out had not weakened.

A few days later, when Houston was opposing a move to alter the terms of the Cherokee land bill in favor of speculators, a member interrupted to ask permission to introduce a request on behalf of the administration. The President desired leave-of-absence to seek medical advice in New Orleans and proposed that Vice-President Burnet act for him during his absence. Houston supported the measure, but fought a proposed $5,500 increase in salary, which had been recommended for Burnet as compensation for his additional duties as acting president. The constitution, Houston pointed out, prohibited raising an official's salary during his term of office. Burnet's supporters argued that the sum they proposed was not an increase in salary, but a deserved donation. In this form the resolution passed.

Houston went back to whittling once more, awaiting the next bold move that he was sure would come from the acting president. Burnet strengthened his political position by replacing some of President Lamar's appointees with his own. In his highly inflammatory message of December 16, 1840, he demanded war on Mexico. Texas proper, he asserted, was bounded by the Rio Grande; but Texas, as defined by the sword, might include the Sierra Madre. He urged that the sword do its proper work.

General Houston opposed resorting to war to push the boundary to the Sierra Madre. It meant an undertaking to conquer thousands of square miles of Mexican territory. The proposal invited worse disasters than Lamar's Santa Fe expedition. Before starting out on new conquests, why did not Texas develop the resources and territory that she already had? He waited in vain for an answer.

Tempers flared and the wrangle went on for days. Members finally declared that the hope of carrying on the government was gone. They would end the farce and go home. A motion to adjourn sine die was carried with a voice vote. Houston's colleagues were leaving when he addressed the speaker and demanded to be heard. A motion to adjourn is not debatable, and Houston did not debate it. He called upon members of the House to reassemble at once, and they turned back from the door and listened to the representative from San Augustine. He told them that their constitution and government were far from perfect but were better than starting from the beginning. As he went on speaking, members resumed their seats. He recalled the sacrifices that the nation had made to get as far as it had. He closed with a motion to adjourn until the following morning at the usual hour, and the motion carried.

Houston may have saved the Republic's government from complete dissolution. The next day the House postponed action on demand for a declaration of war.[1]

A few days before adjournment, Houston wrote to a friend about the solemn conclusions he had reached while whittling. Texas was "in a bad box" that appeared to be "locked upon us." The government could not go on without levying taxes that would be too burdensome for the people to pay.

> What is to become of us, God only can tell. All human wisdom, or at least Texas wisdom seems to fail us ... it seems that every measure proposed by those most able in finance cannot devise a plan by which the nation is to be extricated from its present difficulties.

He could see but one remedy. The people must "raise crops, rear cattle and do everything" they could to "make themselves comfortable in their homes." In spite of the administration's "useless extravagance and unprincipled profligacy... we will still be a people if we cannot be a government... adjournment on Thursday next ... God knows we are doing no good by staying here." [2]

6. *Orange Peel and Bitters*

MARGARET Houston's adjustment to the changed conditions of her life in Texas took months. Other illnesses followed her first attack of malaria. She also experienced troubles that were apparently the result of diet. One of these illnesses occurred in the spring of 1841 at Houston City. While she was recovering and a house at Cedar Point was being prepared for occupancy, she encouraged her husband to attend to his normal duties. He proceeded to look after his political fences.

The campaign for Lamar's successor, which would be decided by the election on September 6, 1841, had been in progress informally since the first of the year. There were no formal party conventions. Nominations were made by county or other groups that met and passed resolutions or by newspapers. The contest had actually been in progress since Vice-President Burnet called Houston a half-Indian. Amused rather than indignant, Houston decided that Texas temperament and demand for excitement required him to go one better, so he called Burnet a hog thief.

In a letter to J. W. Webb on January 29, 1841, James Morgan described the political situation as he saw it. The loss of his buildings and orange grove at Morgan's Point had in no way affected Morgan's saltiness as a correspondent and political observer.

> We have a bad state of affairs here now—Lamar, the poor imbecile could not hold out and had to give up the helm of State to Burnet—who is even more worthless.... Old Sam H. with all his faults appears to be the only man for Texas—He is still unsteady—*intemperate* but drunk in a ditch is worth a thousand of Lamar and Burnet.... Burnet has rendered himself supremely [?] ridiculous is so much disliked & being naturally

[of] turbulent ... disposition that he has become as snarlish as a half starved dog dealing forth anathemas aga'st everybody. ... Report says He challenged Genl Houston because H intimated ... that B was a *Hog thief!*[1]

Morgan's observations on Houston's drinking at this time were based on past performance and not on current events. But this report of Burnet's challenge was correct. Houston had called Burnet various things before. His favorite device was to ridicule Burnet's assumption of dignity by calling him Little Davy or King Wetumka. As a result of the hog thief appellation, Houston received a caller, Branch T. Archer, on a formal mission. Houston described the nature of the visit and how he disposed of it:

It was a verbal challenge, sent on a Saturday night to meet the challenger the next morning. I objected to it, first, on the ground that we were to have but one second, and that was the man who brought the challenge. Another objection was, that we were to meet on Sunday morning, and that I did not think anything was to be made by fighting on that day. The third objection was, that he was a good Christian, and had had his child baptised the Sunday before. The fourth was, that I never fought down hill, and I never would. I must, at least, make character, if I was to lose my life; and therefore I notified him in that way. He seemed to be satisfied with this good-humored answer. ...[2]

Burnet's hatred of Houston was by no means mollified by Houston's method of brushing him off. Previously Houston had attacked Burnet's motives in the Cherokee War, had opposed an unconstitional increase in Burnet's salary, and, with the aid of his supporters, had voted down Burnet's appeal for a declaration of active war against Mexico. To smoldering hate, the brush-off added fury, and this fury added notably to the color and intensity of the campaign.

Houston was given a public dinner by friends at Galveston on Texas Independence Day and another at San Augustine on April 5, 1841. Citizens of Harris County nominated him for President on April 19. Two days later, on the anniversary of San Jacinto, he made a speech at Nacogdoches which was not notably successful because he had not been forgiven for his reproaches in connection with the Cherokee War.

As early as March 31, it was apparent that the campaign would be one of personalities when the Houston *Telegraph and Texas Register* announced for Burnet. The *Telegraph*, (March 31, 1841), still wedded to the idea that only a statesman other than Houston could give a satisfactory character to Texas, set the tone:

> There is one consideration connected with the ensuing presidential election that our citizens should constantly keep in view. The national character is to be sustained, so the private character of the individual elected, should be free from blemish or any degrading vice.... Burnet has been tried in adversity and prosperity, and ever found capable and faithful to the best interests of the people. Why then should we hesitate? By electing a drunkard, we cast the high destinies of our beloved republic upon a die, and leave it to blind chance. Whether our bark of state bound on with her sails swelled to the breeze of prosperity, or whether misguided by the *reeling* helmsman, she founders amid rocks of quicksands, to the ruin of the country.

The *Telegraph* continued to pluck the same string, but showed some slight compassion on May 19, when it called Houston "a noble wreck of humanity—great even in ruins." Newspaper support for Houston's candidacy came from the Colorado *Gazette and Advertiser*, San Augustine *Red-Lander*, and the Austin *City Gazette*. The *Houstonian* of Houston City was founded mainly to support Houston's campaign and passed out of existence soon after the election.

By July, Houston and his wife were at Cedar Point. The two-room house, with lean-to and a separate shed for the servants, was unfinished. It was for summer use only, "as plain as plain can be," but it was their first home and had a fine view of the bay. There was an excellent spring nearby, and Margaret could enjoy the salt air.

Houston's mother-in-law had contributed some furniture to augment the pieces Margaret had bought. The General, too, had bought some things; they were all trucked in by ox cart from Galveston. The bed was comfortable, even though the mattress was filled with Spanish moss. A feather bed would come later—much later.

Margaret sang sweetly and played the piano, harp, and guitar, but she had only her guitar now. Her piano was on the way. She liked housekeeping, was happy putting up draperies with a little help from her husband, and soon had things homelike. Houston, who had roughed it all his life, had more than the average man's interest in the feminine touches that make a house a home. He amiably made himself useful about the house, devoting his skill as an amateur blacksmith to creating home conveniences, putting up shelves, and making hanging devices. He could cut anything out of soft pine or cedar with a jackknife, and used angled branches or roots for hooks to hang up pots, pans, and clothing.

The new husband was short of money—more so than he wanted his wife to know because it would trouble her. The cost of getting their furniture from Mobile and Galveston had used up his ready cash, and he worried about repaying $500 that he had borrowed on a note from General William G. Harding in Nashville. The depth of his feeling about his inability to meet an obligation of this kind is revealed in his letter to Harding on July 17, 1841:

Dear General, Long as my silence has been, I have not either forgotten you nor your kindness to me. From time to time, I did hope to . . . make you the remittance which [you] were so kind as to oblige me with in Nashville of $500. I have offered every sacrifice in property, but there *is no money in Texas,* but our depreciated notes. I have upward of twenty five thousand dollars due me, and some of it for years, and I cannot collect as much as will pay one fourth of my land Tax! . . . I hope soon to be able to pay all my cash debts. If any person in the meantime should be coming to Texas, in whom you can confide, send the note if you think well of it, and I will let you have property (warranted) at any price, rather than not pay you! This is my apology for my remissness toward you, and I hope you will have the kindness to accept it as my feelings have not been less accute [sic] because you have not pressed me.

Then he gave Harding a politician's view of Texas:

We ought to have been most prosperous and happy, had our Rulers acted wisely. All the evils of which Texas has now to complain were brought upon her by ignorance and corruption. Profligacy has sunk our credit, and corruption has consumed the spoils. . . . If the next administration shou'd be composed of men possessing patriotism, integrity and talents, Texas will again lift up its head, and stand among the nations. It ought to do so, for no country upon the Globe can compare with it, in natural advantages. Come and see it! [3]

Then Houston was obliged to describe his financial plight in a letter to Sam Williams of Williams & McKinney, the patriotic Galveston commercial house that had advanced large sums to meet government expenses. It was written at Cedar Point, July 28, 1841, and began with a report of a terrible dry spell that had hit Texas:

PRIVATE!!!

Dear Sam Things move on with me pretty coolly, and very dryly—*drily* because we have had no rain for the last nine weeks, *drily*, because we have no *liquor*, and I do not taste one drop of it, nor will I do it! My health is pretty fine, but Mrs. Houston's is not good, but better than it has been. . . . I hope to see Roberts and Sublette; and get some Cash—I must have it!!! In the mean time; I wish you cou'd lend me sixty or $80.00; If Mr. McKinney can buy me a one horse Buggy strong, for two persons . . . with good Gears; I will be under endless obligations to him. He may give a good price *on time.*—[4]

Houston's statement that he was not drinking liquor appears to have been founded on absolute truth. How was it that a regular, extensive consumer could taper off without repercussions except those concocted by his enemies? The secret may be hidden in some of the old Texas recipes for "bitters." One kind is known to have contained forty per cent alcohol; others somewhat less. Perhaps Houston, who drank bitters, used the forty per cent variety. This would not have violated his pledge to Margaret or disturbed her program for his reformation, and would have permitted him to taper off moderately without excesses or insupportable inconvenience. When the temptation to toss off a drink was strong, he had his hartshorn vial and his new consolation, which he mentioned in a letter to his friend Thomas M. Bagby, a merchant of Houston City:

. . . and I wish you to save me all the Orange Peal which you can with convenience. I need it for bitters. The Doctors commend it. I don't drink hard, but what I do take, I wish it to be palatable.[5]

Watching and hopeful that the power of marriage would continue to sustain Houston's resolution, none of his friends—not a single one so far as can be discovered—reported disappointment, but letter writers and scribblers miles from the scene proclaimed yesterday's unfortunate truths as valid today. Houston's political opponents based their campaign solidly on his reputation for drunkenness and on vices that they continued to represent as a national disgrace.

Dr. Francis Moore, eidtor of the *Telegraph* went further in the campaign of defamation than any one except Burnet, declaring in the issue of July 28, 1841:

> A few days past [Houston] *was brought* to this City in such a brutal state of intoxication, that his own friends were filled with shame and disgust . . . and carried back in the same deplorable condition.

No explanation was offered for such a round-trip performance.

Morgan continued to write from Galveston as if he were Houston's next-door neighbor, although he was completely out of touch with the General's current policy of abstinence. Early in 1841, Morgan had professed doubt of Houston's ability to survive his addiction to ardent spirits. A couple of months later in a letter to his old friend Samuel Swartwout, he wrote that General Houston, if he lived, would assuredly be elected president.

Margaret was not worried about the General's survival. In good spirits, he was working hard with a malicious joy on an extraordinary literary product.

The pro-Houston Austin *City Gazette* charged that Burnet and his friends financed a campaign reissue of a scurrilous pamphlet, "Houston Displayed," [6] which had appeared during Houston's first administration. Since the pamphlet was anonymous and bore no imprint, the *City Gazette* surmised that the publisher was rightfully ashamed of his work.

The widely circulated pamphlet charged Houston with cowardice on the San Jacinto battlefield, but argued that he was not to be blamed for this because he was a deranged, opium-drugged sufferer from delirium. Among other things, he was charged with having sold the Texas consulship at New Orleans for a price. One question asked by the anonymous author was: "If General Houston will sell the place of Consul for a sufficient quantity of champagne to gratify his beastly disposition to intoxication, would he not for gold or silver betray the dearest interests of the country that has confided in him?"

To this the *Texas Sentinel* (July 5, 1841) added that Houston was accustomed to "blaspheme his God, by the most horrible oaths, that ever fell from the lips of man."

Previous to the campaign, Burnet had already published sixty-six newspaper columns of letters signed with his pen name "Publius." Houston had ignored many of them. They were mostly in the vein of the pamphlet "Houston Displayed." Using the same pen name, Burnet revived these productions for campaign purposes, charging Houston with military incompetence, with "beastly intemperance and other vices degrading to humanity."

At Cedar Point, candidate Houston divided his time between enjoyment of his new home life and an attempt to take the initiative in the campaign billingsgate. He composed some effective diatribes, signed "Truth," and published them as letters to newspapers. Historians believe that Burnet had the literary assistance of President Lamar in his compositions, and Houston, although he did the best he could, never quite succeeded in equaling the slanders, bitterness, and vindictiveness of "Publius." Houston was moved by necessity; letting the charges go unanswered might be a serious default in the eyes of the "sovereigns," his favorite name for voters. His real purpose was to restrain Burnet. At the same time, he could see the humor and futility of the proceeding. His "Truth" letters of August 16 and 18, 1841, in the *Houstonian*, adopted a style of mockery and were tinged with malicious humor: A little fellow was running around Texas telling a lot of lies. If there had been a mystery about what his middle initial stood for, it was now all cleared up. G. was for Grog, and Grog, sometimes tipsy himself, made a habit of charging other people with getting drunk.

After all the charges of drunkenness that had been leveled at him, Houston enjoyed describing occasions when, so he charged, to prevent Grog from making an unholy exhibition of himself, several gentlemen had assisted in removing him from Kessler's Round Tent. Kessler's was the best known entertainment and drink emporium in the early days of the boom-town capital. Recently, he reported,

Grog, when presiding over the Texas Senate, had joined in the discussion from the chair until Senator Oliver Jones of Austin County called him to order. Would Grog have misconducted himself in this manner if he had been sober? Then there was that occasion when—

> ... You swelled to a most consequential degree; and really the collar of your shirt, from connection with your imagination, I presume, out-topped your ears, while your step was as lofty and aimless, too, as that of a blind horse! Was there any liquor in this? It appeared so to those who dared to question the indomitable *"sobriety"* of the *illustrious hero* Davy G. Burnet—even some of the soldiers facetiously remarked that the letter "G" in your name stood for "Grog."

After many other charges, Houston raised the more serious question of Burnet's honesty:

> ... You were looked to as a *learned man,* and you obtained a grant of land; ... yet, *you are no land speculator.* I will admit that to be true—but you were *instrumental, in giving rise to the most outrageous fraud ever perpetrated upon mankind.* Yes, Sir, to the amount of millions of dollars. ... It was not *"land speculation,"* for you had no land—*but it was worse;* it was a *base fraud,* if not upon those to whom you sold your *pretended claim,* it enabled them ... to defraud honest mechanics, and others to whom they sold scrip, and who came to Texas to locate it in "Burnet's Grant." They found it valueless, and without means to meet the disappointment, numbers died of want. ... Fie, upon it Davy; be honest, if you do not love Brandy, and don't tell your fibs upon sober men! But I suppose since your *object is defamation,* the truth would not suit your purpose. Now, *about your honesty.* I could inform the public that you had made over all your property to your brother. ... by way of dafrauding just creditors out of their lawful demands against you. *This is true,* and you pretend that it was done for monies long since advanced to you. Is this honest? Has Houston, whom you call the "basest of rascals," ever been guilty of such shameless dishonesty?
> ... You prate about the faults of other men, *While the blot of foul unmitigated treason rests upon you.* You political brawler and canting hypocrite, whom the waters of Jordon could never cleanse from your political and moral leprosy.[7]

374

In the midst of these abusive exchanges, reports came from Austin indicating that a new and more serious crisis for Texas was in the making. Houston toned down his sensational offensive and began a serious discussion of basic issues.

7. *"You Dam Blackguard Indian Drunk"*

DURING the campaign activities of midsummer, Houston received disconcerting news. After returning from New Orleans, President Lamar had moved swiftly in the spring of 1841 to equip his proposed Santa Fe expedition. Because Congress had refused to sanction it, he began secretly but came into the open as his preparations advanced. At his direction, officers withdrew large quantities of supplies and ammunition from the government stores. With amazement, Houston read in the Austin *City Gazette* an appeal for volunteers by Colonel William G. Cooke, one of four commissioners appointed by Lamar to persuade the people of Santa Fe to rebel and unite with the people of Texas.

Houston realized that it would be the duty of the United States minister to inform the secretary of state in Washington that the object of this expedition was to integrate New Mexico into Texas. English and French diplomatic representatives would have to advise their countries of this undertaking. Was it a rational enterprise for Texas in its present state? What would friendly governments think? Yet the General did not make the expedition a major issue in his campaign. He condemned President Lamar's defiance of Congress, promising that, if elected, he would have the matter investigated. In mild terms he declared that the only end he could foresee for the Santa Fe venture was dismal failure.

Mexico, under Santa Anna's heel after a series of cruel repressions, was quiet. Bold Texas voices argued that active war against Mexico would save the Republic. Spoils would pay the national debt. But would "Old Sam" do it? It was well known that he was opposed to war as a way out of the national difficulties. During his two years as President, the country had enjoyed comparative peace and some

375

progress. This time if elected, he would have three years in office by constitutional provision and might even accomplish annexation.

Other matters also occupied the public during these hot campaign days of July, 1841. Money was scarce, prices high, and Lamar's multimillions in red backs were practically worthless. Many voices asked what was to become of the country if it couldn't save itself by war?

After disposing of Vice-President Burnet's attacks, Houston settled down to a few basic issues: frontier defense, sound currency, tranquility, prosperity, and the development of a national character that other nations would be compelled to respect. He recommended that the next Congress and the people adopt as their motto *"fewer officers and more corn fields."* The first part would curtail expenditures; the second would enable the people to put something into the empty treasury. Meanwhile, he was disturbed to learn that, President Lamar's Santa Fe expedition had left Austin.

"Grog's" supporters had one more contemptuous fling just before election day. Candidate Houston culled the result from the Austin, *Texas Sentinel* (August 26, 1841) and showed it to his wife:

> *A hero was travelling—his labors were o'er*
> *But sad was the smile his countenance wore.*
> *For ...*
> *he'd sworn before God 'gainst taking strong drink,*
> *Shall I take to friend opium. Ah! it is worse foe—*
> *By th' Eternal, I have it. To think more would be idle.*
> *The book that I swore on—why, it was not the Bible!*
> *So give me some whisky—'tis the cheer of Gods! ...*

She read it without change of expression and handed it back—untroubled because she knew the spiteful words were untrue.

Houston won the election of September 6, 1841, with 7,508 votes against 2,574 for Burnet.[1] Ed Burleson was elected vice-president over Memucan Hunt. Mrs. Houston was pleased by the outcome on the General's account but not particularly elated on her own. She cared little for social position.

Washington County gave them a victory dinner. An enormous crowd ate thirteen barbecued hogs and two whole beeves, well roasted with lots of honey, potatoes, chicken, and pastries. E. H.

Winfield reported to Ashbel Smith that he was astonished because only cold water was served, and Houston did not touch a drop of ardent spirits during his stay in the county.

Houston gave his top Cabinet post, secretary of state, to Dr. Anson Jones. Another trusted friend, Ashbel Smith, was nominated for Texas minister to Paris with the understanding that he would fill the same post in London as soon as recognition came. Houston made George Hockley Secretary of War and Marine; Texas Senator William Daingerfield, Secretary of the Treasury; George Terrell, Attorney General. James Riley was named minister to the United States, and Gail Borden became collector of the port at Galveston.

Since it was a journey of more than four days from Houston City to Austin, not many citizens of East Texas would be on hand for Houston's inaugural address. So, on November 25, 1841, as President-elect, he made a speech in Houston City that was virtually his inaugural. He told a large and cordial crowd what he thought was wrong with the country and what he would attempt to do:

> But when we look about us and within us, we cannot avoid the melancholy consciousness, that our happiness is impaired by the misfortunes of the country. We perceive our money depreciated, our credit sunk, our political institutions and laws disregarded or suspended.... It is known to you all, that a deplorable laxity, originating at the head, has extended into many portions of our land. Hundreds of men have been riding over the country in bands, consuming the substance of the industrious, arresting, condemning and executing many of our citizens without the sanction of laws: while the President has remained quietly ensconced at Austin, regardless of the cries of the fugitives, pursued by a rabble multitude; neglecting to call out the militia of the country to suppress the insurrection, or to punish the aggressors. Judges shrank appalled from the disgraceful spectacle, unable themselves, for the want of moral courage, to rescue the land from dishonor and blood.... Such a state of things I will never tolerate, while I may have the energy of the people to sustain me in upholding order, law and justice.

He explained that there were reasons for rejoicing because the much talked of "mighty loan" from France "has burst at last."

> I thank God! as to the loan, we have no longer anything to anticipate. We can now have recourse to our industry. Instead

377

of visionary and unauthorized Santa Fé Expeditions—instead of beautiful navies built for the enemy at a heavy expense; I trust the day is coming when the purposes of useful retrenchment will receive their due attention in the councils of the nation. Instead of millions thrown away on swarms of useless loafers ... we shall find the expenses of government reduced to three hundred thousand dollars per annum instead of three millions.

Was it by his wife's request that the President-elect inserted remarks on the subject of temperance? Smiles must have passed over the audience when he said,

In view of the circumstances under which Texas has grown into existence, we must expect many evils to be corrected in the formation of our society. For the want of the sweet attractions of the fireside it has been too usual among us to have recourse to the grog shop, either for the purpose of exhilaration, or to while away the time; or, still more demoralizing, to resort to the faro bank.

It was remarkable on how many occasions since his marriage Houston had seized an opportunity to indorse the views of the Texas Temperance Society. He closed with:

... Often have I met you, and often been greeted by the same warm welcome. It is again renewed under the most flattering circumstances. Ever grateful for your partiality, I may say to you, that I feel a certain degree of self approbation. It is for that we live—it is for that I act.... The approbation of intelligent freemen, displayed in the bestowal of their suffrage, is the highest boon that can be conferred upon the citizens of a republic.[2]

Thus, hardly suspecting the number of new crises in the offing, the extent to which anarchy had gripped the nation, and the violence of the congressional opposition that was in store for him, Houston promised in his turn to give a new character to Texas.

The "President's House" in Houston City had been finished a few weeks before the end of Houston's first term and now was made available for the temporary use of the President and his wife. Houston's increasing dependence on Margaret's understanding and tenderness made it hard for him to separate from her when he left for Austin. But he expected a short session and, because of Margaret's poor health, knew that it would be best to spare her the fatigue of the journey and the risks of Austin's exposed location. Furthermore, Mrs. Lea was expected for a visit and she and Margaret had been invited to stay with the Lubbocks during Houston's absence.

On a cold, windy day, December 13, 1841, salvos of artillery greeted the President-elect when he appeared under a canopy at the rear of the capitol. He faced a crowd of 1,000 persons. As a symbol of economy he wore a linsey-woolsey hunting shirt, an old pair of pantaloons, and an old, wide-brimmed fur hat. He urged the people to realize that the nation's salvation would be found in industriousness and economy.

The presidential ball was attended by visitors from all over the country. Ex-President Lamar was in town but did not attend. A week later when Lamar gave his farewell ball, Houston, by his absence, returned the compliment.

Sam Houston announced that he would have no use for the garish mansion on which Lamar had squandered the people's money. He would not sanction wastefulness by living in it, and made his home at the Eberly House instead.

Isaac Van Zandt of Harrison County led a fairly strong pro-Houston faction in the House. Senator John A. Greer of San Augustine was Houston's floor leader in the Senate. At the outset, pro-Houston members could muster a majority, but their ranks were soon broken. Fiery William L. Cazneau of Travis County (Austin) led the anti-Houston opposition in the House. In the Senate, William H. Jack of Brazos shared the anti-Houston leadership with the one-armed Senator, Dr. Francis Moore, editor of the Houston *Telegraph*.

President Lamar's disastrous adventures with printing-press money left Houston with stronger convictions than ever that just one common sense, rule-of-thumb idea could alleviate the painful consequences. He knew that the country's currency must be backed with reasonable security in order to keep it anywhere near par. He proposed a $350,000 issue of "exchequer" notes to be secured by taxes, duties, and the public lands from which the Cherokees had been expelled. Congress reduced the amount to $200,000 and refused his request to support it with a pledge of the one-time Cherokee lands. Then Congress repealed the principal legislation passed during the previous administration—authorization for a $5,000,000 loan. The legislators rejected Houston's request to float a modest government loan of $300,000. Since income from taxes and duties was not sufficient to meet current expenses, this left the government unable to pay its bills and guaranteed that the new currency would depreciate violently.

The President's economy recommendations were adopted with wild and destructive enthusiasm. The congressmen cut their own pay from five to three dollars a day. Then they were pleased to reduce the President's salary from $10,000 to $5,000 a year. Houston made no public protest. He recommended cutting direct taxes by half. Exuberantly, Congress reduced them so low that the treasurer informed Houston that taxes would not yield enough to be worth the expense of collection. Job holders were cut off indiscriminately, and some necessary offices were abolished. Economy measures forced the curtailment of mail service. Houston was obliged to refer a number of government responsibilities to Congress because the departments, destitute of clerks, could not perform them.

On January 11, 1842 he appealed to the House for appropriations to meet the "indispensable necessities of the [State] Department." Ten days later he asked Congress to relieve the "destitute condition" of the Attorney General's department "for the purpose of enabling the Attorney General to perform the duties required of him by law."

Houston proposed that a line of garrisoned trading posts be erected along the frontier as a defense measure and to promote peace with the Indians. He asked for $20,000 for this project, but Congress passed a law for a grander effort: more numerous posts garrisoned with more men, located far out on the border, miles beyond any settlements, dangerously exposed, and expensive to maintain. But Congress provided no money for the execution of this plan.[3]

Houston considered the capital's position a real threat to the safety of the government's officials and archives. His concern was justified by Comanche raids on the outskirts of the capital during which houses were burned and settlers were scalped. Moreover, dealings with Santa Anna had given him an uncanny understanding of the dictator's mental processes. Nothing would please Santa Anna more than to seize the top officers of the Texas government and parade them in Mexico City; and he would risk much to get possession of his former captor. Before Houston offered a specific proposal for reestablishing the capital in a safer location, he had tried to prepare the way for rational consideration of the measure by "leaking" the administration's viewpoint to the friendly Houston *Morning Star*. In the issue of October 2, 1841, the *Star* writer suggested that readers should consider the appalling consequences if—

> ...the enemy should descend and capture [the capital] and destroy the public archives or murder or carry into captivity the officers of the Government, in what a deplorable condition could our Republic be placed? We should become the laughing stock of the world.

One bill recommended by Houston authorized him to transfer the government archives to a place of safety; another proposed that, by joint vote, the Senate and House should designate a permanent site for the capital. The outlook for passage of both bills was favorable until Representative Cazneau of Austin made an impassioned plea. The tears in Cazneau's eyes, the catch in his throat, the way he beat his breast, and his eloquence moved the House to refrain from passing them. The bills were not defeated, but deadlocked.

The question of the capital's removal became the subject of a great debate. The genial warmth with which the citizens of Austin and other western settlements entered into the argument against Houston's recommendation for a safer location is reflected in an undated letter that President Houston received from Settler John Welsh:

> Sir Old Sam We did heart that you was goin to move the seat of government and the publick papers and that you swore you would do it, and then you come to Austin and found out the boys would not let you do it you sed you never was goin to move it. Now Sam you told a dam lie for you did promise the people in Houston that you would move it, and I heard a man say that you told Hockley not to bring all his servants because you would all go back soon. But the truth is that you are afeard you Dam old drunk Cherokee. We don't thank you becase we would shoot you and every dam waggoner that you could start with the papers you cant do it and we ax you no odds. Travis and Bastrop Fayette Gonzales can bring 1000 Men out and Ned Burleson and Lewis P. Cook have promised that you shant budge with the papers I heard them myself and you

know Burleson and Cook can make you squat you dam black-guard indian drunk. Now old fellow if you want to try Ned Burlesons spunk just try to move these papers, and old Ned will serve you just as he did your Cherokee brother when he took the Hat what you give to your Daddy Bowles You shall hear more from me when I am ready.[4]

Against the attacks of Cazneau and other legislators representing the settlers of western Texas, Houston rallied his forces with the intention of pushing the question of a safer location for the capital and government records to a final decision. But, suddenly, all interest in the seat-of-government issue evaporated. The legislators, the press, the public, and President Houston himself, horrified by the details, became absorbed in the news, rumors, and speculations about the fate of Lamar's Santa Fe expedition.

8. *The Gay Pioneers*

HOUSTON never claimed to know the exact details of the negotiations between "the high contracting parties" involved in the Santa Fe expedition. A cloud of uncertainty still enveloped Lamar's preliminary planning. He appears to have put his trust in red-headed Manuel Arista, commander of Mexican troops along the Rio Grande, who had once lived in Cincinnati, Ohio. Apparently Lamar and Arista discussed uniting Mexico's northern provinces with Texas. Lamar was to head the government of this great realm. General Arista was to be rewarded with a suitable high office.

Evidently, they agreed that the first step would be to unite the people of New Mexico with the people of Texas. A portion of New Mexico lay within the Rio Grande boundary claimed by the Texas Republic, although it had not been occupied. Santa Fe, a central point on an important trade route, was the capital of New Mexico. General Manuel Armijo was governor.

Arista, still loyal to his own country, advised the Mexican government of what was going on. He was instructed to appear to fall in with Lamar's proposals; General Armijo was warned, and Mexican spies were introduced into Lamar's expedition before it set out.

Lamar supporters had argued that the people of Santa Fe would favor uniting with Texas and that commercial revenues to be derived from this association would greatly exceed the cost of the undertaking. Members of Congress did not believe that the Mexican citizens of Santa Fe were as warmly disposed toward Texas as President Lamar maintained; they were also influenced against the project by its cost. Congress twice denied the sanction requested by President Lamar.

Notwithstanding the unequivocal denial of sanction, Lamar, in the early part of 1841, instructed Secretary of the Treasury John C. Chalmers to furnish him $89,000 in drafts on the treasury. Chalmers acceded to the unauthorized demand. That sum and other funds available to Lamar financed his preparations.

Next, he appointed several commissioners headed by Colonel William G. Cooke. Among Cooke's associates were Dr. R. F. Brenham, Samuel Howland and two obscure Lamar political supporters, Rosenbury and Baker. Lamar's instructions to the commissioners were drawn up for him by Acting Secretary of State Samuel Roberts. He informed them that they would meet little opposition. If, however, the authorities of the Santa Fe district attempted to thwart the people's political desires for union with Texas, force was to be used against the officials. In no case was there to be an attempt to coerce the people.

Commissioner Cooke openly solicited volunteers by advertising in the Austin *City Gazette*. He stated that the expedition's object was mercantile but that it must be strongly prepared militarily to protect the traders' merchandise from Indians. The appeal went on:

All who arm, mount and equip themselves will receive the pay of mounted gunmen—will serve six months, or until the return of the expedition, and will be supplied with subsistence, &c. The companies will consist of 56, rank and file, and elect their company officers. The Field and Staff Officers will be appointed by the President. Ten large road wagons will be furnished by the Government to merchants who desire to send their goods to that market, and the troops will secure their transportation.

As this expedition will not only furnish an ample field for adventure on the march, but conduce by a successful result, to the benefit of our common country ... young men [are expected to show] readiness to unite and contribute by their discipline, as well as by their courage, to sustain the interest and glory of our young Republic.[1]

This prospectus affected many people in many different ways. When Houston read it, he was discouraged by the pitfalls into which the lawless officials were leading the country. Feverish with excitement, young men from Texas and a few from the United States responded to the appeal. Mexicans were angered by the boldness of an undertaking whose obvious purpose was to enforce Texan claims to the upper part of the Rio Grande basin. In Santa Fe, Governor Armijo calmly pondered instructions received from Mexico City directing him to make preparations against the invasion and to expect reinforcements.

On June 5, 1841, Lamar wrote a friendly proclamation to the citizens of Santa Fe. It was printed in both Spanish and English, and large quantities were packed in the luggage of the expedition for later distribution. In the proclamation, Lamar disclosed the purpose of the expedition—to annex the Santa Fe territory to Texas—and asked the cooperation of Santa Fe citizens.

We tender to you a full participation in all our blessings. The great River of the North, which you inhabit, is the natural and convenient boundary of our territory, and we shall take great pleasure in hailing you as fellow-citizens, members of our young Republic, and co-aspirants with us for all the glory of establishing a new and happy and free nation.... This communication I trust will be received by you and by your public Authorities in the same spirit of kindness and sincerity in which it is dictated....

This ardent appeal to Santa Fe citizens to commit treason and join Texas closed with a promise that if Lamar's sentiments were welcomed, he would then gladly "explain more minutely the condition of our Country, of the Seaboard and the co-relative interests which so emphatically recommend and ought perpetually to cement the perfect union and identity of Santa Fe and Texas."[2]

For public consumption, Lamar maintained that the expedition was a peace and trade mission, but he put Brigadier General Hugh McLeod in command of the recruits. Five companies, a total of 265 men, assembled at several encampments before finally concentrating in a camp near Austin. In gay spirits and bright new uniforms, the men began calling themselves pioneers.

The commissioners and General McLeod, his officers, and men were all well mounted; as much as $1,000 in depreciated currency had been paid for some of the horses. Ten merchants from San Antonio and their clerks were going along to give credence to the claim that this was a peace and mercantile mission. In addition, there were gamblers and independent adventurers; a young English lawyer, Thomas Falconer; and a forerunner of modern war correspondents, George Wilkins Kendall, a talented editor of the New Orleans *Picayune*.[3]

On the eve of departure, a letter from an unidentifiable source in Santa Fe was circulated (apparently by Lamar's instructions) which stated that two-thirds of the Rio Grande Mexicans, Pueblo Indians, and American traders would unite in welcoming the Texans; that Governor Armijo knew the expedition was coming, and had said he would not resist, and had not the means to do so even if he desired. When Houston heard of this letter, he recognized it immediately as a stratagem. He called it an invitation to death.

Somewhat behind schedule, the expedition left Brushy Creek on June 18, 1841. Kendall of the *Picayune* described the event: Twenty-two wagons carried the expedition's supplies. Fourteen were loaded with miscellaneous goods, two contained General McLeod's personal belongings, five carried the troops' baggage, and one was a doctor's wagon. A field piece with *Mirabeau Buonaparte Lamar* inscribed on the breech was drawn by mules. The men were as gay as though they were participating in a Mardi Gras. The prospect of a tough 1,500-mile campaign across prairie, wilderness, and mountains occasioned no fears. The *Picayune* correspondent caught the true spirit of the venture:

> It was looked upon as nothing more than a pleasant hunting excursion. Such portions of the route as had been previously explored were known to abound with buffalo, bear, elk, antelope and every species of game besides fish and wild honey. The climate ... dry and salubrious. The trip promised to be one of continued interest and delight. But beyond that point the country was a perfect *terra incognita*, untrodden save by wild and wandering Indians, and all were eager to partake of the excitement of being among the first to explore it.[4]

Earlier, Kendall's paper had published a glowing forecast predicting that its editor's trip would be "full of novelty and delight, unmingled with opposing inconveniences." [5]

The commander of the expedition, General McLeod, had helped plan the campaign that had expelled the Cherokees. This seems to have inspired him with confidence that he had mastered the military art. But he was handicapped by the same naïveté and optimism that handicapped Lamar. He did not suspect that his Mexican guide was a spy and his suspicions were not aroused even after the expedition repeatedly lost its way.

The late start contributed to his difficulties from the first. The best pasturage for the animals had been burned by the hot July sun, and cattle taken along for food gave out before the expedition reached the borders of New Mexico. Half starved, the once gay pioneers became sick; when their Mexican guide abandoned them, they were discouraged.

General McLeod detached a group under Commissioner Cooke and sent it on ahead toward distant San Miguel to buy food. Another group under Commissioners Howland, Baker, and Rosenbury was dispatched to contact the Mexicans who were supposed to extend a cordial welcome. Correspondent Kendall undertook a somewhat similar mission with four companions. All three groups were captured.

The hazards that afflicted the main group were as great as those encountered by the detached missions. The men were reduced to eating anything they could find, including insects and reptiles. Harried by Indians, five Texans were killed. In another attack, eighty-three horses were run off, and only mules and draft oxen remained. This put most of General McLeod's force on foot. The great heat and the pioneers' inability to replenish the salt they lost with perspiration, reduced their energy and drove some of them frantic. With few exceptions, they discarded the burden of arms and ammunition, leaving themselves without means of defense.

Informed by spies of the expedition's predicament, Governor Armijo adopted appropriate measures. A once handsome man, he was now described by Kendall as a mountain of fat with a large head, heavy clean shaven jaws, and a bulging lower lip. Known as a

386

gambler, he freely boasted that he had made his start on the road to affluence by stealing sheep. In August, Armijo sent Captain Damasio Salezar to observe closely the approaching Texans. Salezar captured the three commissioners, Howland, Baker, and Rosenbury. Rosenbury was killed trying to escape. Howland and Baker were sent under guard to the prison at San Miguel del Vado.

Salezar turned over to Armijo a bundle of Lamar's printed invitations to the people of Santa Fe which the commissioners had been carrying. The governor's eyes opened wide. Before this he had had only vague reports of its contents. Now he could read for himself President Lamar's offer to Santa Fe citizens of "a full participation in all our blessings." He learned of the pleasure it would be to Lamar to hail the people of Santa Fe as "fellow citizens." Struggling with the rather mangled Spanish translation, but fully aware of the idea back of this "peaceful, mercantile" expedition, governor Armijo did not reciprocate the "kindness and sincerity" with which President Lamar asked the governor's people to join hands with "a new and happy and free nation." He considered the "pioneers" invaders.

Mounted on a gorgeously caparisoned mule, Armijo led 1,000 men —Mexicans armed with guns and machetes and Indians with bows and arrows—to meet the main body of weary Texans. On the road near the Pecos Mission, he encountered Captain Salezar who, in command of 100 Mexican soldiers, was convoying a handful of captured Texans. One of the prisoners was a Captain Lewis. Under questioning, Lewis insisted that he and his companions were American merchants who had lost their way. Armijo seized Lewis by the collar of his dragoon jacket, pointed to the buttons which bore a single star and the word "Texas," and demanded angrily, "What does this mean? I can read—Texas! You need not think to deceive *me*. No merchant from the United States ever travels with a Texas military jacket." [6]

Then the governor asked who could speak Spanish. Lewis, who had lived in Mexico, stepped forward. The governor mounted him on a mule. Lewis' companions were herded on foot thirty miles through the night to the San Miguel prison to keep company with Howland and Baker. From their cell windows, the Texas prisoners saw a blindfolded man beaten and hammered to his knees. He was shot in the back by a squad of soldiers, but he struggled to rise. A corporal shot him with a pistol at such close range that his shirt

387

caught fire. They learned that he was Commissioner Baker, who had escaped and had been recaptured. The prisoners were also forced to witness the execution of Commissioner Howland, who had made his own futile attempt to escape.

Captain Lewis had been allowed to ride comfortably on the mule through the night while his comrades walked. He consented to act as Armijo's interpreter, and was escorted to meet the main body of Texans, now creeping in the direction of Santa Fe. To his fellow Texans, he repeated Armijo's pledges, assuring them that if they surrendered without resistance they would be permitted to return to Texas or to go to the United States. Without firing a shot, the Texans laid down the few rifles they still were carrying. Armijo's men surrounded them, seized their belongings, and tied them together with lariats.

On October 9, 1841, the bells of the little San Miguel church rang out and guns were fired to honor Governor Armijo's great "bloodless" victory. The Texans were marched into the plaza. Deprived of their clothes, they had a blanket apiece to protect them from the freezing cold of the high altitude. Some were without shoes; all were close to starvation.

Their wagons, laden with merchandise and driven by Mexicans, followed them into the plaza. They watched as their cargoes were distributed among the eager people. Ten days later, 187 captives were assembled in the plaza. Seventy-eight of the original 265 were not there. Some had been lost or killed on the way, others had been killed while resisting, a few had escaped, and three had been executed. Commissioner Cooke and his group had passed through the plaza a little earlier on their march, under guard, to Mexico City.

General McLeod was among the survivors assembled in the plaza that day. Stripped of his regimentals, he was clad in ragged clothes made available from garments discarded by Mexicans after they had appropriated the captured luggage. Armijo preserved McLeod's apparel and, for the next ten years, displayed it to visitors, especially those from Texas, as trophies "such as no other Mexican general can exhibit." [7]

The prisoners expected nothing better than summary execution, but at long last they were told that they were to start immediately on foot for Mexico City, 2,000 miles away. Exactly what orders

Governor Armijo gave Captain Salezar concerning the treatment of his charges is not known but can be inferred from an earlier episode. A large group of captives under Salezar's second in command, always referred to by Kendall as Don Jesus, had been marched thirty miles in one day from San Miguel to Governor Armijo's station. When Armijo ordered Don Jesus to march them back to San Miguel that same night, the junior officer protested that the prisoners had already covered a great distance under difficult conditions. Armijo answered:

"They are able to walk ten leagues (thirty miles) more. The Texans are active and untiring people—I know them; if one of them *pretends* to be sick or tired on the road *shoot him down* and bring me his ears! Go!" [8]

Armijo must have given similar orders to Salezar for the march to Mexico City because he followed these instructions precisely, adding additional cruelties devised by his own twisted nature.

The first night out on their return journey the prisoners bivouacked amid the ruins of an old mission on the Pecos road. No food was distributed. A bitter cold wind from the Sangre de Cristo mountains swept down on them. No one slept; they kept moving for warmth.

In the dimness of a cold early morning Salezar appeared with a small basket. The prisoners were overjoyed at the prospect of food. Their custodian tossed a small cake into the air and they scrambled for it while Salezar laughed at their animal-like frenzy. He tossed another and another, but not one for each man—only fifty biscuits in all.

On empty bellies and bare feet, the pioneers trudged along the Galisteo Creek road toward the Rio Grande. One night, they received a pint of meal as a ration for the day. The third day, they reached the Rio Grande at Santo Domingo. Farther downstream, Indian women, touched by their misery, gave them food. Salezar did not interfere with this, since the Texans needed food to keep going. One night when they begged him to give them shelter from the cold, he crowded them all into two small connecting rooms and closed the outside doors. At the point of suffocation, they screamed for release. Salezar released fifty, to sleep on the frozen ground outside.

Governor Armijo had instructed Salezar to keep the prisoners tied to one another at all times lest they escape. But Salezar varied his instructions. He preferred to march them a sufficient distance each day so that they would be too exhausted to attempt escape. In this he succeeded.

They marched several days on a ration of one ear of uncooked corn for each man. Already thin and ragged as scarecrows, they had been paraded through the streets of Albuquerque. At Valencia, each man got a pint of flour but few had strength to cook it. Many collapsed in a stupor of fatigue. The next morning a man died. Captain Salezar had a soldier cut off the dead man's ears so that the proper audit could be made.

A captive, John McAllister—a native of Tennessee and of excellent family—had inflamed, swollen ankles. About to succumb from weakness, he declared he was unable to proceed. Salezar ordered him to quicken his pace and overtake the main body.

"Forward, or I'll shoot you on the spot."

"Then shoot!" replied McAllister, "and the quicker the better!"

Salezar took him at his word. A single ball, says Kendall, sent as brave a man as ever trod the earth to eternity. "His ears were then cut off, his shirt and pantaloons stripped from him, and his body thrown by the roadside as food for wolves." [9]

At Socorro, not from mercy but to keep his prisoners alive, Salezar granted a day's rest. In the morning, another man fell out and was shot. During a two-day march without an overnight stop across a mountain desert to become known as Dead Man's March, Salezar taunted his living scarecrows with what they would experience at Chihuahua. Nearing El Paso, they forded the Rio Grande through ice cold water up to their chins. Their reception in the town was like waking from a dreadful nightmare. The El Paso women could not do enough for the prisoners. They fed them all the meat, eggs, and bread they could eat, and liberal quantities of the delicious Paso wine. The men were allowed to bathe and sleep, were given money for clothes, and were assisted by Padre Ramón Ortiz to write letters home to tell of their kind treatment at El Paso.

Don José Maria Elias Gonzáles, Commanding General of the District of Chihuahua, after talking with the prisoners, lashed out at Salezar for his cruelties and charged him with the murder of three men. The prisoners begged to be allowed to remain in El Paso but the commanding general had contrary orders from Mexico City. After three days' rest, the Texans resumed their march toward Santa Anna's capital. The whole population of El Paso turned out to see them off. General Elias, Padre Ortiz, the *alcalde*, and other leading citizens rode with them part of the first day and wished them a good journey, safe arrival, and prompt liberation.

Later, during their imprisonment in the Castle of Perote—a hideous survival of the Inquisition—some of the prisoners wrote home that their parting from the citizens of El Paso was an affectionate farewell. As long as they lived they would remember the kindness of the Mexicans of El Paso; and many in Texas also would be grateful.

9. *Keeping the Nation Out of War*

LETTERS and news of the outcome of the expedition poured into Texas. The cruelties inflicted on the pioneers obscured the imbecilities of the undertaking. Citizens of the United States, as well as of Texas, flamed with indignation. The Kentucky legislature demanded intervention by the United States to release one of the pioneers, the seventeen-year-old son of General Leslie Combs of Lexington. Maryland and Louisiana joined in eloquent protests. New Orleans held public indignation meetings.

The *Picayune*, ignoring the provocative nature of the expedition, declared on February 4, 1842, "We will calmly tell the aggressor [Mexico] that . . . our country is too proud of its glorious birthright and the rank it holds within the pale of nations, to submit, at this year of its history, to insult and injustice."

But Andrew Jackson was not swept off his feet. He rated the disastrous events on the upper Rio Grande as a wild goose chase that had so dimmed the powers of Texas that it would take three San Jacintos to restore it. Anson Jones wept in verse:

> A chase of silly hopes and fears,
> Begun in folly, closed in tears.[1]

391

Houston moved immediately to assist the captives.[2] He requested Captain Charles Elliot, the British commercial agent at Galveston, to ask the British minister in Mexico City to intervene to prevent their execution. Houston was obliged to concede that the affair had not been authorized by the Texas Congress; but, he argued, the members of the expedition were entitled to honorable treatment as prisoners of war because Governor Armijo had negotiated with them and they had surrendered on promises of safety and liberation. He sent similar appeals by diplomatic channels to the governments of the United States and France.

Enraged at the Mexicans, the Texas Congress sought reprisal. It asked President Houston to approve a bill annexing a vast sweep of Mexican territory: portions of the states of Tamaulipas, Coahuila, Durango, and Sinaloa; and all of New Mexico, Chihuahua, Sonora, and Upper and Lower California. The bill authorized war to accomplish these measures.

Houston, eager to get his opinions before Congress and the people before they committed some act of impetuous folly, sat up all night wondering how he could puncture the dangerous emotions that had inspired this bill. His veto message was a memento of his ability to maintain calm and to act discreetly amidst furor and excitement.

He informed the Congress that he regarded the present moment as the most unfortunate imaginable for going to war. "Our fellow citizens taken at Santa Fe, if they still survive, are prisoners in the City of Mexico, at the *mercy* of the Mexicans. Every possible means at my command has been employed to attain their release and restoration to their friends and country...." If the annexation bill passed the prisoners might be executed before moves for their release could be effective. He cautioned that this was a time when Texas should seek friendly intercourse with all nations instead of resorting to provocative measures.

"So long as we are not on amicable terms with Mexico," he wrote, "so long will we suffer hindrance to our prosperity.... emigration will be impeded, if not entirely prevented.... Texas only requires peace to make her truly prosperous and respectable ... peace will bring with it every advantage."

Then he reminded the legislators that the territory they proposed to annex was "larger than the United States of the North," and actually included two-thirds of the Republic of Mexico. The inhabitants of the area numbered not less than 2,000,000. Nations friendly to Texas would regard it as curious that a people destitute of means to meet their most pressing wants should assume the right to govern a country with a population many times its own. "... I am inclined to believe other nations would regard the measure as visionary—or as a legislative jest inasmuch as it would assume a right which it is utterly impossible to exercise." [3]

Congress turned its rage upon the President. Texans had had their ears cut off and their bodies flung into ditches. Barefoot men had traveled rocky mountain paths to Mexico City and were now in prison or working in sewers—if they had not already been executed. At such a time, Houston dared talk of peace and prosperity and to suggest that a legislative measure annexing a huge slice of Mexican territory was not entirely respectable. Impeach him!

While Congress fumed, Houston grimly considered the situation. Somewhere out there in the general direction of Santa Fe lay an abandoned cannon with *Mirabeau Buonaparte Lamar* inscribed on its breech, the symbol of an insane undertaking. To this was added the painful exhibition by Congress. What could be said for legislators who refused to authorize a small loan to meet government expenses, yet were eager to plunge the nation into a war that would cost millions and keep Texas in turmoil for years?

Congress passed the annexation measure over the President's veto. A joint resolution to enable the President, in case of invasion by Mexico, to employ the army and use the navy in the Gulf was passed by the Senate, but rejected by the House. This left everything as it was before, in total confusion, including the method of enforcing proposed annexation.

On February 5, 1842, without passing revenue bills or granting the President requested authority for a loan, the Texas Congress adjourned. For protection against wintry weather, President Houston put on his poncho-style Mexican blanket, mounted a mule and headed for Houston City—for home and Margaret.

The President's mule was something new. Though mules were less dignified than fine horses, their reputation for slogging through all kinds of weather had persuaded him to try one. On the recommendation of Washington Miller, formerly of Charleston, South

Carolina, who served as secretary of the Texas Senate and as the President's part-time secretary, he had bought as fine an example of the hybrid as he had ever seen. Chestnut brown, with longish hair, flopping ears, and a stout burliness that made him equal to carrying the weight of a well-set-up man of six-feet two, the mule resembled an overgrown cinnamon bear. The President named him Bruin. Bruin had a methodical approach to his work. He allowed nothing to interfere with his solemn obligations as he conceived them. He covered much ground by the simple procedure of planting one foot in front of another, regardless of mud, bog, sleet, icy rivers to ford, or any other obstacle. Where a horse might step in a hole, strain a tendon, wrench an ankle or knee, or get a branch in its eye, Bruin's superior intuition got him through treacherous places without nudges or guidance, permitting the President to relax and meditate on his problems.

The Santa Fe disaster, followed by clamor for war, brought a new crisis into the affairs of Texas. He knew from experience that "to invade a nation requires everything." To conquer Mexicans in Texas was one thing; to battle with Mexicans in Mexico was quite another. And Texas did not have the means for a war of conquest. His lowest possible estimate of the cost of an invasion with reasonable prospects of success called for $2,500,000 and 5,000 men or more. The men probably would have to serve for several years. Defending Texas required radically less means. If she remained on the defensive, he believed she could never be reconquered.

On the other hand, he could imagine venturesome, bragging volunteers, eager for plunder, storming in from the United States to "assist" Texas. Suppose that, backed by zealous recruits, a campaign south of the Rio Grande succeeded? What then? If victory crowned a war inspired by desire for plunder, what would such a victory do to Texas? The people would find that the nation could support itself by pillage; they would abandon commerce and husbandry. A few thousand victorious troops returning to the country would damage Texas more than an invasion by four times that many Mexicans.

The President was weary of the nagging, quarrelsome, exasperating peace that had followed San Jacinto. Perhaps a greater glory beyond the success of that victory awaited him. He could not fail to realize that he had only to cry, "On to Mexico City to free the Santa Fe prisoners! More revenge for the Alamo and Goliad! A rich harvest awaits us in the Halls of Montezuma!" Every man capable of bearing a rifle would fall in behind him without shoes and without ammunition, ready to fight without second thought.

Entering the outskirts of his namesake city, Houston saw Representative Archibald Wynnes. Wynnes's fine horse looked blown and fagged, but the plodding Bruin seemed eager for more travel. The President took note of this in a letter to Miller on February 15, 1842:

> My dear Miller.... On my arrival I had the happiness to meet my dear Wife in fine health, and not expecting my immediate arrival, so the surprise was quite agreeable. To me, my dear Friend, it was most surely a cause of joy unmingled with regrets.
> I made the trip in two hours less than four days. So you see the *mule* did me honest service.... I was in sight of Wynnes on his arrival, tho' he had started one day sooner than I did! Since my arrival I have met with a gentleman direct from Mexico, who brought dispatches from Colo. Cooke, [one of Lamar's captured Santa Fe Commissioners], and the Santa Fe prisoners! ... I feel that nothing can be done for them at the present.... they will not be treated as harshly as was anticipated, if they should remain in quiet, and by no act of theirs provoke, or irritate the Mexicans!
> Santa Anna will be governed by policy, as he is not yet firmly fixed in power. He will have to consult the prejudices of the Priesthood, and the populace, on whom he is dependent for his powers. If he can be free to consult his wishes, uncontrolled by circumstances, it will be a matter of pride and ambition to acquire the reputation of a humane and generous conqueror! These are my views, tho' I may be mistaken....[4]

Houston read Editor Moore's latest war cry in the Houston *Telegraph* of February 2, 1842:

> ... we can hardly doubt that the least demonstration on the part of our government to commence or sanction offensive operations against Mexico, would be responded to with joyous acclamations throughout the United States, and especially through the broad and populous valley of the Mississippi. Let the mandate but go forth. "Texas has decided to prosecute an offensive war," and she might in all probability remain almost passive and look on with folded arms to see the great work accomplished.

People met publicly to demand war, and Houston refused to act. A committee of bellicose Galveston citizens headed by George William Brown, a lawyer and recent arrival from Virginia, appealed by letter to the President. From Houston's answer we know the nature of their appeal. They wanted him to respond to the will of the people and to use his discretion to make war on Mexico. He answered that it would be "a pleasure to accommodate them" if he could do so "within the limits of my official duties and consonant with the true interests of the nation." But his duties were "defined by the Constitution and laws and [he] should not transcend them." He went on:

> ... No calamity has ever befallen Texas, from the commencement of the Revolution up to the capture of the Santa Fé Expedition, but what has been caused by a disregard of law and subsituting in its place a "wide discretion."

To this he added what had become his basic military policy:

> To defend a country requires comparatively but little means—to invade a nation requires everything.—To conquer Mexicans in Texas is one thing—to battle with Mexicans in Mexico is a different kind of warfare.
> The true interest of Texas is to maintain peace with all nations and to cultivate her soil.... if she should be invaded, the husbandman could be easily converted into the soldier. Then the flag of Texas would be displayed only in defence of her own soil and liberty.... [5]

Houston's enthusiastic part-time secretary, twenty-eight-year-old Washington Miller, was one of those who clamored for war. He appealed to the President by letter to shake off his anti-war attitude. "*Think*, General," he wrote, "and think betimes, of the complexity and grandeur of the movements about to be exhibited to the gaze of astonished millions..." Then Miller went on to describe the "conquest of Mexico" as "a beacon of glory" and concluded, "General, I am not raving. I am in earnest." [6]

With a hundred duties pressing upon him, Houston patiently responded with fatherly advice and a touching plea: "... you have only looked upon the lights of the picture! Remember the lights have their shades! When you contemplate all the difficulties and cast an eye upon the perspective, you will perceive, many objects, which a careless observer would not discover." In the same letter he wrote,

"...few *wise men* are hasty *in great business!* Weak men and silly ones are hasty; *wisdom is the result of reflection!*" And he added: "My friend, I never before felt the want of help so much as at the present moment! Can you not be with me?" [7]

10. *"Kill the Snake"*

HOUSTON'S expectation that Santa Anna would retaliate for the provocative Santa Fe expedition was fulfilled on March 5, 1842, when General Rafael Vasquez crossed the Rio Grande with 1,400 troops. Vasquez made a swift march to San Antonio, and the totally unprepared citizens surrendered without resistance. Promptly withdrawing, Vasquez took 100 prisoners to Mexico, pausing to hold Goliad and Refugio briefly and frightening the wits out of everybody, but, apparently on orders from Santa Anna, doing little damage.

The strike-and-run aspect of the affair left Houston in doubt whether it was the beginning of a serious attempt to reconquer Texas or merely a pin-prick raid. But he could not afford to take chances and promptly ordered defensive moves. He directed that the militia, which could be called out only by the Congress, should be held alert for orders. He sent General Alexander Somervell, the only legally qualified officer for command of the First Brigade, to San Antonio to take charge of all troops engaged in punishing the retreating Mexicans.

Houston cautioned Somervell that his troops probably would want to cross the Rio Grande "without orders and in a tumultuous mass," exposing themselves "to every disaster that can arise from insubordination" such as "the fate of Johnson, Grant and all the disasters in the Spring of '36." Somervell must prevent this.

He informed Somervell that Texas would not be "in position to invade Mexico for 120 days" because rifles, lead, and powder were inadequate. Somervell would have to depend largely upon contributions from the people. The President also made clear his concern for continued productiveness at home. It was vital that "farmers should be sent to their homes at this important season of planting." Later he added: "Be governed by the exigencies of the case and

397

defend our liberties to the knife ... if the invasion promises to be a formidable one, I will be at the army in person...." Finally, he ordered Somervell to send a force of two companies, fifty-six men each, to scout from Corpus Christi to San Antonio and westward.[1]

As a further precaution, he ordered Colonel Alden A. M. Jackson at Galveston to prepare the fort at the east end of the island to repel an assault by sea; and he proclaimed a blockade of the Mexican coast from Tabasco to Brazos Santiago. Commodore Moore's presence with the fleet off Yucatán gave some weight to this measure.

The clamor mounted for all-out war. The Austin *City Gazette*, of March 30, 1842, demanded an "immediate invasion of the northern Mexican provinces ... The Rio Grande should be the theater of every battle; and on the enemy should our men subsist until we have our rights and independence acknowledged."

On April 14, 1842, the President issued a "Proclamation to all Texans." Partial peace, he said, had existed for the last six years. But the recent insult by a Mexican force advancing on San Antonio "compelled Texas to make war; a war not of aggression, but one which the civilized world will justify—not directed against the nationality of Mexico, but a war upon its despots and oppressors."

He also told the public that the last Congress had left the Executive destitute of means for making war. Congress had rejected every defense measure he had recommended; it could have raised millions of dollars by the sale of Cherokee lands, but had refused to do so. Now these lands were unsalable and the treasury was without funds. In any case, he assured the people that he would permit no unauthorized venture similar to the Santa Fe expedition. He cautioned that war procedures must be orderly.

> When the Executive requires troops in the field, under sanction of the Constitution ... he will call upon the people of Texas as a nation, and the object will be national it will not be for spoils or for individual aggrandizement. We will not incur the epithet of marauder, to which our enemies alone are entitled. ... our actions must be such as will elicit the admiration and approbation of the world.[2]

While he was setting standards of national responsibility, some of the men around him favored a course which he regarded as reckless. Secretary of State Anson Jones now had the same delusions he had previously accused President Lamar of having. He wrote to Secretary of the Treasury Daingerfield in Houston City—

I hope to God the President will act with promptness and energy and follow up the *Manifesto* [Houston's "Proclamation to all Texans"] by *deeds* corresponding to the *words* of that instrument. I want to see in the course of six weeks Matamoras, Tampico, and Vera Cruz—in our power and a formadable Army in the valley of the Rio Grande threatening all Northern Mexico, and even Mexico herself. Then, I think, we may *negotiate* and settle the matter in short order.[3]

Like all the other fire-eating advocates of vigorous offensive war against Mexico, Jones had no suggestions to offer as to sources of funds and supplies. Houston knew that muskets, powder, lead, and clothing were non-existent and that transport wagons were in a state of disrepair that made them unusable.

On April 25, accompanied by his wife, the President was in Galveston. From there he issued an address intended for the people of the United States about "Self-appointed Texas Agents." These fraudulent agents were numerous and were posing as representatives of various "committees of vigilance" in Texas. In 1835-1836, he said, persons falsely claiming to represent Texas had received large sums from the American public which they appropriated to their own use. Once more these self-appointed agents were imposing on "our noble and generous friends." No funds or other assistance, he warned, should be rendered any but those agents specifically authorized by the President and the Texas agent at New Orleans.[4]

Two days later on April 27, 1842, Houston wrote to Secretary of the Treasury Daingerfield, saying that because of ill health his wife was leaving with her brother, Martin Lea, to spend some time with her family in Alabama. He said she was reluctant to go lest he "take a fancy to the Rio Grande" and she should see no more of him until the war was over. "This is groundless," Houston said, "but from the impetuosity of our people I do fear some disaster."[5]

On April 30, the day before his wife sailed with her brother for New Orleans, the President appointed Colonel Barry Gillespie general agent of the government in New Orleans, placing him in charge of all transactions in the Mississippi Valley that had to do with Texas. Gillespie was to appoint only subagents worthy of confidence. "To prevent imposition upon our friends in the United States is all important," Houston said. "Correct all abuses which may exist by persons claiming to be agents of Texas. Render all aid in forwarding troops. See that no contribution to this government is expended unless by special order of the President or Secretary of War." [6]

Houston gave Gillespie the same instructions he gave to Daingerfield and Colonel Lewis M. H. Washington, the Texas agent in New Orleans regarding conditions under which volunteers would be acceptable. No volunteers were to be sent to Texas unless they came prepared to serve for six months and had equipped themselves at their own expense with clothing to last for that time, a rifle or musket with 100 rounds of ammunition, a cartridge box, and food for eight days.

Back in Houston, on May 2, the President appointed James Davis Acting Adjutant General of the Army of Texas. On May 5, he ordered Davis to proceed to Corpus Christi to take command of the troops already there and of all that would arrive.

Restless elements in Texas, claiming that the President was not proceeding with war preparations with sufficient vigor, took matters into their own hands. On May 16, Houston wrote to Colonel Gillespie that he wanted him to understand what was going on in the country. Texas, he said, has been placed in a "peculiar situation at this epoch in her history by a *few* disaffected and vindictive enemies —creatures of passion who are using every exertion, not only at home, but abroad, to embarrass the powers of the government." He continued:

> Meetings have been called for no other purpose than to set at defiance the authorities of the country, and for the avowed intention of raising a force and advancing to the frontier in contempt of the Executive and under leaders of their own creation. . . . These incendiaries would not, I presume, exceed twenty in number; but they are composed of men who have some smartness, some means, and possess all the attributes of mischief. . . . They are not men who shared in the toils of the Revolution. They are men who have no principle but self; and aside from that feel no affections.[7]

These agitators, he made it clear, were demanding war for their own purposes—spoils and possibly glory.

When the agitators demanded that Texas take "splendid" hazards, the President was obliged to write a humiliating letter to an Indian agent, Colonel L. B. Franks. He thanked him for good work done recently without pay when it was vital to keep the Indians at peace. Payment could not be made at this time "because there is not one dollar in the treasury ... we are all in great straits ... we shall have to suffer and do the best we can." Would Colonel Franks please continue at his post and wait for his due "until a better day dawned?" [8]

A captain solicited Houston's help to fit out a corps. The President replied that he would have been glad to cooperate but he had neither the money nor the necessary equipment.

When M. E. Holiday of Parkersburg, Virginia, inquired about sending a volunteer company organized by himself, the President answered that the company would be welcome only on condition that its men were "armed and provisioned for six months." If war came, he added, it would be because the Mexicans provoked it and in that case they must take the consequences. Any reimbursement for Holiday's company must come from the enemy. "The rules of honorable warfare will be observed." [9]

The unreadiness of Texas to support a war was emphasized by an urgent appeal to the President from the commander at Corpus Christi. Sugar and coffee for the troops could not be obtained unless President Houston personally guaranteed payment. Houston's credit was better than his government's. He dispatched the required pledge for $250 in haste.

Insubordination was rampant on the frontier. Burleson, without orders, had gathered three cavalry companies and dashed to San Antonio. He appealed to a force of volunteers and militia who, eager to follow him below the Rio Grande to avenge the Vasquez raid, elected him commander. When General Somervell arrived, he was informed by the volunteers that their leader had already been chosen. He displayed his orders, but Burleson refused to give up the command. The troops declared they would serve only under Burleson. While this wrangle went on, Vasquez' force herded the 100 Texas prisoners off toward the Rio Grande without losing a man.

Somervell, a man of mild temperament, had a nice sense of honor and was loyal to the President, but he was not firm enough for a situation of this kind and withdrew without attempting to oust

Burleson. Then Burleson, appreciating the extent of his own insubordination, also withdrew. The troops had no commander.

Twenty-five hundred roistering militia and volunteers preyed upon the limited food supplies of the frontier and announced their determination to raid Mexico and take spoils before they disbanded. This insurrection had to be dealt with, and Houston called on Major Thomas G. Western, who had redeemed himself by good behavior after his earlier bad conduct. Houston sent Western to the army with a letter he was to read or show to the troops. No copy was to be made lest it fall into the hands of Santa Anna's spies:

> I positively command . . . that [not a soldier] go on [to Mexico] without orders from the government. . . .
>
> We have to rely upon the United States for assistance, and cooperation in the invasion of Mexico. Without their aid, we are not in a condition to make war or have such means as will be required for our success.
>
> If the people of the United States once learn that the laws and the government are disregarded in Texas, we will get no help from them. No one will sustain a cause that has no head and no rule of action. They will remember the fate of those who fell with Fannin. . . .
>
> The excitement of a few men at this time will injure Texas much. . . . Anarchy has never achieved anything useful, great or glorious. Obedience to law, order and subordination, will secure all that is desirable for free men to possess.[10]

The troops grumbled but they did not go to the Rio Grande.

In spite of emphasis and constant repetition, Houston's orders concerning the equipment of volunteers were disregarded by Texas representatives in New Orleans. Swarms applied to go, but they were improperly clad, had no arms, and could not provide themselves with eight days' provisions. They were eager to fight and were looking for spoils. Colonel Gillespie and his associate, Colonel Washington, decided that it would be too bad for Texas to be deprived of the services of such eager fellows, so they sent them to Corpus Christi in defiance of orders.

On May 31, Houston wrote to Colonel Washington in New Orleans:

Texas is in a most deplorable situation. The introduction of emigrants contrary to orders, without supplies, has reduced us to our present calamitous condition. Orders were sent by every steamer to command or suggest.... [that they must come equipped as previously specified].

I wish no violation of orders. There is no excuse.... No plan can be executed, when once designed, unless its details are carried out.

The troops sent to Galveston are in a starving condition; and they have to be quartered out on the bay shore to obtain food and water. The drill and duties of a soldier are neglected; and their expense to the country for transportation from point to point will increase the national burthen.

The orders of the Government shall be obeyed, and no excuse, even the most plausible, will be accepted.... evils resulting from a disregard of orders have become intolerable. They must cease.[11]

Unequipped volunteers continued to pour in. They complained of hard conditions and poor rations, resisted authority, and charged that they had been deceived by the government. They refused to obey orders, raided the surrounding territory, and stole horses. Having received reports of these events, the President sent Adjutant General James Davis a letter on June 15, in which he expressed unbounded indignation:

The troops are to blame and not the government for the want of supplies. They would come to Texas in violation of my orders.... They were not deceived by our government.... The Government has already done more than it was able to do ... I have advanced about $450 on my individual account. Others have done likewise ... malcontents have dared to charge the nation with bad faith and with practicing deceit upon them. The assertion is a foul calumny....

We are not so dependent as to submit to mutiny and disorder by those who degrade the character of soldiers.... nor do we wish to submit our national reputation to those who are not capable of appreciating our condition, or to those willing to add additional misfortunes to those which we are now bound to endure. We expected, if volunteers came to our aid, that they would act as friends, and not as enemies....

Subordination ... shall be established in the army.... there

is a point ... where matters must be remedied, and at it we have
arrived....

You will ... place in irons those men who stole horses; ...
punish them as a court martial may think proper. ... I fear, my
dear friend, you have temporized too long. It is easier to break
an egg than kill a serpent. ... you must now kill the snake.[12]

The snake that Houston dreaded more than any other was insubordination. He had learned his lesson. Disillusioned with the volunteers, he pondered the need for a new military policy. Texas must
not risk its future on the volunteers. He had to find a way to control
them and guide Texas into calmer consideration of its necessities.

11. *A Veto against National Folly*

ANGRY Congressional representatives from the west took the President's call for a special session to meet in Houston on June 27, 1842,
as equivalent to a change of the capital's location without their consent. They announced that they would not attend, but their eagerness
for war and participation in legislation to bring it about caused them
to reconsider. Congress met with its full membership in attendance.

The President's message, read on the morning of the opening day,
urged Congress to use its authority to remove the government records from the frontier capital to a point of safety and convenience
for the transaction of public business. He left the choice of a new
site to the legislators. He asked for a law defining insurrection so
that he could deal effectively with citizens who "obstructed the Executive in the performance of his constitutional duty." Everyone knew
that he referred to Austin's angry citizens who had prevented the
President from removing the records. Western members were incensed by his designation of this interference as an insurrection. The
request provoked an uproar but no legislation.

Houston described how lack of funds had put the executive department in a helpless condition and he respectfully implored support
for the civil government.

The Government cannot exist without revenue ... the pittance afforded its officers and agents is utterly insufficient; and some of the most active and efficient officers have retired and others have notified the Executive of their intention to do so ... the means placed in the Executive's hands at this time for the conduct of government does not exceed one sixth of the amount annually allowed to his predecessor for the administration of the civil departments.

He told Congress that punishment of the Vasquez raiders had been frustrated by lack of discipline and the conflict over the command. He intimated that his hopes of assistance from volunteers had been disappointed. So far the volunteers had been sustained by private contributions. This could not go on.

He said that the general rendezvous of volunteers on the frontier would occur between July 20 and 28. If Congress "should think proper to desire the invasion should not take place, it is important the fact should be immediately known...."

Should the Honorable Congress deem it unwise to invade Mexico and think proper to place at the disposition of the Executive an amount comparatively trifling, with power to establish such regulations as he may think proper, he will be able to maintain such a force on the Southwestern frontier as will rescue it from alarm and danger; unless produced by a regular and formidable invasion.[1]

His message was an invitation to Congress to join him in toning down the war fever, but it did not have the desired effect. Congress did not like it. The war agitators were still provoking the country to a feverish pitch. The President was severely criticized for apathy.

In May, 1842, from Galveston, Colonel Morgan reported to his friend Swartwout in the United States that it would be difficult to restrain the volunteers. They were almost uncontrollable, so keen were they to get into Mexico. Morgan believed that if Congress passed a war bill the President would be compelled to accept it and lead the march south. Many members of Congress felt the same way.[2]

On a torrid July day, the sweating congressmen passed a bill for an offensive war against Mexico. The measure authorized the President to conscript one-third of the population to carry arms, to sell ten million acres of land to finance the undertaking, to put himself at the head of the army and proceed across the Rio Grande. The western members who backed the bill believed that the people were so eager for war that they would turn against the President if he refused to act; they might even eject him from office. One motive for the measure was to "fix Old Sam!"

Texans rejoiced at the war measure and its prospect of revenge and victory. Few believed Houston could refuse to assume authority and follow instructions. Pinckney Henderson was one of the few who hoped he would refuse. He wrote Ashbel Smith that he hoped an invasion of Mexico would not be undertaken and that the Old Chief would get his way, which would be fortunate for the country.

Houston made no public comment. His view seemed to be that the bill was equivalent to appropriating ten million acres of blue sky and conferring dictatorial powers on the north wind.

Congress sent a delegation urging him to sign the measure. Houston refused to disclose his intention, saying that he had the act under consideration. Then he began a campaign to educate the people on the true condition of the country. Partial means to this end were two separate messages he sent to the Senate and the House, in which he stated that the country, in desperate need of a sound currency, faced a crisis because the Congress had not acted upon his earlier recommendations. To the Senate he said: "It is in vain to suppose that any nation can exist without a currency and without means. We have *none*—we must have *some*, or we sink!" [3]

Then to the House of Representatives on the same day, asking enactment of the measures previously recommended:

> . . . Wreck and ruin are fearfully conspicuous on every hand. The period in which we could rely upon credit unsupported and the ink and paper of our statute books, has passed away. We must now turn to something tangible and substantial. It is in the power, and it is the province of the Congress to provide relief. Will they do so? . . . [4]

Congress did nothing about the currency, but demanded to know what measures he had taken to protect the frontier. Houston answered that he had issued appropriate orders for a company to patrol the Rio Grande, but for lack of means it had been impossible to sustain the force for more than a few days. It was the Executive's intention to rout the enemy back across the Rio Grande whenever they appeared; but Houston would be compelled to rely on private citizens to supply guns, lead, powder, food, horses, and mules. Although the country had many patriots they could not be expected to sustain this burden for long.

Congress was having difficulty in putting the President on a hot spot. When they poked at him he responded with something that reddened their faces. The way to fix him was to quit and go home. July 23 was posted as the adjournment date. If the President did not veto the measure before then it would become law.

Reports circulated that the President would veto the war bill. Memucan Hunt wrote him that if he would rally the choicest spirits of the land he would find himself at the head of an army no Mexican force could withstand, and he would be the idol of camp and country. This was followed by an intimation that the President would have to accept the bill and lead the country to war or he could expect to be put out of office by the new Congress that would be elected on September 5.

Excitement over the President's reported intention to stand in the way of war brought threats against his life. Angry and desperate men flocked to the capital, circulating talk about revolution and assassination. Roistering volunteers collected in the streets. After dark, groups paraded past the President's house. Friends suggested a guard, a proposal Houston dismissed as unnecessary.

Houston's supporters asked him not to hazard a veto because it would end in ruining him and his country. Assassins lurked around his dwelling, and friends ceased to call on him. Even his Cabinet officers talked of resigning rather than risk reprisals.

Margaret was home from her visit to Alabama. In his *Memoir*, Houston (writing in the third person) recalled the support he received from her at this time:

> He stationed no guard around his house. . . . The blinds in the windows of his dwelling were wide open, and he was often seen walking across his parlor . . . his wife . . . calmly . . . sustained him by her placid and intellectual conversations. Long after the lights had been extinguished through the town, and sullen, desperate armed men gathered in secret meetings, the gay voice of his

wife, mingling with the tones of her harp and the piano, was heard coming forth from the open windows of Houston's dwelling.[5]

Almost the only public support the beleaguered President received at this time came from Galveston *Civilian*, whose editor wrote on July 18, 1842:

> The war Bill has not yet been acted upon by the Executive, and if I am allowed to prophesy, it will be vetoed, and if so it will elevate Gen. Houston so far above all his enemies that henceforward he will be invulnerable to the shafts so lavishly aimed at him.—His refusal to accept the almost unlimited powers vested in him will display his superior strength of mind in refusing what his enemies have so loudly declared was his only object and desire—the complete control of the purse and sword.[6]

On July 22, one day before Congress was scheduled to adjourn, Houston sent in his veto message. It was an appeal to the people to reject precipitate leadership and to understand his reasons for trying to keep the country out of war. He described the huge effort necessary for a successful invasion. It required "a force whose term of service will not be less than one year and whose numbers should not be less than 5000 men."

Six months would be necessary to complete the training of the troops. If they were enlisted for less than a year no time would be afforded for operations. Five thousand men returning to the settlements of Texas, disorganized and exasperated, would be more formidable than four times their number of the enemy invading Texas.

Here, of course, he was referring to the refractory volunteers, and many members of Congress resented it. He pointed out that the volunteers who had arrived in the country had come "in violation of the express [stipulations] of the Executive as to their clothing and supplies of provisions."

> They did not bring with them the means necessary to their subsistence for even a short time. There have not been public means to sustain them. Private resources are now exhausted— liberality [of individuals] is worn down; and if the few who are now here cannot be sustained for the want of public means, how could the Executive call for, receive and support an emigration of five thousand?

He again reviewed his experience with volunteers over the past six years. There was danger in their presence if they could not be put into "instant service."

> Heretofore a few [volunteeers] have assumed the right of dictating to the Executive; and if five thousand were assembled they would feel confident in their numbers and power. Not only the Executive but the nation would be at their mercy; for [an insubordinate] armed force is more dangerous to the liberties of a country than all the external enemies that could invade its rights.

Instead of means for an enterprise of this grand scope the Congress had provided the Executive with ten million acres of land which he was expected to convert into cash. But at this very time, he pointed out, "hundreds of thousands of acres of scrip heretofore issued by the Government of Texas can be obtained in quantities in the United States, at a price not exceeding twenty-five dollars for 640 acres." It could not be supposed that "hypothecation or sale of ten million acres of land" would furnish funds in the needed amount.

Moreover, if he approved the bill a considerable time for preparation must elapse before it could be carried out.

> A war of invasion would be the theme of continued conversation—a state of feverish excitement would exist . . . general incertitude would pervade every class, and discontent would be universal. The question would be asked, what is the Executive doing? . . . The Executive has indeed a show of power but he is helpless and destitute for the want of means.

Further, it was doubtful if Congress had the right to give the Executive the powers tendered him in the bill.

> If it would be wrong to clothe an individual with powers, who might, by their exercise, bring ruin upon his country; it is equally at war with principle that a man should exercise powers improperly granted, though it were intended for the salvation of his country.
>
> If the Executive were to sanction the exercise of the powers granted by the bill, he would consider it an act of war against all his hopes and desires for [the country's] future and permanent welfare. . . . I can never sanction the adoption of a principle

at war with the conviction of my mind, the practice of my life and the liberties of my fellow men.[7]

The veto threw the House of Representatives into a commotion. But the next day, Congress adjourned without an attempt to override it. That same day the Houston *Morning Star* conceded that popular clamor would be raised against the veto, but it implored citizens to defer judgment until passion and prejudice had subsided.

But the storm broke. Threats to get the President out of the way by assassination were renewed. A delegation of townspeople who begged Houston to take command and lead the country to war went away enraged because he advised them that the real need of the country was to plant corn.

In his diary the President's friend, Adolphus Sterne, now postmaster at Nacogdoches, apostrophized his country:

> Oh—dear Texas, have I worn chains for thee, to see *such* fellows try to fatten on thy ruin! Confound all demagogues— all Political gamblers, god grant that Texas belong to the great union of the Land of Washington—if it does not soon I'll give up hopes of ever seeing this a happy country!!! [8]

But gradually the terms of the veto message caught up with the bare fact; the people perceived that they had been saved from costly folly. Morgan, who had agitated for war, reported to Ashbel Smith in August that the excitement caused by the veto, had died away and Old Sam, he believed, was more popular than ever.

Then in the heat of mid-August, the President received a letter from Nashville in Jackson's pathetically shaky handwriting. Houston had sent him a copy of the veto and the aging General had read it. "...I wish to God I had strength enough to go into the subject fully..." Jackson wrote. "All my debilitated and feeble strength will permit me, is to assure you I approve your veto fully." Then he succeeded in writing a long letter praising the position Houston had taken.

> If you had not vetoed this bill, it would have led to the destruction of your country and the disgrace of all concerned ... as the attempt under your present situation must have inevitably failed. ...
>
> P.S. I hope your Congress had not the design in passing this

bill to disgrace you, regardless of the great injury an offensive war would entail upon the republic, if not destroy it by making Texas an easy conquest for St. Anna after your failure and all your resources consumed. By your veto you have saved your country and yourself from disgrace. *Stand on the Defensive.* A. J.[9]

The letter gave Houston the assurance that the friend to whom he was devoted beyond all others understood that by his veto message he had made character for Texas.

12. *"The Burden in the Heat of the Day"*

ANGERED by Houston's attack on the volunteers, his stand on defense, and his naval policy, the President's old and trusted friend, George Hockley, Secretary of War and Marine, resigned. Hurt, Houston asked him to withdraw his resignation:

I ... would have been glad to have had a personal interview ... I dislike to witness any change in old friendships. . . . My wishes are influenced by friendly personal feelings ... Should these sentiments not be reciprocated by you then the course which you have adopted will be the proper one to pursue.

In addition to writing to Hockley, Houston tried to prevent the break by asking another friend, Attorney General George W. Terrell, to intervene. Hockley is "a tried friend and I value him!" he wrote Terrell. "He is a prime officer, and I respect him for all his high qualities, but if either his feelings, or his duty to himself demand of him a course not in accordance with my wishes and desires, I must do the best I can. . . . Occasional jars will test the solidity of a building: And Heaven knows that my poor Wigwam 'gets several'." [1]

But Hockley refused to read the letter delivered by Terrell and adhered to his statement that he could not stay in office and see the "interests of the country are sacrificed to opinions" that were "not in my estimation founded upon enlightened, liberal and just ground." [2]

411

In years to come the friendship was renewed, but it never was as close as before.

More public officials, long unpaid and doubting the country's future, offered their resignations. Among them was Gail Borden, collector of customs at the port of Galveston. The efficient Borden could not be spared. Houston responded with an appeal that kept Borden at his post:

> This I know; you have as much interest in the country as I have, and if you think the country can dispense with your services, every useful officer may think so too; and I will come to the same conclusion as to myself. What will be the consequences? Anarchy!!! ... This I have looked to, and have made my sacrifices to duty.... I hope ... you will continue to ... bear your share of "the burden in the heat of the day." "Blessed are they who continue to the end, and do not faint by the way...."
> Heaven bless you. Thine truly, Sam Houston.[3]

On September 8, 1842, three days after the election of the seventh Congress, Richardson Scurry, a Houston stalwart in that body, wrote to the President, saying that he was worried because Houston's eastern supporters in the new Congress would be outnumbered by his western opponents. To conciliate the westerners, Scurry suggested that the President compromise on the location of the capital. If considerations of safety did not permit restoring the seat of government to Austin, why not hold the next session at Washington-on-the-Brazos? Scurry considered it unwise to bite off the nose to spite the face; and that, he thought, was what convening Congress at Houston would amount to. Scurry had been with Houston on the long retreat and had fought as a first sergeant with the artillery at San Jacinto. A loyal supporter, his opinions always commanded Houston's respect. After some thought, Houston adopted Scurry's suggestion.

Since the birthday of the Republic the capital had been on wheels, rolling from Washington, where it was born, to Harrisburg, to Morgan's Point, to Galveston, to Columbia, to Houston, to Austin, and then back to Houston. Now after it had been located for one session —all of twenty-nine days—in Houston City, it was time to move back to the place of its origin.

Houston sent an emissary to Washington to see what arrangements could be made. The town fathers, led by Judge John Lockhart, agreed to furnish free transportation for all government property, and to provide accommodations for government offices without rent if existing buildings could be suitably remodeled. Until the necessary new houses could be put up, the Houstons and Secretary Miller would stay in the Judge's home. Other government officers and employees would live with private families.

On September 20, when the government's belongings were packed and the Houstons' personal things were ready to go, an excited messenger rode up to the President's house. Delayed several days by high water, he brought news that, nine days before, Santa Anna had delivered his second thrust in revenge for the Santa Fe expedition. One of the Mexican's commanders, Colonel Adrian Woll, had raided San Antonio with 1,400 men.

Woll's troops had appeared suddenly at night in a dense fog. The town was awakened at daylight by a cannon shot, followed by martial music. The fog obscured the Mexican soldiers until they were actually in the public square. Fifty Texans assembled and fired on the invaders until the fog lifted. Then the Texans were completely surrounded and forced to surrender. In addition, Woll carried off the judge and jury panel of the district court and three lawyer-congressmen who were in town to try cases. One lawyer, James Robinson, had taken over as governor after the General Council had deposed Governor Smith. Without waiting for authority from Congress, Houston ordered two regiments of militia and any United States volunteers still in the country to assemble at San Antonio. He warned Gail Borden to have the Galveston defenses ready for any possible attack by sea. Then he ordered General Somervell to prepare for a possible march to the Rio Grande.

The country had quieted down after digesting the President's reasons for vetoing the war bill. Now its zest for war flared again, whipped up by newspapers that exhorted every man who could shoulder a rifle to hasten to the aid of western citizens. The Houston *Morning Star*, September 17, 1842, eagerly forecast that one timely decisive blow might defeat Santa Anna's contemplated campaign.

The country waited in vain for a ringing appeal from the President. His hand was forced, but, still playing down the crisis to abate hysteria, Houston issued suitable "Orders to the Country" for dealing with the situation. He activated two regiments of militia and volunteers, and directed Somervell to take command. The enemy was to be driven from the country and fellow citizens were to be rescued. *"Expedition, energy, order, united with subordination,* will ensure success." [4] He was eager to punish Woll, but he wanted to keep the country from becoming involved in all-out war. While the excitement was increasing in intensity, the President and the departments went ahead with their removal plans.

On the morning of September 28, Houston City was abandoned by the government for the last time. Six wagons, each drawn by three yoke of oxen, transported the government's property and the Presidential home furnishings, including Mrs. Houston's harp and piano. Margaret rode with one of the loads, the President on Bruin. Bruin, as usual was good at his work, leaving Houston free to spend his traveling time in analyzing events.

BOOK VI

WORLD STATESMAN ON THE BRAZOS

1. *The New Strategy*

BY 1842, growth and some dignity had come to the village of shanties and barracks, now known as "Old Washington," which had cradled the Texas Republic. It stood in a post oak grove on a bluff, its houses beyond sight of the River of the Arms of God. Main Street lay 500 feet back from the bluff. Its most important building was Independence Hall, a weatherbeaten barracks where the declaration of independence had been signed and Houston had taken the oath as Commander in Chief. Not far from it, an office had been built for the President—a one-room shack that smelled pleasantly of new wood and fresh carpentering and contained a rough desk, a couch, and a chair.

Independence Hall and the President's office were surrounded by numerous saloons and gambling parlors that were open for business both day and night. How gamblers could have money, even specie, when nobody else had any, was a mystery. Between 50 and 100 "floaters"—gamblers, and horse racers—mingled with some 400 established inhabitants, including four lawyers and four doctors.

Judge and Mrs. Lockhart cordially welcomed President Houston and his wife on October 2, 1842. They had provided a comfortable bedroom-sitting room with a small fireplace and a large mahogany bed which Mrs. Lockhart had brought from Alabama. A fine four-poster, it was equipped with a marvel of comfort—a feather-filled mattress. A side door had been cut into this room so the President and his wife would not have to go in and out through the house.

Soon after President Houston moved into his new office on Main Street, the government was plunged into a new crisis by events that followed General Woll's raid of September 18 on San Antonio. A force of 600 men under two well-known Indian fighters, Jack Hays and "Old Paint" Caldwell, had pursued Woll from San Antonio, tracking him down some six miles away on the Salado River. A battle was imminent when a dispute arose over command. The supporters of "Old Paint" won the argument, but meanwhile Woll's mounted troops escaped, receiving only a few parting shots from Hays's battalion.

While this was taking place, Captain Nicholas Dawson's regiment of volunteers, coming from the east on foot to join Caldwell and Hays, had been cut off by Mexican cavalry. Half the regiment was killed and the survivors negotiated a surrender with the understanding that they would be treated as prisoners of war. An escaped survivor related that after the prisoners had been disarmed, they were lined up and shot. Another case of perfidy by one of Santa Anna's commanders was entered on the record as the Dawson massacre.

Again Texas flamed with martial fever. Houston remained calm, believing as firmly as ever that a formidable invasion of Texas was not likely. He was convinced that Santa Anna had settled on a definite policy of keeping the frontier stirred up to prevent Texas from developing prosperous industry and to curtail its growth by discouraging immigration. He also believed that an invasion of Mexico by Texas invited far greater risks than were warranted by any possible gain.

West Texas seethed with anger against its pacifistic President. Vice-President Burleson collected a few hundred volunteers to join him in a Mexican invasion. He fumed and threatened, but could not get the President's authority to go to the Rio Grande. He thought it best not to go without authorization.

Congressmen, editors, and sundry firebrands demanded a march on Mexico City to free the Santa Fe prisoners and those taken in the recent raids. The President believed that they failed to comprehend the difficulties and consequences of such an undertaking. The ill-equipped troops would have to march more than a thousand miles through Mexico's mountains, canyons, arroyos, and forests. In letters to government officials and friends, he appealed for discretion. He could not publish the facts about the government's inability to supply wagons, weapons, and ammunition because this would aid the enemy.

But another aspect of the matter was equally disturbing to the President. As he saw it, the test and proof would come when some rash commander, without executive sanction and in rebellion against restraining orders, induced troops to follow him across the river. The consequences, he feared, would be as horrible as those of the Santa Fe expedition.

Houston finally decided it would be wise to retaliate with the same kind of pin-prick raid that Santa Anna used. Under the constitution, the only man available to him to command such a venture was Brigadier General Alexander Somervell. Somervell had served as lieutenant colonel of the First Regiment during the withdrawal from Gonzales. He followed instructions without argument, although he was not always happy about the Commander in Chief's orders which called for restraint and cunning instead of bold attack. Houston believed him to be trustworthy.

On October 13, 1842, the President had ordered Somervell to proceed to the southwestern frontier and select the most eligible position on the Cibolo, or elsewhere, for training. He was to organize and drill all troops who solemnly declared their "resolve to be obedient to orders, and, if required, to cross the Rio Grande." Along with these orders went a warning:

> ...The greatest care and economy must be observed... or starvation will be the consequence.
>
> ...conduct all your movements with secrecy; for this reason, San Antonio [overrun with Mexicans] is not deemed a proper place for concentration.... the enemy should be kept in ignorance of our designs....
>
> When the force shall have assembled, if their strength and condition will warrant a movement upon the enemy, it is desirable that it should be executed with promptness and efficiency.
>
> A plan of the organization for the army will be forwarded to you....[1]

The next communication to Somervell informed him of something he must already have suspected. The government's military resources were at rock bottom. The secretary of war, acting on Houston's instructions advised Somervell that the government could supply "no Rifle Powder, and but a small quantity of Lead." Only a few hundred pounds of the metal remained in the public store at Galveston. Supplies of ammunition had been sent by individuals, but the President doubted "whether it has, or will ever reach Head Quarters." It had to be collected by Somervell's quarter masters.[2]

This was to be a people's campaign, not ordered but permitted by the President in response to popular clamor. A dangerous expedient under any circumstances, it was to have a definitely limited objective. Previously Houston had instructed Somervell to be governed by the rules of humane warfare and not to cross the river if there was the slightest doubt of his being unable to recross. He was to venture no general or partial action unless victory was certain. Somervell was not to try to achieve an overwhelming victory. If he liked, he could capture some goods, horses, and cattle, but the President feared that if Somervell took a great quantity of property, the people of Texas, pacified sufficiently just now to go to work, would be inspired by military success to leave the plough, turn to adventuring and guerrilla warfare and, in the end, sustain a loss of character with no profit.

In short, Somervell's campaign was to show the world that Texans were able to occupy not only the country they claimed but also country beyond; and that they could maintain themselves in Mexico a least as long as Mexican raiders ventured to stay in Texas, which was a matter of a few days. In orders and letters, as well as in secret instructions to Somervell, the President emphasized that the consequences would be serious if the fate of war went against Texas. It would discourage the people and affect foreign governments. These possibilities were the cause of his great anxiety.[3]

On Main Street, the President was most frequently seen in a linsey-woolsey, checked hunting shirt, loose pantaloons of coarse cotton, a smoky broad-brimmed hat, and russet shoes without strings. A tight shoe irritated his old ankle wound and his unusually high instep. He deliberately chose plain clothes because they linked him with the common people, but on suitable occasions he liked to dress in a coat lined with bright yellow silk and a shirt with a ruffled front.

His renown as the victor of San Jacinto and twice-elected Chief Executive of the country he had liberated, reached the Sultan of Turkey. Impressed, the Sultan sent him a full suit of clothes. With some hesitation, the President tried on the fez to satisfy his wife's curiosity. She thought it funny. Sensitive about anything that made him appear ridiculous, he never put it on again and refused to try on, even experimentally, the large and baggy trousers that terminated in soft leather shoes and had several yards of material to wind around the waist. However, he loved the long robe of flaming red silk which reached almost to his ankles and wore it constantly in his office.

The preceding summer, having delayed action for two years while exerting pressure on Texas to outlaw slavery, England had ratified a treaty recognizing the new Republic. Captain Charles Elliot, who had served as British commercial agent at Galveston in the interim, was now chargé d'affaires in Texas. Formerly an officer in the British Navy, he had commanded British forces in the opium war with the Chinese government (1837-1841). A conscientious officer, he had offended commercial interests in the opium trade, and consequently his government had permitted him to transfer to an entirely different service.

Elliot was able, intelligent, sincere, and deeply interested in the success and prestige of this new country. He admired the President and keenly appreciated the many facets of his character. He reported to his government that Houston, after a stormy career, had made "a new connextion with a young and gentle woman brought up in the fear of God." He had "conquered" her "no doubt . . . by a glowing tongue. . . ." While she "in good revenge [made] conquest of his habits of tremendous cursing, and passionate love of drink." [4]

Houston was fond of Elliot and considered him a talented and fine gentleman. In November 15, 1842, Elliot, who was enjoying the relative comforts of Galveston, reported to his friend, Undersecretary of Foreign Affairs William Addington, in London:

> . . . the President has convened Congress to assemble at Washington on the Brazos, where there are 12 or 13 Wooden shanties. . . .
> The President writes to me in a private Note a few days since, that He finds things at Washington rather raw and as He has been accustomed to the elaborate comforts of an Indian wigwam, I presume he must be living in a commodious excavation.

Elliot visited the President at the capital. Although the Houstons made things pleasant for him, he was not favorably impressed by their surroundings. It was Elliot's responsibility to report on the character of men in other countries with whom Her Majesty's agents had dealings. He supplied the British Foreign Office with what possibly may be the most penetrating thumbnail sketch ever made of the Texas President:

> Whatever General Houston has been, it is plain that He is the fittest man in this Country for his present station. His education has been imperfect, but he possesses great sagacity and penetration, surprising tact in his management of men trained as men are in these parts, is perfectly pure handed and moved in the main by the inspiring motive of desiring to connect his name with a Nation's rise. Adverting to his general safe and reasonable policy with respect to Mexico, it must certainly be admitted that He sometimes says and writes what appears to be capricious and contradictory. But the truth is that He knows his own people thoroughly, and when He seems to be running with them, He is probably satisfied that opposition would only provoke their precipitate purposes. With hard fare at the point of assembly, skilful delays on the part of the President, and an abundant measure of mutual laudation, the fit passes away innocently enough.

After Elliot's visit to the capital, Margaret Houston went to Grand Cane on the Trinity River where her brother Vernal was developing a plantation and where her lively and amusing sister, Antoinette Bedloe, was visiting. There was no reason to suspect that the General could not get along without her. She had every reason to believe that, with the aid of his bitters and orange peel, he had overcome his weakness. The President accompanied her to Grand Cane but did not stay long. All circumstances of an episode that occurred after his return to the capital are not available, but main details have been certified by the testimony of a member of the Lockhart family.

It is certain that although Judge Lockhart's wife was the sturdy pioneer type she clung to the niceties she had known during her old life in Alabama. It is also certain that the President was chewing tobacco at this time, probably to help keep down his recurrent thirst for something more flavorsome than bitters. Sitting on Mrs. Lockhart's clean porch, the President sometimes exerted himself to spit a curve in the wind without achieving complete success in avoiding the railing. On other occasions, he may have been too casual in his efforts. In Mrs. Lockhart's opinion, if the President took proper precautions he could manage to expectorate over the rail with unfailing regularity. Houston accepted her rebuke with graciousness and affability, and mended his ways.

It seems that within the next day or two, the President passed Hatfield's saloon. The proprietor waylaid him; he was proud to have received in his last shipment from New Orleans several gallon jugs of extra fine Madeira and wished to give the President one. Houston declined to accept it as a gift, but was glad to find something out of the ordinary as a token for the wife of his host. When he reached home, the children said Mrs. Lockhart was at a neighbor's. He wanted to make a presentation speech when he gave her the wine, so, awaiting her return, he placed the jug on the floor of his room by the door into the Lockhart's section of the house.

Exactly what happened early in the evening can only be surmised. The President made a practice of reading official reports in bed. One can imagine that his eye may have wandered from the page to rest contemplatively upon the jug. Did that Madeira justify Hatfield's high recommendation? Probably he had no intention of taking a drink, but the question deserved an answer. He broke the hard wax around the cork, tipped the jug to wet his finger, and tasted the wine. The test seemed to support Hatfield's recommendation, but it was not conclusive. He poured a little into a tin cup. No doubt about it; Mrs. Lockhart would be delighted. Satisfied, he went back to bed, but irresistibly his eye wandered toward the jug. His next sample was a deep draught of the excellent Madeira. At some time around 2 A.M., he had disposed of a substantial portion of the gallon.

Somehow or other the notion seized the President that one of the posts on Mrs. Lockhart's fine old mahogany bed interfered with his breathing. He went out to the lean-to where his servant, Frank, slept and told him to bring an ax. Then he ordered Frank to chop off, evenly with the frame, the righthand post at the foot of the bed that had been brought at much expense and trouble from Alabama.

Judge Lockhart was awakened from sound sleep by the crashing blows of Frank's ax. Lockhart knew there were men in the West who had threatened to assassinate the President for removing the capital from the frontier. Alarmed, he rushed into Houston's room, saw the wreckage, and exclaimed, "Thank God, General, are you all right?"

The President maintained his dignity, but his slightly erratic articulation disclosed the true situation. Judge Lockhart took the ax from Frank, sent him back to his quarters, and urged the General to get into bed. Satisfied, now that he had got rid of the offending bedpost, the General promptly complied.

This seems to have been Houston's last binge; careful search has not revealed any episode of similar magnitude. John Washington Lockhart, eighteen years old at the time of the incident, grew up to be a physician with a considerable reputation. In his reminiscences, *Sixty Years on the Brazos*, published in 1930, he gave a kind of clinical report of the affair. He described Margaret, Houston's restraining influence, as "tall, handsome, with a fine figure, weight 115 pounds, intelligent, well educated, modest, unassuming...." Dr. Lockhart felt that Houston had more or less controlled his habit, but the compulsion to drink had not left him. His wife, rather than his will power, was responsible for his ultimate victory. Dr. Lockhart concluded that Mrs. Houston "gained complete control over the General... without her protecting arm he could not resist temptation. If she had not been absent he would not have succumbed. It did not last long, for he soon followed her to Grand Cane and once with her, temptation fled." [5]

Houston always maintained, and truthfully so far as the facts can be ascertained, that never for one hour was he ever incapacitated by drink for the performance of any public or private duty. He conceded that he drank heavily at times, but insisted that the extent of it was "exaggerated a hundredfold." It is at least possible that since the President was under strain from overwork, fatigue, anxiety for his nation, bad diet, intermittent attacks of malaria and dysentery, alcohol did in some way contribute to his endurance and survival.

Demands for help for the needy poured in upon a President whose salary was in arrears and who, short of flour and bacon at this very time, was asking "trust" for these items from John M. Bagby, a merchant in Houston City.

Bagby was a friend as well as a creditor. Virginia-born and raised in Tennessee, he had been a respected business man in Houston City since its founding, forwarding goods from the coast to the interior. He had never held political office and would not accept one. He knew "the curse of grief" that had fallen upon his friend, Houston, and was just the man to understand and sympathize with the tribulations of the Texas President. In one letter, Houston appealed to Bagby to send a consignment of flour and bacon on trust immediately "or I perish." In another, he described a burden that afflicts the chief executive of all states whose people are the sovereigns. Friends, acquaintances, job seekers, the curious, the exhibitionists, and the garrulous flocked to the capitol and crowded his one-room office.

> ... I have in the discharge of my duties perplexities which no one can appreciate, unless they were to be with me all the time. From my uprising to my down lying at night, I have rarely one hour thro' the day to pass in company with Mrs. Houston. Some call on business, some through curiosity, and others... "to spend the time." Now, this last is cruel to me ... they ought to reflect when they are consuming [my time] that it is of some value to me and to the country. I can't say to them—that wouldn't be kindness—so you may judge my unenviable condition—My mind abstracted—I would think ought to indicate my unfitness for company—but no. I have to endure the "auger" and I may screw and twist as much as I please! Oh! what charming wretchedness—... When it will be otherwise, I cannot well guess. ...⁶

The President's wife dropped in to remind him that when he wrote to Bagby there was something to ask on her account. He added this: "Mrs. H. says, 'Do ask Mr. Bagby if he sent the Cambric Linnen.' I say—'no, Madam, but I will request him to read my three last letters'—please do peruse them Bagby... that you may see how much I want of everything!!!"

2. *Proof of the Pudding*

HOUSTON was troubled by the slowness of Somervell's preparations for a cautious raid beyond the Rio Grande. He sent the general a letter of mild reproach through Acting Secretary of War M. C. Hamilton on November 19, 1842:

> ... It was not the design of the Government to keep an undisciplined and disorganized army stationed on the frontier

425

merely for the purpose of consuming the little substance remaining [to] a population already nearly reduced to starvation.[1]

Somervell had violated orders by making San Antonio his point of rendezvous, and this contributed to the delay. No supplies were available there, and he was subjected to interference by disorderly elements and spies from the town. In this same letter, Houston rebuked him for disregarding orders and reminded him that it was his "discretion to determine whether the strength and condition of the force . . . would [warrant] your leading them into the enemy's country." If he decided to go he was to "act with promptitude so as to relieve the frontier of the burden of supporting them."

Another cause of anxiety came to the President's attention—the character of Somervell's subordinates. Thomas Jefferson Green and William S. Fisher were to function as captains in Somervell's force. Green was infamous for his attempt to kidnap Santa Anna from the *Invincible* during a crucial time for Texas. Fisher had served the President well during his first administration. As acting secretary of war, he had furloughed the volunteers who were yielding to Felix Huston's blandishments. Fisher himself had soon followed the volunteers out of the country. Since then he had spent most of his time in New Orleans trying to raise money for a Mexican filibuster with spoils as its object. Houston knew that Somervell would need men of spirit and did not interfere with his choice of captains, hoping that the general would be equal to controlling them.

General Somervell might well have complained of lack of support from the government, but refrained because he understood the conditions under which the President labored. Clothing, food, powder, and guns were inadequate and slow in coming. The troops fretted about being poorly mounted, but were reassured by the expectation of seizing better animals from the enemy. They objected to the training and drill that was intended to make them into a disciplined force. Many had come from the United States as volunteers without bringing the specified equipment. All they owned was on their backs, and they were hungry for spoils.

Prodded by the President, Somervell finally started for the Mexican border with his ill-equipped and disorderly 750 men on November 22, 1842. On December 7, they encamped three miles from Laredo, going into the town the next day. The people of Laredo were all

Mexicans by birth, but lived on soil claimed by Texas and they desired to be considered Texas citizens. They greeted the troops as friends, and the Texans accepted their simple hospitality but complained about being improperly fed.

When General Somervell ordered withdrawal, the troops readily obeyed. He marched them a mile back up the river and camped on shore. A few men asked permission to return to Laredo just to look the place over; they had behaved so well on their first visit that Somervell granted it. Many others went along without leave. On this second visit, they seized everything they could lay their hands on. Later, President Houston was informed that some of the men had "stripped women." Witnesses charged that Thomas Jefferson Green was present and made no effort to restrain the troops. One disgusted witness reported that Green encouraged them with shouts of "Rake them down, boys; rake them down." [2]

The troops brought back to camp as motley an assortment of pillage as ever came within the lines of a civilized force: bed clothing, cooking utensils, horses, saddles, sheep, poultry—even women's undergarments and children's tiny dresses. Somervell ordered the men to gather it all up and restore it to the alcalde of Laredo. They did so with much grumbling but no real disorder.

After Somervell restored discipline, he told his troops that he intended to cross the river. Those who did not wish to leave the soil of their own country were free to return home. Two hundred announced their intention to return, some saying that they were disgusted with the pillaging of Laredo and wanted nothing more to do with the outfit.

The remaining troops marched downstream to the mouth of the Salado River opposite the town of Guerrero and crossed the Rio Grande in flatboats on December 15. The horses swam or were forded. On the way to Guerrero, the Texans encountered 300 cavalrymen under General Antonio Canales who retreated without a skirmish. Unopposed, they marched three miles to Guerrero, took possession of the town without resistance, and camped nearby for three days.

Somervell's command had been on the river for eleven days. He knew the position of the enemy's troops and believed they were concentrating in numbers that made a longer stay imprudent. If his force regained Texas soil without accident, he would have accomplished the mission that had been secretly assigned to him by the President.

The general marched his men back to the river and recrossed, ordering the flatboats destroyed. Presently he learned that a number of boats had been hidden, and he had reason to suspect that other insubordinate actions would follow. On December 19, 1842, he issued an order intended to circumvent them, instructing the troops belonging to the Southwestern Army to be ready to march at ten o'clock the next morning for Gonzales, where they would be disbanded.

Some three hundred and sixty men refused to go, declaring their intention to invade Mexico and choosing Fisher and Green to lead them. Somervell and his followers left for Gonzales. Fisher and Green moved down the river. It was exactly the kind of venture the President dreaded.

The river was swollen with rain. Commanding the flatboats that had been secreted, Green wore a feather in his hat and his flagship flew a red banner with a Lone Star. "Commodore" was hilariously added to his two other titles, "Captain" and "General."

The mounted troops, leading the horses of their comrades who were in the boats, went by land under Fisher's command. Land and naval forces camped together on shore that night, raiding ranches for provisions and forage. Two days before Christmas they camped on the Texas side of the river approximately opposite the Mexican town of Mier, which was inland seven miles from the river. In this region of the lower river, Mier was second in size to Matamoros and could be expected to yield rich spoils.

A patrol returned from Mier, reporting that General Canales had recently evacuated it and General Pedro de Ampudia was supposed to be on his way there with a larger force. Fisher and Green advanced on the town and occupied it without resistance, handing the scared little mayor—they called him "Don Juan"—a written requisition for all government supplies stored there, including cannon, muskets, powder, and lead. To deceive him about the size of their force, they demanded five days' rations for 1,200 men; large amounts of flour, sugar, and coffee; 200 pairs of coarse, strong shoes; 100 pairs of pantaloons; and 100 blankets. Don Juan shrugged helplessly and acquiesced. His people had suffered heavily from levies for the Mexican army, but they would bring what they had.

A small oversight threw the Fisher-Green calculations out of gear. They neglected to order a wagon train for the mass of supplies that piled up. Transporting them to the river had to be postponed for twenty-four hours. In the meantime, scouts reported that a force under General Ampudia was coming closer. Fisher and Green rode back to spend the night at their camp by the river. They took Don Juan with them as a hostage and left five Texans behind to guard the supplies.

Scouts returned from Mier on Christmas Day to report that Generals Ampudia and Canales had arrived with 750 soldiers and two cannon. They had captured the five-man Texas guard and the accumulated supplies.

In a council of war, the Texans voted unanimously in favor of attack. Having crossed the river by four o'clock in the afternoon, they pressed on and neared the town by twilight. Mexican pickets fired on them and ran. Semi-darkness and a cold drizzle covered their approach as they climbed the craggy bluff opposite the town. Sixty-foot-wide Alcantro Creek flowed at the base of the bluff. Since Mexicans were guarding the shallow fords above and below the town, the Texans had to climb down the forty-foot bluff and cross the icy creek in water to their waists. Scouts on both flanks engaged the Mexicans guarding the fords.

They stormed up a steep street that opened on the plaza, fired on the Mexican artillery, and took shelter behind houses to reload. They forced their way into stores and dwellings, found crowbars, and tunneled through the walls from house to house. Fifty yards from the plaza, they fired on the artillery through ports broken in the walls.

In the morning, Ampudia's soldiers took to the rooftops, and the Texans broke through roofs to fight them. They saw the Mexican cavalry capture eight Texans who had been left to guard the camp on the Alcantro bluff. The Mexican fire slackened; then the Mexicans charged and the Texans beat them back. Fisher was hit by a bullet that split his thumb from tip to base and entered the joint. An excruciatingly painful wound, it sickened him. He vomited and was unable to command. After that, "Commodore" Green gave the orders.

Actual fighting at Mier lasted seventeen hours. The Mexicans did not resume their fire, and the Texans believed that victory was near. A Dr. Sinnickton, one of the Texans captured on the bluff, came with a white flag. Instead of announcing the Mexican surrender as the Texans expected, he brought a demand from Ampudia—surrender or death! If they surrendered, they would be treated as prisoners of war. None would be sent to Mexico City but "all [would] be kept on the frontier until an exchange or pacification could be effected."

While the Texans were talking things over, the Mexicans infiltrated and bettered their position. Green argued for a fighting retreat to the river. Fisher, sick and white, had lost his will to fight. He shrank from the toll that retreat would exact. As a freebooter he had soldiered with Ampudia south of the Rio Grande and would vouch for the Mexican general's honor.

When the main body of Texans had stacked their arms in the plaza, they were joined by the prisoners captured on the bluff. These men said that Ampudia and his officers had had horses ready and saddled for their escape if their surrender demand was rejected. Of the 261 Texans in the battle, 16 had been killed and 30 severely wounded. The Texans claimed that more than 700 Mexicans were dead. The score was excellent, but the game was not played out.

Generals Canales and Ampudia marched their prisoners to Matamoros, and paraded them through the streets under triumphal arches. Children cavorted with paper banners: "Glory and Gratitude to the Brave Canales" and "Eternal Honor to the Immortal Ampudia." The prisoners were paraded in other river towns, Camargo, Reynosa, and Guadalupe. Tied together with lariats, they started for Mexico City by way of Monterrey and Saltillo.

At Haciendo Salado, 100 miles beyond Saltillo, Captain Ewing Cameron led an attack on the Mexican guard one morning just after daybreak. With a number of companions, he seized horses and weapons. Leaving five dead and several wounded behind, they escaped on the road leading to Texas by way of Monclava.

Fearing capture, they left the highway for a mountain road that they hoped would lead to the Rio Grande; instead it led to blinding sun, exhausting heat by day and chill at night, starvation, and despair. They killed their horses for meat and drank the blood of their mules to quench maddening thirst. Some of the men drank their own urine. They scooped up earth and held it to their bellies and throats for coolness. After five days of this, they went toward the smoke of a campfire and found themselves back in the hands of their captors. Five of their number had died, three had vanished, and four, it was believed, had managed to make the river.

The recaptured men were marched back to Haciendo Salado chained in pairs by the wrists. Santa Anna had instructed General Canales to execute one in every ten of the prisoners taken in the Mier battle. Black beans (representing ten per cent of the total number of Texans captured) were added to a pot of 159 white beans (the total number of prisoners). Under a guard of dragoons in crossbelts and shakos, the prisoners advanced two-by-two to draw their lots of life or death. Officers came first.

The black beans had been put on top and were not mixed with the white beans. Canales had hoped thus to get rid of officers, particularly the leaders, Green and Fisher, and Cameron, because he had engineered the escape. But the officers delved deep into the pot and each came up with a white bean. Captain Cameron appealed to his captors to kill him and spare his companions. The request was denied. Cameron and General Canales had clashed in a border raid two years before, and now Canales intended to have Cameron shot before he reached Mexico City; he had no reason to grant a favor to a vicious Texan whose life was already condemned.

The cavalcade of the doomed was led into an adjoining courtyard and shot. Some Mexicans fired as many as fifteen shots to kill one man. A Mexican soldier fainted from the horror of the slaughter.

The next morning when the survivors resumed their march to Mexico City they passed the sickening litter of the execution. Canales announced that if any one of the prisoners tried to escape all would be shot. He told the prisoners they should wait until they were confined in Mexican prisons and then see if they could escape the executioners who would be awaiting them there. A month later when the exhausted, footsore captives approached Mexico City, Canales received an order for Cameron's execution, probably solicited by him from Santa Anna. Although Cameron had drawn a white bean the order was carried out. The remaining Texans were confined in various Mexican prisons, the largest number in the gloomy castle of Perote on the highway to Veracruz.[3]

3. *"She Cannot Long Stand"*

NEWS of the disaster came to President Houston in fragments. His hope was defeated that a successful raid would demonstrate to foreign powers that Texas had the same strike-and-run ability as Mexico. He had desired to point out to the United States as well as to England and France that Texans could take care of themselves and were disciplined and courageous. Somervell's "bloodless" seizure of Guerrero would have sufficed.

He was still hoping that the news would not be as bad as first reported when Somervell came in person to confirm it. Disgusted and bitter, Somervell announced his resignation from the army. Houston, believing that he had loyally done the best he could to get the men back from Guerrero in good order, rewarded him with an appointment as collector of customs for the Port of Calhoun.

The President perceived that his plain duty was to do what he could for the Mier prisoners. But a much larger question was involved. How could the country be saved from the consequences of such disgraceful episodes? Obviously, Texas must rid itself of the lawless adventurers. How? He believed that unless some fortunate turn of events occurred in the near future, Texans might be expected to achieve "aspects of sublimity"—Houston's ironic phrase for "catastrophe," a word the President abhorred in connection with his country. Somehow the anticipated disaster must be averted.

The sultan's red robe hung neglected on a hook whittled out of an oak crotch. In his linsey-woolsey pantaloons and Mackinaw shirt, Houston sat at his desk, trying to find answers to his problems. Disorder reigned in Texas. In the west, citizens had risen in outright insurrection against the Executive's authority.

Early in October, 1842, he had ordered Land Office Commissioner Thomas Ward to prepare the government archives for removal from Austin to Washington. In retaliation, a local grand jury, with an anti-Houston editor as foreman, had indicted the President for "moral treason." [1] As an insult to the Executive, a gang had taken Ward's horse and shaved its mane and tail. Congressman Cazneau had seized the records and held them for a time under guard.

The President had sent Captain Thomas Smith with twenty men to recover the records. They had almost finished loading the documents in wagons when "Ma" Eberly took a hand. Mrs. Evangelina Eberly had lost her boarding house in the flames when Mosely Baker burned San Felipe in 1836. She was going to see to it that her profitable Austin hostelry would not lose its clientele of congressmen and government officers. She gave the alarm by firing a six-pounder cannon that had been mounted on the government grounds after the Cherokee War. Her random shot hit the General Land Office Building, and a mob gathered to threaten the government agents.

"Ma Eberly's Rebellion" had been praised by the press as an example of courageous patriotism. It had also served as a subject for rollicking humor, brought ridicule upon the Executive, and weakened the authority of the government.

Houston concluded that a further struggle with West Texas over the archives would result in civil war. He would not risk this. He would stand on his published statement that, no matter what hardships or evil befell the country from the loss of the archives, the Executive would make no further attempt to prevent their destruction. The responsibility must fall upon the people who had supported the insurrectionists, not upon the President.

In the east, a condition approaching civil war had arisen in Shelby County. Escaped convicts, accused murderers, horse thieves, gamblers, forgers, counterfeiters, and land thieves had flocked across the boundary of the United States. Many of these desperadoes had settled north of the old Camino Real and were pursuing their customary way of life among the Republic's decent inhabitants. A Louisiana fugitive, Charles Jackson, blamed his defeat in a congressional election on land-fraud schemers and threatened an exposé of the Land Office. When his opponent, Joseph Goodbread, threatened to run him out of the country, Jackson killed him. During Jackson's trial, Judge John M. Hansford suddenly quit the bench and left town after issuing an order to the Harrison County sheriff:

> . . . Sir, Being unwilling to risk my Person in the Court House any longer where I see Myself Surrounded by Bravoes and Hired Assassins and no longer left free to Preside as an impartial Judge at the Special Term of the Court Called for the Trial of Charles W. Jackson, I order you to adjourn Court.[2]

Friends of Jackson and Goodbread were now organized in two gangs, the "Regulators" and the "Moderators." The declared purpose of each was to prevent crime, but they fought like bandits; ambushed, waylaid, robbed, and murdered individuals and burned homes. Many persons not involved with either gang were forced to take sides. If this kept up, every man in four counties would have to join one side or the other in self-defense.

This situation forced a humiliating truth upon the President. The Republic did not have a reliable force to put down this factional warfare. If the militia was called out, the "volunteers" would rush to join, to take sides, and agitate. Conceivably, they might precipitate a worse crisis than the gang war itself. For the time being, Houston could only keep an eye on the situation, hoping that the decent people of the region would bring it under control.[3]

Other disorders had to be taken into account. Lawless volunteers, who had been discharged but who had not returned to the United States or found employment, had organized into bands and called themselves Soldiers of the Republic. Claiming that they were authorized to "impress" supplies for the government, they had raided settlers, taking beeves, horses, weapons, household goods, and provisions.

The "volunteers" could bring tragedy to barefooted and bareheaded settlers who lived in crude log cabins and ate the same fare for breakfast, dinner, and supper. The impoverished settlers had to be satisfied with corncake, a little fried beef, and black coffee. At night they climbed up on their scaffoldings to sleep on ox hides under a minimum of coverings. What the "impressment" crews took from families of this kind could decide whether these families survived in the Promised Land.

On the economic front the shadows were equally dark. Adverse weather and clouds of insects had damaged the harvest and the cotton crop had failed. The newspapers recorded numerous foreclosures and sheriff sales; the property of prominent people was going up for auction. Town lots in Houston, worth two thousand dollars in boom days, were now being taken for non-payment of taxes and were bringing from ten cents to two dollars. Villages and town sites that had been laid out with resounding names—Rome, Pompeii, Geneva, Trinidad—had not come into existence or had been abandoned.

Congress had discarded what the President regarded as his sound-

434

est recommendations for stabilizing the currency. It had refused him the power to collect imposts, and the currency had collapsed. Virtually all transactions were now carried on by barter: cotton for sugar and coffee, bacon for boots, corn for calomel and whiskey, beef for brandy.

Then, too, world sentiment had turned against Texas because of its military misfortunes. Not since San Jacinto had this nation, which liked to call itself a "fighting Republic," come out on top in any sizable conflict with Mexicans. The Santa Fe fiasco and the Mier disaster, the pin-prick successes of Vasquez and Woll and the Dawson Massacre all suggested that Texas could not hold its own. Newspaper editors in the United States and England were interpreting events this way.

Annexation might be the only solution. The outlook for it was disheartening. The President had to decide whether to go on pressing for it or seek an alternative.

In March, 1843, President Houston received a most discouraging communication from the Texas minister in Washington, D. C. During a debate on a proposed commercial treaty with the Texas Republic, a number of United States senators had spoken most disrespectfully of the new nation. Their opinions, as summarized by Minister Van Zandt, were:

> ...Texas is rent and torn by her own internal discords; she is without a dollar in her treasury; her numbers are small; her laws are set at defiance by her citizens; her officers, both civil and military, cannot have their orders executed or obeyed; Mexico is now threatening to invade her with a large land and naval force; she cannot long stand under such circumstances; the chances are against her. She will either have to submit to Mexico, or come under some other power.[4]

Houston himself could not have given a more accurate description. But he deplored the senators' failure to note that a relatively few were responsible for a large proportion of the afflictions of the Texans' unhappy land. Above all, he regretted the harshness and lack of sympathy for a struggling people undergoing a long and painful ordeal.

Back in April, 1842, when he had thought it time to renew serious annexation efforts, the abolitionists—among them William Lloyd Garrison of the *Liberator*—had kicked the sand from under him. The New York *Journal of Commerce* had expressed the hope that Texas might be "equal to her crisis." In the *Liberator*, Garrison had said:

> It is thus that, in a single sentence, may be comprehended all conceivable profligacy of spirit and inhumanity of heart.... It is impossible for an honest man to wish success to Texas. All who sympathize with that pseudo-Republic hate liberty and would de-throne God." [5]

The anti-Texas agitation of the abolitionists had been so violent that the Southern supporters of annexation had drawn back. Both Whigs and abolitionists were seizing every opening to pour abuse upon Texas, denouncing it as a den of iniquity populated with the dregs of society. This, as President Houston saw it, was far from being the complete truth. The Yankees who poured their scorn upon Texas totally ignored the country's large numbers of hard-working settlers who labored for the security of their families. Always they overlooked the fact that the "dregs of society" in Texas had seeped across the boundary, coming from the bottom drawer of the self-righteous United States.

All through 1842, the newspaper editors of the United States had shown themselves to be indifferent to the acquisition of Texas. When they did mention annexation they were inclined to echo Garrison. One such echo had come from the Salem, Massachusetts, *Observer:* "We have territory enough and bad morals enough and slavery enough without adding thereto by such a union." [6]

Annexation was impossible while such opinions held sway in the United States. Was it possible to separate the question of annexation from the slavery issue? Perhaps it could be brought home to statesmen on the Potomac that they were living in a fool's paradise, ignoring some basic factors that had nothing to do with slavery. It was true that their big, undeveloped country had no pressing need for land, which Texas could offer in plenty. But the Colossus *did* need security on its southwestern frontier. Could its statesmen be awakened to an appreciation of where their true interests lay by making them realize that other nations were not averse to befriending Texas? There might be hazard in the gamble; it called for boldness and skill.

4. *The Architect of Annexation*

HOUSTON turned toward a closer understanding, conceivably an alliance, with England. But in his own mind he did not shut out the possibility of annexation. In fact, he could see how a move toward England might stimulate a mood entirely different from the cantankerous one that had so far prevailed in the United States. It had to be a two-handed game.

On January 24, 1843, he was fully persuaded that he could accomplish most for his country by taking a strong if somewhat devious hand in power politics. He wrote to his friend, Charles Elliot. Well aware that his immediate responsibility as Chief Executive was to do what he could in behalf of the Mier prisoners, he began:

> . . . I am constrained to solicit the kindness of you, should it not be out of the line of your official action that you would address her Majesty's Minister in Mexico and, bad as matters are, make this *representation*.
>
> It is true the men went [to Mier]. . . . This much is granted. But the Mexican officers, by proposing terms of capitulation to the men, relieved them from the responsibility which they had incurred; and the moment that the men surrendered in accordance with the proposals of capitulation, they became prisoners of war, and were entitled to all immunities as such. Upon this view of the subject, I base my hopes of their salvation, if it should be speedily presented through the agency of her Majesty's Minister to the Mexican Government.
>
> . . . This view of the subject seems to me the only feasible one which has presented itself to my mind.[1]

When Captain Elliot had visited Washington-on-the-Brazos, Houston had assured him of his intention to pursue a conciliatory policy toward Mexico. He wanted Elliot to know that this policy remained the same:

> . . . You are aware also that I have suffered no change to take place in my opinions as to what course Texas should pursue

relative to Mexico. Although I seemed to those who could not estimate accurately my acts, to have yielded my opinions or wishes, it never was the case. The madness of Texians enforced upon me (silence because I was *weary*, and I foresaw that sooner or later the evil must be done) acquiescence to what must insure disaster. That has come, and now the only plan that can be adopted is one which will avert future evils to this unhappy country.

This was all that he could find to say in behalf of the prisoners of Mier, but, without a line of transition, he played his first card in the game of power politics, making the move he had determined upon after prolonged meditation:

There is a subject now mooting in Texas, which, it seems to me, will appeal directly to Her Majesty's Government: I mean the subject of "annexation to the United States." Some of our journals are much in favor of the measure. The Eastern portion of Texas contains but few dissenting voices to the measure. I find, from the incertitude of our position, that nine-tenths of those who converse with me, are in favor of the measure upon the ground that *it will give us peace*. Upon this point of our national existence, I feel well satisfied that England has the power to rule.

He pointed out that annexation to the United States was now being advocated more than in any previous period. He had received appeals for cooperation looking toward this step. (This was true, but these appeals had come from Texas, not the United States.) He confidently predicted that "with President Tyler from the South, Clay from the West and Van Buren and Webster from the North" annexation soon would be an issue with both major political parties of the United States and with all Presidential aspirants. After describing the great commercial advantages that "the Yankees will not be blind to," he offered the first step in his shrewd plan:

...To defeat this policy [of the United States], it is only necessary for Lord Aberdeen to say to Santa Anna: "Sir, Mexico must recognize the independence of Texas." Santa Anna would be glad of such a pretext. He could then say to the Mexicans: "You see how I am situated; and I cannot go to war with the United States and France." This state of things would be desirable with him, in my opinion, as it would leave him free to establish his power and a dynasty. . . .

Here was a plain intimation that Texas would prefer independence to annexation if England could bring about peace.

"In all these matters," he concluded, "I may be mistaken, but I am honest in my convictions that Texas and England would both be beneficiaries by this course. Time will tell the tale."

Soon after Captain Elliot received the President's letter he had an important dinner guest in Galveston, Texas Secretary of the Treasury, William Daingerfield. Congenial, the two men lingered long over their wine after dinner. Captain Elliot declared his belief that the question of peace and the recognition of Texas by Mexico would be solved by President Houston within six months.

Daingerfield expressed astonishment at this optimism. He either inferred or learned from Elliot that Elliot's conviction was based on a recent letter from Houston. Elliot thought that, before annexation could be accomplished, Mexico would make peace under pressure from England, or perhaps from England and France jointly. Then Texas would have no reason to surrender its independence for the sake of annexation by the Yankees. He offered to bet Daingerfield that this would be the outcome.

Because of his position in the Texas government, Daingerfield thought such a wager would be improper and he declined. But he understood perfectly the shrewdness with which Houston had forged Elliot's convictions. He immediately wrote to the President, urging him to hit Her Majesty's diplomatic representative again with the same annexation stick. Then he wrote to Secretary of State Anson Jones summarizing his letter to the President. "I have written to the President to 'hit him agen' on the subject of *annexation.* . . ." [2]

Delighted with the result of his strategy, Houston believed that he had belabored Her Majesty's representative sufficiently for the time being. It seemed more appropriate to apply the stick to the rump of the stubborn northern neighbor. Encouraged, he made three moves simultaneously.

He instructed Texas Minister Van Zandt to drop substantial hints in Washington that Texas affairs were entering "an interesting phase." The English and French were definitiely anxious to secure peace and stabilize commercial relations with Texas and Mexico. These events would naturally be followed by a treaty of alliance between Texas and her European friends. Of course this would not contravene the Monroe Doctrine! It would merely represent a step toward the stability and future of Texas.

Houston was taking no chances that the government leaders on the Potomac would fail to realize that this was their great hour to accomplish annexation. After sending word by Van Zandt that was calculated to open their eyes, he wrote to American Chargé Judge Joseph Eve with the same objective. "Even the *oldest settlers*, even some of the original 'Three Hundred' are as anxious for [annexation] as any that I meet with," he told Eve, ... if it should become a political *lever* [in the United States] both of the political parties will seize hold of, or grasp at the handle! ..." [3]

Then Houston inspired Miller, his brainy private secretary, to write to American President John Tyler. On January 30, 1843, Miller wrote a long letter to President Tyler. In a tone of uneasy alarm, he described the nefarious activities of Her Majesty's able and experienced chargé, Captain Elliot. Was it not reasonable to suppose, he asked, that Captain Elliot had been sent to Texas to turn a trick for England? Elliot's object Miller suggested was obviously to counteract the interest and policy of the United States and to plant British power in a favorable soil. Of course, the people of Texas, including President Houston, were virtually unanimous in favor of annexation, but with England jealous of the growing commercial and sea power of the United States there was always a danger that British dictation over Mexico might lead to British dominance in Texas and control of trade in the Gulf of Mexico.

Houston read over Miller's letter. Would Yankee statesmen be too blind to see the point and fail to act on it? The urgency of Miller's message reminded Houston of the youthful eagerness with which Miller had once urged him to undertake the conquest of Mexico.

The time was favorable for the consummation of the work, Miller stated. He implored President Tyler to complete it before peace with Mexico was achieved. If Tyler failed with the Senate, the fault would not be his, and the loss of the country would be charged not to him but to that body.

It was cruel to pummel Tyler with the annexation stick while the other end of it was vigorously fanning the rump of the British Empire. Over a period of time, Tyler would become familiar with the ever recurring refrain: *act now before it is too late.* It would haunt him for months to come; he would receive it in letters from the Texas representative in London, from Texas agents in Washington, and by implication from his own representatives in Texas. In time, he would come to believe that he was the one true architect of annexation.

Miller closed his letter to President Tyler on a lofty note, pointing out that destiny had raised Tyler to his exalted position as the appropriate agent for this great work. Finally, he padded the stick with the same gracious appreciation that President Houston had expressed through others to the foreign ministers of England and France. He assured Tyler that General Houston entertained enthusiasm for the annexation measure and cordial feelings for the President. The General had heard of Tyler's friendly inquiries and statements concerning himself and reciprocated them.

5. *Two Fathers*

Seeds planted in President Tyler's mind had to have time to germinate. Time must be allowed for Elliot's report on President Houston's new attitude on annexation to cross the ocean. In March, 1843, while Houston was patiently waiting for his power play to yield results, a band of Lipan and Toncahua Indians came to the capitol bearing a letter from one of the President's red brothers, Chief Flacco. Flacco's expressions of grief about the murder of his son had been interpreted on paper by Indian Agent Benjamin Bryant, and the Chief had signed it with his mark.

... I am in bad health and fild with sorrow on account of the death of my son   I wish you would giv me all the information

you can   I sent you a musstang stalion . . . Sence the death of
my Sone I wish my name alltered & call Senior Yawney   I dislike to hear the name of Flacco. . . .[1]

Houston was hoping for the birth of a son in late spring and was
deeply touched by the sorrow of a father who could not bear to
hear his own name mentioned because it was also the name of his
lost son. He wrote to Bryant at once:

> . . . Of [young Flacco's murder] I know nothing, only it is
> said that Mexicans from the Rio Grande killed him. . . . When I
> get new particulars of his death, I will write you and you can
> inform his father of the facts. If the Lipans and Toncahuas will
> go out to take satisfaction for his death, tell them by no means
> to harm women and children. The warrior scorns to hurt a
> woman or a child, and only fights with men. I will never shake
> hands with a red brother who has stained his hands with the
> blood of women and children. He is a "squaw" and a coward
> himself.[2]

That night after an exhausting day in his office, the President
wrote Flacco a letter in the rhythmic pattern and picturesque im-
ages that came spontaneously when he addressed his red brothers.
In it, he mourned the death of the young chief.

My Brother:
> *My heart is sad!*
> *A cloud rests upon your nation.*
> *Grief has sounded in your camp;*
> *The voice of Flacco is silent.*
> *His words are not heard in council;*
> *The chief is no more.*
> *His life has fled to the great Spirit,*
> *His eyes are closed;*
> *His heart no longer leaps*
> *At the sight of the buffalo.*
> *The voices of your camp*
> *Are no longer heard to cry*
> *"Flacco has returned from the chase."*
> *Your chiefs look down upon the earth*
> *And groan in trouble.*
> *Your warriors weep.*
> *The loud voices of grief are heard*

442

From your women and children.
The song of birds is silent,
The ears of your people
Hear no pleasant sound,
Sorrow whispers in the winds,
The noise of the tempest passes
It is not heard.
Your hearts are heavy.
The name of Flacco brought
Joy to all hearts.
Joy was on every face,
Your people were happy.
Flacco is no longer seen in the fight,
His voice is no longer heard in battle,
The enemy no longer
Makes a path for his glory.
His valor is no longer
A guard for his people.
The might of your nation is broken.
Flacco was a friend to his white brothers.
They will not forget him;
They will remember the red warrior.
His father will not be forgotten.
We will be kind to the Lipans.
Grass will not grow
On the path between us.
Let your wise men give counsel of peace,
Let your young men walk in the white path.
The gray headed men of your nation
Will teach wisdom.

Thy brother,   Sam Houston [3]

One of Flacco's kinsmen carried the President's letter to Bryant with a request for him to take pains in translating it because the President believed it would console *Señor* Yawney. Along with his threnody, Houston sent gifts, four plugs of tobacco for *Señor* Yawney and eleven shawls for *Señora* Yawney.

The President thoughtfully read a letter from Texas Minister Van Zandt in Washington dated April 21, 1843. Acting on instructions, Van Zandt had approached Secretary of State Daniel Webster asking

443

for support—specifically for "interposition along with the French" —against Mexican raids. He reported Webster's testy reply:

> ... Sir; your affairs assume so many different *phases* that it is impossible one day to tell what will be the appearance on the next. If your Government would take the advice of its friends, to remain at home, unite among yourselves, confine your soldiers to your own territory, and to the defense of your own soil, suppress insubordination, prevent marauding parties upon the frontier and consolidate your energies, then Sir, we might be able to do something effective.[4]

What Webster had said about the many rapidly shifting "phases," panics, and crises could not be denied, but he had been unkind. His words were surly and hostile. He seemed entirely oblivious that the government on the Brazos, trying to do exactly what he recommended, faced insuperable obstacles in controlling those misguided and violent spirits who had left Webster's own country to use Texas soil as a springboard for profitable adventure.

Webster's sharpness called for a resourceful counter. To Her Majesty's minister, President Houston poured out his resentment and indignation against the United States without mentioning Webster. Anyhow, it was time to hit Elliot again with the annexation stick and with a number of other sticks that Houston had in his woodshed. He told Elliot that he thought the course being pursued by the United States was not difficult to understand. For Texas "not to be completely subservient" was "regarded by the United States as rebellious and ungrateful." American political parties had not yet decided what capital to make out of Texas. Meanwhile, they did not want England to bring about peace, for if that happened, it would naturally inspire in Texans "feelings of kindness" and a sense of obligation to England.

Burning with resentment, Houston now saw before him a single road. Webster and other short-sighted American statesmen blocked the road to annexation. The alternate road was independence, paved with hopes for peace enforced by England and for growth and an extended Texas empire sheltered by the friendliness and power of this same ally. Houston confided to Captain Elliot:

> ... All movements on the part of the U. States would seem to indicate that they have an eye to a rupture [with England] at

some period not remote. But I need not suggeset this to a gentleman of your observation. The genius as well as the excitability of that people, united to a bold and generous daring, impel them to war. Their love of Dominion, and the extension of their territorial limits, also, is equal to that of Rome in the last ages of the Commonwealth and the first of the Caesars.

The Continent of North America is regarded by the people of the U. States as their birth-right to be secured by policy, if they can, by force if they must. Heretofore Texas has been looked upon as an appendage to the U. States. They cannot realize that we now form two nations. Therefore, every act done in reference to us and by any power of which they are jealous, or for which they do not cherish kind national feelings, is regarded as an unauthorized interference and necessarily provokes their denunciation.

This is the case at present in relation to England. British influence and every ridiculous humbug which their crazed imaginations can start, are conjured up and marshalled in fearful array for the purpose of alarming Texas, exciting disorder, producing disrespect towards England, and compelling us to look to the U. States as our only hope of political salvation. They are willing to see Texas tantalized by every annoyance until, in a fit of dispair, she is compelled to identify herself with them, and by some act of good fortune become incorporated with them—though they cannot precisely point out the means.

Even this did not dissipate the steam of his indignation; it went on for pages. He applied the annexation stick without padding. Texas, he said, had once shown an unexampled unanimity for annexation. Humbly supplicating, Texans had been kept waiting "in the outer porch of [the American] capital" for many months. "Our solicitations were heard with apathy . . . with politic indifference. . . . [until] I directed our Minister to withdraw the proposition. . . . from a sense of national dignity."

No doubt, he added, the United States again was waiting for Texas to come "soliciting the boon." But times had changed. Once there had been "but one question to ask: Shall the Annexation . . . take place? As it is, there are two: First, Is Texas *willing* to be annexed? Second, in that case, shall it be annexed?" He continued:

... This renders the matter more complicated and produces feelings of excitement and irritibility that induce the leading

445

journals of certain sections of that Country to traduce and vilify the authorities of Texas in a very unbecoming manner.

Then followed a declaration of the stand to which, by slow degrees, the apathy and indifference of the United States had driven him.

It is not selfishness in me to say that I desire to see Texas occupy an independent position among the Nations of the earth, to which she is justly entitled by her enterprise, daring, sufferings and privations. . . . if her independence be steadily [speedily?] recognized in Mexico, heaven will direct and carry out her destiny to a glorious consummation. Every day that it is delayed affords to demagogues a theatre for mischief, and when repose should refresh her, factious political incendiaries are marching about with their torches of discord. I am weary of this state of things. All that Texas requires to make her healthy and vigorous is a respite from execution.[5]

After thoroughly digesting every word, Captain Elliot forwarded the letter as enclosure No. 1 in a secret dispatch to Undersecretary Addington in London. Eventually it would come to the attention of Her Majesty's Secrectary for Foreign Affairs, the Right Honorable Lord Aberdeen.

President Houston asked a favor of Colonel William Bryan, Texas consul at New Orleans. Would Bryan forward a substantial shipment of sundries and house furnishings? The President felt happy to be able to ask this favor of an old friend because he knew that Bryan would take a personal interest and see that the shopping was done "as economically as possible." The list included "two sett" guitar strings for Mrs. Houston, a quantity of household provisions, fine cambric linen, large silk pocket handkerchiefs, silk and cotton socks, and a handsome pocket knife for whittling. The most expensive article requested was a "four-seated barouche with tongue, double harness, whip and all complete" to be sent to Galveston and forwarded to the capital from there.

The President specified quantities of "fine handsome Callico, and coarse ditto and furniture calico and Dimity." For upholstery and draperies, Bryan should take care that none "exhibit Turkey Gobblers, Peacocks, Bears, Elephants, wild Boars or Stud Horses!!! Vines, Flowers or any figure of taste you can select."

446

Checking over the list the President lingered thoughtfully over one item: "4 Bolts of linen Diaper." When he wanted people to know something, he told them; when he did not want them to know he was as close-mouthed as he was about his diplomacy. He added two underscored words to the item so that it read: "4 Bolts of linen Diaper *for Towels*." [6]

Evidently the device failed. According to legend somebody in New Orleans wrote to Minister Van Zandt in Washington, D. C. and somebody else wrote to Ashbel Smith in London. Versailles and Whitehall knew that the President's wife was expecting almost as soon as the ladies in her own home town knew. But only ladies at the capital knew that the event was expected in June, or possibly May.

Houston wanted Texas to be a good place for his "posterity" to grow up in, but agitation for an invasion of Mexico continued for months in the wake of the Mier expedition. After reading an inflammatory pro-war editorial in the *Telegraph*, he reached for his pen and wrote to George Hockley on May 13, 1843. The relationship between the two men had greatly improved since Hockley's resignation the previous September. The letter reflected the President's distress over consequences of the Mier expedition. It clarified his military views which he hoped would contribute further to improved understanding between himself and his old friend:

> I see by the "Santa Anna Telegraph," [the Houston *Telegraph and Texas Register*] that its editor [Dr. Francis Moore] ... is not satisfied with the number of our prisoners in Mexico. He thinks there ought to be more in the power of Santa Anna. Nothing less than the destruction of Texas will satisfy the wretch. . . .
>
> To hurry men from one act of indiscretion to another seems to be the sole object of the seditious monsters who would ruin a country which they had never assisted in emancipating.

Texas, he added, could defend itself, but it had only the means to exist. Very few individuals were "in a state better than that of pinching necessity!" The most lamentable aspect of the situation was that those who wanted invasion had an eye on plunder. "Success can never attend armies that war for plunder," he assured Hockley. "Such principles would dissolve the best army in the world and

447

disgrace the noblest cause." He drew a picture of what must be anticipated even by a man of ability who dared to lead an army beyond the Rio Grande.

> ... if, by prudence he were to gain a victory, it would cause the ruin of the army. Many would insist that each had won the victory, and they must have a new election for a "commander-in-chief." Each pretender would have his partizans. All could not be first, and those who had lost their favorite would leave the main body, or break off with their favorite *leader*. The army would be dissolved, and the men would roam for plunder, with their arms neglected and ammunition lost or injured, and so be surprised by the enemy and added to the sad catalogue of those now confined in loathsome prisons in Mexico. Heaven may save our country from such evils; but I assure you, my dear Hockley, they do seem to be pending over us as a nation.[7]

In another letter to Hockley, he summed up everything with a typically Houstonian apothegm—When one's hand was in the lion's mouth it was unwise to hit the lion on the nose.

A squalling infant, Sam Houston, Jr., was added to the President's household on May 25, 1843. He promptly began making conventional use of the "4 Bolts of linen Diaper *for Towels*" shipped by Colonel Bryan.

For once the President was living on such fat as the land could provide, with Mrs. Lea in the role of provider. Happily, all her funds were not tied up in depreciated Texas real estate or notes. With United States money she bought a milk cow. Margaret's health was not good, and Mrs. Lea planned to have her grandchild weaned as soon as possible.

A stage now made the thirty-hour trip between the capital and Houston City three times a week, and Mrs. Lea could bring in provisions without help from her son-in-law. When Houston expressed his embarrassment over her replenishing the family larder, Mrs. Lea answered that it was all right for the President of the Republic to starve if patriotic motives compelled it, but her grandchild was not old enough to undergo the deprivations of Valley Forge. For the good of his health, she suggested that the President "eat now and pay later," whenever the bankrupt Republic caught up with the arrears of his salary.

6. *"Did I Turn Traitor Then?"*

JAMES ROBINSON was a swarthy man, with snapping dark eyes and a mustache that needed wax. He was addicted to the unpleasant habit of slashing his boot with whatever he had in his hand, a whip or switch. As a member of the pre-San Jacinto General Council he had helped to frustrate Houston's attempt to systematically defend Texas, had been a leading advocate of the raid on Matamoros, and had been captured in Woll's raid on San Antonio.

Robinson had been confined miserably in the Castle of Perote along with the prisoners of the Santa Fe and the Mier expeditions. Seeking any means of release, he wrote an ingeniously false letter to dictator Santa Anna assuring him that his fellow Texans were eager for reunion with the mother country and for the restoration of Santa Anna's liberal and orderly regime. Santa Anna fell for this bait and sent the hungry, flea-bitten Robinson to Texas with peace proposals.

Santa Anna's letter was addressed to "whom-it-may-concern," and was delivered by Robinson to President Houston. The dictator affably promised that if Texas acknowledged the absolute sovereignty of Mexico, he would free all prisoners and grant amnesty for the past acts of the Texas government.

At first President Houston was indignant and astonished, then he was amused and gratified. He believed that Santa Anna was catching at straws, and he ridiculed the dictator's peace proposal as "a curiosity to file away for after times." There was a way to use the incident to the advantage of Texas. He wrote a letter and had Robinson copy it in his own hand over his own signature. Robinson informed Santa Anna that the peace proposals had "caused less stir than I had anticipated." Prompted by Houston, Robinson added a subtle contribution to Santa Anna's fears:

> ...I found the people much engaged in the cultivation of their farms, except those who are very anxious for an invasion of Mexico, and many who are in favor of an invasion are improving their farms and planting their crops so as to be ready

449

for any action the government of this country may think it necessary ... to take. ... I find that your Excellency and myself were mistaken when we suspected that Texas was torn to pieces by factions. It is not so. ... There are some factious men in Texas, and they have some papers at their command. ... The whole number of men, of any prominence of character, engaged in this opposition, would not exceed some thirty to thirty-five in the Republic.

Then Robinson courteously asked leave to present some suggestions for His Excellency's consideration. If Santa Anna would release all Texas prisoners and declare an armistice for some months, it would have a good effect on the people of Texas. After all, Texans could not consider his proposals free of "passion and excitement" when many of them had a friend or an acquaintance imprisoned in Mexico.

He observed that many individuals in Texas "were exciting the people in favor of war beyond the Rio Grande." The President had authority to "accept the services of forty thousand volunteers which could be landed on the borders of the Rio Grande." He added that "General Rusk is raising a large expedition to cross the Rio Grande," although this undertaking might be delayed.

"I would think," Robinson went on, "from what I have heard since my return that Houston would prefer peace, if it could be on terms perfectly honorable to Texas. ... but ... it is possible that he may unite all the influence he may have with those in favor of prosecuting the invasion of Mexico. ... I think she [Texas] would be easily able to raise from her own citizens an army of ten thousand men, besides volunteer immigrants. ... I will not be so presumptuous as to advise your Excellency about anything; but ... I feel bound to inform you of such facts as result from my observation." [1]

The Robinson-Houston letter was sent to Mexico City by courier, and Robinson cautiously remained well out of Santa Anna's reach. Houston immediately supplemented the letter with one to Captain Elliot. He suggested that now would be a good time for Her Majesty's Minister in Mexico City to offer his services as mediator for making an armistice. The minister, Richard Pakenham, presented this suggestion to Santa Anna.

Texas, of course, was perilously weak and unready for any kind of military venture, but the Houston-Robinson letter inspired Santa Anna with uneasy visions of 40,000 volunteers from beyond the Sabine and 10,000 Texans on the rampage in Mexico. Houston's verbal thrusts in the Robinson letter had the same effect as his prowess in battle. Santa Anna crumbled and agreed to appoint peace commissioners to meet with Texans south of the Rio Grande. At last, after seven uneasy years the Lone Star Republic could hope for recognition of her independence by the "mother country."

On June 15, 1843, President Houston acknowledged Attaché Elliot's congratulations on two events, the birth of Sam, Jr., and Santa Anna's consent to an armistice. The President, cheerful enough to don the sultan's red robe again, answered promptly that the value of the armistice was "greatly enhanced" by his having a son. "A son of mine without a country would cut but a shabby figure and indeed, his father would have toiled in vain."

"Mrs. H. Unites with me in salutations to your lady and yourself," he added. "Mrs. H. and the boy are doing well. He is stout, and I hope will be useful to his kind. May he be anything but a loafer, an agitator, or—in other words—a demagogue." He closed his letter with expressions of ironical regret for the adventurers who had hoped to become heroes by invading Mexico: "Poor fellows! they have great cause to hate 'John Bull.' He has by his interference blighted all their hopes of immortal fame, and now they will have to *leave, loaf, steal, starve* or make a living by honest means!" [2]

Minister Pakenham did no more in behalf of Texas than act as go-between in arranging armistice discussions, but President Houston publicly credited England with "noble assistance" and remained silent about his own contribution. His twofold purpose was to create a more favorable attitude in Texas toward England and to remind the United States that Texas had the support of equally powerful and far more helpful nations.

The new United States Chargé d'Affaires, General William Sumter Murphy, who had succeeded Judge Eve in 1843, reported to Washington all the details he had learned of the thickening romance between England and Texas with Texas-Mexican peace a probable result. It had the effect of the proverbial red rag flaunted before the eyes of a bull. Specifically, it made President Tyler, now a man without a party and in need of a political issue, think harder than ever that annexation might be the basis for restoring his failing prestige.

To the people of Texas—the hard-working settlers, the conservative merchants, all those citizens not blindly zealous for a campaign of plunder south of the Great River—the promise of a formal suspension of hostilities brought joy. On September 7, 1843, the Texas correspondent of the New Orleans *Picayune* reported that the masses were applauding Sam the First to the skies. But the correspondent did not join in the rejoicing. Gloomily he predicted that to bring priest-ridden Mexico to a right sense of things and obtain peace, it would be necessary to batter down some of her towns.

Ashbel Smith wrote to Houston from London that the armistice had helped the cause of Texas there. In Texas the anger of the partisans of aggression rose gradually at first, then swept on like a tidal wave. The President's political enemies began a well-organized campaign of detraction. They accused him of using the assistance of a "monarchical nurse" to bring about an armistice. On the other hand, they described the truce, still to be worked out by a treaty, as Houston's first step to submit Texas to Mexican sovereignty; according to them, he had been bribed by Santa Anna to take this step. Simultaneously, they charged that Houston had sold out to England and had received a bribe to make Texas a British colony.

Then the editors of the New Orleans *Picayune* heard that English statesmen had demanded the abolition of slavery in Texas as the price of British assistance; the *Picayune* staff were convinced that Houston had committed Texas to pay this price. Since the end of slavery in Texas would affect adversely the slave interests of the entire South, the *Picayune* launched a campaign to impeach the Texas President. Its writers announced that they had always thought Sam Houston honest, that out of "charity" they still clung to this hope, but that his actions "indicated anything but purity of purpose. If honest, he is demented and the people over whom he presides should no longer suffer themselves to be disgraced by the mad acts of an imbecile or a lunatic." The *Picayune* would not recommend violent measures but an "inspired people" such as the Texans could certainly "devise some constitutional means to rid themselves of an incubus so destructive of their interests."

The *Picayune* offered Texas a specific program for getting rid of the President, recommending General Burleson, Vice-President of Texas, as "certainly an honest man." Let Burleson call Congress together even if he did not have "full authority so to do." In an emergency so pressing "he might assume a point . . . and have Houston impeached at once, either as a traitor or an imbecile. One or the other of these charges can certainly be sustained." Such a proceeding undoubtedly would have beneficial results. "Should the Vice President pursue this course," according to the *Picayune*, "he would be justified by nine-tenths, aye, a greater proportion of the people, and would rid Texas of the only impediment which now stands in the way of a successful prosecution of the war against Mexico, and the attainment, at no distant period, of a full and unconditional independence." [3]

West Texas, still smarting because of the removal of the capital and the President's attempt to get possession of the archives, acted upon the *Picayune's* advice. With violent speeches and editorials, they drummed for a convention to meet on July 17, 1843, at La Grange and to demand the condemnation and impeachment of the President. Six delegates from six counties turned up for the La Grange convention. Though small, it was a red-hot affair; the members denounced the President for all kinds of far-fetched lapses and villainies, particularly for taking bribes from Mexico and England. The proceedings lacked prestige because of the small attendance, but their influence spread. The Houston-haters organized a spate of public meetings that echoed all the charges and denounced him violently while the pro-war editors kept up their fire.

Political conditions in Texas were bad enough, but physical conditions were even worse and exacerbated the inhabitants' already inflamed tempers. Dusty but passable roads and trails usually came as the benefit of a dry season and afforded great relief from the mud of spring and fall. But in the summer of 1843, prolonged rains made the roads quagmires and a curse for all who had to travel, producing great numbers of broken wagons and fabulous amounts of profanity. Travelers reported the necessity of swimming their horses across rivers that were usually fordable in summer.

Visitors in Texas filled their letters with references to omnipresent fleas. One wrote from Galveston: "You sometimes *think* you are troubled with fleas but you have no cause for compaint . . . they prevail universal throughout this City—no place is exempt from their ravages." [4]

In the wet season, mosquitoes were bred far in excess of the usually adequate supply. Travelers reported that in 1843, mosquitoes kept them in a blistered state. It would be more than fifty years before the mosquito would be identified as the source of malaria. The "fevers," with their violent chills were expected every spring and summer, and wet years brought more sickness than others. Along the Brazos, Guadalupe, Colorado, and Trinity Rivers people were hard hit. Thousands were attacked by a disease known as bilious fever. Dysentery, called bloody flux or the summer complaint, was rampant and especially virulent.

Added to these evils were those caused by an inadequate diet. The standard Texas diet consisted of corn bread, frequently described as "cooked sawdust," beer, beans, potatoes, and whiskey. Vegetables and milk were almost totally lacking. Scurvy and rickets were common. Editor Moore, in the July 1, 1840 issue of *The Houston Telegraph* published a warning about the fare in hotels.

> The ill-cooked, unwholesome food which is so often furnished at our taverns is a fruitful source of disease. The heavy sodden doughballs, which in the shape of "hot rolls" are served so plentifully at the hotels, are of themselves sufficient to create the worst of remittent fever, and should be shunned by the hungry traveler as he would shun a charge of grapeshot; indeed, we believe the grapeshot of the Mexicans have committed less havoc among our citizens than these vile doughballs.[5]

Moore was a leader of what might be called the intelligentsia. He was rated as a statesman by some, although not by President Houston. Trained as a geologist and medical man, Dr. Moore had only one arm. For malaria he recommended calomel, castor oil, salts, senna, and mustard seed poultices that would make a blister on the stomach. A diet of mush, molasses, and rice would also help, he said.

Houston wrote a letter of heartfelt congratulations to Dr. Irion who was now the father of a son, Samuel Houston Irion. Houston concluded by observing: "To be President of Texas is losing business to a man of sensibility or sense." [6]

Another note of discouragement appeared in his letter to E. L. R.

Wheelock, a West Pointer who was now a Texas business man. "What can one man do when so many combine to thwart his efforts, disregard the laws, and bring ruin upon our citizens? ... If the people do not now, they will ere long understand my policy and do me justice.... I [cannot be] governed by the jargon and discord of public clamor. May God save us from the poison and blight of faction...." [7]

Answering a letter from a committee of Montgomery citizens who proffered an invitation to a barbecue so that they might express their confidence in him, he accepted and said that in the recent past "the idle, the lazy, the wild visionaries or wilder speculators without capital, and those who are insubordinate to the laws have clamorously urged a war of invasion without means, a plan as destructive to individual happiness as it must have proved to national honor and prosperity. Peace will disappoint those mad projects." [8]

At last he accepted an invitation to address a meeting in his home territory. The Huntsville Presbyterian Church was jammed that afternoon.

He told the audience that his political enemies would have been willing to torture him if they had had him in their power. He said he had been attacked because he had not explained all confidential diplomatic negotiations with foreign countries. But how could he do that without sacrificing the interests of Texas? He defended England and France as active and interested friends and said the United States had been dilatory. Then he made an earnest plea for trust and confidence on the ground of his past service to the state:

Every arrow has been shot that ... could wound, and [the arrows were] poisoned by rancor and malice. Have I deserved this, my countrymen? ... I am a traitor to my country; "*bribed by Santa Anna's gold.*" I am denounced as a villain, a drunkard, a blackguard and a wretch.... I cannot but view them [these charges of treason and other vices] with astonishment. I have been before the citizens of Texas for ten years. I was here four years before they [his accusers] became citizens, and aided them in becoming citizens.... In those dark days, when all were reduced to despair; when many were fugitives, fleeing from their homes, did I turn traitor then? ... Would I, think you, sell my country now for what would make me a prince for the rest of my days? Gray hairs have marked this head, bronzed when your

455

revolution began. These hairs have told that fifty summers have passed over my head.... When the history of your country shall be written, can you take a page or chapter identified with its advancement to freedom and prosperity, and wipe out the name of *Houston* and leave no blank there? ... What motive could incite *me* to betray my country? What! acknowledge Santa Anna's supremacy! I well remember Santa Anna's visit to Texas. On that occasion I sent him home. Yes, I freed the captive bird from his cage and sent him home; and the act of liberation told him this was the natural burial ground of tyrants and butchers of mankind.[9]

He told another audience in the old capitol at Houston that before he "designed an act, or raised an arm" his one consideration was—"will this benefit my country?" If it would, he did it. He did not do it "to be honored," but in the hope that if the country prospered what little he had would become valuable. Then, if he had a plentiful posterity, no matter how humble and obscure, they would at least be able to say "my father served the state." [10]

He closed on that note. Men and women cheered and surged around him, openly weeping. Perhaps these citizens represented a majority of the nation, those who believed that in spite of the charges against him, their President had not sold them out.

7. *Closer to England*

ASHBEL Smith knew that his Chief's intention was to promote annexation by playing England against the United States. From London, he helped this game along by informing President Tyler that the British were eager for abolition of slavery in Texas and would do what they could to obtain a foothold there. This added significance to the letter Houston's secretary had written to the American President and stimulated Tyler's growing conviction that annexation was the issue he needed to improve his own political prospects. Tyler had avoided the ticklish question, but now he acted. It was obvious that Secretary of State Daniel Webster, facing difficulties with his Massachusetts following, could not carry his state for Tyler in the coming election even if Tyler could be nominated. Webster willingly resigned, and his successor, Abel Upshur, instituted a change in policy that was favorable to Texas.

From Washington, D. C., Van Zandt informed President Houston that Upshur was zealous for annexation and spoke of the subject at every interview. Houston instructed Van Zandt to make it appear that the President of Texas considered it inadvisable to pursue the subject of annexation since he preferred to occupy himself exclusively in settling affairs with Mexico.

In mid-October of 1843, Upshur again took up the matter with Van Zandt. He said that unless the views of the administration underwent an unexpected change, he would be prepared to make a proposition whenever Van Zandt had proper powers to meet it. He assured Van Zandt that President Tyler was ready to present the matter in the strongest manner to Congress. Van Zandt forwarded this information to Texas on October 16, and stated: "I am of opinion, that at no time since the question was first presented to this government, have there been so many circumstances combining to secure the favorable action of the Senate of the United States." [1]

This was welcome news to Houston, but he still was skeptical. For seven long years Northern statesmen had been changing their views. Privately he reminded friends that he could not bring about annexation until the willingness for it existed in the United States. The one way that he could see to accomplish it was to inflame the jealousy and ambition of the United States.

With his provocative policy just beginning to show results, was it time to edge closer to the United States? After analyzing the ambiguities in which Upshur wrapped his invitations to talks on annexation, Houston decided that his best response would be to say nothing. It was not long before Van Zandt told him that Upshur did not take kindly to being ignored. Peremptorily the secretary of state proposed that annexation discussions begin and sharply indicated that he expected a definite answer.

Houston directed Van Zandt through Secretary of State Jones to inform Upshur that before Texans would participate in annexation discussions, they must have assurance that the United States Senate would ratify a treaty. "The President thinks," he wrote, . . . "it would not be politic to abandon the expectations which now exist of a

457

speedy settlement of our difficulties with Mexico, through the good offices of other powers, for the very uncertain prospect of annexation to the United States ... [If the proposed treaty failed] Texas would be placed in a much worse situation than at present. ...." In that case, he pointed out, Texas could not hope for assistance from England or France and in view of "our consequent supposed dependence upon the United States might again return the apathy and indifference towards us which has always untill now characterized that Government." [2]

Upshur's answer came as promptly as the slow means of communication permitted. He declared that interference by foreign powers in the affairs of the country on the southwestern border of the United States would mean war. President Houston, believing that the U. S. Senate was not prepared to accept an annexation treaty, calmly signed a proclamation releasing all Mexican prisoners in accord with a similar undertaking by Mexico.

Texans continued to be excited about the President's apparently pro-British leanings. Houston decided that it was advisable to take the Texas Senate partially into his confidence. On January 20, 1844, he made a brief appearance before an executive session of the Senate and revealed the essence of his foreign policy. He told the senators that if, at this time, "... any effort were made on the part of this government to effect ... annexation, which is so desirable, and it should fail in meeting responsive and corresponding action on the part of the United States, it might have a seriously prejudicial influence upon the course which England and France might otherwise be disposed to take in our favor. And a failure on our part after a decided expression could not but be mortifying to us, and ... diminish our claims to the confidence of other nations." He assured them that the status of annexation was the best that was possible at the time. "If we evince too much anxiety it will be regarded as importunity, and the voice of supplication seldom commands ... great respect." [3]

At Nashville, Andrew Jackson heard that his one-time comrade in arms had pro-British leanings. He wrote to assure Houston that he remained his friend and that he would never believe that Houston could be seduced by England. Furthermore, Jackson was refuting every slander he heard in connection with Houston's alleged intrigue with the British.

But Jackson received positive assurance from Washington, D. C., that Sam Houston was upsetting officialdom by his partiality for the British. Only five days elapsed before his trembling hand traced another and more urgent epistle to Houston:

> ... if you will achieve this annexation your name & fame will be enrolled amongst the greatest chieftains of the age.... Now is the time to ... have the treaty of annexation laid before the United States Senate where I am sure it will be ratified. Let the threats of Great Britain & Mexico then be hurled at us,—if war the[y] wish our fleet and army will freely fight them.... I am scarcely able to write.... the Theme only inspires me with strength ... Let me hear from you if only three lines.[4]

A letter to Jackson was nothing less than a state document. Its contents would become known to important persons as a matter of course. For the sake of his ambivalent policy, Houston could not write a letter that might cause Jackson to cease pleading for annexation by pouring out voluminous communications to newspapers and officials. For the time being, Houston had to face both ways even before his old friend; he could not run the risk of allaying Jackson's anxiety.

He reminded Jackson that the behavior of the United States toward Texas had been "peculiar and difficult," and that it justified him in adopting any course that would guarantee security to his country. But he had made no commitment that would prevent him from taking the most desirable course for the nation's future welfare. "So far as I am concerned," he added, "... I am determined upon immediate annexation to the United States."

He no sooner made this concession than he yanked it back. He did not believe that the "measure would be as advantageous to Texas ... as it is indispensably necessary to the United States. Texas, with peace, could exist without the United States, but the United States can not, without great hazard to the security of their institutions, exist without Texas.... With lower tariff than the United States Texas would invite the commerce of all nations to her ports ... and drive the manufactures of the United States from her markets."

459

He drew a persuasive picture of the nation Texas would be after fifty years of peace. Then in conclusion, he undertook to inspire the Old Chief with new incentives to continue that stream of pro-annexation letters he had been sending to editors and statesmen:

> Now, my venerated friend, you will perceive that Texas is presented to the United States, as a bride adorned for her espousal. But if. . . . she should be rejected, her mortification would be indescribable . . . this is the third time she has consented. Were she now to be spurned, it would forever terminate expectation on her part, and it would then not only be left for the United States to expect that she would seek some other friend, but all Christendom would justify her in a course dictated by necessity and sanctioned by wisdom. . . . That you may live to see your hopes in relation to it crowned with complete success, I sincerely desire. In the event that it speedily takes place, I hope it will afford me an opportunity of visiting you again at the Hermitage with my family. It is our ardent desire to see the day when you can lay your hand on our little boy's head, and bestow upon him your benediction. . . .[5]

Houston realized that the sick Jackson might be upset and bitterly disappointed if he failed to comprehend his friend's strategy. Out of love and reverence for the Old Chief he sent the letter by personal messenger, the reliable Washington Miller. Miller knew all the motives and feelings that underlay this document, and he was authorized to disclose them if it seemed necessary.

United States Chargé Murphy received new dispatches from his government and showed them to Houston. The President was encouraged to believe that, after all, an annexation treaty might pass the United States Senate, but caution was necessary. If annexation talks became serious, Mexico would break off peace negotiations and even might try to launch a formidable effort to reconquer Texas. This possibility was in Houston's mind when he instructed Van Zandt to request that a United States naval squadron be stationed in the Gulf and a military force posted on the Texas border while the annexation treaty was under discussion.

He asked Murphy, who was in Galveston, to press this same request and to come to Washington-on-the-Brazos for an exchange of thought on Texas-American relations. At about the same time he appointed J. Pinckney Henderson "special minister" to assist Van Zandt at Washington, D. C. in drawing up a treaty of annexation. He asked Henderson to come to the Texas capital at once for instructions: "You will then be on your way to Washington City. . . . Matters are quite ripe. . . . The lions are all stirred up, and the menagerie is quite full. . . . Matters appear about right, if they will only advance. You will be somewhat amused when you come to see all. . . ." [6]

Henderson and Murphy happened to travel together from Houston to Washington-on-the-Brazos. Murphy showed Henderson instructions that he had received from Washington, D. C. These made it plain that President Tyler had definitely promised to send an adequate fleet to the Gulf and troops to the border. Delighted, when Henderson reached the capital, he wrote to Thomas Rusk: "All things really prove the *very great* desire of the U. S. to annex us. You would be amused to see their jealousy of England. Houston has played it off well & that is the secret of our success if we do succeed." [7]

Judge Andrew Hutchinson, a Texan back from a trip to the United States, wrote to Washington Miller that Houston's action since July of 1842 had seemed so mysterious that Hutchinson doubted the President's sanity. But now the tangled threads unraveled. Jealousy of England had spread from the St. Lawrence to the Gulf and if, in consequence, Texas should become part of the Union, President Houston need not regret the suspicions and accusations that had been hurled at him.

A definite pledge to protect Texas while annexation talks were pending came eventually from Upshur's successor, Secretary of State John C. Calhoun. Calhoun wrote to Van Zandt and Henderson on April 11, 1844:

> . . . I am directed by the President to say, that the Secretary of Navy has been instructed to order a strong naval force to concentrate in the Gulf of Mexico to *meet any emergency;* and that similar orders have been issued by the Secretary of War to move the disposable military forces on our southwestern frontier for the same purpose. . . . I am further directed by the President to say, that during the pendency of the treaty of annexation, he would deem it his duty to use all the means within his power by the Constitution to protect Texas from all foreign invasion. . . .[8]

Murphy brought President Tyler's proposed treaty of annexation to the Texas capital for signing. Calhoun's assurances of military protection accompanied it. Houston read the letter and the treaty in Murphy's presence. Murphy reported with elation the President's warm approbation of the generous policy that now seemed to guide the councils of the northern neighbor.

President Houston and his secretary of state signed the treaty, which then had to be ratified by the United States Senate. In the Senate, Tyler's treaty encountered heavy going. Twelve congressmen joined John Quincy Adams in a blunt threat of secession if annexation went through. "No act of Congress, or treaty of annexation," the signers of the threat declared, "could impose the least obligation upon the several states of this Union, to submit to such an unwarrantable act, or to receive into their family and fraternity such misbegotten and illegitimate progeny." If Tyler's "nefarious project" succeeded "it would be identical with dissolution." [9]

In May, 1844, Houston went to his namesake city to be able to get news from the United States as much as thirty hours sooner than he could get it on the Brazos. Straight from his heart, he wrote to Murphy in Galveston. He hoped his message would be made known to the government and legislators on the Potomac before unfavorable action was taken on the treaty. If annexation failed this time, he told Murphy, it would not work to the detriment of Texas, but the United States would surely be "embarrassed." "All our ports will soon become great commercial marts and places; now scarcely noted upon our maps, they will be built up and grow into splendid cities." A European influence would spread in Texas. "The present moment is the only one that the United States will ever enjoy to annex Texas."

He expressed dissatisfaction with the pending treaty because Texas "surrendered everything and would get nothing except protection."
... Yet, "I am intensely solicitous to see the matter consummated and my country at rest." If the treaty was defeated, he said, "You may depend upon one thing—the Glory of the United States has already culminated. A rival power will soon be built up, and the Pacific as well as the Atlantic will become component parts of Texas, in thirty years from this date."

This statement foreshadowed what he regarded as reasonable realities. For the benefit of the politicians on the Potomac, he drew a verbal map of an Anglo-Hispanic empire embracing all Texas; the friendly northern provinces of Mexico, Chihuahua, and Sonora that had asked to be annexed to Texas; Upper and Lower California, and the Pacific Northwest. Through Murphy, he assured the American statesmen that this empire he visualized would make a clean sweep of "seceded" Southern states all the way from the Atlantic: Florida, the Carolinas, Virginia, Tennessee, Arkansas, and others.

> The Oregon region in Geographical affinity will attach to Texas. By this coalition or Union, the barrier of the Rocky Mountains will be dispensed with, or obviated.... England and France ... would not be so tenacious on the subject of Oregon as if the U States were to be the sole possessor of it.... all the powers, which either envy or fear the U. States, would use reasonable exertions to build us up, as the only rival power which can ever exist on this continent, to that of the U States....

It was a reasonable as well as a frightening hypothesis. Only annexation could prevent the coming of this rival and presumably hostile power. If the gentlemen on the Potomac would look at the map of North America they would see that this was no bugbear; only population would be needed. "You may laugh at these suggestions but ... these matters, will be of most grave and solemn national import. I do not care to be identified with them. They are the results of destiny over which I have no control."

In case Murphy should fail to deliver this combined threat and prophecy to his government with sufficient speed, Houston sent a copy to Henderson and Van Zandt. In a covering letter, he wrote, "The statesmen of that country appear to be united in opinion adverse to our admission.... We must therefore regard ourselves as a nation to *remain forever separate*." [10]

Once again all of Houston's skill in power politics failed to overcome opposition on the Potomac. John Quincy Adams and other abolitionists prevailed. On June 8, 1844, the treaty was rejected by the Senate, 35 to 16. Pennsylvania was the only Northern state whose two senators supported it. The only New Englander to vote for it was Woodbury of New Hampshire. All other votes in favor of ratification were from Southern states. Adams expressed the belief that the vote was a deliverance from an awful conspiracy by the special interposition of Almighty God.

Texans were dumfounded and bitter. But the editors of the Houston *Morning Star* moved back in line to support the President. They said editorially that the rejection of the treaty by the United States Senate had produced "only mortification and disgrace" and urged Houston to cultivate England and France as he was already doing.

Houston announced publicly that Texans must now consider themselves free from "all involvements and pledges." He instructed Smith in London to bring the matter at once to the consideration of the British and French Cabinets. Smith was to "ascertain what offers (if any) they are disposed to make, based upon an assurance from Texas that she will maintain her National unity...." If England or France, singly or jointly, showed a disposition to enter into negotiations on this subject, "... it is the wish of the Government to be informed of it through you as early as possible and that their agents here should be instructed to enter at once upon those negotiations with full powers to conclude the same." [11]

8. *Triumphant Old Fox*

ON June 24, 1844, George Gordon, Earl of Aberdeen, sat at his huge carved desk in the British Foreign Office. It was the same room and the same desk where Lord North had signed the papers that had conceded independence to the American colonies. Reports from Captain Elliot about the extraordinary character who presided over the Texas Republic were among the papers before him. In a general way they were reassuring. Aberdeen noted Elliot's comment that Houston's intellectual processes meandered like Texas rivers but always flowed onward till they reached the sea.

Houston's language, for all its humor and eloquence, was appropriate to the crude country that he governed. A man of great self-confidence, perhaps an egotist, he sometimes expressed himself violently for calculated effect. He was genial to the commonest of his fellow citizens. On occasion he did not hesitate to allude to himself

Sam Houston in His Early Thirties

Courtesy
U. of Texas Library

Dr. Ashbel Smith

Courtesy
Tom Green County Historical Society

Dr. Robert Irion

Courtesy
U. of Texas Library

Thomas J. Rusk

Courtesy
U. of Texas Library

J. Pinckney Henderson

FOUR TEXAS PATRIOTS

General Antonio López de Santa Anna

Executive Mansion Houston 1837-38
Republic of Texas
Sam Houston, President

Executive Mansion, Republic of Texas

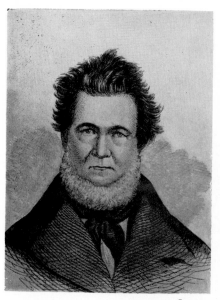

David G. Burnet

Sam Houston

Mirabeau B. Lamar

Anson Jones

FOUR PRESIDENTS, REPUBLIC OF TEXAS

Margaret Lea Houston
at about the time of her marriage

Courtesy
Brady Collection National Archives

Sam Houston about 1862

Courtesy
U. of Texas Library

Houston about 1848

Courtesy
Bettmann Archive

Houston, U.S. Senator, in 1856

Houston's Favorite Home, Huntsville

Steamboat House, Huntsville
built about 1858, Houston's last home

Jeff Hamilton, servant and faithful friend to Houston
at Texas Centennial Exposition, 1936

as "Old Sam." But he also wore the dignity of one who could rule himself as well as his country. Apparently, Elliot had said, nothing in human nature escaped this man's observation. Houston veered his course and turned as the prejudices and feelings of his people required. He used his faults and abilities and those of others to accomplish his ends. And, Elliot added, Houston evidently was determined to maintain the independence of his country. Elliot had also said that Houston was "perfectly pure handed and moved in the main by the inspiring motive of desiring to connect his name with a nation's rise." [1]

What troubled Aberdeen was that Houston had made definite gestures to invite annexation. Because of this, Aberdeen had withdrawn his confidence from the Texas envoy, but recently Minister Smith had clarified the situation. He had stated positively that public feeling had obliged Houston to trim his sails. Smith had expressed his conviction that if Mexico recognized Texas, and Spain made a treaty permitting trade with Cuba, Texans would not care to join the ambitious and arrogant Yankees. Aberdeen had let himself be reassured, but not without recurrent uneasiness.

He fumbled with a long, ivory-handled paper cutter when the Texas envoy was announced. Smith was calling in response to Aberdeen's invitation of the day before. Aberdeen told Smith that earlier advice from Washington, D. C., led him to expect imminent news that the Senate had defeated President Tyler's annexation treaty. As soon as the rejection was official, he was prepared to propose that Great Britain, France, Texas, the United States, and Mexico join in a Diplomatic Act. A tentative draft of the document had been prepared, and Smith could have a copy. It provided: (1) for peace, with Mexico formally recognizing Texas independence; (2) for the establishment of Texas boundary limits; and (3) for a pledge by Texas to maintain her independence, excluding forever the possibility of annexation.

Lord Aberdeen assured Smith that if Mexico or the United States would not agree to participate, the other nations would accomplish it among themselves. England and France were prepared to use force against Mexico, if necessary, and the United States, if she refused to sign the Act, would be obliged to stand aside or face hostilities. Of course, Aberdeen implied, the Texas minister should understand that England could not afford to counsel Mexico to make peace as a

465

preliminary. This would only serve to remove obstacles to annexation, the equivalent of beating the bush for the United States to catch the bird. But peace assuredly would follow if Texas joined Britain and France in the Act.

Smith's eyes crinkled with satisfaction and astonishment. He could imagine Houston's delight when the President learned that England and France were facing up to a move in favor of Texas that might even mean war. After the interview, Smith went to the Texas legation on St. James's Place and wrote a long dispatch on Aberdeen's response to Houston's query about what Britain and France would do, if anything. He said that he believed the British sincerely desired to foster the interests of Texas as long as it remained independent; Aberdeen was prepared to take all proper steps to achieve peace between Mexico and Texas if such action would prevent the annexation of Texas to the United States.

While Smith's dispatch about the proposed Diplomatic Act was crossing the Atlantic, Texas seethed with a presidential campaign. Under the constitution, Houston could never again be the executive. An anti-Houston coalition attempted to persuade ex-President Lamar to run. But with "Old Sam" campaigning against him, Lamar knew he could easily be defeated on his record of failures and wild miscalculations. Burnet refused to run for equally impressive reasons. There was some evanescent talk of J. Pinckney Henderson to succeed Houston, so Anson Jones and Ed Burleson contested the issue in a campaign as bitter and scandalous as that of 1841. Vice-President Burleson's supporters persistently charged that Secretary of State Jones was prosecuting negotiations with England to give her a monopoly of commerce and forever exclude Texas from the Union.

The country was eager to know where Houston stood with reference to his successor, but he withheld open support of Jones until a month before the September election. That left just enough time to get his views before the people.

Having arranged to be asked whether he was opposed to Jones, Houston took the opportunity to recite Jones's services: army surgeon in 1836, minister to the United States in 1838, two terms as senator, and secretary of state. Houston clinched his answer by saying, "He has concurred in my policy ... I have confidence ... he would consult the true interests of the country, ... carry out the policy [to] best promote its honor and prosperity." [2]

With that, Jones was as good as elected, even though he was not personally popular. Houston's retirement reminded common folk that they were losing a leader who had kept them out of adventurous warfare and a vote for Jones was a vote for "Old Sam."

The returns were not all in on September 28, 1844, when breezy James Morgan wrote an accurate forecast from his home in Galveston to Samuel Swartwout in New York. "Dr. Anson Jones is certainly elected to the Presidency—... He had no popularity of his own—rode in on 'Old Sam's' shadow ... 'Old Sam' can beat the D---l himself when he trys, and make anyone President." [3]

When Smith's summary of Aberdeen's proposed Diplomatic Act arrived soon after the election, Houston studied it carefully. He told Secretary of State Jones, now president-elect, to direct Smith to sign the Act. Three days later, learning that Jones had not complied, he repeated his instructions. Again, after another two days, he found that Jones had "not got around to it." Before leaving the capital to attend a series of Indian councils, he gave Jones a written order to instruct Smith to give the British government whatever pledges were necessary for it to complete the proposed arrangement for settling difficulties with Mexico as soon as possible.

Jones ignored the order. He distrusted Houston's motives and suspected him of wanting to defeat annexation or of breaking down Jones's administration.

Jones ardently favored Texas independence. For two years he had known that the President was using every conceivable device to stir the United States to jealousy of England. It was characteristic of a strange streak in his make-up to suspect that the man who had made him President wanted to ruin him.

Without informing the President, Jones instructed Smith to pack up and come home. When Smith arrived, Jones told him that he wanted the honor of concluding the Diplomatic Act for his own administration. The negotiations would take place in Texas and Smith would conduct them as secretary of state. [4]

But events forged ahead and took an entirely different turn.

During that same autumn of 1844, another Presidential campaign was in progress beyond the Sabine. It had been going on since March, accompanied by an almost hysterical change in the American attitude toward annexation. Houston's policy of arousing fear of England had succeeded beyond expectation. Yankee statesmen were doing more than scratching their heads; they were actively seeking means to still their own disquiet about the threat on the southwest border, and the people of the United States were as excited as their leaders. On March 26, 1844, just before the defeat of the annexation treaty, the Philadelphia *Ledger* had struck the note of alarm:

> Let us suppose that Britain seeks a colonization, or offensive and defensive alliance with Texas, and then ask what, in such a contingency, is our duty? Our reply is annexation: with the consent of Mexico if it can be obtained, and without such consent, if it be not obtainable.

Two days after the failure of the annexation treaty, on June 8, 1843, President Tyler had started a new move to accomplish annexation by means of a joint Senate and House resolution, thus bypassing the complicated negotiations involved in a treaty. His message to the House on the subject urged prompt action on this question of "vast magnitude." Acquiring Texas would give "a new impulse of immense importance to the commercial, manufacturing, agricultural and shipping interests of the Union." Tyler's preachment to the House echoed some of the most telling points that Houston had driven home in his instructions to Van Zandt and Henderson. Tyler said that annexation "is to encounter a great ... hazard of final defeat if something is not *now* done to prevent it."

Hints of pending agreements such as Aberdeen had proposed in his Diplomatic Act had reached Tyler from "persons of first respectability and citizens of Texas." These personages concurred in the belief held by General Jackson and by Tyler himself, "that instructions have already been given by the Texan Government to propose to the Government of Great Britain, ... to enter into a treaty of commerce and an alliance offensive and defensive." [5]

Before the party candidates were chosen, Martin Van Buren, who held few firm beliefs but was unwavering in his anti-slavery stand, announced his opposition to bringing a new slave state into the Union. The South promptly turned against him. His friend, Andrew Jackson, cried out in a letter from Nashville that he was quite sick, and had been ever since reading Van Buren's letter. He could not bear the thought of Great Britain having a Canada on the west as she had on the north.

Old Hickory called James K. Polk and his friends to The Hermitage and told them that Van Buren had killed himself politically. Now Polk was the man; the party must have a candidate from the southwest who stood for annexation. The campaign was hardly under way when Cassius M. Clay described the issue as he saw it: Polk, slavery, and Texas were being opposed by Henry Clay, Union, and liberty.

In Whig processions, a flag draped in black and a girl dressed in mourning symbolized Texas. Clay-inspired orators made much of the evils that would follow annexation. But in Democratic parades, the Republic was represented in a way that Houston would have liked to see—as a pure, fair, sweet maiden of the village green decked out in white and flowers.

Daniel Webster was the King Canute of the occasion. He urged that bank, tariff, and other pressing issues should not be lost sight of for the sake of acquiring Texas. His breath was wasted. The rising tide of anger, fear, and jealousy of England controlled the campaign.

On the Brazos, lame-duck President Houston read with satisfaction newspaper accounts that disclosed how United States politicians were reacting to the fire he had built under them. Some of these newspapers carried articles reprinted from the British press. If Houston himself had written them, they could not have been better designed to support his policy.

According to the London *Times*, "Human nature has been lowered by the depravity of the American people." The Democratic leaders had been "reduced to simulate political crimes which they had not the resolution to attempt." That "vanity which in America supplies the place of pride" had led Tyler to reach for Texas to crown his reign. The "extraordinary injustice" of annexation was surpassed only "by the matchless impudence of the arguments used in defense of it."

The British government had referred a neat question to Her Majesty's advocate general. Could annexation be checked by an appeal to international law? The advocate general unhesitatingly replied that a state had the right to surrender its sovereignty and annex itself to another power unless it had engaged not to do so. This settled the matter, but the argument still was good enough for press propaganda. The London *Post* harped on it, adding fuel to American indignation: "As the country it is proposed to annex has been acknowledged by foreign powers, she possesses no right to join the United States."

Lord Aberdeen hardly bothered to veil his threats. If the United States proceeded with annexation plans, he would "do that which was consistent with his duty as a minister of the Crown and what the public service might require."

Some old insults were raked up and reprinted. In the London *Atlas:* "America, in all the length and breadth of its continent, the United States inclusive, must be content to submit to British sur-veillance, and, when necessary, to British control." The London *Times* correspondent in New York described the reactions of an infuriated people, warning that the Yankees' mood was such that, if they discovered Great Britain was intriguing against them, "the project of annexation would be promptly carried into execution by an overwhelming majority.... Every native-born American who drives a cart,"—believing England's object was to break up the Union —would flock to the defense of the Constitution. "Be not mistaken ...I tell you solemn truths." [6]

Fear of England brought the dying Jackson into action again. He was hardly able to hold his pen, but within a matter of weeks he sent F. P. Blair, editor of the Washington *Globe*, twenty long outpourings on the necessity of annexing Texas to protect the southwestern frontier from British attack. Then he took a hand in the campaign strategy of his party, writing Candidate Polk that Clay should be lashed severely for rejecting Texas so that he could get aboli-tion votes.

At the outset of the campaign, Clay had called the annexation proposal idle and ridiculous if not dishonorable. Now, attacked by Polk, he discovered that he had no real personal objections to acquir-ing Texas, assuming it could be done on fair terms, honorably, with-out war, and with the common consent of the Union. His party resented his change from the position on which it had backed him, and the change cost him votes.

As the campaign progressed, the voters became more obsessed with danger of foreign interference and more impatient with the slavery argument as a reason for not annexing Texas. President Hous-ton's hope of separating the annexation question from the slavery issue actually came to pass on November 4, 1844. Polk's election was accepted as a popular mandate for annexation.

In his valedictory before a large audience at Jones's inauguration, December 9, 1844, the retiring Texas President pursued the same old cautious policy. He warned his countrymen that Texas already had been spurned twice by the United States and that even now the government should proceed on the assumption that Texas was to remain independent. "If Texas goes begging again for admission into the United States she will only degrade herself. They will spurn her again from their threshold, and other nations will look upon her with unmingled pity."

Then he discussed what might occur as a result of Polk's election.

"If the United States shall . . . ask her [Texas] to come into her great family of States, you will then have other conductors, better than myself, to lead you into the beloved land from which we have sprung—the land of the broad stripes and bright stars. But let us be as we are until that opportunity is presented, and then let us go in, if at all, united in one phalanx. . . ."

He followed this admonition with a prophecy. "If we remain an independent nation, our territory will be extensive—unlimited. The Pacific alone will bound the mighty march of our race and empire." He took note of Mexico's attitude: ". . . she still maintains the attitude of nominal hostility . . . the vain-glorious and pompous gasconade so characteristic of that nation would indicate that she is not quite ready to acknowledge the independence we have achieved."

He was heartened by the Lone Star Republic's "brightening prospects" with "its resources developing, its commerce extending and its moral influence in the community of nations increasing. . . . A poor and despised people a few years ago, borne down by depressing influences at home and abroad, we have risen in defiance of all obstacles, to a respectable place in the eyes of the world. One great nation is [about to invite] us to a full participancy in all its privileges, and to a full community of laws and interests. Others desire our separate and independent national existence, and are ready to throw into our lap the richest gifts and favors." [7]

Four days later, writing from the Texas capital to General Jackson, Houston said that he, too, accepted Polk's election as conclusive evidence that the American people desired annexation, and he assured the Old Chief that he would not interpose any obstacle to its consummation. He wrote that just before he retired from office, it had been his pleasure to receive Jackson's nephew, Major Andrew Jackson Donelson, as chargé d'affaires from the United States. Come spring, he hoped to visit at The Hermitage with his wife and son. They would not stay away from Texas for long because they desired to "settle down and improve a comfortable home for after life. In the meantime, I beseech you to feel assured of our unabated affection, and most earnest prayers for your health and happiness. Tomorrow morning I shall leave here for home, some hundred and Sixty miles distant." [8]

The ex-President joined his family at Grand Cane four days before Christmas. His home had recently been improved. The cottage stood on a rolling elevation in the midst of a green prairie, interspersed with islands of trees and silver lakes, gleaming in the sunlight. It had never seemed so beautiful.

He turned his thoughts to plans for developing his plantation at Raven Hill near Huntsville, some fifteen miles from Washington-on-the-Brazos. He was ready to go back to one of the original enterprises that had brought him to Texas—cattle raising—and had ideas about cross-breeding Durhams with Texas longhorns to get a better type of animal that could flourish under conditions in Texas and provide more meat.

Houston wrote to President Jones on December 21, 1844, about his joyous meeting with his family. He found his mind "falling back into a channel where the current flows in domestic peace and quiet without care about Government matters . . . That you may not only be successful, but more glorious in your administration than any predecessor, is my ardent desire." [9]

On his desk he found a poem of twenty stanzas written by his wife to tell him how happy she was about his retirement from public office. In part, it read:

> Dearest, the cloud hath left thy brow,
>   The shades of thoughtfulness, of care
> And deep anxiety; and now
>   The sunshine of content is there.

472

God hath crowned thy years of toil
  With full fruition, and I pray
That on the harvest still His smile
  May shed its ever gladdening ray.

This task is done. The holy shade
  Of calm retirement waits thee now.
The lamp of hope relit hath shed
  Its sweet refulgence o'er thy brow.

****

Far from the busy haunts of men,
  Oh, may thy soul each fleeting hour
Upon the breath of prayer ascend
  To Him who rules with love and power.[10]

Margaret scarcely could have foreseen that the years ahead would be more turbulent than any they had yet known.

9. *A Few Cheers for a Hero*

AFTER Polk was elected on the annexation issue, President Tyler's friends urged him to capture prestige by pushing the measure himself without waiting for action by the incoming administration. He had failed before in an attempt to annex by treaty. The outlook for winning a two-thirds majority in the Senate for ratification of a new treaty was equally dim now. So in his December, 1844 message to Congress, Tyler proposed a compromise. He asked for a joint House and Senate resolution proposing terms of annexation to Texas. There was reason to hurry now because it was well understood that Aberdeen and Houston were up to something, and if Sam Houston meant business—as Aberdeen certainly did—the consequences could be serious.

Seven resolutions were introduced and each was debated, some with acrimony. A large section of the country's populace grew angry over the delay, and the taunts of the British press continued. Although Texas had been independent for nine years, Mexico still claimed all Texas territory. Mexican leaders declared that annexation would mean war. In February, when the annexation resolution offered by Representative Milton Brown, a Tennessee Whig, was passed by the House, 120 to 98, the Mexican minister to the United States was called home.

Despite Mexico's step toward war, the Senate debated the Brown resolution. A furious debate was in progress when the London *Morning Post's* denunciation of American "designs" on Texas was circulated. The *Post* characterized the intention to annex as "merely a development of the savage instinct of the strong to tyrannize over the weak.... Some day this Republican monster must be checked."

The editor of the *New York Courier and Enquirer*, weary of fulminations from abroad, switched to support of the administration. The *Pennsylvanian*, which up to now had given no space to the issue, carried an item stating: "We are just beginning to awake to the vitality of the Texas [annexation] question." [1]

When the Senate met on the night of February 27, 1845, every senator's position was known, but eager spectators surged into the galleries and an overflow crowd thronged the lobbies. A hush came over the assemblage, followed by a swelling murmur. Spectators were telling each other that they were about to witness the most important act since the nation's birth.

The resolution was read section by section. If Texas leaders acted favorably on it, Texas would be admitted to the Union with a republican form of state government, subject to certain conditions: the United States would adjust all boundary disputes; Texas' public lands would be retained by Texas and income from them would be used to pay debts; new states, four at most, with the consent of Texas, would be formed from the new territory and slavery would be prohibited in any new states that fell north of the Missouri Compromise line.

At nine o'clock the resolution squeaked through, 27 to 25. The galleries cheered. Guns on Capitol Hill boomed a salute to the turbulent nation beyond the Sabine.

Fourteen of the affirmative votes came from slave states and thirteen from free states. Slave-state senators naturally favored expansion of slave territory. Abolitionist senators, although opposed to the acquisition of more slave territory, were dominated by fear of a neighbor nation that was oriented toward England. Some abolitionist senators said they were not able to withstand the pressure of three presidents, one in the White House, a President-elect, and an ex-President in Nashville.

According to the *National Intelligencer* the annexation resolution "passed by chance." This surely was a superficial view. There had been nine years of controversy, violent enthusiasm, indifference followed by frustration, threats of secession by New England's spokesmen, and threats of war by three nations, Mexico, England, and France. The issue had dominated one Presidential campaign to the exclusion of almost every other question. Mexico had now taken the posture of a nation that definitely intended war. Houston's empire-of-destiny dream had found partial fulfillment by a close shave—two Senate votes—but certainly not by chance.

Which individual deserved most credit would always be a question. Tyler claimed that he accomplished annexation. Calhoun and his friends stressed his part, the South Carolinian had seen to it that inflammatory material from British sources got to Jackson in Nashville, thus stimulating Jackson's powerful support. Houston said that if any one man deserved more credit than another it was Jackson. The importance of Houston's role became clearer with time. His game with England and France and with Jackson and the United States had curious consequences. Texans now had the privilege of choosing either annexation or permanent national independence. If they chose the latter, England and France guaranteed the maintenance of peaceful relationships between Texas and other nations, particularly Mexico.

Lord Aberdeen had been advised by his minister in Washington that if the proposals in his Diplomatic Act became known they would raise a storm in the American press and precipitate instantaneous annexation. Although Aberdeen had abandoned the Act, he had not discarded its purpose. By other means, he undertook to frustrate annexation, insure the continued independence of Texas, and maintain trade and friendship between Texas and England. He instructed Captain Elliot to use every effort to prevent Texas from entertaining any proposal for annexation until the British govern-

475

ment had time to persuade the Mexican government to acknowledge the independence of the Texas Republic.

The French government sent similar instructions to its minister, Alphonse de Saligny. Elliot and de Saligny induced President Jones and Secretary of State Ashbel Smith to sign preliminary terms for a treaty between Texas and Mexico which would be sponsored and defended by Britain and France. This protocol committed the Texas government to delay annexing the Republic to any other country for ninety days. The Jones administration also agreed not to refer any "offer of annexation" for popular approval within the same period, and to submit all territorial and other disputes between Texas and Mexico to arbitration. These agreements, preliminary to a treaty, would not be binding if the people of Texas preferred annexation. In behalf of Mexico, the proposed treaty would provide full recognition of Texas independence, permanent peace between Mexico and Texas, amnesty, and an agreement for Mexican acceptance of boundary limits to be determined by arbitration.

Captain Elliot hurried to Mexico City with this proposal just as the United States annexation proposal was brought to Texas by Andrew Jackson Donelson. When Donelson presented the American offer to President Jones, he was astonished to find himself coldly received. President Jones postponed acting on the offer, refusing to call the Texas Congress into special session for a reason which, as yet, was unknown to Donelson and the public. Jones favored independence, or at least he wished to insure Captain Elliot the full ninety days for negotiating with Mexico and returning to Texas with the result.

All this time, Texans, in the dark as to what was going on behind the scenes, expressed tumultuous joy. Every county held a mass meeting to voice hearty approval of the American offer, and numerous other public demonstrations followed. But when the Texas government was slow to act, joy changed to bewilderment, then to suspicion, and finally to anger.

Puzzled by his cool reception and President Jones's lack of enthusiasm for the American offer, Donelson sought the assistance of ex-President Houston. Nobody in Washington-on-the-Brazos knew where Houston was, so Donelson went to Huntsville where he learned that Houston had gone to East Texas to look after some

476

property interests. Donelson sent him a copy of the annexation resolution and asked when he would be available to discuss it. Houston replied that his return would be delayed until the spring high waters receded.

By the time Houston reached Huntsville he had made a thorough study of the American resolution which he regarded as a hasty, inadequate document with many defects that promised bad consequences for Texas. He incorporated his objections in a long letter on April 9, 1845 to Donelson, protesting that the terms were "dictated, the conditions absolute" and hardly a sound basis "when two nations were entering a compact.'" A Congressional resolution was the wrong approach, he argued. The problems involved should be negotiated by commissioners from each republic. He considered some of the annexation terms to be unfair to Texas. He pointed out that Texas was required to cede to the United States huge amounts of property, ports, harbors, and barracks which were all part of the Texas national debt. Texas or somebody would have to pay for them after they were transferred to the United States.[2]

Houston knew that the people of Texas were eager to accept the American proposal, regardless of its shortcomings which they thought they could deal with later. But after nine years of pinprick war from south of the Rio Grande and capricious behavior, surly insults, and flat rejections from the United States, he was unwilling to trust his country's future to chance and caprice.

Disappointed with Houston's coolly analytical approach, Donelson paid a second visit to Huntsville. He was unable to persuade Houston to modify any of his criticisms but obtained a statement from him that could be used in support of annexation. Even so, it was far from being a glowing indorsement of the American proposal by which this would be accomplished.

Donelson wrote to his wife in Nashville and asked her to tell "Uncle Andrew" that he had not received the support he had hoped for from Houston. At the same time, he sent an optimistic letter to the U.S. State Department. Since Houston had already assented to annexation, Donelson said, he considered the annexation question settled as far as Texas was concerned.

Politicians, eager to undermine ex-President Houston's influence with the people, charged that he was opposing annexation and was responsible for proposals from England and France. It was true that Houston's tactics had contributed to this outcome, but when the American proposal came through, he dismissed Anglo-French maneuvering with the observation that the time was inopportune for proposals from Britain. This did not end the attacks of his political rivals. They claimed that his criticisms of the annexation resolution were an attempt to prevent its consummation. Again, they denounced him as a traitor.

Many groups, eager to hear the ex-President defend himself— always a racy event—invited him to address them. He declined, commenting that his successful annexation policy needed no defense. His restraint provoked his enemies further, and the virulence of their charges disturbed Donelson. He wrote to Houston's former private secretary, Miller, now editor of the *Texas National Register*, urging him to connect Houston with annexation in a favorable light. Houston had been in favor of the measure previously and no harm could come of his seeking better terms for Texas. Donelson said that he himself would not forget the testimony borne by General Jackson to Houston's motives and acts.

Houston wrote to Donelson that he was not disturbed by the attacks of his enemies because he was certain that nine-tenths of the solid people of Texas rendered him thanks for what he had done.

To prevent Houston from achieving the same position of honor and influence in the state that he had held in the Republic, rival politicians and newspaper editors drummed up an extraordinary charge. According to them, the man who had once signed a treaty of annexation (unratified) and had sought this end for years, had been opposed to it all along.

When Houston retired, he had planned to take his wife and son to Alabama to visit his in-laws and to Nashville to see Jackson. Deciding that first he must meet the treason charge and clarify his position on annexation, he accepted an invitation to address a gathering in the Houston Methodist Church. The meeting probably took place in early May; the exact date is unknown. This was his opportunity to restate his attitude. His speech was a salute to a nation that was about to extinguish itself. He again told the story of the revolution and of San Jacinto. The crowd loved it. He voiced not a trace of regret but rejoiced wholeheartedly over the anticipated union of Texas with the United States.

478

The most powerful Texas newspapers were aligned against him and not one reported this speech, although some had sent reporters to hear it. What he said on this occasion was important later because of politicians who accused him for decades of his "villainous" opposition to annexation and of "blood betrayal" because he had endeavored to annex Texas to Mexico. It so happened that William F. Weeks, the first shorthand reporter in Texas, was in the audience. It was not until thirty years later that his transcript was published.

"I can truly rejoice with you, my fellow citizens," Houston said, "that . . . we are permitted to turn from the anxious checkered past, and behold the bright and cheering future. That our annexation to the mother country is assured . . . there . . . can be no doubt. I consider the benefit to be derived . . . great beyond the power of language to describe . . . when we are able to say to the civilized world that we have secured a permanent and stable government beyond all possibility of failure, numberless emmigrants with large possessions of servants and money will flock to our shores."

He turned on his vilifiers:

Will my fellow citizens forgive me for lowering myself sufficiently to notice these creatures? [Yes, yes, go on from the audience.] . . .

The lying scribbler of the *Telegraph* [Dr. Francis Moore] is a one armed man. You never would forgive me for abusing a cripple, but I must confess that one arm can write more malicious falsehoods than any man with two arms I ever saw. His one arm is more prolific for evil than the traditional bag that had seven cats and every cat had seven kits. The idea that such men should accuse me of being disloyal to the interests of the South . . . I who first saw light of day in Old Virginia, educated in Tennessee at the feet of Andrew Jackson, and was taught in my infancy to love the South and all her institutions, social, religious and political. . . .

When he hesitated, the audience shouted, "Go on! Go on!" For the first time publicly, he lifted the veil from his foreign policy tactics:

These men in retailing their slanders are compelled to tell some truths. I did direct our minister at Washington to withdraw the application of Texas for annexation and commence paying court to England and France, for reasons that public policy has heretofore forbid an explanation.... Supposing a charming lady has two suitors. One of them she is inclined to believe would make the better husband, but is a little slow to make interesting propositions. Do you think if she was a skillful practitioner in Cupid's court she would pretend that she loved the other 'feller' best? [Laughter and applause].

If ladies are justified in making use of coquetry in securing their annexation to good and agreeable husbands, you must excuse me for making use of the same means to annex Texas to Uncle Sam. [Laughter and cheers].[3]

Who deserved the credit for bringing about annexation? Houston bestowed some on Jackson, on Tyler, and others, reserving a good measure for himself. In his *Memoir* (p. 253) he attributed the success of his annexation policy to a letter of instructions that he sent to Texas agents, Henderson and Van Zandt on April 16, 1844.

This letter was an excellent example of Houstonian finesse. In it, for the benefit of both the Texas agents and the United States Government, he predicted the attitude of England and France if Texas agreed to remain "separate forever from the United States." He added, "Texas has *done all* that *she could do* to obtain annexation, and you may rely upon this fact, in the event of a failure, that Texas will *do all* that it *should do.*" This was nothing less than a declaration that if annexation failed Texas would go for permanent independence and seek the fullest possible alliance and partnership with England and France. He severely criticized the United States Government for not keeping its promises regarding the annexation of Texas. He assured the Texas agents that France and England were prepared to act effectively—"if we do not permit ourselves to be trifled with, and duped by the United States."

By implication the ministers were authorized to impart the contents of this letter to the United States Government. Then Houston suggested the circumstances under which Henderson and Van Zandt might "leak" the contents of this letter and possibly obtain valuable information from other diplomats:

A Diplomatic agent may eat and sleep enough for health, and may drink generously with the Diplomatic agents of other countries; provided, he can induce them to take two glasses to his one. Men are fond to be thought knowing, as well as wise, and when listened to with attention, frequently impart knowledge, at a wine table, which they would not dream of in the forenoon of the day. You can instruct yourselves much by the "course intimated." [4]

10. *End of the Agony*

AFTER giving his speech, Houston took his family to Galveston where they sailed for New Orleans. There, late in May, 1845 before an overflowing audience in the Arcade, he made a speech strongly favoring annexation. In the same hall, he gave a well-attended temperance lecture. He wrote to Polk, assuring him that Texas was now virtually a part of the Union, but also expressing his anxiety over Texas boundary claims and other problems resulting from the inadequacy of the annexation resolution.

Houston received news that General Jackson was dangerously ill. He dropped everything and set out at once for Nashville with his family. He wanted Jackson to see Margaret and little Sam. Above all, he wanted to obtain Jackson's blessing for his son.

The steamer went aground, causing a two-day delay for repairs and detaining the Houstons while Jackson lay dying at The Hermitage. Jackson had been critically ill for several months, afflicted with agonizing headaches, severe intestinal hemorrhage, bleeding at the lungs, a painful racking cough, dropsical swellings, and frequent diarrhea. One lung seemed to have been consumed entirely; the other was diseased. His condition was unquestionably aggravated by his treatment—bleeding and large doses of calomel.

As death approached, Jackson faced his departure from this world like a general who knows the battle is lost but is determined to manage his retreat in good order. His conduct under the most intense suffering and his thoughtful kindness for family, friends, and servants illustrated the resolution and will power of the man who had inspired Houston's devotion ever since Horseshoe Bend.

For a long time Jackson had been so weak that he could hardly hold a pen. Yet, when he got hold of one and ink flowed on paper, renewed life surged in his veins. He scratched away and dispatched powerful epistles to Sam Houston and President Polk; also to his long time friend, Francis P. Blair, editor of the Washington *Globe*, and to other individuals and newspapers, writing urgently on annexation and a variety of topics. He arranged credit for his farm, placed orders for provisions, gave instructions for management. After a turn for the worse in his condition, the general took communion with his family present. Afterward he said, "Death has no terrors for me. When I have suffered sufficiently, the Lord will take me to himself. . ."

A few days later he sat for a portrait painter, George P. H. Healy, an American art student from Paris. Healy had been commissioned by Louis Philippe to do a painting to hang in the royal gallery beside Washington. On May 29, Jackson received thirty visitors, took all by the hand, and bade them farewell. The next day Healy showed him the finished portrait. Jackson said it convinced him Healy stood at the head of his profession. "I feel very much obliged to you, sir, for the very great labor you have been pleased to bestow upon it," the dying man said.

A family friend, William Tyack, observed that in the midst of the worst paroxysm of pain, not a murmur, not a groan escaped Jackson's lips. On Sunday, June 1, the general asked his family to cease watching by his bedside and go to church. Some of the family did go. Through an open window the general spoke to them, "This is apparently the last Sabbath I shall be with you. God's will be done; he is kind and merciful."

On Monday he received a letter from his nephew, A. J. Donelson, chargé d'affaires to Texas, relating the extraordinary activities of the British agent, Charles Elliot. In spite of great pain, Jackson discussed the matter calmly with Tyack.

One of Jackson's physicians, Dr. Esselman, had to perform an operation to relieve the dying man's distress from rapidly increasing water in the abdomen. Although the general was given opiates, he could not sleep. His prayers to God to sustain him in the hour of dissolution were overheard.

On Friday, June 6, he gave more directions about farm affairs and talked about Texas and the futility of sacrificing Oregon territory to Britain. The news from Texas was good. Relieved, the general said, "All is safe at last." He praised his old friend and companion-in-arms, Sam Houston, and said that the United States owed this outcome to him. He dictated a strongly phrased letter to President Polk urging him to act resolutely on Texas and Oregon affairs.

On Sunday Jackson fainted while being lifted from a chair into his bed. Family and friends gathered. They believed him to be dead. But Jackson, still master in his own house, opened his eyes. "My dear children," he said, "do not grieve for me; it is true I am going to leave you; I am well aware of my situation."

After addressing farewells to all his family—his adopted son, his daughter-in-law, his daughter-in-law's widowed sister, and all the grandchildren—he gave an impressive lecture on the subject of religion, spoke for nearly half an hour, and closed with this: "My dear children, and friends, and servants, I hope and trust to meet you all in heaven, both white and black." He repeated "both white and black."

Sunday afternoon he rested more easily. By Major William B. Lewis, who stayed close to his bedside, he sent farewell messages to Sam Houston, Colonel Benton, Francis Blair, and other friends.

At half past five when the general had not spoken for some time his son whispered, "Father, how do you feel? Do you know me?"

"Know you? Yes, I know you. I would know you all if I could see. Bring me my spectacles."

They gave him his spectacles and he asked about two members of the family who were not there. All day a crowd of servants had been looking in through the windows. The general heard their sobs and groans.

"What is the matter with my children?" he asked. "Have I alarmed you? Oh, do not cry. Be good children and we will all meet in heaven."

He did not speak again. He closed his eyes and breathed easily. From then until the end came at about six o'clock on June 8, 1845, he suffered no pain.[1]

Half an hour later the Houstons, dashing from Nashville to The Hermitage in a coach, encountered Dr. Esselman who told them of the Old Chief's passing. They drove on to The Hermitage at a slower pace. The coach circled the banjo driveway and stopped in front of the house. With young Sam in his arms and Margaret beside him, Houston was shown into the chamber where Jackson lay on a couch. He knelt and laid his head on his Old Chief's breast.

A sister of Sam, Jr., Nettie Houston Bringhurst, recalled many years later an incident that survived as a family legend. It was said that, while kneeling, Houston drew Sam, Jr. to his side and said, "My son, try to remember that you have looked on the face of this great man." Since Master Sam was only two weeks past two years of age, it may seem a little unlikely that he did.[2]

At midnight, in a guest room at The Hermitage, Houston wrote to President Polk, lamenting that the delay on the river had prevented him from "administering, if I could, some comfort in the closing scene of the Old Chief's eventful life." [3]

After Jackson's funeral—he was buried in the garden beside Rachel—the Houstons were guests in the Donelsons' home. The Major was still in Texas but his charming wife, Emily, was a most cordial hostess. Many barbecues and other social events honored the Houstons.

Pausing in Alabama on their return trip to Texas, the Houstons visited some of the General's in-laws. He made several more pro-annexation speeches. The *Alabama State Review* praised his "faultless form" and his "large experience and intimate knowledge of men." He had "a fine manly voice and a manner that was eloquence itself." At fifty-two he moved "with a firm elastic tread and the erect carriage of a young Indian Chief." He appeared to be in much better health, "than when he was here in 1840," the year that Houston and Margaret were married.[4]

In the Mexican capital, Captain Elliot exerted the pressure of the empire he represented. After some hesitation, the dictator who recently had succeeded Santa Anna, General Mariano Paredes Avrillago, ordered his Foreign Minister, Luis Cuevas, to sign the protocol. Racing back to Texas, Elliot delivered it to President Jones on June 3, 1845, when Houston was still in Nashville. The next day, Jones announced the news to his fellow countrymen. They could have peace with recognition by Mexico if Texas would agree never to unite with the United States; this peace and independence would be backed by England and France. He proclaimed amnesty and the end of hostilities between Texas and Mexico.

Texas received this news with resentment and anger. True annexationists did not wish their hope to be deferred by analysis of the American offer or by the discussion of any proposal from elsewhere. Numerous editorials, all of the same tenor, declared that Mexico's objective was to lie and deceive and to dupe the people of Texas. The

Texans' excitement and anger compelled the president to call a special session of Congress for June 16. The Congress promptly voted down the peace and independence offer from Mexico and unanimously supported annexation.

The American offer stipulated that annexation must be ratified by a people's convention elected for that special purpose and to draw up a state constitution. President Jones set the date for such a convention which asssembled at eight o'clock on the morning of July 4, 1845, in the old capitol at Austin. Thomas Rusk was elected chairman. A prayer was offered by a clergyman and this was followed by an impressive moment of silent devotion.

After electing a secretary, the convention took note of the fact that a chair was empty. It was the chair reserved for one of the delegates from Montgomery County, Sam Houston. When someone explained that he was absent on a visit of piety to The Hermitage, the convention officially recorded its approval of this filial pilgrimage. An alternate had been elected, but out of recognition of loyalty and past service the convention refrained from declaring the former President's seat vacant.

Chairman Rusk then appointed a committee of fifteen to prepare an ordinance of assent to the American offer. The vote for the ordinance by the whole convention lacked one of being unanimous. The delegates stood up and shouted in a long, moist-eyed demonstration of joy. All signed the document, including the dissenter. After voting to wear crepe for a month in memory of Andrew Jackson, the convention recessed. The next day it turned to the business of writing the state constitution.

On the second Monday in October, 1845, the people voted overwhelmingly in favor of the new constitution. Houston arrived soon afterward, having left Margaret and Sam with relatives in Alabama. They would rejoin him a few weeks later. Violent attacks from the anti-Houston faction greeted him. The demonstration of hostility was impressive since his opponents controlled most of the press.

In addition to boundary limits and the debt question, numerous matters of great importance remained to be agreed upon between the new state and the Union. Houston, with his executive and legal experience, his prestige and influence, and his skill as a negotiator, was the obvious man to head the Texas delegation to the United

States Senate. Prevention of this assignment became the object of a bitter campaign in which Houston again was denounced as a traitor. With the support of the Georgia faction, Mirabeau Buonaparte Lamar was actively seeking the position. This combination made it inevitable that Houston should be accused of disloyalty. The old familiar charges were dusted off. The allegation that he had murdered the Mier prisoners by neglecting diplomatic intervention was trotted out.

Only one new indictment was brought: Houston had debauched the Texas treasury. The one-armed Dr. Moore of the *Telegraph* joined the chorus, denouncing Houston in the issue of October 22, 1845 for scheming to annex Texas to Mexico, "a bloody betrayal of the people of Texas."

Houston received many invitations to answer his defamers at dinners and mass meetings. On November 5, 1845, the *Telegraph* published one invitation signed by seven persons. The seven persons desired to give Houston public evidence of their continued regard for his civil and military services and expressed their undiminished confidence in his integrity and patriotism.

But Houston was weary of slashing at the Hydra of political venom. He remembered when he had written that it was not a paying business to be president of Texas, and he had learned all he needed to know about the ingratitude of republics. Furthermore, there was no occasion to answer Moore, Lamar, or Burnet; he knew from previous experience that, given enough rope, they always hanged themselves. So he declined the invitation, beginning his letter with tongue-in-cheek:

> To vindicate myself against charges that have been made, that I was ever opposed to annexation, has not been my course of life. If the accusations have resulted either from ignorance or malignity, I can pity their authors.— . . . I have deemed it unnecessary either to become clamorous, or troublesome, in support of a measure which originated under my administration, and was conducted under my directions, until my term as Executive expired in December last.[5]

Ashbel Smith returned from Europe after numerous embarrassments that he had foreseen. Lord Aberdeen had spurned explanations. When it was necessary to consult French Foreign Minister Guizot on some details about closing the Texas legation in Paris, the door of the French foreign office refused to budge. However, admission was finally achieved by the intercession of the United States ambassador.

Smith and others consulted Houston about his willingness to go to the United States Senate. As usual, when confronted with an invitation to continue in public service, he referred to his dreams of enjoying plantation life and building a home "for the after time." But the habit of public service was deeply imbedded, and he no doubt would have been greatly disappointed if not called upon. Finally he announced the conditions of his acceptance—"should my friends and the true friends of the country be satisfied that my services are of paramount importance in the Senate to all others, and really necessary. . . ." [6]

A politically astute legislator, Jesse Grimes, declared to Ashbel Smith that Houston was the one man who could unite Texas opinion, but Grimes feared Houston would be beaten if not paired with the right man. Smith, believing that General Houston's popularity was greater than ever, considered his election certain but did not hazard a guess as to who the other senator would be.

In December, 1845, President Polk transmitted the new Texas constitution to the Congress and asked for the passage of an act admitting Texas as a state. On December 10, Representative Stephen A. Douglas, Chairman of the House Committee on Territories, reported a joint resolution declaring Texas a state that would share equal rights with the original states.

Still the struggle was not won. The American people's "united and joyous welcome" hoped for by Houston was conspicuously lacking. Protests and petitions had poured in from Massachusetts, Rhode Island, and Connecticut. In the House of Representatives, Rockwell of Massachusetts tried to get the "admission" message recommitted for an amendment prohibiting slavery, but the annexationists had the strength on December 16, to force it through 141 to 56.

Senator Daniel Webster opened the subject wide and pleaded earnestly on anti-slavery grounds against admission. Senator J. M. Berrien, a Southern Whig, responded, "The pledge of this Government has been given, and it must be redeemed." Even Webster could not refute this. On December 22, the Senate passed the measure, 31 to 14.[7]

On December 29, 1845, the United States Congress approved the Texas state constitution. That day Texas became the only independent country ever received into the Union. In Texas, United States laws were formally extended, federal courts and postal routes were established, and a state government was created with J. Pinckney Henderson as governor.

On February 19, 1846, members of the Texas legislature, other elected officials, and citizens gathered in front of the old capitol at Austin for the obsequies of their nation. President Jones rose to the occasion with an eloquent oration. "The Lone Star of Texas" he said, ". . . has culminated, and following an inscrutable destiny has passed on and become fixed forever in that glorious Constellation which all free men . . . must reverence and adore—the American Union.

"The final act in this great drama is now performed. The Republic of Texas is no more." [8]

The press reported tears in the eyes of listeners who had suffered and bled to win freedom and establish a government.

Members of the legislature had heard from their constituents, and Ashbel Smith's prediction proved correct. Two days after the flag came down, the legislature elected ex-President Houston and his long-time associate Thomas Rusk as the first senators from Texas, 60 votes for Houston and 70 for Rusk with a few scattered complimentary votes for others.

During August, while the convention had been writing the new state constitution and while Houston was still in Alabama, President Jones had discovered that he was in difficulty. He unquestionably preferred independence to annexation, but actually had done nothing to defeat the will of the people. He simply had insisted that the British-backed Mexican offer as well as the American proposal be passed on by the Texas congress. To many this broadmindedness had the aspect of treachery. Jones never had been popular. As Jim Morgan said, he had ridden into office on the shadow of "Old Sam." Now Jones became aware of growing hostility. Charges that he had connived with Houston to betray Texas by trying to frustrate annexation would continue to depress him through the years. Houston thrived on controversy; for Jones it had tragic consequences.

488

Jones retired to his home in Barrington, where he lived the life of a planter and country doctor. He read over his diaries with their many sly entries attacking his "friend" Houston, his own letters, his indorsements on letters, and his state papers. They persuaded him that he was the true hero of annexation. Not Jackson, not Calhoun, not Tyler, and above all not Houston, but he, Jones, had brought it about. His soul cried out with agony against Old Sam's getting credit for the good deeds of another. In time, he felt compelled to attack his former chief. He wrote long newspaper articles about misrepresentations on the subject of annexation. This way lay madness. Jones could not impair Houston's sturdy character and basic popularity with the people.

Jones's failure to convert Texas to the belief that he was annexation's unrecognized hero deepened his bitterness. It undoubtedly contributed to the aftermath which did not come until 1858. That year when he sought a place in the United States Senate, hoping to succeed Thomas Rusk, the old charge that he had not been a one-hundred-per-cent-annexationer rose to haunt him. He was defeated by J. Pinckney Henderson. Sensitive, humiliated, brooding, he let his sick brain take control. On January 9, 1858, he met a friend in front of the Old Capitol Hotel in Houston. This, he said, was where his career had begun and this was where it might be ended. Then he went inside and up to his room, put a revolver to his temple, and blew out his brains, a victim of his own tragically twisted character.

To the citizens of the new state, annexation brought both regret and joy. Colonel James Morgan, who had come to Texas to speculate in lands and had found home and country there, grieved over the change. To Anson Jones he had written on March 28, 1845:

> It seems that 'the long agony is over' and Texas is to be tacked on to the fag end of the U States, a little behind *Arkansas*.... Worse than all, we shall be annexed with the Curses of fully one-half of the people of the U.S., who have been deriding us and abusing us for Cutthroats, villains, and bestowing upon us every vile epithet... and [are] at it yet! Just, too, as our Independence was about being acknowledged by Mexico! ... Well, all my projects, I fear, are knocked in the head—and I shall die for want of excitement of some kind.[9]

Colonel Morgan was completely mistaken; he lived to a ripe old age and never suffered from lack of excitement.

BOOK VII

AN APOSTLE OF A GREATER AMERICA

1. *An Ex-President Supports a President*

S ENATOR-ELECT Houston came into Washington aboard a
jolting train from Pittsburgh on Saturday, March 28,
1846. From Houston City he had traveled more than 2,600 miles
over bayou and river to Galveston, across the Gulf to New Orleans,
up the Mississippi and Ohio Rivers to Pittsburgh, and by train to
the capital.

As he entered Brown's Hotel, the familiar sign bearing the gaudy
likeness of Pocahontas creaked on its fastenings above the doorway.
It was a reminder of bygone days when he had visited the capital in
behalf of his red brothers and the ration contract that had precipitated the flogging of Stanberry. The hotel had been known as the
Indian Queen in those days and genial Jesse Brown had presided over
the bar. Houston missed Jesse as a friend, but he did not miss the
bartender's services. The Senator-elect was no longer a drinking man.

He rested late on Sunday and did not go to church. Late in the
afternoon he put on his new blue military coat, lined in red, and a
cap in the military style; picked up his gold-headed stick, and walked
up Pennsylvania Avenue to pay his respects to President Polk. The
avenue was one of the city's partially paved thoroughfares; both
sides were lined with saloons and gambling houses. Oil lamps,
lighted only when Congress was in session, hung from the buildings
or from posts at street corners.

This sprawling city, populated by 40,000 whites, 8,000 free Negroes, and 2,000 slaves was larger but not very different from the

capital in Texas. Northern visitors deplored a corral near the Capitol where droves of Virginia-bred Negroes awaited shipment to Southern markets. This disgraceful spectacle was sometimes referred to as a "Negro livery stable." All efforts to uproot slavery from the District of Columbia had failed, and the capital remained a center of the trade in human chattels.

When Houston arrived at the White House he saw that many improvements had been made since Jackson's day. The lawns had been regraded, walks had been graveled, and trees planted. The pillared portico facing Pennsylvania Avenue had been completed, giving the northern façade the appearance it has today. In the rear, a marsh extended to the Potomac. Beyond, where the Washington Monument would eventually rise, the sky was empty. The front of the Treasury had been finished; the Smithsonian Institution had been started; and the State, War, and Navy Departments each occupied two-story dwellings. In the distance, the Capitol stood under a low dome; it did not have the wings that were added later.

In his diary, President Polk recorded the satisfaction that he derived from Houston's visit. "At six o'clock this evening General Sam Houston, late President of Texas and now a Senator in Congress, called. I was much pleased to see him, having been with him in Congress twenty years ago and always his friend. I found him thoroughly Democratic and fully determined to support my administration." [1]

The sick and lonely man in the White House, already suffering from the intestinal malady that hastened his death three months after he left office, had good reason to welcome the support of the new senator. Polk, elected by a narrow popular majority, had little party backing and could not count on dependable support in either house of Congress. Courageous and determined, he had come to the office with a definite program: to buy California if he could, complete the annexation of Texas, and settle the old dispute between the United States and England over the Oregon boundary. He had pledged himself to fight for the Oregon boundary at 54° 40′ N, all the way up the coast to the southern boundary of Alaska. Polk, though responsible for conducting the nation's foreign affairs up to the point of treaty ratification, had asked Congress to grant him specific authority to notify England that the treaty providing for joint occupation of the Oregon territory would be abrogated one year hence, as permitted by one of its provisions.

Congressmen had lashed themselves into a fury over this sensible move to show the world that the nation was united on an important international question. Senator John C. Calhoun was using all his prestige against war, which, he implied, was inevitable if notice of intended treaty abrogation (a year in advance) was given without qualification. The qualification which he demanded was that the United States accept the forty-ninth parallel instead of fifty-four forty as the boundary.

A new revolution in Mexico had sparked a demonstration of patriotic anger against the United States under the whiplash of Mexican dictatorship. The Mexicans had announced that war would follow the annexation of Texas. When the Mexican minister had packed up and had gone home, the American minister in Mexico City had been asked to leave the country.

President José Joaquín Herrera had refused to receive John Slidell, the peace commissioner sent by Polk to negotiate an agreement on a compromise boundary line between Texas and Mexico. Dictator Mariano Paredes y Arrillaga, having succeeded Herrera, had hustled troops to the northern border. American troops were already on the border in keeping with the pledge of protection that had been given to Sam Houston's Republic. Now, with politicians noisily using a confused and alarming situation for their own purposes, the country uneasily faced the possibility of war on two fronts.

Polk was calm and determined, although facing opposition from Whigs, violent abolitionists, and snipers in his own party. Undaunted by the complexities of his situation, he nonetheless was dumfounded by the stream of vituperation that poured on him.

On Monday, March 30, 1846, Houston's junior colleague, Thomas Rusk, introduced him to the Senate. The senators courteously welcomed Houston, but with nothing that resembled a demonstration. Houston and Rusk drew lots to satisfy the constitutional requirement that one-third of the Senate should be elected every two years, one-third every four years, and one-third every six years. By Senate order three pieces of paper, exactly the same size, numbered one, two and three, were placed in a box. Number 1 represented a term to March 3, 1847; Number 2, to March 3, 1849; Number 3 to March 3, 1851. Rusk drew the longest term and Houston the shortest. The short term did not disappoint him because he was never averse to having his constituency pass upon his stewardship.

Some senators may have wondered if Houston's fame would dim certain hard-won senatorial reputations. Others surely speculated about how a self-educated frontiersman could hope to hold his own in company with such as Calhoun, a Yale graduate, and Daniel Webster, who had been trained at Exeter and Dartmouth. In his early forties when he was called upon to control the impetuous young Vikings, Houston's appellation, "Old Sam," had suggested patriarchal wisdom and influence. At fifty-three, he was among coevals and seniors.

Senator Calhoun sat on the Democratic side of the aisle. He was tall, gaunt, and emaciated and had a great mass of hair, angular, somewhat harsh features, and brilliant dark blue eyes. He never lost his self-control in debate; when most bitterly denounced, he sat motionless and intractable, monolithic in his cadaverous yet somehow imperial reserve.

Webster, with his massive overhanging forehead and great speculative eyes, sat on the Whig side. In the lobby, he often walked with his hands behind his back, serene in contemplation. His attitude had given rise to a saying, "No one can be as wise as Daniel Webster looks, not even Webster." He usually wore a dress coat of fine material, spotless linen, silk stockings, and slippers or pumps tied with a bow over the instep.

The presiding officer, Vice-President George Mifflin Dallas, was exactly Houston's age. Calhoun, Webster, Thomas Hart Benton, and Lewis Cass, all were ten years his senior. John J. Crittenden of Ohio was five years older than Houston. There were younger men too: Reverdy Johnson of Maryland, graceful, eloquent, and sparkling in repartee, was fifty; cautious, undistinguished John Bell of Tennessee, forty-nine; cheerful and wily Simon Cameron, forty-seven.

Senator Houston's unpretentious attire set him apart from his colleagues who favored long-skirted coats, watch fobs with heavy seals, and beribboned eyeglasses. Their dignified demeanor sometimes relaxed in the excitement of debate or after a visit to the nearby "Hole in the Wall." Not infrequently they stepped up to the vice-president's desk and delicately refreshed themselves from a gold-mounted snuffbox containing the common supply furnished at public expense.

Observers reported that tobacco juice often trickled onto the red carpet.

The small Senate chamber, now known as the old Supreme Court Chamber, had purple hangings and four tiers of seats for sixty members. A railing at the rear discouraged visitors from strolling out on the floor. A circular gallery, extending all around the room and over the presiding officer's chair, accommodated spectators. The chamber was heated by four fireplaces and two smoky Franklin stoves fed with hickory wood. The air became stale and fetid in winter. Shivering senators sat with their hats on and occasionally wore blankets pinned at their throats. In unseasonable weather, Senator Houston wore a bright Mexican serape to protect his back and chest from drafts.

Listening to the debate on the question of giving notice to England, Senator Houston deplored the unwholesome relationship between the Congress and the President. For once, Calhoun and Webster were on the same side of an argument and were mutually against Polk, but for different reasons. There had been an implied bargain between Northern and Southern legislators that the South would back the North in claiming the whole of Oregon if Texas was admitted to the Union, but Calhoun did not recognize it. Slavery could not prosper in Oregon and if the territory was brought into the Union, it would add to the overbalance of free against slave territory. This unquestionably was one of the motives that prompted Calhoun to oppose the President.

As for Webster, he knew so little about the question on which he spoke with assumed authority that he described Oregon as "a poor country, no way important to England, . . . and of very little consequence to the United States." He expressed the conviction that sooner or later its settlers would establish a great independent Pacific Republic beyond the Rockies. This possibility did not disturb him. In the Senate he criticized President Polk with ponderous sarcasm: "The Executive seems to be for negotiation, and yet is against anything but the whole of Oregon. . . ." [2]

Some jingoistic editors were demanding that the United States declare war if England did not grant the boundary at fifty-four forty. Other editors were proclaiming that abrogation of the treaty would provoke war. In the midst of the excitement, the hothead, Lewis

497

Cass, introduced a resolution looking toward preparation of the army and navy for war and predicting the outbreak of hostilities at any moment. These outcries, in the light of actual facts, were nonsensical.

Polk actually had offered to give up claims to fifty-four forty and to accept the forty-ninth parallel as the boundary. With language that Polk regarded as disrespectful, the British minister, Richard Pakenham, had refused to send the proposal to his government. Polk was now doing the only thing he could do: in a horse-trading situation he retreated to his original position—fifty-four forty—and demanded abrogation of the treaty in the hope that England would see the necessity of compromise. The partisanship and demagoguery of Polk's opposition is emphasized by the known fact that Calhoun had inside information about England's attitude toward Polk's demand for settlement of the Oregon question. From Louis McLane, the American ambassador in London, he personally received the judgment that Polk's tough stand on the Oregon matter had made a strong impression in England that would tend toward peace. Foreign Minister Aberdeen, said McLane, did not look with disfavor on the United States Congress giving notice of abrogation. An interest in reciprocal trade was springing up in England.

McLane also had written to Secretary of State James Buchanan commending Polk for his strong position and declaring that settlement would not be difficult unless one side or the other was determined on war. In spite of McLane's assurances, Calhoun devoted his giant intellect to persuading his jittery countrymen that the notice Polk desired to give, if unqualified, must bring on war. He was as fiery in his anti-war speeches as the editors and firebrands who were still shouting fifty-four forty or fight.

Webster, aspiring to go to England as ambassador, naturally desired to be popular there. Prompted by a good purpose—peace—he was nevertheless operating behind the Executive's back by communicating directly with James McGregor, a friend who was a member of the British Parliament from Glasgow. Webster evidently was not worried about the impropriety of his actions; he even weakened Polk's bargaining position by informing his British correspondent that the forty-ninth parallel would be accepted by the United States if England made a positive offer.

Senator Houston was reluctant to take the floor so soon after his advent, but the more familiar he became with the background of the acrimonious debate and the aspersions being cast on Polk, the more pained he was with the recriminations of his fellow legislators and the more sympathetic he was toward the President. On Monday, April 13, 1846, when he had been a member of the Senate exactly two weeks, he announced that he would speak on the Oregon question two days later. That Wednesday he presented a spectacle never seen before and not likely to be seen again: a repatriated citizen, who had recently completed his second term as the President of a Republic, arose in the United States Senate to plead with his colleagues to show patriotic restraint, if not magnanimity, and to treat the Executive with common decency and fairness. The calmness with which he advanced his reasoning was impresssive:

> If we ... admit the opinions of gentlemen who have spoken on this question, war, with all its calamities, is inevitable if the measure [notice to Britain] is adopted. But this does not seem to be the question. Is it wise policy in this government to pursue this course? Is it necessary for the preservation of our rights? ...
>
> Were we to be restrained from action in a crisis like the present by any considerations as to the possibility of war ... the public interest would be liable to suffer deeply. If we never dare to adventure action, we can achieve nothing ... I am not in favor of precipitate action, but for a calm, deliberate, and firm course of procedure.
>
> No less than twenty-eight years have rolled round without producing a satisfactory result. ...
>
> I think it is idle to anticipate an agreeable termination to our negotiations with England upon the subject of Oregon, unless it is brought about by giving this notice.[3]

No one listened more attentively than the senator from South Carolina. Houston's first words revealed that he would not be among Calhoun's following; Calhoun had taken the position that giving unqualified notice might lead to war. Webster, too, knew that the newcomer was challenging the propriety of his position. Alerted, he ceased to pace in the lobby and came into the chamber to listen.

Senator Houston pleaded earnestly for support of the Executive's "calm and deliberate but firm procedure." The Executive had been charged with "shirking his duty and embarrassing the Congress" by referring this question to them. But, Senator Houston pointed out, the American people had "made a decision on it." Because fifty-four forty had been "a leading topic in the last Presidential canvass ... I believe that the President would have fallen short of his duty if he had not claimed that our right to the whole of Oregon was unquestionable," he said.

Had the President claimed the country only as far as forty-nine, do you not believe that many who now denounce his ... claim to the whole territory, would have been found ready to denounce him for compromising the honor and interest of the country, and as guilty of a shameless abandonment of American rights?

He too desired peace, but questioned how it was to be obtained: ". . . by permitting this question to fester in the public mind of both countries? . . . I venture this opinion, . . . that had the co-ordinate branches of the government cooperated with the Executive with the promptitude, and in the spirit in which he acted, to-day everything had been tranquil, England quiet, and the public mind in the United States calm, serene, and unexcited. . . . But when Great Britain finds that the policy of the Executive is opposed or denounced by American statesmen, her presses at once change their tone. This very opposition is sufficient to inspirit England to beard this country into a war—embarrass the Executive of the nation—I mean the measures of the Executive, not the man. I do not know that he can be embarrassed . . . By the efficient cooperation of the coordinate branches of the Government, I doubt not but that he will be able to bring this matter to a happy consummation and thus avert the evils of war so much deprecated in this chamber. . . ."

Houston urged that notice be given "respectfully and with the utmost decorum, but I would leave its qualification, if any, with the Executive." He closed with an announcement that he would vote in favor of giving notice "because I believe it necessary to enable the Executive to secure harmony in our foreign relations. If peace is to be preserved, I believe this is the measure to insure it. If war springs from it, it will be because war was inevitable in any event. My vote in favor of the measure will be an earnest that I have not sought to embarrass the Executive, or failed to strengthen his hands while [he is] toiling for the honor, the interest, and the glory of his country."

Next day, with a qualifying amendment proposed by Senator Calhoun, the Senate authorized the President to give notice "at his discretion." On April 25, 1846, Houston wrote to Ashbel Smith: "I sustain the President in his course ... out & out. I prefer, *our cause,* to that of a Foreign Power. Some argue to the contrary." [4]

To another Texas friend, John Hemphill, he wrote, "... at least three gentlemen have their eyes on the White House, Cass, Calhoun and Allen. This is a most unfortunate state of things ... All that I desire is the prosperity of the nation. Parties at this time can embarrass our affairs, and humble us to Great Britain. Would to God, that we could act as one man." [5]

Without the aid of inside information from London, Houston had correctly estimated the situation. Far from being bent on war, Lord Aberdeen wrote out a new treaty with his own hand before Polk's formal notice of intention to abrogate even reached him. Polk forwarded the treaty to the Senate: the Oregon boundary would be 49° to the sea, all of Vancouver Island would become British territory, and free navigation of the Columbia River would be permitted the Hudson's Bay Company until its charter expired in 1859.

The satisfaction that Calhoun and Webster derived from the positions they had taken is difficult to estimate. Calhoun was credited with averting a war that had never really been a serious threat. Webster celebrated ratification of the treaty with his English friends who regarded it as a victory. On June 15, 1846, the day the treaty was signed, Webster was one of seven men who attended a dinner given by British Minister Pakenham at the British Embassy. The dinner featured "good wine, good taste, good manners," and "the joyful event was toasted again and again." [6]

Houston, the repatriated citizen of a "foreign country" had set the keynote of his entire thirteen years in the Senate. His service was based on invaluable experience and rare traits of character: his rough and ready tutelage in war and in Congress under Jackson, his victory over Santa Anna and the Texas Vikings, his struggle to keep a weak and impecunious nation afloat, his dealings with foreign diplomats, and his ability to bear up under malignant attack. Thus equipped, he was to prove equal and sometimes superior to any man in the Senate.

On the evening of June 15, 1846, while Webster was toasting the outcome of the Oregon dispute with his British friends, Houston was writing to his three-year-old boy: "My dear Son, Your Father loves you, and hopes you are a good boy.... You ought as a good and

dear son, to love your dear Ma more than all others and next to her
...your dear Grand Ma.... You should love me, too, and when I
do good, you should do like me.... My Son, Sam! Thy devoted
Father, Sam Houston." [7]

2. *Hitting the Lion on the Nose*

ON March 28, 1846, two days before Houston took his seat
in the Senate, the citizens of Matamoros were startled to see American troops encamped across the Rio Grande at Port Isabel, General
Zachary Taylor's new supply depot. Other troops aboard ships bearing into the depot, were singing:

> *Oh, say were you ever on the Rio Grande?*
> *Way, you Rio.*
> *It's there that the river runs down golden sands.*
> *For we're bound for the Rio Grande.*[1]

The troops had been assembled in accord with President Tyler's
pledge to protect Texas while annexation terms were being completed. Taylor sailed with the Third Regiment for Corpus Christi on
July 23, 1845 under orders from Polk.

When the Mexican government changed hands in January, 1846,
Polk once more had sent John Slidell to Mexico with new offers of
negotiation, compromise, and financial compensation. Again the
Mexican government refused to negotiate, and Slidell returned home.
This left Texas open to harassment or invasion. An uncertain but
disturbing amount of activity by Mexican troops along the Rio
Grande was reported. On February 3, 1846, Taylor was ordered to
move from Corpus Christi to the Rio Grande as soon as weather permitted. When they arrived at Port Isabel, his troops beheld Mexicans
swarming on the tiled roofs of their homes in Matamoros and staring
back from across the river.

Taylor's representative, General William J. Worth, crossed the
river to Matamoros on March 28 with a flag of truce and talked with
José Antonio Mexia's representative, General R. D. de la Vega. An
American lieutenant read to de la Vega a statement in French from

Taylor. It said that his troops were on the left bank of the river to take peaceful possession of Texas as far as the Rio Grande. Taylor said he was acting on orders from President Polk and expressed the hope that the Mexican commander would not regard the intrenchment as an occasion for hostilities.

After de la Vega had listened to this statement, which had been translated into Spanish, he asked if General Taylor proposed to remain on the left bank of the river. Worth answered that Taylor would remain there until he received contrary orders from the United States government. When Worth was refused permission to see the American consul at Matamoros, he ended the parley with a warning, "I have to state that a refusal of my demand to see the American consul is regarded as a belligerent act; and in conclusion I have to add, the commanding general of the American forces on the left bank of the river will regard any passage of any armed party of Mexicans in hostile array across the Rio Grande as an act of war, and pursue it acccordingly." [2]

General Taylor erected defenses which he called "Fort Texas." When Mexican troops crossed the river a few miles below the fort, he assumed that Mexico's commander was prepared to risk war, a conclusion in which he was eminently correct. On April 12, 1846, General Pedro de Ampudia, Mexia's successor, sent word to Taylor that unless he withdrew within twenty-four hours to the far bank of the Nueces River it would be taken to mean that he had provoked war. Taylor did not withdraw, but asked the commanders of United States warships off Point Isabel to blockade the mouth of the Rio Grande. Ampudia charged that the blockade was an act of hostility.

General Manuel Arista, an abler and more daring general than Ampudia, was put in command on the right bank. From Mexico City, the dictator Mariano Paredes y Arrillaga, wrote to his new commander that he must take the initiative and that hostilities should begin. On April 23, Paredes announced to his Congress that a defensive war had begun.

Arista was the general who had outsmarted Lamar during the Santa Fe expedition. He believed that he knew Americans and he had no fear of them. His orders were to locate and attack the American army wherever he found it. He sent a large cavalry force under

Captain Torrejon across the river above Taylor's fortification. This force was reported to Taylor to number 2,500 men, probably a gross exaggeration.

Taylor sent a squadron of dragoons, 63 men, under Captain Seth B. Thornton to scout the area. A Marylander, known for his recklessness in courting danger, Thornton proceeded sixteen miles up the river to the Carricito Ranch. Thornton's lack of caution while questioning Mexicans at the ranch resulted in the corral gates being closed on him and his men. Surprised by Torrejon, the Yankees were sitting ducks. Sixteen were killed, including Thornton and Captain William J. Hardee, a West Pointer. Forty-seven prisoners were sent to Matamoros.[3]

The Mexicans would have done well to heed Houston's basic strategic doctrine. Repeatedly, he had warned those of his countrymen who were eager to invade Mexico: *"My rule is, when my hand is in the lion's mouth, not to strike him on the nose!"*[4] Some analysts have suggested that Mexico ventured into war under the impression that the United States was weak and divided. This belief is supposed to have been encouraged by the bitterness and excitement that prevailed in the United States during the period when annexation was under discussion. The Mexicans' error was in assuming that a violently divided country would be unable to unite sufficiently to fight a successful war. They seemed to disregard completely the possible influence of Sam Houston, who had been at war with Mexico, one way or another, for the past decade.

On April 26, 1846, General Taylor informed the United States government, "Hostilities may now be regarded as commenced."[5] President Polk was more remote from his commanding general on the Rio Grande than today's President is from a submarine under the polar ice cap. He did not receive General Taylor's report until May 9, 1846, at six o'clock, two weeks after Torrejon's raid had occurred. That evening, he called in a number of senators, among them Sam Houston, who urged vigorous action.

In his message to Congress on May 11, Polk stated that American blood had been spilled by Mexicans on American soil. This assertion was correct in view of treaties and the sequence of events, but ownership of the soil where the episode occurred was still in dispute.

Polk did not ask for a declaration of war, but said that since war existed regardless of efforts to avoid it, the United States was called upon by every consideration of duty and patriotism to vindicate the rights and interests of the country.

In a surge of patriotic fervor, the House of Representatives passed a resolution declaring that war existed, and authorized a call for 50,000 volunteers. It looked as if President Polk easily would have his way. But when the House war resolution came up in the Senate, Senator Calhoun argued for delay. He feared that a precedent might be set by which a President could maneuver the country into a war without a constitutional declaration by Congress. Houston anticipated that the Senate might become entangled in one of those factional fights that had delayed action on the Oregon question. As a member of the Military Affairs Committee, he made a restrained three-minute speech urging that the "state of things required prompt action—not discussion." He concluded by saying he hoped the question would be put. But Calhoun insisted on delay and the Senate did not vote.[6]

On May 12, Houston tried again. He presented the "true position" of the United States in relation to Mexico. His conviction, he said, was that the United States and Mexico "were actually in a state of war."

> ... War had existed for ten years between Mexico and Texas; and it had been declared in advance on the part of Mexico, when the question of the annexation of Texas to the United States was agitated, that if that annexation took place the war would not only be continued against Texas, but war would be proclaimed also against the United States... Texas having in the meantime become a portion of the United States, the Government of the United States was now placed in the situation occupied heretofore by Texas in relation to Mexico. War, therefore... unquestionably existed between Mexico and the United States.... The United States was therefore, placed precisely in the situation in which Texas had been for the last ten years, subject to the aggressions, incursions, inroads, attacks, and outrages of the Mexican forces, acting in obedience to the commands of the constitutional authorities of the Mexican Government....[7]

The next day, May 13, 1946, the Senate passed the war bill by a vote of 40 to 2.

3. A Voice of Confidence

NEW ENGLAND abolitionists professed to see an extension of slavery in war with Mexico. Representative Joshua Giddings of Ohio, a stalwart with massive head, flowing white hair, and deeply lined face, supported the New England position. When an administration bill for war expenses was introduced in the House, Giddings denounced the war as "against an unoffending people . . . I shall vote against the bill under consideration and all others calculated to support the war." [1] This example inspired further bitter partisan opposition and President Polk and all his works were savagely assailed. Houston continued to come to the President's support.

The news of General Taylor's victories over greatly superior forces at Palo Alto on May 8, 1846, and Resaca de la Palma on May 9, did not reach Washington until two weeeks after Polk signed the war bill. A dozen of Taylor's men were killed and some 50 wounded in the two days of fighting; 2,300 Mexicans were killed or wounded and General Arista lost a great quantity of supplies, mules, and baggage. General de la Vega was captured by the Americans. To a mild degree, Taylor's victories awakened the martial spirit of the country; outside of New England, the war showed signs of becoming popular. Hit on the nose, the lion lashed its tail a bit; it took a tentative hold, but one that could scarcely be called a bite, on the hand that had been thrust into its mouth.

Back in Texas during the late summer and early autumn of 1846, Senator Houston explained to his constituents that the excitement over Oregon and the Mexican War had made it impossible to accomplish much in matters particularly affecting their state. Delayed on his return journey to Washington by a steamboat accident on the Mississippi, he took his seat in the Senate some two weeks after the session resumed.

The political atmosphere was clouded; the attacks on President Polk continued. Senators charged that the Mexican war was "Polk's war" and that he alone was responsible for it. Some asserted that the territory of Texas stopped at the Nueces River and did not go to the

Rio Grande; hence the armed forces of the United States had advanced through disputed territory to a position they had no right to occupy. In other words, the boundary of Texas was in question. The abolitionists violently opposed pressing the war. Doubts were expressed that victory could be achieved. Senator Calhoun declared that the nation's objectives had already been achieved, that active war should cease, and that the country should go on the defensive and wait until Mexico sued for peace.

Then, in February, 1847, Polk asked the House for an appropriation of $3,000,000 to enable him to negotiate a treaty with Mexico. The terms were such that the money could be used for financing war operations or finagling with Mexican plotters. Houston spoke in support of this measure on February 19, 1847. He defended President Polk and dealt with most of the basic issues of the war as he himself saw them. With various interruptions, he was on his feet for several hours. On the question of the President's sole responsibility for bringing on the war, the reporter paraphrased Houston:

> ... He [Senator Houston] could not for a moment agree with some honorable members of this body, that the present war was a war of the Executive of the United States. He could not agree that it was a war brought on by the President ... and only by him. It was a war which grew out of circumstances, which are now known to the world. It was known before Texas was annexed, that war would result. That was predicted again and again. It was declared by the Mexican Minister to this court, that war would be the instantaneous consequence of annexation. It was also declared by Mr. Bocanegra, the Mexican Secretary of State for Foreign Relations, to Mr. Thompson, our Minister at Mexico.... Mexico then declared war prospectively against the United States ... from the moment annexation took place, these two nations were towards each other as belligerents....[2]

He discussed the boundary questions as no one else could have done; he had created that boundary himself and had won recognition of it by the United States and the nations of Europe:

> ... Was, then, the President justified in marching the troops to the frontier of Texas? ... He was justified on every principle that could actuate a nation, and by self-respect, to occupy the territory as far as the Rio Grande. That territory had been

understood to belong to Texas... in 1836 when she defined her boundaries [by a law that Houston himself wrote],... she claimed the Rio Grande to be her boundary. This was before... recognition. She was entitled to that boundary, and she had assumed and declared it....

But who had now set up this assumption of right to the country lying between the Nueces and the Rio Grande? Was it Mexico? Mexico never fixed the boundaries at the Nueces. Mexico contended for no division of the territory; with her it was either all Mexican or none. If Texas did not belong to the United States to the Rio Grande, no territory belonged to her beyond the Sabine....

This was an argument which never could be disposed of by logic. Houston went on to say that President Polk had not transcended his power or duty in marching an army to the Rio Grande but would have been negligent of his duty had he not done so.

Houston saw the war as one who had been a principal actor in the events leading up to it. It was obvious that Mexican dictators proposed to continue to harry Texas, now part of the United States, just as they had done during its independence. They not only refused to give up their claims of sovereignty over Texas, but were taking a position, theoretical and tactical, that would permit them to hang onto the flank of the United States until they succeeded in reannexing Texas or were beaten in the field. As much as Polk himself, Houston was dumfounded by the lack of understanding displayed by the administration's opponents.

Next he dealt with the new position taken by Senator Calhoun. Calhoun had pleaded with the Senate to recognize that the nation's war aims had been achieved. Invasion had been repelled, Calhoun said; the United States had firm control of the Rio Grande and held sufficient Mexican territory to enforce an indemnity for costs, repudiated debts, and injuries to American citizens. Houston vigorously protested Calhoun's proposal. He said that the honorable gentleman was not allowing for the peculiar fighting conditions down there and for the stubbornness of Mexico's leaders. To sustain a defense line on the Rio Grande as proposed, he said, would require at least 10,000 well-equipped men and greater cost than an invasion of Mexico itself would require. It would take millions of dollars for transportation alone.

During the previous summer on August 6, 1846, a farmer and a Democratic representative from Pennsylvania, David Wilmot had offered an amendment to an appropriation for war expenditures. Known as the Wilmot Proviso, it stipulated that slavery should "forever be excluded" from any territory acquired by treaty with Mexico. The House passed it. The North agitated for it, and the South flamed with anger. Senator Butler of South Carolina called it "treason." Senator Calhoun said the South would secede rather than submit.

Profoundly disturbed by the violence and threats provoked by the proviso, Houston had not seen the necessity at the time of declaring his position on the amendment or on slavery. The proviso had been filibustered to death at the end of the session. But the slavery question was continually intruding on all discussions relating to the war. On February 19, 1847, in the same speech, Houston took his stand on the slavery issue. He deplored its existence. The violence with which its adherents and opponents attacked each other alarmed him. He pleaded for calm and common sense. "Discussion of this subject is premature," he said. "It is not a question that necessarily grows out of the war. This calamity [slavery] was not brought on by ourselves but by our ancestors."

This was the second time he formally declared his attitude on slavery. The first had been when he gave his presidential message to the Texas legislature in May, 1837. Earnestly he pleaded with his fellow senators to avoid angry discussion of this question until the proper time came to consider it. The account of his remarks by the reporter continues:

> The question [slavery and disunion] was not raised for our good. Why, was not the North dependent on the South? And was not the South dependent on the North? Would it not be to each a suicidal act? and to both destruction? Disunion! It was a monster; and if he could, he would seize upon its mane, drag it forth, and inspect its scales, and if it had a penetrable spot, he would strike it to the vitals.
>
> He relied on the intelligence of the country to avoid that agitating question. He would postpone it. It was an evil which ought not to be invited; but when it shall come, let it be managed with the judgment of reasonable men, and not by passionate excitement.

Following early victories, the war had progressed slowly and the Americans had suffered a variety of setbacks. General Taylor's inefficiency as an organizer and his neglect of camp sanitation was causing the death of thousands from diphtheria, yellow fever, and smallpox. Politicians, journalists, and many citizens questioned the ability of the nation to win the war. Houston stoutly maintained that victory could be achieved:

> ... We *can* conquer Mexico. ...
> Penetrate into the interior with your arms. March on! And if you inflict a shock on the mind of Mexico, follow it up with rapidity, and you will be able to dictate peace in the halls of Montezumas, or wherever else you please, even on the sacrificial stone in her capital.

Behind this plea was the avenging spirit of one who had had long experience with the dictators of Mexico—dictators who frequently misled their own people. Houston demanded the most energetic measures against the Mexican despots, but spoke with sympathy and pity for the people and urged military measures to protect them:

> ... Let them know we are not warring against the rights of their citizens—against the oppressed people of Mexico, nor their priesthood, nor their religion. Show them that you will respect their temples, treat their images with deference, and, however much you may differ from their religious opinions, teach them that they will be entitled to freedom of thought, and the most perfect liberty. Show them that you only intend to chastize their tyrants, and oppressors.

Polk's request for the $3,000,000 appropriation passed the Senate by a liberal margin; and there were signs that the views of the administration as presented by Houston were taking hold of the country at large.

4. *The Fateful Victories*

AFTER the adjournment on March 4, 1847, Houston hurried home without waiting for the brief special session that followed. His old friend, Dr. Ashbel Smith, had removed a breast cancer for Margaret, who was staying with her brother, Vernal, at Grand Cane. Houston found his wife doing well after the operation and promptly wrote to Smith to thank him for his skill and his kindness to Margaret.

This was the summer of General Winfield Scott's fateful victories, which followed those of General Taylor. Taylor had dramatically reported a smashing triumph in a two-day battle at Buena Vista, February 22 and 23, 1847, over the greatly superior forces of Santa Anna. There were those who said that the victory was produced by the abilities and courage of Taylor's junior officers and of the troops rather than by Taylor himself. Some were mean enough to say that the credit belonged to the general's horse, Old Whitey, and that the horse should have had the nomination for the Presidency which the Whigs tendered Taylor one month later. Anyhow, the war in the northern Mexican theater was over. The scene shifted to even more phenomenal successes in another theater.

In early April, General Scott began a 250-mile march from Veracruz to Mexico City. With a force of 10,000 men, he intended to take a metropolis of 100,000 inhabitants. Scott made a distinction between the Mexican people and their oppressors, probably without knowing that Houston had argued for this policy in the Senate. He issued friendly proclamations. On April 11, he addressed one "To the Good People of Mexico," declaring the Americans to be "not your enemies, but the enemies, for a time, of the men who, a year ago, misgoverned you and brought about this unnatural war between the great Republics." [1]

Though authorized to do so, Scott did not seize Mexican supplies for sustenance. Believing, as did Houston, that the sure road to victory was through friendliness with the people, he paid for what he took. He required his army to respect the Mexicans' religion and their religious symbols. The clergy, disgusted with the tyrannies and brutalities of the dictators, urged non-resistance. Scott's own policy and the attitude of the clergy contributed substantially to his success. The *señoritas* also welcomed the troops with extended arms.

Scott defeated Santa Anna at Cerro Gordo on April 18, 1847. By the end of April, his troops occupied San Carlos de Perote, where prisoners from the Santa Fe expedition and the Mier fiasco had been confined. Six weeks from the time Scott left Veracruz, his army was on the great plateau of Mexico, a mile and a half above sea level within 200 miles of the capital. After a considerable delay he pushed on. Outnumbered, he stormed the defenses of Mexico City and entered the capital on September 13, 1847. This virtually ended the war—but not quite. Even after their city was taken, the Mexican dictatorship would not make peace. Difficult negotiations took the place of actual warfare. Peace would not come until General Scott took the defeated government, which was threatened by rival factions, under his protection.

In the United States, sounds of dissension could be heard above the rejoicings over Scott's victories. Americans turned themselves into a committee of the whole and started cracker barrel debates on how much, if any, territory should be taken from Mexico. In Kentucky, Henry Clay sponsored a convention that declared itself for peace without annexation of any territory. In Springfield, Massachusetts, Webster cried again that the war was unnecessary and unjust. As always, he was opposed to the acquisition of new territory by treaty and saw no necessity for the formation of new states.

When news of this agitation reached Senator Houston in Texas, he took action to combat the "no new territory" campaign. On December 25, 1847, he addressed a meeting at Huntsville, Texas, and proposed a set of resolutions that he had composed. According to his resolutions, the war had been brought on by Mexico, the almost unanimous declaration of war by the United States Congress was "the echo of public sentiment throughout the nation," and the "doctrine of 'no territory' was the doctrine of 'no indemnity.'" If this doctrine were sanctioned, it would be a "public acknowledgment that our country was wrong and...the war...unjust...and degrading to our national character." On the question of slavery, he resolved that, "we abide by the...Federal constitution; that no State has any right to interfere with the domestic institutions of a sister State; and that all interference on this subject by Congress or individuals is unfortunate for the peace of the Union, and still more unfortunate for the happiness of the slave." [2]

The resolutions were unanimously adopted. Armed with them, Houston returned to Washington for the first session of the Thirtieth Congress which convened in December, 1847.

He saw two important new faces among his colleagues. Mississippi had sent tall, austere Jefferson Davis, who was still on crutches from a wound received at Buena Vista. Illinois had sent swarthy, energetic Stephen A. Douglas; the stocky man with the giant head and strong intellect had been promoted from the House of Representatives by his constituents for his forthright support of Polk on the Oregon controversy.

In the House of Representatives there was a new member from Illinois: Abraham Lincoln, a tall, sallow-faced, awkward man had drawn a poor seat in the back row among the Whigs. Near him sat frail Alexander H. Stephens from Georgia, the future vice-president of the Confederacy. On both sides of the aisle were able, strong-willed men who one day would oppose the awkward man from Illinois during the crisis that was fast approaching. Whether or not Congressman Lincoln had read Houston's speeches on the boundary question, he did not agree with Houston's position. He knew too little about the causes of the Mexican War and the boundary issue to depart from the Whig "party line." On January 3, 1848, he voted for a resolution assailing the war as "unnecessarily and unconstitutionally begun by the President of the United States." [3]

The resolution failed, and a few days later Lincoln introduced resolutions of his own. He charged that Polk's claims to the "disputed" territory were "the sheerest deception," that the American boundary was not at the Rio Grande, and that the only citizens "whose blood had been shed [before war actually began] were soldiers advancing into disputed territory." He demanded that Polk indicate the "exact spot" where the first blood was shed. Lincoln had not investigated the subject, and his speech and resolutions merely rehashed old Whig views. Polk totally ignored him.

The Democratic Illinois *State Register* exclaimed, "Thank Heaven, Illinois has eight representatives who will stand by the honor of the nation. Would that we could find Mr. Lincoln in their ranks doing battle on the side of the country as valiantly as did the Illinois volunteers on the battlefields of Buena Vista and Cerro Gordo. He will have a fearful account to settle with them, should he lend his aid in an effort to neutralize their efforts and blast their fame." [4]

Lincoln, choosing not to modify his position, continued voting in support of all Whig resolutions designed to make political capital by condemning the origin and conduct of the war. But, along with most Whigs, he took the realistic view when it came to supply bills and the annexation of territory, voting for them as they came up. And when a radical anti-expansionist group pressed a resolution demanding peace without indemnity and the withdrawal of the American army to the east bank of the Rio Grande, he refused to vote for it.

In the Seventh Illinois District, because of his demand that Polk indicate the exact spot where blood had first been shed, Lincoln was nicknamed "Spotty," a stigma he would find it hard to live down. Alarmed by the outcry, his law partner, William H. Herndon, implored him to fall in line with public opinion. Lincoln vigorously defended his course, but still without investigating the boundary question and events on the border. As Herndon feared, Congressman Lincoln was reproved by his constituency, which refused to return him for a second term. Retiring to his law practice, he had time to think about the course of national events.

A strong nationalist, Senator Douglas struck out boldly in support of Houston's position. He did not specifically attack Lincoln, but assailed the position that Lincoln had supported. Said Douglas: "America wants no friends, acknowledges the fidelity of no citizen who, after war is declared, condemns the justice of her cause or sympathizes with the enemy. All such are traitors in their hearts; and would to God they would commit such overt acts for which they could be dealt with according to their deserts." [5]

Lincoln's indictment of the war had made no particular impression upon Houston. Lincoln was then an obscure figure, generally regarded as a somewhat queer fish and a droll westerner of not more than ordinary ability. At this time, too, Houston was preoccupied with preparing speeches to support the administration and to counteract the "no indemnity" propaganda of more outstanding figures than the man from Illinois. The Huntsville resolutions now became his mandate for his prophetic role in the concluding act of the annexation drama.

Thomas Jefferson had had the vision of a great free and independent empire spreading across the western half of the continent. John C. Calhoun appreciated the grandeur of westward expansion, but feared the acquisition of more territory where climatic conditions would discourage slavery. The dynamics of manifest destiny did not sing for Clay and Webster; if they had controlled the nation's future, San Antonio, San Diego, Los Angeles, and even Seattle might be foreign soil today.

In some respects, the shadow of Andrew Jackson fell upon Sam Houston. They shared the same faith in the sovereignty of the people, the vitality of the Constitution, and the indestructibility of the Union. But Jackson had believed that the nation's territory and population should be concentrated; he favored the annexation of Texas not because he shared the expansionist dream but because he feared that England might become established on the southwestern threshold of his country. Thus, Houston was not indebted to his Old Chief for his vision of an invigorated nation expanding its boundaries across the southern portion of the continent "from the sunrise to the sunset ocean." These words of his measured a dream long cherished. When the annexation of Texas was in doubt, he had warned the United States that unless Texas was received into the Union the glory of the "American nation" had culminated and the states could expect to share the continent with a hostile Anglo-Spanish rival. Now, hoping to obliterate this menace for all time, he ceased to be Polk's defender and, in his own right, became a passionate advocate of the necessity of the war and the justice of a huge indemnity.

Houston's views and proposals, appraised in the light of today's standards, would have to be rated imperialistic. He may have been an imperialist, but he was something more—the boldest and most vocal of all American imperialists of all time. Like that ancient goddess, Nemesis, he now stood for the most fearful retributive justice. During a decade of Mexican vacillations and badgering, of refusals to make a reasonable peace and of cruel reprisals, he had endured ceaseless anguish under constant threats of invasion and reconquest. By the force of his personality, he had held the Lone Star Republic together until it was commonly known as "Houston's Republic." No wonder that now, a repatriated American, he pleaded with his fellow citizens to give no heed to the no indemnity advocates.

In February, 1848, he dropped his duties in the Senate and went on a speaking tour to combat the anti-expansionists of New England. He was mildly heckled in Boston and Hartford, but in New York on Washington's birthday, addressing a Democratic rally under Tammany auspices, he was constantly interrupted by explosive applause.

... I sympathize, indeed, with Mexico. I have no antipathy to gratify against her, but while I can divest myself of all hard feelings towards her, I cannot divest myself of a holy devotion to my country, and her righteous cause; and I must spurn the man who would prove recreant to the cause of his country, and espouse that of an alien. [Three cheers called for, and rapturously given.] I cannot regard as fellow-citizens the men who array themselves against the cause of their country, who defame its armies and the glory they have acquired for the nation; who array themselves against the administration of their country, and seek to strengthen the hands of the enemy. Such people do not reflect, or they have forgotten all wisdom of the mind. Impelled by faction, they are the enemies of their country's cause—... while they reserve all their feelings and piety for "poor Mexico" and care nothing at all about ... their own country....

As surely as tomorrow's sun will rise ... so certain, it appears to my mind, must the Anglo-Saxon race pervade the whole southern extremity of this vast continent, and the people whom God has placed here in this land, spread, prevail, and pervade throughout the whole rich empire of this great hemisphere.— The manner of the consummation of this grand result, I cannot predict; but there is an instinct in the American people which impels them onward, which will lead them to pervade this continent, to develop its resources, to civilize its people, and receive the rich bounties of the creating power of divine Providence....

I do not think the war with Mexico is such a calamity as it has been deplored to be.... The ways of Providence are inscrutable; but I think we may see the finger of God in this war, giving success to our arms, and crowning our forces with victory. I do not deplore it ... I say, the Divine Being has been evidently carrying out the destiny of the American race. We give to the Mexican liberal principles; we elevate them far above

516

what their tyrants have done; and the day will come when they will bless the Americans as their friends and liberators until time shall cease....[6]

At the time Houston made this speech, he did not know the outcome of negotiations in Mexico. On February 2, 1848, the Mexican commissioners had finally ventured to sign a treaty of peace at Guadalupe Hidalgo, a suburb of Mexico City, after General Scott assured them protection from their discontented fellow countrymen. The treaty had been prepared by Secretary of State James Buchanan and submitted by Nicholas P. Trist, Chief Clerk of the State Department. It provided that the Rio Grande from its mouth to its intersection with the southern boundary of New Mexico was to be the international boundary. From there the line was to go to the Pacific to a point some fifty miles south of San Diego. As a consideration, the United States agreed to pay the $15,000,000 Polk had offered before the war and, in addition, to pay the debts that Mexico admittedly owed American citizens.

Some senators of both parties were unable to see "the finger of God" in the Treaty of Guadalupe Hidalgo. Daniel Webster declared that he wanted nothing to do with that Trist paper. Jefferson Davis wanted a boundary farther south to include most of four Mexican states beyond the Rio Grande. Houston objected to the treaty because it did not take enough territory.

The ceded territory comprised more than half of the land area possessed by Mexico when she first contracted for colonization with Moses Austin. It was greater in area than both Germany and France at that time; with Texas it included about 900,000 square miles. Was the vast territorial indemnity just or unjust? The victory cost many millions of dollars and many thousands of lives, although more men died from disease than from wounds. Of the 78,718 officers and men who served, 1,733 were killed in action, 4,152 were wounded, and 11,550 died from disease or accident.[7]

Commentators outside the Senate offered their observations on the treaty. William Tecumseh Sherman scornfully declared that the terms were as liberal as if Mexico had proposed them after winning the war. According to the *Journal des Debates* in Paris, this was sparing a foe who lay in the dust.

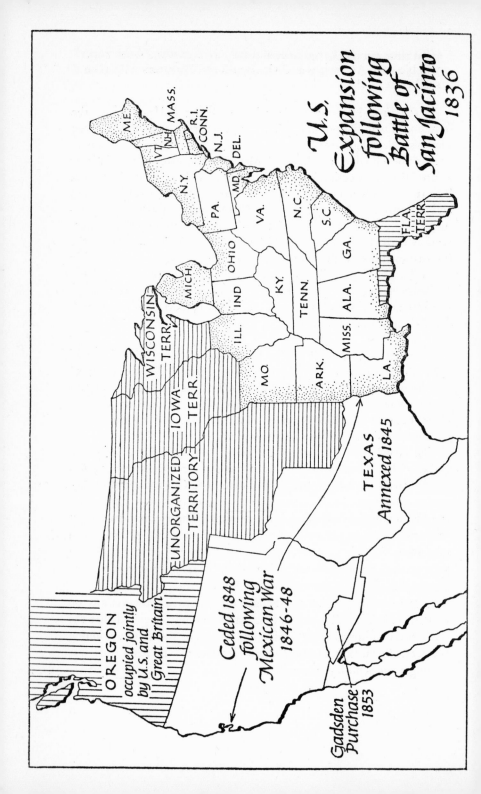

U.S.
Expansion
following
Battle of
San Jacinto
1836

MAINE
MASS.
N.H.
VT.
R.I.
CONN.
N.Y.
N.J.
PA.
DEL.
MD.
VA.
N.C.
S.C.
GA.
FLA. TERR.
OHIO
KY.
TENN.
ALA.
MICH.
IND.
ILL.
MISS.
WISCONSIN TERR.
IOWA TERR.
MO.
ARK.
LA.
UNORGANIZED TERRITORY

TEXAS
Annexed 1845

Ceded 1848
following
Mexican War
1846-48

OREGON
occupied jointly
by U.S. and
Great Britain

Gadsden Purchase
1853

On March 10, 1848, the Senate finally ratified the "Trist paper" 38 to 14, with negative votes equally divided between Whigs and anti-Polk Democrats. The Mexican government made it final in May, and by June American troops were singing on their way back across the Gulf to New Orleans.

While the negotiators had been haggling over the treaty in Mexico City, one James W. Marshall had found some bits of yellow metal at John A. Sutter's place on the American River in California. Sutter was not happy about this, fearing that it would interfere with his agricultural and industrial projects. Mexicans, searching the California mountains, had found traces of gold, but they had neglected the fields nearer the coast where Sutter's land stood. Word of the find did not become widely spread before the treaty was signed and, providentially, California belonged to the United States. Conceivably, had the magnitude of the discovery been known, the Mexicans would have balked at relinquishing California.

By May, 1848 the Americans had taken over California, and the news of Marshall's find thrilled the world. Rumors filled the news columns, and Polk mentioned the discovery in a message to Congress. The English and Irish heard of it and contributed a stream of immigrants. By late August of 1849, 400 wagons had passed through El Paso on the way to the gold fields. Soon Sutter's mill was surrounded by gold seekers washing gravel in dishpans and skillets.

The Forty-niners abandoned every vocation to pursue a quick fortune. They took the northern, the mid-continent, and the southern routes. Some went by clipper ships from eastern ports to Panama and traversed the jungle. Others sailed around the Horn; many went up the Rio Grande and overland through Camargo and Mier. On the way they fought, drank, gambled, and died of starvation, fever, and thirst.

No one knew how many started, how many fell by the way, or how many arrived. Colonizing brought some 40,000 Puritans to New England in the seventeenth century; in the ten years after 1850, California's population jumped from 92,000 to 380,000. It was the site of the world's biggest voluntary migration up to that time. Discovery of Sutter's gold accelerated the trend that Houston believed had long been indicated by the finger of God. The shape and form of this continental expansion under the Stars and Stripes instead of Mexican colors, was one of the many direct and indirect consequences of Houston's victory at San Jacinto, of his shrewd diplomacy while President of the Texas Republic, and of his resounding demands as an American imperialist.

BOOK VIII

TRUE VOICE OF THE SOUTH UNHEEDED

1. *The Battle with Calhoun*

SENATOR CALHOUN, always alert to the best interests of the South, carefully dissected the bill for organizing the vast Oregon territory when it came up for debate in August, 1848. The territory included three present-day states, Washington, Oregon, and Idaho as well as parts of Montana and Wyoming. In part, the bill reaffirmed the Missouri Compromise of 1820 which prohibited slavery north of latitude 36° 30′, along the southern boundary of Kansas. Senator Calhoun denounced the reaffirmation as evidence of Northern tyranny and an intention to throttle the South's economic power.

Calhoun, who did not comprehend the significance of industrial progress in the North, believed that the future prosperity of the South depended upon slavery. He held that slavery had benefited the Negro and was best for blacks and whites under prevailing circumstances. He maintained that the Negro received more care and other benefits and had less exacted from him than was the case with white laborers in most countries. He had fearlessly stated that the existing relationship between the two races in the South formed a durable foundation for free political institutions.

He had expressed these views in the Senate as early as 1837. Now, in 1848, he regarded the possibility of emancipation as a catastrophe for the South. He was convinced that if the North could not be persuaded or forced to acknowledge that slavery was morally right, secession must occur before the North became powerful enough to frustrate it. He warned his fellow senators in a dry, menacing manner that if they enacted the anti-slavery features of the Oregon territory bill without compromise they would put the slavery issue beyond compromise.

Calhoun's language and implications brought the Texas senator to his feet on June 2, 1848. Houston expressed completely divergent views, declaring that he would not regard it "inconsistent with the slave holding interests of the country if citizens of Oregon territory should inhibit slavery." As a Southerner, he himself would be "the last man to wish to do anything to prejudice the interests of the South," but he did not think that on all occasions Southerners were justified in agitating this issue.

> I am not one who feels disposed to croak . . . whenever this question is alluded to, believing that a crime is at hand, and that the Union is about to be dissolved. I have too much confidence in the integrity, intelligence and patriotism, not only of gentlemen upon this floor but of the people of this Union.[1]

After an all-night wrangle, the sleepy senators passed the bill at ten o'clock Sunday morning, August 13, 1848, by a vote of 29 to 25. The bill included an indorsement of the Missouri Compromise and received the affirmative votes of Houston and Thomas Hart Benton of Missouri. The evening before the vote President Polk had rejected Calhoun's plea that he veto the measure if it passed.

At home in Texas after the Senate adjourned, Houston read newspaper accounts of an inflammatory speech delivered by Senator Calhoun in Charleston. The South's defeat on Oregon, Calhoun said, was the more lamentable because it had been accomplished by the vote of two Southern senators, whom he denounced for defection from the South. Houston thus found himself represented as an enemy of the South; it could be that Calhoun was trying to drive a wedge between him and his Texas constituency. In his speech, Calhoun urged South Carolina not to participate in the coming Presidential election, but to take the lead in organizing a Southern Party to deliver an ultimatum to the North. He advised the Southern states to secede if the North remained unyielding and explained his major fear: the North would be able to frustrate secession if the South delayed such action.

The pro-slavery politicians and newspaper editors in Texas needed no more than a hint from Calhoun to attack Houston as a traitor for his Oregon vote. In speeches during the summer, he defended himself on the ground that his vote was squarely in line with his obligations and senatorial oath. He pointed out that Texans had specifically subscribed to the Missouri Compromise when they acted favorably upon the annexation resolution. For the moment, he refrained from mentioning Calhoun. Instead of retaliating sharply and immediately, Houston held his fire and made an intensive study of Calhoun's career from beginning to end. He examined his adversary's motives and objectives, giving special attention to Calhoun's position on tariff and secession issues. When the appropriate time came, Houston would be ready to fight.

After spending a few precious weeks with his family from mid-September to mid-November, 1848, Houston returned to Washington. On December 3, he wrote to his wife saying that he had had a headache for two days. He might have added that he was suffering from acute distress because regional animosities had been sharpened by the recent election of a Whig, Zachary Taylor to the Presidency. Taylor would take office in March, 1849.

When Calhoun reached Washington for the session of 1849, he, too, was ill. In bed, he prepared his call for a caucus of Southern legislators and completed a draft of "An Address of the Southern Delegates in Congress to their Constituents," commonly known as the "Southern Address." He hoped to persuade a caucus of Southern delegates to adopt the viewpoint put forth in the address. At length, he reviewed the wrongs which he believed the South had suffered at the hands of the North. He repeated his old charge that if the North was permitted to "monopolize all the Territories" it would soon have a majority power among the states and be able to emancipate the slaves by constitutional amendment. Then the slaves would be given the vote. With this alliance, the North would complete its domination of the South. The blacks and profligate whites who united with them would "be raised above the whites of the South in the political and social scale."

To forestall this course of events, Calhoun urged the immediate formation of a new Southern Party. Cautiously, he denied that the purpose of this move was "to cause excitement." No! It was merely to warn Southerners "of a deep-seated disease which threatens great danger to you." A final exhortation to unity closed the appeal:

> If you become united, and prove yourselves in earnest, the North will be brought to a pause, and to a calculation of consequences; and that may lead to a change of measures, and the adoption of a course of policy that may quietly and peaceably terminate this long conflict between the two sections. If it should not, nothing would remain for you but to stand immovably in defense of rights, involving your all—your property, prosperity, equality, liberty, and safety.... We hope, if you should unite with anything like unanimity, it may of itself apply a remedy to this deep-seated and dangerous disease; but, if such should not be the case, the time will then have come for you to decide what course to adopt.[2]

The time will then have come for you to decide what course to adopt. That was the snapper in the tail of the whip.

Eighty Southern legislators (Houston and Rusk of Texas and Benton of Missouri were not among them) responded to Calhoun's call and met in secret session in the Senate chamber. Calhoun clashed violently with heavy-set, strong-willed Robert Toombs of Georgia, who was still a dedicated Union man, although he became a militant secessionist within a year under the influence of Calhoun's persuasive principles. After Calhoun pleaded for hours, thirty-two Whigs and Democrats refused to sign what they regarded as an inflammatory and imprudent appeal. But Calhoun had his way just the same; forty-eight of the 121 congressmen from the slave-holding states, did sign. Forty-six of these were Democrats.

The Address was made public the next day, and Calhoun hurried to the White House to complain to President Polk about Southern senators who had refused to share in the movement and had used influence against it. Polk recorded in his diary that Calhoun spoke in excited terms of Texas members and declared that they had "betrayed the South."

The President answered that he would give "no countenance to any movement which tended to violence or the disunion of the States." Disputes should be settled in Congress, not in mass meetings with addresses to "inflame the country." In his diary he recorded his belief that Calhoun was bent on pressing the issue and did not even "desire that Congress should settle the question at the present session." [3]

When Houston read the Southern Address, he was struck by one of its sentences: "What then we do insist on, is, not to extend slavery, but that we shall not be prohibited from migrating with our property, into the Territories of the United States, because we are slaveholders."

To Houston, this was tortuous nonsense. Calhoun did not want to extend slavery; he merely wanted Southerners to be allowed to take slaves as property into the new territories! Houston believed he knew what had prompted the Address—Calhoun's ambition for the Presidency. On January 31, 1849, he wrote to Henderson Yoakum, one of his neighbors in Huntsville:

> Ah! we have had a Southron convention here—a second act (or so intended by Mr. Calhoun) of nullification. Rusk and myself smoked Johnny and would not indorse [sign the Address] for him. We are not done with him yet—but I think he has *nearly done with himself* . . . Whiggery has nothing to do with the question. It is "the Union" or "disunion." You know that I am as unionfier as General Jackson was, and cannot look with one grain of allowance upon any fanatical project while selfish and unholy ambition is to be gratified at the expense of the Republic. We [Texans] were among the last to come into it, and being in, we will be the last to get out of it. [4]

2. The Incurable Discord

CALHOUN's Southern Address was Houston's cue for action. On Texas Independence Day, March 2, 1849, he made public "An Address to My Constituents" which he had been preparing for six months. It began:

> To My Constituents: Soon after the close of the last session of Congress, my conduct in relation to an important public measure was called in question by Mr. Calhoun. In a speech at Charleston, he assumed that, but for my defection, as he was pleased to consider, and that of another Senator (Mr. Benton) from a slaveholding state, the bill organizing the Government of

Oregon would have been defeated, and thus another victory for the South, over the North, achieved.

It has always been my purpose to respond to this accusation, so evidently designed to injure me in the good opinion of my immediate constituents and the people of the whole South. In the hope that some proper occasion might take place during the session of Congress which would render retaliation proper, I forebore making it a matter of especial notice before the Senate, while I resolved not to let it pass unheeded. My motto is, "In time," not in haste. It evinces too much eagerness for oppugnation, and too little consideration for an opponent, who speaks as the representative of the whole South, to rush into a contest without examining well his position.

This cleared the decks, brought the action into focus, and set up another phase of the battle Houston would wage against Calhoun as long as Calhoun lived. Only on the surface was Houston's address to his constituency a reply to Calhoun's attack on his Oregon vote. Basically, it went much deeper. Houston's purpose was to combat and destroy Calhoun's generally accepted "leadership of the whole South." He raised the question whether Calhoun was or ever had been the true representative of the South's best interests, and warned that the South Carolinian intended to bring on a revolution that would break up the Union.

Senator Calhoun, in issuing what Houston called a "Papal bull" against two Senators for their Oregon vote, had presumed to speak as "the representative of the whole South." But by what authority did he "assume the character of guardian?" Houston asked in his address. It must be either "by virtue of divine right" or "the result of the voluntary submission" of those "over whom he presumed to assert his authority." And if by submission, then this submissiveness must be "founded on unlimited confidence in the sanctity, the unselfishness, the consistency of his principles and patriotism or [it must be] tendered him as a tribute of devout gratitude for extraordinary services rendered."

What, then, were these services? And did Calhoun actually have the confidence of the South? If he did, did he deserve it? "Has he ever represented . . . the true interest, the true glory, or the true feeling of the South in its domestic policy?" As Houston saw it, the answer to this question must be negative because of Calhoun's shifting attitudes on the tariff and his responsibility for the nullification crisis during the administration of Andrew Jackson.

Houston reminded his constituents that Calhoun had assisted in "imposing the first tariff yoke upon the South." Calhoun had contributed to the establishment of an iniquitous measure of "fraudulent minimums and other covert contrivances to build up the wealth" of Northern monopolies.

Houston described how, during Jackson's administration, Calhoun had urged "the South to redress itself through revolutionary convulsions" and had "phrenzied the hotheads of the South by incessant agitation ... Surrounded by well-instructed lieutenants he had been ready to take the field when South Carolina passed the ordinance of nullification." The firm actions of Houston's Old Chief—sending a force of warships to Charleston harbor and "certain whisperings" of this "very earnest old gentleman" about "the pains and penalties of treason"—had brought Calhoun and his supporters "to a stand, then to a retreat."

Houston declared that in both the tariff and the nullification crises, "The whole South, was made the sacrifice of the political game in which Mr. Calhoun's ambition [for the Presidency] had engaged him." Then he explained the connection between the Southern Address and Calhoun's Presidential aspirations:

> ... This vigilant guardian of Southern rights, who ... was ever ready to barter them, to attain his selfish ends, is now laboring to make more intense than ever the excitement of the question of slavery ... both at the north and south upon new and most ultra grounds. ... He cared nothing for consistency, principle or precedent. He wanted to create a new excitement at the North to reproduce at the South. His abstract resolutions for extending slavery every where, not being sufficient, the new question [introduction of slavery into California] ... is seized upon to create and inflame a state of incurable discord between the two sections of the Union by the arraignment of the North upon charges made by a Southern caucus, which he would have tried before a Southern convention. To embody this engine of revolution, has ever been in the scope of Mr. Calhoun's dismembering machinations. ... agitation in the North is looked to by Mr. Calhoun as an indispensable preliminary to effectuate his *revolutionary movements at the South*. ... in his late address he renews the idea that the North's interference with Southern

rights *"would be, among independent nations, just cause of war,"* and makes the effort to *"place the several States in the relation to each other of open enemies."*

He closed his indictment with expressions of pride that Calhoun's "long cherished and ill-concealed designs against the Union" had motivated "the denunciation aimed at me."

> ... —if opposition to all the schemes of mad fanaticism at the north and mad ambition at the south, which would embroil the country in civil war, provoke assault upon me, there is no man living who will give them a heartier welcome. It is some evidence that I stand in the way of the rash assailants and the deep plotters who would, to subserve their own unhallowed ambition, put in jeopardy the welfare and liberties of my country....
>
> I would lay down my life to defend any one of the States from aggression, which endangered its peace or threatened its institutions. I could do no more for the Union, but I wish to do more; for the destruction of the Union would be the ruin of all the States.... It is nature that teaches to cling to the Union. It is the best security against every ill that the weak have to apprehend. This feeling has been impressed upon my heart by the instruction and example of the great man whom, when a boy, I followed as a soldier ... and from whom as a statesman I never separated, until I wept over his yet warm remains at the Hermitage. The great trophy of his history will be the stern purpose with which he maintained the watchword of his administration, "The Federal Union, it must be preserved." [1]

Houston's attempt to destroy Calhoun's position as the leader of the South provoked cold hostility in the South Carolinian and brought invectives from his supporters. It was to have a moderating effect on the Nashville Convention, called to take action in support of Calhoun's Address, but its main consequence affected Houston himself. His six months of concentrated study of Calhoun's philosophy and leadership gave him profound insight into what was taking place. From the time he presented his answer to the Southern Address, he never wavered from his belief that Calhoun must be combated because, as Houston saw it, the South Carolinian's object was to make discord between the North and South incurable.

In February, 1849, Calhoun and his supporters had persuaded Senator Isaac P. Walker, a young, easily influenced Democrat of

Wisconsin, to propose an apparently innocuous amendment to an appropriation bill. The amendment provided for extending the laws of the United States over all the territory conceded by Mexico after the war. The joker was that Mexican law, which prohibited slavery, still prevailed in the new territory. The substitution of federal laws would open the door for slavery in all of that vast territory before national policy on this issue had been decided. Unaware of the significance of the amendment, the Senate adopted it. Senator Houston, deceived for the moment by its apparent innocence, was among those who voted for it.

Then Webster, in a clash with Calhoun, exposed its significance. The question of reconsidering the vote came up on Saturday, March 3, 1849, the day after Houston released his carefully prepared attack on Calhoun. The debate ran on into a tempestuous all-night session during which members exchanged curses and blows. Several were grossly intoxicated after repeated visits to the bar. Houston, the former "Big Drunk," took the floor to plead for orderly procedure. He said that he had "waded through scenes of anarchy and turbulence," but never had witnessed order reduced to chaos as on this occasion. He suffered "anguished feelings" to see Senators "agitated and discomposed." When order was restored, he remarked, "I will not rebuke the Senate. Every Senator upon this floor is capable of instructing and teaching me. But I can express my joy at the return of system and order." He followed this with an appeal to the Senate to reconsider its hasty action and withdraw its approval of the Walker amendment. He asked for an opportunity to change his vote.[2]

Congress adjourned on Sunday morning at six o'clock without providing a civil government for either California or New Mexico. Houston, already packed, hurriedly left for home without waiting to see the inauguration of the victor of Buena Vista.

Houston was the only Southern contemporary of Calhoun who dared publicly to expose the hidden labyrinths in the career of the South's great idol. As a result, his visit to his home was disrupted by the attacks of Calhoun's followers. He was upbraided for demagogism and classed with fools and traitors from slave states. James Gadsden, a South Carolinian and active ally of Calhoun, taunted him with having a defective education and branded him as one of the fanatics and fools who supported Northern oppression of the South.

Always tolerant of slighting remarks about his education, Houston answered that this was "an incidental misfortune, arising from my circumstances in early life." Then he condemned Calhoun's gloomy theories about Northern tyranny: "In my humble judgment, the course pursued by Mr. Calhoun, and the abolitionists, tend to the same end . . . the destruction of the Union, and the degradation of the country . . . to the control of reckless demagogues . . . to a condition of anarchy, weakness and civil commotion." [3]

3. *"They Must Stand Firm to the Union"*

AFTER an absence of seven years, seventy-three-year-old Henry Clay was returned to the Senate by a unanimous vote of the Kentucky legislature for the never-to-be-forgotten Thirty-first Congress. Preparing for his role as compromiser, Clay, on January 29, 1850, announced his intention to introduce certain resolutions that he hoped would quell the talk of disunion. He did not go into details in this first brief speech, but Houston knew that Clay could not win support for compromise until the bitterness engendered by Calhoun's agitation for secession was alleviated.

The blind submissiveness of some Southern senators to the South Carolinian made Houston's problem exceedingly delicate. He realized that if he took a stand for conciliation it would anger Southern extremists and possibly provoke serious political consequences for himself. This in no way altered his determination, but it led him to adopt a discreet tactical approach. He discussed what he intended to say with at least one newspaper correspondent in whom he had confidence. A few days before he spoke, it was reported in the press that Houston would make a Union speech but would forbear attacking Calhoun.

Eager crowds climbed Capitol Hill to hear Houston. He had hardly begun when Senator Samuel A. Foote, a Whig of Mississippi, interrupted to ask for suspension of the rules so that the people who had overflowed into the corridor from the galleries might be admitted to the floor. The crowd flocked in, and the chamber was packed. Ladies sat on stools between the senators' desks.

Calhoun was absent, and it was rumored that his death was imminent. Houston expressed regret for the South Carolinian's absence, especially since it was necessary for him to refer to Calhoun's position on important issues. "No one feels more sympathy for his physical sufferings than myself." Then Houston presented his theme that national discord was not incurable but could be alleviated by restraint and self-sacrifice:

> But I call upon the friends of the Union from every quarter, to come forward like men, and to sacrifice their differences upon the common altar of their country's good, and to form a bulwark around the Constitution that cannot be shaken. It will require manly efforts, sir; and they must expect to meet with prejudices ... that will assail them from every quarter. They must stand firm to the Union, regardless of all personal consequences. Time alone can recompense them for their sacrifice and their labors; ...

Historians of the period have remarked that during the years of the rising storm there were no proposals for an amicable conference between Northern and Southern leaders to formulate terms of compromise without publicity or excitement. But in his speech of February 8 Houston made exactly that suggestion:

> ... I have no doubt that this question might be easily adjusted, if gentlemen would encourage such disposition and feeling as doubtless actuate a large portion, if not all, of this body; if they would come up to the work, I have no doubt six Senators here could be designated, without reference to party, [or section], ... who would act as a committee of conference, and sit down together as wayfaring men, and produce satisfactory reconciliation, thereby diffusing universal peace, and calming the agitated waves that are lashing at the base of our Capitol, and speak comfort and solace to millions of freeman.

Partisanship and selfish ambition, he said, stood in the way of conciliation and compromise. "It is our great misfortune that opinion is manufactured here, to be disseminated throughout the country, ... to effect certain private or political ends." He opposed "this manufacture of opinion for home consumption—for the creation of a factitious popularity for members of this body...." Too many men were speaking on the subject "not to calm or allay excitement... but to irritate and increase it.... If, instead of saying that... the North has done such and such things, which are aggressive—if it were simply said that the *abolitionists* of the North had done it, and not the people, the fact would be correctly stated. If the fanatics of the North, ... were spoken of as a contemptible minority, far less harm would be done, ... it is wrong to malign the numerous friends of the South in the North by confounding them with the fanatics. ...They can do little by their own exertions... if they are not aided in their efforts to destroy the peace of the country by politicians who desire to manufacture capital for themselves. I do not hold the great North responsible for all this.... [nor] those men who are patriotic and sincere friends of the Union."

He regretted the constant threats emanating from his own region, particularly the movement to hold a convention of Southern states to denounce the North and to proclaim formally the right of secession. He assigned to the South, and specifically to the absent South Carolinian, a share of responsibility for the excited state of the country:

> ... the Southern Address ... was, in my estimation, not calculated to attain any valuable end.... I ... saw it was an affair and a part of the policy [of] the distinguished gentleman, the author of the address. He believed that it would not only be masterly, but masterful in the end. I believed it calculated to do no good, but that it would excite the southern people, and only drive them perhaps further on the road of separation from their northern friends, ... I knew we had fast and tried friends in the North, and that it was our duty to stand by them and sustain them ... some of them had been immolated ... and sacrificed for their devotion to the Union and the rights of the South. I believed also that the Southern Address was calculated to create sectional parties in the country, and that if we once created such parties, it would be an easy matter to dissolve this Union into sections also.

He outlined what he considered to be the basic difficulties:

> The North contend that they have a right to interfere with the subject of slavery; hence the Wilmot proviso. The South contend that the North has no such right—no right to interfere

534

with . . . slavery anywhere; and hence . . . does not possess this power as applicable to the Territories, [having] no power arising from the terms of the union between North and South— none growing out of the Constitution by which they are bound together.

As a possible solution, he suggested that the Missouri Compromise line might be extended to the Pacific coast. If this was done it might end the conflict. Slavery should be prohibited north of that line, and territories south of it should have a right to slavery if they desired. The Congress had no right "to impose upon states asking for admission to the Union any condition whatever, other than that of having a republican form of government."

Assuming that the North accepted this proposal "what would her sacrifice be? The sacrifice of fanaticism? . . . of a disposition to carry on a crusade against the right of their brethren of the South?" Did not the spirit of conciliation require the North "to discountenance a few fanatics who are rabid upon the subject of abolition?"

> . . . I beseech those whose piety will permit them reverently to petition, that they will pray for this Union, and ask that He who buildeth up and pulleth down nations will, in mercy, preserve and unite us. For a nation divided against itself cannot stand. I wish, if this Union must be dissolved, that its ruins may be the monument of my grave, and the graves of my family. I wish no epitaph to be written to tell that I survive the ruin of this glorious Union.[1]

Houston's effort to reconcile North and South found approval in New England and New York, but it was resented violently by some of his Southern colleagues. His stand was denounced in Texas and throughout the South, with a few exceptions, notably New Orleans. J. Pinckney Henderson, now an outright defender of the slave interests, lashed out at his old friend. To Ashbel Smith, Henderson denounced Clay's effrontery for proposing to yield to the North under the guise of compromise. He declared that Houston had outraged his state and the feelings of the whole South by submitting to the dictates of abolitionists.

After giving his speech, Houston left the capital on a hurried trip to Texas. His unexplained departure in the midst of national uproar provoked suggestions from some quarters that he had deserted his post to avoid accounting to his Southern colleagues for his stand. The truth was that a difficult domestic situation, largely the result of his being away from home during the greater part of the year, had developed into a crisis. His wife, again pregnant, had sprained her ankle. The house servants needed disciplining. The inefficient farm manager had let the pigs and cattle get into poor condition. Margaret's ward, Virginia Thorne, had eloped with the overseer, Thomas Gott. With the aid of local officials who were hostile to Houston, Gott had managed to get himself appointed Virginia's guardian. Houston, assisted by his attorney, Henderson Yoakum, managed to straighten out these matters during a brief stay in Huntsville.

Six days after Houston's eloquent plea for conciliation and compromise, Clay had introduced his eight compromise resolutions. He asked his fellow senators to consider them not as individual measures, but as a system. The resolutions dealt with such vexing problems as admission of California to statehood without slavery, establishing systems of government for territories acquired from Mexico, settlement of the Texas western boundary, the end of slave trade in the District of Columbia, and a more stringent Fugitive Slave Law.

Again a vast crowd had surged up Capitol Hill, this time with the hope of hearing the Kentuckian urge Congress to accept his controversial measures. He supported each of his proposals with equal firmness and declared that the Southern states had no right to secede. Realizing that his proposals were weighted against the South, he urged the North to take a magnanimous attitude toward his proposal for a stronger Fugitive Slave Law.

Clay's proposals were promptly attacked by the Taylor Administration and by Calhoun's followers. Expectations were intense when on Monday, March 4, 1850, Calhoun took his seat in the Senate. For weeks, severe illness had confined him to his rooms in a boarding house across the street from the capitol. Feeble, his cheeks sunken, his hair whitened, his steps uncertain, he entered the chamber on the arm of a South Carolinian, General James Hamilton. But his fire was still there, glowing intensely from brilliant flashing eyes; his straight-cut lips were firm and grim. Senators were shocked by his appearance. An impromptu welcoming delegation of friends and antagonists of the past several decades surged around him, among them Webster, Douglas, Clay, and Jefferson Davis. Houston was not there because of his absence on a grave domestic errand.

With his cloak drawn close around him, Calhoun waited for the hour assigned for his address, 1 p.m. He rose and, with an effort, stood as erect as at any time during his decades in public office, managing to make himself distinctly audible. With customary courtesy he thanked his colleagues for their consideration and announced that he had put his remarks in writing and would ask the senator from Virginia to read them. Sinking into his seat, he was able to sit stiffly upright. James M. Mason rose and read from a manuscript. It was a gripping moment. The speech was recognized as perhaps the last effort of a dying man obliged to listen to his own words as a spectator. Mason's voice rang out with boldness and challenge; but the speech was dry rationalism—bitter, hard, uncompromising, defiant, and strongly "disunionist." He demanded a constitutional amendment to restore and maintain the former balance between the two sections. If this was not forthcoming, the states should "agree to separate and part in peace." This demand was accompanied by his customary threat: if the North would not permit a peaceful separation, the South would know how to act when faced with the demand for "submission or resistance." [2]

After Houston's glowing appeal to North and South for tolerance and magnanimity and after Clay's proposals, Calhoun's speech was vastly out of keeping with what the situation called for. He did not offer one helpful suggestion. Had Calhoun made an earnest effort to suggest a solution, he would have unhorsed the abolitionists, deprived them of their cause, and won the respect and sympathy of the North and the whole world. Had he supported conciliation, the "incurable" discord might have been cured, and the "irrepressible conflict" repressed.

After Calhoun's speech was read, Webster delivered his famous Seventh of March Speech. He reviewed the slavery struggle and the causes of bitterness between the sections and discussed the futility of a rupture. Earnestly and eloquently, he followed the example of Houston and Clay in appealing to the North for tolerance. Although he was a New Englander, Webster deplored the inflammatory attitude of the abolitionists. He supported Clay's demand for a more stringent Fugitive Slave Law. His courage brought upon him the same kind of curses and defilement from Massachusetts that Houston received from Texas. Webster surely knew that he was sacrificing his last chance for the Presidency. But he had done much to turn back the rising tide of sectional hate and had contributed to the ultimate preservation of the Union by postponing the great conflict for a decade. By that time, the North was sufficiently strong and united to win. Houston and Clay had been strong front runners who had prepared the way for Webster's influence.

Calhoun's personal role in the battle of the statesmen was ended. On March 31, 1850, the bells in the South tolled their requiem for the great secessionist. Senate seats and desks were removed from the chamber so that Calhoun could lie in state. Butler, Rusk, and Webster delivered eulogies. But rugged old Thomas Hart Benton bluntly refused to raise his voice in praise of the departed. His reason: Calhoun was dead but his vicious principles would live after him.

During the week after his return to Washington in April, Senator Houston received word that his fourth child and third daughter had been born on April 9. He was now 57. He wrote to his wife that he was glad to hear that it was a little daughter, "tho' I would have been equally gratified if it had been a son." Young Sam, the father feared, would regard another sister as a personal injustice.[3]

Partly as a result of Houston's counsel, disunion sentiment in the South was declining at the time of Calhoun's death. But Calhoun had fiery young disciples who joined with his older followers in supporting his scheme for a Southern convention to demonstrate the South's ability as a "united power" to stand against the North. Houston denounced the enterprise with characteristic vigor as "a piece of ridiculous flummery." When the convention met in Nashville in June, it fizzled. Only nine states sent delegates, and the tone of the resolutions was moderate and conciliatory.

The Great Debate went on, its bitterness intensified by President Taylor's open opposition to Clay's moderate proposals. Houston again spoke in support of the proposals and used personal persuasion on members of the Senate and House. Then President Taylor, after attending a Fourth of July celebration at the foot of the unfinished Washington Monument, contracted typhoid fever and died within a few days.

After a month-long argument, a consolidated measure embracing all of Clay's proposals was outmaneuvered and the eight proposals were stricken from the bill. But Senator Douglas, Chairman of the Committee on Territories, promptly forced rescue of the "components" of the Kentuckian's compromise system. Houston fought for the claim of Texas to the Rio Grande boundary that he had recommended in his memorandum to the provisional government immediately after the battle of San Jacinto. This would have given Texas a large part of New Mexico, but in the end, Texas had to be content with a mere 33,333 more square miles of territory than Clay's original proposal provided. This provision was supplemented by ten million dollars, enough to pay off the state's public debt. Houston planned the strategy and was supported by Senator Rusk. Decisive majorities passed other separate parts of the defeated compromise, including the California bill and the stringent Fugitive Slave Law. Houston voted in favor of each.

By September, 1850, the Great Debate was over. Jubilation marked the end of the contest. Except for the Fugitive Slave Law, the differences that had threatened to split the Union seemed to have ended. To Daniel Webster, everything seemed changed; it was hard to believe that anyone had ever thought of disunion. Now Webster could sleep at night, comforted by the hope that disunion sentiments had been put down for a long time.

On the other hand, Senator Jefferson Davis complained that the balance between the sections had been destroyed in favor of the North. Douglas appealed for an end of the slavery discussion. Just before Christmas he told the Senate he had determined never to make another speech on the question. If the subject was dropped, he believed the Compromise would be recognized as a final settlement.

Houston, too, expressed himself on the outcome, but he probed the situation deeper and peered farther into the future than Webster. On January 24, 1851, he wrote to John Letcher, a strongly pro-Union Democrat of Virginia who later became governor of the state. Houston said he believed that the anti-slavery agitation in the free states was largely subsiding, and that the demogogues who were participating in it were deserting its ranks. But he foresaw the day when it would be renewed:

It may be asked whether a contingency might not arise when the duty every man owes to the fireside and homes of his family and friends would require him to surrender the Union. Undoubtedly such a sad spectacle might possibly be presented. Gross injustice, rank oppression, and persevering tyranny, might produce it, but I think that day will never come.... When it does, if ever, it will *be a law unto itself.* It will have to be met not by the evasive hypocrisy of secession, or nullification, or sectional conventions, but in the bold and manly spirit that actuated our fathers in the revolution—... In the mean time let us all ... contribute our utmost ... to subdue fanaticism and violence, to resist sectional encroachments, to restore kind and harmonious feeling, and to cherish those expansive sentiments of patriotism in which the constitution and the Union originated, ... [4]

4. *Conflict with Douglas*

AFTER the compromise bill was passed, the country settled down to a period of relative calm. Senator Houston had hoped that it would be so, but the surface tranquility had not deceived him into believing that Calhoun's separatist principles finally had been disposed of. His vote to admit California as a free state aroused much resentment in Texas. In October, 1851, he explained this vote in a speech at Huntsville.

One Texas newspaper reported that his argument was convincing and masterly but this was not the general opinion. Although his votes for the compromise measures stirred up violent opposition, it was not sufficiently strong to cause a political reverse. On January 16, 1852, a resolution nominating him for the Presidency passed the Texas House of Representatives. The unexpectedly large group of twenty-one dissenters signaled the growing discontent with Houston's position.

In January, 1853, the Texas legislature re-elected him to the Senate for the third time. Three out of 21 senators and 12 out of 67 House members voted against him. The opposition to his stand for compromise was strong and steady, but he was holding his own, and his eloquence could still move a hardy Texas audience to tears.

When the overwhelmingly Democratic Thirty-third Congress met in December, 1853, it was generally assumed that the major differences between North and South had been settled, except for the Fugitive Slave Law. Then Senator Stephen A. Douglas presented the country with an issue, imbedded in the Kansas-Nebraska Bill, that aroused bitterness in both sections, halted further reconciliation, and put the country on the road to war.

In the previous session, a bill to organize the Nebraska Territory had been introduced in the House of Representatives. Senator Augustus C. Dodge of Iowa introduced an identical bill in the Senate soon after the Thirty-third Congress assembled. When the bill was referred to Senator Douglas' Committee on Territories, it contained no mention of the Missouri Compromise. But when the committee reported it to the Senate it contained a new section permitting the people of Nebraska to choose whether they would admit or exclude slavery. By implication, this plainly overrode the Missouri Compromise restriction against the extension of slavery north of latitude 36° 30′. It foreshadowed an immense triumph for slavery partisans and would amount to a complete surrender to the demand of Calhoun and his followers for "equal rights" in the whole national domain.

The provision that questions concerning slavery in the territories and in new states should be left "to the people residing therein through their appropriate representatives" was the first clear enunciation of the principle of popular sovereignty. But slavery partisans were still unsatisfied. Senator David R. Atchison of Missouri, presiding over the Senate since the sudden death of Vice-President William R. King, brought pressure to bear on Douglas. Atchison, a follower of Calhoun, desired specific repeal of the Missouri Compromise and had the cooperation of four influential Southern senators: Archibald Dixon of Kentucky, Andrew P. Butler of South Carolina, James Mason, and R. M. T. Hunter, both of Virginia.

Senator Dixon argued along with Douglas that the Missouri Compromise should be repealed or slaveholders would not venture to take slaves into the new territory. A Whig, lawyer, and prosperous slaveholding planter, Dixon offered an amendment specifically repealing the Compromise. Douglas sent the bill back to committee. The revised measure that he reported to the Senate on January 23, 1854, divided the Nebraska Territory into two territories, Kansas and Nebraska; provided for their admission as states; and specifically repealed the Compromise slavery restriction.

That such a measure should have the support of Senator Douglas was most extraordinary. Five years before, he had told his Illinois constituency that the Missouri Compromise was held as sacred in the hearts of the American people, and no ruthless hand should ever be reckless enough to disturb it. Why did he now upset a principle that he had indorsed?

Some of the factors that influenced him are known; others are not and probably never will be. Douglas was eager for the construction of a transcontinental railroad by a northern route because it would benefit his Illinois constituents. If the road was not to follow a Southern route, the Nebraska territory had to be organized promptly to establish its definite relationship to the United States. To accomplish this, Douglas needed the support of Southern senators—those same senators who found the Compromise slavery restriction an affront to their pride and interests. He may have persuaded himself that the principle of popular sovereignty would re-invigorate and unite the Democratic party.

Then, too, if he succeeded in putting through the Kansas-Nebraska Bill with its repeal of the Missouri Compromise, it was not unreasonable to expect that he would become the Presidential candidate for the reunited party. Certainly he must have believed that the issues at stake justified his change, but he knew—and said—that the repeal of the Compromise would "raise a hell of a storm." [1]

Senator Salmon P. Chase of Ohio, leader of the extreme anti-slavery faction and an active aspirant for the Presidency, led Northern opposition against Douglas. He was supported by William H. Seward, another Presidential aspirant, and by Charles Sumner. Houston was unhappy to find himself on the same side as these outspoken abolitionists. Three years before he had warned of dangers to come if senators continued to manufacture opinion on slavery and to use the issue for personal political ends. He regarded Chase and Seward as chief offenders in this connection. They were what he called "higher law" men because Chase had argued that slavery had been condemned by a law of sublime origin. Therefore, Chase contended, any procedures—constitutional or otherwise—were permissible against slavery.

The brilliant, satirical, and eccentric Seward had locked arms with Chase in teaching the country that it was not bound by the Con-

542

stitution in dealing with slavery, but by a law of sublime origin. Seward had referred to this law in the Senate, March 11, 1850, when he opposed Clay's compromise measures; his later attempts to explain it away left Southerners unappeased and convinced that they must be ready to protect themselves against Northern lawlessness. Houston listened closely to all that was said and carefully formulated his own views.

Douglas answered the attacks of Chase and Seward in a vitriolic speech calculated to cloak the fact that he, too, was bidding for the Presidency. He charged Chase with having sold honor and conscience for a political advantage. A powerful debater who was quick to seize advantage, Douglas confirmed his title as the most aggressive pugilist in American legislative history. He fought with innuendoes and insults, emitted clouds of irrelevancies, lacerated his opponents with savage scorn, and demoralized them by the unscrupulous adroitness of his attack.

It seemed probable that Douglas' opponents would lose the contest when Houston came to their support. Rumors of his intention appeared in the press while he was preparing for the event. A full week before he spoke, the correspondent of the Richmond *Enquirer* wrote:

> I hear that General Sam Houston ... will vote against the Nebraska bill. Incredible as it may be, there is no doubt of the fact....
>
> Nothing can justify this treachery; nor can anything save the traitor from the deep damnation which such treason may merit.... The man who deserts at this crisis ... will be consigned to a proper fate. The South, with a blush of shame, and the North with secret delight, will alike look without sympathy to the execration of a man who is destitute either of the power to benefit or to injure. 'Hissing, but stingless,' let the viper crawl on.[2]

Houston began his speech on February 15, 1854, with a reference to the *Enquirer's* correspondent. He was not angry with this man, and would think badly of himself should he descend to the level of bitterness disclosed in this newspaper article. He was fully aware of Southern agitation against him, and, in the venom of this particular writer, he detected something prophetic. "He says that I am opposed to this bill. Yes, sir, I am...."

The provision to repeal the Missouri Compromise, he said, excited his repugnance because he had long "stood upon" this measure. The people of the South, although not its politicians, had sustained him. "Why?" he demanded. "Because it was regarded as a solemn compact, and because they are proud, chivalrous, just, and generous. I adopt no new course ... it is one which I have maintained since Texas ... formed one star of our constellation." He could not have failed to know the source and nature of the pressure that had been exerted on Douglas, but he chose to ignore it.

> I do not ... pretend to know, the origin of this measure. I do not conceive that there was the slightest necessity for its introduction; ... and when I saw the question of repeal come up ... I foresaw ... the agitation which must be renewed ... as one of the greatest misfortunes that could happen to us.... Sir, the consequences [of the Missouri Compromise] are too magnificent to be contemplated, too wide and expanded to be embraced at a glance.... it has been of vast importance to the prosperity, and glory of this country from that time to the present.... It is a compact, a solemn compact.... What is there which will give sanctity to the last compromise if you strip the former of all respect ... and trample it under foot? The word of one section of the Union should be kept with the other.

Throughout the debate Douglas was in his seat early in the morning and remained until the last word was spoken late in the afternoon. Attentive, he did not interrupt the Texas senator, but made mental notes for his reply. Houston went on speaking with conviction and accurately forecast coming events:

> ... sir, if it were opposing the whole world, with the conviction of my mind and heart, I would oppose to the last by all means of rational resistance the repeal of the Missouri compromise.... I deem it essential to the preservation of this Union, and to the very existence of the South. It has heretofore operated as a wall of fire to us. It is a guarantee of our institutions.... Repeal it, and you are putting a knife to the throat of the South, and it will be drawn. No event of the future is more visible to my perception than that, if the Missouri compromise is repealed, at some future day the South will be overwhelmed.
> ... I do not wish to be regarded as for the South alone.... I

am for the whole country. If I am, it is sufficient without re-hearsing it here. But, sir, my all is in the South. . . . My life has been spent there. Every tendril that clusters around my heart, every chord that binds me to life or hope, is there; and I feel that it is my duty to stand up in behalf of her rights . . . for her safety and security.

Then he spoke directly to his Southern colleagues:

The day, I fear, must come in the progress of our country—though God forbid that it ever should—that great trials and emergencies will grow up between the North and the South. The South is in a minority. She cannot be otherwise. . . . If the South accede to the violation of a compact as sacred as this, they set an example that may be followed on occasions when they do not desire it. . . . If you regard it as a sacred instrument, one to be esteemed and adhered to, you will find that its benefits will inure to you. But if you tear it up and scatter it to the winds, you will reap the whirlwind; . . .

In closing he reaffirmed his intention to resist every attempt to infringe upon or repeal the Compromise. "We are not acting alone for ourselves, but are trustees for the benefit of posterity. . . . those who come after us . . . are to be affected by the action of this body upon this bill. . . . They are either to live in after times in the enjoy-ment of peace, of harmony, and prosperity or [in] anarchy, discord, and civil broil. We can avert the last. I trust we shall. . . . so far as my efforts can avail, I will resist every attempt to infringe or repeal the Missouri Compromise." [3]

The date of this prophetic warning was February 15, 1854.

Three days later, Douglas replied to Houston in his most savage mood, raging against the notion that the Compromise had sacred aspects. Finally, he undertook to end the debate by obtaining an agreement for the Senate to vote on the measure on March 3. The debate on March 3 and 4 and the decision it led to proved to be one of the most fateful in the nation's history.

5. *Profile of a Patriarch*

SENATOR HOUSTON adopted the tone of a patriarch as he closed his speech of February 15, 1854. He reminded the Senate: "...thirty years ago I occupied a seat in the other end of the capitol...I have seen many changes...Mr. Pleasanton, the Fifth Auditor, is the only officer left of all who were then attached to the Federal Government....Ten Presidents have filled the Executive chair. Out of nearly three hundred...in the Senate and House... but three remain." These three were Representative Thomas Hart Benton, Senator Edward Everett of Massachusetts, and himself.

He quoted a poem descriptive of one who had seen friends around him "fall like leaves in wintry weather."

> *I feel like one*
> *Who treads alone*
> *Some banquet hall deserted;*
> *Whose lights are fled,*
> *Whose garlands dead,*
> *And all but he departed.*[1]

His emotional reference to past glories of the Union was prompted by a desire to soften the hard attitude of some of his colleagues who were against reconciliation between the North and South.

This patriarchal approach, appropriate to his experience, was barely justified by his age. After eight years in the Senate, he lacked two weeks of being sixty-one years old. Time, to be sure, had left its mark; twinges of pain reminded him of the days and nights when he had slept on the cold, wet ground or in drafty cabins in Arkansas and Texas. His shoulder wound opened and drained at times and never would entirely heal. Occasionally, his wounded leg bothered him and, limping slightly, he bore down heavily on his walking stick. He suffered from recurrences of malaria.

With all of these infirmities, he still was a striking figure, tall and inspiring, ready with hearty laughter and possessed of a strong sense of the comic. His facial appearance changed from time to time depending upon whether he happened to be wearing sideburns, close cropped or flowing, or a full beard. In general, he seemed to favor sideburns when matters were reasonably placid; in times of stress he let his beard grow.

The patriarchal note became prominent in all of Houston's relationships. Although he was absent from home eight or ten months of the year, he was a devoted father and experimented with a method of remote control for correcting and encouraging his children as they grew older. From Sam, Jr., he received a childish scrawl on June 17, 1852:

> Dear pa   mama has just read me what she wrote about me and I will try to be a better boy. My little mocking bird which I told you about is dead   my pony is doing well. God bless you Your affectionate son   Sam Houston, Jr.[2]

The busy Senator hastened to answer without waiting for Sunday, his regular day for writing home. Overlooking his wife's account of Sam's derelictions, he thanked his son for two "charming" letters. "You made me happy," he wrote on July 19, 1852, "because you told me all were well, and that you were happy. I hear all your matters with much pleasure." Then, as he did whenever possible, he contributed to his son's training by giving him a small responsibility, "Tell Joshua to have the filly in good order and well rubbed. I may ride her to court." He closed with a paternal injunction: "I hope you are obedient to your Ma, and studious. . . . When you say your prayers think how kind God is to all of us that he allows us to be happy." Across the margin of the page, he wrote, "I am sorry that your poor little pet died." [3]

Young Sam's behavior improved, then suffered a relapse. He annoyed his sisters and behaved selfishly. On February 2, 1853, Houston had disciplined his son with a carefully thought-out letter to his seven-year-old daughter, Nannie.

> My Dear Daughter, I send you a comic Newspaper. I intend to send you some pretty ones soon, & to my Dear Mag, also. I have sent them to my Son up to this time, but I do not intend to send him any more until he writes me, and asks for them. He has made my heart *sad*; I am fearful that he is too *selfish*, either to be happy himself, or to try to make others happy. I delight, my Daughter, that you try to make others happy, and thereby make yourself happy.

Kiss your Grandma, your Ma, & little Sisters for me. If Sam is *penitent*, you *may* kiss him for me!

P. S. I send your Dear Ma, and you, some evergreens from the *Tomb of Washington*.

This letter went to Texas addressed on the envelope to "Miss Nannie Lea Houston, care of her Dear Mother." [4]

On Sunday mornings and frequently in the evenings, Houston attended service at the Reverend G. W. Samson's fashionable E Street Baptist Church. He always occupied the same pew, well down front to the right of the middle aisle. During the long sermon, he whittled soft pine sticks into toys for children and heart-shaped souvenirs for ladies, leaving a mound of shavings for the sexton to clean up.

Offering one of these souvenirs to a lady, he would say with a gallant bow, "Madam, permit me to present you with my heart." Jefferson Davis' beautiful wife, Varina, received one. Kate, the proud daughter of Senator Chase, recorded in her diary after a visit to the Senate gallery that she wished Senator Houston would give her one of his famous hearts. Some thought the Senator's distribution of such souvenirs was ridiculous. The curious speculated on why he whittled in church; was he like an old lady who must always have her knitting handy? Actually, he had fallen back on a habit that helped him to concentrate and to resolve his problems; the Senator was engaged in a mighty struggle to decide whether he was fit to join the church and to take communion.

Back in March, 1846, the second Sunday after Houston's first appearance in Washington as a senator, Mr. Samson looked up from his pulpit and saw a tall form draped in a brightly colored serape coming down the center aisle. After the service, Houston told Samson that he had come out of respect for "one of the best Christians on earth," his wife. Samson expressed the hope that soon obligations even deeper than those that bound him to his wife would bind him to the House of God.

The struggle to see things the way Margaret and Mr. Samson hoped he would was prolonged and prayerful. L. D. Evans, a Texas congressman, lived in a room just under Houston's at Brown's Hotel; he knew every night and morning when Houston went to bed or arose because he heard the thump when the Senator knelt to pray.

At morning service, Houston fixed the parson's discourse in his mind so that he could abstract it in his Sunday afternoon letter to his wife. He strongly approved a sermon on the text, "Better is he that ruleth his spirit than he that taketh a city." It strengthened his convictions regarding his need and duty, but still he grieved Mr. Samson by his inability to announce his faith. For the benefit of his distinguished auditor, Samson preached on before-the-flood examples of saving faith—Abel, Enoch, and Noah; then, more significantly, on four characters of the patriarchal period—Abraham, Isaac, Jacob, and Joseph. But when new believers were invited to come forward, Senator Houston remained seated, deeply absorbed in his whittling.

His difficulty stemmed from recollections of a hell-fire-and-brimstone sermon that he had heard when he was a boy; eternal damnation had been promised those who unworthily took communion. Years would pass before a Texas clergyman would have the wit to explain that the preacher had misinterpreted Paul's denunciation of the Corinthians because they abused communion as an occasion for gluttony. A stern realist in military matters, diplomacy, and statesmanship, Houston was suspicious about authoritarian doctrine that could not be subjected to rational anlaysis. Mr. Samson directed Houston's attention to Nelson's *Cause and Cure of Infidelity*, which the Senator bought and later gave to many persons who expressed skepticism of Christianity. Just as he had preached temperance when he was a hard drinker, he spread the Christian doctrine to unbelievers before he accepted it for himself.

Still unsure of his true religious convictions, Houston maintained the habit of kneeling in prayer night and morning. Across the distance that separated them, he and Margaret united in imploring the Almighty to preserve the Union and to grant them another son. Some two years before, on January 20, 1852, they had been disappointed in this hope for the fourth time. On that date their fifth child and fourth daughter, Antoinette Power, was born.

In June, during the rugged session of 1854, Margaret was pregnant again, and Houston tore open every letter from home with feverish haste. Nannie's latest letter to her father made no mention of a new arrival. He answered it on June 16, 1854, expressing pleasure that she was able to write so well: "I love you very much, and I am more

549

than happy that you love me ... I know you love your Ma & little sisters as well as your brother ... you have little quarrels, but they are soon over and dont reach the heart. ..." [5]

Although he would not hear of it for several weeks, the long-awaited candidate for the honored name, Andrew Jackson Houston, was born on June 21, 1854. As soon as word reached him, the General wrote to tell his wife of his overwhelming gratitude to her and to God.

The long-delayed coming of his second son had something to do with clarifying Senator Houston's religious convictions. Perhaps it proved to him the power of prayer. He told Mr. Samson that he was ready to profess his faith.[6] On November 19, 1854, the convert waded into Rocky Creek, near Independence, Texas, and was baptized by the Reverend Rufus C. Burleson. When he knelt at the pulpit rail of the Independence Baptist Church, the tower bell—a gift from Mrs. Lea which had been cast from the family silver and inscribed with her name—tolled the tidings. His conversion was a national event that was noted in a number of church periodicals.

The Senator informed his wife soon after he joined the church that his pocketbook as well as himself had been baptized. He canceled the interest on a loan that he had made to a clergyman because he realized people sometimes forgot that a minister must eat like other people. He also agreed to pay half the salary of the pastor of the Baptist church in Independence.

One day, the Senator drove into Huntsville in his buckboard. Noticing a crowd in front of T. & S. Gibbs General Store, he tied his horse to a hitching post and went to investigate the cause of the excitement. A slave owner named McKell had put a small, scared black boy, Jeff, on the auction block. To save the auctioneer's fee, McKell was selling his own property. Soliciting bids, he called out to the passersby that he had a little nigger for sale cheap; a strong and willing worker, eight years old, who would make a husky field hand.

Jeff was actually thirteen, but McKell cut back his age to conceal his lack of growth. After one look at the quivering youngster, Houston asked McKell if he had had an offer. Yes, a man named Moreland had bid five hundred dollars, but he had had to go home to get the money and the sale was still open. Houston chided McKell for being willing to sell the child to an abusive, vile-tempered man like Moreland and offered cash if McKell would knock fifty dollars off the price. McKell agreed, and Houston told Jeff to come along with him and not be scared any more. He had a little boy at home, he said, who would enjoy having Jeff for a playmate.

In Gibbs's store, he had the proprietor feed the boy and furnish him with a complete outfit. As he was leaving the store, Houston told Jeff not to cry but to eat his biscuit and candy; Uncle Joshua would soon come to take him to his new home.

Jeff Hamilton lived to be one hundred and ten years old, and to the last he had a clear memory.[7] Among his most vivid recollections was the manner in which he earned his place as a member of the Houston family. Jeff was put in charge of leading Old Pete, the stallion, to the pond for water. Old Pete was gentle and well-behaved if treated kindly, but a bad actor if provoked. The Senator cautioned Jeff that he must never strike Pete. Jeff, by then a well-fed, healthy, and mischievous youngster, had an unbounded curiosity to know what Old Pete would do if he was struck.

One day, thirteen-year-old Nancy Elizabeth came skipping along with a willow switch in her hand as Jeff led Old Pete to the pond. Jeff told Miss Nannie to give Old Pete a crack on the nose, which she did. The consequences were immediate. Old Pete reared, and Miss Nannie jumped back and fell into the pond. Jeff plunged in after her; then some of the other domestics came to help.

Houston investigated the circumstances when he reached home, questioning his wife, Nannie, and the servants who had been eye-witnesses. He told Jeff that his deliberate violation of instructions called for discipline, which he administered in the stable with a switch about the size of the one Miss Nannie had used on Old Pete.

Houston's affection for his own children left room for unswerving devotion to the "children of the forest," and in his patriarchal years he tried to protect and defend them. Again and again the Senator from Texas pleaded with his colleagues in behalf of the Indians. He confessed that he had little hope of persuading his fellow senators to act with greater justice toward the Indians. Yet, accepting the risk of being called a bore and a fanatic, he persisted. He tried in vain to save the treaty rights of the Cherokee nation from destruction by Senator Douglas' Nebraska bill. Before that, on March 3, 1853, he had pleaded:

...Send honest men to pay their annuities; and when they come amongst you, set them the example of hospitality and good faith, and they will emulate your example, and you will make them the equal of yourselves. They have claims upon you. . . .

The Indian no longer . . . stands in the contemplation of some broad river flowing at his feet, or contemplates the beautiful lawns, with lofty trees protecting him from the vertical sun . . . You circumscribe him within a little space of country, embracing but a few square miles, and tell him that these are the limits of his domain; and the Indian is left with the reflection that he has no guarantee for his safety.

I call upon my country to raise the Indian from [his] unhappy lot . . . [we] should at least . . . place honest men in positions of trust . . . to rescue them from the harpies and cormorants that have hung around them.

. . . You will find in the Indian character the germs of integrity, as you find [them] in the corresponding classes of our society in the transaction of business. You will find them generous, noble, faithful, daring and chivalrous. You will find their chiefs elevated in their condition and feeling, and as chivalrous as the proudest man that adorns the annals of Christendom. I call upon you to do justice to them, and protect them.[8]

These were the events, the thoughts, and the deeds; the character and integrity, the domestic happiness and comfort that sustained Houston the man while he fought his battles as Houston the Senator. His religion, his relations with his family, the manner in which he treated human beings whose skins were more deeply tinted than his own—all these contributed to making him a durable statesman who had the strength to pursue an unpopular course despite the opposition of the mob.

6. "This Much I Am Bound to Declare—"

WHILE the Douglas bill was advancing to final discussion and vote, a hurricane of public opinion swept the North. From week to week, the protest gathered force; there were effigy burnings, mass meetings, parades, editorials, pulpit orations, and resolutions of condemnation. One of the first protests had come from conservative business men. They were soon joined by the Northern clergy; then by physicians, lecturers, authors, and mechanics. Never had so many groups united to form a solid front of opposition to a national measure. The excitement in Boston's Faneuil Hall did not exceed that in Philadelphia and Cleveland. On February 2, 1854, the New York *Tribune* correspondent wrote from Cleveland that Ohio could be regarded as a unit against the treasonable scheme in the Senate, and he predicted that any congressman who dared vote for the bill would be hounded from the state, and politically destroyed. A pro-Douglas meeting in Quincy, Illinois, was taken over by Douglas opponents who enacted resolutions condemning the senator for bringing on this agitation.

Pulpits of the Northern clergy resounded with the indignation of Theodore Parker, James Freeman Clarke, and lesser known but equally fervent men. A pastor in Pittsfield, Massachusetts said the bill would establish new breeding grounds for black livestock. Douglas responded to such statements by attacking his opponents in the Senate. He charged that Chase and Sumner were representing free socialism and the interests of the Negro.

The South was comparatively calm, but not at ease. Opinion was divided because limited means of communication prevented the people from fully realizing what was going on in the North. A newspaper correspondent in Georgia explained that Southerners were lethargic about the measure because they would receive no real benefit from it. A contrary opinion was expressed in the Richmond *Enquirer*; since Southerners were unanimously supporting the measure, it was absurd to say they were indifferent to it. Most Southern Democratic newspapers were behind the bill, but there were notable exceptions. The editor of the New Orleans *Bulletin,* concluded that if the struggle over the bill went on two or three months longer, Southern members of the national legislature would drop it.

Southern politicians did not share this opinion; they had no intention of dropping the bill. Senator Albert G. Brown of Mississippi defended it on the ground that slavery was of divine origin, a social and political blessing. Andrew P. Butler of South Carolina sought to vindicate both the bill and the slave system by saying that the African race had not produced an outstanding astronomer, statesman, general, or poet. James M. Mason of Virginia charged that enemies of the bill feared that its ratification would end their vocations as anti-slavery agitators; if the bill passed, they would expire, howling like fiends. Five free-state legislatures in session in early 1854 passed condemning resolutions; five avoided commitments. Five slave states—Texas, Maryland, Alabama, Louisiana, and Kentucky—adjourned without action on the issue.

When the bill came up for debate on March 3, 1854, John Bell, a Kentucky Whig, attacked it. Other members from both sides did the same in long and bitter speeches. It was the beginning of an all-night session, during which members frequently left the floor to visit the Hole in the Wall for food and drink. The scene was similar to the all-night session in 1849, when Webster and Calhoun had struggled about opening the door to slavery in all territory taken from Mexico and Houston had rebuked the Senate for permitting orderly procedure to degenerate into chaos. But passions were stronger and conduct less respectable on this occasion. Senator William P. Fessenden of Maine angered Southern senators who were supporting Douglas, and a fistic encounter between Butler and Fessenden was narrowly averted. Senator Weller of California and other senators showed the effects of the liquor they had consumed. When Weller began delivering irrelevant, bombastic remarks, Douglas silenced him by telling him to sit down and not mix in a fight that was Douglas' own.

Douglas was not able to get the floor until half an hour before midnight, when he demanded that the vote be taken. It seemed obvious that he and his supporters would win. In an attempt to forestall a vote and postpone action on the measure until tempers cooled, Houston addressed the chair. "It is now half-past eleven o'clock," he pointed out, "I cannot see any particular necessity for going on tonight, and therefore we might as well adjourn."

"No! No!" several senators cried.

It was obvious that a motion to adjourn would be rejected. Houston addressed the chair again. "Then I give notice that I shall take the floor after the Senator from Illinois gets through." [1]

Douglas spoke for three hours, raging against the notion that there was anything sacred about the Compromise and launching a devastating attack on his opponents. He displayed vigorous flashes of temper that were possibly accentuated by fatigue. He accused Senator Chase of slander, forgery, and falsehood, implying that Chase and Sumner had obtained their Senate seats through a corrupt bargain and a dishonorable coalition. Chase and Sumner interrupted him, and he verbally snapped them down. He did not attack Houston, presumably desiring not to emphasize the fact that one of the most effective voices raised against him was from the South.

Douglas claimed that he had long stood for the principle of popular self-government and that the repeal of the Missouri Compromise was merely incidental to this noble purpose. He asserted, but did not attempt to prove, that Kansas was in no danger of becoming slave territory, although Missouri slaveholders already were boasting that they would soon have control of Kansas.

The New York *Tribune* correspondent wrote that it was impossible to give more than a faint idea of Douglas' vulgarity and violence. Senator Everett described his speech as ungentlemanlike and coarse.

As dawn slanted into the chamber which was lighted dimly by a circle of flickering candles, Houston again cautioned his Southern colleagues.

> Mr. President, I can not believe that the agitation created by this measure will be confined to the Senate Chamber. I can not believe, from what we have witnessed here to-night, that this will be the exclusive arena for the exercise of human passions and the expression of public opinions. *If the Republic be not shaken, I will thank Heaven for its kindness in maintaining its stability....*
>
> ... what is to be the effect of this measure if adopted? The South is to gain nothing by it; for honorable gentlemen from the South, and especially the junior Senator from Virginia [Mr. Hunter], characterize it as a miserable, trifling little measure. Then, sir, is the South to be propitiated or benefited by ... a miserable trifling little measure? ... Will it allay the agitation of the North? Will it preserve the union of these States? ... It is to be the most ruinous and fatal to the future harmony ... of the country....
>
> This is an eminently perilous measure, and do you expect me to remain here silent, or to shrink from ... my duty in admonishing the South of what I conceive the results will be? ... The discharge of conscious duty prompts me often to confront the

united array of the very section of the country in which I reside, ... in which my affections rest. ...

Depend upon it, Mr. President [if this bill passes], there will be a tremendous shock; it will convulse the country from Maine to the Rio Grande. The South has not asked for it. I, as the most Southern Senator upon this floor, do not desire it. If it is a boon that is offered to propitiate the South, I, as a Southern man, repudiate it. I reject it. I will have none of it. ...

The South, as a community, only desire their rights under the Constitution and existing compromises.

Houston argued that Douglas' popular sovereignty principle had never been applied in any one of numerous cases involving the territories. He conceded that the Compromise might not be constitutional technically. But it was sufficient for him, and should be for others because it had stood for more than thirty years, "with the approbation of our wisest and ablest statesmen ... strange that unconstitutional law should have remained so long in force amid all the agitation, excitement and bitterness between North and South; and this is the first proposition ever made to repeal it. Have we to yield ... without any excuse for it when we see that discord will run riot over the land?"

He reminded the senators that he had made the first address in support of Clay's compromise proposal. His suggestion that six senators be selected without regard to party or section, to compose an address and disseminate it to harmonize the country had met with no response. Nevertheless, peace and harmony subsequently had been obtained. There was no better way to preserve it than by rejecting the current measure. When he closed his eyes to the scenes around him he could cherish the consolation that he had left his children in a peaceful, happy, prosperous, and united community. But when he opened his eyes, his hopes were less sanguine and his anxieties increased. If this measure passed, his youngest child would not live to see the end of the agitation that it would excite. "... I adjure you ... *Maintain the Missouri Compromise! Stir not up agitation!* Give us peace!

"This much I am bound to declare—in behalf of my country, ... upon the decision which we make upon this question, must depend *union or disunion*." [2]

The chamber still was echoing with his plea when the roll call began a little before 5 A.M., March 5. Houston was the only Southern Democrat who voted "No." John Bell, a Kentucky Whig, voted the same way. The bill, soon to be proved a costly and fateful error, passed 37 to 14.

Though his warning went unheeded, Houston regarded it as the most forceful, most eloquent, and best-reasoned of his life. His desk was flooded with letters of appreciation from the North and West. The South completely failed to understand that the basis of his opposition to the measure was its inherent but unperceived threat to his section. For his independence and courage, he was castigated by the South as a whole, and denounced and disciplined by the most powerful forces in his state.

The harvest of the Kansas-Nebraska Bill was all that Senator Houston had predicted. Northerners bitterly resumed their agitation for abolition. Some Southerners openly opposed the bill, but the majority were indifferent to it and to the storm that was gathering in the North.

Anything that threatened the expansion of slavery also threatened the profits and the way of life of the dominant class in the South. Houston was regarded as such a threat. His insistent demand for settlement of the slavery issue within the Union incited his political antagonists to fury. With few exceptions the Southern press damned him as a traitor. Twenty Texas counties passed formal resolutions of condemnation.

In a speech at Nacogdoches, May 11, 1855, Houston took notice of the anger his stand had evoked.

> ... I do not expect to ride on a railroad in Texas. If I do not get rode (sic) on a rail, I shall come off well; and sometimes considering the attacks that are made upon me, and the circumstances by which I am surrounded, I have good reasons to expect the latter.[3]

Old political enemies, pro-slavery advocates, and anti-Union enthusiasts united in a campaign to force his resignation from the Senate. Anson Jones returned to the limelight when he charged that Houston had opposed annexation. Lamar and Burnet renewed their old friendship and apparently consulted on preparing pamphlets to attack Houston.

557

Houston responded to the Burnet-Lamar barking with the patience of an old mastiff annoyed by a couple of insolent puppies. In a speech at Austin, November 23, 1855, he told the story of the butting ram who didn't know when to give up. When the farmer went out to find his ram, he found only a fragment of the tail; but this fragment, true to the character of the ram, rose up from the ground and made menacing gestures. "So," Houston informed his audience, "whether or not, my political enemies have butted themselves all away, except the tail, I grant that they are still in motion." [4]

Even Houston's oldest friends, Henderson, Lubbock, and Ashbel Smith, failed to speak up for him. The campaign to force his retirement from the Senate, though his term would not expire until 1859, was spearheaded by W. S. Oldham and Louis T. Wigfall. Journalists on the Clarksville *Standard*, the Austin *City Gazette*, and the Galveston *News*, joined in a chorus to make Houston's stand on the Kansas-Nebraska Bill a reason for the legislature not to return him to the Senate. Others insisted that it was time for him to resign.

The campaign succeeded in part. The Texas Legislature took a vote and served notice on Houston that when his term expired he would not be returned to the Senate. On December 8, 1855, the Dallas *Herald* demanded that he resign at once from a position that he had forfeited by misrepresenting his fellow citizens. Houston ignored the demand.

7. *"Leave Him to Me!"*

SENATOR DOUGLAS claimed credit for getting the Kansas-Nebraska Bill through, and no one has ever cared to dispute him for that honor. During the verbal battles in which men were staking their futures, their reputations, and their consciences, the Little Giant had exerted all of his power as a behind-the-scenes parliamentary operator. The efforts of Chase, Sumner, Bell, and others were no match for the relentless ingenuity of the chairman of the Committee on Territories. Douglas, though stunned by his opposition and the nation-wide resentment against him, was proud of his victory and boasted that speeches had had nothing to do with it; he had achieved his triumph by using the power, authority and brute force of a dictator.

After Douglas' success in the Senate, the issue was transferred to the House of Representatives where it was debated with equal acrimony. Senator Benton's constituency had demoted him to the lower house in reprisal for his opposition to the slavery interests. He foresaw, as did Houston, that now he would be penalized again for opposing a measure; it would mean the loss of his chance to return to the Senate.

Houston had been lifted to eloquence by his convictions and his desire to save his country from a ruinous course of action; Benton was inspired to savagery and wit. With unrestrained contempt, Benton caricatured Douglas' aspirations for the Presidency. He demanded four hours for his address and declared that if they were not granted he would talk in the rotunda or—if the size of the crowd warranted it—on the Capitol grounds. He was granted the time, during which he ranted against the bill:

> It is a see-saw bill.... the up-and-down game of politicians, played at the expense of the peace and harmony of the Union. ...It is an amphibological bill, stuffed with monstrosities, hobbled with contradictions, and badgered with a proviso....a silent, secret, limping, halting, creeping, squinting, impish motion, conceived in the dark and midwifed in a committee-room.[1]

Benton's power in the House failed to change the course of events. His colleagues passed the bill on May 22, 1854, 113 to 100.

While the House was debating the bill, waves of anger and resentment surged within the Senate chamber. Northern clergymen, aroused by religious periodicals and resolutions adopted by numerous church organizations, entered the contest with a petition, dated March 1, three days before the Senate passed the bill. It was signed by 3,050 New England clergymen who protested repeal of the slavery restriction "in the name of the Almighty God." A committee of preachers delivered the resolution to Senator Edward Everett of Massachusetts who presented it to the Senate on April 14. After hearing the petition, Mason of Virginia and Butler of South Carolina denounced the clergymen in stinging language for usurping spiritual functions for the purpose of agitation. Douglas assailed the memorial in a bitter, scurrilous speech that skirted the bounds of decency.

> It is presented by a denomination of men calling themselves preachers of the gospel, who have come forward with an atrocious falsehood and an atrocious calumny against the Senate, desecrated the pulpit, and prostituted the sacred desk to the miserable and corrupting influence of party politics. I doubt whether there is a body of men in America who combine so much profound ignorance on the question upon which they attempt to enlighten the Senate as this same body of preachers.[2]

Outraged, Senator Sumner rose to protest. Houston immediately cried out to him, "Sumner, don't speak, don't speak! leave him to me!"

"Will you take care of him?" Sumner asked.

"Yes, if you will leave him to me." [3]

Understanding the reason behind Houston's request, Sumner sat down. Douglas had implied that the petition was a trick supported only by abolitionists and that it would receive no sympathy in the South. Houston intended to make it clear that Southern sentiment— as he represented it—was on the side of the petitioners.

Taking the floor, Houston declared that the ministers shared equal rights with other citizens to petition the Senate on any subject. The clergymen thought that passage of the Kansas-Nebraska Bill was a breach of faith. He himself had made the same charge although he had carefully refrained from accusing individual senators of corrupt or selfish motives. He said that the number of signatures on the petition suggested that a large proportion of Americans believed there was "something wrong with this bill"; he could detect no foundation for the assertion that the ministers had sent the memorial "to manufacture political capital."

Looking into Douglas' angry face, he exclaimed:

> ... Sir, it [the protest] comes from the country. I told you that there would be agitation, but it was denied upon this floor. Is not this agitation? Three thousand ministers of the living God upon earth—His viceregents—send a memorial here upon this subject; and you tell me that there is no excitement in the country! Sir, you realize what I anticipated. The country has to bear the infliction. Sir, the *coup d'état* was not successful....

Ministers have a right to remonstrate.... Because they are ministers of the Gospel they are not disfranchised of political rights and privileges.... they have a right to spread their opinions on the records of the nation.... they have a right to... investigate our conduct, and, if they do not approve of it, to express their opinions in relation to it.

Mason of Virginia angrily interrupted the Texas senator to say that the petition invoked the vengeance of Almighty God upon the Senate. Houston denied that the petition contained any such appeal.

There is no invocation contained in the memorial. It is a respectful protest, ... and not one word is contained in it derogatory to the Senate ... there is no invocation of wrath or vengeance upon the members of this body. It is a respectful protest, in the name of the Almighty God.

Douglas broke in to denounce the petition for its abolitionist character. Houston answered that the bill was the source of the agitation, not the clergymen. "The memorial impugns the action of no one." Then Douglas shifted his ground, protesting that the petition referred to the Kansas-Nebraska Bill as "immoral."

"Surely," Houston answered, "that ought not to insult Senators. They are not such paragons of morality that they cannot bear to have their moral character questioned ... I pray we may never have another such protest in this body.... If we wish to avert calamitous effects we should prevent pernicious causes."

During this heated exchange a number of New England clergymen sat in the gallery closely following everything that was said on the floor. Among them were signers of the petition who were also members of the committee that had delivered it to Senator Everett. They were deeply moved by Houston's earnestness. In years to come his defense of the preachers' right to petition had consequences of prodigious importance to him and all members of his family. How surprised he would have been if he could have foreseen a connection between his defense of the clergymen and what happend on a bloody battlefield eight years later in 1862.[4]

8. *"Why Need I Want the Presidency?"*

DURING two full terms and part of a third in the Senate, Houston was frequently mentioned as a Presidential possibility; several times he had genuine prospects of nomination by his party. As early as 1851, in Huntsville, he had received a letter from a New Yorker, Nicholas Dean, who asked what he could do as an old friend to assist Houston in becoming President. In answer, Houston drew a verbal self-portrait of a man well satisfied with the prospect of retirement and on May 8, 1851, he disposed of Dean's offer of political aid in a somewhat offhand way:

> You wish to know, how you can serve. Well, really you know best and I am willing to trust all matters to you! If you wish to open a correspondence with gentlemen in Texas, I would name Hon. H. Stuart of Galveston, and Col. H. Yoakum of this place as two gentlemen quite suitable. Also Col. Ebenezer Allen of Galveston, ... It will gratify you, I am sure, when I affirm that I have not written a letter on politics since we parted, nor will I, unless I intend it for the public eye, and I do not expect to write any for that purpose!!! [1]

No one was closer to the inner workings of Houston's mind with regard to the Presidency than Henderson Yoakum, his close friend and attorney. Yoakum had many conversations with him on the subject and did not doubt that Houston desired to occupy the high station. But Houston's attitude was that of a man whose strong sense of destiny made him feel that what will be will be; hence he did not yearn for the office as did Clay, Calhoun, and Webster.

On October 11, 1854, at a meeting of the Democratic General Committee of New Hampshire, Houston was placed in nomination as "the people's candidate" for the Presidency in the election of 1856. New Hampshire was President Pierce's own state. The orator, Edmund Burke, who had been one of President Pierce's campaign managers in the election of 1852, had broken with the occupant of the White House and was a thoroughgoing Houston man. In a speech addressed to the people of the whole nation, Burke announced that the committee's decision to support Houston was the only way to check the demoralization of the Democratic Party. Burke and the committee believed that nominations by caucuses and conventions were obsolete and that the choice of Presidents should be restored to the people. They presented Houston to the nation as a "citizen of the Republic, distinguished alike for his abilities, experience in public affairs, and unquestionable statesmanship."

They also believed that Houston's stand on the Kansas-Nebraska Bill "placed him in a position which will command the confidence of the patriotic men of the North, and should commend him to the confidence of the South." In conclusion, the committee urged the party and all the people to rally around Houston for a "glorious triumph in 1856" and recommended the formation of San Jacinto clubs in every state and town in the Republic.[2]

In the meantime, Houston gave his total energy to the problems that confronted him in the Senate, enjoying respite when he could by returning to Texas and his family. Houston's plantation at Raven Hill (so called after his Cherokee name) was fourteen miles from Huntsville. His wife wrote to him in Washington, saying that during his long absences she was restless, impatient, and lonely, even though she had the children with her and was visited often by her mother and Houston's favorite sister, Eliza. After Houston had served a year in the Senate, his family had moved into town where they would have neighbors. They lived in a one-and-a-half story "dog run" house which had an open breezeway. Houston cherished this home more than any other he ever had.

A cabin of squared logs with a stone chimney was built in the yard near the house and was intended for Houston's law office. But he did little practice in the cabin. He whittled, scattered his pipes and papers, read, and wrote. His main furnishings were a chair with turned posts and a worn seat of cowhide tanned with the hair on it, and a large pine table he had owned when he was President of the Republic. The walls of the cabin were lined with his modest law library and his old classical favorites, among them the worn copy of *Caesar's Commentaries* that he had carried in his saddle bag in Lone Star days. In his dictionary, he ringed the word "temporize" with heavy pencil and wrote "out" in the margin.

Houston continued to buy land in Texas and to visualize his future there, not in the White House. He could foresee the time when, if all went well, he would be worth perhaps one hundred and fifty thousand dollars. He had preferred conservative investments to speculations of the kind that made men enormously rich. As President of the Texas Republic, he could have amassed great wealth in lands that had fallen into the hands of others. He might have become the owner of half a million dollars in Texas liabilities at a time when they were worthless, anticipating (as others had) that they would be redeemed by the ten million dollar boundary settlement from the United States Treasury. But he had never invested a dollar in soldiers' scrip or in Texas stocks, and he had never speculated in currency or other government liabilities. Had he done so he would not have been condemned because such practices were part of the generally accepted code of his day. In matters involving conflict of interest, he was guided by his own sense of honor.

Close inspection of his operations shows his eagerness to buy land at fair or bargain prices. He was generous, even reckless, in making loans on poor security to people in trouble. As a result, a large portion of his assets, when inventoried, had to be rated "doubtful." Charles Elliot, in his correspondence with the British Foreign Office, had described the President of the Texas Republic as pure-handed. Some of Houston's political opponents had scanned his record for years in search of irregularities and had found nothing that served their desire to discredit him.

With considerable exaggeration, he had been called a second Washington, but certain similarities are obvious. He frequently referred to Washington's standards of virtue and integrity and shared the first President's belief that a man's achievements were worthless unless they were characterized by honesty.

For more than a decade, Houston's self-appointed, would-be press agent, Charles Edwards Lester, energetically pressed the General's cause. More than once Lester complained that Houston did not show himself throughout the nation and make himself known to "hundreds of thousands of men." "Your friends . . . seem to think you are more insensible on the subject than they themselves," Lester complained.[3]

Finally yielding to persuasion, Houston exposed himself to the electorate, lecturing on temperance and scientific progress. He discussed political subjects forthrightly and even sought an invitation from the stronghold of abolitionism to discuss slavery from the

Southern point of view. The date agreed upon for this mission was Washington's Birthday, 1855. He was to speak in Tremont Temple in Boston before the Anti-Slavery Society. The fervent abolitionist, William Lloyd Garrison, was scheduled to answer him.

When Houston boarded a train in New York on his way to Boston, a letter from an old friend, possibly Thomas Rusk, was put into his hands. This correspondent seems to have advised him to abandon the trip lest he jeopardize his chances for the Presidential nomination. From New Haven, Connecticut, on February 20, Houston wrote to "Dear General," thanking him for his interest:

> ... I appreciate your advice ... but I must go on ... to be honest and fear not is the right path.
> I would not conceal an [one] honest opinion for the Presidency. If I were, [to do so] I would not enjoy the office, ... I know it will be a risk, but it is for the harmony of the Union, if perchance I may benefit it.[4]

He told the crowd that jammed the Temple that he had come unsolicited—"I may say undesired." He was there "to vindicate the South against the responsibility sought to be cast upon it for that for which it was not responsible." With slavery he was himself "involved by destiny, not by choice." He would not discuss the abstract principles of freedom and slavery. "I take it as I find it ... not a contrivance of mine nor of my ancestors...." At the time of the Revolution, he reminded them, there was not one of the colonies which did not hold slaves and "recognize it as a right institution." Liberty was won by slave owners who later had divested themselves of slaves.

In the South, the climate, soil, and industry demanded a class of laborers that had been expelled from the North where institutions had changed. His audience responded with cheers and laughter when he asked, "But do you believe that if it had not been for the influx of foreign labor, you would have had these railroads? Would the Americans, sons of the Revolution, have done the digging and all the other work that has been done here?

"But suppose the railroad projects had taken place before you emancipated your slaves.... Do you think that if railroads had been started then, emancipation would have been begun? You would have had Negroes at work building railroads to this day." Apparently they agreed with him for they again burst into applause and laughter.

He went on: "Had there been an influx of foreign immigration at the South, do you believe they would have continued to hold slaves? No! . . . These are the things the North should look to. Your slaves became unprofitable and were thrown off."

His major points were (1) hastening the end of slavery was not worth the dreadful strife that would result if politicians and agitators continued their clamor; and (2) if the South were let alone to regulate its institutions, time would erase the slavery problem. He reminded his audience that this second proposition had been in effect at the beginning of the last Congress ". . . no jarring sound had been heard until a voice [cried], 'Nebraska! Nebraska!' That was the note of discord. Whence? From the South? [A voice, "No!"] I, too, deny it . . . the South never demanded it, nor did *all* the South acquiesce in it either. [Applause] . . . Not one legislature of the whole South, not one executive [had] exhibited an uneasiness under the Missouri Compromise. Not one. It came from the North . . . the injury was done *to* the South . . . It put the knife to her throat. . . ." [5]

He won his audience completely when he said that he respected them for the respect they had shown him. They interrupted with applause, cheers, and laughter. There were no boos. Every individual in that audience had at some time been inflamed by such men as William Lloyd Garrison and Wendell Phillips; but for this one moment, at least, they could visualize the unknown Southland, cursed with its awful burden. For once, they must have recognized the other side of the story.

Houston's success at Boston was evanescent, more significant as a revelation of the man than for any permanent result. Southerners were too proud and too blind to ask for sympathy and received little in the North except during that brief hour when Houston held his Tremont Temple audience in the hollow of his hand. They cheered him wildly at the close of his appeal for tolerance toward perpetuation of the Union "while time shall last." But in Texas and elsewhere in the South, he was condemned for venturing to address an abolitionist audience and was charged with catering for the Presidency.

Houston unquestionably desired the Presidency, but he wanted it on his own terms without compromise. He made no move to capture it by equivocation or by hedging in either the North or the South. He undoubtedly believed that, if elected, he could heal the breach and save the Union. On May 11, 1855, in a speech at Nacogdoches he answered the charge that he was "catering" for the office. "Why need I want the Presidency? I have twice been President, and although not on as large a theatre as the U. S., yet the future will show that no President of the United States has ever had the opportunity of doing as much for his country as I could have done for Texas." [6]

9. Rejected and Alone

In 1856, in some parts of the country—although not in Texas —Houston's prestige was rising. A New Jersey convention of the newly established Republican Party cheered his name. His more moderate approach to the slavery problem was gaining favor. Some important politicians agreed that if Houston could be nominated— and few believed he could be—he would be elected.

Houston continued to attend to routine business in the Senate and occasionally made speeches outside. The Baltimore *Sun* reported his lecture of April 7, 1856. His subject: "Danger to which this country is exposed from war, bigotry and fanaticism." In relation to fanaticism, the *Sun* reported, ". . . he characterized the Abolitionists of the North, and the Disunionists of the South as coming under that head. . . . He conjured the rising generation to grow up with a love for the union of the states. He was frequently applauded." [1]

In the spring of 1856, Houston's friend, Representative Nathaniel P. Banks of Massachusetts, was elected Speaker of the House. On April 17, ten days after his Baltimore speech reproaching fanaticism, the Texas senator attended a party given by Speaker Banks and met a mild-tempered lady, who was generally regarded by Southerners as a fanatic and a demon. The lady was Harriet Beecher Stowe, whose *Uncle Tom's Cabin* would one day be credited with destroying slavery. Houston made no comment on Mrs. Stowe's views, but in a letter to his wife, written in the Senate the day after Banks's party, he said:

> Last night I went to a party at Speaker Banks, and saw "Uncle Tom's Cabin," alias Madam Beecher Stowe. She is certainly a hard subject to look on. I was at the Party an hour; ate an ice cream and left. It is the first and only Party I have been at this season, and I think it will be the last.[2]

In this same year, 1856, five years before Sumter was fired on, the first armed conflict of the Civil War occurred at Lawrence, Kansas, where Missourians fought to hold the state for slavery against free soil immigrants and abolitionists from the North. The Dred Scott decision, declaring the Missouri Compromise void and denying Congress the right to prohibit slavery in the territories, opened the West to slavery.

In November, the Democrats elected indecisive James Buchanan, a Pennsylvanian with Southern leanings, to the Presidency. In the House of Representatives, pistols were drawn and a South Carolina congressman, Preston S. Brooks, angered by Senator Sumner's verbal attack on silver-haired Senator Butler of South Carolina, cudgeled the Massachusetts statesman into insensibility at his desk.

The fevers of bitter antagonism between North and South rose and fell. From Washington on March 1, 1857, weary of bitterness and commotion, Houston wrote his wife another sunny letter in which he joyfully contemplated his reunion with his family and the end of his public career two years hence:

> My Dear: After two night sessions I did not go to church today....
> Today is pleasant and betokens spring. When I reflect on the distance from this to where you are and our flock, I feel that I am indeed an exile, interdicted from all that is dear to me....
> I have felt exile in other lands and from other homes, but then I was an exile that combined no wish or hope of return. In my present case, there is blended both desire and hope. Desire to be with you and hope that the day is not distant that it will be the case! Our sunny home appears to me more bright and lovely than it has ever done in the realizations of the past. So many, so bright are the joys to my fancy ... that I can scarcely contain myself....

He finished his letter with an enraptured picture of his life as it would be among his children, "ruddy and noisy, with their thousand antics and childish pleasures," and with his wife—"you, my Dear, a kind Mother looking on each one as a nonpareil and half vexed for fear I will not say as much as you wish in their bountiful behalf...." [3]

Houston's hope of peace in the midst of his family was long delayed. In May, 1857, the state Democratic convention at Waco divided violently for and against Houston. Hardin R. Runnels, a strong-jawed, morose, stubborn man who was an ardent disciple of Calhoun, was nominated for governor. Houston thought matters over and asked his wife what he should do. While the matter was pending, a political opponent declared that Houston dared not run for governor because "he would be met at every cross-road [and] he would be killed off." Again Houston consulted his wife. She told him to run. He agreed and entered the race. [4]

He told Ashbel Smith that his purpose was "to regenerate the politics of the State," and he had written Rusk, "The people want excitement, and I had as well give it to them as anyone." [5] He had no party, no organization, no campaign fund. Most newspapers were against him. One young Nacogdoches editor, Eber W. Cave, later his Secretary of State, came out in his support.

Houston covered the state by buggy and stage. Jeff was now big and strong enough to drive the Senator's deep-chested sorrel mare, Horseshoe; and on some trips he accompanied his master as driver and friend.

In Brenham, local officials questioned Houston's right to speak in the courthouse. Houston told the crowd that perhaps he did not have the right to speak there because he had not contributed toward the purchase of a single brick in the courthouse. He invited any man who wanted to hear what he had to say to join him on a nearby hillside, adding that he had a right to speak on the soil of Texas because he had shed his blood on it.

He used all his art and skill in the sixty-seven speeches he delivered between Montgomery and San Antonio. In June, he invaded Henderson's territory and campaigned in Harrison and Cass counties. From north Texas, he advanced across central Texas and was in Cameron and Waco by July 13. It was a heavy schedule.

His success in rousing pro-Union sentiment prompted the Democratic Central Executive Committee to denounce him as a "traitor-knave" and to urge the defeat of all traitors. They assured the electorate that by voting against Houston they would do credit to themselves. About this same time, another disciple of Calhoun and a baiter of the North on the slavery issue, Louis T. Wigfall, recommended tar and feathers for Houston.

Goaded to fury by the "traitor-knave" charge, Houston bade good-by to tolerance and magnanimity. He gave few explanations of his Kansas-Nebraska vote and no longer pleaded for reconciliation between sections. He took his stand on a platform that had one solid plank: Sam Houston and the open book that was his thirty-year record in public office. He turned loose all his powers of invective and ridicule, classing all his antagonists as thieves, rascals, and assassins. In this group he included Runnels, Wigfall (always referred to as "Wiggletail"), Judge William S. Oldham, the entire Democratic State Central Executive Committee, and all the other "conspirators at Waco."

His resentment of the traitor charge prompted him to refuse to appear on the same platform with his detractors. Wigfall and his old friends Henderson, Lubbock, and Oldham trailed him, speaking in opposition wherever he spoke. At Tyler, he closed his speech with a warning that Wiggletail would follow him, and he advised his audience not to waste time listening to him unless they were fond of lies. While Wigfall was speaking, Houston sat on a hotel porch near the court house. When the crowd dispersed after Wigfall's speech, he greeted them with upraised hands and reminded them that he had warned them they would hear nothing but lies.

One sultry afternoon he spoke at Lockhart on a long platform in a grove near Storey's spring. He wore a long coarse linen duster, loose trousers of some rough material, no vest, low shoes (characteristically unlaced), and his shirt collar open to bare the grizzled mop of hair on his chest. Houston's erect bearing, his commanding voice, his gestures, and composure reminded a lawyer in the audience, Alexander W. Terrell, of an Old Testament prophet. Until this campaign, Terrell had taken no active part in politics. The Waco convention had made him a member of the party's Central Executive Committee, and he had been persuaded to announce himself as a candidate for district judge. Without his knowledge, his name had been attached to the Central Committee's broadside calling Houston a "traitor-knave." Now he was an active candidate in the field backed by an organization that vilified a man whom he respected and admired.

While Houston was speaking, Judge Oldham drove up. Terrell moved through the audience and joined him. Oldham took two volumes of the *Congressional Globe* from a large pair of saddlebags. He was prepared to read from Houston's Kansas-Nebraska speeches to support the traitor-knave accusation. When the audience in front showed signs of curiosity about what was going on behind the platform, Senator Houston restrained them, "Be still, my friends, be still. I will report the cause of this commotion."

Taking a step to the rear of the platform, he looked over, then turned to the audience and informed them, "It's only Oldham, only Oldham. I'll tell you what he is doing." After another look he faced his audience and said in louder tones: "He is opening some books, but they are not the bank books that he stole and sank in the White River, Arkansas." Terrell saw Oldham bite his cigar in two.

Then Houston reminded his audience that Oldham's name was attached to that defamatory broadside issued by the Central Committee. "They say they are going to handle me without gloves." He paused, then drew a pair of heavy buckskin gauntlets from the pocket of his duster. With mock gravity he put them on. "This paper is too dirty for me to handle *without gloves*." He read the portion that classed him with "traitor-knaves" and urged voters to remember that "all traitors should be defeated." Throwing the paper to the floor with a gesture of disgust he exclaimed, "Sam Houston a traitor to Texas! I who in defense of her soil moistened it with my blood!" He took several steps, artfully limping on his San Jacinto leg. "Was it for this that I bared my bosom to the hail of bullets at the Horseshoe and rode into a bullet at San Jacinto—to be branded in my old age as a traitor?"

It was powerful and effective melodrama. Terrell beheld the wave of sympathy that swept over the audience; as old soldiers brought out the red bandanas to wipe tears of indignation and sympathy from their eyes, he was moved to tears himself. With his gauntlets on, Houston picked up the paper from the platform. "Let me read you the names of this executive committee who declare me to be a traitor-knave," he thundered. "Oldham, who stole and ran away to

571

Texas and still has not landed in a penitentiary; John Marshall, a vegetarian who would not eat meat, [not even good Texas steer], and one drop of his blood would freeze a frog...." Then he came to A. W. Terrell, who, horrified but admiring, drank in every word of the denunciation aimed at himself by the man whose patriotism and achievements inspired his wonder and approbation.

"They tell me," cried Houston, "that this young scapegrace wants to be a judge! A pretty looking judge he would make, this slanderer of a man old enough to be his father!" Terrell decided then that when the time came he would speak out, but this was not the time.[6]

Houston had the organization on the run, desperate, sending out frantic appeals. As the campaign drew to a close, he was gaining ground with Unionist sentiment rallying around him. Considering the odds, the issue, and the organization of his opponents with the solid Democratic press behind them, the outcome of the early August election was remarkably close: 32,552 for Runnels against 28,678 for Houston.

Young Terrell won his judgeship. Immediately after the election he published a letter in the *State Gazette*, declaring that the Democratic committee had placed his name on the "traitor-knave" address without consulting him. While he indorsed all the committee's "political reasons for the defeat of General Houston" he would "never have signed the address which called him a 'traitor-knave' for his services to the country as a patriot were known to all men." Terrell inclosed this publication in a letter to Houston, stating that he had delayed making this correction "until I was elected, so my motive could not be questioned." [7]

Houston answered that in a long and eventful career he had never received anything from a political opponent that pleased him more; he hoped soon to know Terrell personally. Terrell called on him at once, establishing a close and unbroken friendship. Later, in a fateful hour, Houston turned to him as his confidant and adviser.

Having demonstrated against a powerfully organized opposition that a large proportion of Texas voters approved of "Old Sam," or of his pro-Unionist record, or of his vote against the Kansas-Nebraska bill, or of all three, Houston took his defeat good-naturedly. Ashbel Smith failed to come to his defense against the traitor charge, but Houston bore no grudge. He yearned for reminiscence with old timers. He wrote Smith on August 22, 1857, "Oh, I do

want some one who has seen other days in Texas, to talk with! . . .
If you come to see me, I bind myself to make you laugh." [8]

The Democratic press hailed his defeat as his political death. On
August 29, 1857, the Dallas *Herald* misstated the election returns
and ridiculed Houston for his loss of influence in Washington now
that a popular majority of 10,000 voters of his own state was recorded against him. On November 14, the Texas *State Gazette*
reported that Houston would present a sad spectacle in Congress
where he would be deserted and alone, condemned by the people of
Texas, and looked upon as holding to his office solely to earn his
per diem allowance.

Displaying no chagrin over his defeat, Houston served as a delegate to the Baptist convention in Huntsville in October, 1857. He
renewed the note covering his loan to Brother Baines, his pastor,
and again knocked off the interest. He had reason to be generous.
The Houstons knew that the future held the possibility of another son.

On the day that Houston returned to the Senate in Washington
he met Francis P. Blair, Jr., in the corridor of the Capitol and gave
him his usual hearty greeting. Blair's father had been a member of
Andrew Jackson's kitchen cabinet and had defended Dred Scott
before the Supreme Court. A former slave owner, young Blair was
now a leader of the free-soilers of Missouri. He noticed Houston's
handsome, spotted-skin waistcoat and laid his hand on it, asking
whether it had been a wild cat, panther, or tiger. Houston answered
that it was leopard. He chose to wear it next his bosom because,
according to the Scripture, a leopard could not change his spots.

In March, 1858, Senator Clay of Alabama twitted Houston in a
scathing speech, saying that Houston's action concerning the Missouri Compromise had cost him the support of his constituency.
Houston retorted by deploring the extremes of viewpoint between
North and South as represented by his colleague's bitterness. Then
he entertained the Senate with his good-natured account of the
chastisement and reproof visited upon him by the legislature, press,
and some of the people of Texas:

> . . . I grant him [Clay] . . . that I have received an earnest and
> gratifying assurance from my constituents that they intend to

relieve me of further service here. I say gratifying, for in the recent election, they beat me; and it is gratifying because I had every disposition to retire on the fourth of March next from public life. How it was brought about, I cannot exactly tell . . . [it] was enough to break down any old gray horse [Laughter] . . . and so I was defeated. . . . But I am very much obliged to my State, because they have not disowned me in beating me— they have only preferred another. I have this further assurance, that I made the State of Texas, but I did not make the people; and if they do wrong, the State still remains in all its beauty, with all its splendid and inviting prospects, with nothing on earth to surpass it in its climate, soil, and production—all varied and delightful. It remains the same beautiful Texas. I made it a State, but I did not make its people. They came there, and they are there; but the State remains, and I am a proud citizen of it.

The gentleman says that he loves Alabama, because he was born there. Sir, I, too, love Alabama; I have endearments of the most delicate character connected with Alabama . . . it was there, in Alabama [at Horseshoe Bend], that I kindled camp-fires, sat by them, and kept vigils . . . and I watered it with the richest blood of youth that flowed in these veins. Ought I not to love the South? Yes, sir, I cherish every manly sentiment for the South; and I am determined that while I live in it, none of the fraternal bonds which bind it to this Union shall be broken.[9]

He wrote his wife that he longed to throw off the harness of public service and submit himself to petticoat rule. To Nat Young, a friend in Delaware, he wrote that he was looking forward to retirement from the cares of public life. Not since the halcyon days that he and Young had shared in Nashville had he been so delighted with his prospects. God had granted him and his wife six fine children, two boys and four girls, and he wished to be home to render them all the aid in his power.

His letters told Margaret of his anxiety for her safety and assured her of his prayers and his hope that he would get home in time for the birth of their new child. But again he failed to make it; Margaret came through safely and, at sixty-five, Houston became the father of another boy, William Rogers, born May 25, 1858. When he went home late in June, the father saw the new arrival for the first time.

He spent a busy summer trying to persuade all within reach of his voice that doom awaited the South unless it changed its course. He had little to say about the Southern League and its drive for States' Rights, but he was credited by the *Southern Intelligencer* with telling a friend that it was too late for Southerners to act and that they must rely on the magnanimity of the North. When Northerners laid a finger on the rights of the South, as they had not yet done, then would be the time to repel insult.

Francis Lubbock was present in November, 1858 when the legislature unanimously elected Judge John Hemphill to succeed Houston in the Senate. During the last governorship campaign Lubbock had not contradicted the charge that his old sponsor was a traitor-betrayer, but he was moved to say of this scene long after the event: "... in noting the unanimous way in which Houston was shelved in this contest, a feeling of sadness came over me, from personal regards for the man." [10]

Back in Washington for his final session, Houston seized the opportunity, in a speech favoring the Southern route for the Pacific railroad, to warn once more against disunion and to characterize secession as "rebellion." He urged Northern men to cease their agitation against the South's institutions; to let time take its course. All states had equal rights; there was no such thing as "Southern rights," he said. Senator Alfred Iverson of Georgia denied this contention with scornful invective.

A thrill of expectation gripped the foreign diplomats, members of the House, and visitors who flocked to the galleries to behold the Texas lion take his leave of the Senate. Beaming with amiability, he turned to Iverson:

... as a Union man, I have ever maintained my position, and I ever shall. I wish no prouder epitaph to mark the board or slab that may lie on my tomb than this: 'He loved his country, he was a patriot; he was devoted to the Union.' If it is for this that I have suffered martyrdom, it is sufficient that I stand at quits with those who have wielded the sacrificial knife.[11]

On February 28, 1859, four days before what Houston called "the termination of his political life," he defended himself in an hour-long address against an attack by a Lamar-Burnet man, Dr. N. D. Labadie. Labadie repeated the old disproved libels about Houston's alleged cowardice and opium-eating before and during the battle of San Jacinto. Houston made his last appearance in the Senate the occasion for a lengthy refutation. His colleagues listened enthralled by his narrative of what happened on that day. This led naturally into his farewell.

> ... never again shall I address the President of this body.... I know the high and important duties that devolve upon Senators.... My prayers will remain with them, that light, knowledge, wisdom, and patriotism may guide them, and that their efforts will be perpetually employed for blessings to our country; that under their influence and their exertions the nation will be blessed, the people happy, and the perpetuity of the Union secured to the latest posterity.[12]

No Texas lament for the passing of Houston from the scene where he had been one of the dominant figures for thirteen years touched as vibrant a chord as that struck by an editorial writer of the Washington *Evening Star* on March 11, 1859.

> This distinguished man left Washington yesterday afternoon for his home in Texas. Up to the hour of his departure, his rooms were crowded by his friends calling to take leave of him. No other public man ever made more ... sincere friends here, nor was severance of a gentleman's connection with American public affairs ever more seriously regretted than in his case.

BOOK IX

THE PEAK AND THE VALLEY

1. *A Dead Lion Comes to Life*

Houston returned to Texas fully determined, at sixty-six, to retire from public life. How would it be this time? Since he was vigorously opposed by the most powerful elements in Texas—the slaveholders and the extreme advocates of secession—it was unlikely that his retirement would be interrupted by another call to public office.

In the late spring of 1859, a Galveston newspaper reported that the veteran warrior and statesman was visiting his Cedar Point home, was satisfied to retire, and had no thought of running for governor. Another newspaper writer hoped that the people were waking up and that they would remedy the injustice done General Houston and place him in the position to which he was entitled by his past services. A citizen of Waco joined in, urging Texans to put the Old Chief to work where he could stay the tide of disunion, rebuke sectionalism, war upon Black Republicanism, and expose corruption in high places.

Uneasy forebodings assailed Houston when a strong minority of delegates to the Democratic convention at Houston City demanded a plank that favored reopening the African slave trade; his "evening glow" might not be as peaceful as he had hoped. Party managers realized that this proposal would arouse violent opposition in Texas and probably cost the party the election. Expediency dictated that the resolution be beaten, and it was. Then the Democrats renominated Hardin R. Runnels, a strong advocate of slavery with secessionist leanings, for governor. This ended Houston's pastoral anticipations, and he promptly announced that he had yielded to the inclinations of his friends who believed that, as governor, he could save the people of his state.

As an independent candidate, he would oppose the philosophy of men of the North who preached that a "higher law" demanded the prompt extermination of slavery regardless of the Constitution and the laws. He would also oppose those in the South who favored re-opening the African slave trade regardless of laws against it. Runnels championed the radical pro-slavery element in Texas, although he was not saying much about it because the resuscitated lion was sharpening his claws for the conflict.

Again Houston had no party, no organization, no campaign fund. He was truly in the fight for the cause, and apart from that, he did not want the job. He meant to restate his well-known views, and if the people wanted him they could have him; if not, he would look contentedly after his hillside flock and the "formidable increase of his lambs."[1]

After his defeat by Runnels two years before, Houston had been ridiculed and abused in the press. This had gone so far that one fair-minded man, P. W. Kittrell, who was opposed to Houston politically, protested that there was no necessity to kick the dead lion. But a dead lion he was not. Suddenly his vitality and strength were demonstrated not by his activity in the campaign but by the spontaneous support of the people who were opposed to resumption of the slave trade and breaking up the Union.

He did little traveling and made only one campaign speech. On July 9, 1859, in Nacogdoches, he reviewed his principles and policies. He said that he was a Democrat of the old school—"an old Fogy"— and would advance no modern improvements on the principles of the founding fathers. He declared, ". . . my conscience has not permitted me to stand aloof from my fellow citizens in this emergency. . . . I have been with Texas in six troubles and in seven I will not desert her." The cramped signatures on letters that had come from people all over the state urging him "to once more face calumny and abuse for their sake" told him that the hands of the letter writers were "hard." But "their honest words were those of free men who would not submit to dictation."

"At their call," he said, "I have quit my flocks and herds, and am ready again to throw all my energies into the scale of the common weal."

He reminded his audience of the services that he had rendered to Texas in the United States Senate. For one thing, the state had received ten million dollars for releasing its claim to New Mexico territory. This and other receipts from the federal government had "paid the last cent of the debt of the [Texas] Republic, . . . I helped do this; but when you were giving me such hard licks two years ago did you think of that?"

Some who cheered him were not in sympathy with his views. Their cheers were for the man who could be depended on for plenty of excitement; they would vote against him as they had done before, inspired by his antagonists to believe that his stand against the African slave trade and against secession made him "a traitor to the South."

He condemned the Houston Convention for discussing the reopening of the African slave trade and for "resolutions providing for the agitation of that subject." He wished to God, he said, that they had called it by some other name. To reopen the African slave trade would be ruinous. "I do not go to the results that will accrue to the African. I will not discuss its morality. That is a question with which I have nothing to do. . . . It may be that the African will be benefitted; but it will be death to the Whites." He demanded that Texans support impartial observance of the laws; those against the African slave trade, the Fugitive Slave Law, and the Dred Scott Decision. "Whenever the will or prejudice of individuals becomes the tribunal for the adjudication of Constitutional rights the Government will fall," he declared.

He assured them that the purpose of the men advocating illegal resumption of the African slave trade was to "bait the South on to hasten a dissolution of the Union. Since 1835 the struggle for disunion has been going on. That is what this means. The moment you ask the North to concede it will be the signal for bitterness and strife. We can't live in fellowship. We must have a dissolution and then follows civil war."

With passionate conviction he appealed to his hearers to stand by the Union and reject the advocates of secession:

... If we depart from the constitution ... We will have civil war without end. Make a Southern Confederacy, and there would be a Northern one. These men who have shown a disregard for the struggles of our fathers, will care but little for Union, when their chief end is attained ... The scenes that would ensue, I will not shock you by relating. God when He intends to destroy men first makes them mad.... He has maddened these men. Mark me, the day that produces a dissolution of this [Union] will be written in history in the blood of humanity. All that is horrible in war will characterize the future of this people. Preserve Union and you preserve Liberty. They are one and the same, indivisible and perfect.

He added a brief but powerful appeal, "Let me exhort you, then, to stand by the Constitution and the Union. Confide in one another in the hour of danger. Rely upon yourselves when demagogues would mislead you. Maintain those reserved powers which are essential to preserve your liberties against centralization, and they will withstand the shock of centuries." [2]

Most of the state's powerful newspapers attacked Houston for his pro-Union stand. Enemies, prodded by Burnet and Lamar, raked up old charges of cowardice and immorality. The secessionist radicals pressed hard on the traitor-to-the-South charge. Houston responded to the "traitor" charge with light irony far different from the flaming wrath he had displayed in 1857.

Confronted by a Houston-stimulated wave of popular sentiment in favor of the Union and constitutional procedures, the "new school" Democrats were forced to straddle. Runnels announced that he did not believe there was any cause to dissolve the Union, at least not for the time being.

Resenting charges of betrayal and cowardice against their former commander, Houston's San Jacinto comrades gathered around him. They strengthened a state-wide wave of sentimental affection for the man who, after giving his best years to Texas, was now denounced as the South's worst enemy. In the August election he won over Runnels by about the same modest margin by which Runnels had defeated him two years before—33,375 for Houston and 27,500 for Runnels. The champions of slavery suffered their first reverse at the polls in eleven years. Houston became the only man ever to be elected governor of two American states. He spoke briefly at barbecues given in his honor in September at Huntsville and Montgomery, and was repeatedly applauded when he denounced "the plan for a Southern Confederacy."

Runnels declared that Houston's election was an irreparable blow to Southern interests. The new Texas legislature, overwhelmingly Democratic and pro-slavery, quickly displayed its hostility toward the victorious candidate. An appropriation for needed furnishings for the executive mansion was blocked because such expenditures would indicate undeserved deference and respect for the newly elected Governor. One member suggested that a man who had lived in a wigwam was not entitled to civilized luxuries at public expense. The House debated whether to permit the use of its chamber for an inaugural ball.

In response, the Governor-elect announced that he believed the legislature did not represent the will of the people. He made his own arrangements for his inaugural. His address was delivered from the front of the capitol to an immense and enthusiastic crowd on the sloping lawn. The correspondent of the San Antonio *Daily Herald* reported on December 27, 1859:

> Then burst forth the mighty heart of the people with a great throb; all former applause was weak [compared] with that which now made the old capitol building shake to its center. Long continued was this spontaneous outburst of feeling, while the hero of San Jacinto . . . stood like a mighty Hercules in their midst.

This was like old times. Houston went on to discuss calmly the angry recriminations that followed John Brown's October, 1859, raid on Harper's Ferry. He urged his audience to distinguish between the acts of crazy individuals such as John Brown and those of the whole Northern people, pointing out that the acts of fanatics did not truly represent the Northern masses. "We should meet their clamor with the contempt of a people who fear no invasion of their rights, and . . . lend our endeavors toward quenching it altogether. . . . Half the care—half the thought which has been spent to meet sectionalism with sectionalism, bitterness with bitterness, and abolition by disunion, would have made this people today a happy, united and hopeful nation." [3]

In his formal message, January 13, 1860, he again stressed the necessity for tolerance: "... notwithstanding the ravings of deluded zealots, or the impious threats of fanatical disunionists, the love of our common country still burns with the fire of the olden time in the hearts of the American people. Nowhere does that fire burn with more fervor than in the hearts of the conservative people of Texas. ... Texas will maintain the Constitution and stand by the Union. It is all that can save us as a nation. Destroy it and anarchy awaits us." [4]

He had been in office about a month when the South Carolina legislature passed a resolution declaring that any state had the right to secede. South Carolina's Governor forwarded to Governor Houston an invitation for Texas to send delegates to a "Southern Convention." He forwarded the resolutions to the legislature with a vigorous message of dissent. "The Union was intended to be a perpetuity," he declared. After a lengthy discussion he recommended "resolutions dissenting from the assertion of the abstract right of secession, and refusing to send deputies ... and urging upon the people of all the States, North and South, the necessity of cultivating brotherly feeling, observing justice, and attending to their own affairs." [5]

Adroit parliamentary tactics by pro-Houston minorities in both houses averted favorable action on South Carolina's invitation. This outraged Senator Iverson of Georgia, who earnestly urged "some Texas Brutus" to "rise and rid his country of the hoary-headed incubus." [6] It was not the first time extremists had suggested that assassins dispose of Houston.

Letters and newspapers brought to Texas tales of exciting scenes in the national House of Representatives. Thaddeus Stevens of Pennsylvania charged the South with trying to intimidate the free states. In response, Congressman Martin J. Crawford jibed, "I have this to say,—and I speak for Georgia,—'We will never submit to the inauguration of a black Republican President.'" Congressman William Barksdale of Mississippi gave the scene its climax. "The army," he warned, "which invades the South to subjugate her will never return. Their bodies will enrich the soil."

In the Senate Robert Toombs of Georgia was equally bellicose, declaring that the South had just cause for war. Addressing freemen of Georgia, he exclaimed, "Defend yourselves; the enemy is already at your doors . . . meet him at the doorsill, and drive him from the temple of liberty, or pull down its pillars, and involve him in a common ruin." [7]

Houston could visualize these scenes of anger and passion. There were nights when his anxiety over the gathering storm prevented sleep. He saw it as the coming of the hurricane whose seeds had been sown by John C. Calhoun. He could recall having once agreed with Thomas Hart Benton that although Calhoun was dead, his principles would live on. Now the prophecy was fact.

Despite his ceaseless anxiety, the Governor found consolation in his family. The executive mansion, partly furnished by the Houstons, made a sumptuous setting for family gatherings and social entertainments. Margaret managed some gay parties to divert her husband from office cares and the threats on the national horizon. Her lively and amusing sister Emily was a frequent visitor. She had married Charles Power after her prosperous husband, William Bledsoe, died. Power had made a fortune in the mines of Brazil.

All the children were at home except Sam, Jr., who was boarding with friends in Bastrop while attending the Allen Military Academy. Past sixteen, Sam was nearly six feet tall. His sisters attended public school in Austin, and their mother gave them lessons in Latin and music at home. The Governor often warned his children to make the most of their educational opportunities, so they would not grow up with regrets as he had done.

Margaret's health was excellent except for frequent attacks of asthma. She was anticipating another increment to the Governor's "planned posterity." At sixty-seven, he still hoped to round out his brood with the sextet of brothers he had promised Sam, Jr. If the next little Houston turned out to be a boy, he and Margaret would have only two more to go.

During the busy January days just after taking office, he had found time to write letters to Sam, Jr., that were always affectionate and sometimes instructive.

Don't smoke, nor chew . . . [or] carry concealed weapons . . . I look upon you as the one on whom my mantle is to

585

fall. . . . It is natural that I should desire you to wear it worthily, aye nobly, and to give [it] additional lustre. Remember your Creator in the days of your youth . . . & my Dear boy, never associate with those who . . . sneer at the teachings of the Bible.[8]

Houston gave Sam the news of his girl friends, Tula Clay, Miss Rosa, Maggie Willis, Maggie Ragsdale, and Miss Oldham; and stressed the importance of studying languages, history, geography, grammar, and penmanship. On April 7, 1860, he wrote to Sam that the pressure of work still compelled him to eat dinner in his office. Mother's health was improving; little Willie was better; the girls were all learning well. "Mr. Pendleton sends regards & says he met Miss Oldham on the street this morning, and she looked as blooming as a Pink and as attractive as a Swamp Cabbage. Things that are familiar to you at Bastrop would be news to us at home.

"Maggie Ragsdale has not been at our house for some time. She is one of the sweetest girls I have seen in Austin. I think she sends 'regards to your son.' Andrew is the cleverest fellow in the world, if he can do as he wishes. He had been hugging the dogs the other day, and that night I had to get up, take off his flannels, turn them inside out and shake them in the Hall, as I think the Fleas would have nearly eaten him up otherwise. Since then I think he has not been so familiar with the dogs." [9]

2. "Your Sons and Brothers Will Be Herded Like Sheep"

In the huge pine-board "Wigwam" hastily thrown together in Chicago, Illinois, to house the Republican Presidential convention, ten thousand persons assembled at ten o'clock Friday morning, May 18, 1860—delegates, press, professional politicians, excited spectators. In two days, routine business had been disposed of. Nominations began at once. Many of Abraham Lincoln's enthusiastic supporters had obtained admission by bogus tickets. On the second ballot Seward picked up 11 votes, Lincoln gained 79. Chase and Bates trailed along making no headway.

Tally pencils clicked off 231½ votes for Lincoln. Joseph Medill, editor of the Chicago *Tribune*, having taken his seat amid the Ohio delegation, whispered to the delegation's chairman, David Cartter, that if he would throw the Ohio delegation to Lincoln, Chase could have anything he wanted.[1] Cartter, who stuttered, bounced up and stammered, "I-I a-a-rise Mr. Chairman, to a-a-nounce—" He announced a change of four votes from Chase to Lincoln.[2]

Banners, canes, hats, and handkerchiefs went into the air as the crowd yelled wildly. Telegraph wires chattered the news across the country. A cannon on the roof fired. River boats whistled.

Sagging in a chair in the office of the Springfield *Journal*, Lincoln waited, distraught. He had been jittery for three days, and his nerves had not been calmed by the messages received from Chicago. On May 14, he had received from Nathan M. Knapp a short letter intended to reassure: "Be not too Expectant but rely upon our discretion. Again I say brace your nerves for any result." On May 16, Norman B. Judd, a long time Lincoln associate in political campaigns and on the Illinois Eighth Judicial District, had sent a telegram: DON'T BE FRIGHTENED KEEP COOL THINGS IS WORKING   JUDD.

And now a telegram was thrust into his hand: VOTE JUST ANNOUNCED—WHOLE NO 466—NECESSARY TO CHOICE 234—LINCOLN 354—ON MOTION OF MR. EVARTS OF NY THE NOMINATION MADE UNANIMOUS AMID INTENSE EXCITEMENT. The word came that Hannibal Hamlin would be his running mate. In another wire, delegate Knapp exclaimed, WE DID IT GLORY TO GOD.[3]

In April, 1860, in the Democratic convention at Charleston, South Carolina, Stephen A. Douglas had polled a majority, but fell short of the required two-thirds majority. The extreme pro-slavery bloc bolted and later picked John C. Breckinridge.

The National Union party, meeting at Baltimore on May 10, gave 57 votes to Sam Houston on the first ballot against 68½ for John Bell, a moderate Union man from Kentucky. After compliments to Houston by a Kentucky spokesman, the Kentucky delegation's strength went to Bell. Bell was finally nominated with elderly Edward Everett of Harvard for vice-president, making the ticket solid Whig. Thus there were three candidates in the field to divide the strength of those who were opposed to Lincoln, the "Black Republican."

On May 17, 1860, the day before Lincoln was nominated, Houston wrote to one of his active supporters, John H. Manley:

... I have noticed in the proceedings of the late Baltimore Convention, that my name was submitted to that body and balloted for ... while I appreciate the regard manifested for me by the numerous gentlemen who voted for me on that occasion, the use of my name was entirely unauthorized by me, and opposed to my well known opinions. In a letter written March 25, 1860, I said:

"If my name should be used in connection with the Presidency, the movement must originate with the people themselves, as well as end with them. I will not consent to have my name submitted to any convention, nor would I accept a nomination, if it were tendered me, and procured by contrivance, trick, or management."

Houston had been nominated at San Jacinto on April 21, 1860 by a group of enthusiastic supporters who were fully informed on all his views. To this group he told Manley he had responded: "... if the independent masses of the country deem my name important, in connection with the Presidency, they have a right to use it." [4]

On May 30, 1860, the New York *Herald* gave most of its front page to the story about Houston's San Jacinto nomination, his acceptance, and a mass meeting that had taken place the day before in Union Square. Leaders of the meeting were from many states, including New York, Tennessee, California, and Texas. The meeting had all of the characteristics of the usual campaign rally: speeches, banners, songs, a huge picture of Houston in military uniform, and slogans:

THE PEOPLE'S CANDIDATE FOR PRESIDENT, GENERAL SAM HOUSTON. A GREAT MAN.

FOR PRESIDENT, GENERAL SAM HOUSTON. AN HONEST MAN NO PLATFORM NEEDS; HE FOLLOWS RIGHT, AND GOES WHERE JUSTICE LEADS.

More than one New York newspaper expressed the belief that Houston might be the solution to the ugly problem before the nation. [5]

There was a small popular ground swell for Houston, and some good men were for him; but, to get a nomination that was worth more than a testimonial, Houston needed a platform and sound organization and management.

As Lincoln's campaign progressed, resentment grew steadily in the South. The world into which Governor Houston's eighth child and fourth son, Temple Lea Houston, was born August 20, 1860, seethed with threats of revolution.

A shrewd interpreter of political trends, Houston noted with alarm that in early local elections Maine and Vermont rolled up significant Republican majorities. He foresaw Lincoln's election and feared the consequences. With the exception of himself and Alexander H. Stephens of Georgia, most influential Southerners believed in the right to secede even though many feared the result. During his battle with Calhoun, Houston had endeavored to demolish the conception that secession was a right. But angry Southern leaders had adopted Calhoun's reasoning as gospel. The Governor saw daily evidence that they would succeed in popularizing their secession sentiment. Could he save Texas from blindly following the advocates of this doctrine? What arguments would persuade the people to oppose it?

As the Presidential election drew near, Texas was rocked by violent excitement. Terrible stories circulated—secret caches of arms had been discovered, the capital was in flames, kegs of powder had been found under houses, thousands of Negroes were engaged in insurrectionary plots, and wells had been poisoned. Town after town was reported to be in ashes. By the time one report was proved false, stories equally exciting about other communities were afloat.

Governor Houston left his sick bed to address a Union mass meeting during the last week of September. "Whipsters and demagogues," he told them, "are making capital out of the misfortunes of the people." He conceded that some property had been burned; that here and there, a case of insubordination had been found among the Negroes. Occasionally, attempts had been made to run a Negro off and sell him. ". . . We all know how every occurrence has been magnified by the disunion press and leaders and scattered abroad, and for no other purpose than to arouse the passions of the people and drive them into the Southern Disunion movement."

Pleading for a renewal of vows of fidelity to the Constitution and for an interchange of sentiments of devotion to the whole country, he said:

The error has been that the South has met sectionalism with sectionalism.... Because a minority at the North are inimical to us, shall we cut loose from the majority, or shall we not rather encourage the majority to unite and aid us?

... Let past differences be forgotten in the determination to unite against sectionalism....

But if, through division in the ranks of those opposed to Mr. Lincoln, he should be elected, we have no excuse for dissolving the Union. The Union is worth more than Mr. Lincoln, and if the battle is to be fought for the Constitution, let us fight it in the Union and for the sake of the Union. With a majority of the people in favor of the Constitution, shall we desert the Government and leave it in the hands of the minority? ...

Secession or revolution will not be justified until legal and constitutional means of redress have been tried, and I can not believe that the time will ever come when these will prove inadequate....

But, ... we have a new party in our midst.... what they call a Southern constitutional party.... and yet there is scarcely one of them but will tell you that, notwithstanding the fact that Mr. Lincoln may be elected in the mode pointed out by the Constitution and by a constitutional majority, they will not submit. You hear it from the stump, you read it in their papers and in their resolution, that if Mr. Lincoln is elected the Union is to be dissolved. Here is a constitutional party that intends to violate the Constitution because a man is constitutionally elected President....

What do these men propose to give you in exchange for this Government? All are ready to admit their ability to pull down, but can they build up? I have read of the glory of a Southern Confederacy, and seen the schemes of rash enthusiasts; but no rational basis has been presented.... But where are their Washingtons, their Jeffersons, and Madisons? ... Look at the men who are crying out disunion, and then ask yourselves whether they are the men you would choose to create a new government? ...

Democrats, you remember! Whigs, you remember! how Clay and Webster aided Jackson to put down nullification and secession! Will you stand back now, when both are openly avowed by sectionalists North and South!

... Let the people say to these abolition agitators of the North, and to the disunion agitators of the South, "You cannot dissolve this Union. We will put you both down; but we will not let the Union go!" [6]

Unionists rose and cheered. According to the Dallas *Herald* of November 7, 1860, the Governor's speech was the last "expiring kick (political) of the Old Hero." Resolutions against Houston's "sentiments of servility" were passed by a secessionist mass meeting. A number of Unionists were hanged in effigy, but they did not hang the Old Hero. He knew perfectly well that he was taking a fateful road. Whatever the outcome he had no choice but to follow where it led. He and Margaret agreed that everything must be risked for the sake of his basic principle: "... to be honest and fear not is the right path...."

On November 7, 1860, when the Governor wrote to Sam, Jr., he did not yet know the result of the national election the day before. All he knew was that the secessionist candidate Breckinridge had carried the city of Austin over the moderate Bell by an exceedingly narrow margin. This encouraged him to hope that the final returns would support him on the Union issue. "... The fire eaters got their chunk put out," he informed his son. "The price of liberty is blood, and if an attempt is made to destroy the Union, or violate the Constitution, there will be bloodshed to maintain them. The Demons of Anarchy must be put down and destroyed. The miserable Demagogues & Traitors ... must be silenced, and set at naught." [7]

Houston's hope that the fire-eaters had sustained a nation wide setback was soon dispelled. News came of the election of Lincoln, whose three opponents had out-polled him by a million votes. South of the Potomac, Lincoln had won not a single electoral vote and in some states not a single popular vote. He would be that sinister thing, "a sectional President."

Six Southern governors and almost every senator and congressman from the deep South had declared in favor of secession if Lincoln was elected. After the election, South Carolina took the lead in calling for a secession convention. Governor Joseph E. Brown of Georgia recommended that the state legislature approve an appropriation of a million dollars to arm the state. Senator Robert

Toombs, later to be the Confederacy's secretary of state, had come home from Washington in anticipation of this event. Toombs had been a strong Union man, but now was an ardent advocate of secession. He was famous as an able parliamentarian and debater. On the evening of November 13, 1860, he addressed the Georgia legislature in support of Governor Brown's request.

"I ask you," he roared, "to give me the sword; for if you do not give it to me, as God lives, I will take it myself ..." He called upon them to buy arms. "... throw the bloody spear into this den of incendiaries and assassins." [8]

On the evening of November 14, Alexander H. Stephens, later to be vice-president of the Confederacy, pleaded with the legislators not to heed his life-long friend, Toombs. Stephens urged loyalty to the federal Constitution and begged his auditors to realize that nothing had happened to justify breaking up the Union. Lincoln had been elected in accord with constitutional procedure; to rebel against him would desecrate the national charter. Stephens conceded that the South did not like things Lincoln had said, but could not make a war on a President for his words. Only direct acts would justify extreme measures. In the past ten years the only transgression of the North against the South had been its failure to enforce the Fugitive Slave Law. This error, Stephens said, would be corrected and it did not justify secession. Stephens' appeal to reason was disregarded by the Georgia legislature and ignored in Texas and the rest of the South. Toombs's advice to hurl the bloody spear spread like fire from a brand cast into straw.

A committee of secessionists called on Governor Houston at Austin, demanding an immediate session of the legislature to follow the example of South Carolina and Georgia in preparing for secession. The Governor played for time, taking the matter "under advisement." Soon, others came with similar petitions. Houston's old friend Ashbel Smith, whose home was not far from the Houston summer residence at Cedar Point, was a member of one of these delegations. This time the Governor thought it advisable to act.

On November 28, in conformance with a law passed during the Kansas crisis, he sent an invitation to all Southern governors to meet for a conference in Austin. On December 3, 1860, he issued "An Address to the People of Texas," explaining that a convention such as the South Carolina governor had proposed, or any other action, was unnecessary until the other states answered his invitation for a conference of conciliation. "...the fearful calamity of disunion now impending, calls for the united action of the Southern States so that it may, if possible, be averted," he counseled in vain. Not a single governor responded to his appeal or even acknowledged it.[9]

Angered by Houston's delaying tactics, particularly by his ignoring their appeal for a special session of the legislature, a committee of some sixty prominent men met on December 3, 1860, in Attorney General George M. Flournoy's office in Austin. They called for an election of delegates by the people to meet on January 28, 1861, to decide on the course Texas should take.

In answer to this challenge, the governor took the stump. In Galveston, he was refused permission to use a hall. Friends, fearing for his safety, asked him not to speak. He disregarded them and stepped out through an open window onto a balcony of the Tremont House. His commanding appearance silenced roars of anger which gave way to cheers from the crowd that thronged the street.

A Northerner in the crowd that day wrote admiringly "an old man of seventy years, [he was sixty-eight] on the balcony ten feet above the heads of the thousands assembled to hear him, where every eye could scan his magnificent form, ... straight as an arrow, with deep-set and penetrating eyes, looking out from heavy and thundering brows, a high forehead, with something of the infinite intellectual shadowed there, crowned with white locks ... and a voice of the deep basso tone, which shook and commanded the soul of the hearer, adding to all this a powerful manner, made up of deliberation, self-possession, and restrained majesty of action, leaving the hearer impressed with the feeling that more of his power was hidden than revealed. Thus appeared Sam Houston on this grand occasion, equal and superior to it.... He paralyzed the arm of the mobocrat by his personal presence...."[10]

His remarks were as fearless as his presence. He told the dissenters exactly what he believed they had to look forward to:

> Some of you laugh to scorn the idea of bloodshed as a result of secession, and jocularly propose to drink all the blood that will ever flow in consequence of it. But let me tell you what is coming on the heels of secession. The time will come when your

fathers and husbands, your sons and brothers, will be herded together like sheep and cattle at the point of the bayonet; and your mothers and wives, and sisters and daughters, will ask, 'Where are they?' and echo will answer, Where? You may, after the sacrifice of countless millions of treasure and hundreds of thousands of precious lives, as a bare possibility, win Southern independence, if God be not against you; but I doubt it. I tell you that . . . the North is determined to preserve this Union. They are not a fiery, impulsive people as you are, for they live in colder climates. But when they begin to move in a given direction, where great interests are involved, . . . they move with the steady momentum and perseverance of a mighty avalanche; and what I fear is, they will overwhelm the South with ignoble defeat, and I would say Amen to the suffering and defeat I have pictured, if the present difficulties could find no other solution, and that, too, by peaceable means. I believe they can. Otherwise I would say, 'Better die freemen than live slaves.' [11]

While he was speaking, a horse in a team nearby grew restive and attempted to kick itself out of the harness. The Governor paused to say, "Let old Dobbin alone. He is trying a little practical secession!" The horse finally "choked himself down" and the teamster commenced beating him.

"See how it works!" the Governor exclaimed promptly. "That's secession for you!" The horse after being well beaten was got to his feet and the teamster began putting on the broken harness. The Governor pointed the moral. "See in what a fix he is brought back into the Union!" [12]

They cheered him for that, and again when he said that whatever his State did his sympathies would go with her. "And as Henry Clay, my political opponent on annexation, said, when asked why he allowed his son to go into the Mexican war, 'My country, right or wrong,' so I say, My State, right or wrong."

After Houston spoke, a small group of Unionists voted to indorse his plan for the meeting of Southern governors and disapproved the convention proposed by the secessionists. The next day Houston spoke in his namesake city to a crowd, eager to join the secession movement and resenting his gloomy forecasts. They interrupted repeatedly with, "Three cheers for Georgia!" "Three cheers for Toombs!" "Three cheers for Yancey!" "Three cheers for South Carolina!" But they could not shout him down.

594

About half the counties of the state responded to the call of the secessionist committee to elect convention delegates. Most of the 174 delegates were for slavery and secession. Soon after this election, a single member of the legislature called on his fellows to meet in extra session for the admitted purpose of taking Texas out of the Union. Fearing that he would have a runaway legislature on his hands, Houston reluctantly bowed to the inevitable. On December 17, he called the legislature into extra session January 21, 1861. This would give Houston time to exert his influence on the legislature before the convention assembled one week later.

With rising passions threatening civil war within the state, the Governor decided to trim sail a bit. In a speech at Waco on New Year's Day, he announced that he would yield to the demand for secession if the people voted for it in a fair election. If the people did demand secession, then he believed Texas "would unfurl again the banner of the 'lone star' to the breeze, and reenter upon a national career." [13]

The Governor's proposal for a separate Republic instead of affiliation with the other seceding states, angered the secessionist leaders. Houston's friends urged him to leave town and get beyond the Brazos without delay, but he refused to go. That night a keg of powder exploded behind the hotel where he was sleeping.

The Governor's opponents were jubilant when they heard that South Carolina had seceded on December 20. Undoubtedly this drastic step was the result of a people's movement. Citizens of Charleston had crowded the streets, cheering for a Southern Confederacy; palmetto flags appeared at windows and on public buildings and a group of young men, after marching around John C. Calhoun's grave, vowed to give their lives, fortunes, and sacred honor to the cause of South Carolina's independence.

Each night the distracted Texas Governor knelt to appeal to the Almighty. "Dear Heavenly Father," he prayed, "I beseech thee cast out of my mind the dark forebodings of the coming conflict...." He still hoped that some act of reconciliation by the North would avert the impending disaster. But nothing that was being said or done anywhere in the North or in the South supported this hope. Frightened men in both sections appealed to Persident-elect Lincoln to appease the South with a conciliatory declaration. For a time Lincoln kept his own counsel. Then he gave a statement of his views to

Senator Lyman Trumbull of Ohio to be presented with discretion to a Republican rally. The statement was misinterpreted. Secessionists took it to be a threat, and Republicans charged weakness. As Houston had complained in Texas, Lincoln complained in the North that the trouble was in men's minds: " 'Party malice' and not 'public good' possesses them entirely." [14]

Lincoln issued no more public statements about compromise, but to individuals he disclosed frankly what was in his mind. "Whatever springs of necessity from the fact that the institution is amongst us," was not his great concern. But as for popular sovereignty on slavery in the territories south of the Missouri Compromise line, he was inflexible. Since 1854 he had believed that extension of slavery into the territories would be followed immediately by filibustering and demands for its further extension.

He urged Senator Lyman Trumbull to stand firm, telling him that the tug had to come and that it would be better if it came now than later. He wrote to Congressman Elihu B. Washburne, urging him to hold firm too. Lincoln did not believe that compromise meant peace. So he assumed responsibility for blocking compromise, hoping during the four months intervening between his election in November, 1860 and his inauguration in March, 1861, that a rebirth of loyalties, old traditions, and Union sentiment in the Southern states would avert secession and hence war.[15]

In Texas, Houston saw no hope for concessions that would turn away the wrath of the secessionists who surrounded him. His dream of keeping Texas in the Union was fading.

3. *"Texas Is Lost"*

THE special session of the legislature called by the Governor met in confusion and tumult on January 21, 1861. Houston's message added to the fury of his opponents and to the discomfiture of his few remaining friends who held positions of influence. Ignoring the hand-picked "revolutionary" convention scheduled to meet a week later, he recommended that the legislature call "a convention of delegates fresh from the people." He reminded them that the people were "the tribunal of last resort" and that no action should be considered final until it had been submitted for their approval. "While deploring the election of Messrs. Lincoln and Hamlin," he said, "the Executive yet has seen in it no cause for the immediate and separate secession of Texas."

Already four Southern states had "declared themselves no longer members of the Union" but—

> ... The Executive has not yet lost the hope that our rights can be maintained in the Union, and that it may yet be perpetuated. Between constitutional remedies and anarchy and civil war he can see no middle ground. All the glorious associations of our past history prove that hitherto we have been capable of self-government ... let us keep proudly in the ascendant the great principle upon which rests the idea of American liberty....
> May a kind Providence guide you aright.[1]

The press denounced his message as "submissive" and not in accord with the "people's demand" for speedily leaving the Union. Some argued that the Governor should be impeached, but the necessity for such action vanished when the legislature declared that the delegates already chosen comprised "a people's Convention."

On the day the Governor read his message to the legislature, Margaret wrote to her mother, saying that the outlook was gloomy. She reported that her husband seemed cheerful and hopeful by day, but in the watches of the night she heard him praying for the distracted nation. She could not shut her eyes to dangers that threatened and thought it likely that the Houston family would be reduced to poverty. But her faith sustained her and she was certain that the Lord would go with them wherever they went.

Plans for a Confederacy were maturing rapidly. On January 21, the same day that Houston addressed the Texas legislature, the two senators from Alabama, Clement C. Clay and Benjamin Fitzpatrick, made fiery farewell speeches in Washington. Their state had passed an ordinance of secession and they announced their intention to "sustain her actions and her fortunes." For himself and the people of Alabama, Clay disclaimed "the godlike virtue which teaches us to love our enemies and to bless them that curse us."

Senator Jefferson Davis of Mississippi announced his resignation. He hoped for peaceful but separate relations between the states. If the contrary occurred, "we will trust the God of our fathers, ... and in our firm hearts and strong hands, we will vindicate the right as best we may."

In taking leave of the Senate on February 4, 1864, John Slidell of Louisiana, predicted a sure success for the new venture because the seceding states contained within themselves "elements of greatness." Those states that would not join the South, he said, would be regarded "as enemies in war, in peace friends.... You will find us ready to meet with you the outstretched hand of fellowship, or in the mailed panoply of war, as you will it; elect between these alternatives."

Senator Judah P. Benjamin, later to hold posts in the Confederate Cabinet, walked out saying, "... better, far better, the wildest anarchy, with the hope, the chance, of one hour's inspiration of the glorious breath of freedom, than ages of hopeless bondage and oppression, to which our enemies would reduce us." [2]

Earlier in January, Senator John J. Crittenden of Kentucky had offered a compromise measure that was a total surrender to previous demands of the Southern states. His proposed permanent amendments to the Constitution would guarantee slavery forever in the slave states and the District of Columbia, continue the domestic slave trade, indemnify slave owners for runaways, and extend the Missouri Compromise line to the Pacific.

Senator Toombs ridiculed the proposal. "The Union is already dissolved," he declared. He expressed contempt for the origin of the Union; talk of it being cemented by the blood of brave men was "nonsense." Had he lived when the United States Constitution was formed he would have voted against it. Its adoption had injured the South. Mr. Lincoln had deprecated the Southern demand that the North must "cease to call slaveholding wrong, and join them in calling it right, and this must be done thoroughly, done in acts as well as words."

"I say so too," Toombs exclaimed. "... I will have these rights in the Union, or I will not stay in it." [3]

Twice before Northern Democrats and Whigs had voted down the same territorial concession which Crittenden proposed anew. Now, with the support of the South, senators might have passed his proposals, but six Southern senators refused to vote for them. Senator Andrew Johnson of Tennessee said that the compromise proposals failed because these six senators "wanted no compromise. ... I believe more, Mr. President, that these gentlemen were acting in pursuance of a settled and fixed plan to break up and destroy the government...." [4]

Little was heard in Southern states about Crittenden's conciliatory proposals; but the telegraph flashed the words of defiance with which Southern senators quit their posts—words that fanned the flames. To Governor Houston they brought more dark forebodings. The brief remarks of courtly Senator Crittenden were not featured in the Texas press. With a pathetic note, he sought to mitigate bitterness and hate, expressing the fervent "hope that the Union which was the glory of the fathers, will not become the shame of their children." [5]

Oran M. Roberts, associate justice of the Texas Supreme Court, was elected president of the Secessionist Convention when it met in the chamber of the House of Representatives at Austin, January 28, 1861. The next day the delegates passed a resolution declaring in favor of secession. An ordinance of secession was to be prepared and voted on at noon, February 1.

To preserve a situation in which he still might exert influence against secession, Houston recognized the "legality" of the convention and assured one of its committees that if the secession ordinance was submitted to the vote of the people he would abide by it.

Some sixteen years before, Houston had retained Oran Roberts, then a young attorney, to look after some of his private business interests. Although he knew the Governor well, Justice Roberts let himself be persuaded that Houston would acquiesce in the secession movement if he beheld the magnitude of his opposition with his own eyes. He overlooked Houston's record for never permitting opposition to influence him to retreat from a position based on principle. So Roberts sent a committee to the Governor with a courteous invitation to attend the session of February 1. On that day, at noon, the ordinance taking Texas out of the Union would be voted on. The ordinance fixed February 23 for the balloting by the people with the provision that if the result favored secession Texas would leave the Union on March 2, the anniversary of the Texas Declaration of Independence from Mexico and of Sam Houston's birth.

The galleries were crowded when the Governor, amid thunderous, hopeful applause, was escorted to a seat at Roberts' right. Houston's face was expressionless, showing no trace of gratification for the demonstration. Grim and motionless, he listened to the reading of the ordinance. It had been agreed that no discussion would be permitted before voting.

The roll was called alphabetically, and each of the first seventy delegates responded with a hearty, "Aye." One of the seventy, T. Jefferson Chambers, disregarded the no discussion rule before casting his vote. He advanced down the aisle, pointed a finger at the convention's guest of honor, and declared him a traitor. Delegate William P. Rogers, Houston's cousin, took the floor and forced an apology from Chambers. Houston remained impassive.

Houston's long-time supporter, Thomas Hughes of Williamson County, was the first to shout, "No!" when his name was called. A startled murmur, then loud protests and hisses swept the chamber. Houston ignored this, too, while Roberts banged for order. James W. Throckmorton, leader of a small pro-Houston minority in the Texas Senate, was the next to defy the rule of no discussion.

A flicker of approval crossed Houston's face, but it faded quickly and he was again impassive as delegates and galleries hissed. Throckmorton angrily turned on them shouting that when the rabble hissed, patriots might well tremble!

The convention's final vote fell only a little short of the unanimity desired. The ordinance passed by a vote of 167 to seven. Immediately after the result was announced, Attorney General Flournoy conducted a bevy of ladies down the aisle toward the platform. They unfurled and triumphantly waved a Lone Star flag; delegates and spectators in the galleries went wild.

Governor Houston still remained impassive as Texans rushed joyfully toward the terrible destiny he had foretold. He left the chamber without a word, deep in sorrow for what he saw ahead for Texas and the South.

Step by step the convention managers extended their control over the state government and the destiny of the people. After passing the secession ordinance, they demanded that the Legislature surrender its authority and "recognize" the convention's "supreme and sovereign power." The legislature refused, but granted the convention the right to submit the secession ordinance to the people. Houston doubted that the people would be allowed to express their will without interference. However, he had no choice but to acquiesce in a procedure he, himself, had proposed. He announced that he would make no speeches and would leave the people free to decide for themselves how they should vote.

Soon after the Governor formally announced the election date, secessionists spread reports in the press and by word of mouth that Houston had reversed his stand and now favored quitting the Union. In open letters to friends, he reasserted his true position. The following, written on February 20, 1861, appeared in the Austin *Southern Intelligencer* just before the election:

> You say that it is reported that I am for secession. Ask those who say so to point to a single word of mine authorizing the statement. I have declared myself in favor of peace, of harmony, of compromise, in order to obtain a fair expression of the will of the people....
> I still believe that secession will bring ruin and civil war. Yet, if the people will it, I can bear it with them.... far less concession than was made to form the Constitution would now preserve it. Thus believing I cannot vote for secession.... My views are of record.... If I err ... my countrymen will forgive me, as they have forgiven me for many other things I have done. I am willing, even, to be called a submissionist for their sake.[6]

News reached Texas that Jefferson Davis, at Montgomery, Alabama, had been chosen Provisional President of the new Confederate States of America. Equally exciting reports came from Georgia, Florida, and Louisiana. Federal property was being seized—forts, post offices, custom houses, a mint, and sub-treasuries with gold stocks enough to finance the new government for many months. Fort Sumter still remained in federal hands, but the *Star of the West*, entering Charleston harbor with provisions, had been fired on and had turned back.

Texas secessionists, without waiting for results of the referendum, prepared to follow the example of other Southern states in seizing federal property. The convention authorized Roberts to appoint a nineteen-member "Committee of Public Safety," which would have almost unlimited powers. The committee appointed William S. Oldham, W. P. Rogers, and T. D. Devine a subcommittee to confer with Governor Houston on the disposition of federal property within the state. Oldham, the most influential member, had been antagonistic to Houston ever since Houston had voted against the Kansas-Nebraska Bill. Oldham had signed the Democratic State Committee's denunciation of Houston as a traitor-betrayer. All three members of the committee had voted for the secession ordinance.

On February 4, Governor Houston received the committee courteously and treated them as gentlemen whose word could be trusted. When they asked what he proposed to do about Federal property within the state, he pledged them to secrecy and answered that it was not within his power to seize and dispose of such property while Texas was still in the Union because his oath to support the United States Constitution was binding. He assured them he would never be instrumental in the shedding of fraternal blood. When they inquired what he would do if Texas seceded, he asked them to promise that they would take no action that would conflict with his authority. Then he confided that if the popular vote favored secession, he would see that all U. S. troops were removed from the State at the earliest possible moment.

This was not what the committee wanted and they decided they were absolved from their pledge of secrecy. They promptly reported his confidential information to the convention managers. This was the basis of the Governor's later charge that he had been betrayed.

At about this time, the Committee of Public Safety learned that Colonel Charles A. Waite had been ordered to relieve the Federal Commander of the Department of Texas, General David E. Twiggs, whose loyalty was suspect. A native of Georgia and a graduate of West Point, Twiggs was an ardent secessionist; Waite was a loyal Union man.

An outfit of Texas troops, hastily organized under Colonel Ben McCulloch, went to San Antonio. McCulloch had fought under Houston at San Jacinto. At San Antonio, by prearrangement, General Twiggs surrendered to McCulloch without resistance eleven hundred Union soldiers, the United States arsenal and barracks, and federal stores and equipment worth about three million dollars.

Houston denounced Twiggs as a traitor, and the general was promptly dismissed from the U. S. Army.

At two o'clock on the afternoon of February 16, 1861, a few hours after General Twiggs's surrender, Colonel Robert E. Lee, in his heavily loaded carryall, drove up in front of the Read House in San Antonio. He learned of Twiggs's surrender from a group of McCulloch's men who wore crude red military symbols on their shirts and coats. They made Colonel Lee a "prisoner of war." Lee took off his uniform and put on civilian clothes. When he tried to arrange with McCulloch for transportation to the coast, he was promised assistance if he would resign his United States commission and join the Confederacy. Otherwise he would not be allowed transportation for his luggage. Colonel Lee refused, declaring that he owed allegiance to the United States and not to the revolutionary authorities of Texas.

Lee had been on duty with troops in the Department of Texas for several months. On January 23, 1861, he had written to his son in Washington about the crisis:

> Secession is nothing but revolution. The framers of our Constitution never would have exhausted so much labor, wisdom, and forebearance in its formation, and surrounded it with so many securities, if it was intended to be broken by every member of the confederacy at will. It is intended for *perpetual union*, as expressed in the preamble, and for the establishment of a *government*, not a compact. . . . It is idle to talk of secession. Anarchy would have been established, and not a government, by Washington, Hamilton, Jefferson, Madison, and all the other patriots of the Revolution.[7]

At Fort Mason, on February 4, Lee had received orders from the United States War Department to report to Washington by April 1. He was on his way to Washington when McCulloch's men seized him. After surrendering to McCulloch and asserting his allegiance to the United States, Lee went to a warehouse to arrange for storage of his belongings until he could provide for their release and forwarding. He was accompanied by a friend, Charles Anderson, brother of Major Robert Anderson who commanded at Fort Sumter. Lee's views on secession had changed since he had written to his son. On the way to the warehouse, he is reported to have said to Anderson:

> ... I still think, ... that my loyalty to Virginia ought to take precedence over that which is due the Federal Government. And I shall so report myself at Washington. If Virginia stands by the old Union, so will I. But if she secedes (though I do not believe in secession as a constitutional right, nor that there is sufficient cause for revolution), then I will still follow my native state with my sword, and if need be with my life. I know you think and feel very differently, but I can't help it. These are my principles, and I must follow them.[8]

Lee demonstrated his principles a few weeks later in Washington, D. C., when he declined the command of the federal army and resigned from the service of the United States.

In a carriage drawn by four white horses, Jefferson Davis rode to his inaugural ceremony which was conducted in front of the pillared capitol at Montgomery, Alabama, on February 19, 1861. Six states had already seceded. Four days later, Texans went to the polls for a disorderly referendum. Conditions at the time were described by an unnamed Union observer:

> The whole State was in a blaze of excitement. Arbitrary arrests, broils, murder and hanging were the order of the day, and under the pressure large numbers of Union men were giving way, and the secessionists were receiving daily accessions to their strength. The people were either deceived into secession, led into it, or forced into it.[9]

The campaign had been going on for only two weeks. A Waco vigilance committee had announced that it would hang every Lincoln sympathizer who kept on talking. Conservatives were directed to leave town or shut up. Twenty-seven counties, including some of the most populous, submitted no official figures. Seventeen counties voted against secession and eighty-one for it. In eighty counties reporting, 34,794 voted for secession and 11,255 against it. With the election machinery in the hands of the secessionists, charges of unfair dealing were inevitable. Charges were made regarding miscounting and refusal to receive ballots from voters suspected of Union sympathies.

By March 3, the official tally was completed: 46,129 for secession and 14,697 against it. Governor Houston was at home with his family when the news, spreading throughout the capital, was greeted with ringing bells and thunder of cannon. His face turned ashen; his jaw set and the cords of his neck tightened and throbbed. Nancy Elizabeth, then fifteen, later told her children of the anguish on her father's face as he said to her mother, "Texas is lost." Another member of the family heard him say his heart was broken.[10] Others said he was never the same afterward. Something had happened that he could not visualize. It was almost, they said, as if he had received his death blow—numbing grief beyond expression. Regardless of consequences to himself, he had stood by his principles in refusing to take an oath in which he did not believe; and in so doing he had ascended to his highest peak, a kind of martyrdom. Now, with Texas quitting the Union amid sounds of jubilation, he descended into his deepest valley of despair.

4. "Have All the People Gone Mad?"

SENATOR LOUIS T. WIGFALL of Texas, awaiting news that his state had seceded, had remained in Washington after most of his Southern colleagues had left. On March 3, 1861, the day before Lincoln's inauguration, he had blamed the desperate state of the nation's affairs on the indecision and irresolution of the outgoing Buchanan administration.

"We shall learn tomorrow from the eastern front of the capitol that we have a Government," retorted Senator Lyman Trumbull of Ohio, "and that will be the beginning of the maintenance of the Union."

Angered, the Texas senator leaped to his feet to present a bitter challenge. "The *Star of the West* swaggered into Charleston harbor," he shouted, "received a blow planted full in the face, and staggered out. Your flag has been insulted; redress it if you dare. You have submitted to it for two months, and you will submit forever.... We have dissolved the Union; mend it if you can;

cement it with blood; try the experiment.... This Federal Government is dead." [1]

Some twenty-four hours later, the huge crowd facing the east front of the Capitol heard the opening words of Abraham Lincoln's inaugural address. His introduction was coldly received, but the sombre cloud which seemed to hang over the audience began to fade when he said, "I hold ... that the Union of the states is perpetual! ... I shall take care, as the Constitution itself expressly enjoins upon me, that *'the laws of the Union shall be faithfully executed in all the states!'* " Then the cloud dissolved into wild enthusiasm when, with uplifted eyes, he solemnly pledged, "The power confided to me will be used to hold, occupy, and possess the property and places belonging to the government."

"I am loathe to close," he said, finally. "We are not enemies, but friends. We must not be enemies. Though passion may have strained, it must not break our bonds of affection....

"The Mystic chords of memory, stretching ... to every living heart and hearthstone, all over this broad land, will yet swell the chorus of the Union, when again touched, as surely they will be, by the better angels of our nature." [2]

While Lincoln was appealing to the "better angels," the imps of perversity had taken over in Texas. Without waiting for the result of the popular referendum, the convention had voted to annex Texas to the Confederate States of America and had dispatched seven delegates to Montgomery.

A few days later, when Governor Houston announced the result of the secession referendum, the convention voted a second time to annex Texas to the Confederacy. But the question put to the people by the referendum was whether Texas should withdraw from the Union, not whether it should join the Confederacy. On March 6, 1861, Governor Houston reminded the convention that it had been authorized only to submit the secession question to the people: "... it was understood," he said, "that the performance of that act would terminate the existence of the Convention."

He said that when the legislature met on March 18, he would recommend that it "call a new Convention directly from the people, which will fairly represent their wishes and opinions, ... to make such changes in the Constitution of the States as her present and future relations to the world at large may require." [3] His strategy was obvious to the managers of the convention. They knew that since Texas was out of the Union, Houston wanted his state to resume its former Lone Star nationality. This was far from what the convention wanted.

The Confederate government was equally precipitate in its readiness to take over Texas affairs before the people had a chance to decide on their own future. Before the seven Texas delegates reached Montgomery, Jefferson Davis' Secretary of War, Leroy Pope Walker, wrote to Governor Houston that the "Confederate states assumes control of all military operations in Texas." Through his Secretary of State, Eber W. Cave, Houston informed Walker that the convention had no authority to send delegates to Montgomery; he himself had not communicated with the convention since the submission of the ordinance "except to deny its authority," and Texas was in no way subject to the control of the convention or its president. "The people alone have any right to say what form of government they will have," he added. "There are requirements due to the national pride and dignity of a people who have just resumed their nationality ... and [these] do not sanction the course pursued in annexing them to a new government without their knowledge or consent." [4]

His purpose now was to persuade Texans to resume their nationality instead of joining the Confederacy. But already the legislature was virtually abolished; the convention and its Committee of Public Safety were supreme. It was apparent that they could be restrained only by force, and this raised the specter that appalled Houston— Texas plunged into its own civil war.

Angered by the Governor's stubborn resistance to their authority, the convention managers adopted a prompt reprisal. On March 14, 1861, by a vote of 109 to 2, the delegates resolved that all state officers must take an oath of allegiance to the Confederate government on the following day. The resolution carried the implied threat that any officer declining to take the oath would be removed.

All members of the convention who were state officers took the oath. Houston did not. On the evening of March 15, George W. Chilton, on order from the convention, went to the executive mansion with the convention's ultimatum. What occurred was later described by Nannie to her son, Temple Houston Morrow.

After dinner, the Negro servants cleared away the food and dishes. Margaret brought the family Bible and laid it before her husband at the head of the table. The servants sat along the wall of the dining room while the Governor read a chapter and made a few remarks. Then all knelt in prayer. At eight o'clock, about twenty minutes after prayers, Chilton arrived. He delivered the convention's message and asked the Governor to answer immediately whether or not he would appear at noon the next day to take the oath. The Governor understood the convention managers' purpose. They wanted him out of the way before the legislature convened on Monday. Their object was to forestall his anticipated appeal for the restoration of the state's constitutional government.

Evading a direct answer, he told Chilton that the time allowed him for making so important a decision was too short. Chilton, on his own authority, agreed that the Governor could have until noon on Saturday, March 16, 1861, to notify the convention of his decision and could take the oath at some later time. Chilton, of course, could give no assurance that the convention would accept this modification of its instructions.

Governor Houston needed no time to make up his mind about the oath, but he did need time to shape his strategy. The temper of the convention was at fever heat. Citizens had been murdered through the reckless intervention of the Committee of Safety. Property had been seized. What happened to him was of small account, but he must give careful thought to the evils that his refusal might bring upon his wife and eight children. The Governor kissed the younger children good night and told his wife that he was going upstairs to think things out.

In his bedroom, he removed his coat and vest and then his shoes so that he would not disturb the rest of the household. In his socks, he walked the floor of his room and the upper hall for an hour. Taking an oath to support a government that was opposed to the Union would taint every act of courage and principle of his long public career. Did the safety of his family require him to violate his principles? When he went downstairs Margaret was waiting to hear his decision.

"Margaret, I will never do it," he said.[5]

Margaret had written to her mother that, as a result of the Governor's course, they "might be rendered unto poverty." To her husband, she made the same comment that she had made many times before: he must do what he believed to be right, and the spirit of the Lord would watch over them.

He spoke of the many difficult times that they had passed through together. He put his arms around her and kissed her. Somehow or other they would come through again. He only hoped that the worst of their misfortunes would be his removal from office, which he was certain would follow. Then he went back upstairs to work on a message to the people explaining why he would not take the Confederate oath. Margaret slept little. All night the light burned in the General's study. He was still working on his address when dawn broke over the eastern hills.

In the morning, a curt message from Justice Roberts informed Houston that his agreement with Chilton was not acceptable to the convention. The Governor must present himself at the capitol on Saturday, March 16, at noon to take the oath.

When Houston arrived at the capitol, the delegates were surging in and out of the House chamber and through the corridors. A large crowd of curious and excited persons, some hostile and some sympathetic, thronged the lobby. Houston did not go to the lobby, report his presence to the officials, or go to his office; entering the basement through a separate entrance, he sat down, took out his jackknife, and began whittling a piece of soft pine.

In the lobby upstairs, the convention's secretary, R. P. Brownrigg, announced that all persons whose names were called should present themselves immediately to take an oath of loyalty to the Confederate government.

"Sam Houston!"

The bearer of the name did not move except to whittle off a long clean shaving from his white pine stick.

"Sam Houston!"

Four times his name was called. Four times a long clean shaving fell to the basement floor. William Baker, an anti-slavery Presbyterian minister of Austin and one of a group of spectators who gathered in the basement, later recalled "the old Governor sitting in his

609

chair, silent, immovable, sorrowfully meditating...and whittling steadily on...." [6]

Secretary of State Cave, who had supported Houston in both his gubernatorial campaigns, also refused to respond when his name was called. He was the only member of the state government to follow the example of his chief.

Swift retaliation followed the Governor's silent defiance. Roberts called the convention into session. None of the delegates protested an ordinance declaring the offices of governor and of secretary of state to be vacant. It passed unanimously. The authors of the ordinance disingenuously asserted that Houston's ouster was "ordained by the people of Texas;" Lieutenant Governor Edward Clark was "hereby required and authorized" to exercise the powers of the governor. Cave was ordered to turn over his papers and seal to his successor, who had not yet been named.

While this judgment was being enacted, Houston was in the executive office completing his long Address to the People which he had begun but had not finished the night before.

> ...Fellow-Citizens, in the name of your rights and liberties, which I believe have been trampled upon, I refuse to take this oath....In the name of my own conscience and manhood,...I refuse to take this oath....I love Texas too well to bring civil strife and bloodshed upon her. To avert this calamity, I shall make no endeavor to maintain my authority as Chief Executive of this State, except by the peaceful exercise of my functions. When I can no longer do this, I shall calmly withdraw from the scene, but still claiming that I am its Chief Executive....
>
> ...think not that I complain at the lot which Providence has now assigned me. It is perhaps but meet that my career should close thus. I have seen the patriots and statesmen of my youth, one by one, gathered to their fathers, and the government which they had created, rent in twain; and none like them are left to unite it once again. I stand the last almost of a race, who learned from their lips the lessons of human freedom. I am stricken down now, because I will not yield those principles, which I have fought for and struggled to maintain. The severest pang is that the blow comes in the name of the State of Texas. [7]

The convention managers hoped that Houston's ouster would forestall his submitting a message to the legislature. But after working over it for two days, he submitted a long and memorable document on Tuesday, March 18, 1861. He pointed out to the legislators that as the state's executive he had "obeyed the action taken by the people" when they voted for withdrawal from the Union. He refused to support annexation to the Confederacy because it had not been submitted to the people. For this he had been dispossessed of his office.

He vividly described the "high-handed, arbitrary" and "unconstitutional" acts of the convention and its Committee of Public Safety. He denounced the convention's "bluster and bravado," specifying many ways in which the rights of the people had been violated by the convention and its Committee of Public Safety. After building his case against "the usurpers," he pleaded with the legislators to resist usurpations: "... you are called upon to exercise the powers delegated to you by your constituents to interpose in behalf of their rights, and to avert these evils."

In conclusion, he referred to the executive's power to call out the militia, but said that because he believed the calamities of civil war within the state would be greater than the endurance of this usurpation for a time, he would make no violent effort to overthrow it. Driven to retirement in defiance of the constitution, he asserted that he still was the Governor elected by the people.[8]

When the convention managers learned the contents of Houston's message, they agreed that something must be done to prevent him from stirring up the people with his charges of usurpation. While they were thinking up their next move, Houston called four loyal friends, strong Unionists, to meet at the executive mansion. This meeting was virtually a council of war. The consultants were Benjamin H. Epperson, who had supported Houston for the presidency and who was the youngest member of the group; James W. Throckmorton, one of the seven members of the convention who had dared vote against taking Texas out of the Union; David B. Culberson, who later served in the United States Senate, and George W. Paschal, editor of the *Southern Intelligencer* and head of the Union Party of Texas.

Houston told them that he had received from Abraham Lincoln an offer of military support to help keep Texas in the Union. He had sent back word by Lincoln's messenger, Colonel Frederick West Lander, that he did not desire such assistance. He had instructed Lander to tell Lincoln that it was advisable to recall all United States forces from Texas, and had offered the opinion that the Union party of the whole South would collapse if coercion was attempted.

Houston's position had been so widely misrepresented by Southern newspapers that Lincoln apparently distrusted the accuracy of the report brought back by Lander. Lincoln sent a letter by a second messenger, George H. Giddings, a Texan who had been in Washington in connection with his mail contract for the route between San Antonio and San Diego. Paschal and the son of David B. Culberson later wrote articles describing what happened at this conference, but neither of them gave the exact terms of Lincoln's proposal. Houston said later that Lincoln had tentatively offered 70,000 troops. It also appears that Lincoln's letter suggested making Houston a major general of the United States Army, to take charge of all government property in Texas and to recruit 100,000 men.

After discussing Lincoln's proposals, Governor Houston polled his chosen advisers, beginning with the youngest. Epperson favored accepting the offer. Throckmorton opposed it on the ground that secession was inevitable. Culberson and Paschal supported Throckmorton.

Houston thanked them. "Gentlemen, I have asked your advice and will take it, but if I were twenty years younger I would accept Mr. Lincoln's proposition and endeavor to keep Texas in the Union." [9] Then he stepped to the fireplace and burned Lincoln's letter.

Paschal, in his review of the meeting, suggested that "Houston was too old and his family too young," to justify acceptance of the offer.[10] But other reasons also influenced Houston's decision. The offer had come too late; acccepting it at this time would surely have ignited a civil war in Texas. Houston also believed that no show of force now could prevent war between the North and South. The geographical position of Texas might protect the state from many of the horrors to come, but if he accepted Lincoln's offer, Texas would become a theater of war to be overrun and devastated.

Rumors of an intrigue between President Lincoln and Governor Houston excited Texas. In a speech at Galveston on April 19, 1861, and in a letter to the Galveston *Civilian* on September 12, Houston denied participation in any such activity. He said that calumnies heaped upon him by the Texas press had misled Lincoln as to his true position.

The calumnies and misunderstandings continued, bringing new hardships to Houston and his family. The convention managers, having decided upon a form of retaliation for the deposed Governor's defiance, notified him that he must vacate the executive mansion within twenty-four hours. Friends came to help the Houstons with their packing. They worked on the evening of March 18, and all the next day. After the task was finished, the Governor and his wife were sitting with their friends and helpers when a knock came at the door. Houston opened it and discovered a large party of men outside.

Margaret's first thought was that the convention had sent a force to hasten eviction. But these men were friends of the Governor, and they were armed. Most of them stayed back in the shadows. Several spokesmen came forward to tell Houston that they were prepared to disperse the convention and to reinstate him in office if he gave the word. They believed the people would support them.

Those inside did not hear all of Houston's answer to his callers, and he never disclosed the conversation or hinted at the identity of his supporters. For decades after the war, embittered secessionists cherished such resentment toward him, that none of the night visitors ever ventured to reveal his connection with the episode. What took place that night was described some thirty years later in the Galveston *Daily News* "By a Friend Who Was Present." The words attributed to Houston are compatible with his acts and characteristic mode of expression.

My God, is it possible that all the people are gone mad? Is it possible that my friends would be willing to inaugurate a war that would be infinitely more horrible than the one inaugurated by the secessionists? Do you know, my friends, that the civil war now being inaugurated will be as horrible as his Satanic Majesty could desire? And after condemning them for their folly and their crimes would you be willing to deluge the capital of Texas with the blood of Texans, merely to keep one poor old man in a position for a few days longer. . . .

His voice rose and vibrated with earnestness. "No. No!! go tell my deluded friends that I am proud of their friendship, of their love and loyalty, and I hope to retain them to the end. But say to them that for the sake of humanity and justice to disperse, to go to their homes and to conceal from the world that they would have been guilty of such an act." [11]

The deposed Governor could see more clearly into the future than the friends who offered armed support that night. For his restraint, Texas would owe him a debt of gratitude that was hardly acknowledged and never repaid.

Sam Houston's critics have commented that his course as Governor was "mysterious." The record itself dispels the mystery. When the choice was between the Union and secession or the Confederacy, he favored the Union with passionate intensity. But after the Union was disrupted and war became an actuality, his loyalty returned to Texas—not to Texas as part of the Confederacy, but to the Texas that he had helped build as a nation. He looked to the day when he could take Texas out of the Confederacy and again run up the Lone Star emblem. It was a thought to cherish until the time was ripe to reveal it. In time, he did reveal it; on that the record is clear.

Horace Greeley, sometimes strongest in his opinions when he knew least about what went on, declared that if Houston had shown either principle or courage he could have kept Texas in the Union. As Greeley saw it, Texas was lost because Sam Houston's lack of courage and leadership had made Texans sheep without a shepherd. That was the other side of the demagogue and traitor charge.

On the other hand, Charles Anderson praised Houston for his fearlessness. He pointed out that as a result of Houston's resolute stand, Texas had distinguished itself by being the only Southern state even to pretend to take the vote of the people on the secession issue. He lauded Houston's energy, shrewdness, calm, and courage in carrying out his plan as far as he could; he could detect no flaw in the design or execution of that plan.

Later John G. Nicolay and John Hay, Lincoln biographers, said that Houston's refusal of Lincoln's offer was the end of his public career. But they were mistaken. Before his career ended, he had many other acts of fortitude and courage to perform that brought him to the summit of his own particular Calvary.

BOOK X

LAST DREAMS

1. "Kill Him!"

I N his sixty-eighth year, deposed as Governor and reviled by the secessionist press, General Houston began the last of his many pilgrimages. The roads that he would travel from now on, from Austin to Independence, to Galveston, to Cedar Point, and to Huntsville were all familiar. But he had new relationships to establish with neighbors and friends, with the new state government, and with what he referred to as "the so-called Confederate Government." Above all, he had to face a troublesome situation with seventeen-year-old Sam, Jr., an eager disciple of secession. Sam had been given instructions to go to the summer home at Cedar Point after the close of school at the Allen Military Academy in the spring of 1861.

With his wife and seven other children, Houston quit the executive mansion within thirty-six hours after the warning of eviction. The family went by stage to Independence, a placid village where his wife's mother had a comfortable home. Their household furnishings would follow later by wagon.

Before the roads improved sufficiently to move the family to Cedar Point, Houston set out alone on a business trip to Galveston. From there, he planned to go to Cedar Point to have a fatherly talk with Sam. On the day before Easter Sunday, the ex-Governor interrupted his journey to Galveston with a stop-over at Brenham, probably because he was averse to traveling on the Sabbath on business. A strict observer of the day, he was even unwilling to write to his wife concerning business matters when he was absent from home on the Sabbath. On the street in Brenham, he met an old friend, Hugh McIntyre, a wealthy, influential planter and slave owner. McIntyre said that he and a number of his friends, all of whom had a high regard for the governor personally, were troubled about his refusal to take the Confederate oath. Would he meet with them in the court house and explain his attitude? His answer was that he had no desire to speak. He was averse to arousing passion and clamor.[1]

When other friends joined McIntyre, Houston remained firm in his refusal. But when a report reached him that if he spoke against secession, it would be regarded as "treason to the Confederacy" and he would be roughly dealt with, he accepted McIntyre's invitation.

That Sunday afternoon, March 31, 1861, when he rose to speak, the crowd overflowed the courthouse. Some of them leaped to their feet, shook their fists, and hissed and shouted, "Put him out! Don't let him speak! Kill him! Kill him!"

McIntyre leaped up on a table at the front of the platform, whipped out a big Colt, swept it menacingly at the disturbers, and demanded silence. No one cared to put his threat to the test. When the mob had quieted, McIntyre laid down the law:

> I and 100 other friends of Governor Houston have invited him to address us. We will kill the first man who insults or in any way attempts to injure him. I myself think Governor Houston ought to have taken the oath of allegiance to our Confederate Government, but he thought otherwise. He is honest and sincere, and he shed his blood for Texas independence. There is no man alive who has more right to be heard by the people of Texas. Now, fellow citizens, give him your close attention; and, you ruffians, keep quiet, or I will kill you.

Looking out of his old lion's face with a quizzical expression, Houston took the floor and appraised the crowd. He began in his usual conciliatory manner, explaining that he had intended to remain silent on the great issues confronting the country—

> ... but old soldier comrades who fought with me at San Jacinto, and other dear friends, insist that I shall explain the reason why I refuse to take the oath of allegiance to the Con-

federate Government, and why I have been deposed from the Governorship of our beloved State. The earnest solicitations of my old soldier comrades outweigh my desire to remain silent until the whirlwind of passion and popular clamor have subsided and the voice of reason can be fairly heard.

... It has always been the invariable rule of my life never to form an opinion or verdict upon any great public question until I have first carefully and impartially heard and considered all the evidence ... upon both sides, and when I have thus formed my verdict, no fear of popular condemnation can induce me to modify or change such verdict. I have never permitted popular clamor, passion, prejudice nor selfish ambition to induce me to change an opinion or verdict which my conscience and judgment has once formed and tells me is right.

As he spoke these impressive, calming words the burden of years fell away and he stood at his full majestic height. His resonant voice rang out in a direct and unequivocal challenge:

... The Vox Populi is not always the voice of God, for when the demagogues and selfish political leaders succeed in arousing public prejudice and stilling the voice of reason, then on every hand can be heard the popular cry of 'Crucify him, crucify him!' The Vox Populi then becomes the voice of the devil, and the hiss of mobs warns all patriots that peace and good government are in peril.

McIntyre was uneasy as Houston paused, waiting for the effect of his words. But the crowd remained quiet and did not interrupt. The Governor bore down on the matter of mobs.

I have heard the hiss of mobs upon the streets ... of Brenham, and friends have warned me that my life was in great peril if I expressed my honest sentiments and convictions.
But the hiss of the mob and the howls of their jackal leaders can not deter me nor compel me to take the oath of allegiance to a so-called Confederate Government.

There was a stir, but no disorder, nor hisses. Houston continued:

I protest against surrendering the Federal Constitution, its Government and its glorious flag to the Northern abolition leaders and to accept in its stead a so-called Confederate Government whose constitution contains the germs and seeds of decay which must and will lead to its speedy ruin and dismemberment if it can ever secure any real existence. Its seeds of ruin and decay are the principle of secession which permits any one or more of the Confederate States to secede from the parent Confederate Government and to establish separate governments....

And still the audience was quiet. McIntyre relaxed, concluding that the Old Warrior could say anything that was on his mind without provoking a demonstration.

One S. A. Hackworth was in the audience. He had a sharp ear and a keen memory. Nothing that the deposed Governor said was lost upon him. He was stirred by Houston's words and fascinated by the manner in which Houston held the close attention of those who had come determined to make him keep still or to injure him. The Governor's precise statements bit into his brain like acid on an etcher's plate. He followed closely as Houston explained at length how the Southern people had been misled by "designing demagogues" and why he could not subscribe to an oath that would make him disloyal to "the best government that ever existed for men." In unmistakable language that inspired Hackworth to record it, Houston told them where he stood and where they were going:

... Our galaxy of Southern Presidents—Washington, Jefferson, Monroe, Jackson, Taylor, Tyler and Polk cemented the bonds of union between all the States which can never be broken.... All our Northern Presidents have been equally patriotic and just to the South. Not a single Southern right has been violated by any President or by any Federal Administration. President Lincoln has been elected, because the secession Democratic leaders divided the Democratic party and caused the nomination of two separate Presidential Democratic tickets and nominees.

Both branches of Congress are Democratic; therefore it will be impossible for President Lincoln's administration to enact or enforce any laws or measures that can injure Southern rights.

Having dispelled the mob spirit with his firm precision of statement, he proceeded to discuss fearlessly the most inflammatory subject—whether the Southern people were being misled, jockeyed, and deceived by radical slavery and revolutionary advocates. No franker discussion of this burning issue ever occurred during the war that followed or afterward.

... I believe a large majority of our Southern people are opposed to secession, and if the secession leaders would permit our people to take ample time to consider secession and then hold fair elections the secession movement would be defeated by an overwhelming majority. But the secession leaders declare that secession has already been peaceably accomplished and the Confederate Government independence and sovereignty will soon be acknowledged by all foreign governments. They tell us that the Confederate Government will thus be permanently established without bloodshed.

The secession leaders also tell us if war should come that European Nations will speedily come to our relief, and aid us to win our independence because cotton is King and European commerce and civilization can not long exist without cotton, ... Gentlemen who use such false and misleading statements forget or else are ignorant of the facts that commerce and civilization existed a long period of time before cotton was generally known and used.

They also forget or else are ignorant of the fact that the best sentiment of Europe is opposed to our systems of negro slavery. They also tell us if war comes that the superior courage of our people with their experience of the use of firearms, will enable us to triumph in battle over ten times our number of Northern forces. Never was a more false or absurd statement ever made by designing demagogues. I declare that Civil War is inevitable and is near at hand. When it comes the descendants of the heroes of Lexington and Bunker Hill will be found equal in patriotism, courage and heroic endurance with descendants of the heroes of Cowpens and Yorktown. For this same reason I predict that the civil war which is now near at hand will be stubborn and of long duration. ...

Houston's voice vibrated with the power of his emotion as he forecast that the "principles of secession must inevitably lead to discord, conspiracy and revolution, and at last anarchy and utter ruin:"

Then, oh my fellow countrymen, the fearful conflict will fill our fair land with untold suffering, misfortune and disaster. The soil of our beloved South will drink deep the precious blood of our sons and brethren. In earnest prayer to our Heavenly Father, I have daily petitioned him to cast out from my mind the dark foreboding of the coming conflict. My prayers have caused the light of reason to cast the baleful shadows of the coming events before me. I cannot, nor will I close my eyes against the light and voice of reason. The die has been cast by your secession leaders, whom you have permitted to sow and broadcast the seeds of secession, and you must ere long reap the fearful harvest of conspiracy and revolution.[2]

Transfixed by the boldness of his gloomy conclusion and Cassandra-like forecast, the crowd heard him to the end without remonstrance. When he finished, no hisses broke the thoughtful silence of the audience. McIntyre and his friends were sobered and subdued, but gave no evidence of being convinced.

Hackworth was so impressed that immediately afterward he wrote down the words that had burned into his memory, and submitted them to Editor Rankin of the Brenham *Enquirer*. Rankin, who had been present, complimented him upon his accuracy, but he found it "inexpedient" to print Hackworth's version of Houston's remarks. In its issue of April 3, 1861, the *Enquirer* briefly noted that such a meeting had taken place on March 31; that Governor Houston had been threatened by a "howling mob" and that "a brave secession leader" had addressed them stating that he would protect General Houston while he made any remarks he thought fitting.[3]

Though he had faced many other hostile demonstrations this was the nearest Houston ever came to delivering himself to the hands of lynch law. Few, if any, statesmen have ever similarly predicted their undesirable futures with such uncanny insight and precision to a hostile mob. But for Houston there was no special novelty in this occasion; he was accustomed to hostile demonstrations. The views he expressed were exactly in keeping with his former practice—never, in a pinch, to hit soft. No statesman has ever been more frequently accused of demagoguery than Houston, although the charge was contrary to the facts. He often used his powers of leadership and his eloquence in support of unpopular causes. He had held to his strategy during the Forty Days and Nights campaign despite the rage of subordinates and the outcries of the people. He risked his popularity and political future to avert Santa Anna's execution, which would have disgraced Texas. He opposed Lamar and the land speculators after the Cherokee war, disregarded threats of assassination in 1842 when he vetoed the war bill, contended against the most powerful and popular leader of the South when he stood against Calhoun, accepted hate and ridicule after he voted against the Kansas-Nebraska Bill, and took on the governorship in 1859 when he was elected by a slight margin of pro-Union votes. His stand against the secession convention had kept him in practice as a spokesman of unpopular causes. He knew that if he went against his convictions his name would be an "honored" one in the Confederacy, but this he refused to do.

His speech at Brenham may be regarded as the dark climax of a career guided by principle and conscience.

2. *Young Sam Goes to War*

AT the end of the spring term, Houston's war-minded stripling, Sam, Jr., had gone directly to Cedar Point, where his father joined him. Sam feared that the impending conflict would be over before he could get into it. To distract him from this idea, his father arranged to keep him busy at the ranch.

While on this trip to Cedar Point to see Sam, Jr., Houston went to Galveston. There, on April 19, 1861, (approximate date) he made a speech at the Tremont House which should not be confused with a previous one delivered at the same place before Texas had voted for secession. On this second occasion, he was again urged not to speak, this time by four friends, Messrs. Sydnor, Stuart, Nichols, and McLean. If he did speak, they advised him not to say anything against the Convention, the state government, or the government of the Confederate States. In a half-hour talk briefly summarized in the Houston *Telegraph* of April 23, 1861, he denied reports that he had intrigued with Lincoln. He "advised the people now, no matter what were the causes that had brought on this state of affairs, to counsel wisely and to be united."

He "declared that Mr. Lincoln had been precipitate and foolish in steps that he had taken." The same report said he was listened to quietly "with now and then some cheers and laughter." When Mr. Sydnor called for three cheers for Houston, only a part of the large audience responded. As in the case of his previous talk at Galveston, no verbatim report of the speech was ever printed. The editors of *Writings* believe this was because "all the newspapers of this time were afraid of losing popularity if they printed Houston's speeches." [1]

After his return to Independence, friends and neighbors asked Houston to advise them on their conduct in the distressing situation. On May 10, 1861, he told a large audience gathered in the Baptist church that it was no longer a question of whether he or the Convention had been right:

> ...I was conservative, [and] so long as there was a hope of obtaining our rights, and maintaining our institutions, through an appeal to the sense and justice and the brotherhood of the Northern people, I was for preserving the Union. The voice of hope was weeks since drowned by the guns of Fort Sumter. It is not now heard above the tramp of invading armies. The mission of the Union has ceased to be one of peace and equality, and now the dire alternative of yielding tamely before hostile armies, or meeting the shock like freemen, is presented to the South....
> The time has come when a man's section is his country. I stand by mine. All my hopes, my fortunes, are centered in the South. When I see the land for whose defence my blood has been spilt, and the people whose fortunes have been mine through a quarter of a century of toil, threatened with invasion, I can but cast my lot with theirs and await the issue.... The trouble is upon us.... Whether we have opposed this secession movement or favored it, we must alike meet the consequences.... Better meet war in its deadliest shape than cringe before an enemy whose wrath we have invoked.

He told them that it would be necessary for the South not only to equal the North in courage but also in ability to organize and to yield obedience when obedience was called for. He felt obliged himself to yield obedience, and he closed on that note:

> ...I have ever been conservative; I remained conservative as long as the Union lasted; I am now a conservative citizen of the Southern Confederacy, and giving to the constituted authorities of the country, civil and military...an honest obedience... regarding this the first duty of a good citizen. [2]

624

From Independence he communicated constantly with Sam at Cedar Point, sending instructions that he hoped would keep his son's mind off war. "Keep the Hoes in the corn, if it is too wet to plow.... If it is too wet to do anything in the corn, put up a cow pen; also one for the goats—a brush pen will do for the goats.... Keep the [field] hands busy. I intend to be satisfied with whatever you may do. You must think for yourself, as I cannot be there ... while the rain continues.... I do not wish you or the hands to be exposed."

On May 22, 1861, again writing to his son, he deplored the rainy weather that prevented the family's departure for the Point. "... I am distressed to be thus detained. Though all is kindness, I do not like to eat our friends out of House and home at one visit." Then he quickly passed on to matters of far greater concern:

> ... We have no news of interest, in the *Sensation Extras*. They lie to suit the market. Do you, my son, not let anything disturb you; attend to business, and when it is proper, you shall go to war, if you really wish to do so. It is every man's duty to defend his Country; and I wish my offspring to do so at the proper time and in the proper way. We are not wanted or needed out of Texas, and we may soon be wanted and needed in Texas. Until then, my son, be content.

Not the Confederacy, but Texas was his country, and he wanted it to be his son's as it was his own. As sons will, however, Sam thought differently.

Late May or early June found all the Houstons at the Point. The hot-blooded youths of Galveston and vicinity were drilling in a nearby camp in expectation of a call from the Richmond government. Sam pleaded to be allowed to join them. His father felt obliged to consent, but continued to remind him that his first loyalty was to Texas.

On July 23, 1861, Houston wrote to his son at the camp.

> ... The men and arms are all leaving this quarter of the theatre in the great Drama, which is playing, and is to be played. ... If Texas is attacked she must be in her present isolated condition. She can look for no aid from the Confederacy, and must either succumb or defend herself....

625

... if Texas did not require your services, and you wished to go elsewhere, why then all would be well, but as she will need your aid, your first allegiance is due to her and let nothing cause you in a moment of ardor to assume obligation to any power whatever, without my consent. If Texas demands your services or your life, in her cause, stand by her.

He added a touching reminder. "Houston is not, nor will be a favorite name in the Confederacy! Thus, you had best keep your duty and your hopes together, and when the Drill is over, come home.... When will you be home, my son! Thy Devoted Father, Sam Houston." [3]

On July 21, 1861, two days before the anxious father besought his son to come home, the meeting of two amateur armies at Manassas had resulted in a smashing victory for the Confederacy. The first news to reach Richmond was of defeat, but this had changed to news of how the Confederates had forced the Federals to retreat in panic. Texas was spared the false news of disaster, and the first word that came was glorious. Jubilant dancing in the streets was in progress when General Houston made one of his frequent trips to his namesake city where he often went to transact business, see a doctor, or get the latest news from Richmond and Washington. In shaggy country clothes, he was a lonely and despised figure as he thumped his way along Main Street with his long, gold-headed staff.

In the glittering bar of the Capitol Hotel he sat unobserved, drinking his customary innocuous ginger beer. Suddenly he heard his name ridiculed as belonging to a false prophet and a coward who had predicted the South's defeat. A braggart announced that it would be a pleasure to run a sword through Houston's traitorous heart. This was more than Houston could take in silence. He stepped toward the speaker and stiffened up, holding his arms spread wide as if baring himself for the blow. "Here is the heart of Sam Houston and whoever says it is the heart of a coward or traitor lies in his teeth!" [4]

These were fighting words, but a belated sense of decency and respect for an aging warrior whose courage and sacrifice for Texas were beyond dispute, silenced his critic. Houston stalked from the bar into the street, his cane thumping, his stoop gone, his head up.

A few days later as he sat on the balcony of the City Hotel, a few score recruits guided by a sergeant on their way to enlist in the Second Texas Infantry paused and informally saluted him. He talked to the youngsters in a fatherly way, telling them some things that he thought they needed to know as soldiers. A bystander sneered that Confederate recruits risked contamination when they listened to a snake in the grass who had refused to take the oath.

The General answered with moderate words of deep feeling. As an old soldier, he said, he had a feeling for boys going off to war that only soldiers could understand; he honored them. This did not mean that he thought this war was right or reasonable. Manassas had brought a belief in a quick, easy triumph. It might be followed by emblems of sorrow. But these recruits had his blessing. He wanted them to go into battle with it, and he would pray "that they may be brave, trust in God and fear not." [5]

When Houston reached Cedar Point, he found that Sam had arrived ahead of him. Sam told his father he had been among the recruits who had received the blessing. He asked forgiveness for disobedience. He was now a member of Captain Ashbel Smith's Company C, Second Texas Infantry, Colonel Moore, commander. He had enlisted "for during the war."

Sorrowfully, but without reproach and with a certain pride, the General granted forgiveness. Then he consoled Sam's grief-stricken mother, who did not believe in this or any other war and was desperately certain that her son would never come back. The General reminded her that they must approve the spirit that the boy had shown, even though they both disapproved the cause to which he was attached. Texas was *their* country; the Confederacy was Sam's.

While Sam's mother was trying to adjust herself to the manliness of a son determined to play his part in his country's cause, Texas was rejoicing in the humiliation of the North at Manassas and enjoying the delusion that final victory was near. But the North went on to constructive plans for better organization and improved discipline, while the Southern general, Joseph E. Johnston, complained that "our army was more demoralized by victory than that of the United States by defeat." [6]

General Houston did not share the prevailing opinion that Manassas was the forerunner of early victory to be easily achieved. He continued to believe that the North would be slow to gather momentum, but that when it did organization and discipline might make it invincible.

Sam had already gone to join his regiment when Captain Ashbel Smith, his commander and his father's old friend, called at Cedar Point to say farewell before he joined his command. The General and the captain talked less of the war than about old days in Texas. Margaret took the opportunity to ask a favor. Sam had gone off to camp without the Bible that she had bought and inscribed for him. Would it be too burdensome for the captain to take it to him?

3. *Shiloh Shadows*

HOUSTON owned Cedar Point and the farm at Raven Hill where his rams propagated, but he had always thought of Huntsville as his permanent home and had planned to spend his retirement years there. In 1857, however, he had sold his Huntsville property in order to clean up odds and ends of debts incurred during his first futile campaign against Runnels for the governorship. After the sale, the Huntsville property changed hands several times. In 1861, soon after he left office, he tried unsuccessfully to buy it back. Then he rented what was known as the Steamboat House. In 1858, Dr. Rufus W. Bailey, president of Austin College, had built it to resemble a stern-wheeler, the popular mode of river travel. A piazza ran the entire length of the house on one side. The second floor was reached by a stairway from outside. The view from the house was pleasant, even though it included the village burial ground and the low drab buildings of the state penitentiary.

Warm weather came early to Texas in the spring of 1862. During the last days of February, Houston sat in the sun or sometimes sought the shade, sitting on a bench under an oak in the side yard of his rented home. The hardships of his early life were telling on him now; inactivity and the sun's intense heat were congenial. Although he reached eagerly for every item of war news, about all he knew for certain was that the Second Texas was still in training on Galveston Island. Since Manassas, Maj. Gen. George B. McClellan had been engaged in reorganizing the Union Army. It was known that, in the West, Federal armies were slowly taking shape. Even so, General Houston did not know if Lincoln was enough of a statesman to meet the crisis.

Then the Second Texas was ordered to Missouri. Its ultimate destination was the Confederate concentration near Corinth, Mississippi. Margaret received this news with despair, and wrote to her aged mother in Independence:

> My beloved Mother,
> Since Gen'l Houston's return I have had no spirit to write to any of you on account of my deep affliction from my dear boy being sent to Missouri. My heart seems almost broken. . . . I left nothing undone that was in my power, to prevent his going, but my weaknesses gave him an opportunity of displaying traits of character that made his father's heart swell with pride . . . . When I first heard the news, I thought I would lie down and die, but it is strange how life will cling to such a poor emaciated frame as mine. . . . I did not love him more than the rest of my children, but he absorbed all my anxiety, all my hopes and fears.

She gave her mother the family news and signed herself, "Ever thy affectionate daughter, M. L. Houston." [1]

On Saturday, April 5, 1862, General Houston wrote to his old political antagonist, Williamson S. Oldham, who was now a Texas senator in the Confederate Congress. Houston was not in the least embarrassed to ask Oldham's support for a lieutenant's commission for his son. He informed Oldham that Sam, "18 years of age, 6 feet high, and rather a well made and good looking boy had refused a situation of Brevet Lieutenant if he would consent . . . to be stationed at Galveston." But Sam had "preferred the glory of an active, and immediate campaign." "He is a very good scholar, his habits are good, and he is ardently devoted to the cause in which he is engaged, as well as to the life of a soldier." [2]

We do not know what Private Sam Houston, Company C, Second Texas, may have been doing on this particular Saturday to merit his father's confidence in his soldierly qualities. His regiment had just arrived with a large force brought up by General Albert Sidney Johnston to join Beauregard's heavy concentration at Corinth. Sam's reminiscences of the ensuing battle of Shiloh begin with Sunday morning, April 6, 1862.

General U. S. Grant's headquarters were at Savannah on the Tennessee River nine miles from Shiloh (Pittsburg Landing), Tennessee. There the main body of his army was waiting for General Don Carlos Buell to come up with the 20,000 men of his Army of Ohio. On April 5, Grant went to the front to investigate reports of heavy firing. Finding everything quiet, he returned to Savannah. General William T. Sherman reported heavy picket firing, but said, "I do not apprehend anything like an attack on our position." Grant then notified General H. W. Halleck, at St. Louis, "I have scarcely an idea of an attack being made."

At dawn on April 6, Sam was one of the tide of men in gray who plunged forward, screeching the rebel yell, in a surprise attack that crumpled the Federal right. Sam entered a camp that the Yankees had obviously abandoned in haste and burned his hand fishing a three-pound piece of beef from a camp kettle. But the beef was worth it; he and his comrades enjoyed a second breakfast at Federal expense as they pushed on after the Yankees.

Sam's regiment captured a Union battery and three thousand men of a reserve brigade. Captain Ashbel Smith fell wounded, and a bullet plowed into Sam's knapsack. That night, Sam's regiment fell back to rest. As Sam remembered it, "We lay down in order of battle, dead weary.... The remainder of Sunday night was a blank ... it rained terribly...." He awoke shivering to find his clothes and blanket drenched.

Day was breaking on April 7 when the order came, "Forward, double quick! March!" The Federals were on the move. Sam's brigade moved out, extending across the field with unbounded confidence because of the victory the day before. "Where are the Yankees?" Sam kept asking himself.

Company C was within a rod of the field's eastern boundary when the fence ahead became a wall of flame. The Confederate line wilted. The earth swarmed with Yankees who were so close to Sam that he could see the ornaments on their caps; he remembered observing in this terrible moment that the immediate adversary of the Second Texas was the Third Iowa Infantry. Struck in the groin with a Minié ball, he fell. The Yankees swept over him, and he lay in a pool of blood behind the Northern lines, growing weaker hour by hour. He would lose consciousness and then regain it long enough to wonder dazedly what his family were doing at Cedar Point and to wish that he could see them before he died. The field was strewn with wounded men, and the air was alive with their outcries of suffering. A Federal surgeon took a hurried look at Sam and passed on. Sam was barely conscious, just able to realize that he had been passed up as a case beyond help.

Late in the afternoon a Yankee chaplain crossed the field and saw a crumpled and apparently lifeless figure. Kneeling, the chaplain believed he saw signs of life in the still form. He picked up a small battered Bible, part of the contents of the soldier's knapsack that were strewn on the ground. A bullet had passed through the Bible, cutting every leaf at the binding. On the flyleaf, the chaplain read: *Sam Houston, Jr. from his mother. March 6, 1862.* He knelt and asked, "Are you related to General Houston of Texas who served in the United States Senate?"

"My father," the gray-clad figure answered weakly.

The chaplain's mind swept back to 1854 when he had been one of the ministers who petitioned the United States Senate not to repeal the Missouri Compromise. He had been deeply moved by Senator Houston's defense of the right of the ministers to petition. Now he hastened across the field and returned with a surgeon, who believed that he had already examined this soldier. The surgeon thought that Sam's femoral artery had been cut; he had no means to check the blood. On second examination, the surgeon found that he had been mistaken about the artery. Coagulation had stopped the bleeding. The chaplain got a litter, and Sam was carried off the field.[3]

Southern newspapers listed General Houston's son among the "dead and missing" and Sam's name was struck from the rolls of Company C. The General and his wife were torn between grieving for their loss and praying that their boy was not suffering from unattended wounds. Southern women, who had gone to Corinth to nurse, were writing letters home, and others were writing diaries. One of them, Kate Cumming, wrote in April 1862:

... Gray-haired men—men in the pride of manhood—beardless boys—Federals and all, mutilated in every imaginable way, lying on the floor, just as they were taken from the battle-field; so close together that it was almost impossible to walk without stepping on them. . . .

There is no end to the tales of horror related about the battle-field. They fill me with dismay. . . .

I daily witness the same sad scenes—men dying all around me. I do not know who they are, nor have I time to learn. . . .

The doctors seem to think that the enemy poisoned their musket balls, as the wounds inflamed terribly. Our men do not seem to stand half so much as the Northerners. Many of the doctors are quite despondent about it, and think that our men will not be able to endure the hardships of camp life. . . .[4]

Reports of this kind had to be lived with, but they destroyed Margaret's morale. In a letter to Francis Lubbock, now governor of Texas, Houston referred to harrowing scenes of "unutterable anguish that I have witnessed in my domestic circle." Nonetheless, Houston and Margaret would not give up hope of Sam's survival. In May, Margaret heard from Anson Jones's widow, who enclosed a letter from a Confederate soldier, Jim Hageman. Hageman told his mother that Sam had been taken prisoner. He did not indicate how he knew this. The merest hearsay, it was accepted by Sam's parents as additional reason to hope.

The anxious weeks passed into months. September came, and streams of soldiers on their way to Galveston, or coming home wounded or on furlough, flowed past the Cedar Point house as they had since spring. So it did not seem unusual when, one evening, a stranger turned into the walk that led to the house. He was pale and ragged and supported on two crutches made of saplings. His eyes were sunk in their sockets, the skin was taut over his cheek bones, and his rumpled hair hung down over the collar of a dirty jacket. The Houston children in the yard did not know him. A dog barked. Margaret came out to greet this unprepossessing stranger. Tears blinded her as she threw her arms around him. Then the children also began to cry. Old Joshua, strong and able, came around the corner of the house from the flower bed he was tending. He picked up the boy, carried him inside to the guest room, and laid him on the bed. Sam's mother told one of the servants to bring soup from the pot on the kitchen hearth, but Sam fell asleep before the soup arrived. Joshua helped Margaret remove his clothes, and they bathed him while he slept. Jeff, too, was there to lend a hand.

Somehow General Houston learned of or sensed his son's return and he came galloping back from a visit to a neighbor, his San Jacinto crutch banging from his saddle horn. Inside the house, he put his arm around Sam and told him that all morning something had told him his son was alive and would come home safe.

When Sam awoke after a good sleep his father and mother were sitting on either side of his bed, each holding one of his hands. He told them something about the hardships of the journey home; of his sojourn in a Federal prison, Camp Douglas; and of his exchange.

Later, he gave his mother the shattered Bible and told his parents about the chaplain who had rescued him from the battlefield. The chaplain had looked after Sam until his recovery was assured. If he had written to tell the family that their son was safe and a prisoner, his letter never reached them. Houston thought he remembered a minister coming to see him after his Senate speech defending the clergy's right to petition, but he had forgotten his name. While he was in the Yankee field hospital, Sam must have learned the minister's name, but he could not recall it either.

Nannie Houston was sixteen years old when her brother returned from Camp Douglas. Sam's Bible was passed on to her, and later she gave it to her son, Temple Houston Morrow. On Sunday, March 5, 1939, the Dallas *Morning News* carried an article by Temple Morrow. He announced that he was presenting the Bible to the Houston Memorial Museum at Huntsville and he related the story of his uncle's homecoming and of his rescue by the Yankee chaplain. Then he appealed for any information that might lead to the discovery of the chaplain's name. The appeal brought no response.

4. Last Stand against Tyranny

IMMEDIATELY after Shiloh, the government of Jefferson Davis put conscription into effect. General Louis Hebert, commander of the Department of Texas, declared martial law and administered it with a heavy hand. Having created numerous provost marshals, Hebert gave them dictatorial authority to order army officers and their troops to assist in enforcing his decrees. Some marshals ran amuck under this regime and committed many atrocities that were not directly traceable to orders from the top.

Whites and blacks, suspected of Unionist sympathies, were "converted" by halters around their necks. Poor white settlers from the North were hanged by mobs on suspicion that they had caused fires in stores. Women and men were hung up by their thumbs until they disclosed where they had concealed specie. One observer reported that, because rope was scarce, hanging victims were formed into a queue to await their turn when their predecessors had ceased to twitch.

The most ruthless atrocities were perpetrated against the German settlers near San Antonio by the "partisan rangers" under a Provost Marshal Dunn. Loyal to the Union, these Germans had supported Governor Houston in his struggle to keep Texas from seceding. In retaliation, the partisans raided their homes and farms, destroyed their crops, burnt their orchards, overturned their beehives, smashed their furniture and houses, sent women and children in one direction and drove the men in another, never to be reunited.

A band of Germans abandoned their homes and set out for the Rio Grande, hoping to escape into Mexico. Dunn's rangers surprised the Germans in camp, ran off their horses, and wounded two score men during a fight. When the sun was shining on the wounded the next day, the captors asked them if they would like to be moved into the shade. The prisoners gratefully accepted and were carried into the woods. Soon rifle shots were heard. No one asked what had happened to the wounded men.

Vague reports of these disorders reached Houston. They confirmed his prophetic fears that if Texas seceded anarchy would flourish. In a letter to Governor Francis Lubbock, he criticized the way Hebert was sweeping up thousands of conscripts and, almost before they knew the meaning of, "Forward march," was shipping them across the Mississippi despite loud protests from some of them. He also denounced the terms of the proclamation by which General Hebert announced to the people of Texas the scope of the authority granted him by the Richmond government:

> . . . he abrogates all the powers of your Excellency . . . ignores the Bill of Rights, the Constitution and the Laws, and arrogates

to himself *undefined and unlimited* powers.... he has created Provost Marshals, who are authorized to remove all citizens upon suspicion, out of the State, without trial; and called in the military to aid in the execution of the Provost Marshal's pleasure or will....

Martial Law may be proclaimed ... when a city is besieged, or a neighborhood.... Will any one say that any part of Texas was besieged when this extraordinary document was issued ... ?

Ironically, he asked, "Are such things necessary to aid the glorious cause of the independence of the South? ... I understand the Confederacy not to be a *Union*, but a *League* of the States, each one *absolutely sovereign in itself*, and with a right to secede from the Confederacy whenever it may think so to do."

The Confederate government, he argued persuasively, "... does not seem to ... be exercising *Confederate* powers, but *Central* and *absolute* powers." He used liberal underscoring to emphasize his outraged state of mind:

> ... It may be said that this is not the time to discuss these matters. My answer is, that the time to discuss the principle of liberty is whenever the *rights* of the *citizen* are *invaded*, or the *laws trampled under foot!* Acquiescence to usurpation is— SLAVERY! Is necessity urged in behalf of such things? My answer is *necessity* is the plea of *tyrants*, and the exercise of *unrestrained will* is the throne of Despotism! If the question is asked what can be done *now*, I would answer, let everything that has been that is inconsistent with the Constitution and the laws, be revoked by their author or authors, and the Governor be left free to exercise his functions....[1]

Perhaps Houston hoped that in remembrance of their old association Lubbock would at least acknowledge his letter. But his patient waiting for response was not rewarded. Before Hebert's heavy hand was removed from authority over Texas, between 50,000 and 65,000 Texas volunteers and conscripts were enlisted in the Confederate Army.

In September, 1862, while Sam was at home convalescing and his father was futilely trying to change the course of events in Texas, General Lee retreated south from the crippling day-long battle of Antietam. President Lincoln decided to accept the less-than-complete victory as the basis for acting upon his earlier resolution to announce partial emancipation as soon as a military success was achieved.

Northern newspapers published the preliminary proclamation on September 23, 1862. It stated that on January 1, 1863, all persons held as slaves in any state then in rebellion against the United States "shall be then, thenceforward and forever free." The Texas newspapers carried the news in October, just when Houston's family was preparing to leave Cedar Point to return to Huntsville for the winter. Sam had already returned to his regiment.

Lincoln's proclamation reminded Houston of his own warning to the Southern leaders, long before Fort Sumter, that the first shot in a sectional war would be the death-knell of slavery. After the usual prayer and Bible reading on Sunday morning, he sent word by Old Joshua that as soon as the servants had finished breakfast they were all to come to the front door. He joined them there with Margaret and all the children. His manner was grave and impressive as he wiped his spectacles, then took a newspaper from his pocket.

"I want you all to listen closely as I read," he said. He read the proclamation slowly and explained what it meant. The slaves had all heard of emancipation, and the rumor had passed among them that somehow the war would set them free. "But I don't propose to wait until January to give my people their freedom," the General declared. "The laws of Texas, of the Confederacy and of Almighty God give me the right to free them whenever I want to, and I am glad to be able to do it. You all and each one of you are now free."

Gasps, murmurs, groans, and sobs greeted the announcement. Jeff, who later described the scene, said that the General and his wife, all the children except baby Temple, and all the slaves were in tears.

The General wiped his eyes and continued, "I am your friend and you are my friends. I shall always help you when I can. If you want to stay here and work for me I will pay you good wages as long as I am able." [2]

Uncle Joshua told the General that he was going to stay right on and work for him just as he always had. Aunt Eliza, who from Jeff's description, appears to have been a camp-meeting type, moaned and swayed. Hysterical, she picked up two-year-old Temple in her

636

arms and cried out that she wasn't going to be freed, didn't want 'mancipation, and would stay with the children. Like Jeff, Aunt Eliza had been bought by General Houston out of pity. Living in Huntsville at the time, he had passed through the public square, on one corner of which stood the slave block. A Negro woman who had a little daughter was put up at auction and sold, but the child was not. Feeling sorry for the child, he had bought her and taken her home. As a nursemaid she had acquired a proprietary interest in the family. Unwilling to abandon them, she continued with the Houstons as long as she lived. On the day she was granted her freedom, she was about thirty-four years old.[3]

General Houston was the first Southerner to accept Lincoln's edict as a law for his personal guidance. "The throne of despotism," as he called it, was already tottering, and he was not averse to giving it a nudge that might hasten its collapse.

Because Houston had resisted secession and refused to take the Confederate oath, the military authorities suspected he had designs for restoring the Texas Republic. He had given them no other reason for this suspicion. One of Hebert's edicts may have been aimed particularly at keeping track of Houston's movements. It required all citizens of Texas to have passports, even school children when returning from their homes if their schools were as much as one hundred miles distant. One day while Houston was riding in his yellow-wheeled buggy, a Hebert agent stopped him and demanded his credentials. Houston flared up and answered, "San Jacinto is my pass through Texas." [4] He shook the reins over the back of his sorrel trotter, flicked her with the whip, and disappeared in dust down the road.

He wrote a sharp letter to Provost Marshal Frazer:

Having heard through Colonel William J. Mills ... that inquiries have been made ... by you, for persons in Cedar Bayou, who would be most probable witnesses against me. This has left me to infer that ... charges have been lodged against me with you. Now, sir, I request you ... to communicate to me the name of the author, or authors who have ... made any charges against my loyalty to the Government. ... I claim no more than the humblest man in the community, and I am always ready to answer to the Laws of my Country.[5]

His reference to "my Country" is obscure. He did not choose to clarify whether he meant Texas, the United States, or the Confederate States. As in the case of his letter to Lubbock, this communication went unanswered, and the military authorities continued to watch his activities.

By November, when Sam, Jr. was a lieutenant and with the army in Louisiana, Houston was in Independence. Having concluded that Governor Lubbock could not be persuaded to join him in resisting tyranny, he hopefully turned in another direction, pleading his cause with the sage of Goose Creek. Recently promoted, Colonel Ashbel Smith was still at home recovering from his Shiloh wound when General Houston wrote him on November 18, 1862:

> ...I would be most happy to see you. If I were to do so, I would only say "Another man ought not to leave Texas." For this there are a thousand reasons.
>
> If Texas is lost & ruined, what would the Confederacy be without her? She has been its *van* and *rear* guard. Oh, that our Governor would rise from his *lair* and shake the dew drops from his mane!!! And say, "by the Constitution I am the Sovereign of a Sovereign State,—*the people look to me to save it, and they will sustain me in its salvation.*"
>
> If you can, come to see me soon; if not, may God guide, direct, & prosper you, and save our dear country....
>
> Thine Ever, Houston.[6]

Smith's answer was eloquent silence. Probably he sensed that the General had some kind of *coup d'état* in mind; anyhow, he was due back with his command.

Houston sought another confidant in a furloughed Confederate field officer whose name is not given. On November 24, 1862, he wrote to this gentleman:

> Please come to see me at Huntsville, where a warm welcome awaits, and a thousand things to speak of with a comrade who has seen other and better days in Texas.... We must send out no more troops, *not one man!* ... Now, I mean to preserve Texas. It is my duty. Am I not, according to the constitution, the sovereign authority of this state.... The people will uphold me in this and with God's help we will *save Texas.*[7]

There was no response to this appeal either.

By now Hebert's despotism had aroused general resentment that conceivably could become a menace to the Confederacy. Abruptly, the Confederate administration appointed General John B. Magruder, a West Pointer, to succeed Hebert. "Prince John" had served in Texas before the war and had been known as the Beau Brummel of the old army. He would more readily understand how to get along with sensitive Texans. He would also be responsible for dealing with the Federal troops who had seized Galveston.

On January 1, 1863, "Prince John" chased the Federal command out of Galveston and took a considerable number of prisoners. General Houston wrote him a letter of congratulation and hailed the advent of a "new era." The new era that Houston longed for was one in which Texas would shake off the Richmond despotism; but, warily, he had not disclosed all that he had in mind:

> ... We hope that Texas with so gallant a leader as you are, General, will yet show to the world that she is yet capable of defending her own soil, notwithstanding that she has already been drained of her only resources that have been transferred to other battlefields. ... I pray that under the guidance of a Divine Being, you may be enabled to carry out the regeneration of Texas. ... It would give me pleasure ... to call and pay my respects to you, were it not that I have been recently arisen from a sick bed.[8]

As an ally to bring about the new era, the regeneration of Texas, and the suppression of tyranny, Magruder failed him. To the General's indignation, the Richmond government continued to demand and drain Texas of conscripts.

5. *An Undisclosed Hope*

WHEN his health permitted, Houston still made brief trips to his namesake city for the latest war news and sometimes to see a doctor. During one of these visits on March 18, 1863, he was surprised and pleased to be asked to make an address. The people were unhappy about the war; they had been told that this would be a short triumphant war, but its end seemed ever more remote. Would he give them his views?

Many months had passed since Houston's last public appearance. He welcomed the opportunity to re-establish the harmony that had existed between him and the people before his expulsion from office. As he looked from a hotel balcony into the faces of the crowd, he realized that they craved reassurance and consolation. Taxes and levies had impoverished many. They had suffered even as he and Margaret had suffered while Sam's fate had been in doubt.

Should he tell them that he still held the same beliefs he had stood for before secession? Should he tell them again that he believed the people had been misled into a venture that would terminate in greater miseries than any they had yet known? Should he bare his conviction that Texas should not send another man to fight? No, this was not the time for that. A hopeless situation called for such cheerfulness as he could devise. But between his convictions and the people's need for solace there was a vast gulf that somehow must be bridged. He accomplished it by a glowing inconsistency. Desiring to console the people, he went further than he intended in predicting the possibilities of victory:

> ... The country demands the highest energies of the patriot to bear its victorious banners onward to peace and independence. Once I dreamed of empire, as vast and expansive for a united people, as the bounds of American civilization. The dream is over. The golden charm is broken. Let us gather up the links that remain to us, and encircling with them our hearts, swear to resist to the last that worst of all tyranny, fraternal hate. From one nation, we have become two, and well will it be for mankind, if this fact of destiny is soon recognized by our foes and the world. War may still wage, and its march of desolation trample upon the hopes of millions, yet the chain of unity will be broken, and two people yet live, to attest how vain were the dreams of those who believed that the Union was a thing of forever.

Older than his years, Houston was weakening, but he still knew what he was about. This was the nearest he ever came to outright indorsement of Confederate aims, forced upon him by the course of events. But he seemed to be speaking of the people's cause rather than of organized secession. He had come to the point of conceding publicly that there might be two nations where there had been one. What he refrained from saying was that, if there must be two, he hoped there would be three and that the third would be Texas.

Then it must have occurred to him that he was holding out hopes which might be followed by disillusionment, and he drew back:

> ... If we fail of success, want of statesmanship and generalship will be the cause. ... The hopes of the nation have been too often already blasted by the imbecility of educated chieftains, who could lead our armies into danger but knew not how to pluck the victory from it, or extricate them when necessary.

But this would not do either. Again he felt it necessary to qualify, and he went on to praise the South's able generals, Lee, Jackson, Johnston, Magruder, and to speak hopefully of victory. But this hope was restrained. From it he led them to the solid ground of his true convictions. Bluntly, he told them that he feared this talk of victory was futile:

> ... Thus, although I do not look with confidence for these results, nor do I advance them as more than mere probabilities, they certainly indicate that there is discord and discontent in the North. ... Yet I do not trust to these things, nor would I have you do so.

He praised the proud achievement of Texas troops, and again returned to the hope of victory, this time without disparaging it:

> ... Convinced that the separation of the Yankee and the Southern people is fixed and certain, that fanaticism and conservative principles of government cannot harmonize, I long for peace, and with it, the happy dawn of a nation, whose gloomy period has given such evidence of greatness the world may hope for its long and prosperous existence. I trust the day will hasten ... and that we may emerge from the scenes of war, with our liberties unimpaired at home, or tyranny abroad.[1]

He talked for more than an hour. Some noticed that he seemed weak and feeble. He was sixteen days past his seventieth year; his hair was sparse and gray and his upright carriage was assisted by a long, gold-headed staff. His voice at times was still full and vibrant, clear as a bugle, but some of his listeners were struck by the somber undertone of despair beneath the iridescent gleams of hopefulness.

A politician and diarist, William Pitt Ballinger, who had backed Houston for the Democratic Presidential nomination in 1860, correctly appraised the General's motivation. In his diary on March 18, 1863, he complained that Houston's remarks were "flat" because he had deliberately "steered clear" of giving offense.[2] It is certain that on this occasion Houston did not declare the secret hope that he entertained for the future of Texas.

After this effort, Houston went home to Huntsville and was sick for two weeks. By the second of April he had recovered so that he was able to write his will, leaving his remaining estate after debts "to my beloved wife Margaret, and to our children." He expressed his desire for his children to acquire "thorough knowledge of the English language, with a good knowledge of the Latin language." He left the sword that he had worn at San Jacinto to Sam, Jr.; his library, to the disposition of his wife, also his watch and jewelry.

When appraised by the executors, more than twenty notes and claims, some regarded as of doubtful value, totaled $16,748.10. Houston's two-horse wagon was valued at $100; five "head horses" at $500; lands of the estate, whole or partly owned in about a dozen counties, added up to $60,910; the entire estate to $89,288. The actual value, in view of the war going against the Confederacy was uncertain.[3]

Until time had passed and the undisclosed secret was made known to friends, it was not possible to make anything of the many nuances of Houston's address to the people except that, old and weakening, he wanted to be close to them. But the flashes of hope that he offered had a profound effect when the address was printed almost in full in some Texas newspapers. His reappearance in public and this proof that in his feeling for the people he still was the same Old Sam they had always known, had remarkable results. Today, journalists would say that he had staged a phenomenal comeback.

Committees and many individuals demanded his return to the governorship. This, of course, was not because they knew he had in mind any particular plan for Texas. The general idea seemed to be that, with Jefferson Davis commanding a ship of state that showed signs of foundering, why shouldn't the Old Hero again steer the

Texas longboat? One of the remarkable things about the revival of Houston's popularity was that no one suggested he be required to take the Confederate oath of loyalty.

Resuming the governorship was not part of the General's plan for himself or for Texas. He told inquirers that he was not a candidate. Many newspapers, commenting on the rumor that he would run, predicted that if he did the result would be an overwhelming victory. The old General's eyes gleamed with humorous recognition as he read bitter diatribes in the die-hard, anti-Houston press lamenting the recrudescence of his popularity. Finally, partly to assuage the anxiety of his worried opposition, he sent an open letter to the Huntsville *Item.*

Asserting that he was aware of the "agonizing distress" of some newspapers that he might run for Governor, he wished to "relieve them from their painful apprehension." After definitely withdrawing as a candidate he added, "A man of three score years and ten, as I am, ought at least [to] be exempt from the charge of ambition, even if he should be charged with having loved his country but too well." [4]

Although he had no ambition for office, he still cherished a grand project; and he was waiting for the time. Would the time ever come? He still believed that the project was more than a faltering dream.

6. *"All Is Well"*

HOUSTON was losing weight and had a bad cough. He seldom mounted a horse, but used a buggy. When he did ride, he tied his crutch to the pommel of his saddle; his leg and shoulder wounds bothered him constantly. To account for neglecting his correspondence, he explained to a friend that he had been confined in bed for two weeks. But he still could dream, and his dream was bold and far-reaching.

Early in May, 1863, the bells of Houston rang with joyous news, and girls in crinoline danced in the streets. General Grant's column, advancing on Vicksburg, was reported to have been completely crushed. With Vicksburg safe, the Confederacy no longer would be in danger of fatal geographical division by losing control of the Father of Waters. But truth, following fast upon rumor, dampened ardor. Grant, in fact, had driven a wedge between two Confederate generals, Johnston and W. C. Pemberton. Ten days later, Grant settled down to besiege the city.

Grant was shelling Vicksburg around the clock when Houston made another trip to his namesake city in June in response to an invitation from an old friend, Eber W. Cave. As Secretary of State, Cave had been the only member of Houston's official family to join him in refusing to take the Confederate oath. He was now in the Confederate Army.

On March 3, 1863, Houston had acknowledged Cave's cordial invitation and had promised to come when he was able. "I need not write to you about politics as you wrote to me on a former occasion that you had eschewed them. For my own part I cannot for the life of me keep from thinking about them. . . . Yesterday, my friend, I concluded my seventieth year; and now if I am not wise, I may at least claim to have experience which is said to be nature's great teacher." [1]

Wise or not, he had his project in mind when he went to visit Cave. In front of the old Fannin Hotel, he met Judge Alexander Terrell who vividly recalled the circumstances of this meeting in his reminiscences. An Austin newspaper had attributed to Terrell implications that General Houston was a traitor. Terrell told the General that he had made no such attack and no covert references to him of any kind.

"I know, Judge," Houston answered, "you did not refer to me, and if you had it would only have excited regret. I feel that my time is short and I have not a root of bitterness here"—he touched his bosom wih his hand—"toward any being that breathes." Before they parted, he asked Terrell to meet him that evening at Major Cave's home. Terrell understood that a matter of importance was to be discussed. That evening, after some conversation about the war and Vicksburg, Houston abruptly asked his friends' opinion "about Texas sending all her young men to battlefields beyond the Mississippi." "We will soon have no one in Texas but old men and boys to defend our homes," Houston said. The waste of life seemed to him "wicked and unnecessary." [2]

This was not a matter that his host, a Confederate officer, felt disposed to discuss, and he said nothing. But Houston pressed ahead with what he had in mind. He asked Terrell how he thought people in Texas would feel about unfurling the Lone Star flag and calling the boys home, saying hands off to both North and South.

Terrell and Cave inferred that he was seeking their support for a serious effort to separate Texas from the Richmond government. They were shocked, Cave more than Terrell. After silently considering the question Terrell answered emphatically that it would cause the sacrifice of any man who proposed it. Houston turned inquiringly to Cave, whose silence was his answer.

Without another word, the General dropped the subject. If men like Terrell and Cave could see in his proposal only the prospect of a lynching bee, then obviously Texas was not ready. Without the wholehearted indorsement of such men, the majority of Texans could not be expected to support the movement. Houston perceived that the Lone Star appeal had lost its magic, and unless there was magic in his call to rally around that standard it would lead to violence and civil war within a civil war—the thing he dreaded for Texas above all else.

Whether Houston seriously contemplated an attempt to take Texas out of the Confederacy has long been a disputed question. Judge Terrell supplied the answer. Terrell wished to publish the facts about this meeting. Cave believed that doing so would reflect discredit on General Houston. Terrell did not think so, but since the meeting had taken place at Cave's home, he felt obliged to keep the episode secret as long as Cave lived. He withheld his account of the meeting for half a century, then told it in his reminiscences of Houston, concluding his narrative with:

> The idea of a separate republic for Texas was naturally dear to General Houston, but he failed to realize that such a move as he proposed during the madness of the hour would be regarded as treachery to the other Southern States, and would be treated as an act of treason.[3]

It is highly improbable that Houston, in the light of his experience and vigorously phrased but cautious letters about the desirability of a new era in Texas, failed to realize the full purport and risks involved in his proposal. He also knew the enormous cost of such a project if it was undertaken without Texas being ready for it.

One can imagine Houston, sad and lonely, thumping upstairs with his gold-headed cane to the guest room in Cave's house after the disappointing response to his query. Cave and Terrell, who were younger than he, had not lived under the inspiring Lone Star, sharing the struggle for liberty and survival. Those years fostered in the participants and in their descendants an undying love for the turbulent Republic.

Houston's disappointment must have made him feel more solitary than when he had been alone in the United States Senate, deserted by Texas and hated by the whole South. He had once said of himself, "I am almost the last of my race," referring to those Texans who had lived through the hazardous and satisfying task of creating a nation. Now he may well have asked himself, was he the last man who was ready to put the rights and welfare of Texas above all other claims?

In his stocking feet, the General paced his room. Did he suspect that he had struck his last blow for Texas? Everywhere he had looked for encouragement he had been rebuffed—by Lubbock, Smith, and Magruder, and now by Cave and Terrell. Where were Old Ben Milam, Jim Bowie, Davy Crockett, the flaming Travis, and those other desperate men who had startled the world with their defiance and had given Texas her slogan of victory? With a handful of lieutenants like those bold spirits, he might have welded Texas into a nation that would fly the Lone Star again and have brought home the boys he believed should never have gone beyond the Sabine.

It was the end of the last big project and the last grand dream.

The General went to Sour Lake hoping that the baths would help him to recover his health. News of the surrender of Vicksburg reached him while he was there. Margaret wrote, saying that he was not to think of coming home until he was better. They all missed him and he was frequently mentioned in the prattle of the baby, Temple; but they would get along. However, with Vicksburg gone and the Union severed, he could not stand being away from home for long.

After his return to Huntsville in July, he had the same despairing thought that had prompted a passage in his speech in Houston City.

It seemed that the growing bitterness, enhanced by the slaughter, would forever prevent North and South from reuniting. Despair fostered a feeling that his race was run. He did not confide in Margaret how ill he felt, but she sensed it. He did tell Jeff that he thought he had about two weeks to live. A few days later, he was in better spirits and was able to go to the penitentiary to talk with his friend, the director, Major Thomas Carothers, and with some of the Federal prisoners.

He had caught a cold at Sour Lake, and pneumonia developed. Because of the torrid July weather, Dr. Markham had Houston's bed moved downstairs and placed in the center of the room so that he would get whatever air was stirring. Jeff slept on a pallet in the sick room and was up and down all night, giving him medicines. Margaret was close by most of the time, catching a little sleep when she could. Jeff fell asleep one afternoon when fanning the General, and his fan struck the General's face. Awakened, he said, "Margaret, you and that boy go and get some rest . . . no use in both of you breaking yourselves down." [4]

An American giant was dying. How had he achieved his stature? His character had been forged in controversy; a century would not see the end of the contention that had raged around him during his lifetime.

As a frontier boy, he had been a truant from school, although he hungered for learning. Despite an innate sense of responsibility and his love for his widowed mother, he had rebelled against his environment, left home, and gone to live with Indians. When this primitive existence had ceased to satisfy his restless, ambitious nature, he had experimented with a new future, trying his hand at teaching. When his country called, he had enlisted in the ranks, intending to seek advancement and make the army his career.

He had paid for his bravery with agonizing battle wounds and had been rewarded by the attention of Andrew Jackson. Later he had incurred the displeasure of the secretary of war—a disaster of great magnitude for a junior officer. After resigning from the army in his mid-twenties, he had spent three months studying law, then struck off on his own to make his way in this profession that was precisely suitable for an enterprising young man who wanted to make something of himself. He had done well, and his future had begun auspiciously with his election to represent Tennessee in the United States Congress. Later, he had become governor of that state.

The failure of his first marriage had been followed by a scandal that threatened to crush him. Seeking refuge, he had returned to the primitive people he loved, abandoning himself to alcohol and the impracticable dreams it inspired. In desperation, knowing that reality existed somewhere and had to be faced, he had gone to Texas where the challenges were as endless as the vast territory's horizon. He had made Texas and Texas had made him.

How had he managed to link his name forever with the history of the world? At one time, Sam Houston had unwittingly drawn his own dimensions when, deploring the absence of sagacious leaders in the new Republic, he had said that a man was needed who was "brave enough for any trial, wise enough for any emergency, and cool enough for any crisis." He had become that kind of man.

As the outgrowth of a paradoxical combination of great caution and equally great resolution, he had developed an indomitable belief in himself. He had meditated, calculated, and planned with the cool, consummate logic of a master chess player, considering all the odds. When he had finally arrived at strategies he considered most likely to succeed, he had cast aside caution and all regard for personal consequences and followed his plan with the dauntless determination of a born fighter. He was willing to fight on even when he fought alone. This rare synthesis of intellect and fighting heart was the magic formula that had made him great.

It was the genesis of the power that had enabled him as Commander in Chief of the tiny Texas army to stand firm against murmurings of discontent, threats of rebellion, and personal insults. It had helped him to go on and win a battle that never would have been fought if he had not known how to blend caution, masterly planning, and resolute action. Because of it, he had shown himself to be equal to any who practiced the complex art of diplomacy in the nineteenth century; often he had been superior to them. Operating from an obscure, mud-bound capital on the Brazos, he had influenced the course of events in the United States and Europe.

As president of a turbulent republic, self-assurance, supported by reasoned conviction, had enabled him to withstand popular clamor for defiance of law and order which, if heeded, would have replaced constitutional freedom with anarchy. It had sustained him in the

United States Senate when Southerners turned against him because he warned that secession would mean ruin for the region he loved, and for the Union itself. It had supported him when his loyalty to the Union had made him an object of derision and contempt.

Again and again events had tested his leadership, his ability to endure savage opposition and resist questionable counsel, and his will to survive. Few men of his time had experienced such extremes of public adulation and obloquy. But Houston's identification with the fortunes of his native land had been complete. Immersed wholeheartedly in the conflicts of his day, this relatively untutored man—who said experience had been his only university—had developed a keen, sophisticated mind with which he had perceived the shape of the future far in advance of his contemporaries.

Detractors had considered him a devil incarnate; admirers had compared him to Oliver Cromwell, George Washington, and Andrew Jackson. Such comparisons did not explain him and added nothing to his stature. Houston had been as individual as any of the great ones to whom he had been likened, and he had been as different from each as they were from each other.

This man, now lying on the threshold of eternal serenity, had perhaps won his greatest victory when he conquered himself. The impatient youth who had known many excesses had become a gentle, wise, and principled man. Tragedies that would have overwhelmed lesser men had tempered his strength. In each of his crises, his rugged courage prevailed. In the whole span of his public career, he had never indulged in self-enrichment; he had elevated steadfastness of principle and plain everyday honesty to the level of grandeur. In countless numbers, his enemies had leveled every possible accusation at this gigantic target. But his record stands today, as it did then, a challenge to his critics.

Sam Houston's life was failing; but, judged by the battles and principles that he had made his own, he had not failed life.

Margaret heard snatches of feverish murmurings, but could not piece together what seemed to be passing through her husband's mind. She sent a servant to the penitentiary to tell Major Carothers that the General had taken a turn for the worse. Carothers came and brought with him the Reverend Samuel McKinney, only to find the General somewhat better. Perhaps to avoid calling attention to their urgent errand, Mr. McKinney asked if the General's opinions about the war had changed. Houston seemed to revive and spoke with surprising energy, reflecting his youthful infatuation with the thundering lines of the *Iliad* and his mature aversion to disunion.

"My views as to the propriety and possibility of the success of this wicked revolution have undergone no change," he said.[5]

Major Carothers asked what Houston wanted for Jeff. The General said that Jeff had been freed with his other slaves, but he wanted Sam, Jr., to take good care of Jeff and he was sure that Sam would do it. Then, he lapsed into a stupor. When he was again conscious, Mr. McKinney asked him how it was between him and his Maker. The General turned and looked the minister squarely in the face, saying "All is well; all is well." [6]

He fell into a deep sleep. The family gathered about his bed, and Mr. McKinney prayed. The General slept throught most of the night with Margaret constantly beside him. At dawn she read to him from the Bible: "In my Father's house are many mansions; if it were not so, I would have told you. I go to prepare a place for you."

She laid down the Book, clasped his hand, and heard him murmur, "Texas . . . Texas. . . ." And a little later his lips moved again, "Margaret. . . ." [7] Jeff thought he heard his master speak an anguished phrase about his stricken country.

Once before the General had lain on what was supposed to be his death bed. All the family had gathered and farewells had been said. But his fighting spirit had triumphed and he recovered. With trenchant humor, he had asked a friend to break the news gently. "Tell my enemies I am not dead yet." [8] This time there was no salutation for his foes. He died at sunset, July 26, 1863.

His coffin was built by a Union prisoner of war, the ship's carpenter from the *Harriet Lane,* a Federal vessel captured at Galveston. This carpenter had been released from a penitentiary cell by the General's intervention.

It was raining when they buried him in the little Huntsville cemetery easily within view from the oak in the yard of Steamboat House. They put up a plain slab bearing his name and the date. A generation passed before the slab was replaced by a shaft of gray Texas granite twenty-five feet high bearing Jackson's words:

"The world will take care of Houston's fame." [9]

Notes

Notes to Chapter 1

[1] Charles Edwards Lester, *The Life of Sam Houston: The Only Authentic Memoir of Him Ever Published*, p. 21. (Hereafter cited as *Memoir*.) For further details concerning Houston's boyhood and family background see William Carey Crane, *Life of Sam Houston*, pp. 17-20; Oren F. Morton, *A History of Rockbridge County, Virginia*, pp. 256-58.

[2] Marquis James, *The Raven*, p. 29. (Hereafter cited as *Raven*.)

[3] *Memoir*, pp, 21-26.

Notes to Chapter 2

[1] *Memoir*, p. 18.

[2] For character of the Cherokees and their tribal history see Marion L. Starkey, *The Cherokee Nation;* Houston's later life among the Cherokees, Grant Foreman, *Indians and Pioneers; the Story of the American Southwest before 1830;* customs, religion and love-making, James Mooney, "Sacred Formulas of the Cherokees," *Seventh Annual Report of the Bureau of American Ethnology*, 1891.

[3] *Raven*, pp. 19-20.

[4] *Memoir*, p. 23.

[5] *Ibid.*

[6] C. E. Lester, *Sam Houston and His Republic*, p. 13. The same thought appears in *Memoir*, p. 23, in somewhat different words.

[7] *Memoir*, p. 26.

[8] A. M. Williams, *Sam Houston and the War of Independence in Texas*, p. 9.

[9] *Memoir*, p. 27.

Notes to Chapter 3

[1] Houston's complete U. S. Army record as it appears in *Historical Register and Dictionary of the United States Army* (1903): "Samuel

Houston, Va. Army. pvt. and sergt; 7 inf. 24 Mar. to Aug. 1813; ens. 39th inf. 29 July 1813; 3 Lt. 31 Dec. 1813; 2 Lt. 20 May 1814; tr to 1 inf 17 May 1815; 1 Lt. May 1817; resd. 1 Mar 1818; 1st gov. of Tex; died 25 July 1863." (N. B. Houston was not the first governor of Texas.)

2 *Memoir*, p. 303.

3 *Ibid.*, pp. 29-38. For description of the battle from Jackson's viewpoint, see James Parton, *Life of Andrew Jackson*, I, 514-22.

4 Amelia W. Williams and Eugene C. Barker (eds.), *The Writings of Sam Houston, 1813-1863*, I, 5. (Hereafter cited as *Writings*.)

Notes to Chapter 4

1 *Raven*, p. 44.

2 *Writings*, I, 8. For details on Houston's expense account, his letters of protest to Calhoun, see *ibid.*, pp. 9-12.

Notes to Chapter 5

1 Crane, *op. cit.*, p. 33.

2 *Writings*, I, 19.

3 *Ibid.*, p. 16.

4 *Ibid.*, p. 130.

5 Crane, *op. cit.*, p. 35.

6 Parton, *op. cit.*, III, 57.

7 *Writings*, I, 24.

8 *Ibid.*, p. 28.

9 *Raven*, p. 64.

10 *Writings*, I, 113.

11 *Ibid.*, p. 65.

Notes to Chapter 6

1 A. M. Williams, *op. cit.*, p. 33.

2 *Writings*, II, 10.

3 Parton, *op. cit.*, III, 141-44.

4 Marquis James, *Andrew Jackson, Portrait of a President*, p. 174.

5 *Ibid.*, p. 175.

6 See Henderson Yoakum, *History of Texas*, I, 307.

Notes to Chapter 7

1 *Writings*, I, 130.

2 Jo Guild, *Old Times in Tennessee*, p. 278.

3 *Raven*, p. 139.

4 *Writings*, I, 130. See also *ibid.*, pp. 149-50.

5 *Ibid.*, p. 144. Houston's letter to John H. Overton, Dec. 28, 1829, expressed deep-felt gratitude for Overton's visit some eight months after it occurred.

6 *Memoir*, pp. 46-47.

7 *Ibid.*

[8] *Niles' Register*, XXXVI, May 23, 1829, 198.

[9] Llerena B. Friend, *Sam Houston, The Great Designer*, p. 22.

[10] Houston's resignation in the records of the Tennessee State Historical Society, Nashville, is in the small handwriting of a clerk who copied it, but the signature is in Houston's bold hand.

[11] *Writings*, I, 144.

[12] *Memoir*, p. 48.

[13] Nashville *Banner*, Dec. 30, 1907.

[14] Dr. George W. Samson, "Sam Houston's Exile Explained After Many Years," New York *Tribune*, Nov. 13, 1880.

[15] Will T. Hale and Dixon L. Merritt, *A History of Tennessee and Tennesseeans*, II, 379.

[16] A version of Eliza Allen Houston's side of the story, current within the family, differs from the report of the committee to Eliza's father and from all published reports. In the course of research on this book, Mrs. Eleanor Allen Sullivan of Nashville, Eliza's great-niece, was contacted and she made this statement, Jan. 31, 1962:

"The explanation of the separation was so simple the Allen family felt the public would not accept it, and for this reason it was not discussed.

"Aunt Eliza had been fascinated by this man of glamor, the protege of Andrew Jackson, who possibly was headed for the White House. She had gone freely and hopefully into her marriage. No one forced her or over-persuaded her. It is absurd to suggest such a thing. I know the Allens. I am one. It's just one of the things they simply could not have thought of doing.

"In one of the Indian wars Houston had been struck by a poisoned arrow. It left a festering wound which never healed. His uncouthness, plus the running wound, was too much for the girl who had led a sheltered life.

"I regret that the older members of my family would not discuss with any author things which they discussed within the family circle."

[17] Versions of this episode are reported by George Creel, *Sam Houston, Colossus in Buckskin*, p. 38; *Raven*, p. 84; and Georgia J. Burleson (ed.), *Life and Writings of Dr. Rufus C. Burleson*, p. 522.

[18] Burleson, *loc. cit.*

[19] Carroll to Jackson, May 25, 1829, Jackson Papers, LC.

[20] John S. Bassett (ed.), *Correspondence of Andrew Jackson*, IV, 21.

Notes to Chapter 8

[1] Friend, *op. cit.*, p. 23. See also *Writings*, I, 242, n. 3.

[2] *Memoir*, p. 52.

[3] *Writings*, I, 136.

[4] See note 6, Chapter 6, *supra*.

[5] Jackson's Memorandum Book, May 21, 1829, LC.

[6] *Writings*, I, 141-42.

[7] *Ibid.*, p. 140.

[8] *Ibid.,* p. 144.

[9] A. M. Williams, "General Houston's Indian Life," *Magazine of American History,* X (July-Dec. 1883), 403.

[10] *Writings,* I, 151.

[11] For full text of committee report see Guild, *op. cit.,* pp. 269-74.

[12] *Writings,* I, 149-50.

[13] *Raven,* pp. 154-55.

[14] *Writings,* I, 142.

[15] *Memoir,* p. 260.

[16] *Raven,* p. 157.

[17] Wharton's two letters, *Raven,* p. 177.

Notes to Chapter 9

[1] The two European tourists were Alexis de Tocqueville and his traveling companion, Gustave de Beaumont. On the way down the Mississippi Tocqueville questioned Houston about the characteristics and customs of Indians and elicited information that filled eight pages of his notebooks. Houston told Tocqueville that he believed Indians and whites could live side by side in developing the continent because the Indians had fine qualities and excellent institutions and were able to absorb progress; but he did not say he regarded it as a probability. Tocqueville's first impression of Houston was not favorable; he spoke of him as a perfect example of the disastrous consequences of popular sovereignty. His view was modified as a result of their conversations, and he later referred to him as a man of great physical and moral energy. G. W. Pierson (ed.), *Tocqueville and Beaumont in America,* pp. 607-15.

[2] *Writings,* I, 199.

[3] Parton, *op. cit.,* III, 388-89.

[4] *Ibid.,* pp. 389-90.

[5] Crane, *op. cit.,* p. 21.

[6] *Writings,* I, 202-3.

[7] *Ibid.*

[8] Parton, *op. cit.,* III, 391.

[9] *Congressional Globe,* May 9, 1832.

[10] For interrogations of Houston and Stanberry see House Executive Documents, No. 210, 22nd Cong., 1st Sess., Vol. V, Serial 220, p. 1 ff.

[11] Alexander W. Terrell, "Recollections of General Sam Houston," *Southwestern Historical Quarterly,* XVI (1912-1913), 120-36.

[12] *Ibid.,* p. 126 ff.

Notes to Chapter 10

[1] All quotations in this chapter, unless specified otherwise, are from Houston's speech, *Writings,* I, pp. 207-25, *passim.*

[2] The account on the following pages, matter stricken from the record, is based on Terrell's "Recollections," pp. 123-28.

[3] *Writings,* I, 208. See n. 1 above.

⁴ Houston's daughter, Mrs. Nettie Houston Bringhurst, told Marquis James that Edwin Booth called on her in San Antonio in 1888 and told her about his father. *Raven,* p. 442, n. 8.

Notes to Chapter 11

¹ See *Writings,* I, 207-25, for record of the vote, the sentence, and Houston's protest.

² Reports of Committees of U. S. House of Representatives, 1st Sess., 22nd Cong., V, Doc. 502.

³ In the following pages most of the important items of the little known but extensive Houston-Prentiss correspondence during the spring and summer, 1832, are from *Writings,* I, 197-266; other letters are in the James Prentiss Collection, Univ. of Texas Library.

⁴ *Writings,* I, 230.

⁵ Did Jackson lend Houston $500 for his trip to Texas? Augustus C. Buell, (*History of Andrew Jackson,* II, 35, footnote) thinks he did and that the loan was made in Washington. This is doubtful because when Houston was in Washington he believed his deal with Prentiss would go through. James (*Raven,* p. 182) implies the loan had a covert purpose. But Jackson was a friend, he wanted peace among Indians, information about Texas; a loan of this amount does not seem out of order from the Old Chief to a friend who was broke. Nevertheless, the loan stirred overtones of a plot to grab Texas.

⁶ *Writings,* IV, 11.

⁷ *Memoir,* p. 65. For Houston's "confidential Indian mission," James (*Raven,* p. 182) argues that it was "concocted" by Jackson, thus implying some kind of conspiracy in connection with Houston's going to Texas. The seriousness of the undertaking is indicated by Houston's report on his mission to Lewis Cass, U. S. Secretary of War, from Arkansas Territory, July 30, 1833 (*Writings,* II, 15); and to U. S. Acting Secretary of War, John Robb, from Natchitoches, La., Oct. 4, 1833 (*Writings,* II, 18).

⁸ Creel, *op. cit.,* pp. 61-62.

⁹ *Ibid.,* p. 61. I have never discovered where my old friend, George Creel got this material. Friend and James also tell part of this story.

¹⁰ *Writings,* VI, 1-2.

Book II

THE FIVE-POINTED STAR

Notes to Chapter 1

¹ Eugene C. Barker, *Life of Stephen Austin,* p. 89.

² *Ibid.,* p. 173.

³ *Ibid.,* p. 176.

[4] *Ibid.*, p. 178.
[5] A. J. Houston, *Texas Independence*, p. 37.
[6] Barker, *op. cit.*, p. 198.
[7] Justin H. Smith, *War With Mexico*, I, 31-32.
[8] *Ibid.*
[9] Justin H. Smith, *The Annexation of Texas*, 7.
[10] Smith, *War With Mexico*, I, 43.
[11] A. J. Houston, *Texas Independence*, p. 42.
[12] *Ibid.*, pp. 43-44.
[13] Creel, *op. cit.*, p. 74.

Notes to Chapter 2

[1] Barker, *op. cit.*, pp. 77, 269.
[2] *Writings*, I, 274.
[3] *Ibid.*, V, 364-65.
[4] *Ibid.*, pp. 5-6.
[5] *Ibid.*, I, 290. James (*Raven*, p. 210) states that Houston "resumed ... his leisurely plotting," implying that Houston forced the developing revolution to a crisis. No evidence to support this conclusion is offered except an ambiguous gossipy letter by an English excursionist, G. W. Featherstonhaugh, (*Raven*, p. 207).
[6] Barker, *op. cit.*, p. 434.
[7] *Ibid.*, pp. 440-41.

Notes to Chapter 3

[1] *Writings*, I, 231.
[2] A copy of the original portrait, "Houston as Marius," hangs in the Texas State Capitol today. On the west wall of the Senate gallery to the south of the main entrance, it faces the rostrum where the lieutenant governor presides as president of the Senate.
[3] *Writings*, V, 5-6.
[4] *Raven*, p. 211.
[5] Smith, *War With Mexico*, I, 42.
[6] *Ibid.*, I, 47.
[7] *Ibid.*, p. 414, n. 7.
[8] A. J. Houston, *op. cit.*, p. 58.
[9] *Ibid.*, p. 59.
[10] Barker, *op. cit.*, p. 478.
[11] *Ibid.*, pp. 480-81.
[12] *Writings*, I, 302.
[13] *Ibid.*, p. 304.
[14] A. J. Houston, *op. cit.*, pp. 64-65.

Notes to Chapter 4

[1] Barker, *op. cit.*, pp. 482-83.
[2] *Writings*, VII, 24.

[3] Proceedings of the Consultation, pp. 43-49, LC microfilm.
[4] Carleton Beals, *Stephen F. Austin*, p. 201.
[5] Friend, *op. cit.*, p. 63.

Notes to Chapter 5

[1] *Proceedings of the General Council*, Nov. 15, 1835, pp. 12-15, LC microfilm.
[2] A. J. Houston, *op. cit.*, p. 91.
[3] *Ibid.*, p. 81.
[4] For Houston's plan of defense and his intention to command in the field see orders and letters, *Writings*, I, 307-329; also A. J. Houston, *op. cit.*, pp. 149-50.
[5] *Writings*, I, 312-13.
[6] Smith, *War With Mexico*, I, 70.
[7] Houston was generous in support of claims by soldiers and their dependents. But when Barrett's estate entered money claims for his services to the revolution, Houston was roused to fury. On Nov. 29, 1853, in protest against allowance of the claim, he wrote to Texas State Comptroller, John M. Swisher: "D. C. Barrett was, in my opinion, the worst man that was ever in Texas. He was so capable, and all his capability was turned to harm. I attribute to his management the fall of the Alamo, and the destruction of Fannin and Ward. He did all the mischief in his power while he was here, and fled in time of danger.... He surely deserves nothing but the condemnation of the people of Texas for his acts in the Consultation." *Writings*, VII, 24-25. For an opposing view of Barrett's service in the General Council, see Eugene C. Barker, "Don Carlos Barrett," in the *Southwestern Historical Quarterly*, XX, 139-45.
[8] Houston's judgment of Chairman Hanks was even more severe than of Barrett. Houston charged two members of the military committee, Chairman Hanks and a less well known member, Clements, with using their committee authority to "urge and authorize... individuals at San Antonio" to undertake an expedition to Matamoros which was not sanctioned by the government. (*Writings*, I, 347-48.) Although Houston wrote Lieutenant Governor James Robinson indorsing Hanks for sutler, he later learned more about Hanks's activities and revoked his indorsement "as I do most seriously regard him, as the *basest* of all mankind." *Ibid.*, p. 335.
[9] *Ibid.*, p. 321.

Notes to Chapter 6

[1] *Writings*, I, 304.
[2] *Ibid.*, p. 325.
[3] *Ibid.*, p. 330.
[4] *Ibid.*, p. 331.
[5] *Ibid.*, p. 332.
[6] *Ibid.*, p. 352.

⁷ No complete version of Houston's powerful appeal to the soldiers at Goliad exists. It is one of two important "lost" speeches, but fragments in various sources agree in essentials. Extracts here are from the version, "To the Soldiers at Goliad" and "Comrades, Citizens of Texas!" dated Jan. 15 (?), 1836. *Writings*, I, 337.

⁸ *Ibid.*, p. 338.

⁹ *Ibid.*, pp. 339-40.

¹⁰ A. J. Houston, *op. cit.*, p. 97.

¹¹ Proceedings of the General Council, Jan. 9, 1836, p. 239, LC microfilm.

¹² A. J. Houston, *op. cit.*, p. 100.

¹³ After wrecking the provisional government the Council declared the Commander in Chief, Texas agents in the United States, and all Texas officials responsible to Lieutenant Governor Robinson. See W. Roy Smith, "The Quarrel between Governor Smith and the Provisional Government of the Republic," *Quarterly of the Texas State Historical Association*, V, (1902), 325.

¹⁴ A. J. Houston, *op. cit.*, p. 101.

¹⁵ No formal report of these remarks exists. For a brief indirect summary of Houston's talk, see A. J. Houston, *op. cit.*, p. 105.

Notes to Chapter 7

¹ See Colonel William Fairfax Gray's diary, *From Virginia to Texas*, pp. 100-130.

² George P. Garrison (ed.), *Diplomatic Correspondence of the Republic of Texas*, I, 66.

³ On Nov. 11 or 12, 1835, after a resolution by Houston, the San Felipe Consultation had adopted Article XVIII declaring "all grants sales and conveyances of land: illegally and fraudulently made by the Legisature of the State of Coahuila and Texas ... within the limits of Texas null, void and of no effect." This referred to grants which allotted more than half a million acres to a grantee at one stroke. Houston's resolution provided that holders who could prove good faith and money actually paid in obtaining such grants should be reimbursed with ten per cent interest. *Writings*, I, 306-7; H. P. N. Gammel (ed.), *Laws of Texas*, 1822-1897, I, 538.

⁴ Noah Smithwick, *The Evolution of a State*, p. 60.

⁵ Original in Texas State Archives; photostat, LC. Frequently misquoted, this document is somewhat difficult to decipher. This version is from an enlarged facsimile reproduced in George P. Garrison's *Texas, a Contest of Civilizations*, pp. 206-7.

⁶ The little known but important Cherokee treaty negotiated by Houston and Forbes is given in full, *Writings*, I, 358-60.

⁷ *Ibid.*, p. 360.

⁸ A. J. Houston, *op. cit.*, pp. 123-24.

⁹ *Ibid.*, p. 135.

[10] Houston's own description of this address reads: "He spoke nearly an hour. . . . He admonished the Convention of the peril of the country; he advised them to sit calmly, and firmly and coolly pursue their deliberation; to be wise and patriotic; to feel no alarm, and he pledged himself instantly to repair to Gonzalez, where he had heard that a small corps of militia had rallied, and interpose them between the Convention and the enemy; and while they chose to sit in convention, the Mexicans would never approach them unless they marched over his dead body. In the meantime, if mortal power could avail, he would relieve the brave men in the Alamo." *Memoir*, pp. 90-91.

[11] A. J. Houston, *op. cit.*, p. 125.

Book III

FORTY DAYS AND NIGHTS THAT CHANGED THE WORLD

Notes to Chapter 1

[1] Houston spelled "Dickinson" as it appears in this letter; however, Amelia W. Williams says: "A few writers of Texas history spell Almeron Dickerson's name correctly, but the majority write it 'Dickinson.' Several documents to be found among *Comptroller's Military Service Records*, Texas State Library, show this man's signature as written by himself. It is clearly 'Almeron Dickerson,' and at the Alamo from Jan., 1836 to March 6, 1836, he enjoyed the rank of captain of artillery." *Writings*, I, 375, n. 2.

[2] Two versions of the letter to Fannin, with slight variations, are given in *Writings*, I, 362-65.

[3] *Ibid.*, p. 367.

[4] Mrs. Dickerson's account of her experiences varied considerably. Her talk in 1881 with Rev. Walter Raleigh Richardson appears R. M. Green, *Memoirs of Mary A. Maverick*, pp. 135-36. Other accounts: "Adjutant General's Letters Concerning the Alamo, 1875-1878," Texas State Archives (see, "Testimony of Mrs. Hannig Touching the Alamo Massacre," Sept. 23, 1876); interview, San Antonio *Express*, Apr. 28, 1881; another interview with Mrs. Dickerson in an unidentified Ohio newspaper was reprinted in San Antonio *Express*, Feb. 24, 1929.

[5] "Joe," Travis' Negro slave, related his experiences in the Alamo and afterward under examination by the Texas Cabinet. The diarist, William Fairfax Gray, was present when he was interrogated. See Gray, *From Virginia to Texas*, pp. 136-38. For other versions of Joe's testimony see the New Orleans *Commercial Bulletin*, Apr. 11, 1836. An account of the experiences of Ben, Colonel Almonte's Negro orderly, appears in the work of a contemporary historian, Rev. Chester Newell, *History of the Revolution in Texas*, pp. 88-89.

[6] *Memoir*, pp. 95-96.

[7] *Writings*, VI, 5-13.

[8] C. E. Castañeda, translator, *The Mexican Side of the Texas Revolution*, Filisola's "Representation," p. 169.

[9] *Memoir*, p. 106.

Notes to Chapter 2

[1] In the U. S. Senate, Feb. 28, 1859, in refutation of calumnies, Houston told the story of the burning of Gonzales: "On that night, about twelve miles from there [Gonzales], it was announced to the General that the Mexicans would suffer; that a barrel of gin and a barrel of wine had been poisoned with arsenic, and that, as they came to consume it, it would destroy them. I presume no man ever had such feelings of horror at a deed being perpetrated of this kind, from which all the water of the Jordan could not cleanse the reputation of a General." *Writings*, VII, 312.

[2] *Ibid.*, I, 364, n. 5.

[3] *Ibid.*, p. 375.

Notes to Chapter 3

[1] *Writings*, I, 378.

[2] *Ibid.*, pp. 380-81.

[3] *Ibid.*

[4] *Ibid.*, p. 382.

[5] *Ibid.*

Notes to Chapter 4

[1] *Writings*, I, 384.

[2] *Ibid.*, p. 389.

[3] *Ibid.*

Notes to Chapter 5

[1] *Writings*, I, 395. Also see A. J. Houston, *op. cit.*, pp. 170-86, *passim*.

[2] Except as noted the account of the Goliad massacre is based on John Duval, "His Own Story of Escape from the Fannin Massacre at Goliad," *Quarterly of the Texas State Historical Association*, I, 54-57.

[3] Portilla's *Diary* as translated in Yoakum, *op. cit.*, II, 519-20. Yoakum notes, in connection with the massacre, "The Indian Colonel Portilla knew for what purpose he and his Indian command had been sent to Goliad and wrote to Urrea as if the latter knew.... The diary of Urrea, that of Portilla, and the *Manifesto* of Santa Anna, were all manufactured *after* the civilized world had pronounced upon the atrocity of these assassinations." (*Ibid.*, p. 524.)

[4] *Writings*, I, 395-96.

[5] *Ibid.*, pp. 411-12, n. 3.

[6] *Ibid.*, p. 398.

[7] *Ibid.*, IV, 274, n. 2.

Notes to Chapter 6

[1] *Writings,* I, 403.
[2] *Ibid.,* p. 391.
[3] *Ibid.,* pp. 410-11.
[4] *Ibid.,* pp. 409-10.
[5] *Ibid.,* pp. 408-9.

Notes to Chapter 7

[1] *Memoir,* p. 106.
[2] Crane, *op. cit.,* pp. 648-61: translation of "The Battle of San Jacinto ...an Account of the Action written by Colonel Pedro Delgado, of General Santa Anna's Staff." (See Delgado in bibliography.)

Notes to Chapter 8

[1] See note 2, chapter 7, above.
[2] While supplies were being loaded on the *Flash,* the little vessel lay alongside another steamboat, the *Cayuga.* One of the *Cayuga*'s guns was accidentally discharged. It wounded Acting Secretary of War David Thomas, one of Houston's most trusted friends in the government. Three days later Thomas died of blood poisoning. *Writings,* I, 399, n. 2.
[3] High among the factors listed by Santa Anna in his *Manifesto* as responsible for his defeat, was the capture of Miguel Bachiller with dispatches, thus giving Houston "positive information regarding our forces, at a time when [the enemy] was retreating, wondering what it would do, astonished by our operations and triumphs." (Castañeda, *op. cit.,* p. 78 ff.)
[4] *Memoir,* p. 111.
[5] *Writings,* I, 415.
[6] The copy of this letter addressed to "Colonel Rusk, In the Field," dated Harrisburg, Apr. 19, 1836, differs somewhat from copies furnished Hockley and Raguet. It appears in *Memoir,* p. 114, followed by: "(Certified copy from the Department of War, of the Republic of Texas)." Houston also used this version in his review of the San Jacinto battle in a letter to Hamilton Stuart, editor of the *Civilian and Galveston Gazette,* Aug. 25, 1857.
[7] *Memoir,* pp. 112-14.
[8] *Ibid.,* p. 114.
[9] *Ibid.,* pp. 114-15.

Notes to Chapter 9

[1] Quotations from Delgado in this and succeeding chapters are from Delgado's "Account," Crane, *op. cit.,* pp. 648-61.
[2] The artillery of Texans and Mexicans was alike except for size. All cannon were the smooth bore muzzle-loaders. Powder charges in sacks of about one pound were fired by a fuse or hot iron which ignited the powder in the vent. Shot and shell were round. Friction primers were

not in use. Small arms, muzzle-loaded, were fired by a flint and hammer mechanism. Percussion caps had been invented but were not common. For artillery and small arms available in 1863, see A. J. Houston, *op. cit.*, pp. 138-39.

[3] *Memoir*, p. 118.

[4] *Ibid.*, p. 120.

Notes to Chapter 10

[1] *Memoir*, p. 122.

[2] Santa Anna's disaster at San Jacinto did not change Houston's opinion that the Mexican was a kind of genius. In a lecture on Jan. 28, 1851, Houston said of him: "He was no common man; with genius and capacity for greatness, he was, and is an illustrious man. Genius has marked him for her own; but he is not an American, either by education or the moral impulses that make the man. Had he been educated an American, but few rivals would have presented themselves in the last century." *Writings*, V, 267-81.

Notes to Chapter 11

[1] *Writings*, VII, 319.

[2] *Memoir*, p. 124.

[3] See *Writings*, VII, 319 and for further details of the war council see *Memoir*, p. 125; the participants named, *Writings*, II, 202; see also *ibid.*, VII, 319; VI, 189, 448-61.

[4] *Memoir*, p. 126; *Writings*, VI, 456.

[5] From Houston's official report of the battle to the government, Apr. 25, 1836, *Writings*, I, 416-20. In his speech of June 9, 1855, at San Jacinto, Houston said he had only 540 effective men, *ibid.*, VI, 189.

[6] *Memoir*, p. 129 ff. Details of battle preparations and of the action as given in his official battle report of Apr. 25, 1836, were embellished by Houston on various occasions; see *Writings*, V, 273-75; VI, 5-13, 184-91, 448-61; VII, 306-36, 325-26. See also A. M. Williams, *Sam Houston and the War of Independence in Texas*, p. 200; A. J. Houston, *op. cit.*, p. 228.

[7] *Memoir*, pp. 133-34.

[8] *Ibid.*, p. 134.

Notes to Chapter 12

[1] Yoakum, *op. cit.*, II, 146-47. Sylvester's report was accepted by the Commander in Chief, who awarded him a diploma for vigilance and gallantry, *Writings*, I, 435. Houston's report of the capture with some additional details, *Memoir*, pp. 144-45.

[2] *Writings*, VII, 332.

[3] *Memoir*, pp. 145-46.

[4] *Ibid.*, pp. 146-48.

[5] A. J. Houston, *op. cit.*, pp. 234-35.

[6] *Memoir*, pp. 148-49.

[7] *Ibid.*, pp. 153-54.

[8] *Writings,* I, 416-20.
[9] A. J. Houston, *op. cit.,* p. 237.
[10] *Ibid.,* p. 245.
[11] John J. Linn, *Reminiscences of Fifty Years in Texas,* p. 264.
[12] *Writings,* VI, 190.
[13] *Ibid.,* I, 425.
[14] *Ibid.,* p. 426.
[15] *Memoir,* p. 161.
[16] *Writings,* I, 428.

BOOK IV

A RULER OF VIKINGS

Notes to Chapter 1

[1] *Writings,* I, 429.
[2] *Raven,* p. 263.
[3] *Writings,* I, 430.
[4] *Ibid.,* VI, 86.
[5] *Memoir,* p. 69.
[6] *Writings,* I, 434.
[7] Bassett (ed.), *Correspondence of Andrew Jackson,* V, 425.
[8] *Writings,* I, 436-39.

Notes to Chapter 2

[1] *Writings,* I, 446.
[2] *Ibid.,* V, 364-68.
[3] Theodore Roosevelt, *Life of Thomas Hart Benton,* an extract entitled "How Texas Became Independent" in *Great Epochs in American History,* VI, 140.
[4] *Writings,* I, 448-52.
[5] C. W. Raines (ed.), *Six Decades in Texas; or, Memoirs of Francis Richard Lubbock . . . ,* p. 73.
[6] *Writings,* I, 461, 465, 474.

Notes to Chapter 3

[1] The law that established the boundary limits of Texas became a matter of controversy. After the notoriously troublesome character, Thomas Jefferson Green, claimed authorship of the bill, Houston corrected him in a statement in the U. S. Senate. All the evidence, as well as Houston's statement, indicates that he fathered the law and attended to this important matter at the right time. The boundary of Texas and how it was established—by successful revolution, treaty, national law, and recognition eventually by three great powers, United States, France and England—

became of importance in connection with the war with Mexico and the rights of Texas after annexation.

2 *Writings*, I, 469-74.

3 *Ibid.*

4 Two Texans, Collinsworth and Grayson, were first to ask Jackson to intercede between Texas and Mexico. Before he became secretary of state, Stephen Austin suggested to Santa Anna that he appeal to President Jackson to mediate. Santa Anna quickly grasped the idea as a means to achieve his liberation and wrote Jackson on July 4, 1836, declaring "continuation of the war and its disasters would be inevitable if some powerful hand were not outstretched to compel the voice of reason to be heard." This opened the way for later exchanges between Jackson and Houston and the understandings that led to Santa Anna's trip to Washington, D. C., and eventual return home. Santa Anna's letter to Jackson and Jackson's letter to Santa Anna, Sept. 4, 1836, are given in J. D. Richardson, *Messages and Papers of the Presidents*, III, 274-75 and 275-76. For Austin's participation in the affair see Barker, *op. cit.*, pp. 505-9.

5 *Writings*, I, 487.

6 *Ibid.*

7 *Ibid.*, p. 453.

8 *Memoir*, p. 183.

9 George P. Garrison (ed.), *Diplomatic Correspondence of the Republic of Texas*, I, 187-92, *passim*.

Notes to Chapter 4

1 Garrison, *op. cit.*, I, 170.

2 *Ibid.*, p. 193.

3 Barker, *op. cit.*, p. 520.

4 *Ibid.*

5 *Writings*, II, 28.

Notes to Chapter 5

1 Garrison, *op. cit.*, I, 168.

2 *Ibid.*, pp. 152-53.

3 James, *Andrew Jackson*, p. 423.

4 Garrison, *op. cit.*, I, 169.

5 *Ibid.*, pp. 168-72.

6 *Ibid.*, p. 201.

7 *Writings*, II, 74.

8 *Writings*, I, 290-91.

9 Gray, *op. cit.*, II, 219.

Notes to Chapter 6

1 *Writings*, II, 74.

2 *Ibid.*, pp. 82-90.

3 Crane, *op. cit.*, p. 128.

[1] *Writings*, II, 99.
[2] *Ibid.*, pp. 113-14.
[3] See Edmund T. Miller, *A Financial History of Texas*, pp. 31-33 and Aldon S. Lang, "Financial Aspects of the Public Lands in Texas," *Southwestern Political and Social Science Quarterly*, XIII, 1923.
[4] Garrison, *op. cit.*, I, 232-34.
[5] *Ibid.*, I, 255.
[6] J. H. Smith, *The Annexation of Texas*, p. 680.
[7] *Writings*, II, 150-51.
[8] Garrison, *op. cit.*, I, 331.
[9] Herbert Gambrell, *Anson Jones*, pp. 128-29.

[1] Robert Buchanan, *Life and Adventures of Audubon the Naturalist*, pp. 309-10.
[2] Correspondence between the Houston government and Henderson quoted in this chapter, Garrison, *op. cit.*, III, 808-866, *passim*.

[1] *Writings*, II, 184.
[2] *Ibid.*, p. 189.
[3] *Ibid.*, p. 64.
[4] *Ibid.*, I, 465.
[5] *Ibid.*, II, 43-44.
[6] *Ibid.*, p. 228.
[7] *Ibid.*, pp. 63-64.
[8] *Raven*, p. 277.
[9] *Ibid.*, pp. 278-79.
[10] *Ibid.*, pp. 427-28.
[11] *Writings*, II, 244-45.
[12] *Ibid.*, p. 245, n. 2.

[1] *Writings*, II, 180.
[2] See Stanley Siegel, *A Political History of the Texas Republic*, pp. 96-97.
[3] Anson Jones, *Memoranda and Official Correspondence Relating to the Republic of Texas*, pp. 139-40; also W. S. Red's article on William Y. Allen's "Reminiscences of Texas, 1838-1842," *Southwestern Historical Quarterly*, XVIII, 295.
[4] *Raven*, pp. 305-6.
[5] Anson Jones, *loc. cit.*
[6] *Raven*, p. 304.

Notes to Chapter *1*

[1] *Writings,* II, 312.

[2] *Ibid.,* p. 308.

[3] *Ibid.,* IV, 143, 327.

[4] *Raven,* pp. 307-8. The General's confusing Margaret with her sister, Mrs. Bledsoe, not included in the James account, was related to the present writer on Dec. 4, 1961, by Temple Houston Morrow.

[5] Typescript collection of Houston Unpublished Correspondence, Archives, Univ. of Texas Library. Original owned by Mrs. Ruth John Sanders.

[6] Crane, *op. cit.,* p. 253.

Notes to Chapter *2*

[1] *Writings,* II, 273-74.

[2] *Ibid.,* p. 274.

[3] *Ibid.,* p. 269.

[4] Walter F. McCaleb (ed.), *Memoirs of John H. Reagan, LL.D.,* pp. 29-36.

[5] Harriet Smither, "Diary of Adolphus Sterne," *Southwestern Historical Quarterly,* XXXII, 256.

[6] *Writings,* II, 315-62, *passim* for quotations from Houston in the following pages of this chapter.

Notes to Chapter *3*

[1] At the end of Houston's two-year term the Texas Republic had $800,000 in currency in circulation. The Lamar administration repudiated this interest-bearing currency as well as its own large issues of "red backs," by refusing to accept them for duties or taxes. With the decks thus cleared, President Lamar plunged into new issues of currency and had $2,500,000 in circulation at the end of his three-year term. (See E. T. Miller, *A Financial History of Texas,* p. 70; and W. R. Hogan, *The Texas Republic,* pp. 100-101.

[2] Hogan, *op. cit.,* p. 135.

[3] Anson Jones, *The Republic of Texas,* p. 34. Other extracts from Jones's diary in this chapter: *ibid.,* pp. 35-36.

Notes to Chapter *4*

[1] *Raven,* p. 313.

[2] The original ode quoted in full by the *Telegraph and Texas Register,* July 1, 1840, inspired the editor to remark that the comparison of Houston with the Father of His Country was "unmerited."

[3] Friend, *op. cit.*, p. 97.

[4] *Writings*, II, 352.

Notes to Chapter 5

[1] See Proceedings of the Texas House of Representatives, Fifth Cong., First Sess., Dec. 16, 1840, p. 293. LC microfilm. Also, *Memoir*, pp. 202-3.

[2] *Writings*, II, 365.

Notes to Chapter 6

[1] Hogan, *op. cit.*, p. 288.

[2] *Writings*, VI, p. 62.

[3] *Ibid.*, III, 10.

[4] *Ibid.*, II, 369.

[5] *Ibid.*, III, 236.

[6] Austin *City Gazette*, Aug. 11, 1841. This pamphlet was first circulated in 1837. It was dictated by Colonel Robert M. Coleman and written and printed by Algernon P. Thompson at Velasco. Coleman was an inveterate Houston enemy and Thompson was a devoted Lamar man. See *Writings*, II, 262, n. 2.

[7] Houston's "Truth" letters of Aug. 16 and 18, 1841, from the *Houstonian* appear in *Writings*, II, 376-386. Five "Truth" letters were published in the *Houstonian* and in the Galveston *Civilian*. Burnet's more numerous "Publius" letters appeared in the *Telegraph and Texas Register*, Aug.-Sept., 1841. *Writings*, II, 386, n. 3.

Notes to Chapter 7

[1] Friend, *op. cit.*, p. 101. Siegel, *op. cit.*, p. 182, says Houston received 7,915 to Burnet's 3,619.

[2] *Writings*, II, 391-97.

[3] Houston's currency proposals and his appeal for appropriations, *ibid.*, 425, 437, 447.

[4] Gambrell, *op. cit.*, p. 247.

Notes to Chapter 8

[1] Paul Horgan, *The Great River*, II, 571. Lamar's negotiations with Arista are shrouded in mystery because Lamar wanted it that way. During the political campaign of 1841 Houston demanded an investigation of the Santa Fe expedition. Nothing further was heard because of the disaster that befell the expedition. But later, on Dec. 17, 1845, Houston charged Lamar with (1) opening a secret correspondence with Arista, a general of the enemy's army; (2) sending and receiving "commissioners" (apparently Mexican commissioners from Arista) and permitting them to be present at the outset of the ill-fated expedition; (3) not laying before the Texas Congress communications involved in the affair. *Writings*, IV, 432. A "Republic of the Rio Grande" comprising northern Mexican states, Texas, and New Mexico, was proposed in 1839 by General An-

tonio Canales, a Mexican revolutionist; Lamar and his government rejected it. Whether Lamar or Arista reopened the subject is not definitely known, but it is certain that the inception of the Santa Fe expedition was steeped in chicanery. See Siegel, *op. cit.*, pp. 165-66, William C. Binkley, "New Mexico and the Texan Santa Fe Expedition," *Southwestern Historical Quarterly*, XXVII, 85-107; Justin H. Smith, "La republica del Rio Grande," *American Historical Review*, XXV, Oct. 1919-July 1920; and Horgan, *op. cit.*, II, 559-71. Bancroft and Yoakum also discuss the Santa Fe enterprise.

2 Horgan, *loc. cit.*

3 For a detailed account of the expedition from this point on see George W. Kendall, *Narrative of the Texan Santa Fe Expedition.*

4 Kendall, *op. cit.*, pp. 12-13.

5 New Orleans *Daily Picayune*, May 18, 1841.

6 Kendall, *op. cit.*, p. 397.

7 Horgan, *op. cit.*, II, 799.

8 *Ibid.*, p. 577.

9 Kendall, *op. cit.*, p. 534.

Notes to Chapter 9

1 Kendall, *op. cit.*, p. xiv.

2 *Writings*, III, 92. At this time and for years afterward Houston was accused by his political opponents of failure to act in behalf of prisoners captured by Mexico in the Santa Fe and Mier expeditions. Houston's message to Congress shows that he did what he could and explains why he was obliged to act with discretion. For complete details of his efforts to assist all Texas prisoners in Mexico see *ibid.*, p. 300, also 303, n. 2.

3 *Ibid.*, II, 462-65.

4 *Ibid.*, p. 484.

5 *Ibid.*, IV, 73.

6 Siegel, *op. cit.*, p. 197.

7 *Writings*, II, 507.

Notes to Chapter 10

1 *Writings*, II, 492, 505, 509, 510.

2 *Ibid.*, III, 26-31.

3 *Ibid.*, pp. 16-17, n. 6.

4 *Ibid.*, p. 35.

5 *Ibid.*, pp. 37-40.

6 *Ibid.*, p. 41.

7 *Ibid.*, p. 51.

8 *Ibid.*, p. 55.

9 *Ibid.*, IV, 93.

10 *Ibid.*, II, 511.

11 *Ibid.*, III, 62.

12 *Ibid.*, IV, 119-20.

1 *Writings*, III, 74-83.

2 Some of Houston's friends, in revolt against his cautious military policy, supported the war bill. Isaac Van Zandt, a member of the House Military Affairs Committee, implored Houston to sell or pledge millions of acres of land to finance the project without "sordid calculation" whether the policy of aggressive war would be "incompatible with the genius of our institutions." Van Zandt and others believed that individual Texans would subscribe enough to finance the war and that the volunteers whose insubordination Houston feared would make a successful march beyond the Rio Grande. For the psychology of the war proposal, see Gambrell, *op. cit.*, pp. 252-53; terms of the war bill, Siegel, *op. cit.*, pp. 198-99.

3 *Writings*, III, 108-9.

4 *Ibid.*, pp. 110-11.

5 *Memoir*, pp. 209-10.

6 Siegel, *op. cit.*, p. 199.

7 *Writings*, III, 116-24.

8 H. Smither, "The Diary of Adolphus Sterne," *Southwestern Historical Quarterly*, XXXIII, 325.

9 *Writings*, III, 124, n. 2.

Notes to Chapter 12

1 Letters to Hockley and Terrell: *Writings*, IV, 135.

2 *Ibid.*, p. 141.

3 *Ibid.*, III, 147-49.

4 *Ibid.*, VII, 6-7.

Book VI

WORLD STATESMAN ON THE BRAZOS

Notes to Chapter 1

1 *Ibid.*, III, 177.

2 *Ibid.*, p. 193.

3 See Lucy A. Erath, "Memoirs of Major George Bernard Erath," *Southwestern Historical Quarterly*, XXVII, (1923), 37 ff.

4 See E. D. Adams (ed.), *British Diplomatic Correspondence*, pp. 126-27 for quotations from Elliot concerning Houston.

5 J. L. Wallis and L. L. Hill (eds.), *Sixty Years on the Brazos*, pp. 28-158, *passim*.

6 *Writings*, III, 323.

[1] *Writings*, III, 198.
[2] *Ibid.*, VI, 74-93. See also editorial note, *ibid.*, pp. 93-94. For Thomas J. Green's version of the Laredo affair see his *Journal of the Texian Expedition Against Mier*, pp. 56-63.
[3] This account of the Mier disaster is based on Green, *op. cit.*; *Writings*, VI, 74-93; and Horgan, *op. cit.*, II, 592-600.

Notes to Chapter 3

[1] *Telegraph and Texas Register*, Oct. 19, 1842.
[2] Hogan, *op. cit.*, p. 264.
[3] For details of the war between "Regulators" and "Moderators," see John W. Middleton, *History of the Regulators and Moderators;* Yoakum, *op. cit.*, II, 438-40; Houston's "Proclamation against the Regulators," Jan. 31, 1842, *Writings*, II, 459-61.
[4] Smith, *The Annexation of Texas*, pp. 41-42.
[5] *Ibid.*, p. 73.
[6] *Ibid.*

Notes to Chapter 4

[1] Quotations from Houston's letter to Elliot in this chapter are from *Writings*, III, 299-303.
[2] Jones, *Republic of Texas*, pp. 208-9.
[3] *Writings*, III, 322.

Notes to Chapter 5

[1] *Writings*, III, 343. See also *ibid.*, II, 362-63, n. 3.
[2] *Ibid.*, III, 344.
[3] *Ibid.*, pp. 341-42.
[4] Garrison, *op. cit.*, II, 168.
[5] Houston to Elliot, May 13, 1843, *Writings*, III, 385-90.
[6] *Ibid.*, p. 304.
[7] *Ibid.*, IV, 204-6.

Notes to Chapter 6

[1] *Writings*, III, 351-53.
[2] *Ibid.*, IV, 211.
[3] Siegel, *op. cit.*, p. 222.
[4] Hogan, *op. cit.*, pp. 227-28.
[5] *Ibid.*
[6] *Writings*, IV, 202.
[7] *Ibid.*, III, 413.

[8] *Ibid.*, IV, 221.
[9] *Ibid.*, III, 442-55.
[10] *Ibid.*, pp. 455-57.

Notes to Chapter 7

[1] Garrison, *op. cit.*, II, 221.
[2] *Ibid.*, pp. 232-33.
[3] *Writings*, III, 521-23.
[4] *Raven*, p. 346.
[5] *Writings*, IV, 260-65.
[6] *Ibid.*, p. 253.
[7] Friend, *op. cit.*, p. 131.
[8] *Writings*, IV, 536.
[9] Smith, *The Annexation of Texas*, p. 132.
[10] *Writings*, IV, 320-25.
[11] Anson Jones to Ashbel Smith, Garrison, *op. cit.*, III, 1156. Houston's instructions through his secretary of state to Minister Ashbel Smith in London led J. H. Smith to conclude that Houston's prime purpose was to establish a rival nation to the United States with a "predominantly British tone." He denied Houston all idealism, credited him with an ambition to triumph regardless of means as long as he was not found out; and he doubted that Houston sincerely desired annexation. (See J. H. Smith, *Annexation*, pp. 97-99 and 163-65.)

Notes to Chapter 8

[1] Adams, *op. cit.*, pp. 126-27.
[2] *Writings*, IV, 354-57.
[3] Siegel, *op. cit.*, p. 241.
[4] See Ashbel Smith, *Reminiscences*, pp. 62-65.
[5] Smith, *The Annexation of Texas*, p. 283.
[6] *Ibid.*, pp. 303-5 for comments of British press.
[7] *Writings*, IV, 401-5.
[8] *Ibid.*, pp. 406-7.
[9] *Ibid.*, p. 408.
[10] Crane, *op. cit.*, p. 255.

Notes to Chapter 9

[1] Newspaper comment is reported by Smith, *The Annexation of Texas*, pp. 323-25.
[2] *Writings*, IV, 410-17.
[3] *Ibid.*, VI, 5-13.
[4] This letter, *Writings*, IV, 298, differs from the versions in *Memoir*, p. 253 and Crane, *op. cit.*, pp. 359-62. Both *Memoir* and Crane omit the paragraph about the use of wine by diplomats.

[1] Account of Jackson's last days is based on Parton, *Life of Andrew Jackson*, III, 668-78 and George P. A. Healy, *Reminiscences of a Portrait Painter*, pp. 139-47.

[2] *Raven*, p. 357.

[3] *Writings*, IV, 424.

[4] *Ibid.*, VI, 14.

[5] *Ibid.*, IV, 425.

[6] *Ibid.*, VII, 15-16.

[7] *Cong. Globe*, 29th Cong., 1st Sess., 37-60 and 66-101, *passim*.

[8] Gambrell, *op. cit.*, pp. 418-19.

[9] Siegel, *op. cit.*, p. 254.

Book VII

AN APOSTLE OF A GREATER AMERICA

Notes to Chapter 1

[1] Allan Nevins (ed.), *Polk, The Diary of a President*, p. 68.

[2] Claude M. Fuess, *Life of Daniel Webster*, II, 141, n. 1.

[3] See *Writings*, IV, 451-71, for the complete speech quoted here and in the following pages.

[4] *Ibid.*, p. 473.

[5] *Ibid.*, p. 474.

[6] Fuess, *op. cit.*, II, 157-58.

[7] *Writings*, IV, 484.

Notes to Chapter 2

[1] Horgan, *op. cit.*, II, 617.

[2] *Ibid.*, p. 661.

[3] Episodes on the Rio Grande: See *Fifty Years in Camp and Field*, diary of Major General Ethan Allen Hitchcock, W. A. Croffut (ed.); Lloyd Lewis, *Captain Sam Grant*, pp. 136-46; and Horgan, *op. cit.*, pp. 662-79.

[4] *Writings*, IV, 201.

[5] Lloyd Lewis, *op. cit.*, p. 141.

[6] *Writings*, IV, 475-76.

[7] *Ibid.*, pp. 476-77.

Notes to Chapter 3

[1] Charles A. and Mary R. Beard, *The Rise of American Civilization*, I, 606.

[2] *Writings*, IV, 523-47; quotations and extracts in this chapter are from Houston's speech, Feb. 19, 1847.

[1] Lewis, *op. cit.*, pp. 203-4.
[2] *Writings*, VI, 18-20.
[3] For a close study of Lincoln's stand on Mexican War, see Benjamin P. Thomas, *Abraham Lincoln*, pp. 118-21.
[4] *Ibid.*, p. 120.
[5] Beard, *op. cit.*, I, 606-7.
[6] *Writings*, V, 29-36.
[7] Casualty figures are from the office of the Secretary of Defense, Progress and Statistics Division, rev. Sept. 7, 1957.

BOOK VIII

TRUE VOICE OF THE SOUTH UNHEEDED

Notes to Chapter 1

[1] *Writings*, V, 53-56.
[2] Richard K. Crallé, *Works of John C. Calhoun*, VI, 290-313.
[3] Nevins (ed.), *Polk, The Diary of a President*, p. 367.
[4] *Writings*, V, 71.

Notes to Chapter 2

[1] *Writings*, V, 78-88.
[2] *Ibid.*, p. 90.
[3] *Ibid.*, pp. 95-107.

Notes to Chapter 3

[1] *Writings*, V, 119-44. When Houston in the U. S. Senate, Feb. 8, 1850, used this striking imagery, *"A nation divided against itself cannot stand,"* Abraham Lincoln was a frustrated politician in Illinois following closely every word that was said on the slavery question and compiling a mass of newspaper clippings for future use. He may well have been impressed by Houston's striking close. Lincoln's famous "house divided" speech came eight years later on June 16, 1858, before the Springfield Convention that advocated his nomination for senator as the successor to Stephen A. Douglas.
[2] Crallé, *op. cit.*, IV, 542-73.
[3] *Writings*, V, 145-47.
[4] *Ibid.*, pp. 261-67.

Notes to Chapter 4

[1] Benjamin P. Thomas, *Abraham Lincoln*, p. 139.
[2] *Writings*, V, 490.
[3] *Ibid.*, pp. 469-502.

[1] *Writings*, V, 501.
[2] *Ibid.*, p. 349.
[3] *Ibid.*, pp. 347-48.
[4] *Ibid.*, p. 374.
[5] *Ibid.*, VI, 28.
[6] Crane, *op. cit.*, pp. 240-45.
[7] See *My Master*, by Jeff Hamilton as told to Lenoir Hunt, with an introduction by a Houston grandson, Houston Williams. Jeff was about one hundred years old when he was interviewed for the book.
[8] *Writings*, V, 433-40.

[1] *Writings*, V, 504.
[2] *Ibid.*, pp. 504-12.
[3] *Ibid.*, VI, 183.
[4] *Ibid.*, p. 210.

[1] Henry Wilson, *Rise and Fall of the Slave Power*, II, 399.
[2] Wilson, *op. cit.*, p. 393.
[3] Edward L. Pierce, *Memoirs and Letters of Charles Sumner*, III, 366-67.
[4] *Writings*, V, 523-30.

[1] *Writings*, V, 297-99. Houston to Nicholas Dean, May 8, 1851.
[2] *Memoir*, pp. 393-402.
[3] *Writings*, V, 283, n. 3.
[4] *Ibid.*, VI, 166-67.
[5] *Ibid.*, pp. 167-77.
[6] *Ibid.*, p. 183.

[1] *Writings*, VI, 305.
[2] *Ibid.*, pp. 305-6.
[3] *Ibid.*, p. 434.
[4] *Ibid.*, VII, 29.
[5] *Ibid.*, VI, 446, 444.
[6] Alexander W. Terrell, "Recollections of General Sam Houston," *Southwestern Historical Quarterly*, XVI, 119-21.
[7] *Ibid.*
[8] *Writings*, VI, 447-48.
[9] *Ibid.*, VII, 41.
[10] C. W. Raines (ed.), *Memoirs of Francis Richard Lubbock*, p. 224.

[11] *Writings*, VII, 205.

[12] *Ibid.*, pp. 306-35. Houston's farewell to the Senate, "A Refutation of Calumnies."

BOOK IX

THE PEAK AND THE VALLEY

Notes to Chapter 1

[1] Houston was unquestionably sincere in not wanting to campaign again. On Aug. 6, 1859, he wrote Simon Mussina, "I paid no attention to the election... I made one speech at Nacogdoches, as I was there purchasing sheep and cattle.... Had it not been for the love I bear the Union, and my strong devotion to Conservatism, I would never have allowed my name to go before the people for any office on earth... but I afterwards saw that to meet the issues of disunion and the African Slave trade, I must face my foes and make the issue direct." *Writings*, VII, 370.

[2] *Ibid.*, pp. 343-67.

[3] *Ibid.*, p. 384.

[4] *Ibid.*, p. 421.

[5] *Ibid.*, p. 432.

[6] *Raven*, p. 406.

[7] Wilson, *op. cit.*, II, 645-51.

[8] *Raven*, p. 402.

[9] *Writings*, VIII, 7-9.

Notes to Chapter 2

[1] Thomas, *op. cit.*, p. 213.

[2] *Ibid.*, p. 149.

[3] David C. Mearns, *The Lincoln Papers*, I, 234-237.

[4] *Writings*, VIII, 58-60.

[5] *Ibid.*, pp. 60-61.

[6] *Ibid.*, pp. 145-60.

[7] *Ibid.*, p. 184.

[8] Wilson, *op. cit.*, III, 6-7.

[9] *Writings*, VIII, 206.

[10] A. M. Williams, *Sam Houston and the War of Independence in Texas*, p. 353.

[11] *Ibid.*, pp. 354-55.

[12] Jeff Hamilton, *op. cit.*, p. 77.

[13] Charles A. Culberson, "General Sam Houston and Secession," *Scribner's Magazine*, XXXIX (Jan.-June, 1906), 590.

[14] Thomas, *op. cit.*, pp. 227-28, 229-30.

[15] *Ibid.*, p. 227.

[1] *Writings*, VIII, 236-52.
[2] Farewell speeches of Clay, Fitzpatrick, Davis, Slidell, and Benjamin: Wilson, *op. cit.*, III, 154-57.
[3] *Ibid.*, p. 76.
[4] *Ibid.*, p. 82.
[5] *Ibid.*, p. 19.
[6] *Writings*, VIII, 263.
[7] L. E. Chittenden, *Recollections of President Lincoln and His Administration*, pp. 97-98.
[8] D. S. Freeman, *Robert E. Lee*, I, 428-29.
[9] James Pike, *Scout and Ranger*, p. 145.
[10] Henry Bruce, *Life of General Houston*, p. 215, and *Raven*, p. 455.

Notes to Chapter 4

[1] Wilson, *op. cit.*, III, 41-42.
[2] Chittenden, *op. cit.*, pp. 89-90.
[3] *Writings*, VIII, 265-66.
[4] *Ibid.*, pp. 268-71.
[5] Events of the evening of March 15 described by Temple Houston Morrow, *Texas Senate Journal*, Feb. 27, 1945, 49th Legislature, Reg. Sess., 1945, pp. 263-64.
[6] Rev. William Mumford Baker, "A Pivotal Point," *Lippincott's Magazine*, XXVI, (November, 1880), 566.
[7] *Writings*, VIII, 271-78.
[8] *Ibid.*, pp. 278-92.
[9] Culberson, *op. cit.*, p. 587.
[10] George W. Paschal, "Last Years of Sam Houston," *Harper's New Monthly Magazine*, XXXII (1865-66), 633.
[11] *Writings*, VIII, 293.

Book X

LAST DREAMS

Notes to Chapter 1

[1] *Writings*, VIII, 295-300.
[2] *Ibid.*
[3] *Ibid.*, p. 299.

Notes to Chapter 2

[1] *Writings*, VIII, 300.
[2] *Ibid.*, pp. 301-5. *Ibid.*, p. 305.
[3] Houston to Sam, Jr., May 15, 22 and July 23, 1861, *Writings*, VIII, 305, 306, 309.

[4] *Raven*, p. 414.
[5] *Ibid.*, pp. 414, 455.
[6] Robert U. Johnson and Clarence C. Buel (eds.), *Battles and Leaders*, I, 252.

Notes to Chapter 3

[1] Katharine M. Jones, *Heroines of Dixie*, p. 107.
[2] *Writings*, VIII, 315.
[3] "Shiloh Shadows," reminiscences of Sam Houston, Jr., *Southwestern Historical Quarterly*, XXXIV, 329-33.
[4] Katharine M. Jones, *op. cit.*, pp. 107-17.

Notes to Chapter 4

[1] *Writings*, VIII, 316-30.
[2] Jeff Hamilton, *op. cit.*, pp. 100-101.
[3] Temple Houston Morrow in a letter to the author, Dec. 26, 1961.
[4] Alfred M. Williams, *op. cit.*, p. 372.
[5] *Writings*, VIII, 322.
[6] *Ibid.*, p. 323.
[7] *Raven*, p. 424.
[8] *Writings*, VIII, 324.

Notes to Chapter 5

[1] *Writings*, VIII, 327-39.
[2] Friend, *op. cit.*, p. 352.
[3] *Writings*, VIII, 339-44.
[4] *Ibid.*, pp. 346-47, n. 1.

Notes to Chapter 6

[1] *Writings*, VIII, 327.
[2] A. W. Terrell, "Recollections of Sam Houston," *Southwestern Historical Quarterly*, XVI, (1912), 122-23.
[3] *Ibid.*, p. 123.
[4] Jeff Hamilton, *op. cit.*, pp. 118-19.
[5] Bruce, *op. cit.*, p. 215.
[6] Jeff Hamilton, *loc. cit.*
[7] Bruce, *op. cit.*, pp. 217-18.
[8] A. M. Williams, *op. cit.*, p. 371.
[9] Lester, *Life and Achievements of Sam Houston, Hero and Statesman*, p. 157. The quotation is from remarks made by Andrew Jackson when Houston was being abused because he would not permit the trial and execution of Santa Anna. "Let those who clamor for blood clamor on," Jackson said. This was followed by the sentence that became Houston's epitaph.

* * * * *

Houston achieved a desire that he often expressed when addressing Texas audiences or his colleagues in the Senate. He left a strong posterity. All his children grew up, married and had children of their own.

After his death Margaret moved with the children to Independence to be near her mother. In 1867 a yellow fever epidemic struck southern Texas, and Margaret's mother was one of the victims. After nursing her mother through this fatal illness Margaret served as a volunteer nurse in other yellow fever cases and was herself stricken and died. She was buried at Independence. Beside her lies Aunt Eliza who was set free by General Houston in the same ceremony with Jeff and Uncle Joshua. The circumstances of Aunt Eliza's burial beside her mistress were described by Temple Houston Morrow in a letter, Dec. 16, 1961, to the author:

Mrs. Houston [Mr. Morrow's grandmother] gave her [Eliza] to my mother [Nancy Elizabeth Houston Morrow] for a maid. My mother had three sisters and when I was a child Aunt Liza would divide her time between the four, each sister living in a different city. At the time of her last illness she was at the home of my aunt, Mrs. Williams of Houston, Texas.

One night the family physician beckoned Mrs. Williams out of the room and told her Aunt Liza would probably lapse into a coma during the night and pass away and if Mrs. Williams desired to have a last talk with her she should do so at once. Mrs. Williams told Aunt Liza she was going on a long journey and would not be coming back. Aunt Liza replied, "Yes, Miss Maggie, I know I'm going for my feet have already touched the chilly waters of the Jordan." She asked if she could be buried in the family lot at Independence and sleep by the side of 'Miss Margaret', our grandmother.

Aunt Maggie said, "Yes, we'll take you there and put you away next to her." This was done. Anyone who visits Independence will see a little head-stone by the grave of Mrs. Houston which reads, "Aunt Eliza. Faithful unto death." And one who was once a slave-girl has been sleeping through the long years by the side of one who was once the wife of the President of a Republic.

Notes on Special Sources

OF ALL Houston biographies, Marquis James's *The Raven* has been the most durable. Historically, it is not in accord with some important recent judgments based on the publication of more complete records, but it will always command special respect for the authenticity with which it reports family traditions and anecdotes. At the age of eighty-three, one of Sam Houston's two surviving grandsons, Temple Houston Morrow of Lubbock, Texas, explained to the present author (December 4, 1961) the facilities James had in this connection. The Morrows provided office space for James to write up the family interviews and notes on voluminous Houston papers stored in the Morrow trunk. "We gave him everything we had," Morrow wrote. "We held back nothing he wanted to know. We did not ask him to shield the General in any way. I never heard any member of the family criticize James's use of the material we supplied him. The stories we told him were as accurate as we could make them and he reported them correctly."

Mr. Morrow made one request. "I hope the fact will not be overlooked that at the age of fifty-four, nine years before his death, my grandfather made his profession of faith and became a member of the Baptist church of Independence, Texas. From that time on he did not use intoxicants of any kind."

The Writings of Sam Houston, already noted in the preface, is in excess of 2,000,000 words and includes more than 4,000 letters, military and executive orders, communiques, speeches, and documents (1813-1863) with numerous editorial notes and sidelights on secondary characters. It represents the great bulk of Houston's available writings but is not all-inclusive. Some materials are still being withheld by members of the family and by collectors who have refused to permit copying. When these become available, it is not anticipated that they will substantially alter today's knowledge of Houston.

Houston's *Authentic Memoir* (*The Life of Sam Houston, The Only Authentic Memoir of Him Ever Published*) appeared in 1855 when his friends believed he had a chance of winning his party's nomination for the Presidency. Except for minor details, it is identical with *Sam Houston and His Republic*, published anonymously in 1846. In a later work (*The Life of Sam Houston*, 1883), Charles Edwards Lester claimed authorship of the two previous publications. Lester described the joint authorship which produced the *Memoir*. For three months he worked in Senator Houston's private room in Washington "without the intermission of a single day" and with constant direction and assistance from the Senator. Portions were dictated by Houston and taken down verbatim by Lester. Other portions were taken from Houston's writings. At the time, Houston was custodian of the archives from the Texas embassy which had closed following annexation. Lester states that the official records were used for "authentication for every statement." There will always be uncertainty as to where Lester departed from Houston's actual words, but there can be no doubt that the *Memoir* expressed Houston's personal views, convictions, and recollections. Mrs. Houston told William Crane, her husband's first biographer, that the *Memoir* was the only reliable account of him that had been written.

Andrew Jackson Houston's *Texas Independence* (1938) is a work of special interest because it is the product of the son for whose coming Sam Houston and his wife will be found praying in Book VIII, Chapter Five, of the present work. A. J. Houston went further than any previous writer in analyzing and understanding his father's military achievement. He was well qualified for his task of interpretation by two years of training at West Point and two years of service as professor of military science and tactics at St. Mary's University in Texas. He also followed in his father's footsteps in the U. S. Senate by appointment to fill a vacancy created by death, serving briefly from April 21, 1941 until his own death on June 26, 1941. However, with the single exception of General Houston's official report of the Battle of San Jacinto, *Texas Independence* was not documented.

Bibliography

I. Manuscripts

Bell, John, *Papers;* Blair Family *Papers;* Donelson, Andrew Jackson, *Papers;* Houston, Sam, *Letters;* Jackson, Andrew, *Papers;* Jackson, Andrew, *Memorandum Book* with entries for years 1829-1832; Lander, Frederick West, *Papers;* Robert Todd Lincoln Collection of Abraham Lincoln Papers; Monroe, James, *Papers;* Pierce, Franklin, *Papers;* Polk, James K., *Papers;* Van Buren, Martin, *Papers;* Welles, Gideon, *Papers.* (All Library of Congress.)

Houston, Sam, *Unpublished Correspondence;* also letters from various sources in typescript, Archives, University of Texas Library.

II. Public Documents

Microfilm: State Record Series (Texas), Library of Congress. Documents from which these microfilms were made are in the Texas State Library, Austin, except as noted.

Journal of the Consultation, Oct. 16, 1835-Nov. 14, 1835 (Archives Collection, University of Texas Library). Alc.2

Journal of the General Council, Nov. 14, 1835-March 11, 1836 (Archives Collection, University of Texas Library). Alc.2

Ordinances and Decrees of the Consultation. B2.1

Journal of the Senate of the Republic of Texas, 1836-1845. Ala.1

Proceedings of the House of Representatives of the Republic of Texas, 1836-1845. A.1b-1,2,3

Session Laws of the Congresses of the Republic of Texas, 1836-1845. B.2-1&2

Executive Department Journals, 1836-1845. E.1 1,2

Department of State; Letter Books, Foreign Letters, Home Letters, Foreign Legation Letters and Journals, 1836-1845. E.3 1,2

Messages of the Presidents of the Republic of Texas, 1838-1845. D.1 1

Debates of the Annexation Convention, July 4-Aug. 28, 1845. Cs.1

Congressional Globe, 22nd Cong., 1st Sess.; 29th Cong., 1st and 2nd Sess.; 36th Cong., 1st Sess., Parts I and II.

Historical Register and Dictionary of the United States Army. Washington: Government Printing Office, 1903.

Garrison, George P. (ed.). "Diplomatic Correspondence of the Republic of Texas," *American Historical Association Annual*, 1907-1908, 3 vols. Washington: Government Printing Office, 1908-1911.

Gammel, H. P. N. (ed.). *The Laws of Texas, 1822-1897*. 10 vols. Austin: Gammel Book Company, 1898.

Mooney, James. "The Sacred Formulas of the Cherokees," *Seventh Annual Report of Bureau of American Ethnology*, 1885-86. Washington: Government Printing Office, 1891.

Morrow, Temple Houston. "Address by Temple Houston Morrow," *Senate Journal*, 49th Texas Legislature, Reg. Sess., February 27, 1945.

Phillips, U. B. (ed.). The Correspondence of Robert Toombs, Alexander H. Stephens, and Howell Cobb. Vol. II, *Annual Report of the American Historical Association*, 1911. Washington: Government Printing Office, 1913.

Richardson, James D. (ed.). *A Compilation of the Messages and Papers of the Presidents, 1789-1897*. 20 vols. Washington: Government Printing Office, 1896-1899.

Winkler, Ernest W. (ed.). *Journal of the Secession Convention of Texas, 1861*. Austin: Austin Printing Company, 1912.

———. *Secret Journals of the Senate, Republic of Texas, 1836-1845*. Published by the Texas State Library and Historical Commission, 1909-1910.

III. Mexican Documents

Castañeda, Carlos E. (trans.). *The Mexican Side of the Texas Revolution*. Dallas: P. L. Turner Co., 1928.

This work includes translations of a number of important Mexican documents. Among them are the "Manifesto which Santa Anna Addressed to His Fellow Citizens Relative to His Operations During the Texas Campaign and His Capture" (published in Mexico in 1837); "A True Account of the First Texas Campaign and the Events Subsequent to the Battle of San Jacinto," by Santa Anna's personal secretary, Ramón Martínez Caró; "Representation Addressed to the Supreme Government by General Vicente Filisola in Defense of his Honor with Notes on his operations as General-in-chief of the Army of Texas"; and General José Urrea's "Diary of the Military Operations of the Divisions Which Under His Command Campaigned in Texas."

In his *Manifesto* Santa Anna attempted to exculpate himself from responsibility for the disastrous San Jacinto campaign and to place all blame for the outcome on his subordinates' inefficiency, carelessness, and disregard of orders. General Filisola responded to this with his heated address in defense of his honor. Caró sided with Filisola and denounced his chief's *Manifesto* as artful and deceptive.

Crane, William Carey, D.D., LL.D. *Life and Select Literary Remains of Sam Houston of Texas*. Philadelphia: J. B. Lippincott Co., 1885. Appendix pp. 647-61. "Mexican Account of the Battle of San Jacinto by Col. Pedro Delgado, of Gen. Santa Anna's Staff." This account of the battle and a portion of the campaign that preceded it was published in Austin in 1879 in a pamphlet entitled *The Battle of San Jacinto, as Viewed from both an American and Mexican Standpoint; its Details and Incidents as Officially Reported by Major-General Sam Houston, of the Texan Army; also, an Account of the Action written by Colonel Pedro Delgado, of General Santa Anna's Staff.* The portion of the pamphlet described as "from an American standpoint" was General Houston's official report to the Texas government after the Battle of San Jacinto, written nine years before Texas was annexed. The translator of Delgado's contribution is not noted. Its authenticity is attested by the fact that it is quoted at length by General Filisola in his *Memorias* (see below). A portion of it appears in John Linn's *Reminiscences*. The most complete translated version is that in Crane's appendix.

Delgado's vivid and revealing eyewitness report goes further than any other account in exposing the extraordinary deficiencies and indiscretions of the Mexican president general. The charges and counter charges by Santa Anna, Filisola, and Caró in the course of their public washing of dirty linen together with Delgado's account makes it possible to coordinate Mexican activities before and during the battle. There have been various attempts to treat the Battle of San Jacinto and its outcome as a mystery. The several Mexican accounts listed above leave one point beyond dispute. Houston owed a substantial share of his victory to the mercurial and unstable Santa Anna.

Filisola, General Vicente. *Memorias Para la Historia de la Guerra de Tejas por el General de División.* Mexico: Ignacio Cumplido, 1849; a book-length amplification of Filisola's "Representation."

IV. Works by Houston's Contemporaries

Bassett, John Spencer (ed.). *Correspondence of Andrew Jackson.* 7 vols. Washington: Carnegie Institution, 1926-35.

Ben, Perley Poore. *Perley's Reminiscences of Sixty Years in the National Metropolis.* Philadelphia: Hubbard Brothers, 1886.

Benton, Thomas Hart. *Thirty Years View; or, a History of the Working of the American Government for Thirty Years, from 1820 to 1850.* 2 vols. New York: D. Appleton and Company, 1854-56.

Burleson, Georgia J. (ed.). *Life and Writings of Dr. Rufus C. Burleson.* [Waco ? Texas.] Compiled and Published by Mrs. Georgiana Jenkins Burleson, 1901.

Chestnut, Mary Boykin. *A Diary from Dixie.* Isabella D. Martin and Myrta Lockett Avary (eds.). New York: Peter Smith, 1929.

Chittenden, L. E. *Recollections of President Lincoln and His Administration.* New York and London: Harper & Brothers, 1901.

Crallé, Richard K. (ed.). *Works of John C. Calhoun.* 6 vols. New York: D. Appleton and Company, 1854-57.

Croffut, W. A. (ed.). *Fifty Years in Camp and Field;* diary of Major General Ethan Allen Hitchcock, U.S.A. New York: G. P. Putnam's Sons, 1909.

Davis, Jefferson. *The Rise and Fall of the Confederate Government.* 2 vols. New York: D. Appleton and Company, 1881.

Davis, Varina Howell. *Jefferson Davis, Ex-President of the Confederate States of America: A Memoir by His Wife.* 2 vols. New York: Belford Company, 1890.

Duganne, A. J. H. *Camps and Prisons: Twenty Months in the Department of the Gulf.* New York: J. P. Robens, 1865.

Dyer, Oliver. *Great Senators of the United States Forty Years Ago, (1848 and 1849.)* New York: Robert Bonner's Sons, 1889.

Fremantle, Arthur James. *Three Months in the Southern States: April-June, 1863.* New York: John Bradburn, 1864.

Freund, Max (ed.). Gustav Dresel's *Houston Journal, Adventures in North America and Texas, 1837-1841.* Translated from a German manuscript. Austin: University of Texas Press, 1954.

Grant, Ulysses Simpson. *Personal Memoirs of U. S. Grant.* 2 vols. New York: The Century Co., 1895.

Gray, William Fairfax. *From Virginia to Texas, 1835: Diary of Col. Wm. F. Gray Giving Details of His Journey to Texas and Return in 1835-1836 and Second Journey to Texas in 1837.* Houston: Gray, Dillaye and Company, 1909.

Green, Rena Maverick (ed.). *Memoirs of Mary A. Maverick.* Arr. Mary A. Maverick and George Maverick. San Antonio: Alamo Printing Company, 1921.

Green, Thomas Jefferson. *Journal of the Texian Expedition Against Mier.* New York: Harper & Brothers, 1845.

Guild, Josephus Conn. *Old Times in Tennessee, with Historical, Personal, and Political Scraps and Sketches.* Nashville: Tavel, Eastman, and Howell, 1878.

Halstead, Murat. *Caucuses of 1860: A History of the National Political Conventions of the Current Presidential Campaign.* Columbus: Follett, Foster and Company, 1860.

Hamilton, Jeff. *My Master.* Memories of Houston's former slave as told to Lenoir Hunt; foreword by Franklin Williams. Dallas: Manfred, Van Nort & Co., 1940.

Hatcher, Mattie Austin (ed.). *Letters of an Early American Traveller: Mary Austin Holley, Her Life and Her Works, 1784-1846.* Dallas: Southwest Press, 1933.

Healy, George P. A. *Reminiscences of a Portrait Painter.* Chicago: A. C. McClurg and Company, 1894.

Jameson, J. Franklin (ed.). Correspondence of John C. Calhoun, 1899. Vol. II. *Annual Report of the American Historical Association,* 1900.

Jones, Anson. *Memoranda and Official Correspondence Relating to the Republic of Texas, Its History and Annexation—Including a Brief*

Autobiography of the Author. New York: D. Appleton and Company, 1859 (cited in chapter notes as *The Republic of Texas*).

Jones, Katherine M. *Heroines of Dixie. An Anthology: Confederate Women Tell Their Story of the War.* Indianapolis: The Bobbs-Merrill Company, 1955.

Lee, Robert E. *Recollections and Letters of General Robert E. Lee, by his Son, Captain Robert E. Lee.* New York: Doubleday, Page & Company, 1905.

Lester, Charles Edwards. *Sam Houston and His Republic.* New York: Burgess, Stringer & Co., 1846.

————. *The Life of Sam Houston: The Only Authentic Memoir of Him Ever Published.* New York: J. C. Derby, 1855.

————. *The Life and Achievements of Sam Houston, Hero and Statesman.* New York: Hurst and Company, 1883.

Linn, John J. *Reminiscences of Fifty Years in Texas.* New York: D. & J. Sadlier & Co., 1883.

Lubbock, Francis Richard. *Six Decades in Texas,* etc. See Raines, C. W. (ed.) *infra.*

McCaleb, Walter F. (ed.). *Memoirs of John H. Reagan, LL.D.* New York: Neale Publishing Company, 1906.

Muir, Andrew F. (ed.). *Texas in 1837: An Anonymous, Contemporary Narrative.* Austin: University of Texas Press, 1958.

Nevins, Allan (ed.). *The Diary of John Quincy Adams, 1794-1845.* New York: Longmans, Green & Co., 1928.

————. *Polk, The Diary of a President 1845-1849, Covering the Mexican War, the Acquisition of Oregon, and the Conquest of California and the Southwest.* New York: Longmans, Green & Co., 1952.

Newell, Reverend Chester. *History of the Revolution in Texas, Particularly of the War of 1835 & '36; together with the Latest Geographical, Topographical, and Statistical Accounts of the Country.* New York: Wiley and Putnam, 1838.

North, Thomas. *Five Years in Texas; or, What You Did Not Hear During The War from January 1861 to January 1866: A Narrative of His Travels, Experiences, and Observations in Texas and Mexico.* Cincinnati: Elm Street Printing Co., 1871.

Pierce, Edward L. (ed.). *Memoir and Letters of Charles Sumner.* 4 vols. Boston: Roberts Brothers, 1877-93.

Pike, Corporal James. *The Scout and Ranger.* Cincinnati and New York: J. R. Hawley & Co., 1865.

Raines, C. W. (ed.). *Six Decades in Texas; or, Memoirs of Francis Richard Lubbock, Governor of Texas in War Time, 1861-63: A Personal Experience in Business, War and Politics.* Austin: Ben C. Jones and Company, 1900.

Smith, Ashbel. *Reminiscences of the Texas Republic.* Historical Society of Galveston Series, No. 1, December 16, 1875. Galveston: 1876.

Smithwick, Noah. *The Evolution of a State; or, Recollections of Old Texas Days.* Austin: Gammel Book Company, 1900.

Sumner, Charles. *Memoir and Letters of,* See Pierce, Edward L. (ed.) *supra.*

Taylor, Richard, Lieutenant-General in the Confederate Army. *Destruction and Reconstruction: Personal Experiences of the Late War;* edited by Richard B. Harwell. New York: Longmans, Green & Co., 1955.

Wallis, Jonnie Lockhart and Laurance L. Hill (eds.). *Sixty Years on the Brazos: The Life and Letters of Dr. John Washington Lockhart, 1824-1900.* Los Angeles: privately printed, 1930.

Welles, Gideon. *Diary of Gideon Welles.* Boston: Houghton Mifflin Company, 1911.

Williams, R. H. *With Border Ruffians; Memories of the Far West, 1852-1868;* edited by E. W. Williams. New York: E. P. Dutton and Company, 1907.

Yoakum, Henderson. *History of Texas, from Its First Settlement in 1685 to Its Annexation to the United States in 1846.* 2 vols. New York: J. S. Redfield, 1855.

V. Books on Houston, His Times, and the Spirit of Texas

Abernethy, Thomas P. *From Frontier to Plantation in Tennessee.* Chapel Hill: University of North Carolina Press, 1932.

Adams, Ephrain Douglass. *British Interests and Activities in Texas, 1838-1846.* Baltimore: Johns Hopkins Press, 1910.

Bancroft, Hubert Howe. *History of the North Mexican States and Texas.* 2 vols. San Francisco: A. L. Bancroft and Co., 1884.

Barker, Eugene C. *The Life of Stephen F. Austin, Founder of Texas, 1793-1836: A Chapter in the Westward Movement of the Anglo-American People.* Nashville: Cokesbury Press, 1925.

Beals, Carleton. *Stephen F. Austin: Father of Texas.* New York: McGraw-Hill Book Company, 1953.

Beard, Charles A. and Mary R. *The Rise of American Civilization.* One Volume Edition. New York: Macmillan Company, 1930.

Bill, Alfred Hoyt. *Rehearsal for Conflict: The War with Mexico, 1846-1848.* New York: Alfred A. Knopf, Inc., 1947.

Bruce, Henry. *Life of General Houston, 1793-1863.* New York: Dodd, Mead, and Company, 1891.

Buchanan, Robert. *Life and Adventures of Audubon the Naturalist.* New York: E. P. Dutton and Co., 1915.

Buell, Augustus C. *History of Andrew Jackson: Pioneer, Patriot, Soldier, Politician, President.* New York: Charles Scribner's Sons, 1904.

Carr, Clark E., LL.D. *Stephen A. Douglas.* Chicago: A. C. McClurg and Company, 1909.

Coit, Margaret L. *John C. Calhoun.* Boston: Houghton Mifflin Company, 1950.

Crane, William Carey, D.D., LL.D., President of the Baylor University, Independence, Texas. *Life and Select Literary Remains of Sam Houston of Texas*. Two volumes in one. Philadelphia: J. B. Lippincott Company, 1885.

Creel, George. *Sam Houston, Colossus in Buckskin*. New York: Cosmopolitan Book Corporation, 1928.

Curtis, George Ticknor. *Life of Daniel Webster*. 2 vols. New York: D. Appleton and Company, 1870.

DeVoto, Bernard. *The Year of Decision 1846*. Boston: Houghton Mifflin Co., 1943.

Dobie, J. Frank. *Tales of Old-Time Texas*. Boston: Little, Brown & Co., 1955.

——. *The Flavor of Texas*. Dallas: Dealey and Lowe, 1936.

Donald, David (ed.). *Inside Lincoln's Cabinet, The Civil War Diaries of Salmon P. Chase*. New York: Longmans, Green & Co., 1954.

Eisenschiml, Otto, and Ralph Newman. *The American Iliad*. "The First Big Battle of the West: The Battle of Shiloh," pp. 168-203. Indianapolis: The Bobbs-Merrill Company, 1947.

Foreman, Grant. *Indians and Pioneers: The Story of the American Southwest before 1830*. New Haven: Yale University Press, 1930.

——. *Pioneer Days in the Early Southwest*. Cleveland: Arthur H. Clark Company, 1926.

Freeman, Douglas Southall. *R. E. Lee: A Biography*. 4 vols. New York: Charles Scribner's Sons, 1934-35.

Friend, Llerena B. *Sam Houston, The Great Designer*. Austin: University of Texas Press, 1954.

Fuess, Claude Moore. *Life of Daniel Webster*. 2 vols. Boston: Little, Brown & Co., 1930.

Gambrell, Herbert. *Anson Jones, the Last President of Texas*. Garden City, N. Y.: Doubleday and Company, 1948.

Garrison, George P. *Texas: a Contest of Civilizations*. Boston & N. Y.: Houghton Mifflin Co., 1903.

Graham, Philip. *Life and Poems of Mirabeau Buonaparte Lamar*. Chapel Hill: University of North Carolina Press, 1938.

Greeley, Horace. "Houston's Seizure of Texas," an excerpt from Greeley's *American Conflict* in *Great Epochs in American History Described by Famous Writers from Columbus to Roosevelt*, Francis W. Halsey (ed.) in Ten Volumes. Vol. VI, "The Jacksonian Period." 1828-1840. New York: Funk and Wagnalls, 1912.

Hale, Will T. and Dixon L. Merritt. *A History of Tennessee and Tennesseeans*. 8 vols. Chicago and N. Y.: The Lewis Publishing Company, 1913.

Hamilton, Holman. *Zachary Taylor, Soldier of the Republic*. Indianapolis: The Bobbs-Merrill Company, 1941.

Hendrick, Burton J. *Statesmen of the Lost Cause: Jefferson Davis and His Cabinet*. New York: The Literary Guild, 1939.

Hofstadter, Richard. *The American Political Tradition*. "John C. Calhoun: The Marx of the Master Class." New York: Alfred A. Knopf, Inc., 1948.

Hogan, William Ransom. *The Texas Republic: A Social and Economic History*. Norman: University of Oklahoma Press, 1946.

Horgan, Paul. *The Great River, The Rio Grande in North American History*. 2 vols. New York: Rinehart & Co., 1954.

Houston, Andrew Jackson. *Texas Independence*. Houston: The Anson Jones Press, 1938.

Houston, Sam. *The Writings of Sam Houston*. See below, Williams, Amelia W.

James, Marquis. *Andrew Jackson, Portrait of a President*. Indianapolis: The Bobbs-Merrill Company, 1940.

———. *Andrew Jackson, The Border Captain*. Indianapolis: The Bobbs-Merrill Company, 1933.

———. *The Raven: A Biography of Sam Houston*. Indianapolis: The Bobbs-Merrill Company, 1929.

Johnson, Robert Underwood and Clarence Clough Buel (eds.). *Battles and Leaders of the Civil War*. Vol. I (From Sumter to Shiloh). New York: Thomas Yoseloff, Inc., 1956.

Kendall, Geo. Wilkins. *Narrative of the Texan Santa Fe Expedition*. Chicago: The Lakeside Press, R. R. Donnelly & Sons Co., 1929.

Korngold, Ralph. *Thaddeus Stevens*. New York: Harcourt, Brace and Company, 1955.

Lewis, Lloyd. *Captain Sam Grant*. Boston: Little, Brown & Co., 1950.

Mearns, David C. *The Lincoln Papers*. 2 vols. Garden City, N. Y.: Doubleday and Company, 1948.

Middleton, John W. *History of the Regulators and Moderators and the Shelby County War in 1841 and 1842, in the Republic of Texas*. Fort Worth: Loving Publishing Company, 1883.

Miller, Edmund T. *A Financial History of Texas*. Austin: University of Texas Bulletin No. 37, A. C. Baldwin and Sons, 1916.

Moore, John Trotwood (ed.). *Tennessee, the Volunteer State*. 4 vols. Chicago: S. J. Clarke Publishing Company, 1923.

Morton, Oren F. *A History of Rockbridge County, Virginia*. Staunton: McClure Co., 1920.

Nevins, Allan. *Ordeal of the Union*. 2 vols. New York: Charles Scribner's Sons, 1947.

———. *Emergence of Lincoln*. 2 vols. New York: Charles Scribner's Sons, 1951.

Nicolay, John G. and John Hay. *Abraham Lincoln: A History*. 10 vols. New York: The Century Co., 1890.

Parton, James. *Life of Andrew Jackson*. 3 vols. New York: Mason Brothers, 1861.

Perry, George Sessions. *Texas A World in Itself*. New York: McGraw-Hill Book Company, 1942.

Pierson, George Wilson (ed.). *Tocqueville and Beaumont in America.* New York: Oxford University Press, 1938.

Ramsdell, Charles William. "Reconstruction in Texas." *Studies in History, Economics and Public Law Edited by the Faculty of Political Science of Columbia University,* Vol. XXXVI. New York: Longmans, Green & Co., 1910.

Randall, J. G. *The Civil War and Reconstruction.* Rev. ed. Boston: D. C. Heath and Co., 1953.

Rives, George Lockhart. *The United States and Mexico.* 2 vols. New York: Charles Scribner's Sons, 1913.

Roosevelt, Theodore. "How Texas Became Independent," an excerpt from Roosevelt's *Life of Thomas Hart Benton* in *Great Epochs in American History Described by Famous Writers from Columbus to Roosevelt,* Francis W. Halsey (ed.) in Ten Volumes. Vol. VI, "The Jacksonian Period," 1828-1840. New York: Funk and Wagnalls, 1912.

Ross, Ishbel. *Proud Kate* [daughter of Salmon P. Chase]. New York: Harper & Brothers, 1953.

Schouler, James. *History of the United States.* "Steamboat Travel on Inland Waters." New York: Dodd, Mead, and Company, 1880.

Siegel, Stanley. *A Political History of the Texas Republic, 1836-1845.* Austin: University of Texas Press, 1956.

Smith, Justin H. *The Annexation of Texas.* Corrected edition. New York: Barnes & Noble, Inc., 1941.

——. *The War with Mexico.* 2 vols. New York: Macmillan Company, 1919.

Starkey, Marion L. *The Cherokee Nation.* New York: Alfred A. Knopf, Inc., 1952.

Thomas, Benjamin P. *Abraham Lincoln.* New York: Alfred A. Knopf, Inc., 1952.

Webb, Walter Prescott, and others (eds.). *The Texas Handbook.* 2 vols. Austin: The Texas State Historical Association, 1952.

——. *The Great Frontier.* Boston: Houghton Mifflin Co., 1952.

Wiley, Bell Irwin. *The Life of Billy Yank.* Indianapolis: The Bobbs-Merrill Company, 1952.

——. *The Life of Johnny Reb.* Indianapolis: The Bobbs-Merrill Company, 1943.

Williams, Alfred M. *Sam Houston and the War of Independence in Texas.* Boston: Houghton Mifflin Co., 1893.

Williams, Amelia W., and Eugene C. Barker (eds.). *The Writings of Sam Houston, 1813-1863.* 8 vols. Austin: University of Texas Press, 1938-43.

Wilson, Henry. *Rise and Fall of the Slave Power in America.* 3 vols. Boston: Houghton Mifflin Co., 1872.

Wiltse, Charles M. *John C. Calhoun, Sectionalist, 1840-1850.* Indianapolis: The Bobbs-Merrill Company, 1951.

VI. *Newspapers, Periodicals and Articles*

Austin *State Gazette*, 1853-1860.
Charleston *Courier*, 1846-1861.
Charleston *Mercury*, 1844-1848.
Gallatin (Tenn.) *Journal*, Sept. 20, 1828; Feb. 24 and March 3, 1829.
Houston *Morning Star*, April 15, 17, 19, Nov. 5, 1839.
Houston Telegraph and Texas Register, 1838-1845.
Telegraph and Texas Register (Columbia), Sept. 1836-April 1837.
London (England) *Atlas*, 1839-1843.
London (England) *Morning Post*, 1833-1835; 1855-1861.
The Liberator (Boston), 1840-1859.
Nashville *Banner*, 1829.
National *Intelligencer* (Washington, D. C.), 1845-1863.
New Orleans *Picayune* (daily and weekly), 1839-1846.
New York *Herald*, 1860.
New York *Tribune*, 1855-1860; Nov. 13, 1880.
Niles' Weekly Register, 1828-1832; 1846-1859.
Richmond *Enquirer*, 1853-1864.
The Evening Star (Washington, D. C.), 1854-1859.

Baker, Rev. William Mumford. "A Pivotal Point," *Lippincott's Magazine*, XXVI (November, 1880), 559-66.
Barker, Eugene C. "Don Carlos Barrett," *Southwestern Historical Quarterly*, XX (January, 1917), 139-45.
Christian, A. K. "Mirabeau Buonaparte Lamar," *Southwestern Historical Quarterly*, XXIII-XXIV (July-April, 1919-20), 153-70.
Culberson, Charles A. "General Sam Houston and Secession," *Scribner's Magazine*, XXXIX (Jan.-June, 1906), 584-91.
Dobie, J. Frank. "Bowie and the Bowie Knife," *Southwest Review*, XVI (April, 1931), 351-68.
————. "The First Cattle in Texas and the Southwest Progenitors of the Longhorns," *Southwestern Historical Quarterly*, XLII (January, 1939), 171-97.
Duval, John. "His Own Story of Escape from the Fannin Massacre at Goliad," *Quarterly of the Texas State Historical Association*, I (1897), 54-57.
Erath, Lucy A. (ed.). "Memoirs of Major George Bernard Erath." *Southwestern Historical Quarterly*, XXVI (January, 1923), 207-33; XXVI (April, 1923), 255-79.
Harris, Dilue. "Reminiscences of Mrs. Dilue Harris," *Quarterly of the Texas State Historical Association*, IV (1900-1901), 85-127.
Houston, Sam, Jr. "Shiloh Shadows" (Reminiscences), *Southwestern Historical Quarterly*, XXXIV (April, 1931), 329-33.
Jaffa, Harry V. "Expediency and Morality in the Lincoln-Douglas Debates," *The Anchor Review*. Number Two of a Series, 179-204. Garden City, N. Y.: Doubleday and Company, 1957.

Lang, Aldon S. "Financial Aspects of the Public Lands in Texas," *Southwestern Political and Social Science Quarterly*, XIII (June, 1932), 57-68.

Maher, Edward R., Jr. "Sam Houston and Secession," *Southwestern Historical Quarterly*, LV (July-April, 1951-52), 448-58.

Muckleroy, Anna. "The Indian Policy of the Republic of Texas," *Southwestern Historical Quarterly*, XXV (April, 1922), 229-60; XXVI (July, 1922), 1-29; XXVI (October, 1922), 128-48; XXVI (January, 1923), 184-206.

Muir, Andrew F. "The Destiny of Buffalo Bayou," *Southwestern Historical Quarterly*, XLVII (October, 1943), 91-106.

———— (ed.). "Diary of a Young Man in Houston, 1838," *Southwestern Historical Quarterly*, LIII (January, 1950), 276-307.

————. "The Mystery of San Jacinto," *Southwest Review*, XXXVI (May, 1951), 77-84.

"Notes on Texas. By a Citizen of Ohio," *Hesperian; or, Western Monthly Magazine*, I (September, 1838), 350-60; I (October, 1838), 428-40; II (November, 1838), 30-39; II (December, 1838), 109-18; II (January, 1839), 189-99; II (February, 1839), 288-93; II (March, 1839), 359-67; II (April, 1839), 417-26.

Paschal, George W. "Last Years of Sam Houston," *Harper's New Monthly Magazine*, XXXII (Dec.-May, 1865-1866), 630-35.

Reagan, John H. "The Expulsion of the Cherokees from East Texas," *Quarterly of the Texas State Historical Association*, I (1897), 38-46.

Red, W. S. (ed.). "Allen's Reminiscences of Texas, 1838-1842," *Southwestern Historical Quarterly*, XVII (January, 1914), 283-305; XVIII (January, 1915), 287-304.

Smith, Henry. "Reminiscences of Henry Smith," *Quarterly of the Texas State Historical Association*, XIV (July, 1910), 24-73.

Smith, W. Roy. "The Quarrel Between Governor Smith and the Provisional Government of the Republic," *Quarterly of the Texas State Historical Association*, V (1902), 269-346.

Smither, Harriet (ed.). "Diary of Adolphus Sterne," *Southwestern Historical Quarterly*, XXX (October, 1926), 139-55; (January, 1927), 219-32; (April, 1927), 305-24; XXXI (July, 1927), 63-83; (October, 1927), 181-87; (January, 1928), 285-91; (April, 1928), 374-83; XXXII (July, 1928), 87-94; (October, 1928), 165-79; (January, 1929), 252-58; (April, 1929), 344-51; XXXIII (July, 1929), 75-79; (October, 1929), 160-68; (January, 1930), 231-42; (April, 1930), 315-25; XXXIV (July, 1930), 69-76; (October, 1930), 159-65; (January, 1931), 257-65; (April, 1931), 340-47; XXXV (July, 1931), 77-82; (October, 1931), 151-68; (January, 1932), 238-42; (April, 1932), 317-24; XXXVI (July, 1932), 67-72; (October, 1932), 163-66; (January, 1933), 215-30; (April, 1933), 312-16; XXXVII (July, 1933), 45-61; (October, 1933), 136-48; (January, 1934), 215-22; (April, 1934), 320-23; XXXVIII (July, 1934), 53-70; (October, 1934), 149-53; (January, 1935), 213-28.

Terrell, A. W. "Recollections of General Sam Houston," *Southwestern Historical Quarterly*, XVI (October, 1912), 113-36.

Webb, Walter Prescott. "The American Revolver and the West," *Scribner's Magazine*, LXXXI (February, 1927), 171-78.

Wilcox, S. S. "Laredo During the Texas Republic," *Southwestern Historical Quarterly*, XLII (October, 1938), 83-107.

Williams, Alfred M. "General Houston's Indian Life," *Magazine of American History*, X (July-December, 1883), 401-8.

Index

Forbes, John, 163-64, 237, 247, 345
Ford, John, 296
Forsyth, John, 293
Fort Bend, Texas, 197, 204, 207, 211, 214, 217, 219
Fort Defiance, Texas, 187, 190, 200
Fort Gibson, 54-55, 61, 62, 63, 108, 110, 112
Fort Mason, 603
Fort Mims, Alabama, 16
Fort Strother, Alabama, 16, 187
Fort Sumter, 601, 603
Fort Towson, 84
Fort Williams, Alabama, 19
Fossen, John Van, 65
France, 312, 313, 315-17, 319, 328, 333, 377, 438-39, 440-41, 458, 464, 465-66, 480, 484
Franciscans, 365
Franks, L. B., 401
Fredonia, Republic of, 94
Fredonia Rebellion, 92, 99, 110, 111
"Fredonians," 94-95, 111
Fugitive Slave Law, Clay's plea for stronger, 536, 537

Gadsden, James, 531
Gallatin, Tennessee, 38, 42, 45, 59
Galveston, Texas, 92, 209, 217-18, 219, 252, 258-59, 261, 303, 321, 358, 359, 363, 396, 398, 399, 453-54
Galveston Bay and Texas Land Company, 64, 362
Galveston Civilian, 408, 612
Galveston Island, 226
Galveston News, 558, 613
Gaona, Antonio, 183, 194, 219, 250-51
Garrison, William Lloyd, 310-11, 436, 565, 566
Gentry, Tiana Rogers, 60, 83-84
Georgia, 124

Gibbs General Store (Huntsville, Texas), 550-51
Giddings, George H., 612
Giddings, Joshua, 506
Gillespie, Barry, 399, 400, 402
Goliad, Texas, 105, 137, 148, 150, 151, 152, 153, 173, 175-76, 178, 187, 188, 192-93, 199-206, 213, 225-26, 227, 274, 305, 397
Goliad Massacre, The, 199-206, 234, 249
Golladay, Isaac, 26
Gonzales, José Maria, 143, 208, 390
Gonzales, Texas, 125-26, 128, 129, 137, 139, 140, 141, 165, 168, 173, 174, 179-84, 188, 189, 191, 196-97, 203-4, 212, 213, 230, 231, 288, 341
Goodbread, Joseph, 433-34
Gordon, George, see Aberdeen, Lord
Gott, Thomas, 536
Graham, Daniel, 28
Grand Cane, Texas, 338, 422, 424, 472
Grant, James, 130, 148-51, 152, 154, 199, 213, 221, 286, 304
Grant, U. S., 630, 643, 644
Gray, William Fairfax, 158, 160, 161, 165, 296
Grayson, Peter, 269, 313
Greeley, Horace, 614
Green, Duff, 55, 56, 69
Green, Thomas Jefferson ("Dog"), 268-69, 271-72, 273, 426, 427, 428-30
Greer, John A., 379
Grimes, Jesse, 487
Groce, Jared Ellison, 63, 110
Groce's Landing, 192, 197-98, 206, 208, 210, 214, 297
Grundy, Felix, 67, 71
Guadalupe, Mexico, 430

Houston, Sam—(*Cont.*)

711